Triangle Tech Electrical Program

NCCER Contren Modules
Trainee Guide—1st Term Modules—Volume One
Published by Prentice Hall
ISBN: 0-13-169260-7

Contents:

Trainee Workbook Module

9/21/05

Goal Line Cogeneration Power Project

Goal Line is a cogeneration power plant in Escondido, California. A cogeneration power plant produces electricity and steam simultaneously. The combustion turbine at Goal Line burns natural gas and has a capacity of 50 megawatts. Exhaust from the combustion turbine is used produce steam, and compressors use the steam from Goal Line to produce ice at a local ice-skating arena.

26104-05
Electrical Theory One

Topics to be presented in this module include:

Overview

The foundation for successful and safe electrical installations and troubleshooting is a sound understanding of electrical theory. Electrical theory involves the study of atoms, their reactions, and their involvement in electric circuits. Electricians must understand electrical theory to fully understand the roles that voltage, current, and resistance play in electrical systems.

The primary action in any designed electrical circuit or system is the controlled flow of electrons. Electricians must know what electrons are, what makes them flow, how their flow is controlled, and how this flow is used to perform work. In addition, they must know what to expect if an unintentional or catastrophic flow of electrons should occur.

Having a solid understanding of electrical theory enables electricians to complete quality installations and troubleshoot a circuit or electrical system quickly and efficiently. These skills are fundamental for a successful career as an electrician.

Objectives

When you have completed this module, you will be able to do the following:

1. Recognize what atoms are and how they are constructed.
2. Define voltage and identify the ways in which it can be produced.
3. Explain the difference between conductors and insulators.
4. Define the units of measurement that are used to measure the properties of electricity.
5. Explain how voltage, current, and resistance are related to each other.
6. Using the formula for Ohm's law, calculate an unknown value.
7. Explain the different types of meters used to measure voltage, current, and resistance.
8. Using the power formula, calculate the amount of power used by a circuit.

Trade Terms

Ammeter	Nucleus
Ampere (A)	Ohm (Ω)
Atom	Ohmmeter
Battery	Ohm's law
Circuit	Power
Conductor	Protons
Coulomb	Resistance
Current	Resistor
Electron	Schematic
Insulator	Series circuit
Joule (J)	Valence shell
Lo	Volt (V)
Matter	Voltage
Mega	Voltage drop
Micro	Voltmeter
Neutrons	Watt (W)

Required Trainee Materials

1. Paper and pencil
2. Appropriate personal protective equipment

Prerequisites

Before you begin this module, it is recommended that you successfully complete Core Curriculum and Electrical Level One, Modules 26101-05 through 26103-05.

This course map shows all of the modules in *Electrical Level One.* The suggested training order begins at the bottom and proceeds up. Skill levels increase as you advance on the course map. The local Training Program Sponsor may adjust the training order.

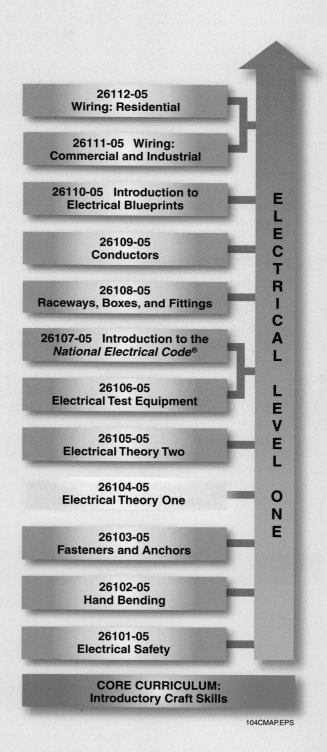

104CMAP.EPS

1.0.0 ◆ INTRODUCTION TO ELECTRICAL THEORY

As an electrician, you must work with a force that cannot be seen. However, electricity is there on the job, every day of the year. It is necessary that you understand the forces of electricity so that you will be safe on the job. The first step is a basic understanding of the principles of electricity.

The relationships among current, voltage, resistance, and power in a basic direct current (DC) series circuit are common to all types of electrical circuits. This module provides a general introduction to the electrical concepts used in Ohm's law. It also presents the opportunity to practice applying these basic concepts to DC series circuits. In this way, you can prepare for further study in electrical and electronics theory and maintenance techniques. By practicing these techniques for all combinations of DC circuits, you will be prepared to work on any DC circuits you might encounter.

2.0.0 ◆ CONDUCTORS AND INSULATORS

2.1.0 The Atom

The atom is the smallest part of an element that enters into a chemical change, but it does so in the form of a charged particle. These charged particles are called ions, and are of two types—positive and negative. A positive ion may be defined as an atom that has become positively charged. A negative ion may be defined as an atom that has become negatively charged. One of the properties of charged ions is that ions of the same charge tend to repel one another, whereas ions of unlike charge will attract one another. The term charge can be taken to mean a quantity of electricity that is either positive or negative.

The structure of an atom is best explained by detailed analysis of the simplest of all atoms, the of the element hydrogen. The hydrogen atom *Figure 1* is composed of a nucleus containing o proton and a single orbiting electron. As the electron revolves around the nucleus, it is held in the orbit by two counteracting forces. One of the forces is called centrifugal force, which is the fo that tends to cause the electron to fly outward as travels around its circular orbit. The second for acting on the electron is electrostatic force. The force tends to pull the electron in toward the n cleus and is provided by the mutual attraction between the positive nucleus and the negati electron. At some given radius, the two forces w balance each other, providing a stable path for electron.

- A proton (+) repels another proton (+).
- An electron (−) repels another electron (−).
- A proton (+) attracts an electron (−).

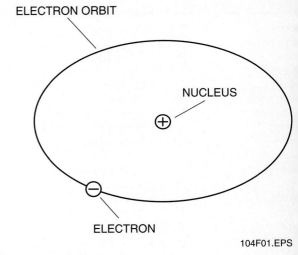

Figure 1 ◆ Hydrogen atom.

104F01.EPS

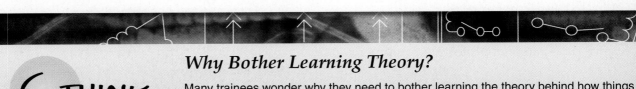

Why Bother Learning Theory?

THINK ABOUT IT

Many trainees wonder why they need to bother learning the theory behind how things operate. They figure, why should I learn how it works as long as I know how to install it? The answer is, if you only know how to install something (e.g., run wire, connect switches, etc.), that's all you are ever going to be able to do. For example, if you don't know how your car operates, how can you troubleshoot it? The answer is, you can't. You can only keep changing out the parts until you finally hit on what is causing the problem. (How many times have you seen people do this?) Remember, unless you understand not only how things work but why they work, you'll only be a parts changer. With theory behind you, there is no limit to what you can do.

Basically, an atom contains three types of sub-atomic particles that are of interest in electricity: electrons, protons, and **neutrons.**

The protons and neutrons are located in the center, or nucleus, of the atom, and the electrons travel about the nucleus in orbits.

Because protons are relatively heavy, the repulsive force they exert on one another in the nucleus of an atom has little effect.

The attracting and repelling forces on charged materials occur because of the electrostatic lines of force that exist around the charged materials. In a negatively charged object, the lines of force of the excess electrons add to produce an electrostatic field that has lines of force coming into the object from all directions. In a positively charged object, the lines of force of the excess protons add to produce an electrostatic field that has lines of force going out of the object in all directions. The electrostatic fields either aid or oppose each other to attract or repel.

2.1.1 The Nucleus

The nucleus is the central part of the atom. It is made up of heavy particles called protons and

neutrons. The proton is a charged particle containing the smallest known unit of positive electricity. The neutron has no electrical charge. The number of protons in the nucleus determines how the atom of one element differs from the atom of another element.

Although a neutron is actually a particle by itself, it is generally thought of as an electron and proton combined and is electrically neutral. Since neutrons are electrically neutral, they are not considered important to the electrical nature of atoms.

2.1.2 Electrical Charges

The negative charge of an electron is equal but opposite to the positive charge of a proton. The charges of an electron and a proton are called electrostatic charges. The lines of force associated with each particle produce electrostatic fields. Because of the way these fields act together, charged particles can attract or repel one another. The Law of Electrical Charges states that particles with like charges repel each other and those with unlike charges attract each other. This is shown in *Figure 2*.

2.2.0 Conductors and Insulators

The difference between atoms, with respect to chemical activity and stability, depends on the number and position of the electrons included within the atom. In general, the electrons reside in groups of orbits called shells. The shells are arranged in steps that correspond to fixed energy levels.

The number of electrons in the outermost shell determines the valence of an atom. For this reason, the outer shell of an atom is called the **valence shell,** and the electrons contained in this shell are called valence electrons *(Figure 3)*. The valence of an atom determines its ability to gain or lose an electron, which in turn determines the chemical and electrical properties of the atom. An

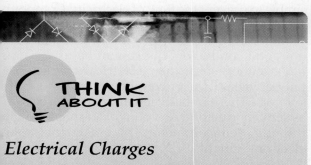

THINK ABOUT IT

Electrical Charges

Think about the things you come in contact with every day. Where do you see or find examples of electrostatic attraction?

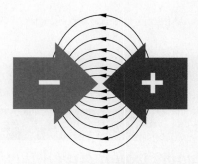

UNLIKE CHARGES ATTRACT

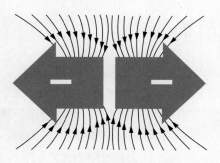

LIKE CHARGES REPEL

104F02.EPS

Figure 2 ◆ Law of electrical charges.

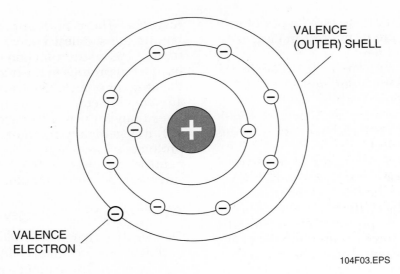

VALENCE (OUTER) SHELL

VALENCE ELECTRON

104F03.EPS

Figure 3 ◆ Valence shell and electrons.

atom that is lacking only one or two electrons from its outer shell will easily gain electrons to complete its shell, but a large amount of energy is required to free any of its electrons. An atom having a relatively small number of electrons in its outer shell in comparison to the number of electrons required to fill the shell will easily lose these valence electrons.

It is the valence electrons that we are most concerned with in electricity. These are the electrons that are easiest to break loose from their parent atom. Normally, a **conductor** has three or less valence electrons, an **insulator** has five or more valence electrons, and semiconductors usually have four valence electrons.

All the elements of which **matter** is made may be placed into one of three categories: conductors, insulators, and semiconductors.

Conductors, for example, are elements such a copper and silver that will conduct a flow of electricity very readily. Because of their good conducting abilities, they are formed into wire an used whenever it is desired to transfer electric energy from one point to another.

Insulators, on the other hand, do not conduct electricity to any great degree and are used when it is desirable to prevent the flow of electricity. Compound such as porcelain and plastic are good insulators.

Materials such as germanium and silicon a not good conductors but cannot be used as insulators either, since their electrical characteristi fall between those of conductors and those of insulators. These in-between materials are classifie as semiconductors. As you will learn later in yo training, semiconductors play a crucial role electronic circuits.

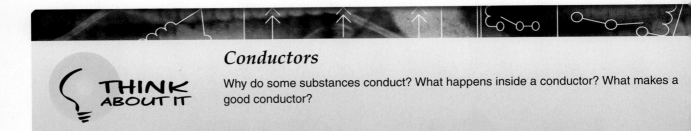

Conductors

THINK ABOUT IT

Why do some substances conduct? What happens inside a conductor? What makes a good conductor?

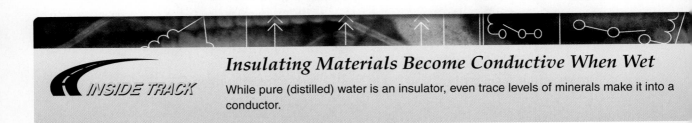

Insulating Materials Become Conductive When Wet

INSIDE TRACK

While pure (distilled) water is an insulator, even trace levels of minerals make it into a conductor.

.0.0 ◆ ELECTRIC CHARGE AND CURRENT

n electric charge has the ability to do the work of
noving another charge by attraction or repulsion.
he ability of a charge to do work is called its po-
ential. When one charge is different from another,
nere must be a difference in potential between
nem. The sum of the difference of potential of all
ne charges in the electrostatic field is referred to
s electromotive force (emf) or voltage. Voltage is
equently represented by the letter E.

Electric charge is measured in **coulombs**. An
ectron has 1.6×10^{-19} coulombs of charge.
herefore, it takes 6.25×10^{18} electrons to make up
ne coulomb of charge, as shown below.

$$\frac{1}{1.6 \times 10^{-19}} = 6.25 \times 10^{18} \text{ electrons}$$

two particles, one having charge Q_1 and the other
narge Q_2, are a distance (d) apart, then the force
etween them is given by Coulomb's law, which
ates that the force is directly proportional to the
roduct of the two charges and inversely propor-
onal to the square of the distance between them:

$$\text{Force} = \frac{k \times Q_1 \times Q_2}{d^2}$$

Q_1 and Q_2 are both positive or both negative,
en the force is positive; it is repulsive. If Q_1 and
2 are of opposite charges, then the force is nega-
ve; it is attractive. The letter k equals a constant
ith a value of 10^9.

.1.0 Current Flow

ne movement of the flow of electrons is called
urrent. To produce current, the electrons are
oved by a potential difference. Current is repre-
nted by the letter I. The basic unit in which curnt is measured is the **ampere**, also called the

amp. The symbol for the ampere is A. One ampere
of current is defined as the movement of one
coulomb past any point of a conductor during one
second of time. One coulomb is equal to 6.25×10^{18} electrons; therefore, one ampere is equal to
6.25×10^{18} electrons moving past any point of a
conductor during one second of time.

The definition of current can be expressed as an
equation:

$$I = \frac{Q}{T}$$

Where:

I = current (amperes)

Q = charge (coulombs)

T = time (seconds)

Charge differs from current in that Q is an accu-
mulation of charge, while I measures the intensity
of moving charges.

In a conductor, such as copper wire, the free electrons are charges that can be forced to move with
relative ease by a potential difference. If a potential
difference is connected across two ends of a copper
wire, as shown in *Figure 4,* the applied voltage

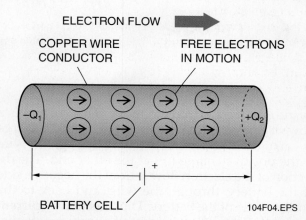

Figure 4 ◆ Potential difference causing electric current.

Units of Electricity and Volta

A disagreement with a fellow scientist over the twitching of a frog's leg eventually led
18th-century physicist Alessandro Volta to theorize that when certain objects and
chemicals come into contact with each other, they produce an electric current. Believing
that electricity came from contact between metals only, Volta coined the term metallic
electricity. To demonstrate his theory, Volta placed two discs, one of silver and the other
of zinc, into a weak acidic solution. When he linked the discs together with wire,
electricity flowed through the wire. Thus, Volta introduced the world to the battery, also
known as the Voltaic pile. Now Volta needed a term to measure the strength of the
electric push or the flowing charge; the volt is that measure.

Law of Electrical Force and de Coulomb

In the 18th century, a French physicist named Charles de Coulomb was concerned with how electric charges behaved. He watched the repelling forces electric charges exerted by measuring the twist in a wire. An object's weight acted as a turning force to twist the wire, and the amount of twist was proportional to the object's weight. After many experiments with opposing forces, de Coulomb proposed the Inverse Square Law, later known as the *Law of Electrical Force*.

The Magic of Electricity

The flow of electrons occurs at close to the speed of light, about 186,000 miles per second. How long does it take the light from the end of a flashlight to reach the floor? If you ran a light circuit from Maine to California and flipped the switch, how long would it take for the light to come on?

Current Flow

Why do you need two wires to use electrical devices? Why can't current simply move to a lamp and be released as light energy?

---

forces the free electrons to move. This current is a flow of electrons from the point of negative charge (−) at one end of the wire, moving through the wire to the positive charge (+) at the other end. The direction of the electron flow is from the negative side of the battery, through the wire, and back to the positive side of the battery. The direction of current flow is therefore from a point of negative potential to a point of positive potential.

3.2.0 Voltage

The force that causes electrons to move is called voltage, potential difference, or electromotive force (emf). One **volt (V)** is the potential difference between two points for which one coulomb of electricity will do one **joule (J)** of work. A **battery** is one of several means of creating voltage. It chemically creates a large reserve of free electrons at the negative (−) terminal. The positive (+) terminal has electrons chemically removed and will therefore accept them if an external path is provided from the negative (−) terminal. When a battery is no longer able to chemically deposit

electrons at the negative (−) terminal, it is said be dead, or in need of recharging. Batteries a normally rated in volts. Large batteries are al rated in ampere-hours, where one ampere-hour a current of one amp supplied for one hour.

4.0.0 ◆ RESISTANCE

Resistance is directly related to the ability of material to conduct electricity. Conductors ha very low resistance; insulators have very hi resistance.

4.1.0 Characteristics of Resistance

Resistance can be defined as the opposition to cu rent flow. To add resistance to a circuit, electric components called **resistors** are used. A resistor a device whose resistance to current flow is known, specified value. Resistance is measured ohms and is represented by the symbol R in equ tions. One **ohm** is defined as the amount of resi ance that will limit the current in a conductor one ampere when the voltage applied to the co ductor is one volt. The symbol for an ohm is Ω.

Voltage

THINK ABOUT IT

Why is voltage called electrical potential? Why are we interested in potential charges—why not simply measure the actual flow of current? Can there be very high potential and no current, or a very small current? What happens when lightning strikes in terms of electrical potential?

Joule's Law

While other scientists of the 19th century were experimenting with batteries, cells, and circuits, James Joule was theorizing about the relationship between heat and energy. He discovered, contrary to popular belief, that work did not just move heat from one place to another; work, in fact, generated heat. Furthermore, he demonstrated that over time, a relationship existed between the temperature of water and electric current. These ideas formed the basis for the concept of energy. In his honor, the modern unit of energy was named the joule.

The Visual Language of Electricity

Learning to read circuit diagrams is like learning to read a book—first you learn to read the letters, then you learn to read the words, and before you know it, you are reading without paying attention to the individual letters anymore. Circuits are the same way—you will struggle at first with the individual pieces, but before you know it, you will be reading a circuit without even thinking about it. Studying the table below will help you to understand the fundamental language of electricity.

What's Measured	Unit of Measurement	Symbol	Ohm's Law Symbol
Amount of current	Amp	A	I
Electrical power	Watt	W	P
Force of current	Volt	V	E
Resistance to current	Ohm	Ω	R

The resistance of a wire is proportional to the length of the wire, inversely proportional to the cross-sectional area of the wire, and dependent upon the kind of material of which the wire is made. The relationship for finding the resistance of a wire is:

$$R = \rho \frac{L}{A}$$

Where:

= resistance (ohms)

= length of wire (feet)

= area of wire (circular mils, CM, or cm²)

= specific resistance (ohm-CM/ft. or microhm-CM)

A mil equals 0.001 inch; a circular mil is the cross-sectional area of a wire one mil in diameter.

The specific resistance is a constant that depends on the material of which the wire is made. *Table 1* shows the properties of various wire conductors.

Table 1 shows that at 75°F, a one-mil diameter, pure annealed copper wire that is one foot long has a resistance of 10.351 ohms; while a one-mil diameter, one-foot-long aluminum wire has a resistance of 16.758 ohms. Temperature is important in determining the resistance of a wire. The hotter a wire, the greater its resistance.

Table 1 Conductor Properties

| Metal | Specific Resistance (Resistance of 1 CM/ft. in ohms) | |
	32°F or 0°C	75°F or 23.8°C
Silver, pure annealed	8.831	9.674
Copper, pure annealed	9.390	10.351
Copper, annealed	9.590	10.505
Copper, hard-drawn	9.810	10.745
Gold	13.216	14.404
Aluminum	15.219	16.758
Zinc	34.595	37.957
Iron	54.529	62.643

4.2.0 Ohm's Law

Ohm's law defines the relationship between current, voltage, and resistance. There are three ways to express Ohm's law mathematically.

- The current in a circuit is equal to the voltage applied to the circuit divided by the resistance of the circuit:

$$I = \frac{E}{R}$$

- The resistance of a circuit is equal to the voltage applied to the circuit divided by the current in the circuit:

$$R = \frac{E}{I}$$

- The applied voltage to a circuit is equal to the product of the current and the resistance of the circuit:

$$E = I \times R = IR$$

Where:

I = current (amperes)

R = resistance (ohms)

E = voltage or emf (volts)

If any two of the quantities E, I, or R are known, the third can be calculated.

The Ohm's law equations can be memorized and practiced effectively by using an Ohm's law circle, as shown in *Figure 5*. To find the equation for E, I, or R when two quantities are known, cover the unknown third quantity. The other two quantities in the circle will indicate how the covered quantity may be found.

Example 1:
Find I when E = 120V and R = 30Ω.

$$I = \frac{E}{R}$$

$$I = \frac{120V}{30\Omega}$$

$$I = 4A$$

This formula shows that in a DC circuit, current (is directly proportional to voltage (E) and inversely proportional to resistance (R).

Example 2:
Find R when E = 240V and I = 20A.

$$R = \frac{E}{I}$$

$$R = \frac{240V}{20A}$$

$$R = 12\Omega$$

Example 3:
Find E when I = 15A and R = 8Ω.

$$E = I \times R$$
$$E = 15A \times 8\Omega$$
$$E = 120V$$

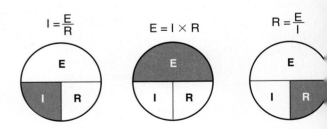

	LETTER SYMBOL	UNIT OF MEASUREMENT
CURRENT	I	AMPERES (A)
RESISTANCE	R	OHMS (Ω)
VOLTAGE	E	VOLTS (V)

104F05.EPS

Figure 5 ◆ Ohm's law circle.

.0.0 ◆ SCHEMATIC REPRESENTATION OF CIRCUIT ELEMENTS

simple electric circuit is shown in both pictorial nd **schematic** forms in *Figure 6*. The schematic di-;ram is a shorthand way to draw an electric cir-uit, and circuits are usually represented in this ay. In addition to the connecting wire, three mponents are shown symbolically: the battery, e switch, and the lamp. Note the positive (+) nd negative (−) markings in both the pictorial nd schematic representations of the battery. The hematic components represent the pictorial mponents in a simplified manner. A schematic agram is one that shows, by means of graphic mbols, the electrical connections and functions the different parts of a circuit.

The standard graphic symbols for commonly sed electrical and electronic components are own in *Figure 7*.

6.0.0 ◆ RESISTORS

The function of a resistor is to offer a particular re-sistance to current flow. For a given current and known resistance, the change in voltage across the component, or **voltage drop**, can be predicted us-ing Ohm's law. Voltage drop refers to a specific amount of voltage used, or developed, by that component. An example is a very basic circuit of a 10V battery and a single resistor in a series circuit. The voltage drop across that resistor is 10V be-cause it is the only component in the circuit and all voltage must be dropped across that resistor. Sim-ilarly, for a given applied voltage, the current that flows may be predetermined by selection of the resistor value. The required power dissipation largely dictates the construction and physical size of a resistor.

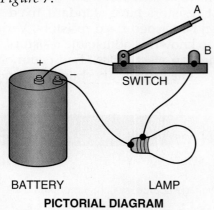

BATTERY   LAMP
PICTORIAL DIAGRAM

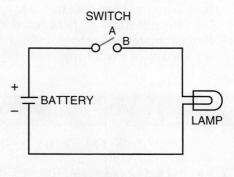

SCHEMATIC DIAGRAM

104F06.EPS

gure 6 ◆ Simple electrical symbols.

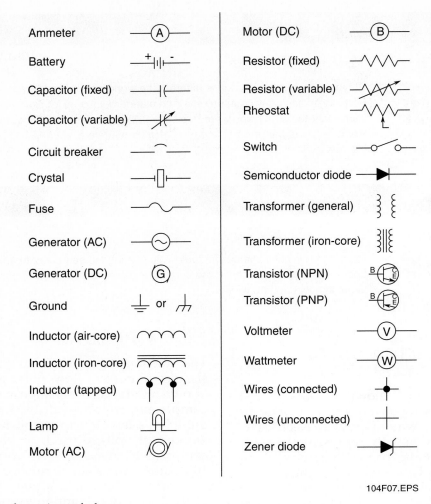

Figure 7 ◆ Standard schematic symbols.

The two most common types of electronic resistors are wire-wound and carbon composition construction. A typical wire-wound resistor consists of a length of nickel wire wound on a ceramic tube and covered with porcelain. Low-resistance connecting wires are provided, and the resistance value is usually printed on the side of the component. *Figure 8* illustrates the construction of typical resistors. Carbon composition resistors are constructed by molding mixtures of powdered carbon and insulating materials into a cylindrical shape. An outer sheath of insulating material affords mechanical and electrical protection, and copper connecting wires are provided at each end. Carbon composition resistors are smaller and less expensive than the wire-wound type. However, the wire-wound type is the more rugged of the two and is able to survive much larger power dissipations than the carbon composition type.

Most resistors have standard fixed values, so they can be termed fixed resistors. Variable resistors, also known as adjustable resistors, are used a great deal in electronics. Two common symbols for a variable resistor are shown in *Figure 9*.

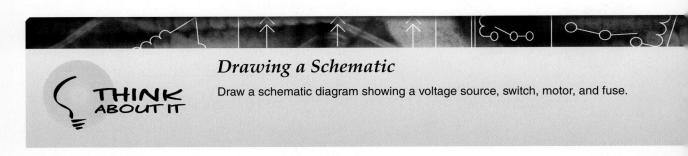

Drawing a Schematic

Draw a schematic diagram showing a voltage source, switch, motor, and fuse.

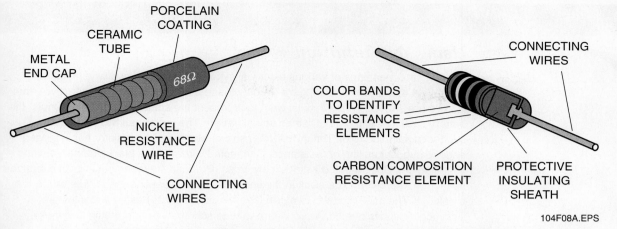

METAL END CAP
CERAMIC TUBE
PORCELAIN COATING
68Ω
NICKEL RESISTANCE WIRE
CONNECTING WIRES

CONNECTING WIRES
COLOR BANDS TO IDENTIFY RESISTANCE ELEMENTS
CARBON COMPOSITION RESISTANCE ELEMENT
PROTECTIVE INSULATING SHEATH

104F08A.EPS

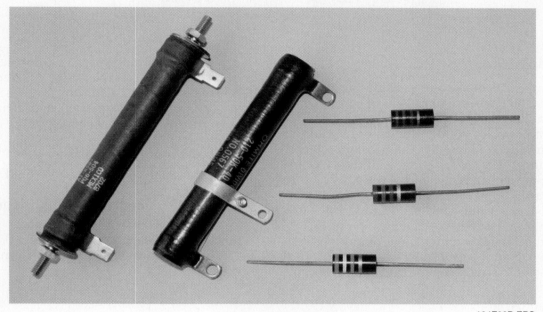

104F08B.EPS

Figure 8 ◆ Common resistors.

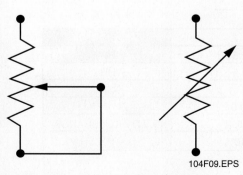

104F09.EPS

Figure 9 ◆ Symbols used for variable resistors.

A variable resistor consists of a coil of closely wound insulated resistance wire formed into a partial circle. The coil has a low-resistance terminal at each end, and a third terminal is connected to a movable contact with a shaft adjustment facility. The movable contact can be set to any point on a connecting track that extends over one (uninsulated) edge of the coil.

Using the adjustable contact, the resistance from either end terminal to the center terminal may be adjusted from zero to the maximum coil resistance.

Another type of variable resistor is known as a decade resistance box. This is a laboratory component that contains precise values of switched series-connected resistors.

 INSIDE TRACK

Using Your Intuition

Learning the meanings of various electrical symbols may seem overwhelming, but if you take a moment to study *Figure 7*, you will see that most of them are intuitive—that is, they are shaped (in a symbolic way) to represent the actual object. For example, the battery shows + and −, just like an actual battery. The motor has two arms that suggest a spinning rotor. The transformer shows two coils. The resistor has a jagged edge to suggest pulling or resistance. Connected wires have a black dot that reminds you of solder. Unconnected wires simply cross. The fuse stretches out in both directions as though to provide extra slack in the line. The circuit breaker shows a line with a break in it. The capacitor shows a gap. The variable resistor has an arrow like a swinging compass needle. As you learn to read schematics, take the time to make mental connections between the symbol and the object it represents.

6.1.0 Resistor Color Codes

Because carbon composition resistors are physically small (some are less than 1 cm in length), it is not convenient to print the resistance value on the side. Instead, a color code in the form of colored bands is employed to identify the resistance value and tolerance. The color code is illustrated in *Figure 10*. Starting from one end of the resistor, the first two bands identify the first and second digits of the resistance value, and the third band indicates the number of zeros. An exception to this is when the third band is either silver or gold, which indicates a 0.01 or 0.1 multiplier, respectively. The fourth band is always either silver or gold, and in

this position, silver indicates a ± 10% tolerance and gold indicates a ± 5% tolerance. Where no fourth band is present, the resistor tolerance is ± 20%.

We can put this information to practical use by determining the range of values for the carbon resistor in *Figure 11*.

The color code for this resistor is as follows:

- Brown = 1, black = 0, red = 2, gold = a tolerance of ± 5%
- First digit = 1, second digit = 0, number of zeros (2) = 1,000Ω

Since this resistor has a value of 1,000Ω ± 5%, the resistor can range in value from 950Ω to 1,050Ω.

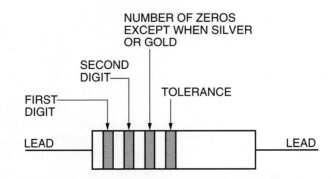

0	BLACK	7	VIOLET	
1	BROWN	8	GREY	
2	RED	9	WHITE	
3	ORANGE	0.1	GOLD	
4	YELLOW	0.01	SILVER	
5	GREEN	5%	GOLD – TOLERANCE	
6	BLUE	10%	SILVER – TOLERANCE	

104F10.EPS

Figure 10 ◆ Resistor color codes.

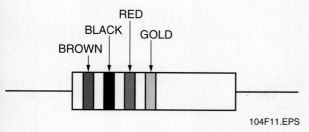

BROWN BLACK RED GOLD

104F11.EPS

Figure 11 ◆ Sample color codes on a fixed resistor.

.0.0 ◆ MEASURING VOLTAGE, CURRENT, AND RESISTANCE

Working with electricity requires making accurate measurements. This section will discuss the basic meters used to measure voltage, current, and resistance: the **voltmeter**, **ammeter**, and **ohmmeter**.

WARNING!

Only qualified individuals may use these meters. Consult your company's safety policy for applicable rules.

.1.0 Basic Meter Operation

When troubleshooting or testing equipment, you will need various meters to check for proper circuit voltages, currents, and resistances and to determine if the wiring is defective. Meters are used in repairing, maintaining, and troubleshooting electrical circuits and equipment. The best and most expensive measuring instrument is of no use to you unless you know what you are measuring and what each reading indicates. Remember that the purpose of a meter is to measure quantities existing within a circuit. For this reason, when the meter is connected to a circuit, it must not change the condition of the circuit.

The three basic electrical quantities discussed in this section are current, voltage, and resistance.

Actually, it is really current that causes the meter to respond even when voltage or resistance is being measured. In a basic meter, the measurement of current can be calibrated to indicate almost any electrical quantity based on the principle of Ohm's law. The amount of current that flows through a meter is determined by the voltage applied to the meter and the resistance of the meter, as stated by $I = E/R$.

For a given meter resistance, different values of applied voltage will cause specific values of current to flow. Although the meter actually measures current, the meter scale can be calibrated in units of voltage. Similarly, for a given applied voltage, different values of resistance will cause specific values of current to flow; therefore, the meter scale can also be calibrated in units of resistance rather than current. The same holds true for power, since power is proportional to current, as stated by $P = EI$. It is on this principle that the meter was developed and its construction allows for the measurement of various parameters by actually measuring current.

You must understand the purpose and function of each individual piece of test equipment and any limitations associated with it. It is also extremely important that you understand how to safely use each piece of equipment. If you understand the capabilities of the test equipment, you can better use the equipment, better understand the indications on the equipment, and know what substitute or backup meters can be used.

7.2.0 Voltmeter

A simple voltmeter consists of the meter movement in series with the internal resistance of the voltmeter itself. For example, a meter with a 50-microamp (μA) meter movement and a 1,000Ω internal resistance can be used to directly measure voltages up to 0.05V, as shown in *Figure 12*. (The prefix **micro** means one-millionth.) When the meter is placed across the voltage source, a current

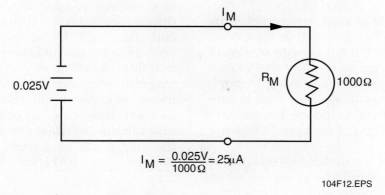

$$I_M = \frac{0.025V}{1000\,\Omega} = 25\mu A$$

104F12.EPS

Figure 12 ◆ Simple voltmeter.

determined by the internal resistance of the meter flows through the meter movement. A voltmeter's internal resistance is typically high to minimize meter loading effects on the source.

To measure larger voltages, a multiplier resistor is used. This increased series resistance limits the current that can flow through the meter movement, thus extending the range of the meter.

To avoid damage to the meter movement, the following precautions should be observed when using a voltmeter:

- Always set the full-scale voltage of the meter to be larger than the expected voltage to be measured.
- Always ensure that the internal resistance of the voltmeter is much greater than the resistance of the component to be measured. This means that the current it takes to drive the voltmeter (about 50 microamps) should be a negligible fraction of the current flowing through the circuit element being measured.
- If you are unsure of the level of the voltage to be measured, take a reading at the highest range of the voltmeter and progressively (step-by-step) lower the range until the reading is obtained.

In most commercial voltmeters, the internal resistance is expressed by the ohms-per-volt rating of the meter. A typical meter has a rating of 20,000 ohms-per-volt with a 50-microamp movement. This quantity tells what the internal resistance of the meter is on any particular full-scale setting. In general, the meter's internal resistance is the ohms-per-volt rating multiplied by the full-scale voltage. The higher the ohms-per-volt rating, the higher the internal resistance of the meter, and the smaller the effect of the meter on the circuit.

7.3.0 Ammeter

A current meter, usually called an ammeter, is used by placing the meter in series with the wire through which the current is flowing. This method of connection is shown in *Figure 13*. Notice how the magnitude of load current will flow through the ammeter. Because of this, an ammeter's internal resistance must be low to minimize the circuit-loading effects as seen by the source. Also, high current magnitudes flowing through an ammeter can damage it. For this reason, ammeter shunts are employed to reduce the ammeter circuit current to a fraction of the current flowing through the load.

To avoid damage to the meter movement, the following precautions should be observed when taking current measurements with an ammeter:

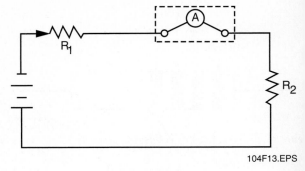

Figure 13 ◆ Ammeter connection.

- Always check the polarity of the ammeter. Make certain that the meter is connected to the circuit so that electrons flow into the negative lead and out of the positive lead. It is easy to tell which is the positive lead because it is normally red. The negative lead is usually black.
- Always set the full-scale deflection of the meter to be larger than the expected current. To be safe, set the full-scale current several times larger than the expected current, and then slowly increase the meter sensitivity to the appropriate scale.
- Always connect the ammeter in series with the circuit element through which the current to be measured is flowing. Never connect the ammeter in parallel. When an ammeter is connected across a constant-potential source of appreciable voltage, the low internal resistance of the meter bypasses the circuit resistance. This results in the application of the source voltage directly to the meter terminals. The resulting excess current will burn out the meter coil.

7.4.0 Ohmmeter

An ohmmeter is used to measure resistance and check continuity. The deflection of the pointer of an ohmmeter is controlled by the amount of battery current passing through the coil. Current flow depends on the applied voltage and the circuit resistance. By applying a constant source voltage to the circuit under test, the resultant current flow depends only on circuit resistance. The magnitude of current will create meter movement. By knowing the relationship between current and resistance, an ohmmeter's scale can be calibrated to indicate circuit resistance based on the magnitude of current for a constant source voltage. Refer to *Figure 14*, a simple ohmmeter circuit.

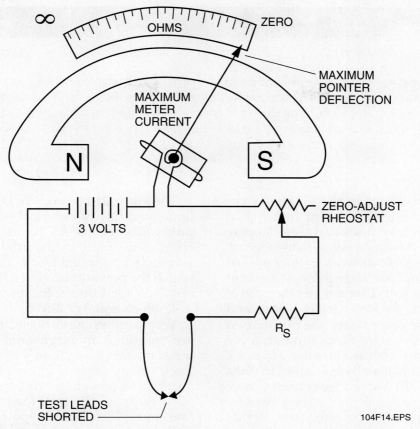

Figure 14 ◆ Simple ohmmeter circuit.

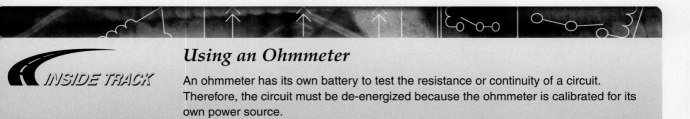

Using an Ohmmeter

INSIDE TRACK

An ohmmeter has its own battery to test the resistance or continuity of a circuit. Therefore, the circuit must be de-energized because the ohmmeter is calibrated for its own power source.

0.0 ◆ ELECTRICAL POWER

ower is defined as the rate of doing work. This equivalent to the rate at which energy is used r dissipated. Electrons passing through a resis- nce dissipate energy in the form of heat. In ectrical circuits, power is measured in units lled **watts (W).** The power in watts equals the te of energy conversion. One watt of power quals the work done in one second by one volt f potential difference in moving one coulomb of harge. One coulomb per second is an ampere; erefore, power in watts equals the product of mperes times volts.

The work done in an electrical circuit can be seful work or it can be wasted work. In both cases, the rate at which the work is done is still measured in power. The turning of an electric motor is useful work. On the other hand, the heating of wires or resistors in a circuit is wasted work, since no useful function is performed by the heat.

The unit of electrical work is the joule. This is the amount of work done by one coulomb flowing through a potential difference of one volt. Thus, if five coulombs flow through a potential difference of one volt, five joules of work are done. The time it takes these coulombs to flow through the potential difference has no bearing on the amount of work done.

Power

We take electrical power for granted, never stopping to think how surprising it is that a flow of submicroscopic electrons can pump thousands of gallons of water or illuminate a skyscraper. Our lives now constantly rely on the ability of the electron to do work. Think about your day up to this moment. How has electrical power shaped your experience?

It is more convenient when working with circuits to think of amperes of current rather than coulombs. As previously discussed, one ampere equals one coulomb passing a point in one second. Using amperes, one joule of work is done in one second when one ampere moves through a potential difference of one volt. This rate of one joule of work in one second is the basic unit of power, and is called a watt. Therefore, a watt is the power used when one ampere of current flows through a potential difference of one volt, as shown in *Figure 15*.

Mechanical power is usually measured in units of horsepower (hp). To convert from horsepower to watts, multiply the number of horsepower by 746. To convert from watts to horsepower, divide the number of watts by 746. Conversions for common units of power are given in *Table 2*.

The kilowatt-hour (kWh) is commonly used for large amounts of electrical work or energy. (The prefix **kilo** means one thousand.) The amount is calculated simply as the product of the power in kilowatts multiplied by the time in hours during which the power is used. If a light bulb uses 300W or 0.3kW for 4 hours, the amount of energy is 0.3 × 4, which equals 1.2kWh.

Very large amounts of electrical work or energy are measured in megawatts (MW). (The prefix **mega** means one million.)

Electricity usage is figured in kilowatt-hours of energy. The power line voltage is fairly constant at 120V. Suppose the total load current in the main line equals 20A. Then the power in watts from the 120V line is:

$$P = 120V \times 20A$$
$$P = 2,400W \text{ or } 2.4kW$$

If this power is used for five hours, then the energy of work supplied equals:

$$2.4 \times 5 = 12kWh$$

Figure 15 ◆ One watt.

Table 2	Conversion Table
1,000 watts (W) = 1 kilowatt (kW)	
1,000,000 watts (W) = 1 megawatt (MW)	
1,000 kilowatts (kW) = 1 megawatt (MW)	
1 watt (W) = 0.00134 horsepower (hp)	
1 horsepower (hp) = 746 watts (W)	

Resistors

Which of the following items are resistors?

- Hair dryer
- Incandescent light bulb
- Switch
- Receptacle
- Circuit breaker

1.0 Power Equation

hen one ampere flows through a difference of
o volts, two watts must be used. In other words,
e number of watts used is equal to the number
amperes of current times the potential differ-
ce. This is expressed in equation form as:

$$P = I \times E \text{ or } P = IE$$

here:

P = power used in watts

I = current in amperes

E = potential difference in volts

e equation is sometimes called Ohm's law for
wer, because it is similar to Ohm's law. This
uation is used to find the power consumed in a
cuit or load when the values of current and
ltage are known. The second form of the equa-
n is used to find the voltage when the power
d current are known:

$$E = \frac{P}{I}$$

e third form of the equation is used to find the
rrent when the power and voltage are known:

$$I = \frac{P}{E}$$

sing these three equations, the power, voltage,
current in a circuit can be calculated whenever
y two of the values are already known.

ample 1:

lculate the power in a circuit where the source
100V produces 2A in a 50Ω resistance.

$$P = IE$$
$$P = 2 \times 100$$
$$P = 200W$$

is means the source generates 200W of power
hile the resistance dissipates 200W in the form of
eat.

ample 2:

alculate the source voltage in a circuit that con-
mes 1,200W at a current of 5A.

$$E = \frac{P}{I}$$

$$E = \frac{1,200}{5}$$

$$E = 240V$$

Example 3:
Calculate the current in a circuit that consumes
600W with a source voltage of 120V.

$$I = \frac{P}{E}$$

$$I = \frac{600}{120}$$

$$I = 5A$$

Components that use the power dissipated in
their resistance are generally rated in terms of
power. The power is rated at normal operating
voltage, which is usually 120V. For instance, an
appliance that draws 5A at 120V would dissipate
600W. The rating for the appliance would then be
600W/120V.

To calculate I or R for components rated in
terms of power at a specified voltage, it may be
convenient to use the power formula in different
forms. There are actually three basic power formulas, but each can be rearranged into two other
forms for a total of nine combinations:

$$P = IE \qquad P = I^2R \qquad P = \frac{E^2}{R}$$

$$I = \frac{P}{E} \qquad R = \frac{P}{I^2} \qquad R = \frac{E^2}{P}$$

$$E = \frac{P}{I} \qquad I = \sqrt{\frac{P}{R}} \qquad E = \sqrt{PR}$$

Note that all of these formulas are based on Ohm's
law (E = IR) and the power formula (P = I × E).
Figure 16 shows all of the applicable power, voltage, resistance, and current equations.

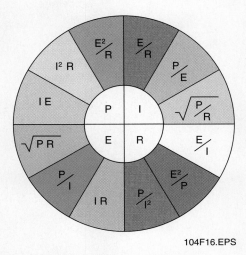

104F16.EPS

Figure 16 ◆ Expanded Ohm's law circle.

Measuring Watts

Electricians are less interested in measuring watts than in measuring amperage and resistance. Who would be most interested in power measurements? What is a common example of a device used to measure watts?

8.2.0 Power Rating of Resistors

If too much current flows through a resistor, the heat caused by the current will damage or destroy the resistor. This heat is caused by I^2R heating, which is power loss expressed in watts. Therefore, every resistor is given a wattage, or power rating, to show how much I^2R heating it can take before it burns out. This means that a resistor with a power rating of one watt will burn out if it is used in a circuit where the current causes it to dissipate heat at a rate greater than one watt.

If the power rating of a resistor is known, the maximum current it can carry is found by using an equation derived from $P = I^2R$:

$$P = I^2R \text{ becomes } I^2 = P/R,$$
$$\text{which becomes } I = \sqrt{P/R}$$

Using this equation, find the maximum curre that can be carried by a 1Ω resistor with a pow rating of 4W:

$$I = \sqrt{P/R} = \sqrt{4/1} = 2 \text{ amperes}$$

If such a resistor conducts more than 2 amperes, will dissipate more than its rated power and bu out.

Power ratings assigned by resistor manufa turers are usually based on the resistors bein mounted in an open location where there is fr air circulation, and where the temperature is n higher than 104°F (40°C). Therefore, if a resistor mounted in a small, crowded, enclosed space, where the temperature is higher than 104°F, the is a good chance it will burn out even before power rating is exceeded. Also, some resistors a designed to be attached to a chassis or frame th will carry away the heat.

Putting It All Together

Notice the common electrical devices in the building you're in. What is their wattage rating? How much current do they draw? How would you test their voltage or amperage?

1. A type of subatomic particle with a negative charge is a(n) _____.
   a. proton
   b. neutron
   c. electron
   d. nucleus

2. A type of subatomic particle with a positive charge is a(n) _____.
   a. proton
   b. neutron
   c. electron
   d. nucleus

3. Like charges _____ each other.
   a. attract
   b. repel
   c. have no effect on
   d. complement

4. An electron has _____ coulombs of charge.
   a. 1.6×10^{-9}
   b. 1.6×10^{9}
   c. 1.6×10^{19}
   d. 1.6×10^{-19}

5. The quantity that Ohm's law does not express a relationship for in an electrical circuit is _____.
   a. charge
   b. resistance
   c. voltage
   d. current

6. The color band that represents tolerance on a resistor is the _____.
   a. 4th band
   b. 3rd band
   c. 2nd band
   d. 1st band

7. A resistor with a color code of red/red/orange indicates a value of _____.
   a. 22,000 ohms
   b. 66 ohms
   c. 223 ohms
   d. 220 ohms

8. An ammeter is placed in _____ with the circuit being tested.
   a. parallel
   b. series

9. The basic unit of power is the _____.
   a. volt
   b. ampere
   c. coulomb
   d. watt

10. The power in a circuit with 120 volts and 5 amps is _____.
    a. 24 watts
    b. 600 watts
    c. 6,000 watts
    d. ¼₄ watt

Summary

The relationships among current, voltage, resistance, and power are consistent for all types of DC circuits and can be calculated using Ohm's law and Ohm's law for power. Understanding and being able to apply these concepts is necessary for effective circuit analysis and troubleshooting.

Notes

Trade Terms Quiz

1. A(n) _____ is an instrument for measuring electrical current.

2. Measured in amperes, _____ is the flow of electrons in a circuit.

3. A(n) _____ is the force required to push a current of one ampere through a resistance of one ohm.

4. Voltage is measured with a(n) _____.

5. One volt applied across one ohm of resistance causes a current flow of one _____.

6. One volt is the potential difference between two points for which one coulomb of electricity will do one _____ of work.

7. A(n) _____ is the common unit used for specifying the size of a given charge.

8. _____ is the driving force that makes current flow in a circuit.

9. The basic unit of measurement for electrical power is the _____.

10. The _____ is the smallest particle of an element that will still retain the properties of that element.

11. The _____ is the center of an atom.

12. Found in the nuclei of atoms, _____ are electrically positive particles and _____ are electrically neutral particles.

13. The outermost ring of electrons orbiting the nucleus of an atom is known as the _____.

14. A(n) _____ is a negatively charged particle that orbits the nucleus of an atom.

15. _____ is any substance that has mass and occupies space.

16. The prefix used to indicate one thousand is _____.

17. The prefix used to indicate one million is _____.

18. The prefix used to indicate one-millionth is _____.

19. Consisting of two or more cells, _____ convert chemical energy into electrical energy.

20. A(n) _____ is a complete path for current flow.

21. Any material that offers very little resistance to current flow is known as a(n) _____.

22. A(n) _____ is a material that offers resistance to current flow.

23. The basic unit of measurement for resistance is the _____.

24. The instrument that is used to measure resistance is called a(n) _____.

25. _____ is a statement of the relationship between current, voltage, and resistance in an electrical circuit.

26. _____ is the rate of doing work or the rate at which energy is used or dissipated.

27. Measured in ohms, _____ is the electrical property that opposes the flow of current through a circuit.

28. A(n) _____ is a component that normally opposes current flow in a DC circuit.

29. A(n) _____ is a drawing in which symbols are used to represent the components in a system.

30. A(n) _____ circuit has only one route for current flow.

31. The change in voltage across a component is called _____.

Trade Terms

Ammeter	Electron	Nucleus	Schematic
Ampere (A)	Insulator	Ohm (Ω)	Series circuit
Atom	Joule (J)	Ohmmeter	Valence shell
Battery	Kilo	Ohm's law	Volt (V)
Circuit	Matter	Power	Voltage
Conductor	Mega	Protons	Voltage drop
Coulomb	Micro	Resistance	Voltmeter
Current	Neutrons	Resistor	Watt (W)

E. L. Jarrell

Associated Builders and Contractors

arlin Layne (E.L.) Jarrell is another prime example of master electrician giving back to the electrical mmunity by teaching and mentoring.

After serving in the United States Army, E.L. went work for Cities Services, now known as CITGO. He ayed at CITGO for 38 years, finally retiring in 1995. was during his employment at CITGO that he first ceived apprenticeship training in the electrical field.

While at CITGO, E.L. worked as a process unit perator before moving to the electrical department. hile there, he worked as a trainee electrician for ree years until he became a first-class electrician. A w years later, he was promoted to temporary pervisor, planning and scheduling shut-down aintenance. In 1983, he took and passed the Block aster Electrician test for the City of Lake Charles, puisiana. In 1997, E.L. became involved with ssociated Builders and Contractors (ABC).

E.L. is currently the Electrical Department Head r the ABC Training Center, where he works in the b, overseeing students doing hands-on electrical ork. During his first semester teaching at the ABC

Training Center, it became clear to E.L. that many students simply had no time to study because they worked 10-hour days, drove over 100 miles to work, and had family obligations. In response, E.L. began an in-class study guide. He encouraged students to form study groups, and he gave students time to study in class.

E.L. was an instrumental member of NCCER's Technical Review Committee, which completely rewrote all four levels of NCCER's Electrical Curriculum. In addition, E.L. is currently a member of both NCCER's National Skills Assessment Written Test Committee and the Performance Verification Packet for Industrial Electricians Committee.

E.L. has decided to give back to the electrical community with his expertise and mentoring. Many of E.L.'s students have become his personal friends. He says, "At this point in my life, I just want to continue being the best electrical instructor that I can be and share some of my knowledge and experience with my students and hope that I can make a difference in their lives and careers."

Trade Terms
Introduced in This Module

Ammeter: An instrument for measuring electrical current.

Ampere (A): A unit of electrical current. For example, one volt across one ohm of resistance causes a current flow of one ampere.

Atom: The smallest particle to which an element may be divided and still retain the properties of the element.

Battery: A DC voltage source consisting of two or more cells that convert chemical energy into electrical energy.

Circuit: A complete path for current flow.

Conductor: A material that offers very little resistance to current flow.

Coulomb: An electrical charge equal to 6.25×10^{18} electrons or 6,250,000,000,000,000,000 electrons. A coulomb is the common unit of quantity used for specifying the size of a given charge.

Current: The movement, or flow, of electrons in a circuit. Current (I) is measured in amperes.

Electron: A negatively charged particle that orbits the nucleus of an atom.

Insulator: A material that offers resistance to current flow.

Joule (J): A unit of measurement that represents one newton-meter (Nm), which is a unit of measure for doing work.

Kilo: A prefix used to indicate one thousand; for example, one kilowatt is equal to one thousand watts.

Matter: Any substance that has mass and occupies space.

Mega: A prefix used to indicate one million; for example, one megawatt is equal to one million watts.

Micro: A prefix used to indicate one-millionth; for example, one microwatt is equal to one-millionth of a watt.

Neutrons: Electrically neutral particles (neither positive nor negative) that have the same mass as a proton and are found in the nucleus of an atom.

Nucleus: The center of an atom. It contains the protons and neutrons of the atom.

Ohm (Ω): The basic unit of measurement for resistance.

Ohmmeter: An instrument used for measuring resistance.

Ohm's law: A statement of the relationships among current, voltage, and resistance in an electrical circuit: current (I) equals voltage (E) divided by resistance (R). Generally expressed as a mathematical formula: $I = E/R$.

Power: The rate of doing work or the rate at which energy is used or dissipated. Electrical power is the rate of doing electrical work. Electrical power is measured in watts.

Protons: The smallest positively charged particles of an atom. Protons are contained in the nucleus of an atom.

Resistance: An electrical property that opposes the flow of current through a circuit. Resistance (R) is measured in ohms.

Resistor: Any device in a circuit that resists the flow of electrons.

Schematic: A type of drawing in which symbols are used to represent the components in a system.

Series circuit: A circuit with only one path for current flow.

Valence shell: The outermost ring of electrons that orbit about the nucleus of an atom.

Volt (V): The unit of measurement for voltage (electromotive force). One volt is equivalent to the force required to produce a current of one ampere through a resistance of one ohm.

Voltage: The driving force that makes current flow in a circuit. Voltage (E) is also referred to as electromotive force or potential.

Voltage drop: The change in voltage across a component that is caused by the current flowing through it and the amount of resistance opposing it.

Voltmeter: An instrument for measuring voltage. The resistance of the voltmeter is fixed. When the voltmeter is connected to a circuit, the current passing through the meter will be directly proportional to the voltage at the connection points.

Watt (W): The basic unit of measurement for electrical power.

Additional Resources

This module is intended to present thorough resources for task training. The following reference works are suggested for further study. These are optional materials for continued education rather than for task training.

Electronics Fundamentals: Circuits, Devices, and Applications, Thomas L. Floyd. New York: Prentice Hall.

Principles of Electric Circuits, Thomas L. Floyd. New York: Prentice Hall.

The NCCER makes every effort to keep these textbooks up-to-date and free of technical errors. We appreciate your help in this process. If you have an idea for improving this textbook, or if you find an error, a typographical mistake, or an inaccuracy in NCCER's *Contren®* textbooks, please write us, using this form or a photocopy. Be sure to include the exact module number, page number, a detailed description, and the correction, if applicable. Your input will be brought to the attention of the Technical Review Committee. Thank you for your assistance.

Instructors – If you found that additional materials were necessary in order to teach this module effectively, please let us know so that we may include them in the Equipment/Materials list in the Annotated Instructor's Guide.

Write: Product Development
          National Center for Construction Education and Research
          P.O. Box 141104, Gainesville, FL 32614-1104

Fax: 352-334-0932

E-mail: curriculum@nccer.org

Craft _____   Module Name _____

Copyright Date _____   Module Number _____   Page Number(s) _____

Description _____

_____

_____

_____

(Optional) Correction _____

_____

(Optional) Your Name and Address _____

_____

_____

Alamo Data Center

Built in Fort Lauderdale, Florida, the Alamo Data Center project was unique because it required stringent clean-room procedures while the electrical work was being done. This was to protect the integrity of the facility and equipment used. Food and drink were prohibited, special uniforms were required, and the electricians were not even allowed to chew gum.

26105-05
Electrical Theory Two

Topics to be presented in this module include:

Overview

Troubleshooting complex electrical or electronic circuitry requires an ad-vanced understanding of electrical theory. When a complex circuit does not re-spond as designed, the electrician or technician must safely locate, determine and repair the problem. To accomplish this task in a relatively short period and with reasonable success, the electrician must apply both fundamental con-cepts, such as Ohm's law, and more advanced concepts, such as Kirchhoff's laws. Studying advanced electrical theory is the only way to know when and where to apply such laws.

Objectives

When you have completed this module, you will be able to do the following:

1. Explain the basic characteristics of a series circuit.
2. Explain the basic characteristics of a parallel circuit.
3. Explain the basic characteristics of a series-parallel circuit.
4. Calculate, using Kirchhoff's voltage law, the voltage drop in series, parallel, and series-parallel circuits.
5. Calculate, using Kirchhoff's current law, the total current in parallel and series-parallel circuits.
6. Find the total amount of resistance in a series circuit.
7. Find the total amount of resistance in a parallel circuit.
8. Find the total amount of resistance in a series-parallel circuit.

Trade Terms

Kirchhoff's current law
Kirchhoff's voltage law
Parallel circuits
Series circuits
Series-parallel circuits

Required Trainee Materials

1. Paper and pencil
2. Appropriate personal protective equipment

Prerequisites

Before you begin this module, it is recommended that you successfully complete *Core Curriculum* and *Electrical Level One*, Modules 26101-05 through 26104-05.

This course map shows all of the modules in *Electrical Level One*. The suggested training order begins at the bottom and proceeds up. Skill levels increase as you advance on the course map. The local Training Program Sponsor may adjust the training order.

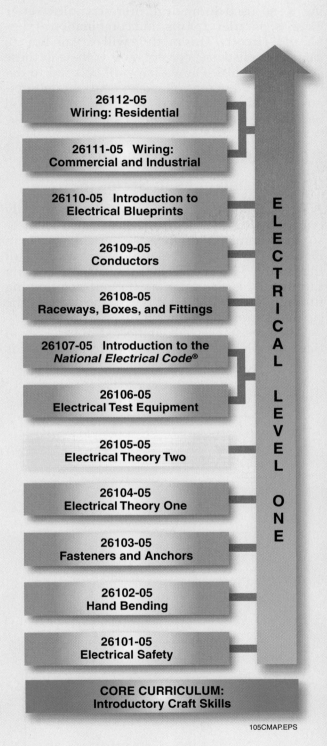

26112-05
Wiring: Residential

26111-05 Wiring:
Commercial and Industrial

26110-05   Introduction to
Electrical Blueprints

26109-05
Conductors

26108-05
Raceways, Boxes, and Fittings

26107-05   Introduction to the
National Electrical Code®

26106-05
Electrical Test Equipment

26105-05
Electrical Theory Two

26104-05
Electrical Theory One

26103-05
Fasteners and Anchors

26102-05
Hand Bending

26101-05
Electrical Safety

CORE CURRICULUM:
Introductory Craft Skills

ELECTRICAL LEVEL ONE

105CMAP.EPS

1.0.0 ◆ INTRODUCTION

Ohm's law was explained in the module *Electrical Theory One*. This fundamental concept is now going to be used to analyze more complex **series circuits**, **parallel circuits**, and combination **series-parallel circuits**. This module will explain how to calculate resistance, current, and voltage in these complex circuits. Ohm's law will be used to develop a new law for voltage and current determination. This law, called Kirchhoff's law, will become the new foundation for analyzing circuits.

2.0.0 ◆ RESISTIVE CIRCUITS

2.1.0 Resistances in Series

A series circuit is a circuit in which there is only one path for current flow. Resistance is measured in ohms (Ω). In the series circuit shown in *Figure 1*, the current (I) is the same in all parts of the circuit. This means that the current flowing through R_1 is the same as the current flowing through R_2 and R_3, and it is also the same as the current supplied by the battery.

When resistances are connected in series as in this example, the total resistance in the circuit is equal to the sum of the resistances of all the parts of the circuit:

$$R_T = R_1 + R_2 + R_3$$

Where:

R_T = total resistance
$R_1 + R_2 + R_3$ = resistances in series

Example 1:

The circuit shown in *Figure 2(A)* has 50Ω, 75Ω and 100Ω resistors in series. Find the total resistance of the circuit.

Add the values of the three resistors in series:

$$R_T = R_1 + R_2 + R_3 = 50 + 75 + 100 = 225\Omega$$

Example 2:

The circuit shown in *Figure 2(B)* has three lamps connected in series with the resistances shown. Find the total resistance of the circuit.

Add the values of the three lamp resistances in series:

$$R_T = R_1 + R_2 + R_3 = 20 + 40 + 60 = 120\Omega$$

2.2.0 Resistances in Parallel

The total resistance in a parallel resistive circuit given by the formula:

$$R_T = \frac{1}{\dfrac{1}{R_1} + \dfrac{1}{R_2} + \dfrac{1}{R_3} + \dfrac{1}{R_n}}$$

Where:

R_T = total resistance in parallel
R_1, R_2, R_3, and R_n = branch resistances

Example 1:

Find the total resistance of the 2Ω, 4Ω, and 8Ω resistors in parallel shown in *Figure 3*.

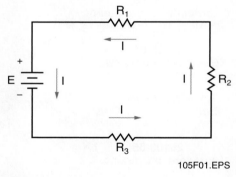

105F01.EPS

Figure 1 ◆ Series circuit.

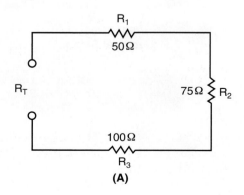

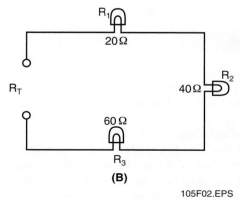

(A)

(B)

105F02.EPS

Figure 2 ◆ Total resistance.

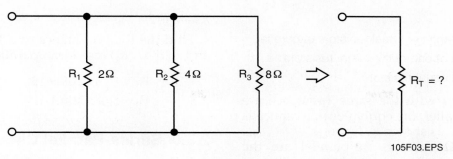

Figure 3 ◆ Parallel branch.

Series Circuits

Simple series circuits are seldom encountered in practical wiring. The only simple series circuit you may recognize is older strands of Christmas lights, in which the entire string went dead when one lamp burned out. Think about what the actual wiring of a series circuit would look like in household receptacles. How would the circuit physically be wired? What kind of illumination would you get if you wired your household receptacles in series and plugged half a dozen lamps into those receptacles?

Write the formula for the three resistances in parallel:

$$R_T = \cfrac{1}{\cfrac{1}{R_1} + \cfrac{1}{R_2} + \cfrac{1}{R_3}}$$

Substitute the resistance values:

$$R_T = \cfrac{1}{\cfrac{1}{2} + \cfrac{1}{4} + \cfrac{1}{8}}$$

$$R_T = \frac{1}{0.5 + 0.25 + 0.125}$$

$$R_T = \frac{1}{0.875}$$

$$R_T = 1.14\Omega$$

Note that when resistances are connected in parallel, the total resistance is always less than the resistance of any single branch. In this case:

$R_T = 1.14\Omega < R_1 = 2\Omega$, $R_2 = 4\Omega$, and $R_3 = 8\Omega$

Example 2:

Add a fourth parallel resistor of 2Ω to the circuit in *Figure 3*. What is the new total resistance, and what is the net effect of adding another resistance in parallel?

Write the formula for four resistances in parallel:

$$R_T = \cfrac{1}{\cfrac{1}{R_1} + \cfrac{1}{R_2} + \cfrac{1}{R_3} + \cfrac{1}{R_4}}$$

Substitute values:

$$R_T = \cfrac{1}{\cfrac{1}{2} + \cfrac{1}{4} + \cfrac{1}{8} + \cfrac{1}{2}}$$

$$R_T = \frac{1}{0.5 + 0.25 + 0.125 + 0.5}$$

$$R_T = \frac{1}{1.375}$$

$$R_T = 0.73\Omega$$

The net effect of adding another resistance in parallel is a reduction of the total resistance from 1.14Ω to 0.73Ω.

2.2.1 Simplified Formulas

The total resistance of *equal* resistors in parallel is equal to the resistance of one resistor divided by the number of resistors:

$$R_T = \frac{R}{N}$$

Where:

R_T = total resistance of equal resistors in parallel

R = resistance of one of the equal resistors

N = number of equal resistors

If two resistors with the same resistance are connected in parallel, the equivalent resistance is half of that value, as shown in *Figure 4*.

The two 200Ω resistors in parallel are the equivalent of one 100Ω resistor; the two 100Ω resistors are the equivalent of one 50Ω resistor; and the two 50Ω resistors are the equivalent of one 25Ω resistor.

When any two unequal resistors are in parallel, it is often easier to calculate the total resistance by multiplying the two resistances and then dividing the product by the sum of the resistances:

$$R_T = \frac{R_1 \times R_2}{R_1 + R_2}$$

Where:

R_T = total resistance of unequal resistors in parallel

R_1, R_2 = two unequal resistors in parallel

Example 1:

Find the total resistance of a 6Ω (R_1) resistor and an 18Ω (R_2) resistor in parallel:

$$R_T = \frac{R_1 \times R_2}{R_1 + R_2} = \frac{6 \times 18}{6 + 18} = \frac{108}{24} = 4.5\Omega$$

Example 2:

Find the total resistance of a 100Ω (R_1) resist and a 150Ω (R_2) resistor in parallel:

$$R_T = \frac{R_1 \times R_2}{R_1 + R_2} = \frac{100 \times 150}{100 + 150} = \frac{15,000}{250} = 60\Omega$$

2.3.0 Series-Parallel Circuits

To find current, voltage, and resistance in seri circuits and parallel circuits is fairly easy. Whe working with either type, use only the rules th apply to that type. In a series-parallel circuit, son parts of the circuit are series connected and oth parts are parallel connected. Thus, in some pa the rules for series circuits apply, and in oth parts, the rules for parallel circuits apply. To an lyze or solve a problem involving a series-parall circuit, it is necessary to recognize which parts the circuit are series connected and which par are parallel connected. This is obvious if the c cuit is simple. Many times, however, the circu must be redrawn, putting it into a form that is ea ier to recognize.

In a series circuit, the current is the same at a points. In a parallel circuit, there are one or mo points where the current divides and flows in se arate branches. In a series-parallel circuit, the are both separate branches and series loads. T easiest way to find out whether a circuit is a seri parallel, or series-parallel circuit is to start at t

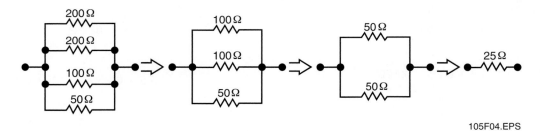

105F04.EPS

Figure 4 ◆ Equal resistances in a parallel circuit.

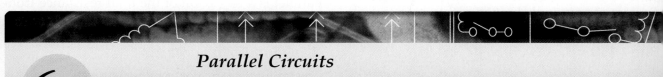

Parallel Circuits

An interesting fact about circuits is the drop in resistance in a parallel circuit as more resistors are added. But this fact does not mean that you can add an endless number of devices, such as lamps, in a parallel circuit. Why not?

Parallel Circuits

Most practical circuits are wired in parallel, like the pole lights shown here.

105PO501.EPS

gative terminal of the power source and trace
e path of current through the circuit back to the
ositive terminal of the power source. If the curnt does not divide anywhere, it is a series circuit.
the current divides into separate branches, but
ere are no series loads, it is a parallel circuit. If
e current divides into separate branches and
ere are also series loads, it is a series-parallel cir-
it. *Figure 5* shows electric lamps connected in se-
es, parallel, and series-parallel circuits.

After determining that a circuit is series-
rallel, redraw the circuit so that the branches
d the series loads are more easily recognized.
is is especially helpful when computing the to-
l resistance of the circuit. *Figure 6* shows resis-
rs connected in a series-parallel circuit and the
uivalent circuit redrawn to simplify it.

2.3.1   *Reducing Series-Parallel Circuits*

Very often, all that is known about a series-
parallel circuit is the applied voltage and the values of the individual resistances. To find the
voltage drop across any of the loads or the current
in any of the branches, the total circuit current
must usually be known. But to find the total current, the total resistance of the circuit must be
known. To find the total resistance, reduce the circuit to its simplest form, which is usually one resistance that forms a series circuit with the voltage
source. This simple series circuit has the equivalent resistance of the series-parallel circuit it was
derived from, and also has the same total current.
There are four basic steps in reducing a series-
parallel circuit:

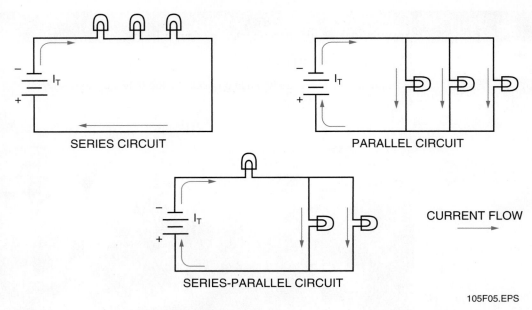

Figure 5 ◆ Series, parallel, and series-parallel circuits.

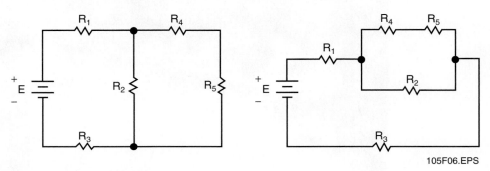

Figure 6 ◆ Redrawing a series-parallel circuit.

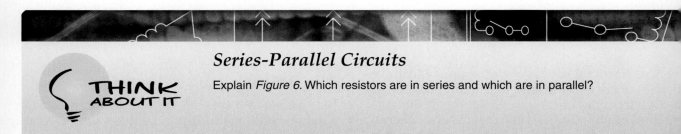

Series-Parallel Circuits

THINK ABOUT IT

Explain *Figure 6*. Which resistors are in series and which are in parallel?

- If necessary, redraw the circuit so that all parallel combinations of resistances and series resistances are easily recognized.
- For each parallel combination of resistances, calculate its effective resistance.
- Replace each of the parallel combinations with one resistance whose value is equal to the effective resistance of that combination. This provides a circuit with all series loads.
- Find the total resistance of this circuit by adding the resistances of all the series loads.

Examine the series-parallel circuit shown *Figure 7* and reduce it to an equivalent seri circuit.

In this circuit, resistors R_2 and R_3 are connecte in parallel, but resistor R_1 is in series with both th battery and the parallel combination of R_2 and R_3 The current I_T leaving the negative terminal of th voltage source travels through resistor R_1 before is divided at the junction of resistors R_1, R_2, and (Point A) to go through the two branches forme by resistors R_2 and R_3.

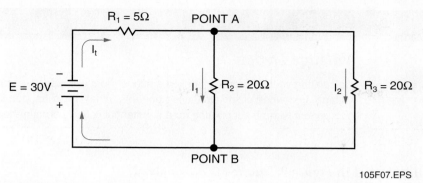

ure 7 ◆ Reducing a series-parallel circuit.

Given the information in *Figure 7*, calculate the
sistance of R_2 and R_3 in parallel and the total retance of the circuit, R_T.
The total resistance of the circuit is the sum of
and the equivalent resistance of R_2 and R_3 in
rallel. To find R_T, first find the resistance of R_2
d R_3 in parallel. Because the two resistances
ve the same value of 20Ω, the resulting equiva-
nt resistance is 10Ω. Therefore, the total resis-
nce (R_T) is 15Ω (5Ω + 10Ω).

4.0 Applying Ohm's Law

4.1 Voltage and Current in Series Circuits

resistive circuits, unknown circuit parameters
n be found by using Ohm's law and the tech-
ques for determining equivalent resistance.
m's law may be applied to an entire series cir-
it or to the individual parts of the circuit.
hen it is used on a particular part of a circuit,
e voltage across that part is equal to the current
that part multiplied by the resistance of that
rt.
For example, given the information in *Figure 8*,
culate the total resistance (R_T) and the total curnt (I_T).
To find R_T:

$$R_T = R_1 + R_2 + R_3$$
$$R_T = 20 + 50 + 120$$
$$R_T = 190Ω$$

To find I_T using Ohm's law:

$$I_T = \frac{E_T}{R_T}$$

$$I_T = \frac{95}{190}$$

$$I_T = 0.5A$$

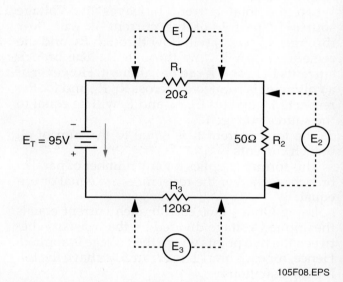

Figure 8 ◆ Calculating voltage drops.

Find the voltage across each resistor. In a series
circuit, the current is the same; that is, I = 0.5A
through each resistor:

$$E_1 = IR_1 = 0.5(20) = 10V$$
$$E_2 = IR_2 = 0.5(50) = 25V$$
$$E_3 = IR_3 = 0.5(120) = 60V$$

The voltages E_1, E_2, and E_3 found for *Figure 8* are
known as voltage drops or IR drops. Their effect is
to reduce the voltage that is available to be applied across the rest of the components in the circuit. The sum of the voltage drops in any series
circuit is always equal to the voltage that is applied to the circuit. The total voltage (E_T) is the
same as the applied voltage and can be verified in
this example (E_T = 10 + 25 + 60 or 95V).

2.4.2 Voltage and Current in Parallel Circuits

A parallel circuit is a circuit in which two or
more components are connected across the same

Voltage Drops

voltage source, as illustrated in *Figure 9*. The resistors R_1, R_2, and R_3 are in parallel with each other and with the battery. Each parallel path is then a branch with its own individual current. When the total current I_T leaves the voltage source E, part I_1 of the current I_T will flow through R_1, part I_2 will flow through R_2, and the remainder I_3 will flow through R_3. The branch currents I_1, I_2, and I_3 can be different. However, if a voltmeter is connected across R_1, R_2, and R_3, the respective voltages E_1, E_2, and E_3 will be equal to the source voltage E.

The total current I_T is equal to the sum of all branch currents.

This formula applies for any number of parallel branches whether the resistances are equal or unequal.

Using Ohm's law, each branch current equals the applied voltage divided by the resistance between the two points where the voltage is applied. Hence, for each branch in *Figure 9* we have the following equations:

$$\text{Branch 1: } I_1 = \frac{E_1}{R_1} = \frac{E}{R_1}$$

$$\text{Branch 2: } I_2 = \frac{E_2}{R_2} = \frac{E}{R_2}$$

$$\text{Branch 3: } I_3 = \frac{E_3}{R_3} = \frac{E}{R_3}$$

With the same applied voltage, any branch that has less resistance allows more current through it than a branch with higher resistance.

Example 1:

The two branches R_1 and R_2, shown in *Figure 10(A)*, across a 110V power line draw a total line current of 20A. Branch R_1 takes 12A. What is the current I_2 in branch R_2?

Transpose to find I_2 and then substitute given values:

$$I_T = I_1 + I_2$$
$$I_2 = I_T - I_1$$
$$I_2 = 20 - 12 = 8A$$

Example 2:

As shown in *Figure 10(B)*, the two branches R_1 and R_2 across a 240V power line draw a total line current of 35A. Branch R_2 takes 20A. What is the current I_1 in branch R_1?

Transpose to find I_1 and then substitute given values:

$$I_T = I_1 + I_2$$
$$I_1 = I_T - I_2$$
$$I_1 = 35 - 20 = 15A$$

2.4.3 Voltage and Current in Series-Parallel Circuits

Series-parallel circuits combine the elements and characteristics of both the series and parallel configurations. By properly applying the equations and methods previously discussed, the values of individual components of the circuit can be determined. *Figure 11* shows a simple series-parallel circuit with a 1.5V battery.

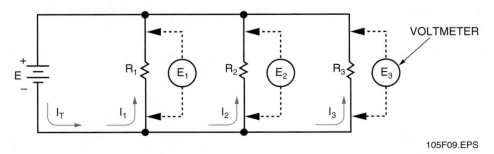

105F09.EPS

Figure 9 ◆ Parallel circuit.

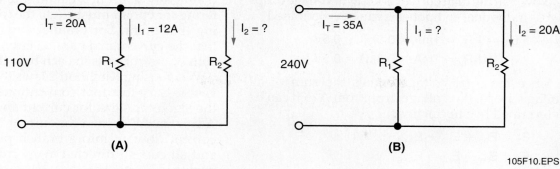

(A)   **(B)**

105F10.EPS

Figure 10 ◆ Solving for an unknown current.

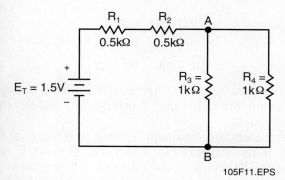

105F11.EPS

Figure 11 ◆ Series-parallel circuit.

The current and voltage associated with each component can be determined by first simplifying the circuit to find the total current, and then working across the individual components.

This circuit can be broken into two components: the series resistances R_1 and R_2, and the parallel resistances R_3 and R_4.

R_1 and R_2 can be added together to form the equivalent series resistance R_{1+2}:

$$R_{1+2} = R_1 + R_2$$
$$R_{1+2} = 0.5k\Omega + 0.5k\Omega$$
$$R_{1+2} = 1k\Omega$$

R_3 and R_4 can be totaled using either the general reciprocal formula or, since there are two resistances in parallel, the product over sum method. Both methods are shown below.

$$R_{3+4} = \cfrac{1}{\cfrac{1}{R_3} + \cfrac{1}{R_4}} = \cfrac{1}{\cfrac{1}{1k\Omega} + \cfrac{1}{1k\Omega}}$$

$$= \cfrac{1}{\cfrac{2}{1,000\Omega}} = \cfrac{1}{0.002} = 500\Omega$$

$$R_{3+4} = \frac{R_3 \times R_4}{R_3 + R_4} = \frac{1k\Omega \times 1k\Omega}{1k\Omega + 1k\Omega}$$

$$= \frac{1,000,000\Omega}{2,000\Omega} = 500\Omega$$

The equivalent circuit containing the R_{1+2} resistance of $1k\Omega$ and the R_{3+4} resistance of 500Ω is shown in *Figure 12*.

Using the Ohm's law relationship that total current equals voltage divided by circuit resistance, the circuit current can be determined. First, however, total circuit resistance must be found. Since the simplified circuit consists of two resistances in series, they are simply added together to obtain total resistance.

$$R_T = R_{1+2} + R_{3+4}$$
$$R_T = 1k\Omega + 500\Omega$$
$$R_T = 1.5k\Omega$$

Applying this to the current/voltage equation:

$$I_T = \frac{E_T}{R_T}$$

$$I_T = \frac{1.5V}{1.5k\Omega}$$

$$I_T = 1mA \text{ or } 0.001A$$

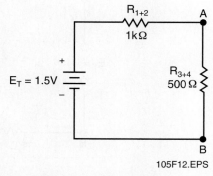

105F12.EPS

Figure 12 ◆ Simplified series-parallel circuit.

Now that the total current is known, voltage drops across individual components can be determined:

$$E_{R1} = I_T R_1 = 1mA \times 0.5k\Omega = 0.5V$$
$$E_{R2} = I_T R_2 = 1mA \times 0.5k\Omega = 0.5V$$

Since the total voltage equals the sum of all voltage drops, the voltage drop from A to B can be determined by subtraction:

$$E_T = E_{R1} + E_{R2} + E_{A+B}$$
$$E_T - E_{R1} - E_{R2} = E_{A+B}$$
$$1.5V - 0.5V - 0.5V = E_{A+B} = 0.5V$$

Since R_3 and R_4 are in parallel, some of the total current must pass through each resistor. R_3 and R_4 are equal, so the same current should flow through each branch. Using the relationship:

$$I = \frac{E}{R}$$

$$I_{R3} = \frac{E_{R3}}{R_3} \qquad\qquad I_{R4} = \frac{E_{R4}}{R_4}$$

$$I_{R3} = \frac{0.5V}{1k\Omega} \qquad\qquad I_{R4} = \frac{0.5V}{1k\Omega}$$

$$I_{R3} = 0.5mA \qquad\qquad I_{R4} = 0.5mA$$

$$0.5mA + 0.5mA = 1mA$$

Therefore, the total current for the circuit passes through R_1 and R_2 and is evenly divided between R_3 and R_4.

3.0.0 ◆ KIRCHHOFF'S LAWS

Kirchhoff's laws provide a simple, practical method of solving for unknown parameters in a circuit.

3.1.0 Kirchhoff's Current Law

In its most general form, **Kirchhoff's current law**, which is also called Kirchhoff's first law, states

that at any point in a circuit, the total current entering that point must equal the total current leaving that point. For parallel circuits, this implies that the current in a parallel circuit is equal to the sum of the currents in each branch.

When using Kirchhoff's laws to solve circuits, is necessary to adopt conventions that determine the algebraic signs for current and voltage terms. A convenient system for current is to consider current flowing into a branch point as positive and all current directed away from that point negative.

As an example, in *Figure 13*, the currents can written as:

$$I_A + I_B - I_C = 0$$

or

$$5A + 3A - 8A = 0$$

Currents I_A and I_B are positive terms because these currents flow into P, but I_C, directed out of is negative.

For a circuit application, refer to Point C at top of the diagram in *Figure 14*. The 6A I_T in Point C divides into the 2A I_3 and 4A I_{4+5}, both rected out. Note that I_{4+5} is the current through and R_5. The algebraic equation is:

$$I_T - I_3 - I_{4+5} = 0$$

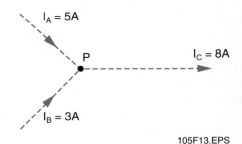

Figure 13 ◆ Kirchhoff's current law.

105F13.EPS

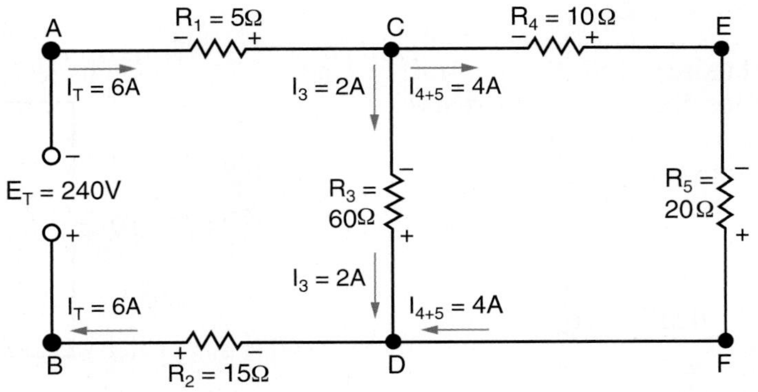

Figure 14 ◆ Application of Kirchhoff's current law.

105F14.EPS

Substituting the values for each current:

$$6A - 2A - 4A = 0$$

[F]or the opposite direction, refer to Point D at the [b]ottom of *Figure 14*. Here, the branch currents into [P]oint D combine to equal the mainline current I_T [r]eturning to the voltage source. Now, I_T is directed [o]ut from Point D, with I_3 and I_{4+5} directed in. The [al]gebraic equation is:

$$I_3 + I_{4+5} - I_T = 0$$
$$2A + 4A - 6A = 0$$

Note that at either Point C or Point D, the sum [of] the 2A and 4A branch currents must equal the [to]tal line current. Therefore, Kirchhoff's cur[re]nt law can also be stated as:

$$I_{IN} = I_{OUT}$$

For *Figure 14*, the equations for current can be [w]ritten as shown below.
At Point C:

$$6A = 2A + 4A$$

At Point D:

$$2A + 4A = 6A$$

Kirchhoff's current law is really the basis for the [pr]actical rule in parallel circuits that the total line [cu]rrent must equal the sum of the branch cur[re]nts.

[3.]2.0 Kirchhoff's Voltage Law

[Ki]rchhoff's voltage law states that the algebraic [su]m of the voltages around any closed path is [ze]ro.

Referring to *Figure 15*, the sum of the voltage [dr]ops around the circuit must equal the voltage [ap]plied to the circuit:

$$E_A = E_1 + E_2 + E_3$$

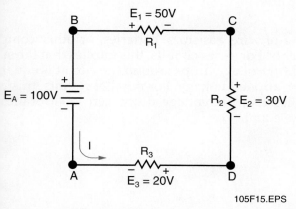

Figure 15 ◆ Kirchhoff's voltage law.

Where:

E_A = voltage applied to the circuit
E_1, E_2, and E_3 = voltage drops in the circuit

Another way of stating this law is that the algebraic sum of the voltage rises and voltage drops must be equal to zero. A voltage source is considered a voltage rise; a voltage across a resistor is a voltage drop. (For convenience in labeling, letter subscripts are shown for voltage sources and numerical subscripts are used for voltage drops.) This form of the law can be written by transposing the right members to the left side:

$$\text{Voltage applied} - \text{sum of voltage drops} = 0$$

Substitute letters:

$$E_A - E_1 - E_2 - E_3 = 0$$
$$E_A - (E_1 + E_2 + E_3) = 0$$

3.3.0 Loop Equations

Any closed path is called a loop. A loop equation specifies the voltages around the loop. Refer to *Figure 16*.

Consider the inside loop A, C, D, B, A, including the voltage drops E_1, E_3, and E_2, and the source E_T. In a clockwise direction, starting at Point A, the algebraic sum of the voltages is:

$$- E_1 - E_3 - E_2 + E_T = 0$$

or

$$- 30V - 120V - 90V + 240V = 0$$

Voltages E_1, E_3, and E_2 have a negative value, because there is a decrease in voltage seen across each of the resistors in a clockwise direction. However, the source E_T is a positive term because an increase in voltage is seen in that same direction.

For the opposite direction, going counterclockwise in the same loop from Point A, E_T is negative while E_1, E_2, and E_3 have positive values. Therefore:

$$- E_T + E_2 + E_3 + E_1 = 0$$

or

$$- 240V + 90V + 120V + 30V = 0$$

When the negative term is transposed, the equation becomes:

$$240V = 90V + 120V + 30V$$

In this form, the loop equation shows that Kirchhoff's voltage law is really the basis for the practical rule in series circuits that the sum of the voltage drops must equal the applied voltage.

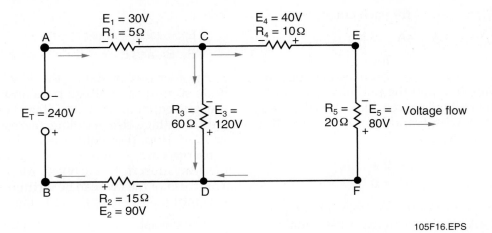

Figure 16 ◆ Loop equation.

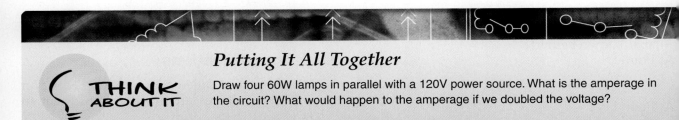

Putting It All Together

THINK ABOUT IT

Draw four 60W lamps in parallel with a 120V power source. What is the amperage in the circuit? What would happen to the amperage if we doubled the voltage?

For example, determine the voltage E_B for the circuit shown in *Figure 17*. The direction of the current flow is shown by the arrow. First mark the polarity of the voltage drops across the resistors and trace the circuit in the direction of the current flow starting at Point A. Then write the voltage equation around the circuit:

$$- E_3 - E_B - E_2 - E_1 + E_A = 0$$

Solve for E_B:

$$E_B = E_A - E_3 - E_2 - E_1$$
$$E_B = 15V - 2V - 6V - 3V$$
$$E_B = 4V$$

Since E_B was found to be positive, the assumed direction of current is in fact the actual direction of current.

In its most general form, Kirchhoff's voltage law (also called Kirchhoff's second law) states that the algebraic sum of all the potential differences in a closed loop is equal to zero. A closed loop means any completely closed path consist-

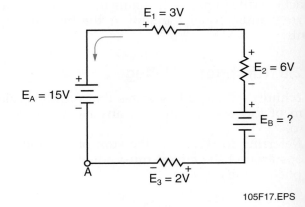

Figure 17 ◆ Applying Kirchhoff's voltage law.

ing of wire, resistors, batteries, or other comp[onents]. For series circuits, this implies that the su[m] of the voltage drops around the circuit is equal [to] the applied voltage. For parallel circuits, this i[m]plies that the voltage drops across all branch[es] are equal.

1. The formula for calculating the total resistance in a series circuit with three resistors is _____.
   a. $R_T = R_1 + R_2 + R_3$
   b. $R_T = R_1 - R_2 - R_3$
   c. $R_T = R_1 \times R_2 \times R_3$
   d. $R_T = \dfrac{1}{\dfrac{1}{R_1} + \dfrac{1}{R_2} + \dfrac{1}{R_3}}$

2. The formula for calculating the total resistance in a parallel circuit with three resistors is _____.
   a. $R_T = R_1 + R_2 + R_3$
   b. $R_T = R_1 - R_2 - R_3$
   c. $R_T = R_1 \times R_2 \times R_3$
   d. $R_T = \dfrac{1}{\dfrac{1}{R_1} + \dfrac{1}{R_2} + \dfrac{1}{R_3}}$

3. The total resistance in *Figure 1* is _____.
   a. $1{,}035\Omega$
   b. 129Ω
   c. 100Ω
   d. 157Ω

4. Find the total resistance in a series circuit with three resistances of 10Ω, 20Ω, and 30Ω.
   a. 15Ω
   b. 1Ω
   c. 20Ω
   d. 60Ω

5. In a parallel circuit, the voltage across each path is equal to the _____.
   a. total circuit resistance times path current
   b. source voltage minus path voltage
   c. path resistance times total current
   d. source voltage

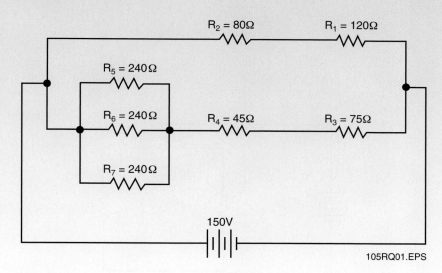

105RQ01.EPS

Figure 1

6. The value for total current in *Figure 2* is _____ amps.
   a. 1.25
   b. 2.50
   c. 5
   d. 10

7. A resistor of 32Ω is in parallel with a resistor of 36Ω, and a 54Ω resistor is in series with the pair. When 350V is applied to the combination, the current through the 54Ω resistor is _____ amps.
   a. 2.87
   b. 3.26
   c. 5.86
   d. 4.93

8. A 242Ω resistor is in parallel with a 180Ω resistor, and a 420Ω resistor is in series with the combination. A current of 22mA flows through the 242Ω resistor. The current through the 180Ω resistor is _____ mA.
   a. 29.5
   b. 40.2
   c. 19.8
   d. 36.4

9. Two 24Ω resistors are in parallel, and a 42Ω resistor is in series with the combination. When 78V is applied to the three resistors, the voltage drop across the 42Ω resistor is about _____ volts.
   a. 55.8
   b. 60.5
   c. 65.3
   d. 49.8

10. Kirchhoff's voltage law states that the algebraic sum of the voltages around any closed path is _____.
    a. infinity
    b. zero
    c. twice the current
    d. always less than the individual voltages due to voltage drop

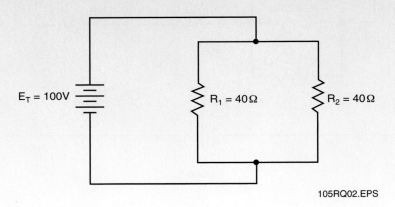

105RQ02.EPS

Figure 2

Summary

...e relationships among current, voltage, resis-
...ce, and power in Ohm's law are the same for
...th DC series and DC parallel circuits. Under-
...nding and being able to apply these concepts is
...cessary for effective circuit analysis and trou-
...shooting. DC series-parallel circuits also have
...ese fundamental relationships. Since DC series-
...rallel circuits are a combination of simple series

and parallel circuits, Kirchhoff's voltage and current laws will apply. Calculating I, E, R, and P for
series-parallel circuits is no more difficult than
calculating these values for simple series or parallel circuits. However, for series-parallel circuits,
these calculations require more careful circuit
analysis in order to use Ohm's law correctly.

Notes

Trade Terms Quiz

1. _____ states that the total amount of current flowing through a parallel circuit is equal to the sum of the amounts of current flowing through each current path.

2. _____ states that the sum of all the voltage drops in a circuit is equal to the source voltage of the circuit.

3. _____ circuits contain both series and parallel current paths.

4. _____ circuits contain two or more parallel paths through which current can flow.

5. _____ circuits contain only one path for current flow.

Trade Terms

Kirchhoff's current law
Kirchhoff's voltage law

Parallel circuits
Series circuits

Series-parallel circuits

James Mitchem

TIC — The Industrial Company

Jim Mitchem serves as a troubleshooter for a large electrical contractor. During his career in the electrical industry, he worked his way up from apprentice to technical services manager.

ow did you become an electrician?
uite by accident. A couple of years after college, I
as working as a relief operator in a plant when the
d electrician retired, creating a vacancy. I liked the
ea that electricians were expected to use their
owledge and initiative to keep the place running. I
plied and was accepted as a trainee.

ow did you get your training?
ook an electrical apprenticeship course by
rrespondence, and I was fortunate enough to work
th good people who helped me along. I worked in
environment that exposed me to a variety of
uipment and applications, and just about everyone
e ever worked with has taught me something. Now
 passing my knowledge on to others.

hat kinds of work have you done in your career?
e worked as an apprentice, journeyman,
strument and controls technician, instrument fitter,
eman, general foreman, superintendent, and
rtup engineer. Each of these positions required that
arn new skills, both technical and managerial. My
perience in many disciplines and types of projects
 given me a high level of credibility with my
ployer and our clients.

Now I act as a technical resource and trouble-shooter for job sites and in-house functions such as safety, quality assurance, and training. I visit job sites to help solve problems and help out with commissioning and startup.

What factor or factors have contributed the most to your success?
There are several factors. Two very important ones have been a desire to learn and a willingness to do whatever is asked of me. I also keep an eye on the big picture. When I'm on a job, I'm not just pulling wire, I'm building a power plant or whatever the project is. I also think it has helped me to remain with the same employer for 18 years.

Any advice for apprentices just beginning their careers?
Keep learning! And don't depend on others to train you. Take the initiative to buy or borrow books and trade journals. Take licensing tests and do whatever is necessary to keep your licenses current. Finally, make sure you know your own personal and professional values and work with a company that shares those values.

Trade Terms
Introduced in This Module

Kirchhoff's current law: The statement that the total amount of current flowing through a parallel circuit is equal to the sum of the amounts of current flowing through each current path.

Kirchhoff's voltage law: The statement that the sum of all the voltage drops in a circuit is equal to the source voltage of the circuit.

Parallel circuits: Circuits containing two or more parallel paths through which current can flow.

Series circuits: Circuits with only one path for current flow.

Series-parallel circuits: Circuits that contain both series and parallel current paths.

is module is intended to present thorough re-
urces for task training. The following reference
orks are suggested for further study. These are
·tional materials for continued education rather
an for task training.

Electronics Fundamentals: Circuits, Devices, and Applications, Thomas L. Floyd. New York: Prentice Hall.

Principles of Electric Circuits, Thomas L. Floyd. New York: Prentice Hall.

CONTREN® LEARNING SERIES — USER FEEDBACK

The NCCER makes every effort to keep these textbooks up-to-date and free of technical errors. We appreciate your help in this process. If you have an idea for improving this textbook, or if you find an error, a typographical mistake, or an inaccuracy in NCCER's *Contren®* textbooks, please write us, using this form or a photocopy. Be sure to include the exact module number, page number, a detailed description, and the correction, if applicable. Your input will be brought to the attention of the Technical Review Committee. Thank you for your assistance.

Instructors – If you found that additional materials were necessary in order to teach this module effectively, please let us know so that we may include them in the Equipment/Materials list in the Annotated Instructor's Guide.

Write: Product Development
National Center for Construction Education and Research
P.O. Box 141104, Gainesville, FL 32614-1104

Fax: 352-334-0932

E-mail: curriculum@nccer.org

Craft _____ Module Name _____

Copyright Date _____ Module Number _____ Page Number(s) _____

Description _____

_____

_____

_____

_____

(Optional) Correction _____

_____

_____

(Optional) Your Name and Address _____

_____

_____

_____

Inn at the Ballpark
Houston, Texas
Renovation $10–99 Million Award Winner
HOAR Construction, LLC

26201-05
Alternating Current

Topics to be presented in this module include:

Overview

The vast majority of your work as an electrician will be with alternating current (AC) circuits, because AC provides the power to operate the appliances and machines in our homes and businesses. Although direct current (DC) was used in the original electrical systems developed by Thomas Edison, the dynamic nature of AC makes it much easier to generate and distribute than DC. On the other hand, circuit analysis is more difficult because, unlike DC, AC does not act the same way in components such as coils and capacitors as it does in resistive components. When circuits contain these AC components, Ohm's law cannot be directly applied. Special formulas must be used to determine the circuit resistance.

Because alternating current is in a constant state of change with regard to polarities and values, its dynamics make it very useful. Induction-dependent components such as transformers, motors, and coils rely on the changing polarity and voltage values of alternating current in order to function.

Objectives

When you have completed this module, you will be able to do the following:

1. Calculate the peak and effective voltage or current values for an AC waveform.
2. Calculate the phase relationship between two AC waveforms.
3. Describe the voltage and current phase relationship in a resistive AC circuit.
4. Describe the voltage and current transients that occur in an inductive circuit.
5. Define inductive reactance and state how it is affected by frequency.
6. Describe the voltage and current transients that occur in a capacitive circuit.
7. Define capacitive reactance and state how it is affected by frequency.
8. Explain the relationship between voltage and current in the following types of AC circuits:
   - RL circuit
   - RC circuit
   - LC circuit
   - RLC circuit
9. Describe the effect that resonant frequency has on impedance and current flow in a series or parallel resonant circuit.
10. Define bandwidth and describe how it is affected by resistance in a series or parallel resonant circuit.
11. Explain the following terms as they relate to AC circuits:
    - True power
    - Apparent power
    - Reactive power
    - Power factor
12. Explain basic transformer action.

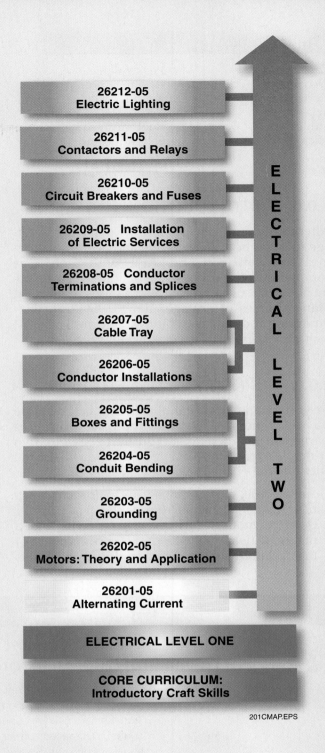

201CMAP.EPS

Prerequisites

Before you begin this module, it is recommended that you successfully complete *Core Curriculum* and *Electrical Level One*.

This course map shows all of the modules in *Electrical Level Two*. The suggested training order begins at the bottom and proceeds up. Skill levels increase as you advance on the course map. The local Training Program Sponsor may adjust the training order.

Required Trainee Materials

1. Pencil and paper
2. Appropriate personal protective equipment
3. Copy of the latest edition of the *National Electrical Code*®

Capacitance
Frequency
Hertz (Hz)
Impedance
Inductance
Micro

Peak voltage
Radian
Reactance
Resonance
Root-mean-square (rms)
Self-inductance

1.0.0 ◆ INTRODUCTION

Alternating current (AC) and its associated voltage reverses between positive and negative polarities and varies in amplitude with time. One complete waveform or cycle includes a complete set of variations, with two alternations in polarity. Many sources of voltage change direction with time and produce a resultant waveform. The most common AC waveform is the sine wave.

2.0.0 ◆ SINE WAVE GENERATION

To understand how the alternating current sine wave is generated, some of the basic principles learned in magnetism should be reviewed. Two principles form the basis of all electromagnetic phenomena:

- An electric current in a conductor creates a magnetic field that surrounds the conductor.
- Relative motion between a conductor and a magnetic field, when at least one component of that relative motion is in a direction that is perpendicular to the direction of the field, creates a voltage in the conductor.

Figure 1 shows how these principles are applied to generate an AC waveform in a simple one-loop rotary generator. The conductor loop rotates through the magnetic field to generate the induced AC voltage across its open terminals. The magnetic flux shown here is vertical.

There are several factors affecting the magnitude of voltage developed by a conductor through a magnetic field. They are the strength of the magnetic field, the length of the conductor, and the rate at which the conductor cuts directly across or perpendicular to the magnetic field.

Assuming that the strength of the magnetic field and the length of the conductor making the loop are both constant, the voltage produced will vary depending on the rate at which the loop cuts directly across the magnetic field.

The rate at which the conductor cuts the magnetic field depends on two things: the speed of the generator in revolutions per minute (rpm) and the angle at which the conductor is traveling through the field. If the generator is operated at a constant rpm, the voltage produced at any moment will depend on the angle at which the conductor is cutting the field at that instant.

In *Figure 2*, the magnetic field is shown as parallel lines called lines of flux. These lines always go from the north to south poles in a generator. The motion of the conductor is shown by the large arrow.

Assuming the speed of the conductor is constant, as the angle between the flux and the

Why Do Power Companies Generate and Distribute AC Power Instead of DC Power?

The transformer is the key. Power plants generate and distribute AC power because it permits the use of transformers, which makes power delivery more economical. Transformers used at generation plants step the AC voltage up, which decreases the current. Decreased current allows smaller-sized wires to be used for the power transmission lines. Smaller wire is less expensive and easier to support over the long distances that the power must travel from the generation plant to remotely located substations. At the substations, transformers are again used to step AC voltages back down to a level suitable for distribution to homes and businesses.

There is no such thing as a DC transformer. This means DC power would have to be transmitted at low voltages and high currents over very large-sized wires, making the process very uneconomical. When DC is required for special applications, the AC voltage may be converted to DC voltage by using rectifiers, which make the change electrically, or by using AC motor-DC generator sets, which make the change mechanically.

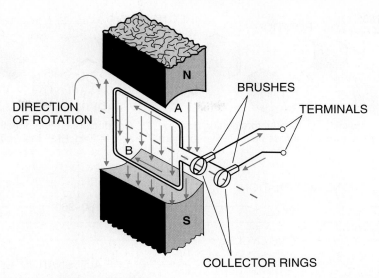

Figure 1 ◆ Conductor moving across a magnetic field.

201F01.EPS

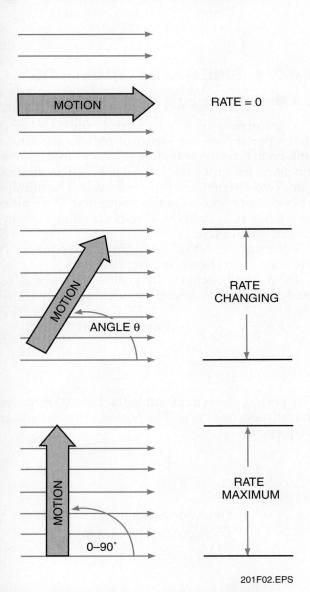

201F02.EPS

Figure 2 ◆ Angle versus rate of cutting lines of flux.

conductor motion increases, the number of flux lines cut in a given time (the rate) increases. When the conductor is moving parallel to the lines of flux (angle of 0°), it is not cutting any of them, and the voltage will be zero.

The angle between the lines of flux and the motion of the conductor is called θ (theta). The magnitude of the voltage produced will be proportional to the sine of the angle. Sine is a trigonometric function. Each angle has a sine value that never changes.

The sine of 0° is 0. It increases to a maximum of 1 at 90°. From 90° to 180°, the sine decreases back to 0. From 180° to 270°, the sine decreases to −1. Then from 270° to 360° (back to 0°), the sine increases to its original 0.

Because voltage is proportional to the sine of the angle, as the loop goes 360° around the circle the voltage will increase from 0 to its maximum at 90°, back to 0 at 180°, down to its maximum negative value at 270°, and back up to 0 at 360°, as shown in *Figure 3*.

Notice that at 180° the polarity reverses. This is because the conductor has turned completely around and is now cutting the lines of flux in the opposite direction. This can be shown using the left-hand rule for generators. The curve shown in *Figure 3* is called a sine wave because its shape is generated by the trigonometric function sine. The value of voltage at any point along the sine wave can be calculated if the angle and the maximum obtainable voltage (E_{max}) are known.

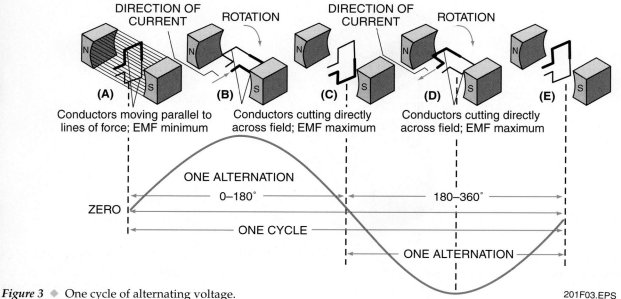

DIRECTION OF CURRENT   **ROTATION**   **DIRECTION OF CURRENT**   **ROTATION**

(A)   (B)   (C)   (D)   (E)

Conductors moving parallel to lines of force; EMF minimum   Conductors cutting directly across field; EMF maximum   Conductors cutting directly across field; EMF maximum

ONE ALTERNATION
0–180°

ZERO

ONE CYCLE

ONE ALTERNATION

180–360°

Figure 3 ◆ One cycle of alternating voltage.

201F03.EPS

The formula used is:

$$E = E_{max} \text{ sine } \theta$$

Where:

E = voltage induced

E_{max} = maximum induced voltage

θ = angle at which the voltage is induced

Using the above formula, the values of voltage anywhere along the sine wave in *Figure 3* can be calculated. Sine values can be found using either a scientific calculator or trigonometric tables. With an E_{max} of 10 volts (V), the following values are calculated as examples:

θ = 0°, sine = 0
E = E_{max}sine θ
E = (10V)(0)
E = 0V

θ = 45°, sine = 0.707
E = E_{max}sine θ
E = (10V)(0.707)
E = 7.07V

θ = 90°, sine = 1.0
E = E_{max}sine θ
E = (10V)(1.0)
E = 10V

θ = 135°, sine = 0.707
E = E_{max}sine θ
E = (10V)(0.707)
E = 7.07V

θ = 180°, sine = 0
E = E_{max}sine θ
E = (10V)(0)
E = 0V

θ = 225°, sine = −0.707
E = E_{max}sine θ
E = (10V)(−0.707)
E = −7.07V

θ = 270°, sine = −1.0
E = E_{max}sine θ
E = (10V)(−1.0)
E = −10V

θ = 315°, sine = −0.707
E = E_{max}sine θ
E = (10V)(−0.707)
E = −7.07V

3.0.0 ◆ SINE WAVE TERMINOLOGY

3.1.0 Frequency

The **frequency** of a waveform is the number of times per second an identical pattern repeats itself. Each time the waveform changes from zero to a peak value and back to zero is called an alternation. Two alternations form one cycle. The number of cycles per second is the frequency. The unit of frequency is **hertz (Hz).** One hertz equals one cycle per second (cps).

For example, let us determine the frequency of the waveform shown in *Figure 4*.

In one-half second, the basic sine wave is repeated five times. Therefore, the frequency (f) is:

$$f = \frac{5 \text{ cycles}}{0.5 \text{ second}} = 10 \text{ cycles per second (Hz)}$$

3.1.1 Period

The period of a waveform is the time (t) required to complete one cycle. The period is the inverse of frequency:

$$t = \frac{1}{f}$$

Where:

t = period (seconds)
f = frequency (Hz or cps)

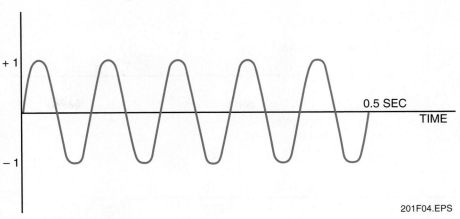

Figure 4 ◆ Frequency measurement.

For example, let us determine the period of the waveform in *Figure 4*. If there are five cycles in one-half second, then the frequency for one cycle is 10 cps ($0.5 \div 5 = 10$). Therefore, the period is:

$$t = \frac{1}{cps}$$

$$t = \frac{1}{10} = 0.1 \text{ second}$$

3.2.0 Wavelength

The wavelength or λ (lambda) is the distance traveled by a waveform during one period. Since electricity travels at the speed of light (186,000 miles/second or 300,000,000 meters/second), the wavelength of electrical waveforms equals the product of the period and the speed of light (c):

$$\lambda = tc$$

or:

$$\lambda = \frac{c}{f}$$

Where:

λ = wavelength (meters)
t = period (seconds)
c = speed of light (meters/second)
f = frequency (Hz or cps)

3.3.0 Peak Value

The peak value is the maximum value of voltage (V_M) or current (I_M). For example, specifying that a sine wave has a **peak voltage** of 170V applies to either the positive or the negative peak. To include both peak amplitudes, the peak-to-peak (p–p) value may be specified. In the above example, the

peak-to-peak value is 340V, double the peak value of 170V, because the positive and negative peaks are symmetrical. However, the two opposite peak values cannot occur at the same time. Furthermore, in some waveforms the two peaks are not equal. The positive peak value and peak-to-peak value of a sine wave are shown in *Figure 5*.

3.4.0 Average Value

The average value is calculated from all the values in a sine wave for one alternation or half cycle. The half cycle is used for the average because over a full cycle the average value is zero, which is useless for comparison purposes. If the sine values for all angles up to 180° in one alternation are added and then divided by the number of values, this average equals 0.637.

Since the peak value of the sine is 1 and the average equals 0.637, the average value can be calculated as follows:

Average value = 0.637 × peak value

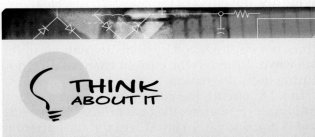

Frequency

The frequency of the utility power generated in the United States is normally 60Hz. In some European countries and elsewhere, utility power is often generated at a frequency of 50Hz. Which of these frequencies (60Hz or 50Hz) has the shortest period?

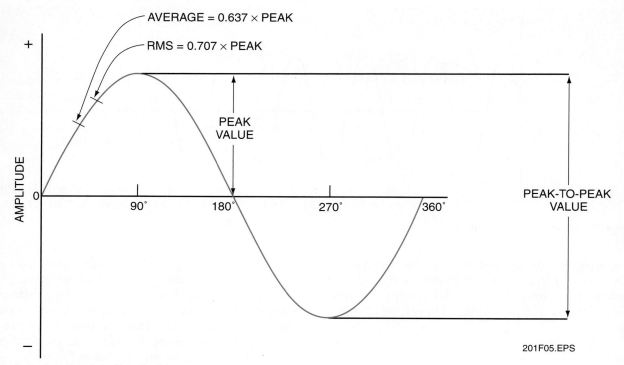

Figure 5 ◆ Amplitude values for a sine wave.

For example, with a peak of 170V, the average value is 0.637 × 170V, which equals approximately 108V. *Figure 5* shows where the average value would fall on a sine wave.

3.5.0 Root-Mean-Square or Effective Value

Meters used in AC circuits indicate a value called the effective value. The effective value is the value of the AC current or voltage wave that indicates the same energy transfer as an equivalent direct current (DC) or voltage.

The direct comparison between DC and AC is in the heating effect of the two currents. Heat produced by current is a function of current amplitude only and is independent of current direction. Thus, heat is produced by both alternations of the AC wave, although the current changes direction during each alternation.

In a DC circuit, the current maintains a steady amplitude. Therefore, the heat produced is steady and is equal to I²R. In an AC circuit, the current is continuously changing; periodically high, periodically low, and periodically zero. To produce the same amount of heat from AC as from an equivalent amount of DC, the instantaneous value of the AC must at times exceed the DC value.

By averaging the heating effects of all the instantaneous values during one cycle of alternating current, it is possible to find the average heat produced by the AC current during the cycle. The amount of DC required to produce that heat will be equal to the effective value of the AC.

The most common method of specifying the amount of a sine wave of voltage or current is by stating its value at 45°, which is 70.7% of the peak. This is its **root-mean-square (rms)** value. Therefore:

Value of rms = 0.707 × peak value

For example, with a peak of 170V, the rms value is 0.707 × 170, or approximately 120V. This is the voltage of the commercial AC power line, which is always given in rms value.

4.0.0 ◆ AC PHASE RELATIONSHIPS

In AC systems, phase is involved in two ways: the location of a point on a voltage or current wave with respect to the starting point of the wave or with respect to some corresponding point on the same wave. In the case of two waves of the same frequency, it is the time at which an event of one takes place with respect to a similar event of the other.

Often, the event is the starting of the waves at zero or the points at which the waves reach their maximum values. When two waves are compared in this manner, there is a phase lead or lag of one

Left-Hand Rule for Generators

Hand rules for generators and motors give direction to the basic principles of induction. For a generator, if you move a conductor through a magnetic field made up of flux lines, you will induce an EMF, which drives current through a conductor. The left-hand rule for generators will help you determine which direction the current will flow in the conductor. It states that if you hold the thumb, first, and middle fingers of the left hand at right angles to one another with the first finger pointing in the flux direction (from the north pole to the south pole), and the thumb pointing in the direction of motion of the conductor, the middle finger will point in the direction of the induced voltage (EMF). The polarity of the EMF determines the direction in which current will flow as a result of this induced EMF. The left-hand rule for generators is also called Fleming's first rule.

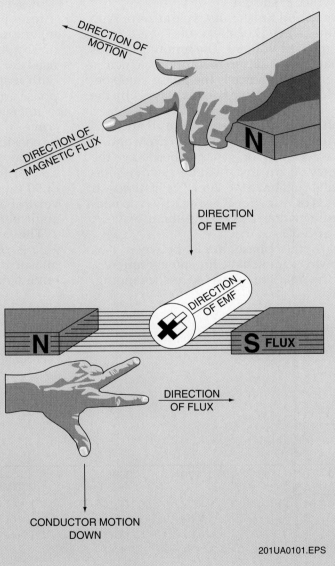

201UA0101.EPS

with respect to the other unless they are alternating in unison, in which case they are said to be in phase.

4.1.0 Phase Angle

Suppose that a generator started its cycle at 90° where maximum voltage output is produced instead of starting at the point of zero output. The two output voltage waves are shown in *Figure 6*. Each is the same waveform of alternating voltage, but wave B starts at the maximum value while wave A starts at zero. The complete cycle of wave B through 360° takes it back to the maximum value from which it started.

Wave A starts and finishes its cycle at zero. With respect to time, wave B is ahead of wave A in its values of generated voltage. The amount it leads in time equals one quarter revolution, which is 90°. This angular difference is the phase angle between waves B and A. Wave B leads wave A by the phase angle of 90°.

The 90° phase angle between waves B and A is maintained throughout the complete cycle and in all successive cycles as long as they both have the same frequency. At any instant in time, wave B has the value that A will have 90° later. For instance, at 180°, wave A is at zero, but B is already at its negative maximum value, the point where wave A will be later at 270°.

To compare the phase angle between two waves, both waves must have the same frequency. Otherwise, the relative phase keeps changing.

Both waves must also have sine wave variations because this is the only kind of waveform that is measured in angular units of time. The amplitudes can be different for the two waves. The phases of two voltages, two currents, or a current with a voltage can be compared.

4.2.0 Phase Angle Diagrams

To compare AC phases, it is much more convenient to use vector diagrams corresponding to the voltage and current waveforms, as shown in *Figure 6*. V_A and V_B represent the vector quantities corresponding to the generator voltage.

A vector is a quantity that has magnitude and direction. The length of the arrow indicates the magnitude of the alternating voltage in rms, peak, or any AC value as long as the same measure is used for all the vectors. The angle of the arrow with respect to the horizontal axis indicates the phase angle.

In *Figure 6*, the vector V_A represents the voltage wave A, with a phase angle of 0°. This angle can be considered as the plane of the loop in the rotary generator where it starts with zero output voltage. The vector V_B is vertical to show the phase angle of 90° for this voltage wave, corresponding to the vertical generator loop at the start of its cycle. The angle between the two vectors is the phase angle.

The symbol for a phase angle is θ (theta). In *Figure 7*, θ = 0°. *Figure 7* shows the waveforms and phasor diagram of two waves that are in phase but have different amplitudes.

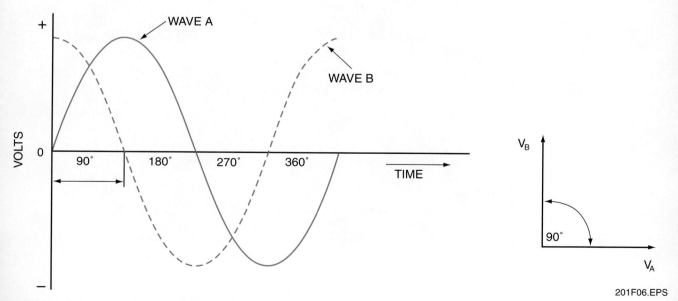

Figure 6 ◆ Voltage waveforms 90° out of phase.

201F06.EPS

RMS Amplitude

The root-mean-square (rms) value, also called the *effective value,* is the value assigned to an alternating voltage or current that results in the same power dissipation in a given resistance as DC voltage or current of the same numerical value. This is illustrated below. As shown, 120 (peak) VAC will not produce the same light (350 lumens versus 500 lumens) as 120VDC from a 60W lamp. In order to produce the same light (500 lumens), 120V rms must be applied to the lamp. This requires that the applied sinusoidal AC waveform have a peak voltage of about 170V (170V × 0.707V = 120V).

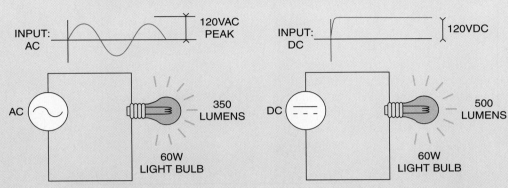

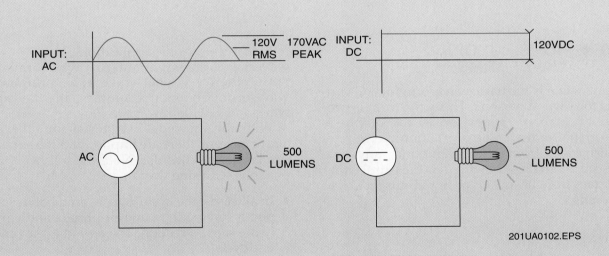

201UA0102.EPS

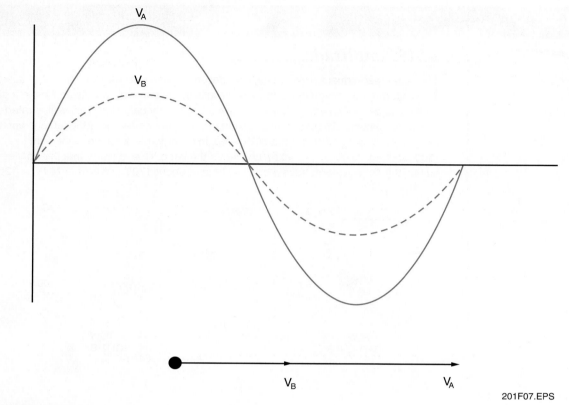

Figure 7 ◆ Waves in phase.

5.0.0 ◆ NONSINUSOIDAL WAVEFORMS

The sine wave is the basic waveform for AC variations for several reasons. This waveform is produced by a rotary generator, as the output is proportional to the angle of rotation. Because of its derivation from circular motion, any sine wave can be analyzed in angular measure, either in degrees from 0° to 360° or in **radians** from 0 to 2π radians.

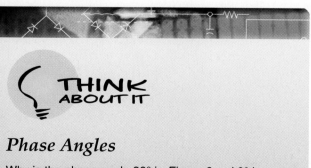

Phase Angles

Why is the phase angle 90° in *Figure 6* and 0° in *Figure 7?* Why is the vector diagram in *Figure 7* shown as a straight line?

In many electronic applications, however, other waveshapes are important. Any waveform that is not a sine (or cosine) wave is a nonsinusoidal waveform. Common examples are the square wave and sawtooth wave in *Figure 8*.

With nonsinusoidal waveforms for either voltage or current, there are important differences and similarities to consider. Note the following comparisons with sine waves:

- In all cases, the cycle is measured between two points having the same amplitude and varying in the same direction. The period is the time for one cycle.
- Peak amplitude is measured from the zero axis to the maximum positive or negative value. However, peak-to-peak amplitude is better for measuring nonsinusoidal waveshapes because they can have asymmetrical peaks, as with the rectangular wave in *Figure 8*.
- The rms value 0.707 of peak applies only to sine waves, as this factor is derived from the sine values in the angular measure used only for the sine waveform.
- Phase angles apply only to sine waves, as angular measure is used only for sine waves. Note that the phase angle is indicated only on the sine wave of *Figure 8*.

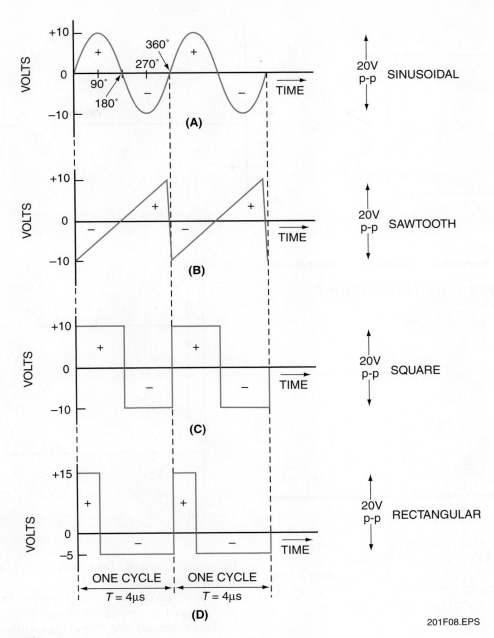

Figure 8 ◆ AC waveforms.

201F08.EPS

6.0.0 ◆ RESISTANCE IN AC CIRCUITS

An AC circuit has an AC voltage source. Note the circular symbol with the sine wave inside it shown in *Figure 9*. It is used for any source of sine wave alternating voltage. This voltage connected across an external load resistance produces alternating current of the same waveform, frequency, and phase as the applied voltage.

According to Ohm's law, current (I) equals voltage (E) divided by resistance (R). When E is an rms value, I is also an rms value. For any instantaneous value of E during the cycle, the value of I is for the corresponding instant of time.

In an AC circuit with only resistance, the current variations are in phase with the applied voltage, as shown in *Figure 9*. This in-phase relationship between E and I means that such an AC circuit can be analyzed by the same methods used for DC circuits since there is no phase angle to consider. Components that have only resistance

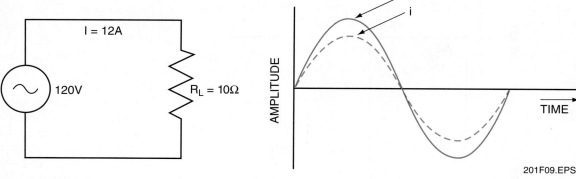

Figure 9 ◆ Resistive AC circuit.

What's wrong with this picture?

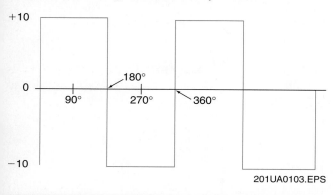

201UA0103.EPS

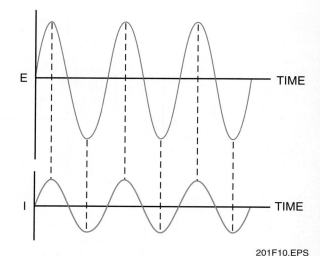

201F10.EPS

Figure 10 ◆ Voltage and current in a resistive AC circuit.

include resistors, the filaments for incandescent light bulbs, and vacuum tube heaters.

In purely resistive AC circuits, the voltage, current, and resistance are related by Ohm's law because the voltage and current are in phase.

$$I = \frac{E}{R}$$

Unless otherwise noted, the calculations in AC circuits are generally in rms values. For example, in *Figure 9*, the 120V applied across the 10Ω resistance R_L produces an rms current of 12A. This is determined as follows:

$$I = \frac{E}{R_L} = \frac{120V}{10\Omega} = 12A$$

Furthermore, the rms power (true power) dissipation is I^2R or:

$$P = (12A)^2 \times 10\Omega = 1,440W$$

Figure 10 shows the relationship between voltage and current in purely resistive AC circuits. The voltage and current are in phase, their cycles

begin and end at the same time, and their peaks occur at the same time.

The value of the voltage shown in *Figure 10* depends on the applied voltage to the circuit. The value of the current depends on the applied voltage and the amount of resistance. If resistance is changed, it will affect only the magnitude of the current.

The total resistance in any AC circuit, whether it is a series, parallel, or series-parallel circuit, is calculated using the same rules that were learned and applied to DC circuits with resistance. Power computations are discussed later in this module.

7.0.0 ◆ INDUCTANCE IN AC CIRCUITS

Inductance is the characteristic of an electrical circuit that opposes the change of current flow. It is the result of the expanding and collapsing field caused by the changing current. This moving flux cuts across the conductor that is providing the current, producing induced voltage in the wire itself. Furthermore, any other conductor in the field, whether carrying current or not, is also cut by the varying flux and has induced voltage. This induced current opposes the current flow that generated it.

In DC circuits, a change must be initiated in the circuit to cause inductance. The current must change to provide motion of the flux. A steady DC of 10A cannot produce any induced voltage as long as the current value is constant. A current of 1A changing to 2A does induce voltage. Also, the faster the current changes, the higher the induced voltage becomes, because when the flux moves at a higher speed it can induce more voltage.

However, in an AC circuit the current is continuously changing and producing induced voltage. Lower frequencies of AC require more inductance to produce the same amount of induced voltage as a higher frequency current. The current can have any waveform as long as the amplitude is changing.

The ability of a conductor to induce voltage in itself when the current changes is its **self-inductance** or simply inductance. The symbol for inductance is L and its unit is the henry (H). One henry is the amount of inductance that allows one volt to be induced when the current changes at the rate of one ampere per second.

7.1.0 Factors Affecting Inductance

An inductor is a coil of wire that may be wound on a core of metal or paper, or it may be self-supporting. It may consist of turns of wire placed side by side to form a layer of wire over the core or coil form. The inductance of a coil or inductor depends on its physical construction. Some of the factors affecting inductance are:

- *Number of turns* – The greater the number of turns, the greater the inductance. In addition, the spacing of the turns on a coil also affects inductance. A coil that has widely-spaced turns has a lower inductance than one that has the same number of more closely-spaced turns. The reason for this higher inductance is that the closely-wound turns produce a more concentrated magnetic field, causing the coil to exhibit a greater inductance.
- *Coil diameter* – The inductance increases directly as the cross-sectional area of the coil increases.

- *Length of the coil* – When the length of the coil is decreased, the turn spacing is decreased, increasing the inductance of the coil.
- *Core material* – The core of the coil can be either a magnetic material (such as iron) or a non-magnetic material (such as paper or air). Coils wound on a magnetic core produce a stronger magnetic field than those with non-magnetic cores, giving them higher values of inductance. Air-core coils are used where small values of inductance are required.
- *Winding the coil in layers* – The more layers used to form a coil, the greater the effect the magnetic field has on the conductor. Layering a coil can increase the inductance.

Factors affecting the inductance of a coil can be seen in *Figure 11*.

7.2.0 Voltage and Current in an Inductive AC Circuit

The self-induced voltage across an inductance L is produced by a change in current with respect to time ($\Delta i / \Delta t$) and can be stated as:

$$V_L = L\frac{\Delta i}{\Delta t}$$

Where:

$$\Delta = \text{change}$$
$$V_L = \text{volts}$$
$$L = \text{henrys}$$
$$\Delta i/\Delta t = \text{amperes per second}$$

This gives the voltage in terms of how much magnetic flux is cut per second. When the magnetic flux associated with the current varies the same as I, this formula gives the same results for calculating induced voltage. Remember that the induced voltage across the coil is actually the result of inducing electrons to move in the conductor, so there is also an induced current.

For example, what is the self-induced voltage V_L across a 4h inductance produced by a current change of 12A per second?

$$V_L = L\frac{\Delta i}{\Delta t}$$
$$V_L = 4h \times \frac{12A}{1}$$
$$V_L = 4 \times 12$$
$$V_L = 48V$$

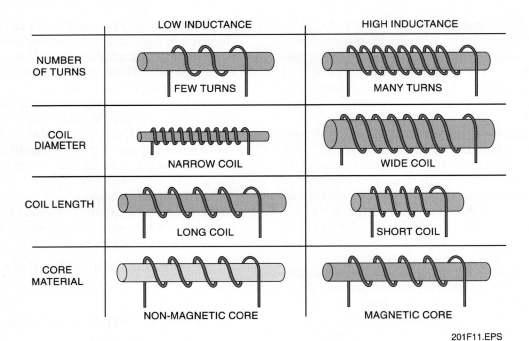

	LOW INDUCTANCE	HIGH INDUCTANCE
NUMBER OF TURNS	FEW TURNS	MANY TURNS
COIL DIAMETER	NARROW COIL	WIDE COIL
COIL LENGTH	LONG COIL	SHORT COIL
CORE MATERIAL	NON-MAGNETIC CORE	MAGNETIC CORE

201F11.EPS

Figure 11 ◆ Factors affecting the inductance of a coil.

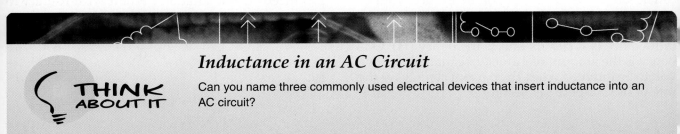

Inductance in an AC Circuit

THINK ABOUT IT

Can you name three commonly used electrical devices that insert inductance into an AC circuit?

The current through a 200 microhenry (µh) inductor changes from 0 to 200 milliamps (mA) in 2 microseconds (µsec). (The prefix **micro** means one-millionth.) What is the V_L?

$$V_L = L\frac{\Delta i}{\Delta t}$$

$$V_L = \left(200 \times 10^{-6}\right)\frac{200 \times 10^{-3}}{2 \times 10^{-6}}$$

$$V_L = 20V$$

The induced voltage is an actual voltage that can be measured, although V_L is produced only while the current is changing. When $\Delta i / \Delta t$ is present for only a short time, V_L is in the form of a voltage pulse. With a sine wave current that is always changing, V_L is a sinusoidal voltage that is 90° out of phase with I_L.

The current that flows in an inductor is induced by the changing magnetic field that surrounds the inductor. This changing magnetic field is produced by an AC voltage source that is applied to the inductor. The magnitude and polarity of the induced current depend on the field strength, direction, and rate at which the field cuts the inductor windings. The overall effect is that the current is out of phase and lags the applied voltage by 90°.

At 270° in *Figure 12*, the applied electromotive force (EMF) is zero, but it is increasing in the positive direction at its greatest rate of change. Likewise, electron flow due to the applied EMF is also increasing at its greatest rate. As the electron flow increases, it produces a magnetic field that is building with it. The lines of flux cut the conductor as they move outward from it with the expanding field.

As the lines of flux cut the conductor, they induce a current into it. The induced current is at its maximum value because the lines of flux are expanding outward through the conductor at their greatest rate. The direction of the induced current is in opposition to the force that generated it. Therefore, at 270° the applied voltage is zero and

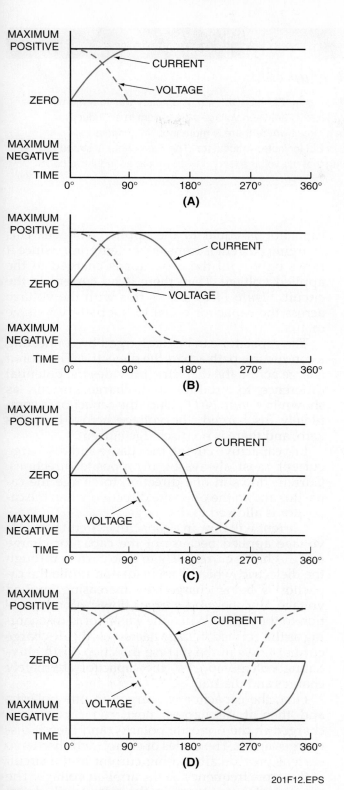

Figure 12 ◆ Inductor voltage and current relationship.

is increasing to a positive value, while the current is at its maximum negative value.

At 0° in *Figure 12*, the applied voltage is at its maximum positive value, but its rate of change is zero. Therefore, the field it produces is no longer expanding and is not cutting the conductor. Because there is no relative motion between the field and conductor, no current is induced. Therefore, at 0° voltage is at its maximum positive value, while current is zero.

At 90° in *Figure 12*, voltage is once again zero, but this time it is decreasing toward negative at its greatest rate of change. Because the applied voltage is decreasing, the magnetic field is collapsing inward on the conductor. This has the effect of reversing the direction of motion between the field and conductor that existed at 0°.

Therefore, the current will flow in a direction opposite of what it was at 0°. Also, because the applied voltage is decreasing at its greatest rate, the field is collapsing at its greatest rate. This causes the flux to cut the conductor at the greatest rate, causing the induced current magnitude to be maximum. At 90°, the applied voltage is zero decreasing toward negative, while the current is maximum positive.

At 180° in *Figure 12*, the applied voltage is at its maximum negative value, but just as at 0°, its rate of change is zero. At 180°, therefore, current will be zero. This explanation shows that the voltage peaks positive first, then 90° later the current peaks positive. Current thus lags the applied voltage in an inductor by 90°. This can easily be remembered using the phrase "ELI the ICE man." ELI represents voltage (E), inductance (L), and current (I). In an inductor, the voltage leads the current just like the letter E leads or comes before the letter I. The word ICE will be explained in the section on **capacitance**.

7.3.0 Inductive Reactance

The opposing force that an inductor presents to the flow of alternating current cannot be called resistance since it is not the result of friction within a conductor. The name given to this force is inductive **reactance** because it is the reaction of the inductor to alternating current. Inductive reactance is measured in ohms and its symbol is X_L.

Remember that the induced voltage in a conductor is proportional to the rate at which magnetic lines of force cut the conductor. The greater the rate or higher the frequency, the greater the counter-electromotive force (CEMF). Also, the induced voltage increases with an increase in inductance; the more turns, the greater the CEMF. Reactance then increases with an increase of frequency and with an increase in inductance. The formula for inductive reactance is as follows:

$$X_L = 2\pi fL$$

ELI in ELI the ICE Man

INSIDE TRACK

Remembering the phrase "ELI" as in "ELI the ICE man" is an easy way to remember the phase relationships that always exist between voltage and current in an inductive circuit. An inductive circuit is a circuit where there is more inductive reactance than capacitive reactance. The L in ELI indicates inductance. The E (voltage) is stated before the I (current) in ELI, meaning that the voltage leads the current in an inductive circuit.

Where:

X_L = inductive reactance in ohms

2π = a constant in which the Greek letter pi (π) represents 3.14 and $2 \times$ pi = 6.28

f = frequency of the alternating current in hertz

L = inductance in henrys

For example, if f is equal to 60Hz and L is equal to 20h, find X_L:

$$X_L = 2\pi fL$$
$$X_L = 6.28 \times 60Hz \times 20h$$
$$X_L = 7,536\Omega$$

Once calculated, the value of X_L is used like resistance in a form of Ohm's law:

$$I = \frac{E}{X_L}$$

Where:

I = effective current (amps)

E = effective voltage (volts)

X_L = inductive reactance (ohms)

Unlike a resistor, there is no power dissipation in an ideal inductor. An inductor limits current, but it uses no net energy since the energy required to build up the field in the inductor is given back to the circuit when the field collapses.

8.0.0 ◆ CAPACITANCE

A capacitor is a device that stores an electric charge in a dielectric material. Capacitance is the ability to store a charge. In storing a charge, a capacitor opposes a change in voltage. *Figure 13* shows a simple capacitor in a circuit, schematic representations of two types of capacitors, and a photo of common capacitors.

Figure 14(A) shows a capacitor in a DC circuit. When voltage is applied, the capacitor begins to charge, as shown in *Figure 14(B)*. The charging continues until the potential difference across the capacitor is equal to the applied voltage. This charging current is transient or temporary since it flows only until the capacitor is charged to the applied voltage. Then there is no current in the circuit. *Figure 14(C)* shows this with the voltage across the capacitor equal to the battery voltage or 10V.

The capacitor can be discharged by connecting a conducting path across the dielectric. The stored charge across the dielectric provides the potential difference to produce a discharge current, as shown in *Figure 14(D)*. Once the capacitor is completely discharged, the voltage across it equals zero, and there is no discharge current.

In a capacitive circuit, the charge and discharge current must always be in opposite directions. Current flows in one direction to charge the capacitor and in the opposite direction when the capacitor is allowed to discharge.

Current will flow in a capacitive circuit with AC voltage applied because of the capacitor charge and discharge current. There is no current through the dielectric, which is an insulator. While the capacitor is being charged by increasing applied voltage, the charging current flows in one direction to the plates. While the capacitor is discharging as the applied voltage decreases, the discharge current flows in the reverse direction. With alternating voltage applied, the capacitor alternately charges and discharges.

First, the capacitor is charged in one polarity, and then it discharges; next, the capacitor is charged in the opposite polarity, and then it discharges again. The cycles of charge and discharge current provide alternating current in the circuit at the same frequency as the applied voltage. The amount of capacitance in the circuit will determine how much current is allowed to flow.

Capacitance is measured in farads (F), where one farad is the capacitance when one coulomb is stored in the dielectric with a potential difference of one volt. Smaller values are measured in microfarads (μF). A small capacitance will allow less charge and discharge current to flow than a larger

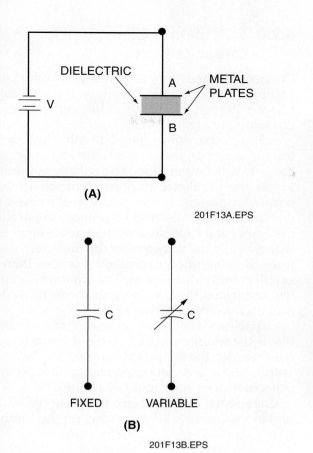

(A)

201F13A.EPS

(B)

FIXED   VARIABLE

201F13B.EPS

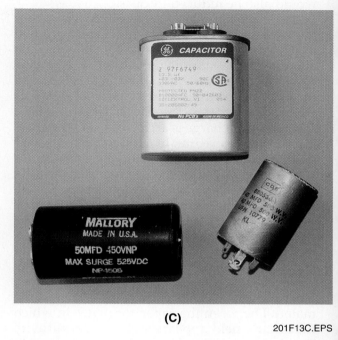

(C)

201F13C.EPS

Figure 13 ◆ Capacitors.

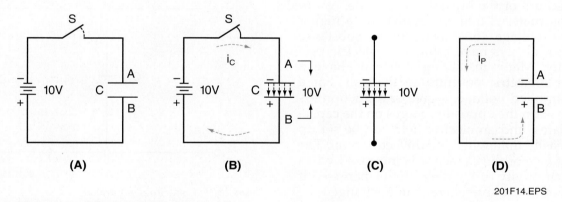

(A)   **(B)**   **(C)**   **(D)**

201F14.EPS

Figure 14 ◆ Charging and discharging a capacitor.

capacitance. The smaller capacitor has more op-position to alternating current, because less current flows with the same applied voltage.

In summary, capacitance exhibits the following characteristics:

- DC is blocked by a capacitor. Once charged, no current will flow in the circuit.
- AC flows in a capacitive circuit with AC voltage applied.
- A smaller capacitance allows less current.

8.1.0 Factors Affecting Capacitance

A capacitor consists of two conductors separated by an insulating material called a dielectric. There are many types and sizes of capacitors with different dielectric materials. The capacitance of a capacitor is determined by three factors:

- *Area of the plates* – The initial charge displacement on a set of capacitor plates is related to the number of free electrons in each plate. Larger plates will produce a greater capacitance than smaller ones. Therefore, the capacitance of a capacitor varies directly with the area of the plates. For example, if the area of the plates is doubled, the capacitance is doubled. If the size of the plates is reduced by 50%, the capacitance would also be reduced by 50%.

- *Distance between plates* – As two capacitor plates are brought closer together, more electrons will move away from the positively charged plate and move into the negatively charged plate. This is because the mutual attraction between the opposite charges on the plates increases as we move the plates closer together. This added movement of charge is an increase in the capacitance of the capacitor. In a capacitor composed of two plates of equal area, the capacitance varies inversely with the distance between the plates. For example, if the distance between plates is decreased by one-half, the capacitance will be doubled. If the distance between the plates is doubled, the capacitance would be one-half as great.

- *Dielectric permittivity* – Another factor that determines the value of capacitance is the permittivity of the dielectric. The dielectric is the material between the capacitor plates in which the electric field appears. Relative permittivity expresses the ratio of the electric field strength in a dielectric to that in a vacuum. Permittivity has nothing to do with the dielectric strength of the medium or the breakdown voltage. An insulating material that will withstand a higher applied voltage than some other substance does not always have a higher dielectric permittivity. Many insulating materials have a greater dielectric permittivity than air. For a given applied voltage, a greater attraction exists between the opposite charges on the capacitor plates, and an electric field can be set up more easily than when the dielectric is air. The capacitance of the capacitor is increased when the permittivity of the dielectric is increased if all the other parameters remain unchanged.

8.2.0 Calculating Equivalent Capacitance

Connecting capacitors in parallel is equivalent to adding the plate areas. Therefore, the total capacitance is the sum of the individual capacitances, as illustrated in *Figure 15*.

A 10µF capacitor in parallel with a 5µF capacitor, for example, provides a 15µF capacitance for the parallel combination. The voltage is the same across the parallel capacitors. Note that adding parallel capacitance is opposite to the case of inductances in parallel and resistances in parallel.

Connecting capacitances in series is equivalent to increasing the thickness of the dielectric. Therefore, the combined capacitance is less than the smallest individual value. The combined equivalent capacitance is calculated by the reciprocal formula, as shown in *Figure 16*.

Capacitors connected in series are combined like resistors in parallel. Any of the shortcut calculations for the reciprocal formula apply. For example, the combined capacitance of two equal capacitances of 10µF in series is 5µF.

Capacitors are used in series to provide a higher voltage breakdown rating for the combina-

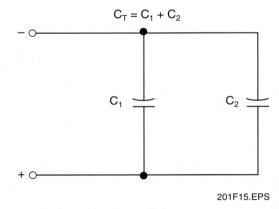

201F15.EPS

Figure 15 ◆ Capacitors in parallel.

Capacitance

The concept of capacitance, like many electrical quantities, is often hard to visualize or understand. A comparison with a balloon may help to make this concept clearer. Electrical capacitance has a charging effect similar to blowing up a balloon and holding it closed. The expansion capacity of the balloon can be changed by changing the thickness of the balloon walls. A balloon with thick walls will expand less (have less capacity) than one with thin walls. This is like a small 10µF capacitor that has less capacity and will charge less than a larger 100µF capacitor.

$$C_T = \cfrac{1}{\cfrac{1}{C_1} + \cfrac{1}{C_2}}$$

Figure 16 ◆ Capacitors in series.

tion. For instance, each of three equal capacitances in series has one-third the applied voltage.

In series, the voltage across each capacitor is inversely proportional to its capacitance. The smaller capacitance has the larger proportion of the applied voltage. The reason is that the series capacitances all have the same charge because they are in one current path. With equal charge, a smaller capacitance has a greater potential difference.

8.3.0 Capacitor Specifications

This specifies the maximum potential difference that can be applied across the plates without puncturing the dielectric.

8.3.1 Voltage Rating

Usually, the voltage rating is for temperatures up to about 60°C. High temperatures result in a lower voltage rating. Voltage ratings for general-purpose paper, mica, and ceramic capacitors are typically 200V to 500V. Ceramic capacitors with ratings of 1 to 5kV are also available.

Electrolytic capacitors are commonly used in 25V, 150V, and 450V ratings. In addition, 6V and 10V electrolytic capacitors are often used in transistor circuits. For applications where a lower voltage rating is permissible, more capacitance can be obtained in a smaller physical size.

The potential difference across the capacitor depends on the applied voltage and is not necessarily equal to the voltage rating. A voltage rating higher than the potential difference applied across the capacitor provides a safety factor for long life in service. With electrolytic capacitors, however, the actual capacitor voltage should be close to the rated voltage to produce the oxide film that provides the specified capacitance.

The voltage ratings are for applied DC voltage. The breakdown rating is lower for AC voltage because of the internal heat produced by continuous charge and discharge.

8.3.2 Leak Resistance

Consider a capacitor charged by a DC voltage source. After the charging voltage is removed, a perfect capacitor would keep its charge indefinitely. After a long period of time, however, the charge will be neutralized by a small leakage current through the dielectric and across the insulated case between terminals, because there is no perfect insulator. For paper, ceramic, and mica capacitors, the leakage current is very slight, or inversely, the leakage resistance is very high. For paper, ceramic, or mica capacitors, R_1 is 100MΩ or more. However, electrolytic capacitors may have a leakage resistance of 0.5MΩ or less.

8.4.0 Voltage and Current in a Capacitive AC Circuit

In a capacitive circuit driven by an AC voltage source, the voltage is continuously changing. Thus, the charge on the capacitor is also continuously changing. The four parts of *Figure 17* show the variation of the alternating voltage and current in a capacitive circuit for each quarter of one cycle.

The solid line represents the voltage across the capacitor, and the dotted line represents the current. The line running through the center is the zero or reference point for both the voltage and the current. The bottom line marks off the time of the cycle in terms of electric degrees. Assume that the AC voltage has been acting on the capacitor for some time before the time represented by the starting point of the sine wave.

At the beginning of the first quarter-cycle (0° to 90°), the voltage has just passed through zero and

Capacitance

Suppose you had a motor with a bad 30μF starting capacitor and no 30μF direct replacement capacitor was available. As a temporary measure, you are authorized to substitute two equal-value capacitors in its place. What size capacitors (μF) should be used if you are connecting them in parallel?

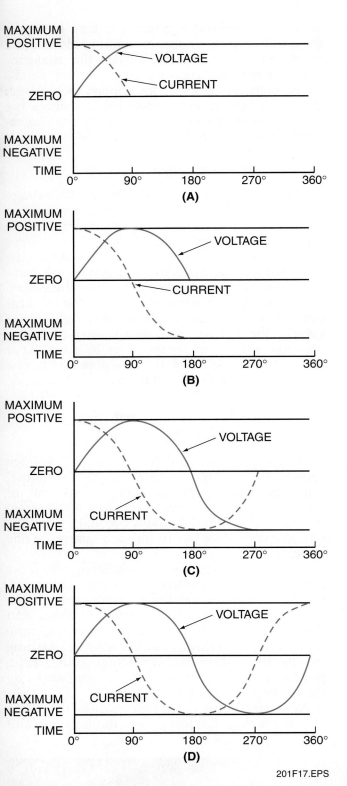

(A)

(B)

(C)

(D)

201F17.EPS

Figure 17 ◆ Voltage and current in a capacitive AC circuit.

is increasing in the positive direction. Since the zero point is the steepest part of the sine wave, the voltage is changing at its greatest rate.

The charge on a capacitor varies directly with the voltage; therefore, the charge on the capacitor

is also changing at its greatest rate at the beginning of the first quarter-cycle. In other words, the greatest number of electrons are moving off one plate and onto the other plate. Thus, the capacitor current is at its maximum value.

As the voltage proceeds toward maximum at 90°, its rate of change becomes lower and lower, making the current decrease toward zero. At 90°, the voltage across the capacitor is maximum, the capacitor is fully charged, and there is no further movement of electrons from plate to plate. That is why the current at 90° is zero.

At the end of the first quarter-cycle, the alternating voltage stops increasing in the positive direction and starts to decrease. It is still a positive voltage; but to the capacitor, the decrease in voltage means that the plate that has just accumulated an excess of electrons must lose some electrons. The current flow must reverse its direction. The second part of the figure shows the current curve to be below the zero line (negative current direction) during the second quarter-cycle (90° to 180°).

At 180°, the voltage has dropped to zero. This means that, for a brief instant, the electrons are equally distributed between the two plates; the current is maximum because the rate of change of voltage is maximum.

Just after 180°, the voltage has reversed polarity and starts building to its maximum negative peak, which is reached at the end of the third quarter-cycle (180° to 270°). During the third quarter-cycle, the rate of voltage change gradually decreases as the charge builds to a maximum at 270°. At this point, the capacitor is fully charged and carries the full impressed voltage. Because the capacitor is fully charged, there is no further exchange of electrons and the current flow is zero at this point. The conditions are exactly the same as at the end of the first quarter-cycle (90°), but the polarity is reversed.

Just after 270°, the impressed voltage once again starts to decrease, and the capacitor must lose electrons from the negative plate. It must discharge, starting at a minimum rate of flow and rising to a maximum. This discharging action continues through the last quarter-cycle (270° to 360°) until the impressed voltage has reached zero. The beginning of the entire cycle is 360°, and everything starts over again.

In *Figure 17*, note that the current always arrives at a certain point in the cycle 90° ahead of the voltage because of the charging and discharging action. This voltage-current phase relationship in a capacitive circuit is exactly opposite to that in an inductive circuit. The current through a capacitor leads the voltage across the capacitor by 90°. A convenient way to remember this is the phrase "ELI the ICE man" (ELI refers to inductors, as previously explained). ICE pertains to capacitors as follows:

$$I = \text{current}$$
$$C = \text{capacitor}$$
$$E = \text{voltage}$$

In capacitors (C), current (I) leads voltage (E) by 90°.

It is important to realize that the current and voltage are both going through their individual cycles at the same time during the period the AC voltage is impressed. The current does not go through part of its cycle (charging or discharging) and then stop and wait for the voltage to catch up. The amplitude and polarity of the voltage and the amplitude and direction of the current are continually changing.

Their positions, with respect to each other and to the zero line at any electrical instant or any degree between 0° and 360°, can be seen by reading upward from the time-degree line. The current swing from the positive peak at 0° to the negative peak at 180° is not a measure of the number of electrons or the charge on the plates. It is a picture of the direction and strength of the current in relation to the polarity and strength of the voltage appearing across the plates.

8.5.0 Capacitive Reactance

Capacitors offer a very real opposition to current flow. This opposition arises from the fact that, at a given voltage and frequency, the number of electrons that go back and forth from plate to plate is limited by the storage ability or the capacitance of the capacitor. As the capacitance is increased, a greater number of electrons changes plates every cycle. Since current is a measure of the number of electrons passing a given point in a given time, the current is increased.

Increasing the frequency will also decrease the opposition offered by a capacitor. This occurs because the number of electrons that the capacitor is capable of handling at a given voltage will change plates more often. As a result, more electrons will pass a given point in a given time (greater current flow). The opposition that a capacitor offers to AC is therefore inversely proportional to frequency and capacitance. This opposition is called capacitive reactance. Capacitive reactance decreases with increasing frequency or, for a given frequency, the capacitive reactance decreases with increasing capacitance. The symbol for capacitive reactance is X_C. The formula is:

$$X_C = \frac{1}{2\pi fC}$$

Where:

$$X_C = \text{capacitive reactance in ohms}$$
$$f = \text{frequency in hertz}$$
$$C = \text{capacitance in farads}$$
$$2\pi = 6.28 \ (2 \times 3.14)$$

For example, what is the capacitive reactance of a 0.05μF capacitor in a circuit whose frequency is 1 megahertz?

$$X_C = \frac{1}{2\pi fC} = \frac{1}{(6.28)(10^6 \text{ hertz})(5 \times 10^{-8} \text{ farads})}$$

$$X_C = \frac{1}{3.14 \times 10^{-1}} = \frac{1}{0.314} = 3.18 \text{ ohms}$$

The capacitive reactance of a 0.05μF capacitor operated at a frequency of 1 megahertz is 3.18 ohms. Suppose this same capacitor is operated at a lower frequency of 1,500 hertz instead of 1 megahertz. What is the capacitive reactance now? Substituting where $1,500 = 1.5 \times 10^3$ hertz:

$$X_C = \frac{1}{2\pi fC} = \frac{1}{(6.28)(1.5 \times 10^3 \text{ hertz})(5 \times 10^{-8} \text{ farads})}$$

$$X_C = \frac{1}{4.71 \times 10^{-4}} = 2,123 \text{ ohms}$$

Note a very interesting point from these two examples. As frequency is decreased from 1 megahertz to 1,500 hertz, the capacitive reactance increases from 3.18 ohms to 2,123 ohms. Capacitive reactance increases as the frequency decreases.

ICE in ELI the ICE Man

INSIDE TRACK

Remembering the phrase "ICE" as in "ELI the ICE man" is an easy way to remember the phrase relationships that always exist between voltage and current in a capacitive circuit. A capacitive circuit is a circuit in which there is more capacitive reactance than inductive reactance. This is indicated by the C in ICE. The I (current) is stated before the E (voltage) in ICE, meaning that the current leads the voltage in a capacitive circuit.

Frequency and Capacitive Reactance

THINK ABOUT IT

A variable capacitor is used in the tuner of an AM radio to tune the radio to the desired station. Will its capacitive reactance value be higher or lower when it is tuned to the low end of the frequency band (550kHz) than it would be when tuned to the high end of the band (1,440kHz)?

9.0.0 ◆ LC AND RLC CIRCUITS

AC circuits often contain inductors, capacitors, and/or resistors connected in series or parallel combinations. When this is done, it is important to determine the resulting phase relationship between the applied voltage and the current in the circuit. The simplest method of combining factors that have different phase relationships is vector addition with the trigonometric functions. Each quantity is represented as a vector, and the resultant vector and phase angle are then calculated.

In purely resistive circuits, the voltage and current are in phase. In inductive circuits, the voltage leads the current by 90°. In capacitive circuits, the current leads the voltage by 90°. *Figure 18* shows the phase relationships of these components used in AC circuits. Recall that these characteristics are summarized by the phrase "ELI the ICE man."

$$ELI = E \text{ Leads } I \text{ (inductive)}$$
$$ICE = I \text{ Capacitive (leads)} E$$

The **impedance** Z of a circuit is defined as the total opposition to current flow. The magnitude of the impedance Z is given by the following equation in a series circuit:

$$Z = \sqrt{R^2 + X^2}$$

Where:

Z = impedance (ohms)
R = resistance (ohms)
X = net reactance (ohms)

The current through a resistance is always in phase with the voltage applied to it; thus resistance is shown along the 0° axis. The voltage across an inductor leads the current by 90°; thus inductive reactance is shown along the 90° axis. The voltage across a capacitor lags the current by 90°; thus capacitive reactance is shown along the −90° axis. The net reactance is the difference between the inductive reactance and the capacitive reactance:

X = net reactance (ohms)
X_L = inductive reactance (ohms)
X_C = capacitive reactance (ohms)

The impedance Z is the vector sum of the resistance R and the net reactance X. The angle, called the phase angle, gives the phase relationship between the applied voltage and current.

9.1.0 RL Circuits

RL circuits combine resistors and inductors in a series, parallel, or series-parallel configuration. In a pure inductive circuit, the current lags the voltage by an angle of 90°. In a circuit containing both resistance and inductance, the current will lag the voltage by some angle between zero and 90°.

9.1.1 Series RL Circuit

Figure 19 shows a series RL circuit. Since it is a series circuit, the current is the same in all portions of the loop. Using the values shown, the circuit will be analyzed for unknown values such as X_L, Z, I, E_L, and E_R.

The solution would be worked as follows:

Step 1 Compute the value of X_L.

$$X_L = 2\pi f L$$
$$X_L = 6.28 \times 100 \times 4 = 2,512 \text{ ohms}$$

Step 2 Draw vectors R and X_L as shown in *Figure 19*. R is drawn horizontally because the circuit current and voltage across R are in phase. It therefore becomes the reference line from which other angles are measured. X_L is drawn upward at 90° from R because voltage across X_L leads circuit current through R.

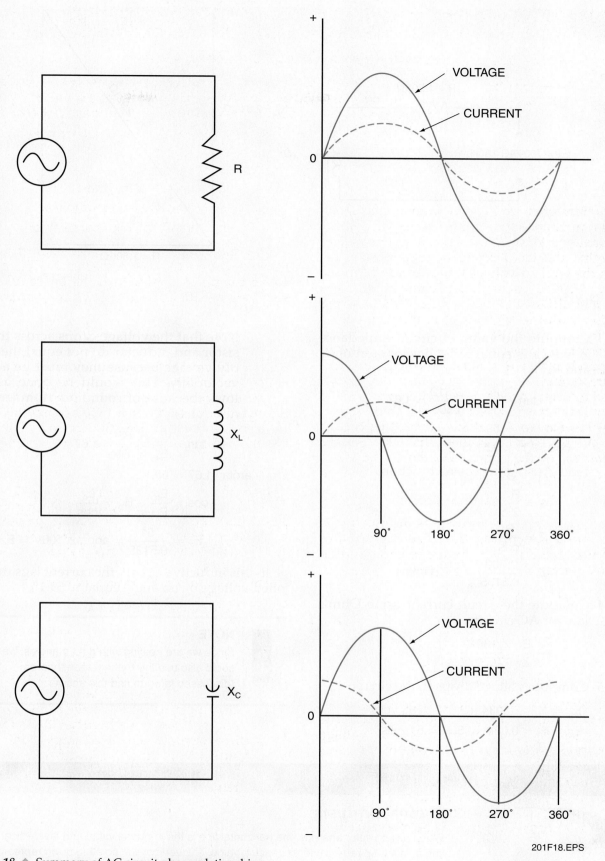

201F18.EPS

Figure 18 ◆ Summary of AC circuit phase relationships.

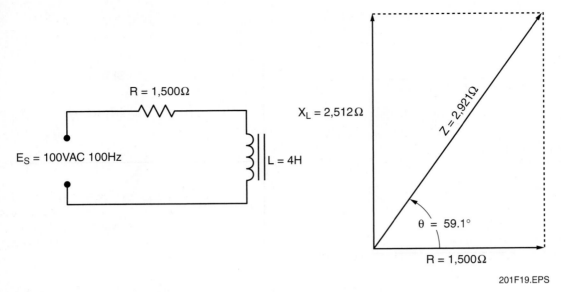

Figure 19 ◆ Series RL circuit and vector diagram.

Step 3 Compute the value of circuit impedance Z, which is equal to the vector sum of X_L and R.

$$\tan = \frac{X_L}{R} = \frac{2,512}{1,500} = 1.67$$

$$\arctan 1.67 = 59.1°$$
$$\cos 59.1° = 0.5135$$

Find Z using the cosine function:

$$\cos = \frac{R}{Z}$$

$$Z = \frac{R}{\cos}$$

$$Z = \frac{1,500}{0.5135} = 2,921 \text{ ohms}$$

Step 4 Compute the circuit current using Ohm's law for AC circuits.

$$I = \frac{E}{Z} = \frac{100\,V}{2.921\Omega} = 0.034A$$

Step 5 Compute voltage drops in the circuit.

$$E_L = IX_L = 0.034 \times 2,512 = 85 \text{ volts}$$
$$E_R = IR = 0.034 \times 1,500 = 51 \text{ volts}$$

Note that the voltage drops across the resistor and inductor do not equal the supply voltage because they must be added vectorially. This would be done as follows (because of rounding, numbers are not exact):

$$\tan = \frac{E_L}{E_R} = \frac{85}{51} = 1.67$$

$$\arctan 1.67 = 59.1°$$

$$\cos = \frac{E_R}{E_Z} \quad E_Z = \frac{E_R}{\cos}$$

$$E_Z = \frac{51}{0.5135} = \text{approx. } 100V = E_S$$

In this inductive circuit, the current lags the applied voltage by an angle equal to 59.1°.

NOTE

Since we are dealing with right triangles, we could also use the Pythagorean theorem (discussed later) to find this answer.

Vector Analysis

When using vector analysis, the horizontal line is the in-phase value and the vertical line pointing up represents the leading value. The vertical line pointing down represents the lagging value.

Figure 20 shows another series RL circuit, its associated waveforms, and vector diagrams. This circuit is used to summarize the characteristics of a series RL circuit:

- The current I flows through all the series components.
- The voltage across X_L, labeled V_L, can be considered an IX_L voltage drop, just as V_R is used for an IR voltage drop.
- The current I through X_L must lag V_L by 90°, as this is the angle between current through an inductance and its self-induced voltage.
- The current I through R and its IR voltage drop have the same phase. There is no reactance to sine wave current in any resistance. Therefore, I and IR have the same phase, or this phase angle is 0°.
- V_T is the vector sum of the two out-of-phase voltages V_R and V_L.
- Circuit current I lags V_T by the phase angle.
- Circuit impedance is the vector sum of R and X_L.

In a series circuit, the higher the value of X_L compared with R, the more inductive the circuit is. This means there is more voltage drop across the inductive reactance, and the phase angle increases toward 90°. The series current lags the applied generator voltage.

Several combinations of X_L and R in series are listed in *Table 1* with their resultant impedance and phase angle. Note that a ratio of 10:1 or more for X_L/R means that the circuit is practically all

Table 1 Series R and X_L Combinations

R (Ω)	X_L (Ω)	Z (Ω) (Approx.)	Phase Angle (θ) (°)
1	10	$\sqrt{101} = 10$	84.3°
10	10	$\sqrt{200} = 14$	45°
10	1	$\sqrt{101} = 10$	5.7°

inductive. The phase angle of 84.3° is only slightly less than 90° for the ratio of 10:1, and the total impedance Z is approximately equal to X_L. The voltage drop across X_L in the series circuit will be equal to the applied voltage, with almost none across R.

At the opposite extreme, when R is 10 times as large as X_L, the series circuit is mainly resistive. The phase angle of 5.7° means the current has almost the same phase as the applied voltage, the total impedance Z is approximately equal to R, and the voltage drop across R is practically equal to the applied voltage, with almost none across X_L.

9.1.2 Parallel RL Circuit

In a parallel RL circuit, the resistance and inductance are connected in parallel across a voltage source. Such a circuit thus has a resistive branch and an inductive branch.

The 90° phase angle must be considered for each of the branch currents, instead of voltage

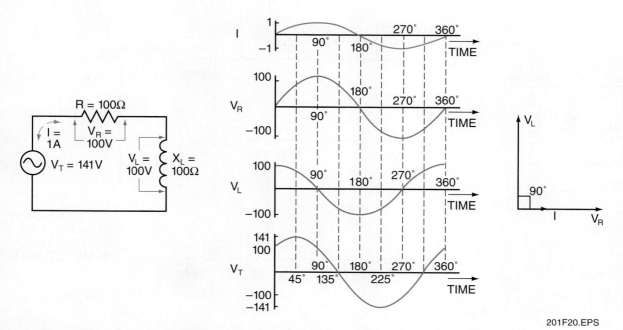

201F20.EPS

Figure 20 ◆ Series RL circuit with waveforms and vector diagram.

drops in a series circuit. Remember that any series circuit has different voltage drops, but one common current. A parallel circuit has different branch currents, but one common voltage.

In the parallel circuit in *Figure 21*, the applied voltage V_A is the same across X_L, R, and the generator, since they are all in parallel. There cannot be any phase difference between these voltages. Each branch, however, has its individual current. For the resistive branch $I_R = V_A/R$; in the inductive branch $I_L = V_A/X_L$.

The resistive branch current I_R has the same phase as the generator voltage V_A. The inductive branch current I_L lags V_A, however, because the current in an inductance lags the voltage across it by 90°.

The total line current, therefore, consists of I_R and I_L, which are 90° out of phase with each other. The phasor sum of I_R and I_L equals the total line current I_T. These phase relations are shown by the waveforms and vectors in *Figure 21*. I_T will lag V_A by some phase angle that results from the vector addition of I_R and I_L.

The impedance of a parallel RL circuit is the total opposition to current flow by the R of the resistive branch and the X_L of the inductive branch. Since X_L and R are vector quantities, they must be added vectorially.

If the line current and the applied voltage are known, Z can also be calculated by the equation:

$$Z = \frac{V_A}{I_{Line}}$$

The Z of a parallel RL circuit is always less than the R or X_L of any one branch. The branch of a parallel RL circuit that offers the most opposition to current flow has the lesser effect on the phase angle of the current.

Several combinations of X_L and R in parallel are listed in *Table 2*. When X_L is 10 times R, the parallel circuit is practically resistive because there is little inductive current in the line. The small value of I_L results from the high X_L. The total impedance of the parallel circuit is approximately equal to the resistance then, since the high value of X_L in a parallel branch has little effect. The phase angle of −5.7° is practically 0° because almost all the line current is resistive.

As X_L becomes smaller, it provides more inductive current in the main line. When X_L is 1/10R, practically all the line current is the I_L component. Then, the parallel circuit is practically all inductive, with a total impedance practically equal to X_L. The phase angle of −84.3° is almost −90° because the line current is mostly inductive. Note that these conditions are opposite from the case of X_L and R in series.

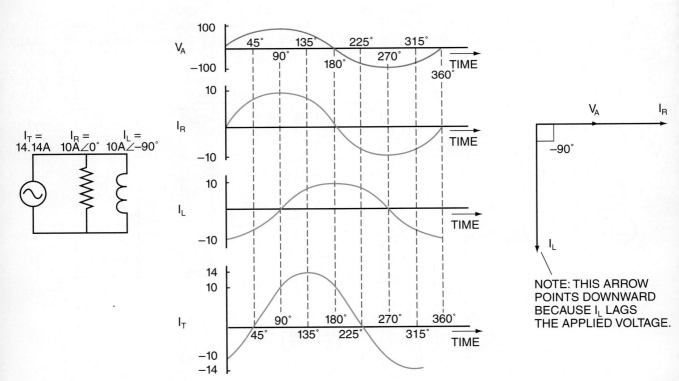

Figure 21 ◆ Parallel RL circuit with waveforms and vector diagram.

Table 2 Parallel R and X_L Combinations

R (Ω)	X_L (Ω)	I_R (A)	I_L (A)	I_T (A) (Approx.)	$Z_T = V_A/I_T$ (Ω)	Phase Angle $(\theta)_I$ (°)
1	10	10	1	$\sqrt{101} = 10$	1	−5.7°
10	10	1	1	$\sqrt{2} = 1.4$	7.07	−45°
10	1	1	10	$\sqrt{101} = 10$	1	−84.3°

9.2.0 RC Circuits

In a circuit containing resistance only, the current and voltage are in phase. In a circuit of pure capacitance, the current leads the voltage by an angle of 90°. In a circuit that has both resistance and capacitance, the current will lead the voltage by some angle between 0° and 90°.

9.2.1 Series RC Circuit

Figure 22(A) shows a series RC circuit with resistance R in series with capacitive reactance X_C. Current I is the same in X_C and R since they are in series. Each has its own series voltage drop, equal to IR for the resistance and IX_C for the reactance.

In *Figure 22(B)*, the phasor is shown horizontal as the reference phase, because I is the same throughout the series circuit. The resistive voltage drop IR has the same phase as I. The capacitor voltage IX_C must be 90° clockwise from I and IR, as the capacitive voltage lags. Note that the IX_C phasor is downward, exactly opposite from an IX_L phasor, because of the opposite phase angle.

If the capacitive reactance alone is considered, its voltage drop lags the series current I by 90°. The IR voltage has the same phase as I, however, because resistance provides no phase shift. Therefore, R and X_C combined in series must be added by vectors because they are 90° out of phase with each other, as shown in *Figure 22(C)*.

As with inductive reactance, θ (theta) is the phase angle between the generator voltage and its series current. As shown in *Figure 22(B)* and *Figure 22(C)*, θ can be calculated from the voltage or impedance triangle.

With series X_C the phase angle is negative, clockwise from the zero reference angle of I because the X_C voltage lags its current. To indicate the negative phase angle, this 90° phasor points downward from the horizontal reference, instead of upward as with the series inductive reactance.

In series, the higher the X_C compared with R, the more capacitive the circuit. There is more voltage drop across the capacitive reactance, and the phase angle increases toward −90°. The series X_C always makes the current lead the applied voltage. With all X_C and no R, the entire applied voltage is across X_C and equals −90°. Several combinations of X_C and R in series are listed in *Table 3*.

9.2.2 Parallel RC Circuit

In a parallel RC circuit, as shown in *Figure 23(A)*, a capacitive branch as well as a resistive branch are connected across a voltage source. The current that leaves the voltage source divides among the branches, so there are different currents in each branch. The current is therefore not a common quantity, as it is in the series RC circuit.

In a parallel RC circuit, the applied voltage is directly across each branch. Therefore, the branch

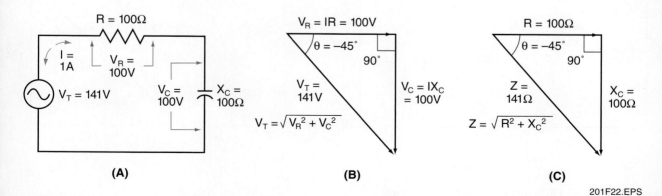

(A)   **(B)**   **(C)**

201F22.EPS

Figure 22 ◆ Series RC circuit with vector diagrams.

Table 3 Series R and X_C Combinations

R (Ω)	X_C (Ω)	Z (Ω) (Approx.)	Phase Angle $(\theta)_Z$ (°)
1	10	$\sqrt{101} = 10$	84.3°
10	10	$\sqrt{200} = 14$	45°
10	1	$\sqrt{101} = 10$	5.7°

voltages are equal in value to the applied voltage and all voltages are in phase. Since the voltage is common throughout the parallel RC circuit, it serves as the common quantity in any vector representation of parallel RC circuits. This means the reference vector will have the same phase relationship or direction as the circuit voltage. Note in *Figure 23(B)* that V_A and I_R are both shown as the 0° reference.

Current within an individual branch of an RC parallel circuit is dependent on the voltage across the branch and on the R or X_C contained in the branch. The current in the resistive branch is in phase with the branch voltage, which is the applied voltage. The current in the capacitive branch leads V_A by 90°. Since the branch voltages are the same, I_C leads I_R by 90°, as shown in *Figure 23(B)*. Since the branch currents are out of phase, they have to be added vectorially to find the line current.

The phase angle, θ, is 45° because R and X_C are equal, resulting in equal branch currents. The phase angle is between the total current I_T and the generator voltage V_A. However, the phase of V_A is the same as the phase of I_R. Therefore, θ is also between I_T and I_R.

The impedance of a parallel RC circuit represents the total opposition to current flow offered by the resistance and capacitive reactance of the circuit. The equation for calculating the impedance of a parallel RC circuit is:

$$Z = \frac{RX_C}{\sqrt{I_R^2 + I_C^2}} \ or \ Z = \frac{V_A}{I_T}$$

For the example shown in *Figure 23*, Z is:

$$Z = \frac{V_A}{I_T} = \frac{100}{14.14\,A} = 7.07\,\Omega$$

This is the opposition in ohms across the generator. This Z of 7.07Ω is equal to the resistance of 10Ω in parallel with the reactance of 10Ω. Notice that the impedance of equal values of R and X_C is not one-half, but equals 70.7% of either one.

When X_C is high relative to R, the parallel circuit is practically resistive because there is little leading capacitive current in the main line. The small value of I_C results from the high reactance of shunt X_C. The total impedance of the parallel circuit is approximately equal to the resistance, since the high value of X_C in a parallel branch has little effect.

As X_C becomes smaller, it provides more leading capacitive current in the main line. When X_C is very small relative to R, practically all the line current is the I_C component. The parallel circuit is practically all capacitive, with a total impedance practically equal to X_C.

The characteristics of different circuit arrangements are shown in *Table 4*.

9.3.0 LC Circuits

An LC circuit consists of an inductance and a capacitance connected in series or in parallel with a voltage source. There is no resistor physically in an LC circuit, but every circuit contains some resistance. Since the circuit resistance of the wiring

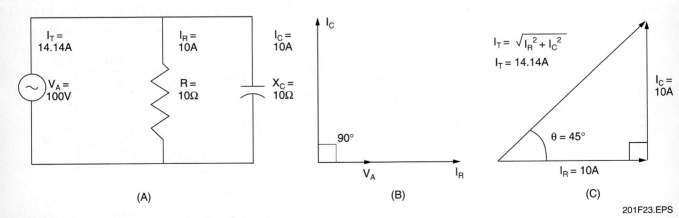

(A)   (B)   (C)

201F23.EPS

Figure 23 ◆ Parallel RC circuit with vector diagrams.

Table 4   Parallel R and X_C Combinations

R (Ω)	X_C (Ω)	I_R (A)	I_C (A)	I_T (A) (Approx.)	Z_T (Ω) (Approx.)	Phase Angle (θ) (°)
1	10	10	1	$\sqrt{101} = 10$	1	5.7°
10	10	1	1	$\sqrt{2} = 1.4$	7.07	45°
10	1	1	10	$\sqrt{101} = 10$	1	84.3°

and voltage source is usually so small, it has little or no effect on circuit operation.

In a circuit with both X_L and X_C, the opposite phase angles enable one to cancel the effect of the other. For X_L and X_C in series, the net reactance is the difference between the two series reactances, resulting in less reactance than either one. In parallel circuits, the I_L and I_C branch currents cancel. The net line current is then the difference between the two branch currents, resulting in less total line current than either branch current.

9.3.1   Series LC Circuit

As in all series circuits, the current in a series LC circuit is the same at all points. Therefore, the current in the inductor is the same as, and in phase with, the current in the capacitor. Because of this, on the vector diagram for a series LC circuit, the direction of the current vector is the reference or in the 0° direction, as shown in *Figure 24*.

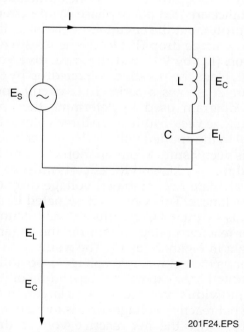

201F24.EPS

Figure 24 ◆ Series LC circuit with vector diagram.

When there is current flow in a series LC circuit, the voltage drops across the inductor and capacitor depend on the circuit current and the values of X_L and X_C. The voltage drop across the inductor leads the circuit current by 90°, and the voltage drop across the capacitor lags the circuit current by 90°. Using Kirchhoff's voltage law, the source voltage equals the sum of the voltage drops across the inductor and capacitor, with respect to the polarity of each.

Since the current through both is the same, the voltage across the inductor leads that across the capacitor by 180°. The method used to add the two voltage vectors is to subtract the smaller vector from the larger, and assign the resultant the direction of the larger. When applied to a series LC circuit, this means the applied voltage is equal to the difference between the voltage drops (E_L and E_C), with the phase angle between the applied voltage (E_T) and the circuit current determined by the larger voltage drop.

In a series LC circuit, one or both of the voltage drops are always greater than the applied voltage. Remember that although one or both of the voltage drops are greater than the applied voltage, they are 180° out of phase. One of them effectively cancels a portion of the other so that the total voltage drop is always equal to the applied voltage.

Recall that X_L is 180° out of phase with X_C. The impedance is then the vector sum of the two reactances. The reactances are 180° apart, so their vector sum is found by subtracting the smaller one from the larger.

Unlike RL and RC circuits, the impedance in an LC circuit is either purely inductive or purely capacitive.

9.3.2   Parallel LC Circuit

In a parallel LC circuit there is an inductance and a capacitance connected in parallel across a voltage source. *Figure 25* shows a parallel LC circuit with its vector diagram.

As in any parallel circuit, the voltage across the branches is the same as the applied voltage. Since

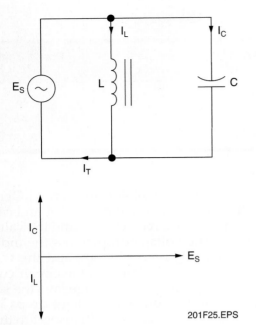

Figure 25 ◆ Parallel LC circuit with vector diagram.

they are actually the same voltage, the branch voltages and applied voltage are in phase. Because of this, the voltage is used as the 0° phase reference and the phases of the other circuit quantities are expressed in relation to the voltage.

The currents in the branches of a parallel LC circuit are both out of phase with the circuit voltage. The current in the inductive branch (I_L) lags the voltage by 90°, while the current in the capacitive branch (I_C) leads the voltage by 90°. Since the voltage is the same for both branches, currents I_L and I_C are therefore 180° out of phase. The amplitudes of the branch currents depend on the value of the reactance in the respective branches.

With the branch currents being 180° out of phase, the line current is equal to their vector sum. This vector addition is done by subtracting the smaller branch current from the larger.

The line current for a parallel LC circuit, therefore, has the phase characteristics of the larger branch current. Thus, if the inductive branch current is the larger, the line current is inductive and lags the applied voltage by 90°; if the capacitive branch current is the larger, the line current is capacitive, and leads the applied voltage by 90°.

The line current in a parallel LC circuit is always less than one of the branch currents and sometimes less than both. The reason that the line current is less than the branch currents is because the two branch currents are 180° out of phase. As a result of the phase difference, some cancellation takes place between the two currents when they combine to produce the line current. The imped-

ance of a parallel LC circuit can be found using the following equations:

$$Z = \frac{X_L \times X_C}{X_L - X_C} \text{ (for } X_L \text{ larger than } X_C)$$

or:

$$Z = \frac{X_L \times X_C}{X_C - X_L} \text{ (for } X_C \text{ larger than } X_L)$$

When using these equations, the impedance will have the phase characteristics of the smaller reactance.

9.4.0 RLC Circuits

9.4.1 Series RLC Circuit

Circuits in which the inductance, capacitance, and resistance are all connected in series are called series RLC circuits. The fundamental properties of series RLC circuits are similar to those for series LC circuits. The differences are caused by the effects of the resistance. Any practical series LC circuit contains some resistance. When the resistance is very small compared to the circuit reactance, it has almost no effect on the circuit and can be considered as zero. When the resistance is appreciable, though, it has a significant effect on the circuit operation and therefore must be considered in any circuit analysis. In a series RLC circuit, the same current flows through each component. The phase relationships between the voltage drops are the same as they were in series RC, RL, and LC circuits. The voltage drops across the inductance and capacitance are 180° out of phase. With current the same throughout the circuit as a reference, the inductive voltage drop (E_L) leads the resistive voltage drop (E_R) by 90°, and the capacitive voltage drop (E_C) lags the resistive voltage drop by 90°.

Figure 26 shows a series RLC circuit and the vector diagram used to determine the applied voltage. The vector sum of the three voltage drops is equal to the applied voltage. However, to calculate this vector sum, a combination of the methods learned for LC, RL, and RC circuits must be used. First, calculate the combined voltage drop of the two reactances. This value is designated E_X and is found as in pure LC circuits by subtracting the smaller reactive voltage drop from the larger. This is shown in *Figure 26* as E_X. The result of this calculation is the net reactive voltage drop and is either inductive or capacitive, depending on which of the individual voltage drops is larger. In *Figure 26*, the net reactive voltage drop is inductive since $E_L > E_C$. Once the net reactive voltage drop is known, it is added vectorially to the voltage drop across the resistance.

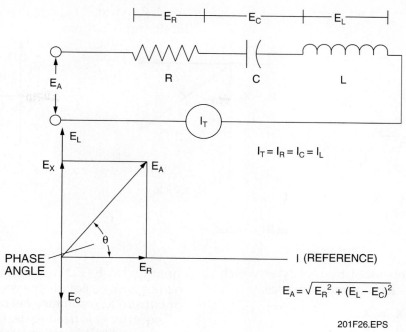

Figure 26 ◆ Series RLC circuit and vector diagram.

$$E_A = \sqrt{E_R^2 + (E_L - E_C)^2}$$

201F26.EPS

The angle between the applied voltage E_A and the voltage across the resistance E_R is the same as the phase angle between E_A and the circuit current. The reason for this is that E_R and I are in phase.

The impedance of a series RLC circuit is the vector sum of the inductive reactance, the capacitive reactance, and the resistance. This is done using the same method as for voltage drop calculations.

When X_L is greater than X_C, the net reactance is inductive, and the circuit acts essentially as an RL circuit. Similarly, when X_C is greater than X_L, the net reactance is capacitive, and the circuit acts as an RC circuit.

The same current flows in every part of a series RLC circuit. The current always leads the voltage across the capacitance by 90° and is in phase with the voltage across the resistance. The phase relationship between the current and the applied voltage, however, depends on the circuit impedance. If the impedance is inductive (X_L greater than X_C), the current is inductive and lags the applied voltage by some phase angle less than 90°. If the impedance is capacitive (X_C greater than X_L), the current is capacitive, and leads the applied voltage by some phase angle also less than 90°. The angle of the lead or lag is determined by the relative values of the net reactance and the resistance.

The greater the value of X or the smaller the value of R, the larger the phase angle, and the more reactive (or less resistive) the current. Similarly, the smaller the value of X or the larger the

value of R, the more resistive (or less reactive) the current. If either R or X is 10 or more times greater than the other, the circuit will essentially act as though it is purely resistive or reactive, as the case may be.

9.4.2 Series Resonance

Recall that:

$$X_L = 2\pi fL$$

and:

$$X_C = \frac{1}{2\pi fC}$$

With X_L and X_C being frequency sensitive, any change in frequency will affect the operating characteristics of any reactive circuit.

The effects of frequency variations on the input voltage of a series RLC circuit are shown in *Figure 27* and summarized as follows:

- As frequency is increased, X_L will become larger and X_C will become smaller. As a result, the circuit becomes even more inductive, θ increases, and the voltage across L will increase.
- As frequency decreases, X_L will become smaller and X_C larger, and θ will decrease toward zero.
- At a certain frequency, X_L will equal X_C. This is referred to as **resonance.**
- A further decrease in frequency will make X_C larger than X_L. The circuit will become capacitive and will increase in a negative direction.

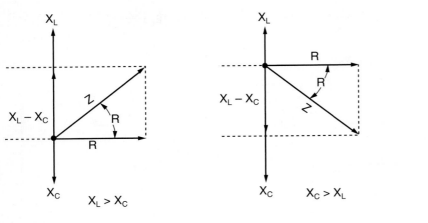

Figure 27 ◆ Effects of frequency variations on an RLC circuit.

To determine the resonant frequency at which $X_L = X_C$ requires only a bit of mathematics:

$$X_L = X_C$$
$$X_L = 2\pi fL$$
$$X_C = \frac{1}{2\pi fC}$$

Therefore, at resonance:

$$2\pi fL = \frac{1}{2\pi fC}$$

or:

$$f_r = \text{resonant frequency} = \frac{1}{2\pi\sqrt{LC}}$$

Figure 27 shows a vector diagram of the resistance and reactance at a frequency when $X_L = X_C$, or resonance. Since X_L and X_C are equal and 180° out of phase, the algebraic sum of X_L and X_C is zero. The only opposition to current flow in the circuit is R. At series resonance:

$$Z = R$$

At frequencies above resonance, X_L is greater than X_C. The circuit becomes inductive and Z increases. At frequencies below resonance, X_C is greater than X_L. The circuit becomes capacitive and Z increases. The point of lowest impedance of the circuit is at resonance. These characteristics are shown in *Figure 28*.

The impedance of a series RLC circuit is minimum at resonance, so the current must therefore be maximum. Both above and below the resonant frequency circuit impedance increases, which means that current decreases. The further the frequency is from the resonant frequency, the greater the impedance, and the smaller the current becomes. At any frequency, the current can be calculated from Ohm's law for AC circuits using the equation $I = E/Z$. Since at the resonant frequency the impedance equals the resistance, the equation for current at resonance becomes $I = E/R$.

The letter Q is used to designate the quality of a tuned circuit. It is an indication of its maximum response as well as its ability to respond within a band of frequencies.

To secure maximum currents and response, the resistance must be kept at a low value. At resonance, R is the only resistance in the circuit. The Q of a circuit is the relationship of the reactance of the circuit to its resistance:

$$Q = \frac{X_L}{R} = \frac{X_C}{R}$$

The bandwidth or bandpass of a tuned circuit is defined as those frequency limits above and below resonant frequency where the response of the circuit will drop to 0.707 of its peak response. If current or voltage drops to 0.707 of its peak value the power drops to 50%.

Bandwidth is frequency above and below resonance where power drops to one-half of its peak value. These are called the half-power points.

If the frequency of an RLC circuit is varied and the values of current at the different frequencies are plotted on a graph, the result is a curve known as the resonance curve of the circuit, as shown in *Figure 29*.

Actually, *Figure 29* shows two curves: one with a high resistance that results in a lower current flow, low Q, and wide bandwidth; and the second with a low resistance that results in high current flow at resonance, high Q, and low bandwidth.

9.4.3 Parallel RLC Circuit

A parallel RLC circuit is basically a parallel LC circuit with an added parallel branch of resistance. The solution of a parallel circuit involve

---

AC Circuits

The photo below shows a simple series circuit comprised of an ON/OFF switch, small lamp, motor, and capacitor. How would you classify this circuit? When energized, which components insert resistance, inductive reactance, and capacitive reactance into the circuit?

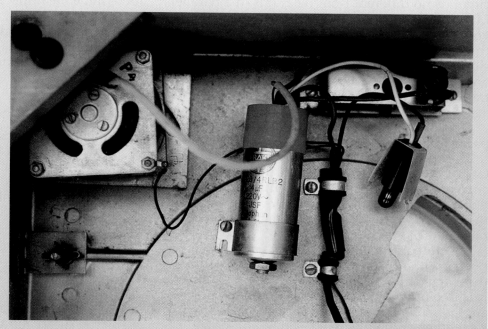

201P0101.EPS

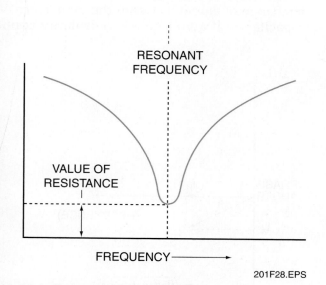

201F28.EPS

Figure 28 ◆ Frequency-impedance curve.

$$Q = \frac{X_L}{R}$$

201F29.EPS

Figure 29 ◆ Typical series resonance curve.

the solution of a parallel LC circuit, and then the solution of either a parallel RL circuit or a parallel RC circuit. The reason for this is that a parallel combination of L and C appears to the source as a pure L or a pure C. So by solving the LC portion of a parallel RLC circuit first, the circuit is reduced to an equivalent RL or RC circuit.

The distribution of the voltage in a parallel RLC circuit is no different from what it is in a parallel LC circuit, or in any parallel circuit. The branch voltages are all equal and in phase, since they are the same as the applied voltage. The resistance is simply another branch across which the applied voltage appears. Because the voltages throughout the circuit are the same, the applied voltage is again used as the θ phase reference.

Figure 30 shows the current relationship in a parallel RLC circuit.

The three branch currents in a parallel RLC circuit are an inductive current I_L, a capacitive current I_C, and a resistive current I_R. Each is independent of the others, and depends only on the applied voltage and the branch resistance or reactance.

The three branch currents all have different phases with respect to the branch voltages. I_L lags the voltage by 90°, I_C leads the voltage by 90°, and I_R is in phase with the voltage. Since the voltages are the same, I_L and I_C are 180° out of phase with each other, and both are 90° out of phase with I_R. Because I_R is in phase with the voltage, it has the same zero-reference direction as the voltage. So I_C leads I_R by 90°, and I_L lags I_R by 90°.

The line current (I_T), or total current, is the vector sum of the three branch currents, and can be calculated by adding I_L, I_C, and I_R vectorially.

Whether the line current leads or lags the applied voltage depends on which of the reactive branch currents (I_L or I_C) is the larger. If I_L is larger, I_T lags the applied voltage. If I_C is larger, I_T leads the applied voltage.

To determine the impedance of a parallel RLC circuit, first determine the net reactance X of the inductive and capacitive branches. Then use X to determine the impedance Z, the same as in a parallel RL or RC circuit.

Whenever Z is inductive, the line current will lag the applied voltage. Similarly, when Z is capacitive, the line current will lead the applied voltage.

9.4.4 Parallel Resonance

A parallel resonant circuit is a circuit in which the voltage source is in parallel with L and C. The characteristics of parallel resonance are quite different from those of series resonance. However, the frequency at which parallel resonance takes place is identical to the frequency at which series resonance takes place. Therefore, parallel resonance uses the same formula as series resonance:

$$f_r = \frac{1}{2\pi\sqrt{LC}}$$

The properties of a parallel resonant circuit are based on the action that takes place between the parallel inductance and capacitance, which is often called a tank circuit because it has the ability to store electrical energy.

The action of a tank circuit is basically one of interchange of energy between the inductance and capacitance. If a voltage is momentarily applied

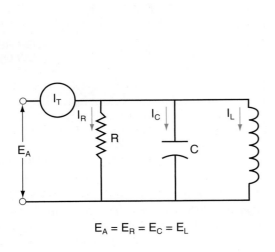

$$E_A = E_R = E_C = E_L$$

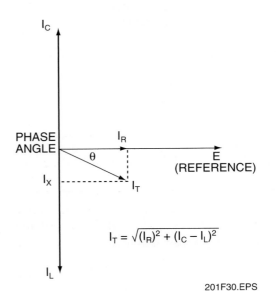

$$I_T = \sqrt{(I_R)^2 + (I_C - I_L)^2}$$

201F30.EPS

Figure 30 ◆ Parallel RLC circuit and vector diagram.

across the tank circuit, C charges to this voltage. When the applied voltage is removed, C discharges through L, and a magnetic field is built up around L by the discharge current. When C has discharged, the field around L collapses, and in doing so induces a current that is in the same direction as the current that created the field. This current, therefore, charges C in the opposite direction. When the field around L has collapsed, C again discharges, but this time in the direction opposite to before. The discharge current again causes a magnetic field around L, which, when it collapses, charges C in the same direction in which it was initially charged.

This interchange of energy and the circulating current it produces would continue indefinitely, producing a series of sine waves, if this were an ideal tank circuit with no resistance. However, since some resistance is always present, the circulating current gradually diminishes as the resistance dissipates the energy in the circuit in the form of heat. This causes the sine wave current to be damped out. If a voltage were again momentarily applied across the circuit, the interchange of energy and accompanying circulating current would begin again.

At resonance, X_L equals X_C, so the two currents I_L and I_C are also equal. Because the two currents in a parallel LC circuit are 180° out of phase, the line current, which is their vector sum, must be zero. Thus, the only current is the circulating current in the tank circuit. No line current flows, therefore the circuit has infinite impedance as far as the voltage source is concerned.

These two conditions of zero line current and infinite impedance are characteristic of ideal parallel resonant circuits at resonance. In practical circuits that contain some resistance, the theoretical conditions of zero line current and infinite impedance are not realized. Instead, practical parallel resonant circuits have minimum line current and maximum impedance at resonance. This is the exact opposite of series resonant circuits, which have maximum current and minimum impedance at resonance.

In the ideal parallel resonant circuit at resonance, the branch currents I_L and I_C are equal, so the line current is zero and the circuit impedance is infinite. Above and below the resonant frequency, one of the reactances X_L or X_C is larger than the other. The two branch currents are therefore unequal, and the line current, which equals their vector sum (or arithmetic difference), has some value greater than zero. Since line current flows, the circuit impedance is no longer infinite. The further the frequency is from the resonant frequency, the greater the difference between the values of the reactances. As a result, the line current is larger and the circuit impedance is smaller.

The principal effect of the resistance in a parallel resonant circuit is that it causes the current in the inductive branch to lag the applied voltage by a phase angle of less than 90°, instead of exactly 90° as in the case of the ideal circuit. As a result, the two branch currents are not 180° out of phase. For simplicity, resonance can still be considered as occurring when X_L equals X_C, but now when the two branch currents are added vectorially, their sum is not zero. This means that at resonance, some line current flows. Since there is line current, the impedance cannot be infinite, as it is in the ideal circuit. Thus at resonance, practical parallel resonant circuits have minimum line current and maximum resistance, instead of zero line current and infinite impedance, as do ideal circuits.

For parallel resonance, Q also measures the quality of a circuit. In parallel resonant circuits, Q depends on circuit resistance. The Q of a parallel resonant circuit is defined as:

$$Q = \frac{X_L}{R} \ or \ \frac{X_C}{R}$$

Recognize this as the same equation used for the Q of a series resonant circuit. As a result, resistance has the same effect on the Q of a parallel resonant circuit as it does on a series resonant circuit. The lower the resistance, the higher the Q of the circuit and the narrower its bandpass. Conversely, the greater the resistance, the lower the Q and the wider the bandpass.

Recall that for every series resonant circuit there is a range of frequencies above and below the resonant frequency at which, for practical purposes, the circuit can be considered as being at resonance. This range of frequencies is called the bandwidth, and consists of all the frequencies at which the circuit current was 0.707 or more times its value at resonance. Parallel resonant circuits also have a bandwidth, but it is defined in terms of the frequency-vs.-impedance curve, and consists of all the frequencies that produce a circuit impedance 0.707 or more times the impedance at resonance. *Figure 31* shows the bandpass or bandwidth as all the frequencies between F_1 and F_2.

Circuit resistance affects the width and steepness of the frequency-impedance curve. Therefore, resistance affects the circuit bandpass. A low resistive circuit causes a steep curve and narrow bandpass. A high resistive circuit causes a flatter frequency-impedance curve and therefore, a wide bandpass.

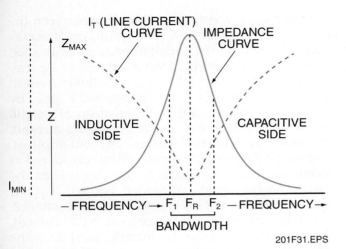

Figure 31 ◆ Tuned parallel circuit curves.

10.0.0 ◆ POWER IN AC CIRCUITS

In DC circuits, the power consumed is the sum of all the I^2R heating in the resistors. It is also equal to the power produced by the source, which is the product of the source voltage and current. In AC circuits containing only resistors, the above relationship also holds true.

10.1.0 True Power

The power consumed by resistance is called true power and is measured in units of watts. True power is the product of the resistor current squared and the resistance:

$$P_T = I^2R$$

This formula applies because current and voltage have the same phase across a resistance. To find the corresponding value of power as a product of voltage and current, this product must be multiplied by the cosine of the phase angle θ:

$$P_T = I^2R \ or \ P_T = EI \cos \theta$$

Where E and I are in rms values to calculate the true power in watts, multiplying I by the cosine of the phase angle provides the resistive component for true power equal to I^2R.

For example, a series RL circuit has 2A through a 100Ω resistor in series with the X_L of 173Ω. Therefore:

$$P_T = I^2R$$
$$P_T = 4 \times 100$$
$$P_T = 400W$$

Furthermore, in this circuit the phase angle is 60° with a cosine of 0.5. The applied voltage is 400V. Therefore:

$$P_T = EI \cos \theta$$
$$P_T = 400 \times 2 \times 0.5$$
$$P_T = 400W$$

In both cases, the true power is the same (400W because this is the amount of power supplied by the generator and dissipated in the resistance. Either formula can be used for calculating the true power.

10.2.0 Apparent Power

In ideal AC circuits containing resistors, capacitors, and inductors, the only mechanism for power consumption is $I^2_{eff}R$ heating in the resistors. Inductors and capacitors consume no power. The only function of inductors and capacitors is to store and release energy. However, because of the

The Importance of Resonance

INSIDE TRACK

A common use of RCL circuits is in resonant filter applications. Because RCL circuits provide a means for frequency selectivity, resonance in electrical circuits is very important to many types of electrical and electronic systems. Series and/or parallel RCL resonant filters are widely used to filter out or reduce the effects of unwanted harmonic frequencies and/or unwanted electromagnetic interference (EMI) signals present in power distribution circuits. Resonant filters are also used to increase the efficiency or power factor of a circuit or system.

In communications, the ability of a radio or television receiver to select a certain frequency transmitted by a certain station, and eliminate frequencies from other stations, is made possible by the use of series and/or parallel RCL resonant circuits.

phase shifts that are introduced by these elements, the power consumed by the resistors is not equal to the product of the source voltage and current. The product of the source voltage and current is called apparent power and has units of volt-amperes (VA).

The apparent power is the product of the source voltage and the total current. Therefore, apparent power is actual power delivered by the source. The formula for apparent power is:

$$P_A = (E_A)(I)$$

Figure 32 shows a series RL circuit and its associated vector diagram.

This circuit is used to calculate the apparent power and compare it to the circuit's true power:

$$P_A = (E_A)(I) \qquad P_T = EI \cos \theta$$
$$P_A = (400V)(2A) \qquad \theta = \frac{R}{X_L} = \frac{100}{173} = 60°$$
$$P_A = 800VA \qquad P_T = (400V)(2A)(\cos 60°)$$
$$P_T = (400V)(2A)(0.5)$$
$$P_T = 400W$$

Note that the apparent power formula is the product of EI alone without considering the cosine of the phase angle.

10.3.0 Reactive Power

Reactive power is that portion of the apparent power that is caused by inductors and capacitors in the circuit. Inductance and capacitance are always present in real AC circuits. No work is performed by reactive power; the power is stored in the inductors and capacitors, then returned to the circuit. Therefore, reactive power is always 90° out of phase with true power. The units for reactive power are volt-amperes-reactive (VARs).

In general, for any phase angle θ between E and I, multiplying EI by sine θ gives the vertical component at 90° for the value of the VARs. In *Figure 32*, the value of sine 60° is 800 × 0.866 = 692.8 VARs.

Note that the factor sine θ for the VARs gives the vertical or reactive component of the apparent power EI. However, multiplying EI by cosine θ as the power factor gives the horizontal or resistive component for the real power.

10.4.0 Power Factor

Because it indicates the resistive component, cosine θ is the power factor (pf) of the circuit, converting the EI product to real power. For series circuits, use the formula:

$$pf = \cos \theta = \frac{R}{Z}$$

For parallel circuits, use the formula:

$$pf = \cos \theta = \frac{I_R}{I_T}$$

In *Figure 32* as an example of a series circuit, R and Z are used for the calculations:

$$pf = \cos \theta = \frac{R}{Z} = \frac{100\Omega}{200\Omega} = 0.5$$

The power factor is not an angular measure but a numerical ratio with a value between 0 and 1, equal to the cosine of the phase angle. With all resistance and zero reactance, R and Z are the same for a series circuit of I_R and I_T and are the same for a parallel circuit. The ratio is 1. Therefore, unity power factor means a resistive circuit. At the opposite extreme, all reactance with zero resistance makes the power factor zero, meaning that the circuit is all reactive.

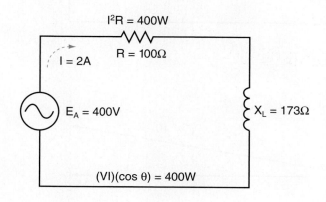
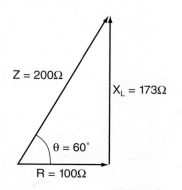

201F32.EPS

Figure 32 ◆ Power calculations in an AC circuit.

The power factor gives the relationship between apparent power and true power. The power factor can thus be defined as the ratio of true power to apparent power:

$$pf = \frac{P_T}{P_A}$$

For example, calculate the power factor of the circuit shown in *Figure 33*.

The true power is the product of the resistor current squared and the resistance:

$$P_T = I^2R$$
$$P_T = 10A^2 \times 10\Omega$$
$$P_T = 1,000W$$

The apparent power is the product of the source voltage and total current:

$$P_A = (I_T)(E)$$
$$P_A = 10.2A \times 100V$$
$$P_A = 1,020VA$$

Calculating total current:

$$I_T = \sqrt{I_R^2 + (I_C - I_L)^2} = \sqrt{10A^2 + (4A - 2A)^2}$$
$$I_T = 10.2A$$

The power factor is the ratio of true power to apparent power:

$$pf = \frac{P_T}{P_A}$$
$$pf = \frac{1,000}{1,020}$$
$$pf = 0.98$$

As illustrated in the previous example, the power factor is determined by the system load. I the load contained only resistance, the apparen power would equal the true power and the powe factor would be at its maximum value of one Purely resistive circuits have a power factor o unity or one. If the load is more inductive than ca pacitive, the apparent power will lag the tru power and the power factor will be lagging. If th load is more capacitive than inductive, the appar ent power will lead the true power and the powe factor will be leading. If there is any reactive loa on the system, the apparent power will be greate than the true power and the power factor will b less than one.

10.5.0 Power Triangle

The phase relationships among the three types c AC power are easily visualized on the power tri angle shown in *Figure 34*. The true power (W) i the horizontal leg, the apparent power (VA) is th

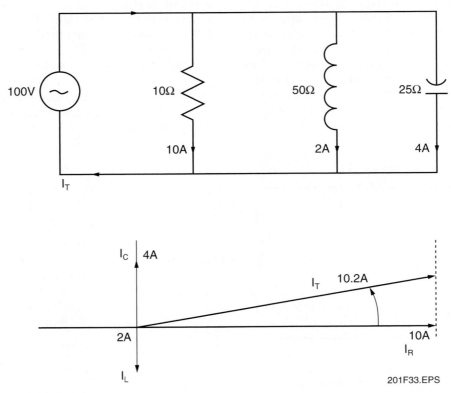

Figure 33 ◆ RLC circuit calculation.

$$P_A = \sqrt{(P_T{}^2) + (P_{RX}{}^2)}$$

$$P_T = \sqrt{(P_A{}^2) - (P_{RX}{}^2)}$$

$$P_{RX} = \sqrt{(P_A{}^2) - (P_T{}^2)}$$

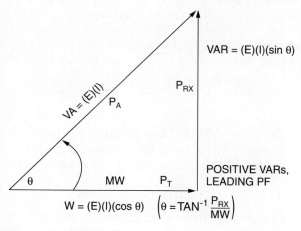

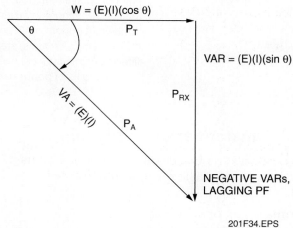

201F34.EPS

Figure 34 ◆ Power triangle.

hypotenuse, and the cosine of the phase angle between them is the power factor. The vertical leg of the triangle is the reactive power and has units of volt-amperes-reactive (VARs).

As illustrated on the power triangle (*Figure 34*), the apparent power will always be greater than the true power or reactive power. Also, the apparent power is the result of the vector addition of true and reactive power. The power magnitude relationships shown in *Figure 34* can be derived from the Pythagorean theorem for right triangles:

$$c^2 = a^2 + b^2$$

Therefore, c also equals the square root of $a^2 + b^2$, as shown below:

$$c = \sqrt{a^2 + b^2}$$

11.0.0 ◆ TRANSFORMERS

A transformer is a device that transfers electrical energy from one circuit to another by electromagnetic induction (transformer action). The electrical energy is always transferred without a change in frequency, but may involve changes in the magnitudes of voltage and current. Because a transformer works on the principle of electromagnetic induction, it must be used with an input source voltage that varies in amplitude.

Power Factor

In power distribution circuits, it is desirable to achieve a power factor approaching a value of 1 in order to obtain the most efficient transfer of power. In AC circuits where there are large inductive loads such as in motors and transformers, the power factor can be considerably less than 1. For example, in a highly inductive motor circuit, if the voltage is 120V, the current is 12A, and the current lags the voltage by 60°, the power factor is 0.5 or 50% (cosine of 60° = 0.5). The apparent power is 1,440VA (120V × 12A), but the true power is only 720W [120V × (0.5 × 12A) = 720W]. This is a very inefficient circuit. What would you do to this circuit in order to achieve a circuit having a power factor as close to 1 as possible?

Transformers

Transformers are essential to all electrical systems and all types of electronic equipment. They are especially essential to the operation of AC high-voltage power distribution systems. Transformers are used to both step up voltage and step down voltage throughout the distribution process. For example, a typical power generation plant might generate AC power at 13,800V, step it up to 230,000V for distribution over long transmission lines, step it down to 13,800V again at substations located at different points for local distribution, and finally step it down again to 240V and 120V for lighting and local power use.

11.1.0 Transformer Construction

Figure 35 shows the basic components of a transformer. In its most basic form, a transformer consists of:

- A primary coil or winding
- A secondary coil or winding
- A core that supports the coils or windings

A simple transformer action is shown in *Figure 36.* The primary winding is connected to a 60Hz AC voltage source. The magnetic field or flux builds up (expands) and collapses (contracts) around the primary winding. The expanding and contracting magnetic field around the primary winding cuts the secondary winding and induces an alternating voltage into the winding. This volt-

age causes AC to flow through the load. The volt age may be stepped up or down depending on th design of the primary and secondary windings.

11.1.1 Core Characteristics

Commonly used core materials are air, soft iror and steel. Each of these materials is suitable fo particular applications and unsuitable for others Generally, air-core transformers are used whe the voltage source has a high frequency (abov 20kHz). Iron-core transformers are usually used when the source frequency is low (below 20kHz) A soft-iron transformer is very useful where th transformer must be physically small yet efficien The iron-core transformer provides better powe transfer than the air-core transformer. Laminate

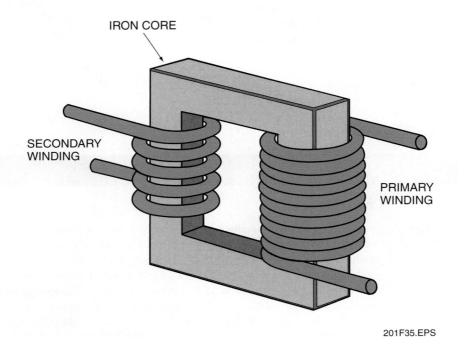

IRON CORE

SECONDARY WINDING

PRIMARY WINDING

201F35.EPS

Figure 35 ◆ Basic components of a transformer.

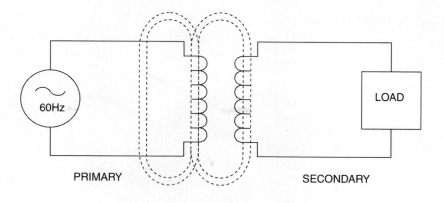

Figure 36 ◆ Transformer action.

...heets of steel are often used in a transformer to ...educe one type of power loss known as eddy cur-...ents. These are undesirable currents, induced ...nto the core, which circulate around the core. ...aminating the core reduces these currents to ...maller levels. These steel laminations are insu-...ated with a nonconducting material, such as var-...ish, and then formed into a core as shown in ...igure 37. It takes about 50 such laminations to ...nake a core one-inch thick. The most efficient ...ransformer core is one that offers the best path for ...he most lines of flux, with the least loss in mag-...etic and electrical energy.

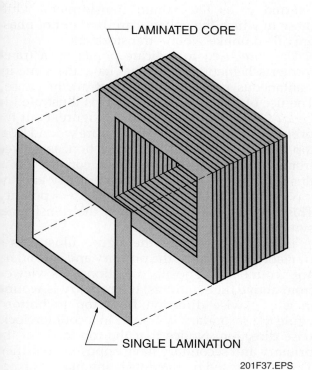

Figure 37 ◆ Steel laminated core.

11.1.2 Transformer Windings

A transformer consists of two coils called wind-ings, which are wrapped around a core. The trans-former operates when a source of AC voltage is connected to one of the windings and a load de-vice is connected to the other. The winding that is connected to the source is called the primary winding. The winding that is connected to the load is called the secondary winding. *Figure 38* shows a cutaway view of a typical transformer.

The wire is coated with varnish so that each turn of the winding is insulated from every other turn. In a transformer designed for high-voltage applications, sheets of insulating material such as paper are placed between the layers of windings to provide additional insulation.

When the primary winding is completely wound, it is wrapped in insulating paper or cloth. The secondary winding is then wound on top of the primary winding. After the secondary wind-ing is complete, it too is covered with insulating paper. Next, the iron core is inserted into and around the windings as shown.

Sometimes, terminals may be provided on the enclosure for connections to the windings. The figure shows four leads, two from the primary and two from the secondary. These leads are to be connected to the source and load, respectively.

11.2.0 Operating Characteristics

11.2.1 Energized with No Load

A no-load condition is said to exist when a voltage is applied to the primary, but no load is connected to the secondary. Assume the output of the sec-ondary is connected to a load by a switch that is open. Because of the open switch, there is no cur-rent flowing in the secondary winding. With the

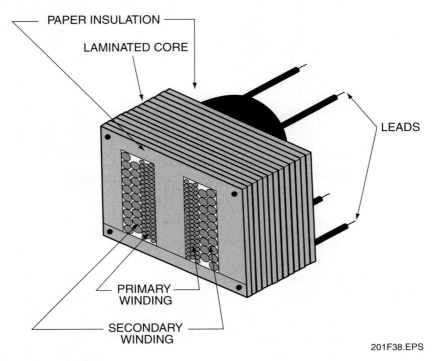

PAPER INSULATION

LAMINATED CORE

LEADS

PRIMARY WINDING

SECONDARY WINDING

201F38.EPS

Figure 38 ◆ Cutaway view of a transformer core.

switch open and an AC voltage applied to the primary, there is, however, a very small amount of current, called exciting current, flowing in the primary. Essentially, what this current does is excite the coil of the primary to create a magnetic field. The amount of exciting current is determined by three factors: the amount of voltage applied (E_A); the resistance (R) of the primary coil's wire and core losses; and the X_L, which is dependent on the frequency of the exciting current. These factors are all controlled by transformer design.

This very small amount of exciting current serves two functions:

- Most of the exciting energy is used to support the magnetic field of the primary.
- A small amount of energy is used to overcome the resistance of the wire and core. This is dissipated in the form of heat (power loss).

Exciting current will flow in the primary winding at all times to maintain this magnetic field, but no transfer of energy will take place as long as the secondary circuit is open.

11.2.2 Phase Relationship

The secondary voltage of a simple transformer may be either in phase or out of phase with the primary voltage. This depends on the direction in which the windings are wound and the arrange-

ment of the connection to the external circuit (load). Simply, this means that the two voltages may rise and fall together, or one may rise while the other is falling. Transformers in which the secondary voltage is in phase with the primary are referred to as like-wound transformers, while those in which the voltages are 180° out of phase are called unlike-wound transformers.

Dots are used to indicate points on a transformer schematic symbol that have the same instantaneous polarity (points that are in phase). The use of phase-indicating dots is illustrated in *Figure 39*. In the first part of the figure, both the primary and secondary windings are wound from top to bottom in a clockwise direction, as viewed from above the windings. When constructed in this manner, the top lead of the primary and the top lead of the secondary have the same polarity. This is indicated by the dots on the transformer symbol.

The second part of the figure illustrates a transformer in which the primary and secondary are wound in opposite directions. As viewed from above the windings, the primary is wound in a clockwise direction from top to bottom while the secondary is wound in a counterclockwise direction. Notice that the top leads of the primary and secondary have opposite polarities. This is indicated by the dots being placed on opposite ends of the transformer symbol. Thus, the

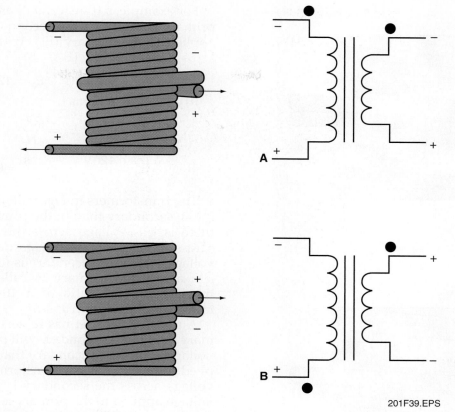

Figure 39 ◆ Transformer winding polarity.

polarity of voltage at the terminals of the transformer secondary depends on the direction in which the secondary is wound with respect to the primary.

11.3.0 Turns and Voltage Ratios

To understand how a transformer can be used to step up or step down voltage, the term turns ratio must be understood. The total voltage induced into the secondary winding of a transformer is determined mainly by the ratio of the number of turns in the primary to the number of turns in the secondary, and by the amount of voltage applied to the primary. Therefore, to set up a formula:

$$\text{Turns ratio} = \frac{\text{Number of turns in the primary}}{\text{Number of turns in the secondary}}$$

The first transformer in *Figure 40* shows a transformer whose primary consists of 10 turns of wire, and whose secondary consists of a single turn of wire. As lines of flux generated by the primary expand and collapse, they cut both the 10 turns of the primary and the single turn of the secondary. Since the length of the wire in the secondary is

approximately the same as the length of the wire in each turn of the primary, the EMF induced into the secondary will be the same as the EMF induced into each turn of the primary.

This means that if the voltage applied to the primary winding is 10 volts, the CEMF in the primary is almost 10 volts. Thus, each turn in the primary will have an induced CEMF of approximately ⅒ of the total applied voltage, or one volt. Since the same flux lines cut the turns in both the secondary and the primary, each turn will have an EMF of one volt induced into it. The first transformer in *Figure 40* has only one turn in the secondary, thus, the EMF across the secondary is one volt.

The second transformer represented in *Figure 40* has a 10-turn primary and a two-turn secondary. Since the flux induces one volt per turn, the total voltage across the secondary is two volts. Notice that the volts per turn are the same for both primary and secondary windings. Since the CEMF in the primary is equal (or almost) to the applied voltage, a proportion may be set up to express the value of the voltage induced in terms of the voltage applied to the primary and the number of turns in each winding. This proportion also

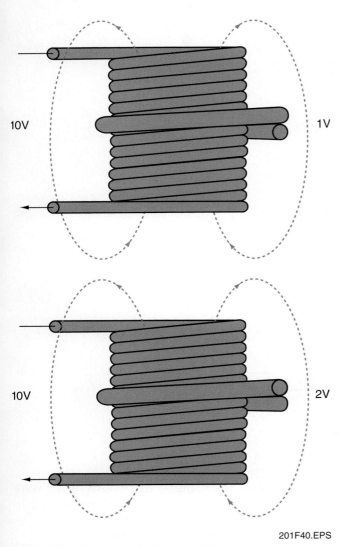

10V   **1V**

10V   **2V**

201F40.EPS

Figure 40 ◆ Transformer turns ratio.

shows the relationship between the number of turns in each winding and the voltage across each winding, and is expressed by the equation:

$$\frac{E_S}{E_P} = \frac{N_S}{N_P}$$

Where:

N_P = number of turns in the primary
E_P = voltage applied to the primary
E_S = voltage induced in the secondary
N_S = number of turns in the secondary

The equation shows that the ratio of secondary voltage to primary voltage is equal to the ratio of secondary turns to primary turns. The equation can be written as:

$$E_P N_S = E_S N_P$$

For example, a transformer has 100 turns in the primary, 50 turns in the secondary, and 120VAC applied to the primary (E_P). What is the voltage across the secondary (E_S)?

$$N_P = 100\,turns \qquad E_P = 120VAC$$
$$N_S = 50\,turns$$
$$\frac{E_S}{E_P} = \frac{N_S}{N_P} \;or\; E_S = \frac{E_P N_S}{N_P}$$
$$E_S = \frac{120\,V \times 50\,turns}{100\,turns} = 60VAC$$

The transformers in *Figure 40* have fewer turns in the secondary than in the primary. As a result, there is less voltage across the secondary than across the primary. A transformer in which the voltage across the secondary is less than the voltage across the primary is called a step-down transformer. The ratio of a 10-to-1 step-down transformer is written as 10:1.

A transformer that has fewer turns in the primary than in the secondary will produce a greater voltage across the secondary than the voltage applied to the primary. A transformer in which the voltage across the secondary is greater than the voltage applied to the primary is called a step-up transformer. The ratio of a 1-to-4 step-up transformer should be written 1:4. Notice in the two ratios that the value of the primary winding is always stated first.

11.4.0 Types of Transformers

Transformers are widely used to permit the use of trip coils and instruments of moderate current and voltage capacities and to measure the characteristics of high-voltage and high-current circuits. Since secondary voltage and current are directly related to primary voltage and current, measurements can be made under the low-voltage or low-current conditions of the secondary circuit and still determine primary characteristics. Tripping transformers and instrument transformers are examples of this use of transformers.

The primary or secondary coils of a transformer can be tapped to permit multiple input and output voltages. *Figure 41* shows several tapped transformers. The center-tapped transformer is particularly important because it can be used in conjunction with other components to convert an AC input to a DC output.

11.4.1 *Isolation Transformer*

Isolation transformers are wound so that their primary and secondary voltages are equal. Their

Turns and Voltage Ratios

What is the magnitude of the voltage and current supplied by the secondary of the transformer in the circuit shown below?

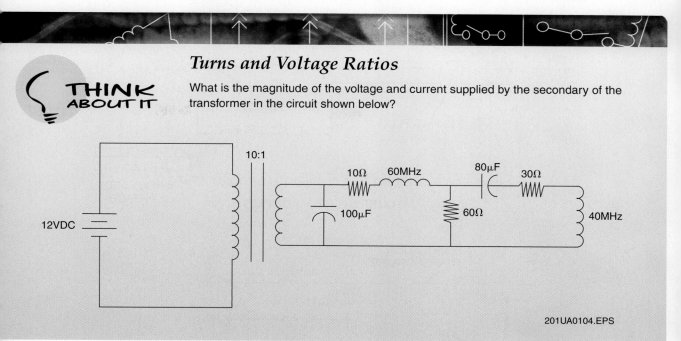

201UA0104.EPS

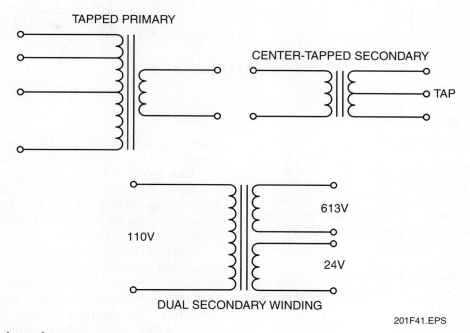

Figure 41 ◆ Tapped transformers.

201F41.EPS

purpose is to electrically isolate a piece of electrical equipment from the power distribution system.

Many pieces of electronic equipment use the metal chassis on which the components are mounted as part of the circuit (*Figure 42*). Personnel working with this equipment may accidentally come in contact with the chassis, completing the circuit to ground, and receive a shock as shown in *Figure 42(A)*. If the resistances of their body and the ground path are low, the shock can be fatal. Placing an isolation transformer in the circuit as shown in *Figure 42(B)* breaks the ground current path that includes the worker. Current can no longer flow from the power supply through the chassis and worker to ground; however, the equipment is still supplied with the normal operating voltage and current.

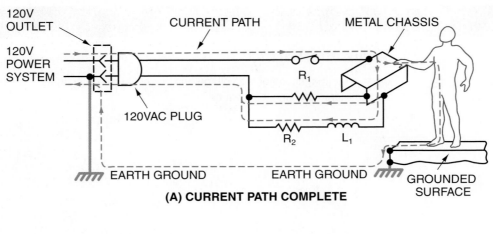

(A) CURRENT PATH COMPLETE

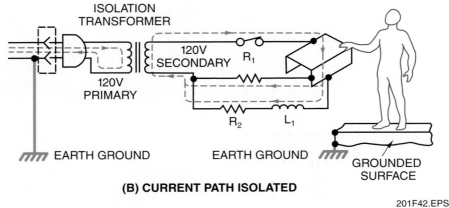

(B) CURRENT PATH ISOLATED

201F42.EPS

Figure 42 ◆ Importance of an isolation transformer.

11.4.2 *Autotransformer*

In a transformer, it is not necessary for the primary and secondary to be separate and distinct windings. *Figure 43* is a schematic diagram of what is known as an autotransformer. Note that a single coil of wire is tapped to produce what is electrically both a primary and a secondary winding.

The voltage across the secondary winding has the same relationship to the voltage across the pri-

mary that it would have if they were two distinct windings. The movable tap in the secondary is used to select a value of output voltage either higher or lower than E_P, within the range of the transformer. When the tap is at Point A, E_S is less than E_P; when the tap is at Point B, E_S is greater than E_P.

Autotransformers rely on self-induction to induce their secondary voltage. The term autotransformer can be broken down into two words: auto, meaning self; and transformer, meaning to change potential. The autotransformer is made of one winding that acts as both a primary and a secondary winding. It may be used as either a step-up or step-down transformer. Some common uses of autotransformers are as variable AC voltage supplies and fluorescent light ballast transformers and to reduce the line voltage for various types of low-voltage motor starters.

11.4.3 *Current Transformer*

A current transformer differs from other transformers in that the primary is a conductor to the load and the secondary is a coil wrapped around the wire to the load. Just as any ammeter is con-

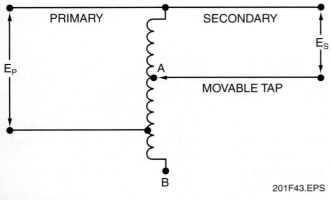

201F43.EPS

Figure 43 ◆ Autotransformer schematic diagram.

nected in line with a circuit, the current transformer is connected in series with the current to be measured. *Figure 44* is a diagram of a current transformer.

Since current transformers are series transformers, the usual voltage and current relationships do not apply. Current transformers vary considerably in rated primary current, but are usually designed with ampere-turn ratios such that the secondary delivers five amperes at full primary load.

Current transformers are generally constructed with only a few turns or no turns in the primary. The voltage in the secondary is induced by the changing magnetic field that exists around a single conductor. The secondary is wound on a circular core, and the large conductor that makes up the primary passes through the hole in its center. Because the primary has few or no turns, the secondary must have many turns (providing a high turns ratio) in order to produce a usable voltage. The advantage of this is that you get an

output off the secondary proportional to the current flowing through the primary, without an appreciable voltage drop across the primary. This is because the primary voltage equals the current times the impedance. The impedance is kept near zero by using no or very few primary turns. The disadvantage is that you cannot open the secondary circuit with the primary energized. To do so would cause the secondary current to drop rapidly to zero. This would cause the magnetic field generated by the secondary current to collapse rapidly. The rapid collapse of the secondary field through the many turns of the secondary winding would induce a dangerously high voltage in the secondary, creating an equipment and personnel hazard.

Because the output of current transformers is proportional to the current in the primary, they are most often used to power current-sensing meters and relays. This allows the instruments to respond to primary current without having to handle extreme magnitudes of current.

11.4.4 Potential Transformer

The primary of a potential transformer is connected across or in parallel with the voltage to be measured, just as a voltmeter is connected across a circuit. *Figure 45* shows the schematic diagram for a potential transformer.

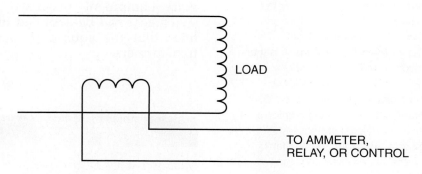

LOAD

TO AMMETER,
RELAY, OR CONTROL

201F44.EPS

Figure 44 ◆ Current transformer schematic diagram.

Isolation Transformers

INSIDE TRACK

In addition to being used to protect personnel from receiving electrical shocks, shielded isolation transformers are widely used to prevent electrical disturbances on power lines from being transmitted into related load circuits. The shielded isolation transformer has a grounded electrostatic shield between the primary and secondary windings that acts to direct unwanted signals to ground.

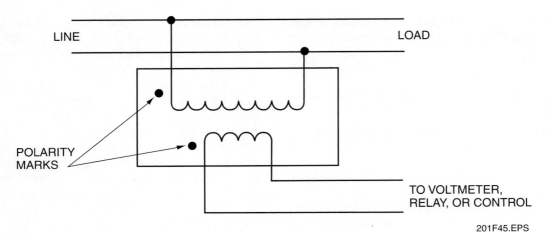

Figure 45 ◆ Potential transformer.

201F45.EPS

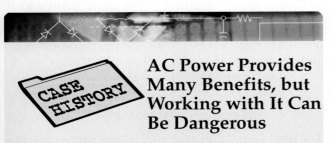
Potential transformers are basically the same as any other single-phase transformer. Although primary voltage ratings vary widely according to the specific application, secondary voltage ratings are usually 120V, a convenient voltage for meters and relays.

Because the output of potential transformers is proportional to the phase-to-phase voltage of the primary, they are often used to power voltage sensing meters and relays. This allows the instruments to respond to primary voltage while having to handle only 120V. Also, potential transformers are essentially single-phase step-down transformers. Therefore, power to operate low-voltage auxiliary equipment associated with high-voltage switchgear can be supplied off the high-voltage lines that the equipment serves via potential transformers.

Putting It All Together

A power company's distribution system has capacitor banks that are automatically switched into the system by a temperature switch during hot weather. Why?

Current Transformers

Although the use of a current transformer completely isolates the secondary and the related ammeter from the high-voltage lines, the secondary of a current transformer should never be left open circuited. To do so may result in dangerously high voltage being induced in the secondary.

Potential Transformers

In addition to being used to step down high voltages for the purpose of safe metering, potential transformers are widely used in all kinds of control devices where the condition of high voltages must be monitored. One such example involves the use of a potential transformer-operated contactor in emergency lighting standby generator circuits. Under normal conditions with utility power applied, the contactor is energized and its normally closed contacts are open. If the power fails, the contactor de-energizes, causing its contacts to close and activating the standby generator circuit.

1. An electric current always produces _____.
   a. mutual inductance
   b. a magnetic field
   c. capacitive reactance
   d. high voltage

2. The number of cycles an alternating electric current undergoes per second is known as _____.
   a. amperage
   b. frequency
   c. voltage
   d. resistance

3. What is the peak voltage in a circuit with an rms voltage of 120VAC?
   a. 117 volts
   b. 120 volts
   c. 150 volts
   d. 170 volts

4. Which of the following conditions exist in a circuit of pure resistance?
   a. The voltage and current are in phase.
   b. The voltage and current are 90° out of phase.
   c. The voltage and current are 120° out of phase.
   d. The voltage and current are 180° out of phase.

5. When the current increases in an AC circuit, what role does inductance play?
   a. It increases the current.
   b. It plays no role at all.
   c. It causes the overcurrent protection to open.
   d. It reduces the current.

6. Which of the following conditions exist in a circuit of pure inductance?
   a. The voltage and current are in phase.
   b. The voltage and current are 90° out of phase.
   c. The voltage and current are 120° out of phase.
   d. The voltage and current are 180° out of phase.

7. The opposition to current flow offered by the capacitance of a circuit is known as _____.
   a. mutual inductance
   b. pure resistance
   c. inductive reactance
   d. capacitive reactance

8. The total opposition to current flow in an AC circuit is known as _____.
   a. resistance
   b. capacitive reactance
   c. inductive reactance
   d. impedance

9. A power factor is not an angular measure, but a numerical ratio with a value between 0 and 1, equal to the _____ of the phase angle.
   a. sine
   b. tangent
   c. cosine
   d. cotangent

10. The two windings of a conventional transformer are known as the _____ windings.
    a. mutual and inductive
    b. high and low voltage
    c. primary and secondary
    d. step-up and step-down

Summary

The process by which current is produced electromagnetically is called induction. As the conductor moves across the magnetic field, it cuts the lines of force, and electrons within the conductor flow, creating an electromotive force (EMF). EMF is also known as voltage. There are three conditions that must exist before a current can be produced in this way:

- There must be a magnetic field through which the conductor can pass.
- There must be a conductor in which the voltage will be produced, and the conductor should be perpendicular to the field.
- There must be motion. Either the magnetic field or the conductor must move.

Several factors control the magnitude of the induced current. Voltage will be increased if:

- The speed with which the conductor cuts through the magnetic field is increased (the faster the conductor cuts through the field, the greater the current pulse)
- The strength of the field is increased (the stronger the field, the greater the current pulse)

- The conductor is wound to form a coil (the voltage increases directly with the number of turns of the coil)

A decrease in voltage occurs as the conductor intersects the magnetic field at an angle less than 90°. The greatest current is produced when the conductor intersects the magnetic field at right angles (perpendicular) to the flux lines.

It should be emphasized that a current may be induced by using the magnetic field of a permanent magnet or the magnetic field of another current-carrying conductor (electromagnet).

The magnetic field is among the reasons why phases of current-carrying conductors should not be separated in a raceway; all phase conductors (including the neutral) should be contained in the same raceway. For example, if phase A is separated from phase B and phase C by a metal enclosure, conduit wall, etc., the magnetic field around the conductors will cut across the conduit, causing the conduit to heat up.

Notes

Trade Terms
Introduced in This Module

Capacitance: The storage of electricity in a capacitor; capacitance produces an opposition to voltage change. The unit of measurement for capacitance is the farad (F) or microfarad (μF).

Frequency: The number of cycles an alternating electric current, sound wave, or vibrating object undergoes per second.

Hertz (Hz): A unit of frequency; one hertz equals one cycle per second.

Impedance: The opposition to current flow in an AC circuit; impedance includes resistance (R), capacitive reactance (X_C), and inductive reactance (X_L). Impedance is measured in ohms.

Inductance: The creation of a voltage due to a time-varying current; also, the opposition to current change, causing current changes to lag behind voltage changes. The unit of measure for inductance is the henry (H).

Micro: Prefix designating one-millionth of a unit. For example, one microfarad is one-millionth of a farad.

Peak voltage: The peak value of a sinusoidally varying (cyclical) voltage or current is equal to the root-mean-square (rms) value multiplied by the square root of two (1.414). AC voltages are usually expressed as rms values; that is, 120 volts, 208 volts, 240 volts, 277 volts, 480 volts, etc., are all rms values. The peak voltage, however, differs. For example, the peak value of 120 volts (rms) is actually $120 \times 1.414 = 169.71$ volts.

Radian: An angle at the center of a circle, subtending (opposite to) an arc of the circle that is equal in length to the radius.

Reactance: The imaginary part of impedance. Also, the opposition to alternating current (AC) due to capacitance (X_C) and/or inductance (X_L).

Resonance: A condition reached in an electrical circuit when the inductive reactance neutralizes the capacitance reactance, leaving ohmic resistance as the only opposition to the flow of current.

Root-mean-square (rms): The square root of the average of the square of the function taken throughout the period. The rms value of a sinusoidally varying voltage or current is the effective value of the voltage or current.

Self-inductance: A magnetic field induced in the conductor carrying the current.

This module is intended to present thorough resources for task training. The following reference works are suggested for further study. These are optional materials for continued education rather than for task training.

Introduction to Electric Circuits, Latest Edition. New York: Prentice Hall.

Principles of Electric Circuits, Latest Edition. New York: Prentice Hall.

CONTREN® LEARNING SERIES — USER FEEDBACK

The NCCER makes every effort to keep these textbooks up-to-date and free of technical errors. We appreciate your help in this process. If you have an idea for improving this textbook, or if you find an error, a typographical mistake, or an inaccuracy in NCCER's *Contren®* textbooks, please write us, using this form or a photocopy. Be sure to include the exact module number, page number, a detailed description, and the correction, if applicable. Your input will be brought to the attention of the Technical Review Committee. Thank you for your assistance.

Instructors – If you found that additional materials were necessary in order to teach this module effectively, please let us know so that we may include them in the Equipment/Materials list in the Annotated Instructor's Guide.

Write: Product Development
National Center for Construction Education and Research
P.O. Box 141104, Gainesville, FL 32614-1104

Fax: 352-334-0932

E-mail: curriculum@nccer.org

Craft _____ Module Name _____

Copyright Date _____ Module Number _____ Page Number(s) _____

Description _____

_____

_____

_____

(Optional) Correction _____

_____

_____

(Optional) Your Name and Address _____

_____

_____

_____

Electrical Test Equipment

26106-05

Durkee Cement Plant Expansion

Ash Grove Cement Company's Durkee Plant Expansion in Durkee, Oregon, was a huge project. The purpose of the expansion was to increase the capacity of the production line. The project used 7,000 cubic yards of concrete, 1,700 tons of structural steel, 425 tons of ductwork and platework, and 14,000 linear feet of piping.

26106-05
Electrical Test Equipment

Topics to be presented in this module include:

Overview

Once electrical systems are installed, they must be tested for proper operatio If a system develops a problem after installation, the cause of the problem mu be located and repaired. The best way to test and troubleshoot an electrical sy tem is to take electrical measurements at various points in the circuit. The measurements are taken using various types of electrical test equipment, cluding ammeters, voltmeters, ohmmeters, and continuity testers, among o ers. If a problem is present, it will show up in the form of an unacceptable val or no value at all.

Electricians must be able to choose the right test equipment and use t equipment correctly. Older test equipment relied on analog meter moveme and scales. Most electrical meters now use digital technology with digital rea outs. Electricians must keep up with changes in testing technology and lea how to make use of the most current test equipment available.

Objectives

When you have completed this module, you will be able to do the following:

. Explain the operation of and describe the following pieces of test equipment:
   - Ammeter
   - Voltmeter
   - Ohmmeter
   - Volt-ohm-milliammeter (VOM)
   - Wattmeter
   - Megohmmeter
   - Frequency meter
   - Power factor meter
   - Continuity tester
   - Voltage tester
   - Recording instruments
   - Cable-length meters
. Explain how to read and convert from one scale to another using the above test equipment.
. Explain the importance of proper meter polarity.
. Define frequency and explain the use of a frequency meter.
. Explain the difference between digital and analog meters.

Trade Terms

il
ntinuity
Arsonval meter
movement

Decibel
Frequency

Required Trainee Materials

. Paper and pencil
. Copy of the latest edition of the *National Electrical Code*®
. Appropriate personal protective equipment

Prerequisites

fore you begin this module, it is recommended
at you successfully complete *Core Curriculum*
d *Electrical Level One,* Modules 26101-05
rough 26105-05.
This course map shows all of the modules in
ctrical Level One. The suggested training order
gins at the bottom and proceeds up. Skill levels
crease as you advance on the course map. The
al Training Program Sponsor may adjust the
ining order.

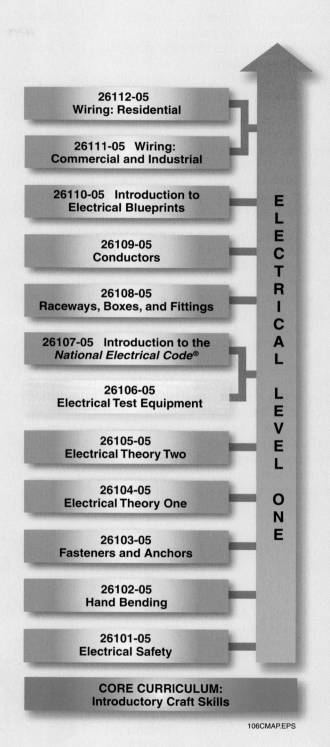

106CMAP.EPS

1.0.0 ◆ INTRODUCTION

The use of electronic test instruments and meters generally involves these three applications:

- Verifying proper operation of instruments and associated equipment
- Calibrating electronic instruments and associated equipment
- Troubleshooting electrical/electronic circuits and equipment

For these applications, specific test equipment is selected to analyze circuits and to determine specific characteristics of discrete components.

The test equipment an electrician chooses for a specific task depends on the type of measurement and the level of accuracy required. Additional factors that may influence selection include:

- Whether the test equipment is portable
- The amount of information that the test equipment provides
- The likelihood that the test equipment may damage the circuit or component being tested (some test equipment can generate enough voltage or current to damage an instrument or electronic circuit)

This module will focus on some of the test equipment that you will be required to use in your job as an electrician. The intent is to familiarize you with the use and operation of such equipment and to provide you with practical experience involving that equipment. Upon completion of this module, you should be able to select the appropriate test equipment and effectively use that equipment to perform an assigned task.

2.0.0 ◆ METERS

The functioning of conventional electrical measuring instruments is based upon electromechanical principles. Their mechanical components usually work on direct current (DC). Mechanical frequency meters are an exception. A meter that measures alternating current (AC) has a built-in rectifier to change the AC to DC and resistors to correct for the various ranges.

Today, many meters are solid-state digital systems; they are superior because they have no moving parts. These meters will work in any position, unlike mechanical meters, which must remain in one position to be read accurately.

2.1.0 d'Arsonval Meter Movement

In 1882, a Frenchman named Arsene d'Arsonval invented the galvanometer. This meter used a stationary permanent magnet and a moving coil (*Figure 1*) to indicate current flow on a calibrated scale. The early galvanometer was very accurate but could only measure very small currents. Over the following years, many improvements were made that extended the range of the meter and increased its ruggedness. The d'Arsonval meter movement is the most commonly used meter movement today.

A moving-coil meter movement operates on the electromagnetic principle. In its simplest form, the moving-coil meter uses a coil of very fine wire wound on a light aluminum frame. A permanent magnet surrounds the coil. The aluminum frame is mounted on pivots to allow it and the coil to rotate freely between the poles

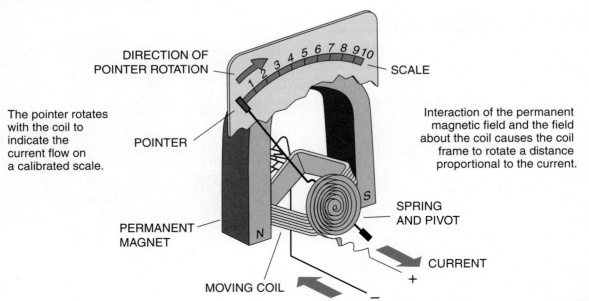

DIRECTION OF POINTER ROTATION

SCALE

The pointer rotates with the coil to indicate the current flow on a calibrated scale.

POINTER

Interaction of the permanent magnetic field and the field about the coil causes the coil frame to rotate a distance proportional to the current.

SPRING AND PIVOT

PERMANENT MAGNET

MOVING COIL

CURRENT

106F01.EPS

Figure 1 ◆ Moving-coil meter movement.

the permanent magnet. When current flows through the coil, it becomes magnetized, and the polarity of the coil is such that it is repelled by the field of the permanent magnet. This will cause the coil frame to rotate on its pivots, and the distance it rotates is determined by the amount of current that flows through the coil. By attaching a pointer to the coil frame and adding a calibrated scale, the amount of current flowing through the meter can be measured.

The d'Arsonval meter movement uses this same principle of operation (*Figure 2*). As the current flow increases, the magnetic field around the coil increases, the amount of coil rotation increases, and the pointer swings farther across the meter scale.

0.0 ◆ AMMETER

The ammeter is used to measure current. Most models will measure only small amounts of current. The typical range is in microamperes, μA (0.000001A) or milliamperes, mA (0.001A). Very few ammeters can measure more than 10mA. To increase the range to the ampere level, a shunt is used. To measure above 10mA, a shunt with an extremely low resistance is placed in series with the load, and the meter is connected across the shunt to measure the resulting voltage drop proportional to current flow. A shunt has a very large wattage rating in order to carry a large current.

The meter is connected in parallel with the shunt (*Figure 3*). Shunts located inside the meter case (internal shunts) are generally used to measure values up to 30 amps; shunts located away from the meter case (external shunts) with leads going to the meter are generally used to measure values greater than 30 amps. Above 30 amps of current, the heat generated could damage the meter if an internal shunt were used. The use of a shunt allows the ammeter to derive current in amps by actually measuring the voltage drop across the shunt. Ammeter connections are shown in *Figure 4*.

Never connect an ammeter in parallel with a load. Because of the low resistance in the ammeter, this will cause a short circuit, probable damage to the meter and/or circuit, and personal injury. When connecting an ammeter in a DC circuit, you must observe proper polarity. In other words, you must connect the negative terminal of the meter to the negative or low potential point in the circuit, and connect the positive terminal of the meter to the positive or high potential point in the circuit (*Figure 5*). Current must flow through the meter from minus (−) to plus (+). If you connect the meter with the polarities reversed, the meter coil will move in the opposite direction, and the pointer might strike the left retaining pin. You will not obtain a current reading, and you might bend the pointer of the meter.

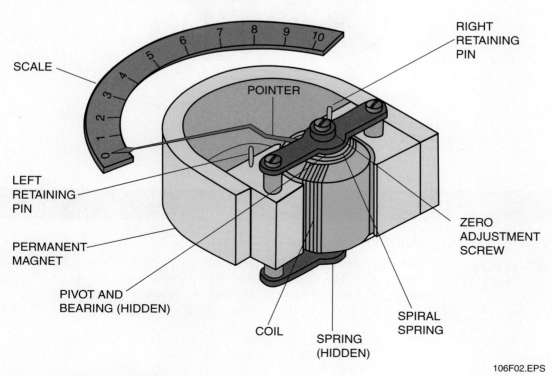

SCALE

RIGHT RETAINING PIN

POINTER

LEFT RETAINING PIN

PERMANENT MAGNET

PIVOT AND BEARING (HIDDEN)

ZERO ADJUSTMENT SCREW

COIL

SPRING (HIDDEN)

SPIRAL SPRING

106F02.EPS

Figure 2 ◆ d'Arsonval meter movement.

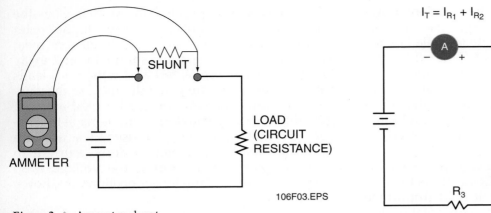

$I_T = I_{R_1} + I_{R_2}$

Figure 3 ◆ Ammeter shunt.

106F03.EPS

Figure 4 ◆ Ammeter connections.

106F04.EPS

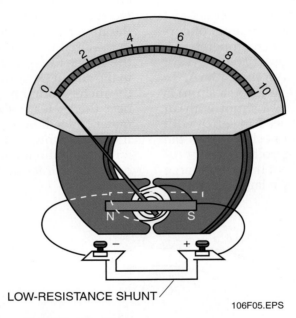

LOW-RESISTANCE SHUNT

106F05.EPS

Figure 5 ◆ DC ammeter.

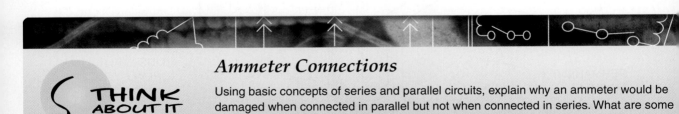

Ammeter Connections

Using basic concepts of series and parallel circuits, explain why an ammeter would be damaged when connected in parallel but not when connected in series. What are some practical examples of connecting an ammeter in series with a load?

THINK ABOUT IT

It is not very practical to use an ammeter that is only one range; therefore, a multirange ammeter needs to be discussed. A multirange ammeter is one containing a basic meter movement and several shunts that can be connected across the meter movement. See *Figure 6*.

A range switch is normally used to select the particular shunt for the desired current range. Sometimes, however, separate terminals for each range are mounted on the meter case. Some multirange ammeters have only one set of values on the scale, even though they measure several different current ranges. For example, if the scale is calibrated in values from 0 to 1 milliamp (mA), and the range switch is in the 1mA position, read the current directly. However, if the range switch is in the 10mA position, multiply the scale reading by 10 to find the amount of current flowing through the circuit. See *Figure 7*.

Other current meters have a separate set of values on the calibrated scale that correspond to the different positions of the range switch. In this case, be sure that you read the set of values that correspond to the position of the range switch (*Figure 8*).

The range of this 1mA meter movement has been extended to measure 0–10mA, 0–100mA, and 0–1A by using multiple shunts.

RANGE SWITCH

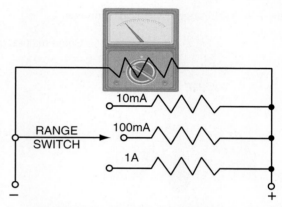

A range switch provides the simplest way of setting the meter to the desired range.

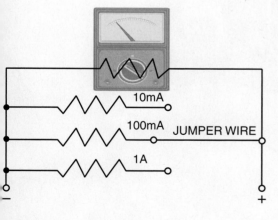

JUMPER WIRE

When separate terminals are used to select the desired range, a jumper must be connected from the positive terminal to connect the shunt across the meter movement.

106F06.EPS

Figure 6 ◆ Multirange ammeter.

Measuring Amperage

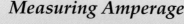

A common example of measuring amperage is checking for a balanced flow of current on the two legs of a service entry.

Some multirange current meters have only one set of values marked on the scale.

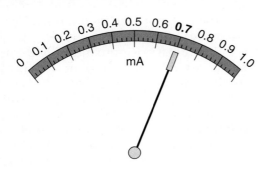

RANGE SWITCH

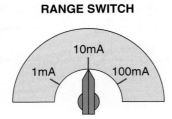

To find the current flowing in the circuit, multiply the scale reading by the range switch setting: current = 0.7 × 10mA = 7mA.

106F07.EPS

Figure 7 ◆ Multirange single-scale ammeter.

Some multirange current meters have a set of values for each range switch position

RANGE SWITCH

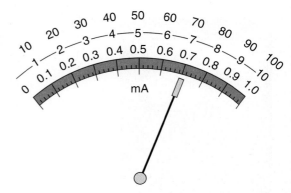

To find the current flowing in the circuit, read the meter scale that corresponds to the position of the range switch: current = 7mA.

106F08.EPS

Figure 8 ◆ Multirange multiscale ammeter.

When measuring AC current at levels greater than one ampere, a clamp-on ammeter is often used. This meter also measures DC. The clamp-on ammeter may have a mechanical movement or a digital readout. These meters clamp over the wire and do not break the insulation. This type of ammeter senses current flow by measuring the magnetic field surrounding the conductor. When using this type of ammeter, be sure to measure only one conductor at a time. This type of meter will often measure up to 1,000 amperes at 600 volts. A digital clamp-on multimeter being used to measure current is shown in *Figure 9*.

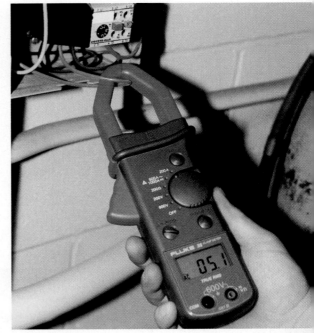

106F09.EP

Figure 9 ◆ Clamp-on multimeter being used to measure current.

0.0 ◆ VOLTMETER

he basic current meter movement already cov-
ed, whether AC or DC, can also be used to mea-
re voltage (electromotive force or emf). The
eter coil has a fixed resistance, and, therefore,
hen current flows through the coil, a voltage
op will be developed across this resistance. Ac-
rding to Ohm's law, the voltage drop will be di-
ctly proportional to the amount of current
wing through the coil. Also, the amount of curnt flowing through the coil is directly propor-
nal to the amount of voltage applied to it.
erefore, by calibrating the meter scale in units
voltage instead of current, the voltage in a cir-
it can be measured.

Since a basic current meter movement has a low
il resistance and low current-handling capabili-
s, its use as a voltmeter is very limited. In fact,
e maximum voltage that could be measured
th a one milliamp meter movement is one volt
gure 10).

The voltage range of a meter movement can be
tended by adding a resistor, called a multiplier
sistor, in series. The value of this resistor must

be such that, when added to the meter coil resistance, the total resistance limits the current to the
full-scale current rating of the meter for any applied voltage (*Figure 11*).

Voltmeters must be in parallel with the circuit
component being measured. On the higher ranges,
the amount of current flowing through the meter
is much lower due to its very high total resistance.
However, an inaccurate reading will result if the
voltmeter is placed in series rather than in parallel
with a circuit component. When connecting a DC
voltmeter, always observe the proper polarity. The
negative lead of the meter must be connected to
the negative or low potential end of the component, and the positive lead to the positive or high
potential end of the component. As was the case
when using an ammeter, if you connect a voltmeter to the component with opposing polarities,
the meter coil will move to the left, and the pointer
could be bent. In an AC circuit, the voltage constantly reverses polarity, so there is no need to observe polarity when connecting the voltmeter to a
component in an AC circuit.

Since the voltage across the meter coil resistance
is proportional to the current flowing through the
coil, the 1mA current meter movement can
measure voltage directly by calibrating the meter
scale in the units of voltage that produce the
current through the coil.

$$E = I_R R_M = 0.001 \times 1000 = 1V$$

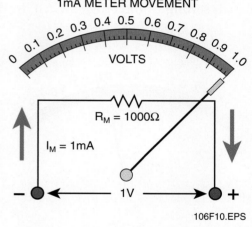

ure 10 ◆ 1mA meter movement.

By connecting a multiplier resistor
in series with the meter resistance,
the range of a basic meter movement
can be extended to measure voltages
higher than the $I_M R_M$ voltage drop
across the meter coil.

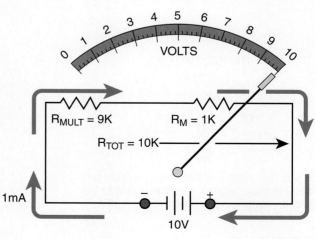

ure 11 ◆ Adding multiplier resistor.

Voltmeters

THINK ABOUT IT

Again using basic circuit theory, explain why a voltmeter must be connected in parallel with the circuit. What would you be measuring if the voltmeter were connected in series?

As with ammeters, it is impractical to have a voltmeter that will only measure one range of voltages; therefore, multirange voltmeters also need to be discussed. To make a voltmeter capable of measuring multiple ranges, an electrician needs several multiplier resistors that are switch-selectable for the different ranges desired. Reading the scale of a voltmeter is as simple as reading the scale of an ammeter. Some multirange voltmeters have only one range of values marked on the scale, and the scale reading must be multiplied by the range switch setting to obtain the correct voltage (*Figure 12*).

Other voltmeters have different ranges on the scale for each setting of the range switch. In this case, be sure that you read the set of values th correspond to the position of the range swit (*Figure 13*).

Some digital voltmeters are autorangir These types of voltmeters do not have a ran switch. The internal construction of the meter self will select the proper resistance for the cu rent being detected. However, when using voltmeter that is not autoranging, always sta with the highest voltage setting and work dov until the indication reads somewhere betwe half-scale and three-quarter scale. This will giv more accurate reading and will prevent dama to the voltmeter.

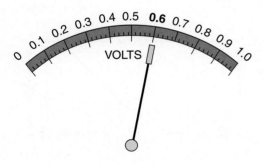

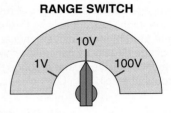

RANGE SWITCH

To find the voltage across a component, multiply the scale reading by the setting of the range switch: voltage = 0.6 × 10 = 6.0V.

106F12.EPS

Figure 12 ◆ Multirange single-scale voltmeter.

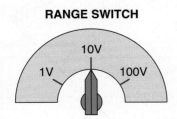

RANGE SWITCH

To find the voltage across a component, simply read the meter scale that corresponds to the position of the range switch: voltage = 6V.

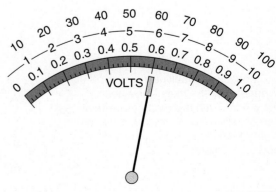

106F13.EPS

Figure 13 ◆ Multirange multiscale voltmeter.

0.0 ◆ OHMMETER

n ohmmeter is a device that measures the resistance of a circuit or component. It can also be used locate open circuits or shorted circuits. Basially, an ohmmeter consists of a DC current meter ovement, a low-voltage DC power source (usualy a battery), and current-limiting resistors, all of hich are connected in series (*Figure 14*).

This combination of devices allows the meter to lculate resistance by deriving it using Ohm's w. Before measuring the resistance of an unnown resistor or electrical circuit, the test leads e shorted together. This causes current to flow rough the meter movement and the pointer dects to the right. This means that there is zero resistance present across the input terminals of the ammeter, and when zero resistance is present, e pointer will deflect full scale. Therefore, fullale deflection of an ohmmeter indicates zero resistance. Most ohmmeters have a zero adjustment nob. This is used to correct for the fact that as the tteries of the meter age, their output voltage deeases. As the voltage drops, the current through e circuit decreases, and the meter will no longer flect full scale. By correcting for this change before each use, the internal resistance of the meter, ong with the resistance of the leads, is lowered d nulled to deflect the pointer full scale.

After the ohmmeter is adjusted to zero, it is ady to be connected in a circuit to measure retance. The circuit must be verified as deergized by using a voltmeter prior to taking a ading with an ohmmeter. If the circuit were energized, its voltage could cause a damaging curnt to flow through the meter. This can cause damage to the meter and/or circuit as well as personal injury.

When making resistance measurements in circuits, each component in the circuit can be tested individually by removing the component from the circuit and connecting the ohmmeter leads across it. Actually, the component does not have to be totally removed from the circuit. Usually, the part can be effectively isolated by disconnecting one of its leads from the circuit. However, this method can still be somewhat time consuming. Some manufacturers provide charts that list the resistance readings that should be obtained from various test points to a reference point in the equipment. There are usually many parts of the circuit between the test point and the reference point, so if you get an abnormal reading, you must begin checking smaller groups of components, or individual components, to isolate the defective one. If resistance charts are not available, be very careful to ensure that other components are not in parallel with the component being tested.

6.0.0 ◆ VOLT-OHM-MILLIAMMETER

The volt-ohm-milliammeter (VOM), also known as the multimeter, is a multipurpose instrument. It is a combination of the three previous meters discussed: the milliammeter, the voltmeter, and the ohmmeter. One common analog multimeter is shown in *Figure 15*. There are many different models of this basic multimeter. To prevent having to discuss each and every meter, one version will be explained here. Any controls or functions on your meter that are not covered here should be reviewed in the applicable owner's manual.

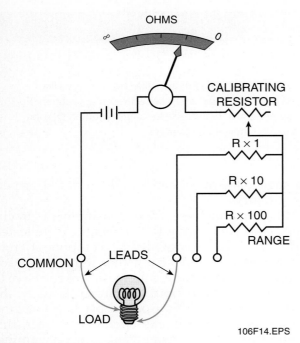

Figure 14 ◆ Ohmmeter schematic.

The typical volt-ohm-milliammeter is a rugge accurate, compact, easy-to-use instrument. T instrument can be used to make accurate me surements of DC and AC voltages, current, res tance, **decibels,** and output voltage. The outp voltage function is used for measuring the A component of a mixture of AC and DC voltag This occurs primarily in amplifier circuits.

This meter has the following features: a 0 volt DC range, 0–500 volt DC and AC ranges TRANSIT position on the range switch, rubb plug bumpers on the bottom of the case to redu sliding, and an externally accessible battery a fuse compartment.

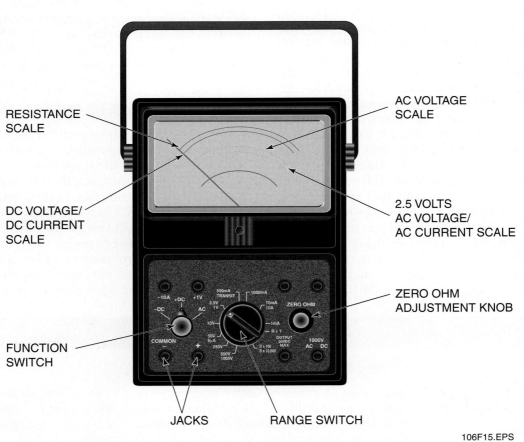

Figure 15 ◆ Multimeter.

1.0 Specifications

The specifications of the example multimeter are:

DC voltage:
 Sensitivity: 20KΩ per volt
 Accuracy: 1¾% of full scale

AC voltage:
 Sensitivity: 5KΩ per volt
 Accuracy: 3% of full scale

DC current:
 250mV to 400mV drop
 Accuracy: 1¾% of full scale

Resistance:
 Accuracy: 1.75° of arc
 Nominal open circuit voltage 1.5V (9V on the 10KΩ ohm range)

Nominal short circuit current:
 1Ω range: 1.25mA
 100Ω range: 1.25mA
 10KΩ range: 75mA

Meter frequency response:
 Up to 100kHz

6.2.0 Overload Protection

In the example multimeter, a 1A, 250V fuse is provided to protect the circuits on the ohmmeter ranges. It also protects the milliampere ranges from excessive overloads. If the instrument fails to indicate, the fuse may be burned out. The fuse is mounted in a holder in the battery and fuse compartment. A spare fuse is located in a well between the + terminal of the D cell and the side of the case. Access to the compartment is obtained by loosening the single captivating screw on the compartment cover. To replace a burned-out fuse, remove it from the holder and replace it with a fuse of the exact same type. When removing the fuse from its holder, first remove the battery.

In addition to the fuse, a varistor protects the indicating instrument circuit. The varistor limits the current through the moving coil in case of overload.

The fuse and varistor will prevent serious damage to the meter in most cases of accidental overload. However, no overload protection system is completely foolproof, and misapplication on high-voltage circuits can damage the instrument. Care and caution should always be exercised to protect both you and the VOM.

Getting to Know Your VOM

VOMs are available in both digital and analog versions. Many beginning electricians find it helpful to get to know the operation of one type of VOM very well, then move on to other types once they have mastered the basics.

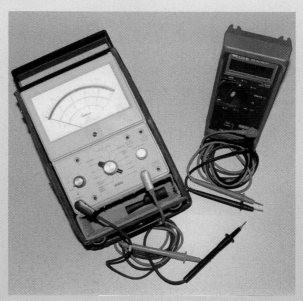

106PO601.EPS

Check Your Connections

When using a VOM, make sure your leads match the function. The meter can be in the voltage function and even display volts, but if the leads are in the amp jack, the meter will short circuit if connected to a voltage source.

Beside the actual steps used in making a measurement, some other points to consider while using a multimeter are:

- Keep the instrument in a horizontal position when storing and away from the edge of a workbench, shelf, or other area where it may be knocked off and damaged.
- Avoid rapid or extreme temperature changes. For example, do not leave the meter in your truck during hot or cold weather. Rapid and extreme temperature changes will advance the aging of the meter components and adversely affect meter life and accuracy.
- Avoid overloading the measuring circuits of the instrument. Develop a habit of checking the range position before connecting the test leads to a circuit. Even slight overloads can damage the meter. Even though it may not be noticeable in blown fuses or a bent needle, damage has been done. Slight overloads will advance the aging of components, again causing changes in meter life and accuracy.
- Place the range switch in the TRANSIT position when the instrument is not in use or when it is being moved. This reduces the swinging of the pointer when the meter is carried. Every meter does not have a TRANSIT position, but if the meter does, it should be used. Random, uncontrolled swings of the meter movement may damage the movement, bend the needle, or reduce its accuracy.
- If the meter has not been used for a long period of time, rotate the function and range switches in both directions to wipe the switch contacts. Most switch contacts are plated with copper or silver. Over a period of time, these materials will oxidize (tarnish). This will create a high resistance through the switch, causing a large inaccuracy. Rotating through the switch positions will clean the tarnish off and provide good electrical contact.

6.3.0 Making Measurements

CAUTION

When using the meter as a millivoltmeter, care must be taken to prevent damage to the indicating instrument from excessive voltage. Before using the 250mV range, first use the 1.0 range to determine that the voltage measured is no greater than 250mV (or 0.25VDC).

6.3.1 Measuring DC Voltage, 0–250 Millivolts

Step 1 Set the function switch to +DC.

Step 2 Plug the black test lead into the − (COMMON) jack and the red test lead into +50µA/250mV jack.

Step 3 Set the range switch to 50µA (dual position with 50V).

Step 4 Connect the black test lead to the negative side of the circuit being measured and red test lead to the positive side of circuit.

Step 5 Read the voltage on the black scale marked DC and use the figures marked 0–250. Read directly in millivolts.

6.3.2 Measuring DC Voltage, 0–1 Volt

Step 1 Set the function switch to −DC. Plug black test lead into the − (COMMON) jack and the red test lead into the +1V jack.

Step 2 Set the range switch to 1V (dual position with 2.5V).

Step 3 Connect the black test lead to the negative side of the circuit being measured and red test lead to the positive side of circuit.

Step 4 Read the voltage on the black scale marked DC. Use the figures marked 0– and divide the reading by 10.

3.3 Measuring DC Voltage, 0–2.5 Through 0–500 Volts

WARNING!

Be extremely careful when working with higher voltages. Do not touch the instrument test leads while power is on in the circuit being measured.

Step 1 Set the function switch to +DC.

Step 2 Set the range switch to one of the five voltage range positions marked 2.5V, 10V, 50V, 250V, or 500V. When in doubt as to the voltage present, always use the highest voltage range as a protection for the instrument. If the voltage is within a lower range, the switch may be set for the lower range to obtain a more accurate reading.

Step 3 Plug the black test lead into the − (COMMON) jack and the red test lead into the + jack.

Step 4 Connect the black test lead to the negative side of the circuit being measured and the red test lead to the positive side of the circuit.

Step 5 Read the voltage on the black scale marked DC. For the 2.5V range, use the 0–250 figures and divide by 100. For the 10V, 50V, and 250V ranges, read the figures directly. For the 500V range, use the 0–50 figures and multiply by 10.

3.4 Measuring DC Voltage, 0–1,000 Volts

WARNING!

Be extremely careful when working with higher voltages. Do not touch the instrument test leads while power is on in the circuit being measured.

Step 1 Set the function switch to +DC.

Step 2 Set the range switch to 1,000V (dual position with 500V).

Step 3 Plug the black test lead into the − (COMMON) jack and the red test lead into the 1,000V jack.

Step 4 Be sure power is off in the circuit being measured and all capacitors have been discharged. Connect the black test lead to the negative side of the circuit being measured and the red test lead to the positive side of the circuit.

Step 5 Turn on the power in the circuit being measured.

Step 6 Read the voltage using the 0–10 figures on the black scale marked DC. Multiply the reading by 100.

6.3.5 Measuring AC Voltage, 0–2.5 Through 0–500 Volts

WARNING!

Be extremely careful when working with higher voltages. Do not touch the instrument or test leads while power is on in the circuit being measured.

CAUTION

When measuring line voltage such as from a 120V, 240V, or 480V source, be sure that the range switch is set to the proper voltage position.

Step 1 Set the function switch to AC.

Step 2 Set the range switch to one of the five voltage range positions marked 2.5V, 10V, 50V, 250V, or 500V. When in doubt as to the actual voltage present, always use the highest voltage range as a protection to the instrument. If the voltage is within a lower range, the switch may be set for the lower range to obtain a more accurate reading.

Step 3 Plug the black test lead into the − (COMMON) jack and the red test lead into the + jack.

Step 4 Connect the test leads across the voltage source (in parallel with the circuit).

Step 5 Turn on the power in the circuit being measured.

Step 6 For the 2.5V range, read the value directly on the AC scale marked 2.5V. For the 10V, 50V, and 250V ranges, read the red scale marked AC and use the black figures immediately above the scale. For the 500V range, read the red scale marked AC and use the 0–50 figures. Multiply the reading by 10.

6.3.6 Measuring AC Voltage, 0–1,000 Volts

WARNING!

Be extremely careful when working with higher voltages. Do not touch the instrument or test leads while power is on in the circuit being measured.

Step 1 Set the function switch to AC.

Step 2 Set the range switch to 1,000V (dual position with 500V).

Step 3 Plug the black test lead into the − (COMMON) jack and the red test lead into the 1,000V jack.

Step 4 Be sure the power is off in the circuit being measured and that all capacitors have been discharged. Connect the test leads to the circuit.

Step 5 Turn on the power in the circuit being measured.

Step 6 Read the voltage on the red scale marked AC. Use the 0–10 figures and multiply by 100.

6.3.7 Measuring Output Voltage

It is often desired to measure the AC component of an output voltage where both AC and DC voltage levels exist. This occurs primarily in amplifier circuits. The meter has a 0.1μF, 400V capacitor in series with the OUTPUT jack. The capacitor blocks the DC component of the current in the test circuit but allows the AC or desired component to pass on to the indicating instrument circuit. The blocking capacitor may alter the AC response at low frequencies but is usually ignored at audio frequencies.

CAUTION

When using OUTPUT, do not apply it to a circuit whose DC voltage component exceeds the 400V rating of the blocking capacitor.

Step 1 Set the function switch to AC.

Step 2 Plug the black test lead into the − (COMMON) jack and the red test lead into t OUTPUT jack.

Step 3 Set the range switch to one of the range p sitions marked 2.5V, 10V, 50V, or 250V.

Step 4 Connect the test leads across the circuit b ing measured, with the black test lead tached to the ground side.

Step 5 Turn on the power in the test circuit. Re the output voltage on the appropriate A voltage scale. For the 2.5V range, read t value directly on the AC scale mark 2.5V. For the 10V, 50V, or 250V ranges, u the red scale marked AC and read t black figures immediately above the sca

6.3.8 Measuring Decibels

For some applications, mockup audio frequen voltages are measured in terms of decibels. T decibel scale (dB) at the bottom of the dial marked from −20 to +10.

Step 1 To measure decibels, read the dB scale accordance with instructions for measu ing AC. For example, when the ran switch is set to the 2.5V position, read t dB scale directly.

Step 2 The dB readings on the scale are refe enced to a 0dB power level of 0.001 across 600Ω, or 0.775VAC across 600Ω.

Step 3 For the 10V range, read the dB scale a add +12dB to the reading. For the 5(range, read the dB scale and add +26dB the reading. For the 250V range, read t dB scale and add +40dB to the reading.

Step 4 If the 0dB reference level is 0.006W acr 500Ω, subtract +7dB from the reading.

6.4.0 Direct Current Measurements

6.4.1 Voltage Drop

The voltage drop across the meter on all mil ampere current ranges is approximately 250m measured at the jacks. An exception is t 0–500mA range with a drop of approximate 400mV. This voltage drop will not affect curre measurements. In some transistor circuits, ho ever, it may be necessary to compensate for t added voltage drop when making measuremen

4.2 Measuring Direct Current, 0–50 Microamperes

CAUTION

Never connect the test leads directly across voltage when the meter is used as a current-indicating instrument. Always connect the instrument in series with the load across the voltage source.

ep 1 Set the function switch to +DC.

ep 2 Plug the black test lead into the − (COMMON) jack and the red test lead into the +50μA/250mV jack.

Step 3 Set the range switch to 50μA (dual position with 50V).

Step 4 Open the circuit in which the current is being measured. Connect the instrument in series with the circuit. Connect the red test lead to the positive side and the black test lead to the negative side.

Step 5 Read the current on the black DC scale. Use the 0–50 figures to read directly in microamperes.

NOTE

In all direct current measurements, be certain the power to the circuit being tested has been turned off before disconnecting test leads and restoring circuit **continuity**.

Voltage Testing

INSIDE TRACK

Voltage testing covers a very wide range of values. For example, if you test the voltage of a residential oil-fired, hot water furnace, the thermostat circuit will be 24V, the circulating pumps will be 120V, and the ignition transformer output will be 10,000V. Notice that the range of voltages on this one appliance can put you outside the range of many multimeters. The photo shown here depicts a voltage reading being taken of a low-voltage control device.

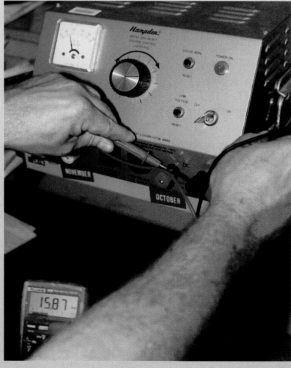

106PO602.EPS

6.4.3 Measuring Direct Current, 0–1 Through 0–500 Milliamperes

Step 1 Set the function switch to +DC.

Step 2 Plug the black test lead into the − (COMMON) jack and the red test lead into the + jack.

Step 3 Set the range switch to one of the four range positions (1mA, 10mA, 100mA, or 500mA).

Step 4 Open the circuit in which the current is being measured. Connect the VOM in series with the circuit. Connect the red test lead to the positive side and the black test lead to the negative side of the part of the circuit you are measuring.

Step 5 Read the current in milliamperes on the black DC scale. For the 1mA range, use the 0–10 figures and divide by 10. For the 10mA range, use the 0–10 figures and multiply by 10. For the 500mA range, use the 0–50 figures and multiply by 10.

6.4.4 Measuring Direct Current, 0–10 Amperes

Step 1 Plug the black test lead into the −10A jack and the red test lead into the +10A jack.

Step 2 Set the range switch to 10A (dual position with 10mA).

Step 3 Open the circuit in which the current is being measured. Connect the instrument in series with the circuit. Connect the red test lead to the positive side and the black test lead to the negative side.

NOTE
The function switch has no effect on polarity for the 10A range.

Step 4 Read the current on the black DC scale. Use the 0–10 figures to read directly in amperes.

CAUTION
When using the 10A range, never remove a test lead from its panel jack while current is flowing through the circuit. Otherwise, damage may occur to the plug and jack.

6.4.5 Zero Ohm Adjustment

When resistance is measured, the VOM batteri furnish power for the circuit. Since batteries a subject to variation in voltage and internal res tance, the instrument must be adjusted to ze prior to measuring a resistance.

Step 1 Set the range switch to the desired ohr range.

Step 2 Plug the black test lead into the − (COI MON) jack and the red test lead into the jack.

Step 3 Connect the ends of the test leads to sho the VOM resistance circuit.

Step 4 Rotate the ZERO OHM control until t pointer indicates zero ohms. If the point cannot be adjusted to zero, one or both the batteries must be replaced.

Step 5 Disconnect the ends of the test leads a connect them to the component bei measured.

6.4.6 Measuring Resistance

CAUTION
Before measuring resistance, be sure power is c to the circuit being tested. Disconnect the component from the circuit before measuring its resistance.

Step 1 Set the range switch to one of the res tance range positions:
- Use R × 1 for resistance readings from to 200 ohms.
- Use R × 100 for resistance readin from 200 to 20,000 ohms.
- Use R × 10,000 for resistance readin above 20,000 ohms.

Step 2 Set the function switch to either the −E or +DC position. The operation is t same in either position.

Step 3 Adjust the ZERO OHM control for ea resistance range.
- Observe the reading on the OHMS sc at the top of the dial. Note that t OHMS scale reads from right to left f increasing values of resistance.
- To determine the actual resistan value, multiply the reading by the fact at the switch position (K on the OHM scale equals one thousand).

ep 4 If there is a forward and backward resistance such as in diodes, the resistance should be relatively low in one direction (for forward polarity) and higher in the opposite direction.

> **CAUTION**
>
> Check that the OHMS range being used will not damage any of the semiconductors.

ep 5 If the purpose of the resistance measurement is to check a semiconductor in or out of a circuit (forward and reverse bias resistance measurements), check the following prior to making the measurement:

- The polarity of the voltage at the input jacks is identical to the input jack markings. Therefore, be certain that the polarity of the test leads is correct for the application.
- Ensure that the range selected will not damage the semiconductor (use R × 100 or below).
- Refer to the meter specifications and review the limits of the semiconductor according to the manufacturer's ratings.
  - If the semiconductor is a silicon diode or conventional silicon transistor, no precautions are normally required.
  - If the semiconductor material is germanium, check the ratings of the device and refer to its specifications.

ep 6 Rotate the function switch between the two DC positions to reverse polarity. This will determine if there is a difference between the resistance in the two directions.

ep 7 The resistance of such diodes will measure differently from one resistance range to another on the same VOM with the function switch in a given position. For example, a diode that measures 80Ω on the R × 1 range may measure 300Ω on the R × 100 range. The difference in values is a result of the diode characteristic and does not indicate any fault in the VOM.

INSIDE TRACK

Current Testing

Levels of current to be tested vary from milliamperes to thousands of amps. In modern communications and consumer electronic devices, you will be measuring for mA. In household circuits you usually test 15A to 50A circuits or higher when testing the service entrance. A high amperage test would be performed on an industrial service entrance, which might go up to 12,000A.

7.0.0 ◆ DIGITAL METERS

Digital meters have revolutionized the test equipment world. Improved accuracy is very easily attainable, more functions can be incorporated into one meter, and both autoranging and automatic polarity indication can be used. Technically, digital multimeters are classified as electronic multimeters; however, digital multimeters do not use a meter movement. Instead, a digital meter's input circuit converts a current into a digital signal, which is then processed by electronic circuits and displayed numerically on the meter face.

A major limitation with many meters that use meter movements is that the scale reading must be estimated if the meter pointer falls between scale divisions. Digital multimeters eliminate the need to estimate these readings by displaying the reading as a numerical display.

With digital meters, technicians must revise the way the indications are viewed. For example, if a technician were reading the AC voltage on a normal wall outlet with an analog voltmeter, any indication within the range of 120VAC would be considered acceptable. But, when reading with a digital meter, the technician might think something was wrong if the meter showed a reading of 114.53VAC. Bear in mind that the digital meter is very precise in its reading, sometimes more precise than is called for, or is usable. Also, be aware that the indicated parameter may change with the range used. This is primarily due to the change in accuracy and where the meter is rounding off.

There are many types of digital multimeters. Some are bench-type multimeters, while others are designed to be handheld. Most types of digital multimeters have an input impedance of 10 megohms and above. They are very sensitive to small changes in current and are therefore very accurate.

An example of a digital meter is shown in *Figure 16*. The internal operation of this meter is basically the same as other digital meters. The following paragraphs discuss the operation and use of this particular meter. For specific instructions, always refer to the owner's manual supplied with your meter.

7.1.0 Features

The example meter offers the following features:

- *Autorange/manual range modes* – The meter features autoranging for all measurement ranges. Press the RANGE button to enter manual range mode. A flashing symbol may be used to show that you are in the manual range mode. Press the RANGE button as required to select the desired range. To switch back to auto range, press the ON/CLEAR button once (clear mode) or select another function.
- *Automatic off* – The example meter turns itself off after one hour of non-use. The current draw while the meter is turned off does not affect battery life. If the meter turns itself off while a parameter is being monitored, press the ON/CLEAR button to turn it on again. To protect against electrical damage, the meter also turns itself off if a test lead is inserted into the 10A jack while the meter is in any mode other than A $=$ or A $\sim$.
- *Dangerous voltage indication* – The meter shows the symbol for any range over 20V. In the autoranging mode, the meter also beeps when it changes to any range over 20V.

106F16.EPS

Figure 16 ◆ Digital meter.

- *Out of Limits (OL)* – The meter displays OL a) a rapidly flashing decimal point (position c termined by range) when the measured value greater than the limit of the instrument or s lected range.
- *Audible acknowledgment* – The meter ackno\ edges each press of a button or actuation of t selector switch with a beep.

Check Your Meter Before Using It

Never assume that a blank meter represents a reading of zero volts. Some digital meters automatically cut off the power to preserve the battery.

Similarly, if you press the HOLD button on some meters when you are reading 0V, it will lock on that reading and will continue to read 0V, regardless of the actual voltage present. Always check the meter for proper operation before using it.

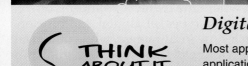

Digital Meters

Most applications do not require the precision of a digital meter. Identify some applications in which precision is important. When wouldn't it be important?

Digital Multimeter Classifications

Newer digital multimeters are rated for safety according to voltage and current limitations and fault interrupting capacity. Never use a multimeter outside of the limits specified by the manufacturer.

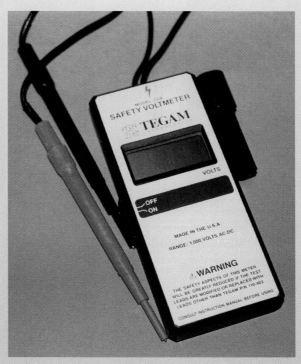

106PO603.EPS

.2.0 Operation

nis section will discuss the use of various con-
ols and explain how measurements should be
ken.

2.1 Dual Function ON/CLEAR Button

ress the ON/CLEAR button to turn the meter on.
peration begins in the autorange mode, and the
nge for maximum resolution is selected auto-
atically. Press the ON/CLEAR button again to
irn the meter off.

7.2.2 Measuring Voltage

Step 1 Select V $\overline{}$ or V $\sim$.

Step 2 Connect the test leads as shown in *Figure 17*.

Step 3 Observe the voltage reading on the display. Depending on the range, the meter displays units in mV or V.

To avoid shock hazard or meter damage, do not apply more than 1,500VDC or 1,000VAC to the meter input or between any input jack and earth ground.

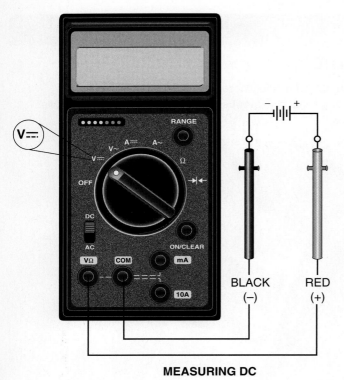

MEASURING DC

MEASURING AC

106F17.EP

Figure 17 ◆ Measuring voltage.

7.2.3 Measuring Current

Step 1 Select A $\equiv$ or A $\sim$.

Step 2 Insert the meter in series with the circuit with the red lead connected to either:
- The mA jack for input up to 200 milliamps
- The 10A jack for input up to 20 amps

Step 3 Make hookups as shown in *Figures 18* and *19*.

Step 4 Observe the current reading.

NOTE

The meter shuts itself off if a test lead is inserted into the 10A jack when the meter is in any function other than A $\equiv$ or A $\sim$.

7.2.4 Measuring Resistance

When measuring resistance, any voltage present will cause an incorrect reading. For this reason, the capacitors in a circuit in which resistance measurements are about to be taken should first be discharged.

Step 1 Select Ω (ohms).

Step 2 Connect the test leads as shown Figure 20.

Step 3 Observe the resistance reading.

7.2.5 Diode/Continuity Test

Step 1 Select →»)) (diode/continuity).

Step 2 Choose one of the following:

- *Forward bias* – Connect to the diode as shown Figure 21(A). The meter will display one of the following: the forward voltage drop (V_F) of good diode (<0.7V), a very low reading for shorted diode (<0.3V), or OL for an open diod
- *Reverse bias or open circuit* – Reverse the leads the diode. The meter displays OL, as shown Figure 21(B). It does not beep.
- *Continuity* – The meter beeps once if the circu resistance is less than 150 ohms, as shown Figure 21(C).

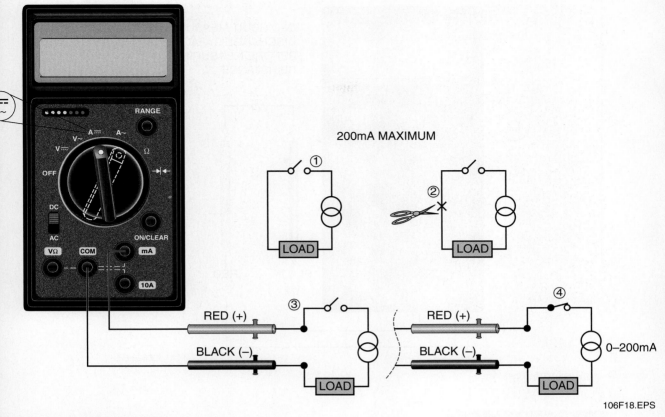

Figure 18 ◆ Measuring current (mA).

200mA MAXIMUM

0–200mA

106F18.EPS

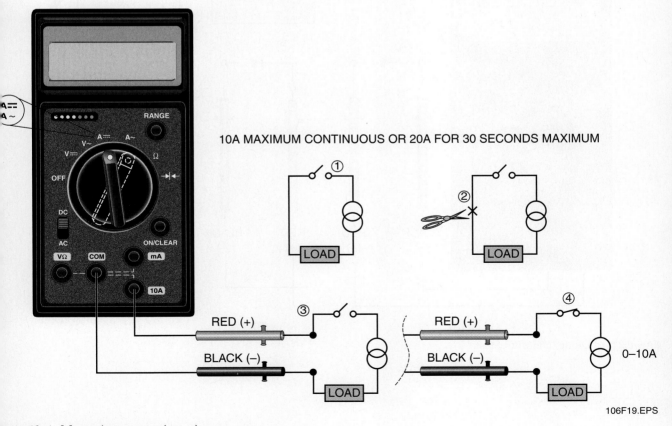

Figure 19 ◆ Measuring current (amps).

10A MAXIMUM CONTINUOUS OR 20A FOR 30 SECONDS MAXIMUM

0–10A

106F19.EPS

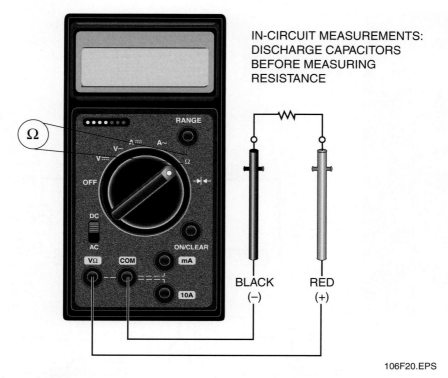

IN-CIRCUIT MEASUREMENTS:
DISCHARGE CAPACITORS
BEFORE MEASURING
RESISTANCE

106F20.EPS

Figure 20 ◆ Measuring resistance.

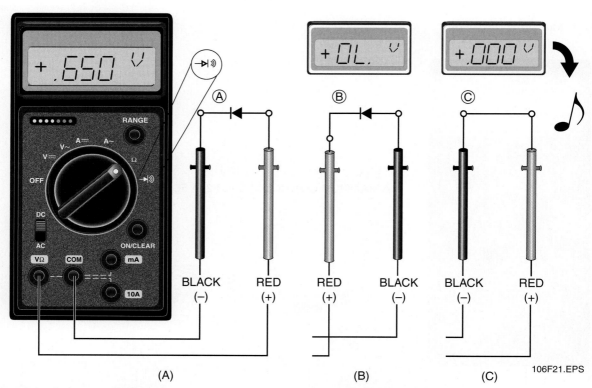

(A)   (B)   (C)

106F21.EPS

Figure 21 ◆ Diode/continuity test.

2.6 Transistor Junction Test

...st transistors in the same manner as diodes by ...ecking the two diode junctions formed be-...ween the base and emitter, and the base and col-...ctor of the transistor. *Figure 22* shows the ...rientation of these effective diode junctions for ...NP and NPN transistors. Also check between ...e collector and emitter to determine if a short is ...resent.

2.7 Display Test

...o test the LCD display, hold the ON/CLEAR but-...n down when turning on the meter. Verify that ...e display shows all segments (see *Figure 23*).

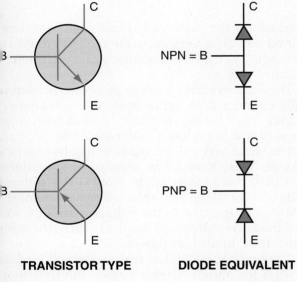

TRANSISTOR TYPE	DIODE EQUIVALENT

106F22.EPS

...gure 22 ◆ Transistor junction test.

106F23.EPS

...gure 23 ◆ Display test.

7.3.0 Maintenance

The following sections discuss the necessary maintenance for a multimeter.

7.3.1 Battery Replacement

Replace the battery as soon as the meter's decimal point starts blinking during normal use; this indicates that <100 hours of battery life remain. Remove the case back and replace the battery with the same or equivalent 9V alkaline battery.

7.3.2 Fuse Replacement

The meter uses two input protection fuses for the mA and 10A inputs. Remove the case back to gain access to the fuses. Replace with the same type only. The large fuse should be readily available. A spare for the smaller fuse is included in the case. If necessary, this fuse must be reordered from the factory.

7.3.3 Calibration

Have a qualified technician calibrate the meter once a year.

Step 1 Remove the case back (*Figure 24*). Turn the meter ON and select V ⎓.

Step 2 Apply +1.900VDC +/−0.0001V to the V-n input (negative to COM).

Step 3 Adjust the DC control through the hole in the circuit board for a display of +1.900V.

Step 4 Select V.

Step 5 Apply +1.900VAC +/−0.002VAC @ 60Hz to the V-n input.

Step 6 Adjust the AC control through the hole in the circuit board for a display of +1.900V.

Step 7 Reassemble the meter.

INSIDE TRACK

Understanding Diodes

A diode is a two-terminal semiconductor device that behaves like a check valve. Forward bias means that you are testing that the diode conducts properly when it is closed. Reverse bias means that current does not flow through the diode.

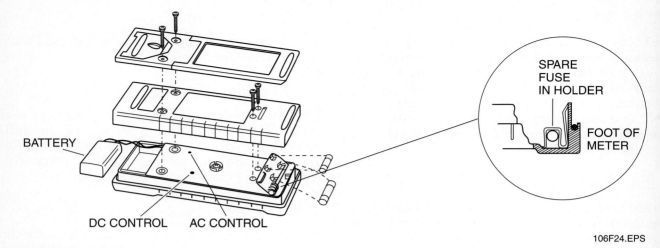

Figure 24 ◆ Meter maintenance.

8.0.0 ◆ WATTMETER

Rather than performing two measurements and then calculating power, a power-measuring meter called a wattmeter can be connected into a circuit to measure power. The power can be read directly from the scale of this meter. Not only does a wattmeter simplify power measurements, but it has two other advantages.

First, voltage and current in an AC circuit are not always in phase; current sometimes either leads or lags the voltage (this is known as the power factor). When this happens, multiplying the voltage times the current results in apparent power, not true power. Therefore, in an AC circuit, measuring the voltage and current and then multiplying them can often result in an incorrect value of power dissipation by the circuit. However, the wattmeter takes the power factor into account and always indicates true power.

Second, voltmeters and ammeters consume power. The amount consumed depends on the levels of the voltage and the current in the circuit, and it cannot be accurately predicted. Therefore, very accurate power measurements cannot be made by measuring voltage and current and then calculating power. However, some watt-meters compensate for their own power losses so that only the power dissipated in the circuit is measured. If the wattmeter is not compensated, the power that is dissipated is sometimes

marked on the meter, or it can easily be dete mined so that a very accurate measurement ca be made. Typically, the accuracy of a wattmeter within 1 percent.

The basic wattmeter consists of two stationa coils connected in series and one movable co (*Figure 25*). The moving coil, wound with mar turns of fine wire, has a high resistance.

The stationary coils, wound with a few turns a larger wire, have a low resistance. The intera tion of the magnetic fields around the differe coils will cause the movable coil and its pointer rotate in proportion to the voltage across the loa and the current through the load. Thus, the met indicates E times I, or power.

The two circuits in the wattmeter will be dar aged if too much current passes through ther This fact is of special importance because the read ing on the meter does not tell the user that the coi are being overheated. If an ammeter or voltmet is overloaded, the pointer will indicate beyon full-scale deflection. In a wattmeter, both the cu rent and potential (voltage) circuits may be carr ing such an overload that their insulation burning, and yet the pointer may only be partwa up the scale. A low-power factor circuit will give low reading on the wattmeter even when the cu rent and potential circuits are loaded to their ma imum safe limits.

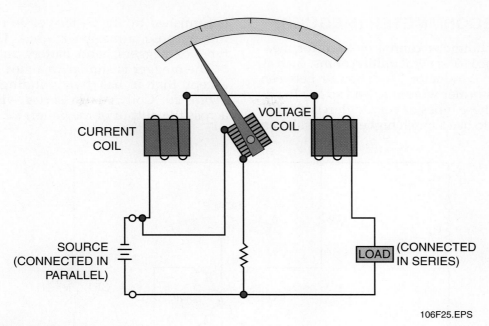

zure 25 ◆ Wattmeter schematic.

106F25.EPS

Wattmeter

Wattmeters are less commonly used than multimeters, since the electrician is usually interested in the existence of electrical potential or the flow of current. The meter used to measure power consumption is the watt-hour meter attached to the service entrance.

106PO604.EPS

9.0.0 ◆ MEGOHMMETER (MEGGER)

An ordinary ohmmeter cannot be used for measuring resistances of several million ohms, such as those found in conductor insulation or between motor or transformer windings, and so on. To adequately test these types of very high resistances, it is necessary to use a much higher potential than is furnished by the battery of an ohmmeter. F this purpose, a megger is used. There are thr types of meggers: hand, battery, and electric.

The megger is similar to a moving-coil met except that it has two windings (coils). S *Figure 26*. Coil A is in series with resistor across the output of the generator.

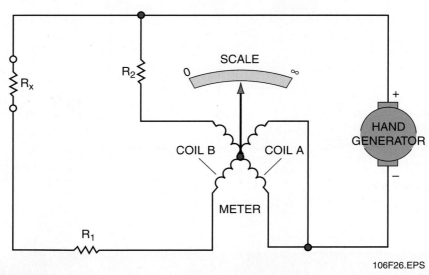

106F26.EPS

Figure 26 ◆ Megger schematic.

Caring for Your Meter

INSIDE TRACK

Like the other meters discussed here, a megger is a sensitive instrument. Treat it with care and keep it in its case when not in use.

106PO605.EPS

This coil is wound so that it causes the pointer to move toward the high-resistance end of the scale when the generator is in operation. Winding is in series with R_1 and R_X (the unknown resistance to be measured). This winding is wound so that it causes the pointer to move toward the low zero-resistance end of the scale when the generator is in operation.

When an extremely high resistance appears across the input terminals of the megger, the current through coil A causes the pointer to read infinity. Conversely, when a relatively low resistance appears across the input terminals, the current through coil B causes the pointer to deflect toward zero. The pointer stops at a point on the scale determined by the current through coil B, which is controlled by R_X.

Digital meggers (*Figure 27*) use the same operational principles. Instead of having a scaled meter movement, these meters give the value of resistance in a digital readout display. The digital readout makes reading the measurement much easier and helps to eliminate errors.

To avoid excessive test voltages, most hand meggers are equipped with friction clutches. When the generator is cranked faster than its rated speed, the clutch slips, and the generator speed and output voltage are maintained at their rated values.

1.0 Safety Precautions

When using a megger, you could be injured or cause damage to the equipment being worked on if you do not observe the following minimum safety precautions:

WARNING!

When a megger is used, the generator voltage is present on the test leads. This voltage could be hazardous to you or the equipment you are testing. *NEVER TOUCH THE TEST LEADS WHILE THE TESTER IS BEING USED.* Isolate the item you are testing from the circuit before using the megger. Protect all parts of the test subject from contact by others.

Use meggers on high-resistance measurements only (such as insulation measurements or to check two separate conductors in a cable). Never touch the test leads while the handle is being cranked.

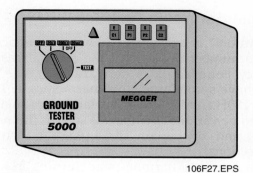

106F27.EPS

Figure 27 ◆ Digital readout megger.

- De-energize and verify the de-energization of the circuit completely before connecting the meter.
- Disconnect the item being checked from other circuitry, if possible, before using the meter.
- After the test, ground the tested circuit to discharge any energy that may be left in the circuit.

10.0.0 ◆ FREQUENCY METER

Frequency is the number of cycles completed each second by a given AC voltage, and it is usually expressed in hertz (one hertz = one cycle per second). The frequency meter is used in AC power-producing devices such as generators to ensure that the correct frequency is being produced. Failure to produce the correct frequency will result in excess heat and component damage.

There are two common types of frequency meters. One operates with a set of reeds having natural vibration frequencies that respond in the range being tested. The reed with a natural frequency closest to that of the current being tested will vibrate most strongly when the meter operates. The frequency is read from a calibrated scale.

A moving-disk frequency meter works with two coils, one of which is a magnetizing coil whose current varies inversely with the frequency. A disk with a pointer mounted between the coils turns in the direction determined by the stronger coil. Solid-state frequency meters are also available.

10.1.0 Phase Rotation Tester

A phase rotation tester is an indicator that allows you to see the phase rotation of incoming current.

10.2.0 Harmonic Test Set

A harmonic is a sine wave whose frequency is a whole number multiple of the original base frequency. For example, a standard 60Hz sine wave may have second and third harmonics at 120Hz and 180Hz, respectively. Harmonics may be caused by various circuit loads such as fluorescent lights and by certain three-phase transformer connections.

The results of harmonics are heating in wiring and a voltage or current that cannot be detected by most digital meters.

11.0.0 ◆ POWER FACTOR METER

The power factor is the ratio of true (actual) pow to apparent power. The power factor of a circuit piece of equipment may be found by using an a meter, wattmeter, and voltmeter. To calculate power factor, divide the wattmeter reading (tr power) by the product of the ammeter and v meter readings (apparent power or EI). The id power factor is 1.

$$\text{Power factor} = \frac{\text{true power (wattmeter reading)}}{\text{apparent power (EI)}}$$

It is not necessary to calculate these reading a power factor meter is available to read power factor directly (*Figure 28*). This meter in cates the equivalent of pure resistance or u power factor, which is a one-to-one ratio.

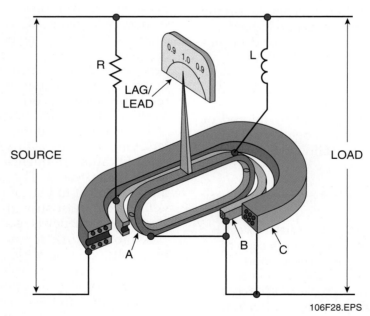

106F28.EPS

Figure 28 ◆ Power factor meter.

2.0.0 ◆ CONTINUITY TESTER

An ohmmeter can be used to test continuity, but this means carrying an expensive, often bulky test instrument with you. Pocket-type continuity testers are just as reliable and much more compact and portable.

There are two types of continuity testers: audio and visual. These are specialized devices for identifying conductors in a conduit by checking continuity.

2.1.0 Audio Continuity Tester

This type of tester is used to ring out wires in conduit runs. At one end of the conduit run, select one wire, strip off a little insulation, and connect that wire to the conduit. At the other end of the conduit run, clip one lead of the tester to the conduit. Touch the other lead to one wire at a time until the audible alarm sounds, which indicates continuity (a closed circuit). Then, put matching tags on the wire. Continue this procedure, one wire at a time, to identify the other wires.

12.2.0 Visual Continuity Tester

This type of tester is useful if you are working in an area where background noise might make it hard to hear the audio tester. The procedure is the same. When the proper wire is tested, the light will come on.

12.3.0 Cable-Length Meter

A cable-length meter measures the length and condition of a cable by sending a signal down the cable and then reading the signal that is reflected back.

13.0.0 ◆ VOLTAGE TESTER

A voltage tester is a simple aid that determines whether there is a potential difference between two points. It does not calculate the value of that difference. If the actual value of the potential difference is needed, use a voltmeter.

13.1.0 Wiggy®

Pocket-type voltage testers are inexpensive and portable. They can easily be carried in your tool pouch, eliminating the need to carry a delicate voltmeter on the job. Simple neon testers are becoming quite popular. Another type is known as a Wiggy® (see *Figure 29*).

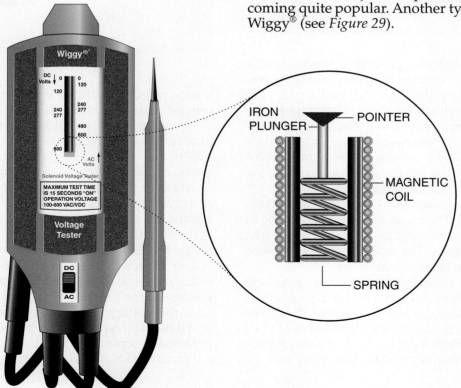

106F29.EPS

Figure 29 ◆ Wiggy® voltage tester.

13.1.1 Principle of Operation

The operation of a Wiggy® is fairly simple. The basic component is a solenoid. When a current flows through the coil, it will produce a magnetic field, which will pull the plunger down against a spring. The spring will limit how far the plunger can be drawn into the cylinder. As the current increases, the plunger will move farther. The amount of current depends upon the potential difference applied across the coil. A pointer on the plunger indicates the potential difference on the scale.

The scale on the tester has voltage indications for AC on one side of the pointer and DC on the other side. The AC scale indicates 120, 240, 480, and 600 volts. The DC scale indicates 125, 240, and 600 volts.

CAUTION

This is an approximation only. If you need to know the actual value of the voltage, use a voltmeter.

CAUTION

To avoid damage to the tester, do not use a Wiggy® above its stated range.

To use a voltage tester, place the probes across a possible source of voltage. If there is voltage present, current flows through the coil inside the tester, creating a magnetic field. The magnetized coil pulls the indicator along the scale until it reaches a point corresponding to the approximate voltage. If there is no voltage, there is no current flow, so the indicator on the scale does not move, and no voltage reading is displayed.

The range of voltage and the type of current (AC and/or DC) that a voltage tester is capable of measuring are usually indicated on the scales that display the reading. The scales for each type of current are marked accordingly.

The methods used to show voltage readings vary from one type of voltage tester to another. For example, there are voltage testers that have lights to indicate the approximate amount of voltage registered. Both lights and scales have relatively broad readout ranges because these voltage

INSIDE TRACK

Know What You're Testing

Remember, voltage testers should only be used to tell whether or not voltage is present. If you need to know the value of the voltage, use a voltmeter.

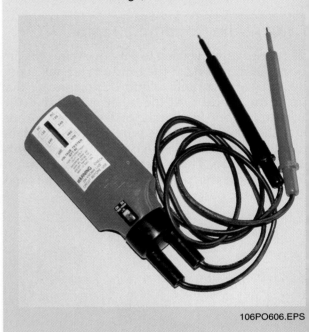

106PO606.EPS

testers can only indicate approximate values, n precise voltage measurements.

A voltage tester should always be checked b fore each use to make sure that it is in good co dition and is operating correctly. The exter check of the tester should include a careful i spection of the insulation on the leads for crac or frayed areas. Faulty leads constitute a safe hazard, so they must be replaced. As a check make sure that the voltage tester is operating co rectly, the probes of the tester are connected to power source that is known to be energized. T voltage indicated on the tester should match t voltage of the power source. If there is no indic tion, the voltage tester is not operating correct and it must be repaired or replaced. It must also repaired or replaced if it indicates a voltage diff ent from the known voltage of the source.

It is essential to check a voltage tester before se. A faulty voltage tester can be dangerous to e electrician using it and to other personnel. For ample, damaged insulation or a cracked casing uld expose the electrician to electrical shock. lso, a faulty voltage tester might indicate that ower is off when it is really on. This would cre- e a serious safety hazard for personnel involved equipment repair. The face plate or the scale on e front of the tester should be checked before a oltage tester is used to be sure that the tester can ndle the amount of voltage that the power urce may contain. Care should be taken when acing the probes of the tester across the power urce. A voltage tester is designed to take a quick ading. If the probes are left in the circuit too ng, the tester will burn out. A voltage tester ould never be connected for more than a few conds at a time.

CAUTION

Do not use a voltage tester in hazardous locations.

Voltage testers are used to make sure that ower is available when it is needed and to make re that power has been cut off when it should ve been. In a troubleshooting situation, it might necessary to verify that power is available in der to be sure that lack of power is not the prob- n. For example, if there were a problem with a ower tool, such as a drill, a voltage tester might used to make sure that power is available to n the drill. A voltage tester might also be used to rify that there is power available to a three- ase motor that will not start.

For safety reasons, it is always necessary to ake sure that the power is turned off before orking on any electrical equipment. A voltage ster can be used for such a test.

Keep the following in mind when using a volt- e tester:

Check the tester before each use.

Handle the tester as if it were a calibrated instrument.

Use good safety practices when operating the tester.

Do not use circuits expected to be above the scale on the tester.

Do not use if damage is indicated to the tester.

Do not use in classified, hazardous areas or in high-frequency circuits.

14.0.0 ◆ RECORDING INSTRUMENTS

The term recording instrument describes many in- struments that make a permanent record of mea- sured quantities over a period of time. Recording instruments can be divided into three general groups:

- Instruments that record electrical quantities, in- cluding potential difference, current, power, re- sistance, and frequency.
- Instruments that record nonelectrical quantities by electrical means (such as a temperature recorder that uses a potentiometer system to record thermocouple output).
- Instruments that record nonelectrical quantities by mechanical means (such as a temperature recorder that uses a bimetallic element to move a pen across an advancing strip of paper).

It is often necessary to know the conditions that exist in an electrical circuit over a period of time to determine such things as peak loads, voltage fluc- tuations, etc. It may be neither practical nor eco- nomical to assign a worker to watch an indicating instrument and record its readings. An automatic recording instrument can be connected to take continuous readings, and the record can be col- lected for review and analysis.

Recording instruments are basically the same as the indicating meters already covered, but they have recording mechanisms attached to them. They are generally made of the same parts, use the same electrical mechanisms, and are connected in the same way. The only basic difference is the per- manent record.

14.1.0 Strip-Chart Recorders

Strip-chart recorders are the most widely used recording instruments for electrical measurement. Their name comes from the fact that the record is made on a strip of paper, usually four to six inches wide and perhaps up to 60 feet long. These can be used to record either voltage or current. A record- ing ammeter is shown in *Figure 30*.

Strip-chart recorders offer several advantages in electrical measurement. The long charts allow the recording to cover a considerable length of time with little attention, and strip-chart recorders can be operated at a relatively high speed to pro- vide very detailed records.

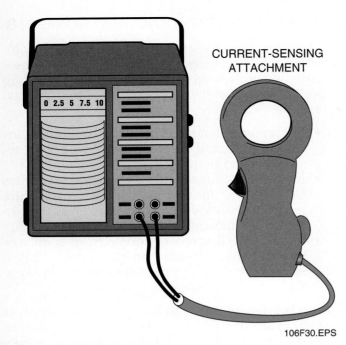

CURRENT-SENSING ATTACHMENT

106F30.EPS

Figure 30 ◆ Recording ammeter.

14.1.1 Typical Strip-Chart Recorder

A typical strip-chart recorder includes the following parts:

- The frame, which supports the other parts
- The moving system, which consists of the parts that move as a direct result of variations in the quantity being measured
- The graphic record, which is the line traced on the chart
- The chart carriage, which consists of the clock mechanism, timing gears, timing drum, chart spool, rewinding mechanism, and writing table
- A scale on the paper strip, which makes it possible to read the values of the quantity being measured
- The inking system, which consists of a special pen with an ink reservoir
- A case, which provides convenience in installation and removal, as well as in replacement of the chart paper

The moving parts used in recording instruments are basically the same as those used in the indicating instrument used to measure the same electrical quantity. However, the parts of a recording instrument are larger and require more power because of the added friction of the pen on the chart paper.

The paper chart is graduated in two directions. In one direction, the graduations correspond to the indicating scale of the instrument. In the other, they indicate time (seconds, minutes, hours, or days depending on the clock mechanism). T time graduations are uniformly spaced becau the chart moves at a constant speed.

The chart carriage includes the entire mech nism for handling the chart paper. At the top, holds the roll of paper. Just above the roll, and rectly beneath the pen, is the writing table. T table is a metal plate that provides a flat surfa under the chart paper at all points on the arc of t pen's motion. This prevents the pen from pu turing or tearing the paper.

The heart of the chart carriage is the clo mechanism, which drives the timing drum. T mechanism may be driven by an electric cloc Some of these mechanisms also contain a mot wound spring clock or a battery-powered clo for a backup in the event of a loss of power.

The timing drum is connected to the clo through a gear unit, which determines the spe of the drum. Drive pins around the timing dru fit into holes at the edges of the chart paper.

The inking system usually includes an inkw containing enough ink for a considerable time.

15.0.0 ◆ SAFETY

In the interest of safety, all test equipment mu be inspected and tested before use. A thorou visual inspection, checking for broken mete or knobs, damaged plugs, or frayed cords important.

Perform an operational check. For example:

- On an ohmmeter, short the probes and ensu that you can zero the meter.
- With an oscilloscope, make sure that you c obtain a trace, and if a test signal is availab connect a test probe and check it.
- A voltmeter can be checked against an AC w receptacle or a battery.

If a meter has a calibration sticker, check to s if it has been calibrated recently. For precise me surements, a recently calibrated meter is a mo reliable instrument.

Every person who works with electronic equi ment should be constantly alert to the hazards which personnel may be exposed, and should a be capable of rendering first aid. The hazards co sidered in this section are: electric shock, bur and related hazards.

Safety must be the primary responsibility of personnel. The installation, maintenance, and eration of electrical equipment enforces a st safety code. Carelessness on the part of the te nician or operator can result in serious injury death due to electrical shock, falls, burns, flyi

jects, etc. After an accident has occurred, investigation almost invariably shows that it could
have been prevented by the exercise of simple
safety precautions and procedures. Each person
concerned with electrical equipment is responsible for reading and becoming thoroughly familiar
with the safety practices and procedures contained in all safety codes and equipment technical
manuals before performing work on electrical
equipment. It is your personal responsibility to
identify and eliminate unsafe conditions and unsafe acts that cause accidents.

You must bear in mind that de-energizing main
supply circuits by opening supply switches will
not necessarily de-energize all circuits in a given
piece of equipment. A source of danger that has
often been neglected or ignored, sometimes with
tragic results, is the input to electrical equipment
from other sources, such as backfeeds. Moreover,
the rescue of a victim shocked by the power input
from a backfeed is often hampered because of the
time required to determine the source of power
and isolate it. Therefore, turn off all power inputs
before working on equipment and tag and lock
out, then check with an operating tester (e.g.,
wattmeter) to be sure that the equipment is safe to
work on. Take the time to be safe when working
on electrical circuits and equipment. Carefully
study the schematics and wiring diagrams of the
entire system, noting what circuits must be de-
energized in addition to the main power supply.
Remember, electrical equipment commonly has
more than one source of power. Be certain that all
power sources are de-energized before servicing
the equipment. Do not service any equipment
with the power on unless absolutely necessary.
Remember that the 115V power supply voltage is
not a low, relatively harmless voltage but is the
voltage that has caused more deaths than any
other medium.

Safety can never be stressed enough. There are
times when your life literally depends on it. The
following is a listing of common-sense safety precautions that must be observed at all times:

Use only one hand when turning power
switches on or off. Keep the doors to switch and
fuse boxes closed except when working inside
or replacing fuses. Use a fuse puller to remove
cartridge fuses, after first making certain that
the circuit is dead.

Your company will make the determination as
to whether or not you are qualified to work on
an electrical circuit.

- Do not work with energized equipment by
yourself; have another person (safety observer),
qualified in first aid for electrical shock, present
at all times. The person stationed nearby
should also know which circuits and switches
control the equipment, and that person should
be given instructions to pull the switch immediately if anything unforeseen happens.
- Always be aware of the nearness of high-voltage
lines or circuits. Use rubber gloves where applicable and stand on approved rubber matting.
Not all rubber mats are good insulators.
- Inform those in charge of operations as to the
circuit on which work is being performed.
- Keep clothing, hands, and feet dry. When it is
necessary to work in wet or damp locations, use
a dry platform and place a rubber mat or other
nonconductive material on top of the wood.
Use insulated tools and insulated flashlights of
the molded type when required to work on exposed parts.
- Do not work on energized circuits unless absolutely necessary.
- All power supply switches or cutout switches
from which power could possibly be fed must
be secured in the OPEN (safety) position and
locked and tagged.
- Never short out, tamper with, or block open an
interlock switch.
- Keep clear of exposed equipment; when it is absolutely necessary to work on it, use only one
hand as much as possible.
- Avoid reaching into enclosures except when
absolutely necessary. When reaching into an
enclosure, use rubber blankets to prevent accidental contact with the enclosure.
- Do not use bare hands to remove hot vacuum
tubes from their sockets. Wear protective gloves
or use a tube puller.
- Use a shorting stick to discharge all high-
voltage capacitors.
- Make certain that the equipment is properly
grounded. Ground all test equipment to the
equipment under test.
- Turn off the power before connecting alligator
clips to any circuit.
- When measuring circuits over 300V, do not
hold the insulated test prods with bare hands.

15.1.0 Use of High-Voltage Protection Equipment

Anyone working on or near energized circuitry
must use special equipment to provide protection
from electrical shock. Protective equipment includes gloves, leather sleeves, rubber blankets,

and rubber mats. It should be noted that this electrical protective equipment is in addition to the regular protective equipment normally required for maintenance work. Regular protective equipment typically includes hard hats that are rated for electrical resistance, eye protection, safety shoes, and long sleeves.

Gloves that are approved for protection from electrical shock are made of rubber. A separate leather cover protects the rubber from punctures or other damage. They protect the worker by insulating the hands from electrical shock. Gloves are rated as providing protection from certain amounts of voltage. Whenever an individual is going to be working around exposed conductors, the gloves chosen should be rated for at least as much voltage as the conductors are carrying.

Rubber sleeves are used along with gloves to provide additional protection. The combination of sleeves and gloves protects the hands and arms from electrical shock.

Rubber blankets and floor mats have many uses. Blankets are used to cover energized conductors while work is going on around them. They might be used to cover the energized main buses in a breaker panel before working on a de-energized breaker. Rubber floor mats are used to insulate workers from the ground. If a worker is standing on a rubber mat and then contacts an energized conductor, the current cannot flow through the body to the ground, so the worker will not get shocked.

15.2.0 General Testing of Electrical Equipment

As stated earlier, personnel must be familiar with the proper use of available test equipment. Also, personnel must be familiar with and use the local instructions governing the testing of electrical circuits to protect both the person and the equipment.

The next section includes an example of instructions from a local utility and covers work permits, test permits, authorized employees for testing, circuit isolation, and relay, instrument, and meter testing. Each topic is discussed individually.

15.2.1 Example Policy—Work Permits or Test Permits

A written work permit must be obtained by an authorized technician or supervisor from the operator in charge before testing equipment under the operator's control. A test permit is required to make a dielectric proof test.

The following must be on the work or test permit:

- Designation of the equipment to be tested
- Scope and limits of tests to be made
- Method of isolation and protection provided

If it is necessary to alter the nature or to exten the scope of tests for which a work permit or te permit has been granted, return the permit to th operator and request a new permit before pr ceeding with the revised tests. When the test completed, return the work permit or test per to the operator, and report whether the results the test were satisfactory or unsatisfactory.

Whenever a work permit or test permit remai in effect beyond the working hours of the pers to whom it was issued and a different person w be in charge of the tests, consult the operator f the proper turnover procedure. The person suming the responsibility for continuance of t work must verify that the items on the work test permit are correct.

If a work permit or test permit is issued for te ing that is to continue over a period of seve days, the permit must be returned to the operat at the end of each working day and picked up the beginning of the next working day.

15.2.2 Example Policy—Authorized Employees for Testing

Only employees authorized to perform oper tions at a given station shall:

- Open, remove, close, or replace doors or cove on electrical compartments.
- Remove or replace potential transformer fus
- Open or close switches.
- Open or close fuse cutouts or disconnecti potheads.
- Make tests for the presence of potential.
- Place or remove blocks and protective tags.
- Apply or remove grounds or short circuits.
- Attach or remove leads to high- intermediate-voltage conductors.
- Make operating tests.
- Test links, fuses, switches associated with ge erators, buses, feeders, transformers, etc. n mally shall be removed, replaced, or operat only under the direct supervision of an autho ized employee when the associated equipme is live or is available for normal operation.

In some cases, when it is necessary for t equipment to remain in service, or in any ca when the associated equipment has been moved from service, the operator-in-charge m authorize the person to whom the work perr was issued to remove and replace test links a fuses and to operate the heel and toe switches a potential switches in low-voltage circuits.

15.2.3 Example Policy—Circuit Isolation

All equipment to be tested that is rated at 350V phase-to-ground or higher must be isolated from all sources of supply by either two breaks, or a single break and a ground, unless test equipment is used that can be operated safely with one break. Where possible, two breaks in series are preferred over one break.

If no potential is to be applied to the equipment, the ground may be applied on the equipment side of the single break.

If a test potential is to be applied to the equipment, the ground has to be on the far side of the single break. If a test potential of less than 400V is to be applied to the equipment, the ground may be replaced with an approved protective discharge gap on the equipment to be tested. The protective gaps and test leads are to be connected or disconnected while the equipment is grounded. If disconnect switches are used to provide the breaks, the switches shall be locked open, and the operating motor fuses removed.

On equipment operating at 350V or less, a test potential may be applied with only a single break. An open truck-type or elevating-type circuit breaker withdrawn or lowered to the disconnect position or a swinging-type disconnect switch shall be considered as a single break.

If any of the following are the only type of disconnecting device available, short circuits and grounds must be applied at the nearest available point to the device.

A disconnect switch with the blade prevented from falling closed by an insulating block placed over the jaw
A disconnect switch in which the separation of the blade and jaw cannot be verified visually
An oil circuit breaker or oil switch having no associated disconnecting device
An oil-filled fusible cutout having no provision for disconnecting the leads

Potential transformers that may become energized from the low-voltage side shall be isolated on that side by opening switches, removing links, removing fuses, or by removing connections temporarily. The low-voltage side of the potential transformer shall also be short circuited and grounded.

Equipment that has been subjected to DC high-voltage tests shall be grounded to discharge the residual voltage before any person is permitted to touch the test cables or any current-carrying part of the equipment tested. If the equipment tested has considerable capacitance, then it should be grounded for at least 30 minutes after the test potential is removed. Equipment of low capacitance should be grounded for a length of time equivalent to the time that the potential was applied.

15.2.4 Example Policy—Clearances

Adequate clearances are to be maintained between energized and exposed conductors and personnel (refer to *NEC Section 110.26*). Where DC voltages are involved, clearances specified shall be used with specified voltages considered as DC line-to-ground values.

If adequate clearances cannot be maintained from exposed live parts of apparatus in the normal course of free movement within the area during test, then access to that area shall be restricted by fences and barricades. Signs clearly indicating the hazard shall be posted in conspicuous locations. This requirement applies to equipment in service as well as to equipment to which test voltages are applied.

Whenever there is any question of the adequacy of clearance between the specific area in which work is to be done and exposed live parts of adjacent equipment, a field inspection shall be made by management representatives of the group involved before starting the job. The result of this inspection should be to outline the protection necessary to complete the work safely, including watchers where needed.

15.2.5 Electrical Circuit Tests

Testing of electrical circuits can be required at new installations or existing installations where wiring has been modified or new wiring has been interfaced with existing circuits. It is broken down into two sections:

- Electrical circuit tests performed on AC relay protection and metering circuits include:
  - Point-to-point wire checks to verify that the wiring has been installed according to the diagram of connections
  - Current transformer polarity, impedance, continuity, and where applicable, tap progression and intercore coupling tests
  - Voltage transformer polarity, ratio, and self-induced high-potential (hi-pot) tests
  - Insulation resistance tests
- Electrical circuit tests performed on control, power, alarm, and annunciator circuits include:
  - Insulation resistance tests
  - Operation tests

An important piece of information is the minimum distance allowed when working near energized electrical circuits because large voltages can arc across an air gap. Personnel must maintain a distance that is greater than that arc distance. This is especially true when using a hot stick to open a disconnect. These distances are listed in *Table 1*.

Table 1 OSHA Table

Voltage Range (Phase-to-Phase) Kilovolts	Minimum Working and Clear Hot Stick Distance
2.1 to 15	2 ft 0 in
15.2 to 35	2 ft 4 in
35.1 to 46	2 ft 6 in
46.1 to 72.5	3 ft 0 in
72.6 to 121	3 ft 4 in
138 to 145	3 ft 6 in
161 to 169	3 ft 8 in
230 to 242	5 ft 0 in
345 to 362	*7 ft 0 in
500 to 552	*11 ft 0 in
700 to 765	*15 ft 0 in

*For voltages above 345kV, the minimum working and clear hot stick distances may be reduced provided that such distances are not less than the shortest distance between the energized part and a grounded surface.

15.3.0 Meter Loading Effects

It is important to understand how a piece of te equipment will affect the circuit to which it is a tached. Even when properly used, a piece of te equipment can put a load on the circuit und testing.

NOTE

Clearances listed in *Table 1* apply to qualified personnel.

An ammeter becomes a part of the circuit whe it is used. Because of this, the meter can som times significantly alter the voltages and currer in the circuit. The following example illustrat how this can happen.

In Circuit A on the left in *Figure 31*, the curre is calculated to be 10µA. To measure this curre using a meter that has an internal resistance 2,000Ω, the meter would be placed as shown Circuit B. The 2,000Ω resistance of the meter ad to the 10,000Ω resistance, reducing the current the circuit to 8.33µA. The presence of the met therefore, alters the current flowing in the circu resulting in an incorrect reading.

A voltmeter can also alter circuit paramete The following example illustrates how this c happen.

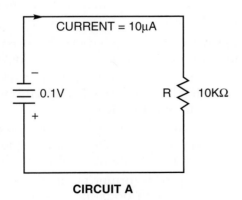

CIRCUIT A

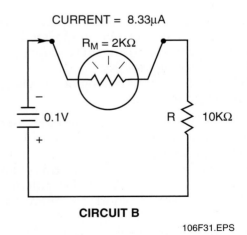

CIRCUIT B

106F31.EPS

Figure 31 ◆ Meter loading—Example 1.

In Circuit A in *Figure 32*, the voltage across the 40,000Ω resistor is to be measured using a voltmeter with a 1,000Ω internal resistance. We can determine the effect that the meter will have on the circuit when it is connected as shown in Circuit B.

Connecting the voltmeter in parallel with the 40,000Ω resistor, as shown in Circuit B, significantly changes the total resistance in the circuit. The parallel combination of 40,000Ω and 200,000Ω is:

$$R = \frac{40,000 \times 200,000}{40,000 + 200,000} = 33,333\Omega$$

Add the 10KΩ resistance in series for a total circuit resistance of 43,333Ω.

Therefore, with the voltmeter in the circuit, the current is:

$$E \div R = I \text{ or } 10 \div 43,333 = 2.31 \times 10^{-4} \text{ A}$$

This current causes a voltage drop across the combination of the meter and the 40,000Ω resistor

$$E = IR \text{ or } (2.31 \times 10^{-4}) \times 33,333 = 7.7V$$

The voltmeter will read 7.7V, whereas the voltage drop across the 40,000Ω resistor without the voltmeter connected is 8V.

In most cases, the current flowing through the voltmeter movement is negligible compared to the current flowing through the element whose voltage is being measured. When this is the case, the voltmeter has a negligible effect on the circuit.

In most commercial voltmeters, the internal resistance is expressed as the ohms-per-volt rating of the meter. This quantity tells what the internal resistance of the meter is on any particular full-scale setting. In general, the meter's internal resistance is the ohms-per-volt rating times the full-scale voltage. The higher the ohms-per-volt rating, the higher the internal resistance of the meter, and the smaller the effect of the meter on the circuit.

Care should be taken when selecting either an ammeter or a voltmeter in which the meter does not load down the circuit under test. Also, realize that the same circuit under test with a different meter will indicate differently due to the separate loading effects of each meter.

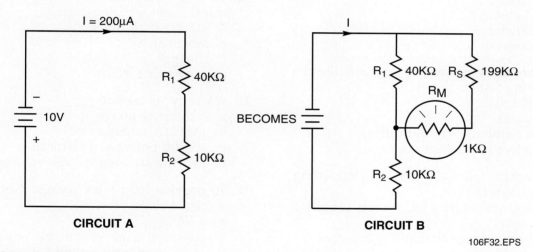

CIRCUIT A   **CIRCUIT B**

106F32.EPS

Figure 32 ◆ Meter loading—Example 2.

Putting It All Together

THINK ABOUT IT

What kind of measuring device would you select or need for the following tasks, and how would you apply the device?

- A short circuit in house wiring
- The output from an AC transformer
- A fuse in house wiring
- A relay

1. An ammeter is used to measure _____.
   a. current
   b. voltage
   c. resistance
   d. insulation value

2. Ammeters use a _____ to measure values higher than 10mA.
   a. multiplier resistor
   b. rectifier bridge
   c. transformer coil
   d. shunt

3. Voltmeters use a _____ to measure values higher than one volt.
   a. multiplier resistor
   b. rectifier bridge
   c. transformer coil
   d. shunt

4. Electromotive force (emf) is measured using a(n) _____.
   a. ammeter
   b. wattmeter
   c. voltmeter
   d. ohmmeter

5. A voltmeter is connected _____ with the circuit being tested.
   a. in parallel
   b. in series
   c. in a sequential configuration
   d. in a looped configuration

6. Which of the following is *not* true regarding an ohmmeter?
   a. It is powered by a DC source, usually a battery.
   b. It contains current-limiting resistors.
   c. It must be used in an energized circuit.
   d. It should be adjusted to zero before each use.

7. All of the following values can be directly measured using a VOM *except* _____.
   a. decibels
   b. voltage
   c. resistance
   d. wattage

8. When in doubt as to the voltage present, always use the _____ range to protect the VOM.
   a. lowest
   b. highest
   c. middle
   d. It does not matter with today's precision instruments.

9. Wattmeters are used to measure _____.
   a. power
   b. voltage
   c. resistance
   d. impedance

10. To check the resistance between motor or transformer windings, use a _____.
    a. standard ohmmeter
    b. wattmeter
    c. megger
    d. power factor meter

11. A Wiggy® is used to _____.
    a. measure wattage
    b. measure impedance
    c. test for potential difference
    d. provide an exact voltage reading

12. To provide long-term voltage monitoring it would be best to use _____.
    a. a VOM
    b. constant supervision by experienced maintenance personnel
    c. a power factor meter
    d. a strip chart recorder

3. The minimum working distance for a 15kV circuit is _____.
   a. 2 ft 0 in
   b. 5 ft 0 in
   c. 7 ft 0 in
   d. 15 ft 0 in

4. Connecting a voltmeter may affect the total _____ in a circuit.
   a. voltage
   b. current
   c. resistance
   d. electromotive force

15. Which of the following is *not* true regarding meter loading?
   a. It may cause different meters to produce different readings.
   b. The higher the ohms-per-volt rating, the smaller the effect of the meter on the circuit.
   c. It may impact both voltage and resistance.
   d. It can be prevented by removing power to the circuit being tested.

Summary

The use of test equipment is an important part of your job as an electrician. Selecting the proper instrument to be used in a specific application will help you to fully perform your task. You will u the information provided by these instruments help evaluate the work being accomplished.

Notes

Trade Terms Quiz

The _____ is used to express a relative difference in power between electric signals.

Used for electromagnetic effects or for providing electrical resistance, _____ are a number of turns of wire.

A _____ uses a permanent magnet and moving coil arrangement to move a pointer across a scale.

Usually expressed in hertz, _____ is the number of cycles completed each second by a given AC voltage.

_____ is an uninterrupted electrical path for current flow.

Trade Terms

Coil
Continuity
d'Arsonval meter movement
Decibel
Frequency

Ed Cockrell

All Star Electric

How did you choose a career in the electrical field?
I was looking for a job that would hold my interest for
more than a year. I studied Electrical Engineering at
Louisiana State University for two years. I was given
an opportunity to work as an electrical helper for a
summer and found it very rewarding.

Tell us about your apprenticeship experience.
I entered an electrical apprenticeship program with
very little idea that it would lead to the position that I
now have. I started work with a very tough ex-marine
as my first journeyman. The first day on the job I
learned some valuable lessons. It left me thinking that
I had chosen the wrong field of work. I had very good
instructors in the classroom, but I found that there
was much to learn in the field. I lucked out and found
an excellent mentor that changed my perception of
the electrical field, my classes, and my possible future.
He taught me that entering into this field would be an
open door to many other options that I had never
thought about. These were to be a foreman,
superintendent, project manager, and potentially an
owner of my own business.

What positions have you held in the industry?
I started as a summer helper; then apprentice,
journeyman, foreman, field superintendent, electrical
designer, project manager, electrical instructor, lead
electrical instructor, and Director of Education for
ABC.

*What would you say is the primary factor in
achieving success?*
Education, luck, and the perseverance to stick with
something that I enjoyed doing.

What does your current job involve?
My job is directing the efforts of some very good
craftpersons (instructors) who are trying to help ou
students become craft professionals. I also create the
budgets and beg for contributions to the school. I
believe that a very important part of my job is to
instill in our students that they determine where the
end up in life by their actions. Becoming a craft
professional is one point along the way, but there a
many more options available to them if they truly
wish to take steps to achieve them.

*Do you have any advice for someone just entering t
trade?*
Stick with it and don't fall into the thought process
that we must only learn from our mistakes. Take tir
to learn from your successes by noting the path to
success. Life is like a grindstone—those who learn t
align themselves with it become sharper, and those
who push head first with little regard for the right
way to do things tend to lose their edge.

Trade Terms
Introduced in This Module

Coil: A number of turns of wire, especially in spiral form, used for electromagnetic effects or for providing electrical resistance.

Continuity: An uninterrupted electrical path for current flow.

D'Arsonval meter movement: A meter movement that uses a permanent magnet and moving coil arrangement to move a pointer across a scale.

Decibel: A unit used to express a relative difference in power between electric signals.

Frequency: The number of cycles completed each second by a given AC voltage; usually expressed in hertz; one hertz = one cycle per second.

Additional Resources

This module is intended to present thorough resources for task training. The following reference works are suggested for further study. These are optional materials for continued education rather than for task training.

Electronics Fundamentals: Circuits, Devices, and Applications, Thomas L. Floyd. New York: Prentice Hall.

Principles of Electric Circuits, Thomas L. Floyd. New York: Prentice Hall.

The NCCER makes every effort to keep these textbooks up-to-date and free of technical errors. We appreciate your help in this process. If you have an idea for improving this textbook, or if you find an error, a typographical mistake, or an inaccuracy in NCCER's *Contren®* textbooks, please write us, using this form or a photocopy. Be sure to include the exact module number, page number, a detailed description, and the correction, if applicable. Your input will be brought to the attention of the Technical Review Committee. Thank you for your assistance.

Instructors – If you found that additional materials were necessary in order to teach this module effectively, please let us know so that we may include them in the Equipment/Materials list in the Annotated Instructor's Guide.

Write: Product Development
National Center for Construction Education and Research
P.O. Box 141104, Gainesville, FL 32614-1104

Fax: 352-334-0932

E-mail: curriculum@nccer.org

Craft   Module Name

Copyright Date   Module Number   Page Number(s)

Description

(Optional) Correction

(Optional) Your Name and Address

Ponnequin Wind Farm

Ponnequin Wind Farm generates electrical power from the wind. The site is located on the plains of eastern Colorado just south of the Wyoming border. It consists of 44 wind turbines and can generate up to 30 megawatts of electricity. Each wind turbine cost about $1 million to build and is capable of generating 700 kilowatts of electricity. The turbines begin operating with wind speeds as low as 7 mph and shut themselves down at speeds over 55 mph. Each turbine weighs nearly 100 tons and stands 181 feet tall. The turbine blades are attached on the top of the turbine and have a diameter of 159 feet.

26101-05
Electrical Safety

Topics to be presented in this module include:

Overview

Electricians work in all areas of a job site. They are exposed to safety hazard that other workers encounter, including hazards that can cause cuts, burn punctures, fall-related injuries, chemical exposure, and other injuries. Mor than other workers, however, electricians risk electrical shock, electrical burn and arc burns because they work with energized circuits and equipment.

Safety regulations and procedures are designed to protect those working i the electrical field, but these regulations are only effective if the electricia knows the hazards and takes the proper precautions to avoid them. For tha reason, the proper use of personal protective equipment and other safety ge is a critical element of the electrician's job.

In order to protect yourself and those around you from injury and possibl death, you must become familiar with the various hazards on the job site, fo low established safety procedures, and always keep safe work practices for most in your mind.

Note: *National Electrical Code*® and *NEC*® are registered trademarks of the National Fire Protection Association, Inc., Quincy, MA 02269. All *National Electrical Code*® and *NEC*® references in this module refer to the 2005 edition of the *National Electrical Code*®.

Objectives

When you have completed this module, you will be able to do the following:

1. Demonstrate safe working procedures in a construction environment.
2. Explain the purpose of OSHA and how it promotes safety on the job.
3. Identify electrical hazards and how to avoid or minimize them in the workplace.
4. Explain safety issues concerning lockout/tagout procedures, personal protection using assured grounding and isolation programs, confined space entry, respiratory protection, and fall protection systems.

Trade Terms

Double-insulated/ungrounded tool
Fibrillation
Grounded tool
Ground fault circuit interrupter (GFCI)
Polychlorinated biphenyls (PCBs)

Required Trainee Materials

1. Paper and pencil
2. Copy of the latest edition of the *National Electrical Code®*
3. Appropriate personal protective equipment

Prerequisites

Before you begin this module, it is recommended that you successfully complete *Core Curriculum*.

This course map shows all of the modules in *Electrical Level One.* The suggested training order begins at the bottom and proceeds up. Skill levels increase as you advance on the course map. The local Training Program Sponsor may adjust the training order.

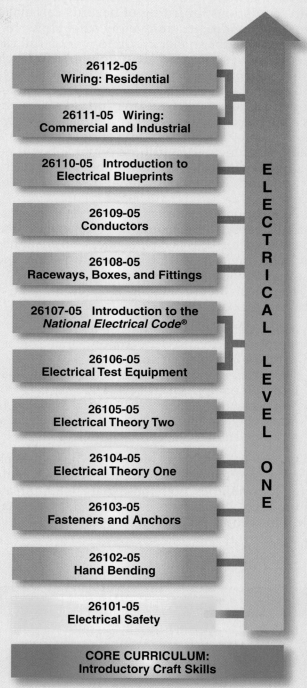

ELECTRICAL LEVEL ONE

26112-05
Wiring: Residential

26111-05 Wiring:
Commercial and Industrial

26110-05 Introduction to
Electrical Blueprints

26109-05
Conductors

26108-05
Raceways, Boxes, and Fittings

26107-05 Introduction to the
National Electrical Code®

26106-05
Electrical Test Equipment

26105-05
Electrical Theory Two

26104-05
Electrical Theory One

26103-05
Fasteners and Anchors

26102-05
Hand Bending

26101-05
Electrical Safety

CORE CURRICULUM:
Introductory Craft Skills

101CMAP.EPS

1.0.0 ◆ INTRODUCTION

As an electrician, you will be exposed to many potentially hazardous conditions that will exist on the job site. No training manual, set of rules and regulations, or listing of hazards can make working conditions completely safe. However, it is possible for an electrician to work a full career without serious accident or injury. To reach this goal, you need to be aware of potential hazards and stay constantly alert to these hazards. You must take the proper precautions and practice the basic rules of safety. You must be safety-conscious at all times. Safety should become a habit. Keeping a safe attitude on the job will go a long way in reducing the number and severity of accidents. Remember that your safety is up to you.

As an apprentice electrician, you need to be especially careful. You should only work under the direction of experienced personnel who are familiar with the various job site hazards and the means of avoiding them.

The most life-threatening hazards on a construction site are:

- Falls when you are working in high places
- Electrocution caused by coming into contact with live electrical circuits
- The possibility of being crushed by falling materials or equipment
- The possibility of being struck by flying objects or moving equipment/vehicles such as trucks, forklifts, and construction equipment

Other hazards include cuts, burns, back sprains, and getting chemicals or objects in your eyes. Most injuries, both those that are life-threatening and those that are less severe, are preventable if the proper precautions are taken.

INSIDE TRACK

Electrical Safety in the Workplace

Each year in the U.S., there are approximately 20,000 electricity-related accidents at home and in the workplace. In a recent year, these accidents resulted in 700 deaths. Electrical accidents are the third leading cause of death in the workplace.

What's wrong with this picture?

101PO101.EF

2.0.0 ◆ ELECTRICAL SHOCK

Electricity can be described as a potential that results in the movement of electrons in a conductor. This movement of electrons is called electrical current. Some substances, such as silver, copper, steel, and aluminum, are excellent conductors. The human body is also a conductor. The conductivity of the human body greatly increases when the skin is wet or moistened with perspiration.

Electrical current flows along the path of least resistance to return to its source. The source return point is called the neutral or ground of a circuit. If the human body contacts an electrically energized point and is also in contact with the ground or another point in the circuit, the human body becomes a path for the current to return to its source. *Table 1* shows the effects of current passing through the human body. One mA is one milliamp, or one one-thousandth of an ampere.

Table 1 Current Level Effects on the Human Body

Current Value	Typical Effects
1mA	Perception level. Slight tingling sensation.
5mA	Slight shock. Involuntary reactions can result in serious injuries such as falls from elevations.
6 to 30mA	Painful shock, loss of muscular control.
50 to 150mA	Extreme pain, respiratory arrest, severe muscular contractions. Death possible.
1000mA to 4300mA	Ventricular fibrillation, severe muscular contractions, nerve damage. Typically results in death.

Source: Occupational Safety and Health Administration

Severity of Shock

In *Table 1*, how many milliamps separate a mild shock from a potentially fatal one? What is the fractional equivalent of this in amps? How many amps are drawn by a 60W light bulb?

A primary cause of death from electrical shock when the heart's rhythm is overcome by an electrical current. Normally, the heart's operation uses very low-level electrical signal to cause the heart to contract and pump blood. When an abnormal electrical signal, such as current from an electrical shock, reaches the heart, the low-level heartbeat signals are overcome. The heart begins twitching in an irregular manner and goes out of rhythm with the pulse. This twitching is called **fibrillation**. Unless the normal heartbeat rhythm is restored using special defibrillation equipment (paddles), the individual will die. No known case of heart fibrillation has ever been corrected without the use of defibrillation equipment by a qualified medical practitioner. Other effects of electrical shock may include immediate heart stoppage and burns. In addition, the body's reaction to the shock can cause a fall or other accident. Delayed internal problems can also result.

2.1.0 The Effect of Current

The amount of current measured in amperes that passes through a body determines the outcome of an electrical shock. The higher the voltage, the greater the chance for a fatal shock. In a one-year study in California, the following results were observed by the State Division of Industry Safety:

• Thirty percent of all electrical accidents were caused by contact with conductors. Of these accidents, 66% involved low-voltage conductors (those carrying 600 volts [V] or less).

NOTE

Electric shocks or burns are a major cause of accidents in our industry. According to the Bureau of Labor Statistics, electrical shock is the leading cause of death in the electrical industry.

• Portable, electrically operated hand tools made up the second largest number of injuries (15%). Almost 70% of these injuries happened when the frame or case of the tool became energized. These injuries could have been prevented by following proper safety practices, using grounded or **double-insulated/ungrounded tools**, and using **ground fault circuit interrupter (GFCI)** protection.

In one ten-year study, investigators found 9,765 electrical injuries that occurred in accidents. Over 18% of these injuries involved contact with voltage levels of over 600 volts. A little more than 13% of these high-voltage injuries resulted in death. These high-voltage totals included limited-amperage contacts, which are often found on electronic equipment. When tools or equipment touch high-voltage overhead lines, the chance that a resulting injury will be fatal climbs to 28%. Of the low-voltage injuries, 1.4% were fatal.

CAUTION

High voltage, defined as 600 volts or more, is almost ten times as likely to kill as low voltage. However, on the job you spend most of your time working on or near lower voltages. Due to the frequency of contact, most electrocution deaths actually occur at low voltages. Attitude about the harmlessness of lower voltages undoubtedly contributes to this statistic.

These statistics have been included to help you gain respect for the environment where you work and to stress how important safe working habits really are.

2.1.1 Body Resistance

Electricity travels in closed circuits, and its normal route is through a conductor. Shock occurs when the body becomes part of the electric circuit (*Figure 1*). The current must enter the body at one point and leave at another. Shock normally occurs in one of three ways: the person must come in contact with both wires of the electric circuit; one wire of the electric circuit and the ground; or a metallic part that has become hot by being in contact with an energized wire while the person is also in contact with the ground.

To fully understand the harm done by electrical shock, we need to understand something about the physiology of certain body parts: the skin, the heart, and muscles.

Skin covers the body and is made up of three layers. The most important layer, as far as electric shock is concerned, is the outer layer of dea cells referred to as the horny layer. This layer composed mostly of a protein called keratin, an it is the keratin that provides the largest percen age of the body's electrical resistance. When it dry, the outer layer of skin may have a resistanc of several thousand ohms, but when it is mois there is a radical drop in resistance, as is also th case if there is a cut or abrasion that pierces th horny layer. The amount of resistance provide by the skin will vary widely from individual individual. A worker with a thick horny lay will have a much higher resistance than a chil The resistance will also vary widely at differe parts of the body. For instance, the worker wi high-resistance hands may have low-resistanc skin on the back of his calf. The skin, like any i sulator, has a breakdown voltage at which ceases to act as a resistor and is simply pun tured, leaving only the lower-resistance body ti sue to impede the flow of current in the bod The breakdown voltage will vary with the ind vidual, but is in the area of 600V. Since most i dustrial power distribution systems operate 480V or higher, technicians working at these le els need to have special awareness of the sho potential.

The heart is the pump that sends life-sustainir blood to all parts of the body. The blood flow caused by the contractions of the heart musc which is controlled by electrical impulses. Th electrical impulses are delivered by an intrica system of nerve tissue with built-in timing mec anisms, which make the chambers of the hea contract at exactly the right time. An outside ele tric current of as little as 75 milliamperes can u set the rhythmic, coordinated beating of the hea

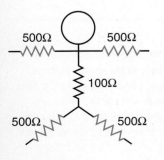

- HAND TO HAND 1000Ω
- 120 VOLT
- FORMULA: $I = E/R$
- 120/1000 = 0.120 AMPS OR 120 MILLIAMPS

101F01.EPS

Figure 1 ◆ Body resistance.

by disturbing the nerve impulses. When this happens, the heart is said to be in fibrillation, and the pumping action stops. Death will occur quickly if the normal beat is not restored. Remarkable as it may seem, what is needed to defibrillate the heart is a shock of an even higher intensity.

The other muscles of the body are also controlled by electrical impulses delivered by nerves. Electric shock can cause loss of muscular control, resulting in the inability to let go of an electrical conductor. Electric shock can also cause injuries of an indirect nature in which involuntary muscle reaction from the electric shock can cause bruises, fractures, and even death resulting from collisions or falls.

The severity of shock received when a person becomes a part of an electric circuit is affected by three primary factors: the amount of current flowing through the body (measured in amperes), the path of the current through the body, and the length of time the body is in the circuit. Other factors that may affect the severity of the shock are the frequency of the current, the phase of the heart cycle when shock occurs, and the general health of the person prior to the shock. Effects can range from a barely perceptible tingle to immediate cardiac arrest. Although there are no absolute limits, or even known values that show the exact injury at any given amperage range, *Table 1* lists the general effects of electric current on the body for different current levels. As this table illustrates, a difference of only 100 milliamperes exists between a current that is barely perceptible and one that can kill.

A severe shock can cause considerably more damage to the body than is visible. For example, a person may suffer internal hemorrhages and destruction of tissues, nerves, and muscle. In addition, shock is often only the beginning in a chain of events. The final injury may well be from a fall, cuts, burns, or broken bones.

2.1.2 Burns

The most common shock-related injury is a burn. Burns suffered in electrical accidents may be of three types: electrical burns, arc burns, and thermal contact burns.

Electrical burns are the result of electric current flowing through the tissues or bones. Tissue damage is caused by the heat generated by the current flow through the body. An electrical burn is one of the most serious injuries you can receive, and should be given immediate attention. Since the most severe burning is likely to be internal, what may appear at first to be a small surface wound could, in fact, be an indication of severe internal burns.

Arc burns make up a substantial portion of the injuries from electrical malfunctions. The electric arc between metals can be up to 35,000°F, which is about four times hotter than the surface of the sun. Workers several feet from the source of the arc can receive severe or fatal burns. Since most electrical safety guidelines recommend safe working distances based on shock considerations, workers can be following these guidelines and still be at risk from arc. Electric arcs can occur due to poor electrical contact or failed insulation. Electrical arcing is caused by the passage of substantial amounts of current through the vaporized terminal material (usually metal or carbon).

 CAUTION

Since the heat of the arc is dependent on the short circuit current available at the arcing point, arcs generated on 480V systems can be just as dangerous as those generated at 13,000V.

The third type of burn is a thermal contact burn. It is caused by contact with objects thrown during the blast associated with an electric arc. This blast comes from the pressure developed by the near-instantaneous heating of the air surrounding the arc, and from the expansion of the metal as it is vaporized. (Copper expands by a factor in excess of 65,000 times in boiling.) These pressures can be great enough to hurl people, switchgear, and cabinets considerable distances. Another hazard associated with the blast is the hurling of molten metal droplets, which can also cause thermal contact burns and associated damage. A possible beneficial side effect of the blast is that it could hurl a nearby person away from the arc, thereby reducing the effect of arc burns.

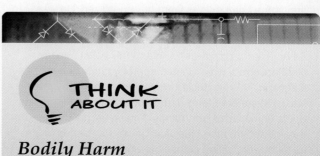

THINK ABOUT IT

Bodily Harm

What factors affect the amount of damage to the body during an electric shock?

3.0.0 ◆ REDUCING YOUR RISK

There are many things that can be done to greatly reduce the chance of receiving an electrical shock. Always comply with your company's safety policy and all applicable rules and regulations, including job site rules. In addition, the Occupational Safety and Health Administration (OSHA) publishes the *Code of Federal Regulations (CFR)*. *CFR Part 1910* covers the OSHA standards for general industry and *CFR Part 1926* covers the OSHA standards for the construction industry.

Do not approach any electrical conductors closer than indicated in *Table 2* unless you are sure they are de-energized and your company has designated you as a qualified individual. Also, the values given in the table are minimum safe clearance distances; if you already have standard distances established, these are provided only as supplemental information. These distances are listed in *CFR 1910.333/1926.416*.

3.1.0 Protective Equipment

You should also become familiar with common personal protective equipment. In particular, know

Table 2 Approach Distances for Qualified Employees— Alternating Current

Voltage Range (Phase-to-Phase)	Minimum Approach Distance
300V and less	Avoid contact
Over 300V, not over 750V	1 ft 0 in (30.5 cm)
Over 750V, not over 2kV	1 ft 6 in (46 cm)
Over 2kV, not over 15kV	2 ft 0 in (61 cm)
Over 15kV, not over 37kV	3 ft 0 in (91 cm)
Over 37kV, not over 87.5kV	3 ft 6 in (107 cm)
Over 87.5kV, not over 121kV	4 ft 0 in (122 cm)
Over 121kV, not over 140kV	4 ft 6 in (137 cm)

the voltage rating of each piece of equipment. Rubber gloves are used to prevent the skin from coming into contact with energized circuits. A separate leather cover protects the rubber glove from punctures and other damage (see *Figure 2*). OSHA addresses the use of protective equipment, apparel, and tools in *CFR 1910.335(a)*. This article is divided into two sections: *Personal Protective Equipment* and *General Protective Equipment and Tools*.

The first section, *Personal Protective Equipment*, includes the following requirements:

- Employees working in areas where there are potential electrical hazards shall be provided with, and shall use, electrical protective equipment that is appropriate for the specific parts of the body to be protected and for the work to be performed.
- Protective equipment shall be maintained in a safe, reliable condition and shall be period

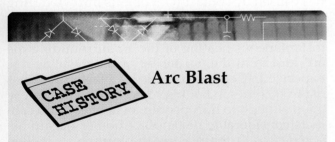

Arc Blast

CASE HISTORY

An electrician in Louisville, KY was cleaning a high-voltage switch cabinet. He removed the padlock securing the switch enclosure and opened the door. He used a voltage meter to verify 0V on the three load phases at the rear of the cabinet. However, he did not test all potentially energized parts within the cabinet, and some components were still energized. He was wearing standard work boots and safety glasses, but was not wearing protective rubber gloves or an arc suit. As he used a paintbrush to clean the switch, an arc blast occurred, which lasted approximately one-sixth of a second. The electrician was knocked down by the blast. He suffered third-degree burns and required skin grafts on his arms and hands. The investigation determined that the blast was caused by debris, such as a cobweb, falling across the open switch.

The Bottom Line: Always wear the appropriate personal protective equipment and test all components for voltage before working in or around electrical devices.

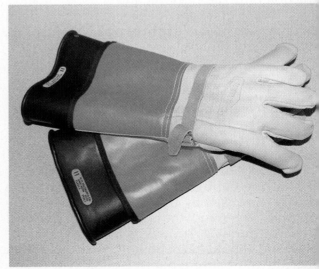

101F02.EF

Figure 2 ◆ Rubber gloves and leather protectors.

cally inspected or tested, as required by *CFR 1910.137/1926.95.*

If the insulating capability of protective equipment may be subject to damage during use, the insulating material shall be protected.

Employees shall wear nonconductive head protection wherever there is a danger of head injury from electric shock or burns due to contact with exposed energized parts.

Employees shall wear protective equipment for the eyes and face wherever there is danger of injury to the eyes or face from electric arcs or flashes or from flying objects resulting from an electrical explosion.

The second section, *General Protective Equipment and Tools,* includes the following requirements:

When working near exposed energized conductors or circuit parts, each employee shall use insulated tools or handling equipment if the tools or handling equipment might make contact with such conductors or parts. If the insulating capability of insulated tools or handling equipment is subject to damage, the insulating material shall be protected.

Fuse handling equipment, insulated for the circuit voltage, shall be used to remove or install fuses when the fuse terminals are energized.

Ropes and handlines used near exposed energized parts shall be nonconductive.

Protective shields, protective barriers, or insulating materials shall be used to protect each employee from shock, burns, or other electrically related injuries while that employee is working near exposed energized parts that might be accidentally contacted or where dangerous electric heating or arcing might occur. When normally enclosed live parts are exposed for maintenance or repair, they shall be guarded to protect unqualified persons from contact with the live parts.

The types of electrical safety equipment, protective apparel, and protective tools available for use are quite varied. We will discuss the most common types of safety equipment. These include the following:

Rubber protective equipment, including gloves and blankets
Protective apparel
Personal clothing
Hot sticks
Fuse pullers
Shorting probes
Eye and face protection

3.1.1 1910.335(a)(1)/1926.951(a) Rubber Protective Equipment

At some point during the performance of their duties, all electrical workers will be exposed to energized circuits or equipment. Two of the most important articles of protection for electrical workers are insulated rubber gloves and rubber blankets, which must be matched to the voltage rating for the circuit or equipment. Rubber protective equipment is designed for the protection of the user. If it fails during use, a serious injury could occur.

Rubber protective equipment is available in two types. Type 1 designates rubber protective equipment that is manufactured of natural or synthetic rubber that is properly vulcanized, and Type 2 designates equipment that is ozone resistant, made from any elastomer or combination of elastomeric compounds. Ozone is a form of oxygen that is produced from electricity and is present in the air surrounding a conductor under high voltages. Normally, ozone is found at voltages of 10kV and higher, such as those found in electric utility transmission and distribution systems. Type 1 protective equipment can be damaged by corona cutting, which is the cutting action of ozone on natural rubber when it is under mechanical stress. Type 1 rubber protective equipment can also be damaged by ultraviolet rays. However, it is very important that the rubber protective equipment in use today be made of natural rubber or Type 1 equipment. Type 2 rubber protective equipment is very stiff and is not as easily worn as Type 1 equipment.

Various classes – The American National Standards Institute (ANSI) and the American Society for Testing and Materials International (ASTM) have designated a specific classification system for rubber protective equipment. The voltage ratings are as follows:

- Class 0   1,000V
- Class 1   7,500V
- Class 2   17,500V
- Class 3   26,500V
- Class 4   36,000V

Inspection of protective equipment – Before rubber protective equipment can be worn by personnel in the field, all equipment must have a current test date stenciled on the equipment, and it must be inspected by the user. Insulating gloves must be tested each day by the user before they can be used. They must also be tested during the day if their insulating value is ever in question. Because rubber protective equipment is going to be used for personal protection and serious injury could result from its misuse or failure, it is important that an adequate safety factor be provided between the voltage on which it is to be used and the voltage at which it was tested.

All rubber protective equipment must be marked with the appropriate voltage rating and last inspection date. The markings that are required to be on rubber protective equipment must be applied in a manner that will not interfere with the protection that is provided by the equipment.

 WARNING!
Never work on anything energized without direct instruction from your employer.

Gloves – Both high- and low-voltage rubber gloves are of the gauntlet type and are available in various sizes. To get the best possible protection and service life, here are a few general rules that apply whenever they are used in electrical work:

- Always wear leather protectors over your gloves. Any direct contact with sharp or pointed objects may cut, snag, or puncture the gloves and take away the protection you are depending on. Leather protectors are required by the National Fire Protection Association's (NFPA) *Standard 70-E* if the insulating capabilities of the gloves are subject to damage. (The standards of the NFPA are incorporated into the OSHA standards.)
- Always wear rubber gloves right side out (serial number and size to the outside). Turning gloves inside out places a stress on the pre-formed rubber.
- Always keep the gauntlets up. Rolling them down sacrifices a valuable area of protection.
- Always inspect and field check gloves before using them. Always check the inside for any debris. The inspection of gloves is covered in more detail later in this section.
- Use light amounts of talcum powder or cotton liners with the rubber gloves. This gives the user more comfort, and it also helps to absorb some of the perspiration that can damage the gloves over years of use.
- Wash the rubber gloves in lukewarm, clean, fresh water after each use. Dry the gloves inside and out prior to returning to storage. Never use any type of cleaning solution on the gloves.
- Once the gloves have been properly cleaned, inspected, and tested, they must be properly stored. They should be stored in a cool, dry, dark place that is free from ozone, chemicals,

oils, solvents, or other materials that coul[d] damage the gloves. Such storage should not b[e] in the vicinity of hot pipes or direct sunligh[t.] Both gloves and sleeves should be stored i[n] their natural shape and kept in a bag or box in[side] their protectors. They should be store[d] undistorted, right side out, and unfolded.

- Gloves can be damaged by many differen[t] chemicals, especially petroleum-based prod[uct]s such as oils, gasoline, hydraulic fluid i[n]hibitors, hand creams, pastes, and salves. [If] contact is made with these or other petroleu[m] based products, the contaminant should b[e] wiped off immediately. If any signs of physic[al] damage or chemical deterioration are foun[d] (e.g., swelling, softness, hardening, stickines[s,] ozone deterioration, or sun checking), the pro[-] tective equipment must not be used.
- Never wear watches or rings while wearin[g] rubber gloves; this can cause damage from th[e] inside out and defeats the purpose of using rub[-] ber gloves. Never wear anything conductive.
- Rubber gloves must be tested every six month[s] by a certified testing laboratory. Always chec[k] the inspection date before using gloves.
- Use rubber gloves only for their intended pu[r-] pose, not for handling chemicals or other wor[k.] This also applies to the leather protectors.

Before rubber gloves are used, a visual inspe[c-] tion and an air test should be made. This shoul[d] be done prior to use and as many times during th[e] day as you feel necessary. To perform a visual in[-] spection, stretch a small area of the glove, check[-] ing to see that no defects exist, such as:

- Embedded foreign material
- Deep scratches
- Pinholes or punctures
- Snags or cuts

Gloves and sleeves can be inspected by rollin[g] the outside and inside of the protective equipmen[t] between the hands. This can be done by squeezin[g] together the inside of the gloves or sleeves to ben[d] the outside area and create enough stress to the in[-] side surface to expose any cracks, cuts, or othe[r] defects. When the entire surface has been checke[d] in this manner, the equipment is then turned in[-] side out, and the procedure is repeated. It is ver[y] important not to leave the rubber protectiv[e] equipment inside out.

Remember, any damage at all reduces the insu[-] lating ability of the rubber glove. Look for signs o[f] deterioration from age, such as hardening an[d] slight cracking. Also, if the glove has been ex[-] posed to petroleum products, it should be consi[d-] ered suspect because deterioration can be cause[d] y such exposure. Gloves that are found to be defective must be turned in for disposal. Never leave a damaged glove lying around; someone may think it is a good glove and not perform an inspection prior to using it.

After visually inspecting the glove, other defects may be observed by applying the air test (Figure 3).

Step 1 Stretch the glove and look for any defects.

Step 2 Twirl the glove around quickly or roll it down from the glove gauntlet to trap air inside.

Step 3 Trap the air by squeezing the gauntlet with one hand. Use the other hand to squeeze the palm, fingers, and thumb to check for weaknesses and defects.

Step 4 Hold the glove up to your ear to try to detect any escaping air.

Step 5 If the glove does not pass this inspection, it must be turned in for disposal.

 CAUTION

Never use compressed gas for the air test as this can damage the glove.

Insulating blankets – An insulating blanket is a versatile cover-up device best suited for the protection of maintenance technicians against accidental contact with energized electrical equipment.

These blankets are designed and manufactured to provide insulating quality and flexibility for use in covering. Insulating blankets are designed only for covering equipment and should not be used on the floor. (Special rubber mats are available for floor use.) Use caution when installing on sharp edges or covering pointed objects.

Blankets must be inspected yearly and should be checked before each use. To check rubber blankets, place the blanket on a flat surface and roll the blanket from one corner to the opposite corner. If there are any irregularities in the rubber, this method will expose them. After the blanket has been rolled from each corner, it should then be turned over and the procedure repeated.

Insulating blankets are cleaned in the same manner as rubber gloves. Once the protective equipment has been properly cleaned, inspected, and tested, it must be properly stored. It should be stored in a cool, dry, dark place that is free from ozone, chemicals, oils, solvents, or other materials that could damage the equipment. Such storage should not be in the vicinity of hot pipes or direct sunlight. Blankets may be stored rolled in containers that are designed for this use; the inside diameter of the roll should be at least two inches.

3.1.2 Protective Apparel

Besides rubber gloves, there are other types of special application protective apparel, such as fire suits, face shields, and rubber sleeves.

Manufacturing plants should have other types of special application protective equipment available for use, such as high-voltage sleeves, high-voltage boots, nonconductive protective helmets, nonconductive eyewear and face protection, and switchboard blankets.

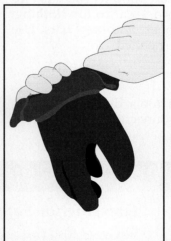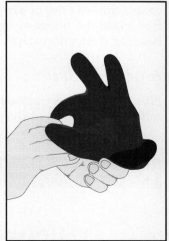

101F03.EPS

Figure 3 ◆ Glove inspection.

All equipment should be inspected before use and during use, as necessary. The equipment used and the extent of the precautions taken depend on each individual situation; however, it is better to be overprotected than underprotected when you are trying to prevent electrocution.

When working with high voltages, flash suits may be required in some applications. Some plants require them to be worn for all switching and rack-in or rack-out operations.

Face shields should also be worn during all switching operations where arcs are a possibility. The thin plastic type of face shield should be avoided because it will melt when exposed to the extremely high temperatures of an electrical arc.

Rubber sleeves are another type of protective apparel that should be worn during switching operations and breaker racking. Sleeves must be inspected yearly.

3.1.3 Personal Clothing

Any individual who will perform work in an electrical environment or in plant substations should dress accordingly. Avoid wearing synthetic-fiber clothing; these types of materials will melt when exposed to high temperatures and will actually increase the severity of a burn. Wear cotton clothing, fiberglass-toe boots or shoes, and hard hats. Use hearing protection where needed.

3.1.4 Hot Sticks

Hot sticks are insulated tools designed for the manual operation of disconnecting switches, fuse removal and insertion, and the application an removal of temporary grounds.

A hot stick is made up of two parts, the head c hood and the insulating rod. The head can b made of metal or hardened plastic, while the in sulating section may be wood, plastic, laminate wood, or other effective insulating material There are also telescoping sticks available.

Most plants have hot sticks available for differ ent purposes. Select a stick of the correct type an size for the application.

Storage of hot sticks is important. They shoul be hung up vertically on a wall to prevent an damage. They should also be stored away fror direct sunlight and prevented from being expose to petroleum products. The preferred method c storage is to place the stick in a long section c capped pipe.

3.1.5 Fuse Pullers

Use the plastic or fiberglass style of fuse puller fc removing and installing low-voltage cartridg fuses. All fuse pulling and replacement operation must be done using fuse pullers.

The best type of fuse puller is one that has spread guard installed. This prevents the pulle from opening if resistance is met when installin fuses.

3.1.6 Shorting Probes

Before working on de-energized circuits that hav capacitors installed, you must discharge the capac itors using a safety shorting probe. When using

horting probe, first connect the test clip to a good ground to make contact. If necessary, scrape the paint from the metal surface. Then, hold the shorting probe by the handle and touch the probe end of the shorting rod to the points to be shorted. The probe end can be hooked over the part or terminal to provide a constant connection to ground. Never touch any metal part of the shorting probe while grounding circuits or components. Whenever possible, especially when working on or near any de-energized high-voltage circuits, shorting probes should be connected and then left attached to the de-energized portion of any circuit for the duration of the work. This action serves as an extra safety precaution against any accidental application of voltage to the circuit.

3.1.7 Eye and Face Protection

NFPA 70-E requires that protective equipment for the eyes and face shall be used whenever there is danger of injury to the eyes or face from electrical arcs or flashes, or from flying or falling objects resulting from an electrical explosion.

3.2.0 Verify That Circuits Are De-energized

You should always assume that all the circuits are energized until you have verified that the circuit is de-energized. Follow these steps to verify that a circuit is de-energized:

Step 1 Ensure that the circuit is properly tagged and locked out *(CFR 1910.333/1926.417)*.

Step 2 Verify the test instrument operation on a known source.

Step 3 Using the test instrument, check the circuit to be de-energized. The voltage should be zero.

Step 4 Verify the test instrument operation, once again on a known power source.

3.3.0 Other Precautions

There are several other precautions you can take to help make your job safer. For example:

- Always remove all jewelry (e.g., rings, watches, bracelets, and necklaces) before working on electrical equipment. Most jewelry is made of conductive material and wearing it can result in a shock, as well as other injuries if the jewelry gets caught in moving components.
- When working on energized equipment, it is safer to work in pairs. In doing so, if one of the workers experiences a harmful electrical shock, the other worker can quickly de-energize the circuit and call for help.

Using a Shorting Probe

Using a shorting probe can be a very dangerous task. Always take the time to use the appropriate personal protective equipment. Remember, you only have one chance to protect yourself.

101PO102.EPS

- Plan each job before you begin it. Make sure you understand exactly what it is you are going to do. If you are not sure, ask your supervisor.
- You will need to look over the appropriate prints and drawings to locate isolation devices and potential hazards. Never defeat safety interlocks. Remember to plan your escape route before starting work. Know where the nearest phone is and the emergency number to dial for assistance.
- If you realize that the work will go beyond the scope of what was planned, stop and get instructions from your supervisor before continuing. Do not attempt to plan as you go.
- It is critical that you stay alert. Workplaces are dynamic, and situations relative to safety are always changing. If you leave the work area to pick up material, take a break, or have lunch, reevaluate your surroundings when you return. Remember, plan ahead.

4.0.0 ◆ OSHA

The purpose of OSHA is "to ensure safe and healthful working conditions for working men and women." OSHA is authorized to enforce standards and assist and encourage the states in their efforts to ensure safe and healthful working conditions. OSHA assists states by providing for research, information, education, and training in the field of occupational safety and health.

The law that established OSHA specifies the duties of both the employer and employee with respect to safety. Some of the key requirements are outlined below. This list does not include everything, nor does it override the procedures called for by your employer.

- Employers shall provide a place of employment free from recognized hazards likely to cause death or serious injury.
- Employers shall comply with the standards of the act.
- Employers shall be subject to fines and other penalties for violation of those standards.

WARNING!

OSHA states that employees have a duty to follow the safety rules laid down by the employer. Additionally, some states can reduce the amount of benefits paid to an injured employee if that employee was not following known, established safety rules. Your company may also terminate you if you violate an established safety rule.

4.1.0 Safety Standards

The OSHA standards are split into several sections. As discussed earlier, the two that affect you the most are *CFR 1926,* construction specific, and *CFR 1910,* which is the standard for general industry. Either or both may apply depending on where you are working and what you are doing. If a job site condition is covered in the 1926 book, then that standard takes precedence. However, if a more stringent requirement is listed in the *1910* standard, it should also be met. An excellent example is the current difference in the two standards on confined spaces; if someone gets hurt or killed, the decision to use the less stringent *1926* standard could be called into question. OSHA's *General Duty Clause* states that an employer should have known all recognized hazards and removed the hazard or protected the employee.

To protect workers from the occupational injuries and fatalities caused by electrical hazards, OSHA has issued a set of design safety standards for electrical utilization systems. These standards are *1926.400–449* and *1910.302–308.* OSHA also enforces the requirements of the *National Electrical Code® (NEC®).*

CFR 1910 must be followed whenever the construction standard *CFR 1926* does not address an issue that is covered by *CFR 1910* or for a preexisting installation. If the *CFR 1910* standard is more stringent than *CFR 1926,* then the more stringent standard should be followed. OSHA does not update all of their standards at the same time, and thus there are often differences in similar sections of the two standards. Safety should always be first, and the more protective work rule should always be chosen.

4.1.1 1910.302–308/1926.402–408 Design Safety Standards for Electrical Systems

This section contains design safety regulations for all the electrical equipment and installations used to provide power and light to employee workplaces. The articles listed are outlined in the following sections.

4.1.2 1910.302/1926.402 Electric Utilization Systems

This article identifies the scope of the standard. Listings are included to show which electrical installations and equipment are covered under the standard, and which installations and equipment are not covered under the standard. Furthermore, certain sections of the standard apply only to uti zation equipment installed after March 15, 1972, and some apply only to equipment installed after April 16, 1981. *Article 1910.302 (1926.402)* addresses these oddities and provides guidance to clarify them.

4.1.3   *1910.303/1926.403*
General Requirements

This article covers topics that mostly concern equipment installation clearances, identification, and examination. Some of the major subjects addressed in this article are:

- Equipment installation examinations
- Splicing
- Marking
- Identification of disconnecting means
- Workspace around electrical equipment

4.1.4   *1910.304/1926.404*
Wiring Design and Protection

This article covers the application, identification, and protection requirements of grounding conductors, outside conductors, service conductors, and equipment enclosures. Some of the major topics discussed are:

- Grounded conductors
- Outside conductors
- Service conductors
- Overcurrent protection
- System grounding requirements

4.1.5   *1910.305/1926.405*
Wiring Methods, Components, and Equipment for General Use

In general, this article addresses the wiring method requirements of raceways, cable trays, pull and junction boxes, switches, and switchboards; the application requirements of temporary wiring installations; the equipment and conductor requirements for general wiring; and the protection requirements of motors, transformers, capacitors, and storage batteries. Some of the major topics are:

- Wiring methods
- Cabinets, boxes, and fittings
- Switches
- Switchboards and panelboards
- Enclosures for damp or wet locations
- Conductors for general wiring
- Flexible cords and cables
- Portable cables
- Equipment for general use

4.1.6 1910.306/1926.406 Specific Purpose Equipment and Installations

This article addresses the requirements of special equipment and installations not covered in other articles. Some of the major types of equipment and installations found in this article are:

- Electric signs and outline lighting
- Cranes and hoists
- Elevators, dumbwaiters, escalators, and moving walks
- Electric welders
- Data processing systems
- X-ray equipment
- Induction and dielectric heating equipment
- Electrolytic cells
- Electrically driven or controlled irrigation machines
- Swimming pools, fountains, and similar installations

4.1.7 1910.307/1926.407 Hazardous (Classified) Locations

This article covers the requirements for electric equipment and wiring in locations that are classified because they contain: (1) flammable vapors, liquids, and/or gases, or combustible dust or fibers; and (2) the likelihood that a flammable or combustible concentration or quantity is present. Some of the major topics covered in this article are:

- Scope
- Electrical installations in hazardous locations
- Conduit
- Equipment in Division 2 locations

4.1.8 1910.308/1926.408 Special Systems

This article covers the wiring methods, grounding, protection, identification, and other general requirements of special systems not covered in other articles. Some of the major subtopics found in this article are:

- Systems over 600 volts nominal
- Emergency power systems
- Class 1, 2, and 3 remote control, signaling, and power-limited circuits
- Fire-protective signaling systems
- Communications systems

4.1.9 1910.331/1926.416 Scope

This article serves as an overview of the following articles and also provides a summary of the installations that this standard allows qualified and unqualified persons to work on or near, as well as the installations that this standard does not cover.

4.1.10 1910.332 Training

The training requirements contained in this article apply to employees who face a risk of electric shock. Some of the topics that appear in this article are:

- Content of training
- Additional requirements for unqualified persons
- Additional requirements for qualified persons
- Type of training

4.1.11 1910.333/1926.416–417 Selection and Use of Work Practices

This article covers the implementation of safety-related work practices necessary to prevent electrical shock and other related injuries to the employee. Some of the major topics addressed in this article are listed below:

- General
- Working on or near exposed de-energized parts
- Working on or near exposed energized parts

4.1.12 1910.334/1926.431 Use of Equipment

This article was added to reinforce the regulations pertaining to portable electrical equipment, test equipment, and load break switches. Major topics include:

- Portable electric equipment
- Electric power and lighting circuits
- Test instruments and equipment

4.1.13 1910.335/1926.416 Safeguards for Personnel Protection

This article covers the personnel protection requirements for employees in the vicinity of electrical hazards. It addresses regulations that protect personnel working on equipment as well as personnel working nearby. Some of the major topics are:

- Use of protective equipment
- Alerting techniques

Now that background topics have been covered and an overview of the OSHA electrical safety standards has been provided, it is time to move on to topics related directly to safety. As we discuss these topics, we will continually refer to the OSHA standards to identify the requirements that govern them.

CFR 1926 Subpart K also addresses electrical safety requirements that are necessary for the practical safeguarding of employees involved in construction work.

2.0 Safety Philosophy and General Safety Precautions

The most important piece of safety equipment required when performing work in an electrical environment is common sense. All areas of electrical safety precautions and practices draw upon common sense and attention to detail. One of the most dangerous conditions in an electrical work area is a poor attitude toward safety.

WARNING!
Only qualified individuals may work on electrical equipment. Your employer will determine who is qualified. Remember, your employer's safety rules must always be followed.

As stated in *CFR 1910.333(a)/1926.403*, safety-related work practices shall be employed to prevent electric shock or other injuries resulting from either direct or indirect electrical contact when work is performed near or on equipment or circuits that are or may be energized. The specific safety-related work practices shall be consistent with the nature and extent of the associated electrical hazards. The following are considered some of the basic and necessary attitudes and electrical safety precautions that lay the groundwork for a proper safety program. Before going on any electrical work assignment, these safety precautions should be reviewed and adhered to.

All work on electrical equipment should be done with circuits de-energized and cleared or grounded – It is obvious that working on energized equipment is much more dangerous than working on equipment that is de-energized. Work on energized electrical equipment should be avoided if at all possible. *CFR 1910.333(a)(1)/1926.403* states that live parts to which an employee may be exposed shall be de-energized before the employee works on or near them, unless the employer can demonstrate that de-energizing

introduces additional or increased hazards or is not possible because of equipment design or operational limitations. Live parts that operate at less than 50 volts to ground need not be de-energized if there will be no increased exposure to electrical burns or to explosion due to electric arcs.

- *All conductors, buses, and connections should be considered energized until proven otherwise*—As stated in *1910.333(b)(1)/1926.417,* conductors and parts of electrical equipment that have not been locked out or tagged out in accordance with this section should be considered energized. Routine operation of the circuit breakers and disconnect switches contained in a power distribution system can be hazardous if not approached in the right manner. Several basic precautions that can be observed in switchgear operations are:
  - Wear proper clothing made of 100% cotton or fire-resistant fabric.
  - Eye, face, and head protection should be worn. Turn your head away whenever closing devices.
  - Whenever operating circuit breakers in low-voltage or medium-voltage systems, always stand off to the side of the unit.
  - Always try to operate disconnect switches and circuit breakers under a no-load condition.
  - Never intentionally force an interlock on a system or circuit breaker.
  - Always verify what you are closing a device into; you could violate a lockout or close into a hard fault.

Often, a circuit breaker or disconnect switch is used for providing lockout on an electrical system. To ensure that a lockout is not violated, perform the following procedures when using the device as a lockout point:

- Breakers must always be locked out and tagged as discussed previously whenever you are working on a circuit that is tied to an energized breaker. Breakers capable of being opened and racked out to the disconnected position should have this done. Afterward, approved safety locks must be installed. The breaker may be removed from its cubicle completely to prevent unexpected mishaps. Always follow the standard rack-out and removal procedures that were supplied with the switchgear. Once removed, a sign must be hung on the breaker identifying its use as a lockout point, and approved safety locks must be installed when the breaker is used for isolation. Breakers equipped with closing springs should be discharged to release all stored energy in the breaker mechanism.

- Some of the circuit breakers used are equipped with keyed interlocks for protection during operation. These locks are generally called kirklocks and are relied upon to ensure proper sequence of operation only. These are not to be used for the purpose of locking out a circuit or system. Where disconnects are installed for use in isolation, they should never be opened under load. When opening a disconnect manually, it should be done quickly with a positive force. Again, lockouts should be used when the disconnects are open.

- Whenever performing switching or fuse replacements, always use the protective equipment necessary to ensure personnel safety. Never make the assumption that because things have gone fine the last 999 times, they will not go wrong this time. Always prepare yourself for the worst case accident when performing switching.

- Whenever re-energizing circuits following maintenance or removal of a faulted component, extreme care should be used. Always verify that the equipment is in a condition to be re-energized safely. All connections should be insulated and all covers should be installed. Have all personnel stand clear of the area for the initial re-energization. Never assume everything is in perfect condition. Verify the conditions.

The following procedure is provided as a guideline for ensuring that equipment and systems will not be damaged by reclosing low-voltage circuit breakers into faults. If a low-voltage circuit breaker has opened for no apparent reason, perform the following:

Step 1 Verify that the equipment being supplied is not physically damaged and shows no obvious signs of overheating or fire.

Step 2 Make all appropriate tests to locate any faults.

Step 3 Reclose the feeder breaker. Stand off to the side when closing the breaker.

Step 4 If the circuit breaker trips again, do not attempt to reclose the breaker. In a plant environment, Electrical Engineering should be notified, and the cause of the trip should be isolated and repaired.

The same general procedure should be followed for fuse replacement, with the exception of transformer fuses. If a transformer fuse blows, the transformer and feeder cabling should be inspected and tested before re-energizing. A blown fuse to a trans-

THINK ABOUT IT

Working on Energized Systems

Some electricians commonly work on energized systems because they think it's too much trouble to turn off the power. What practices have you seen around your home or workplace that could be deadly?

former is very significant because it normally indicates an internal fault. Transformer failures are catastrophic in nature and can be extremely dangerous. If applicable, contact the in-plant Electrical Engineering Department prior to commencing any effort to re-energize a transformer.

Power must always be removed from a circuit when removing and installing fuses. The air break disconnects (or quick disconnects) provided on the upstream side of a large transformer must be opened prior to removing the transformer's fuses. Otherwise, severe arcing will occur as the fuse is removed. This arcing can result in personnel injury and equipment damage.

To replace fuses servicing circuits below 600 volts:

- Secure power to fuses or ensure all downstream loads have been disconnected.
- Always use a positive force to remove and install fuses.

When replacing fuses servicing systems above 600 volts:

- Open and lock out the disconnect switches.
- Unlock the fuse compartment.
- Verify that the fuses are de-energized.
- Attach the fuse removal hot stick to the fuse and remove it.

4.3.0 Electrical Regulations

OSHA has certain regulations that apply to job site electrical safety. These regulations include:

- All electrical work shall be in compliance with the latest *NEC*® and OSHA standards.
- The noncurrent-carrying metal parts of fixed, portable, and plug-connected equipment shall be grounded. It is best to choose grounded tools. However, portable tools and appliances

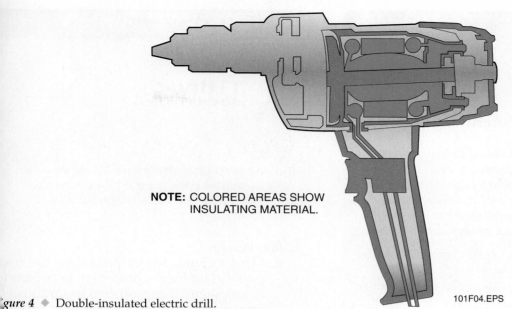

NOTE: COLORED AREAS SHOW
INSULATING MATERIAL.

101F04.EPS

Figure 4 ◆ Double-insulated electric drill.

protected by an approved system of double insulation need not be grounded. *Figure 4* shows
an example of a double-insulated/ungrounded
tool.

Extension cords shall be the three-wire type,
shall be protected from damage, and shall not
be fastened with staples or hung in a manner
that could cause damage to the outer jacket
or insulation. Never run an extension cord
through a doorway or window that can pinch
the cord. Also, never allow vehicles or equipment to drive over cords.

Exposed lamps in temporary lights shall be
guarded to prevent accidental contact, except
where lamps are deeply recessed in the reflec-
tor. Temporary lights shall not be suspended,
except in accordance with their listed labeling.

Receptacles for attachment plugs shall be of an
approved type and properly installed. Installation of the receptacle will be in accordance with
the listing and labeling for each receptacle and
shall be GFCI-protected if the setting is a temporarily wired construction site. If permanent
receptacles are used with extension cords, then
you must use GFCI protection.

Each disconnecting means for motors and appliances and each service feeder or branch circuit at
the point where it originates shall be legibly
marked to indicate its purpose and voltage.

Flexible cords shall be used in continuous
lengths (no splices) and shall be of a type listed
in *NEC Table 400.4.*

Ground fault protection is required when supplying temporary power to equipment used by
personnel during any repair, remodel, mainte-

nance, construction, and demolition activities.
There are two methods for accomplishing this:
an assured grounding program [limited to use
in certain industrial applications only per *NEC
Section 590.6(B)(2)*], or ground fault protection
receptacles or breakers. Each employer will set
the standard and method to be used. *Figure 5*
shows a typical ground-fault circuit interrupter.

4.3.1 OSHA Lockout/Tagout Rule

OSHA released the *29 CFR 1926* lockout/tagout
rule in December 1991. This rule covers the specific
procedure to be followed for the "servicing and
maintenance of machines and equipment in which
the unexpected energization or startup of the machines or equipment, or releases of stored energy,
could cause injury to employees." This standard
establishes minimum performance requirements
for the control of such hazardous energy.

101F05.EPS

Figure 5 ◆ Typical GFCI.

Potential Hazards

A self-employed builder was using a metal cutting tool on a metal carport roof and was not using GFCI protection. The male and female plugs of his extension cord partially separated, and the active pin touched the metal roofing. When the builder grounded himself on the gutter of an adjacent roof, he received a fatal shock.

The Bottom Line: Always use GFCI protection and be on the lookout for potential hazards.

The purpose of the OSHA procedure is to ensure that equipment is isolated from all potentially hazardous energy (for example, electrical, mechanical, hydraulic, chemical, or thermal), and tagged and locked out before employees perform any servicing or maintenance activities in which the unexpected energization, startup, or release of stored energy could cause injury. All employees shall be instructed in the lockout/tagout procedure.

CAUTION
Although 99% of your work may be electrical, be aware that you may also need to lock out mechanical and other types of energy equipment.

The following is an example of a lockout/tagout procedure. Make sure to use the procedure that is specific to your employer or job site.

WARNING!
This procedure is provided for your information only. The OSHA procedure provides only the minimum requirements for lockouts/tagouts. Consult the lockout/tagout procedure for your company and the plant or job site at which you are working. Remember that your life could depend on the lockout/tagout procedure. It is critical that you use the correct procedure for your site. The *NEC*® requires that remote-mounted motor disconnects be permanently equipped with a lockout feature.

GFCIs

Explain how GFCIs protect people. Where should a GFCI be installed in the circuit to be most effective?

I. *Introduction*
   A. This lockout/tagout procedure has bee established for the protection of personn from potential exposure to hazardous e ergy sources during construction, install tion, service, and maintenance of electric energy systems.
   B. This procedure applies to and must be fo lowed by all personnel who may be poten tially exposed to the unexpected startup release of hazardous energy (e.g., electr cal, mechanical, pneumatic, hydrauli chemical, or thermal).

Exception: This procedure does not apply process and/or utility equipment or systen with cord and plug power supply systems whe the cord and plug are the only source of ha ardous energy, are removed from the source, an remain under the exclusive control of the autho ized employee.

Exception: This procedure does not apply troubleshooting (diagnostic) procedures and i stallation of electrical equipment and systen when the energy source cannot be de-energize because continuity of service is essential or shu down of the system is impractical. Addition personal protective equipment for such work required and the safe work practices identified fc this work must be followed.

II. *Definitions*
   • *Affected employee* – Any person working o or near equipment or machinery whe maintenance or installation tasks are bein performed by others during lockout tagout conditions.
   • *Appointed authorized employee* – Any persc appointed by the job site supervisor to c ordinate and maintain the security of group lockout/tagout condition.
   • *Authorized employee* – Any person autho ized by the job site supervisor to use loc

out/tagout procedures while working on electrical equipment.

- *Authorized supervisor* – The assigned job site supervisor who is in charge of coordination of procedures and maintenance of security of all lockout/tagout operations at the job site.
- *Energy isolation device* – An approved electrical disconnect switch capable of accepting approved lockout/tagout hardware for the purpose of isolating and securing a hazardous electrical source in an open or safe position.
- *Lockout/tagout hardware* – A combination of padlocks, danger tags, and other devices designed to attach to and secure electrical isolation devices.

I. *Training*
   A. Each authorized supervisor, authorized employee, and appointed authorized employee shall receive initial and as-needed user-level training in lockout/tagout procedures.
   B. Training is to include recognition of hazardous energy sources, the type and magnitude of energy sources in the workplace, and the procedures for energy isolation and control.
   C. Retraining will be conducted on an as-needed basis whenever lockout/tagout procedures are changed or there is evidence that procedures are not being followed properly.

√. *Protective Equipment and Hardware*
   A. Lockout/tagout devices shall be used exclusively for controlling hazardous electrical energy sources.
   B. All padlocks must be numbered and assigned to one employee only.
   C. No duplicate or master keys will be made available to anyone except the site supervisor.
   D. A current list with the lock number and authorized employee's name must be maintained by the site supervisor.
   E. Danger tags must be of the standard white, red, and black *DANGER—DO NOT OPERATE* design and shall include the authorized employee's name, the date, and the appropriate network company (use permanent markers).
   F. Danger tags must be used in conjunction with padlocks, as shown in *Figure 6*.

√. *Procedures*
   A. Preparation for lockout/tagout:
      1. Check the procedures to ensure that no changes have been made since you last used a lockout/tagout.

101F06.EPS

Figure 6 ◆ Lockout/tagout device.

      2. Identify all authorized and affected employees involved with the pending lockout/tagout.
   B. Sequence for lockout/tagout:
      1. Notify all authorized and affected personnel that a lockout/tagout is to be used and explain the reason why.
      2. Shut down the equipment or system using the normal OFF or STOP procedures.
      3. Lock out energy sources and test disconnects to be sure they cannot be moved to the ON position and open the control cutout switch. If there is no cutout switch, block the magnet in the switch open position before working on electrically operated equipment/apparatus such as motors, relays, etc. Remove the control wire.
      4. Lock and tag the required switches in the open position. Each authorized employee must affix a separate lock and tag. An example is shown in *Figure 7*.
      5. Dissipate any stored energy by attaching the equipment or system to ground.
      6. Verify that the test equipment is functional via a known power source.
      7. Confirm that all switches are in the open position and use test equipment to verify that all parts are de-energized.

Figure 7 ◆ Multiple lockout/tagout device.

101F07.EPS

101PO104.E

8. If it is necessary to temporarily leave the area, upon returning, retest to ensure that the equipment or system is still de-energized.

C. Restoration of energy:

1. Confirm that all personnel and tools, including shorting probes, are accounted for and removed from the equipment or system.

2. Completely reassemble and secure the equipment or system.

3. Replace and/or reactivate all safety controls.

4. Remove locks and tags from isolation switches. Authorized employees must remove their own locks and tags.

5. Notify all affected personnel that the lockout/tagout has ended and the equipment or system is energized.

6. Operate or close isolation switches to restore energy.

VI. *Emergency Removal Authorization*

A. In the event a lockout/tagout device is l secured, and the authorized employee absent, or the key is lost, the authoriz supervisor can remove the lockout/tag device.

B. The authorized employee must be formed that the lockout/tagout device h been removed.

C. Written verification of the action tak including informing the authorized e ployee of the removal, must be recorded the job journal.

CASE HISTORY

Lockout/Tagout Dilemma

In Georgia, electricians found energized switches after the lockout of a circuit panel in an older system that had been upgraded several times. The existing wiring did not match the current site drawings. A subsequent investigation found many such situations in older facilities.

The Bottom Line: Never rely solely on drawings. It is mandatory that the circuit be tested after lockout to verify that it is de-energized.

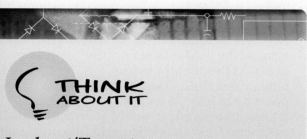

THINK ABOUT IT

Lockout/Tagout – Who Does It and When?

What situations are likely to require lockout/tagout? Who is responsible for performing the lockout/tagout? When would more than one person be responsible?

.4.0 Other OSHA Regulations

here are other OSHA regulations that you need o be aware of on the job site. For example:

OSHA requires the posting of hard hat areas. Be alert to those areas and always wear your hard hat properly, with the bill in front. Hard hats should be worn whenever overhead hazards exist, or there is the risk of exposure to electric shock or burns.

You should wear safety shoes on all job sites. Keep them in good condition.

Do not wear clothing with exposed metal zippers, buttons, or other metal fasteners. Avoid wearing loose-fitting or torn clothing.

Protect your eyes. Your eyesight is threatened by many activities on the job site. Always wear safety glasses with full side shields. In addition, the job may also require protective equipment such as face shields or goggles.

4.4.1 Testing for Voltage

OSHA also requires that you inspect or test existing conditions before beginning work on electrical equipment or lines. Usually, you will use a voltmeter/sensor or voltage tester to do this. You should assume that all electrical equipment and lines are energized until you have determined that they are not. Do not proceed to work on or near energized parts until the operating voltage is determined.

After the electrical equipment to be worked on has been locked and tagged out, the equipment must be verified as de-energized before work can proceed. This section sets the requirements that must be met before any circuits or equipment can be considered de-energized. First, and most importantly, only qualified persons may verify that a circuit or piece of equipment is de-energized. Before approaching the equipment to be worked on, the qualified person shall operate the equipment's normal operating controls to check that the proper energy sources have been disconnected.

Upon opening a control enclosure, the qualified person shall note the presence of any components that may store electrical energy. Initially, these components should be avoided.

To verify that the lockout was adequate and the equipment is indeed de-energized, a qualified person must use appropriate test equipment to check for power, paying particular attention to induced voltages and unrelated feedback voltage.

Ensure that your testing equipment is working properly by performing the live-dead-live check before each use. To perform this test, first check your voltmeter on a known live voltage source. This known source must be in the same range as the electrical equipment you will be working on. Next, without changing scales on your voltmeter, check for the presence of power in the equipment you have locked out. Finally, to ensure that your voltmeter did not malfunction, check it again on the known live source. Performing this test will assure you that your voltage testing equipment is reliable.

In accordance with *CFR 1910.333(b)(2)(iv)/ 1926.417(d)(4)(ii)*, if the circuit to be tested normally operates at more than 600 volts, the live-dead-live check must be performed.

Once it has been verified that power is not present, stored electrical energy that might endanger personnel must be released. A qualified person must use the proper devices to release the stored energy, such as using a shorting probe to discharge a capacitor.

5.0.0 ◆ LADDERS AND SCAFFOLDS

Ladders and scaffolds account for about half of the injuries from workplace electrocutions. The involuntary recoil that can occur when a person is shocked can cause the person to be thrown from a ladder or high place.

5.1.0 Ladders

Many job site accidents involve the misuse of ladders. Make sure to follow these general rules every time you use any ladder. Following these rules can prevent serious injury or even death.

- Before using any ladder, inspect it. Look for loose or missing rungs, cleats, bolts, or screws, and check for cracked, broken, or badly worn rungs, cleats, or side rails.
- If you find a ladder in poor condition, do not use it. Report it and tag it for repair or disposal.
- Never modify a ladder by cutting it or weakening its parts.
- Do not set up ladders where they may be run into by others, such as in doorways or walkways. If it is absolutely necessary to set up a ladder in such a location, protect the ladder with barriers.
- Do not increase a ladder's reach by standing it on boxes, barrels, or anything other than a flat surface.
- Check your shoes for grease, oil, or mud before climbing a ladder. These materials could make you slip.
- Always face the ladder and hold on with both hands when climbing up or down.

- Never lean out from the ladder. Keep your be buckle centered between the rails. If som thing is out of reach, get down and move th ladder.

WARNING!
When performing electrical work, always use ladders made of nonconductive material.

5.1.1 Straight and Extension Ladders

There are some specific rules to follow whe working with straight and extension ladders:

- Always place a straight ladder at the proper ar gle. The distance from the ladder feet to th base of the wall or support should be abou one-fourth the working height of the ladd (see *Figure 8*).
- Secure straight ladders to prevent slipping. U ladder shoes or hooks at the top and bottor Another method is to secure a board to the floe against the ladder feet. For brief jobs, someor can hold the straight ladder.
- Side rails should extend above the top suppo point by at least 36 inches.
- It takes two people to safely extend and raise a extension ladder. Extend the ladder only after has been raised to an upright position.
- Never carry an extended ladder.
- Never use two ladders spliced together.
- Ladders should not be painted because pair can hide defects.

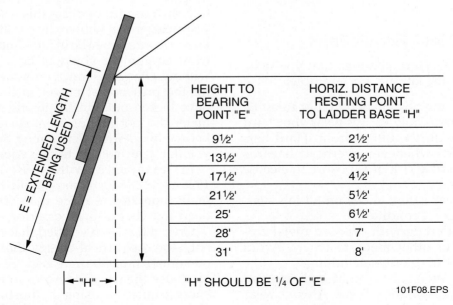

HEIGHT TO BEARING POINT "E"	HORIZ. DISTANCE RESTING POINT TO LADDER BASE "H"
9½'	2½'
13½'	3½'
17½'	4½'
21½'	5½'
25'	6½'
28'	7'
31'	8'

"H" SHOULD BE ¼ OF "E"

101F08.EPS

Figure 8 ◆ Straight ladder positioning.

.1.2 Step Ladders

here are also a few specific rules to use with a tep ladder:

Always open the step ladder all the way and lock the spreaders to avoid collapsing the ladder accidentally.
Use a step ladder that is high enough for the job so that you do not have to reach. Get someone to hold the ladder if it is more than 10 feet high.
Never use a step ladder as a straight ladder.
Never stand on or straddle the top two rungs of a step ladder.
Ladders are not shelves.

WARNING!
Do not leave tools or materials on a step ladder.

Sometimes you will need to move or remove rotective equipment, guards, or guardrails to omplete a task using a ladder. Remember, always eplace what you moved or removed before leavig the area.

.2.0 Scaffolds

Vorking on scaffolds also involves being safe and lert to hazards. In general, keep scaffold platorms clear of unnecessary material or scrap. hese can become deadly tripping hazards or lling objects. Carefully inspect each part of the caffold as it is erected. Your life may depend on ! Makeshift scaffolds have caused many injuries nd deaths on job sites. Use only scaffolding and lanking materials designed and marked for their pecific use. When working on a scaffold, follow ne established specific requirements set by SHA for the use of fall protection. When approriate, wear an approved harness with a lanyard roperly anchored to the structure.

NOTE
The following requirements represent a compilation of the more stringent requirements of both *CFR 1910* and *CFR 1926*.

The following are some of the basic OSHA rules or working safely on scaffolds:

Scaffolds must be erected on sound, rigid footing that can carry the maximum intended load. Guardrails and toe boards must be installed on the open sides and ends of platforms higher than six feet above the ground or floor.

What's wrong with this picture?

101PO105.EPS

- There must be a screen of ½-inch maximum openings between the toe board and the midrail where persons are required to work or pass under the scaffold.
- Scaffold planks must extend over their end supports not less than six inches nor more than 12 inches and must be properly blocked.
- If the scaffold does not have built-in ladders that meet the standard, then it must have an attached ladder access.
- All employees must be trained to erect, dismantle, and use scaffold(s).
- Unless it is impossible, fall protection must be worn while building or dismantling all scaffolding.
- Work platforms must be completely decked for use by employees.
- Your hard hat is the first line of protection from falling objects. Your hard hat, however, cannot protect your shoulders, arms, back, or feet from the danger of falling objects. The person working below depends on those working above. When you are working above the ground, be careful so that material, including your tools, cannot fall from your work site. Use trash containers or other similar means to keep debris from falling and never throw or sweep material from above.

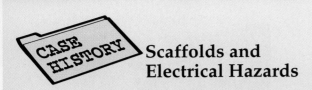

Scaffolds and Electrical Hazards

Remember that scaffolds are excellent conductors of electricity. Recently, a maintenance crew needed to move a scaffold and although time was allocated in the work order to dismantle and rebuild the scaffold, the crew decided to push it instead. They did not follow OSHA recommendations for scaffold clearance and did not perform a job site survey. During the move, the five-tier scaffold contacted a 12,000V overhead power line. All four members of the crew were killed and the crew chief received serious injuries.

The Bottom Line: Never take shortcuts when it comes to your safety and the safety of others. Trained safety personnel should survey each job site prior to the start of work to assess potential hazards. Safe working distances should be maintained between scaffolding and power lines.

What's wrong with this picture?

101PO106.E▶

the load close to your body. Lift by straightenin your legs. Make sure that you lift with your leg and not your back. Do not be afraid to ask for hel if you feel the load is too heavy. See *Figure 9* for a example of proper lifting.

6.0.0 ◆ LIFTS, HOISTS, AND CRANES

On the job, you may be working in the operating area of lifts, hoists, or cranes. The following safety rules are for those who are working in the area with overhead equipment but are not directly involved in its operation.

- Stay alert and pay attention to the warning signals from operators.
- Never stand or walk under a load, regardless of whether it is moving or stationary.
- Always warn others of moving or approaching overhead loads.
- Never attempt to distract signal persons or operators of overhead equipment.
- Obey warning signs.
- Do not use equipment that you are not qualified to operate.

7.0.0 ◆ LIFTING

Back injuries cause many lost working hours every year. That is in addition to the misery felt by the person with the hurt back! Learn how to lift properly and size up the load. To lift, first stand close to the load. Then, squat down and keep your back straight. Get a firm grip on the load and keep

8.0.0 ◆ BASIC TOOL SAFETY

When using any tools for the first time, read th operator's manual to learn the recommende safety precautions. If you are not certain about th operation of any tool, ask the advice of a more e perienced worker. Before using a tool, you shoul know its function and how it works.

Always use the right tool for the job. Incorrect using tools is one of the leading causes of job si injury. Using a hammer as a pry bar or a screw driver as a chisel can cause damage to the tool ar injure you in the process.

9.0.0 ◆ CONFINED SPACE ENTRY PROCEDURES

Occasionally, you may be required to do you work in a manhole or vault. If this is the cas there are some special safety considerations th you need to be aware of. For details on th subject of working in manholes and vaults, ref to *CFR 1910.146/1926.21(a)(6)(i) and (ii)*. Th general precautions are listed in the followir paragraphs.

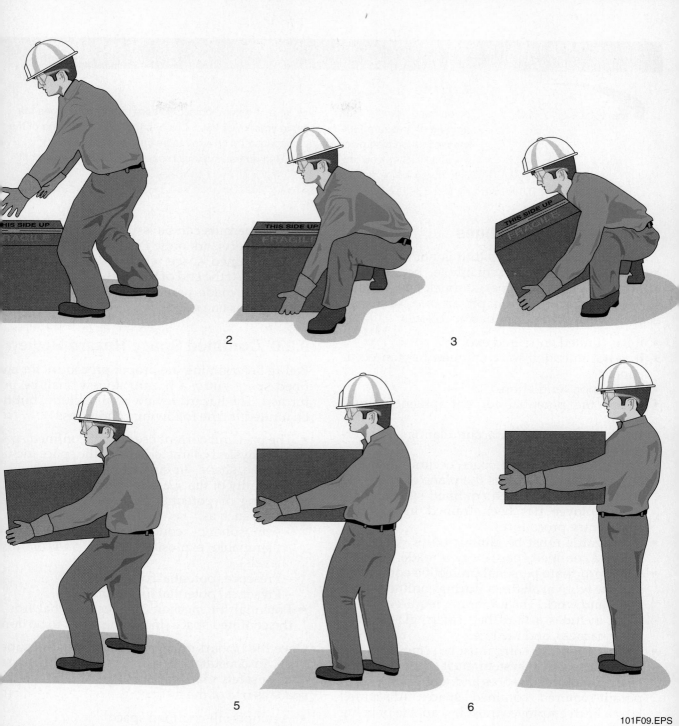

2   3

5   6

101F09.EPS

Figure 9 ◆ Proper lifting.

Lifting

If you bend from the waist to pick up a 50-pound object, you are applying 10 times the amount of pressure (500 pounds) to your lower back. Lower back injuries are one of the most common workplace injuries because it's so easy to be careless about lifting, especially when you are in a hurry. Remember, it is much easier to ask for help than it is to nurse an injured back.

9.1.0 General Guidelines

A confined space includes (but is not limited to) any of the following: a manhole, boiler, tank, trench (four feet or deeper), tunnel, hopper, bin, sewer, vat, pipeline, vault, pit, air duct, or vessel. A confined space is identified as follows:

- It has limited entry and exit.
- It is not intended for continued human occupancy.
- It has poor ventilation.
- It has the potential for entrapment/engulfment.
- It has the potential for accumulating a dangerous atmosphere.
- Entry into a confined space occurs when any part of the body crosses the plane of entry. No employee shall enter a confined space unless the employee has been trained in confined space entry procedures.
- All hazards must be eliminated or controlled before a confined space entry is made.
- All appropriate personal protective equipment shall be worn at all times during confined space entry and work. The minimum required equipment includes a hard hat, safety glasses, full body harness, and life line.
- Ladders used for entry must be secured.
- A rescue retrieval system must be in use when entering confined spaces and while working in permit-required confined spaces (discussed later). Each employee must be capable of being rescued by the retrieval system.
- Only no-entry rescues will be performed by company personnel. Entry rescues will be performed by trained rescue personnel identified on the entry permit.
- The area outside the confined space must be properly barricaded, and appropriate warning signs must be posted.

- Entry permits can be issued and signed by jo site supervisors only. Permits must be kept the confined space while work is being co ducted. At the end of the shift, the entry permi must be made part of the job journal and r tained for one year.

9.2.0 Confined Space Hazard Review

Before determining the proper procedure for co fined space entry, a hazard review shall be pe formed. The hazard review shall include, but n be limited to, the following conditions:

- The past and current uses of the confined spa
- The physical characteristics of the space inclu ing size, shape, air circulation, etc.
- Proximity of the space to other hazards
- Existing or potential hazards in the confine space, such as:
  - Atmospheric conditions (oxygen leve. flammable/explosive levels, and/or tox levels)
  - Presence/potential for liquids
  - Presence/potential for particulates
- Potential for mechanical/electrical hazards the confined space (including work to be don

Once the hazard review is completed, the supe visor, in consultation with the project manage and/or safety manager, shall classify the confine space as one of the following:

- A nonpermit confined space
- A permit-required confined space controlled ventilation
- A permit-required confined space

Once the confined space has been properly cl. sified, the appropriate entry and work procedur must be followed.

3.0 Entry and Work Procedures

Nonpermit spaces – A hazard review checklist must be completed before a confined space is designated as a nonpermit space. The checklist must be made part of the job journal, and a copy of the checklist must be sent to the safety office. A nonpermit confined space must meet the following criteria:

There is no actual or potential atmospheric hazard.

NOTE
Using ventilation to clear the atmosphere does not meet this criterion.

There are no actual or potential physical, electrical, or mechanical hazards capable of causing harm or death.

Documentation using the hazards checklist and entry permit forms, and verifying that the confined space is hazard-free, must be made available to employees and maintained at the confined space while work is conducted. If it is necessary to enter the space to verify that it is hazard-free or to eliminate hazards, entry must be made under the requirements of a permit-required space.

An employee may enter the confined space using the minimum fall protection of harness and anchored life line. Once in the space, the employee may disconnect the life line and reconnect it before exiting.

If the work being done creates a hazard, the space must be reclassified as a permit-required space. If any other atmospheric, physical, electrical, or mechanical hazards arise, the space is to be evacuated immediately and reclassified as a permit-required entry space.

Permit-required spaces controlled by ventilation – A hazard review checklist must be completed before a confined space is designated as a permit-required space controlled by ventilation. The checklist must be made part of the job journal, and a copy of the checklist must be sent to the safety office. A permit-required confined space controlled by ventilation must meet the following criteria:

- The only hazard in the confined space is an actual/potential atmospheric hazard.
- Continuous forced-air ventilation maintains a safe atmosphere (i.e., within the limits designated on the entry permit).
- Inspection and monitoring data are documented.
- No other physical, electrical, or mechanical hazard exists.

An entry permit must be issued and signed by the job site supervisor and be kept at the confined space while work is being conducted.

Atmospheric testing must be conducted before entry into the confined space and in the following order:

- Oxygen content
- Flammable gases and vapors
- Toxic contaminants

Unacceptable atmospheric conditions must be eliminated with forced-air ventilation. If continuous forced-air ventilation is required to maintain an acceptable atmosphere, employees may not enter until forced-air ventilation has eliminated any hazardous atmosphere. Periodic atmospheric testing must be conducted during the work shift to ensure that the atmosphere remains clear. Periodic monitoring must be documented on the entry permit. If atmospheric conditions change, employees must exit the confined space immediately, and atmospheric conditions must be re-evaluated. Continuous communication must be maintained with the employees working in the confined space.

If hot work is to be performed, a hot work permit is required, and the hazard analysis must document that the hot work does not create additional hazards that are not controlled by ventilation only. Hot work is defined as any work that produces arcs, sparks, flames, heat, or other sources of ignition.

A rescue plan using trained rescue personnel must be in place prior to the start of work in the confined space. All employees should be aware of the rescue plan and how to activate it.

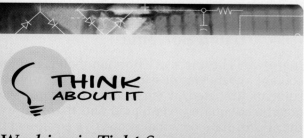

THINK ABOUT IT

Working in Tight Spaces

We routinely work in cramped quarters, from closets to ceiling spaces, without concern. What hazards should we be aware of? What hazards do we typically ignore?

Permit-required confined spaces – A hazard review checklist must be completed before a confined space is designated as a permit-required confined space. The checklist must be made part of the job journal, and a copy must be sent to the safety office. A permit-required space meets the following criteria:

- There are actual/potential hazards, other than a hazardous atmosphere.
- Ventilation alone does not eliminate atmospheric hazards.
- Conditions in and around the confined space must be continually monitored.

An entry permit must be issued and signed by the job site supervisor. The permit is to be kept at the confined space while work is being performed in the space.

Atmospheric testing must be conducted before entry into the confined space and in the following order:

- Oxygen content
- Flammable gases and contaminants
- Toxic contaminants

Unacceptable atmospheric conditions must be eliminated/controlled prior to employee entry. Methods of elimination may include isolation, purging, flushing, or ventilating. Continuous atmospheric monitoring must be conducted while employees are in the confined space. Triggering of a monitoring alarm means employees should evacuate the confined space immediately. Any other physical hazards must be eliminated or controlled by engineering and work practice controls before entry. Additional personal protective equipment should be used as a follow-up to the above methods. An attendant, whose job it is to monitor conditions in and around the confined space and to maintain contact with the employees in the space, must be stationed outside the confined space for the duration of entry operations.

If hot work is to be performed, a hot work permit is required, and the hazard analysis must document the additional hazards and precautions to be considered.

A rescue plan using trained rescue personnel must be in place before confined space entry. The attendant should be aware of the rescue plan and have the means to activate it.

10.0.0 ◆ FIRST AID

You should be prepared in case an accident does occur on the job site or anywhere else. First aid training that includes certification classes in CPR and artificial respiration could be the best insur-

ance you and your fellow workers ever receiv Make sure that you know where first aid is avai able at your job site. Also, make sure you kno the accident reporting procedure. Each job si should also have a first aid manual or booklet gi ing easy-to-find emergency treatment procedure for various types of injuries. Emergency first ai telephone numbers should be readily available everyone on the job site. Refer to *CFR 1910.15 1926.23* and *1926.50* for specific requirements.

11.0.0 ◆ SOLVENTS AND TOXIC VAPORS

The solvents that are used by electricians ma give off vapors that are toxic enough to make pe ple temporarily ill or even cause permanent i jury. Many solvents are skin and eye irritant Solvents can also be systemic poisons when the are swallowed or absorbed through the skin.

Solvents in spray or aerosol form are dangerou in another way. Small aerosol particles or solve vapors mix with air to form a combustible mixtu with oxygen. The slightest spark could cause explosion in a confined area because the mix perfect for fast ignition. There are procedures ar methods for using, storing, and disposing of mo solvents and chemicals. These procedures are nc mally found in the material safety data shee (MSDSs) available at your facility.

An MSDS is required for all materials th could be hazardous to personnel or equipmer These sheets contain information on the mat rial, such as the manufacturer and chemic makeup. As much information as possible is ke on the hazardous material to prevent a dange ous situation; or, in the event of a dangerous s uation, the information is used to rectify t problem in as safe a manner as possible. S *Figure 10* for an example of MSDS informatic you may find on the job.

11.1.0 Precautions When Using Solvents

It is always best to use a nonflammable, nontox solvent whenever possible. However, any tin solvents are used, it is essential that your wo area be adequately ventilated and that you we the appropriate personal protective equipment:

- A chemical face shield with chemical gogg should be used to protect the eyes and sk from sprays and splashes.
- A chemical apron should be worn to prote your body from sprays and splashes. Reme ber that some solvents are acid-based. If th

Section VII — Precautions for Safe Handling and Use

Steps to Be Taken in Case Material is Released or Spilled

Isolate from oxidizers, heat, sparks, electric equipment, and open flames.

Waste Disposal Method

Recycle or incinerate observing local, state and federal health, safety

and pollution laws.

Precautions to Be Taken in Handling and Storing

Store in a cool dry place. Observe label cautions and instructions.

Other Precautions

SEE ATTACHMENT PARA #3

Section VIII — Control Measures

Respiratory Protection *(Specify Type)*

Suitable for use with organic solvents

Ventilation	Local Exhaust	*preferable*	Special	*none*
	Mechanical *(General)*	*acceptable*	Other	*none*
Protective Gloves	*recommended* *(must not dissolve in solvents)*		Eye Protection	*goggles*
Other Protective Clothing or Equipment	*none*			
Work/Hygienic Practices	*Use with adequate ventilation. Observe label cautions.*			

101F10.EPS

Figure 10 ◆ Portion of an MSDS.

come into contact with your clothes, solvents can eat through your clothes to your skin.

A paper filter mask does not stop vapors; it is used only for nuisance dust. In situations where a paper mask does not supply adequate protection, chemical cartridge respirators might be needed. These respirators can stop many vapors if the correct cartridge is selected. In areas where ventilation is a serious problem, a self-contained breathing apparatus (SCBA) must be used.

Make sure that you have been given a full medical evaluation and that you are properly trained in using respirators at your site.

.2.0 Respiratory Protection

otection against high concentrations of dust, st, fumes, vapors, gases, and/or oxygen deficncy is provided by appropriate respirators.

Appropriate respiratory protective devices uld be used for the hazardous material inved and the extent and nature of the work permed.

An air-purifying respirator is, as its name implies, espirator that removes contaminants from air ined by the wearer. The respirators may be divided into the following types: particulate-removing (mechanical filter), gas- and vapor-removing (chemical filter), and a combination of particulate-removing and gas- and vapor-removing.

Particulate-removing respirators are designed to protect the wearer against the inhalation of particulate matter in the ambient atmosphere. They may be designed to protect against a single type of particulate, such as pneumoconiosis-producing and nuisance dust, toxic dust, metal fumes or mist, or against various combinations of these types.

Gas- and vapor-removing respirators are designed to protect the wearer against the inhalation of gases or vapors in the ambient atmosphere. They are designated as gas masks, chemical cartridge respirators (nonemergency gas respirators), and self-rescue respirators. They may be designed to protect against a single gas such as chlorine; a single type of gas, such as acid gases; or a combination of types of gases, such as acid gases and organic vapors.

If you are required to use a respiratory protective device, you must be evaluated by a physician to ensure that you are physically fit to use a respirator. You must then be fitted and thoroughly instructed in the respirator's use.

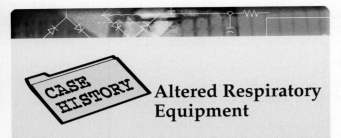

Altered Respiratory Equipment

A self-employed man applied a solvent-based coating to the inside of a tank. Instead of wearing the proper respirator, he used nonstandard air supply hoses and altered the face mask. All joints and the exhalation slots were sealed with tape. He collapsed and was not discovered for several hours.

The Bottom Line: Never alter or improvise safety equipment.

Any employee whose job entails having to wear a respirator must keep his face free of facial hair in the seal area.

Respiratory protective equipment must be inspected regularly and maintained in good condition. Respiratory equipment must be properly cleaned on a regular basis and stored in a sanitary, dustproof container.

WARNING!

Do not use any respirator unless you have been fitted for it and thoroughly understand its use. As with all safety rules, follow your employer's respiratory program and policies.

12.0.0 ◆ ASBESTOS

Asbestos is a mineral-based material that is resistant to heat and corrosive chemicals. Depending on the chemical composition, asbestos fibers may range in texture from coarse to silky. The properties that make asbestos fibers so valuable to industry are its high tensile strength, flexibility, heat and chemical resistance, and good frictional properties.

Asbestos fibers enter the body by inhalation of airborne particles or by ingestion and can become embedded in the tissues of the respiratory or digestive systems. Years of exposure to asbestos can cause numerous disabling or fatal diseases. Among these diseases are asbestosis, an emphysema-like condition; lung cancer; mesothelioma, a cancerous tumor that spreads rapidly in the cells of membranes covering the lungs and body organs; and gastrointestinal cancer. The use of asbestos was banned in 1978.

12.1.0 Monitoring

Employers who have a workplace or work operation covered by *OSHA 3096* (*Asbestos Standard for the Construction Industry*) must perform initial monitoring to determine the airborne concentrations of asbestos to which employees may be exposed. If employers can demonstrate that employee exposures are below the action level and/or excursion limit by means of objective or historical data, initial monitoring is not required. If initial monitoring indicates that employee exposures are below the action level and/or excursion limit, then periodic monitoring is not required. Within regulated areas, the employer must conduct daily monitoring unless all workers are equipped with supplied-air respirators operated in the positive-pressure mode. If daily monitoring by statistically reliable measurement indicates that employee exposures are below the action level and/or excursion limit, then no further monitoring is required for those employees whose exposures are represented by such monitoring. Employees must be given the chance to observe monitoring, and affected employees must be notified as soon as possible following the employer's receipt of the results.

12.2.0 Regulated Areas

The employer must establish a regulated area where airborne concentrations of asbestos exceed or can reasonably be expected to exceed the locally determined exposure limit, or when certain types of construction work are performed, such as cutting asbestos-cement sheets and removing asbestos-containing floor tiles. Only authorized personnel may enter regulated areas. All persons entering a regulated area must be supplied with an appropriate respirator. No smoking, eating, drinking, or applying cosmetics is permitted in regulated areas. Warning signs must be displayed at each regulated area and must be posted at all approaches to regulated areas. These signs must bear the following information:

> **DANGER**
> ASBESTOS
> CANCER AND LUNG DISEASE HAZARD
> AUTHORIZED PERSONNEL ONLY
> RESPIRATORS AND PROTECTIVE
> CLOTHING ARE REQUIRED IN THIS AREA

Where feasible, the employer shall establish negative-pressure enclosures before commencing asbestos removal, demolition, and renovation operations. The setup and monitoring requirements for negative-pressure enclosures are as follows:

A competent person shall be designated to set up the enclosure and ensure its integrity and supervise employee activity within the enclosure.
Exemptions are given for small-scale, short-duration maintenance or renovation operations. The employer shall conduct daily monitoring of the exposure of each employee who is assigned to work within a regulated area. Short-term monitoring is required whenever asbestos concentrations will not be uniform throughout the workday and where high concentrations of asbestos may reasonably be expected to be released or created in excess of the local limit.

In addition, warning labels must be affixed on all asbestos products and to all containers of asbestos products, including waste containers, that may be in the workplace. The label must include the following information:

DANGER
CONTAINS ASBESTOS FIBERS
AVOID CREATING DUST
CANCER AND LUNG DISEASE HAZARD

2.3.0 Methods of Compliance

To the extent feasible, engineering and work practice controls must be used to reduce employee exposure to within the permissible exposure limit (PEL). The employer must use one or more of the following control methods to achieve compliance:

Local exhaust ventilation equipped with high-efficiency particulate air (HEPA) filter dust collection systems
General ventilation systems
Vacuum cleaners equipped with HEPA filters
Enclosure or isolation of asbestos dust-producing processes
Use of wet methods, wetting agents, or removal encapsulants during asbestos handling, mixing, removal, cutting, application, and cleanup
Prompt disposal of asbestos-containing wastes in leak-tight containers

Prohibited work practices include the following:

The use of high-speed abrasive disc saws that are not equipped with appropriate engineering controls

• The use of compressed air to remove asbestos-containing materials, unless the compressed air is used in conjunction with an enclosed ventilation system

Where engineering and work practice controls have been instituted but are insufficient to reduce employee exposure to a level that is at or below the PEL, respiratory protection must be used to supplement these controls.

13.0.0 ◆ BATTERIES

Working around wet cell batteries can be dangerous if the proper precautions are not taken. Batteries often give off hydrogen gas as a byproduct. When hydrogen mixes with air, the mixture can be explosive in the proper concentration. For this reason, smoking is strictly prohibited in battery rooms, and only insulated tools should be used. Proper ventilation also reduces the chance of explosion in battery areas. Follow your company's procedures for working near batteries. Also, ensure that your company's procedures are followed for lifting heavy batteries.

13.1.0 Acids

Batteries also contain acid, which will eat away human skin and many other materials. Personal protective equipment for battery work typically includes chemical aprons, sleeves, gloves, face shields, and goggles to prevent acid from contacting skin and eyes. Follow your site procedures for dealing with spills of these materials. Also, know the location of first aid when working with these chemicals.

13.2.0 Wash Stations

Because of the chance that battery acid may contact someone's eyes or skin, wash stations are located near battery rooms. Do not connect or disconnect batteries without proper supervision. Everyone who works in the area should know where the nearest wash station is and how to use it. Battery acid should be flushed from the skin and eyes with large amounts of water or with a neutralizing solution.

 CAUTION
If you come in contact with battery acid, flush the affected area with water and report it immediately to your supervisor.

14.0.0 ◆ PCBs

Polychlorinated biphenyls (PCBs) are chemicals that were marketed under various trade names as a liquid insulator/cooler in older transformers. In addition to being used in older transformers, PCBs are also found in some large capacitors and in the small ballast transformers used in street lighting and ordinary fluorescent light fixtures. Disposal of these materials is regulated by the Environmental Protection Agency (EPA) and must be done through a regulated disposal company; use extreme caution and follow your facility procedures.

 WARNING!
Do not come into contact with PCBs. They present a variety of serious health risks, including lung damage and cancer.

15.0.0 ◆ FALL PROTECTION

15.1.0 Fall Protection Procedures

Fall protection must be used when employees are on a walking or working surface that is six feet or more above a lower level and has an unprotected edge or side. The areas covered include, but are not limited to the following:

- Finished and unfinished floors or mezzanines
- Temporary or permanent walkways/ramps
- Finished or unfinished roof areas
- Elevator shafts and hoist-ways
- Floor, roof, or walkway holes
- Working six feet or more above dangerous equipment

Exception: If the dangerous equipment is unguarded, fall protection must be used at all heights regardless of the fall distance.

 NOTE
Walking/working surfaces do not include ladders, scaffolds, vehicles, or trailers. Also, an unprotected edge or side is an edge/side where there is no guardrail system at least 39 inches high.

Fall protection is not required during inspection, investigation, or assessment of job site conditions before or after construction work.

What's wrong with this picture?

101PO107.E

These fall protection guidelines do not apply the following areas. Fall protection for these are is located in the subparts cited in parentheses.

- Cranes and derricks (*1926 Subpart N/1910 Su part N*)
- Scaffolding (*1926 Subpart L/1910 Subpart D*)
- Electrical power transmission and distributi (*1926 Subpart V/1910 Subpart R*)
- Stairways and ladders (*1926 Subpart X/19 Subpart D*)
- Excavations (*1926 Subpart P*)

Fall protection must be selected in order of pr erence as listed below. Selection of a lower-lev system (e.g., safety nets) must be based only feasibility of protection. The list includes, but not limited to, the following:

- Guardrail systems and hole covers
- Personal fall arrest systems
- Safety nets

These fall protection procedures are design to warn, isolate, restrict, or protect workers from potential fall hazard.

5.2.0 Types of Fall Protection Systems

The type of system selected shall depend on the fall hazards associated with the work to be performed. First, a hazard analysis shall be conducted by the job site supervisor prior to the start of work. Based on the hazard analysis, the job site supervisor and project manager, in consultation with the safety manager, will select the appropriate fall protection system. All employees will be instructed in the use of the fall protection system before starting work.

1. The most life-threatening hazards on a construction site typically include all of the following *except* _____.
   a. falls
   b. electrocution
   c. being crushed or struck by falling or flying objects
   d. chemical burns

2. If a person's heart begins to fibrillate due to an electrical shock, the solution is to _____ .
   a. leave the person alone until the fibrillation stops
   b. administer heart massage
   c. use the Heimlich maneuver
   d. have a qualified person use emergency defibrillation equipment

3. The majority of injuries due to electrical shock are caused by _____.
   a. electrically operated hand tools
   b. contact with low-voltage conductors
   c. contact with high-voltage conductors
   d. lightning

4. Class 0 rubber gloves are used when working with voltages less than _____ .
   a. 1,000 volts
   b. 7,500 volts
   c. 17,500 volts
   d. 26,500 volts

5. An important use of a hot stick is to _____ .
   a. replace busbars
   b. test for voltage
   c. replace fuses
   d. test for continuity

6. Which of these statements correctly describes a double-insulated power tool?
   a. There is twice as much insulation on the power cord.
   b. It can safely be used in place of a grounded tool.
   c. It is made entirely of plastic or other nonconducting material.
   d. The entire tool is covered in rubber.

7. Which of the following applies in a lockout/tagout procedure?
   a. Only the supervisor can install lockout/tagout devices.
   b. If several employees are involved, the lockout/tagout equipment is applied only by the first employee to arrive at the disconnect.
   c. Lockout/tagout devices applied by one employee can be removed by another employee as long as it can be verified that the first employee has left for the day.
   d. Lockout/tagout devices are installed by every authorized employee involved in the work.

8. What is the proper distance from the feet of a straight ladder to the wall?
   a. one-fourth the working height of the ladder
   b. one-half the height of the ladder
   c. three feet
   d. one-fourth of the square root of the height of the ladder

9. What are the minimum and maximum distances (in inches) that a scaffold plank can extend beyond its end support?
   a. 4; 8
   b. 6; 10
   c. 6; 12
   d. 8; 12

10. Which of these conditions applies to a permit-required confined space, but *not* to a permit-required space controlled by ventilation?
    a. A hazard review checklist must be completed.
    b. An attendant, whose job is to monitor the space, must be stationed outside the space.
    c. Unacceptable atmospheric conditions must be eliminated.
    d. Atmospheric testing must be conducted.

Summary

…fety must be your concern at all times so that …u do not become either the victim of an accident … the cause of one. Safety requirements and safe …ork practices are provided by OSHA and your …mployer. It is essential that you adhere to all …fety requirements and follow your employer's …fe work practices and procedures. Also, you …ust be able to identify the potential safety haz-…ds of your job site. The consequences of unsafe job site conduct can often be expensive, painful, or even deadly. Report any unsafe act or condition immediately to your supervisor. You should also report all work-related accidents, injuries, and illnesses to your supervisor immediately. Remember, proper construction techniques, common sense, and a good safety attitude will help to prevent accidents, injuries, and fatalities.

Notes

1. A life-threatening condition of the heart in which the muscle fibers contract irregularly is called _____.

2. Any tool that has a case made of nonconductive material and that has been constructed so that the case is insulated from electrical energy is a _____ tool.

3. _____ are chemicals often found in liquids that are used to cool certain types of large transformers and capacitors.

4. A _____ will de-energize a circuit or a portion of it if the current to ground exceeds some predetermined value.

5. A _____ tool has a three-prong plug at the end of its power cord or some other means to ensure that stray current travels to ground without passing through the body of the operator.

Trade Terms

Double-insulated/ungrounded tool
Fibrillation
Grounded tool
Ground fault circuit interrupter (GFCI)
Polychlorinated biphenyls (PCBs)

Michael J. Powers

Tri-City Electrical Contractors, Inc.

How did you choose a career in the electrical field?
My father was an electrician and after I "burned out" with a career in fast-food management, I decided to choose a completely different field.

Tell us about your apprenticeship experience.
It was excellent! I worked under several very knowledgeable electricians and had a pretty good selection of teachers. Over my four-year apprenticeship, I was able to work on a variety of jobs, from photomats to kennels to colleges.

What positions have you held and how did they help you to get where you are now?
I have been an electrical apprentice, a licensed electrician, a job-site superintendent, a master electrician, and am currently a corporate safety and training director. The knowledge I acquired in electrical theory in apprenticeship school and preparing for my licensing exams, as well as the practical on-the-job experience over thirty years in the trade, were wonderful training for my current position.

I also serve on the authoring team for NCCER's Electrical Curricula, which has provided me with not only the opportunity to share what I have learned, but also a great way to keep current in other areas by meeting with electricians from a variety of disciplines (we have commercial, residential, and industrial electricians on the team, as well as instructors).

What would you say was the single greatest factor that contributed to your success?
Choosing a company that recognized and rewarded competent, hard workers and provided them with the support and guidance to allow them to develop and succeed in the industry.

What does your current job entail?
I am responsible for safe work practices and procedures through the job-site management team at Tri-City Electrical Contractors, which currently has a workforce of over 1,100. I also assist in developing, delivering, and administering the training program, from apprenticeship to in-house to outsourced training.

What advice do you have for trainees?
Training in all its aspects is the key to your success and advancement in the industry. Any time you are given a training opportunity, take it, even if it might not appear relevant at the time. Eventually, all knowledge can be applied to some situation.

Most importantly, have fun! The construction industry is composed of good people. I firmly believe that construction workers, as a group, are much more honest and direct than any other comparable group. Wait—did I say comparable group? That's a misstatement—there is no comparable group. Construction workers build America!

Trade Terms
Introduced in This Module

Double-insulated/ungrounded tool: An electrical tool that is constructed so that the case is insulated from electrical energy. The case is made of a nonconductive material.

Fibrillation: Very rapid irregular contractions of the muscle fibers of the heart that result in the heartbeat and pulse going out of rhythm with each other.

Grounded tool: An electrical tool with a three-prong plug at the end of its power cord or some other means to ensure that stray current travels to ground without passing through the body of the user. The ground plug is bonded to the conductive frame of the tool.

Ground fault circuit interrupter (GFCI): A protective device that functions to de-energize circuit or portion thereof within an established period of time when a current to ground exceeds some predetermined value. This value is less than that required to operate the overcurrent protective device of the supply circuit.

Polychlorinated biphenyls (PCBs): Toxic chemicals that may be contained in liquids used to cool certain types of large transformers and capacitors.

Additional Resources

This module is intended to present thorough resources for task training. The following reference works are suggested for further study. These are additional materials for continued education rather than for task training.

CFR Parts 1900–1910, Standards for General Industry. Occupational Safety and Health Administration, U.S. Department of Labor.

CFR Part 1926, Standards for the Construction Industry. Occupational Safety and Health Administration, U.S. Department of Labor.

National Electrical Code® Handbook, Latest Edition. Quincy, MA: National Fire Protection Association.

Standard for Electrical Safety in the Workplace, Latest Edition. Quincy, MA: National Fire Protection Association.

The NCCER makes every effort to keep these textbooks up-to-date and free of technical errors. We appreciate your help in this process. If you have an idea for improving this textbook, or if you find an error, a typographical mistake, or an inaccuracy in NCCER's *Contren®* textbooks, please write us, using this form or a photocopy. Be sure to include the exact module number, page number, a detailed description, and the correction, if applicable. Your input will be brought to the attention of the Technical Review Committee. Thank you for your assistance.

Instructors – If you found that additional materials were necessary in order to teach this module effectively, please let us know so that we may include them in the Equipment/Materials list in the Annotated Instructor's Guide.

Write: Product Development
National Center for Construction Education and Research
P.O. Box 141104, Gainesville, FL 32614-1104

Fax: 352-334-0932

E-mail: curriculum@nccer.org

Craft

Module Name

Copyright Date

Module Number

Page Number(s)

Description

(Optional) Correction

(Optional) Your Name and Address

Build America Merit Winner—
Building New

The McCormick Tribune Campus Center and the renovation of the historic Illinois Institute of Technology Commons Building in Chicago, Illinois, was completed by the Gilbane Building Company. This bold and innovative project included the replacement of the Chicago Transit Authority subway track supports, the construction of an elliptical acoustic tube around the elevated subway tracks, and the construction and renovation of the campus center and commons building.

00101-04
Basic Safety

Topics to be presented in this unit include:

Overview

Construction safety has advanced a great deal over the years. There was a time in the industry when very few safety precautions were taken. Workers often worked without hard hats, gloves, eye protection, fall protection, or safety shoes. This resulted in illnesses, injuries, and deaths. Today, with the help of the Occupational Safety and Health Administration (OSHA) and state and local rules and regulations, the construction industry is becoming safer.

Rules and regulations are only a part of what contributes to a safe work environment. Construction workers have the ultimate responsibility for their safety and the safety of others. One way to remain safe is always to use appropriate personal protective equipment (PPE). The type of personal protective equipment will vary depending on your job. For example, a heavy machine operator is not required to wear the same face shield a welder is required to wear.

Proper training is also an essential part of creating a safe work environment. Training must be provided to all workers to ensure that they perform work and use and maintain all tools and equipment safely. When a worker does not know how to use a tool or equipment or has not been properly trained to use personal protective equipment, he or she should immediately tell a supervisor and ask for the necessary training. Safe behavior and safe equipment help to prevent accidents and injury.

Objectives

When you have completed this module, you will be able to do the following:

1. Explain the role that safety plays in the construction crafts.
2. Describe the meaning of job-site safety.
3. Describe the characteristics of a competent person and a qualified person.
4. Explain the appropriate safety precautions to take around common job-site hazards.
5. Demonstrate the use and care of appropriate personal protective equipment (PPE).
6. Properly don and remove personal protective equipment (safety goggles, hard hat, and personal fall protection).
7. Follow the safety procedures required for lifting heavy objects.
8. Describe safe behavior on and around ladders and scaffolds.
9. Explain the importance of hazard communications (HazCom) and material safety data sheets (MSDSs).
10. Describe fire prevention and firefighting techniques.
11. Define safe work procedures to use around electrical hazards.

Key Trade Terms

Apparatus
Arc
Arc welding
Combustible
Competent person
Concealed receptacle
Confined space
Cross-bracing
Dross
Electrical distribution panel
Excavation
Extension ladder
Flammable
Flash
Flashback
Flash burn
Flash goggles
Flash point
Ground
Guarded
Hand line
Hazard Communication Standard (HazCom)
Lanyard
Lockout/tagout
Management system
Material safety data sheet (MSDS)

Maximum intended load
Mid-rail
Occupational Safety and Health Administration (OSHA)
Permit-required confined space
Personal protective equipment (PPE)
Planked
Proximity work
Qualified person
Respirator
Scaffold
Shoring
Signaler
Slag
Stepladder
Straight ladder
Switch enclosure
Toeboard
Top rail
Trench
Trencher
Welding shield
Wind sock

Required Trainee Materials

1. Sharpened pencils and paper
2. Appropriate personal protective equipment

Prerequisites

There are no prerequisites for this module.

This course map shows all of the modules in *Core Curriculum: Introductory Craft Skills.* The suggested training order begins at the bottom and proceeds up. Skill levels increase as you advance on the course map. The local Training Program Sponsor may adjust the training order.

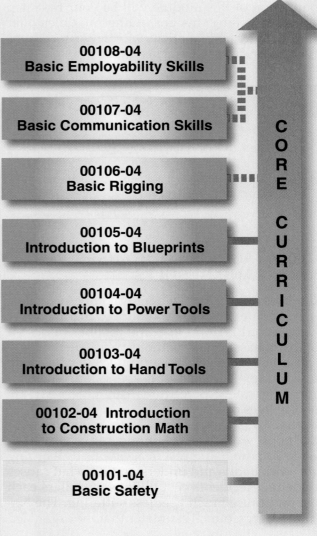

00108-04
Basic Employability Skills

00107-04
Basic Communication Skills

00106-04
Basic Rigging

00105-04
Introduction to Blueprints

00104-04
Introduction to Power Tools

00103-04
Introduction to Hand Tools

00102-04 Introduction to Construction Math

00101-04
Basic Safety

CORE CURRICULUM

101CMAP.EPS

1.0.0 ◆ INTRODUCTION

When you take a job, you have a safety obligation to your employer, co-workers, family, and yourself. In exchange for your wages and benefits, you agree to work safely. You are also obligated to make sure anyone you work with is working safely. Your employer is likewise obligated to maintain a safe workplace for all employees. The ultimate responsibility for on-the-job safety, however, rests with you. Safety is part of your job. In this module, you will learn to ensure your safety and that of the people you work with by adhering to the following rules:

- Follow safe work practices and procedures.
- Inspect safety equipment before use.
- Use safety equipment properly.

To take full advantage of the wide variety of training, job, and career opportunities the construction industry offers, you must first understand the importance of safety. Successful completion of this module will be your first step toward achieving this goal. Other modules offer more detailed explanations of safety procedures and opportunities to practice them.

DID YOU KNOW?
Safety training is required for all activities. Never operate tools, machinery, or equipment without prior training. Always refer to the manufacturer's instructions.

2.0.0 ◆ ACCIDENTS: CAUSES AND RESULTS

Your boss might say, "I want my company to have a perfect safety record." What does that mean? A safety record is more than the number of days a company has worked without an accident. Safety is a learned behavior and attitude. Safety is a way of working. The time you spend learning and practicing safety procedures can save your life and the lives of others.

What causes accidents? Both poor behavior and poor working conditions can cause accidents. You can help prevent accidents by learning safe work habits and understanding what causes accidents. Accidents cost billions of dollars each year and cause much needless suffering. The National Safety Council estimates that the organized safety movement has saved more than 4.2 million lives since it began in 1913. This section examines why accidents happen and how you can help prevent them.

The lessons you will learn in this module will help you work safely. You will be able to spot and avoid hazardous conditions on the job site. By following safety procedures and being aware of the need for safety, you will help keep your workplace free from accidents and protect yourself and your co-workers from injury or even death.

2.1.0 What Causes Accidents?

You may already know some of the main causes of accidents. They include the following:

- Failure to communicate
- Poor work habits
- Alcohol or drug abuse
- Lack of skill
- Intentional acts
- Unsafe acts
- Rationalizing risks
- Unsafe conditions
- **Management system** failure

We will discuss each of these causes in the following sections.

2.1.1 Failure to Communicate

Many accidents happen because of a lack of communication. For example, you may learn how to do things one way on one job, but what happens when you go to a new job site? You need to communicate with the people at the new job site to find out whether they do things the way you have learned to do them. If you do not communicate clearly, accidents can happen. Remember that different people, companies, and job sites do things in different ways.

If you think that people know something without talking with them about it, then you are assuming that they know. Assuming that other people know and will do what you think they will do can cause accidents.

All work sites have specific markings and signs to identify hazards and provide emergency information (see *Figure 1*). Learn to recognize these types of signs:

- Informational
- Safety
- Caution
- Danger
- Temporary warnings

Informational markings or signs provide general information. These signs are blue. The following are considered informational signs:

- No Admittance
- No Trespassing
- For Employees Only

Safety signs give general instructions and suggestions about safety measures. The background on these signs is white; most have a green panel with white letters. These signs tell you where to find such important areas as the following:

- First-aid stations
- Emergency eye-wash stations
- Evacuation routes
- Material safety data sheet (MSDS) stations
- Exits (usually have white letters on a red field)

Caution markings or signs tell you about potential hazards or warn against unsafe acts. When you see a caution sign, protect yourself against a possible hazard. Caution signs are yellow and have a black panel with yellow letters. They may give you the following information:

- Hearing and eye protection are required.
- Respirators are required.
- Smoking is not allowed.

Danger markings or signs tell you that an immediate hazard exists and that you must take certain precautions to avoid an accident. Danger signs are red, black, and white. They may indicate the presence of the following:

- Defective equipment
- Flammable liquids and compressed gases
- Safety barriers and barricades
- Emergency stop button
- High voltage

Safety tags are temporary warnings of immediate and potential hazards. They are not designed to replace signs or to serve as permanent means of protection. Learn to recognize the standard accident prevention signs and tags (see *Table 1*). Other important guidelines regarding communication are covered in the module, *Basic Communication Skills*.

101F01A.EPS

INFORMATION SIGN

101F01B.EPS

SAFETY SIGN

101F01C.EPS

CAUTION SIGN

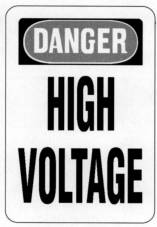

101F01D.EPS

DANGER SIGN

Figure 1 ◆ Communication tags/signs.

Table 1 Tags and Signs

Basic Stock (background)	Safety Colors (ink)	Message(s)
White	Red panel with white or gray letters	Do Not Operate Do Not Start
White	Black square with a red oval and white letters	Danger Unsafe Do Not Use
Yellow	Black square with yellow letters	Caution
White	Black square with white letters	Out of Order Do Not Use
Yellow	Red/magenta (purple) panel with black letters and a radiation symbol	Radiation Hazard
White	Fluorescent orange square with black letters and a biohazard symbol	Biological Hazard

2.1.2 Poor Work Habits

Poor work habits can cause serious accidents. Examples of poor work habits are procrastination, carelessness, and horseplay. Procrastination, or putting things off, is a common cause of accidents. For example, delaying the repair, inspection, or cleaning of equipment and tools can cause accidents. If you try to push machines and equipment beyond their operating capacities, you risk injuring yourself and your co-workers.

Machines, power tools, and even a pair of pliers can hurt you if you don't use them safely. It is your responsibility to be careful. Tools and machines don't know the difference between wood or steel and flesh and bone.

Work habits and work attitudes are closely related. If you resist taking orders, you may also resist listening to warnings. If you let yourself be easily distracted, you won't be able to concentrate. If you aren't concentrating, you could cause an accident.

Your safety is affected not only by how you do your work, but also by how you act on the job site. This is why most companies have strict policies for employee behavior. Horseplay and other inappropriate behavior are forbidden. Workers who engage in horseplay and other inappropriate behavior on the job site may be fired.

These strict policies are for your protection. There are many hazards on construction sites. Each person's behavior—at work, on a break, or at lunch—must follow the principles of safety.

The man pouring the water on his co-worker i Figure 2 may look like he's just having fun by play ing a prank on his co-worker. In fact, what he's do ing could cause his co-worker serious, even fata injury. If you horse around on the job, play prank or don't concentrate on what you are doing, yo are showing a poor work attitude. That can lead a serious accident.

DID YOU KNOW?

Quick Quiz

Look at the man who's trying to play a prank on his co-worker in *Figure 2*. How many things are wrong in this picture? What other safety rules is he breaking?

- No hard hat
- No safety goggles
- No gloves
- Breaking shop rules

DID YOU KNOW?

Stress creates a chemical change in your body. Although stress may heighten your hearing, vision, energy, and strength, long-term stress ca harm your health.

Not all stress is job-related; some stress develops from the pressures of dealing with family and friends and daily living. In the end, your ability to handle and manage your stress determines whether stress hurts or helps you. Use common sense when you are dealing with stressful situations. For example, consider the following:

- Keep daily occurrences in perspective. Not everything is worth getting upset, angry, or anxious about.
- When you have a particularly difficult workday scheduled, get plenty of rest the night before.
- Manage your time. The feeling of always being behind creates a lot of stress. Waiting until the last minute to finish an important task adds unnecessary stress.
- Talk to your supervisor. Your supervisor may understand what is causing your stress and may be able to suggest ways to manage it better.

DID YOU KNOW?

Dull blades cause more accidents than sharp ones. If you do not keep your cutting tools sharpened, they won't cut very easily. When you have a hard time cutting, you exert more force on the tool. When that happens, something is bound to slip. And when something slips, you can get cut.

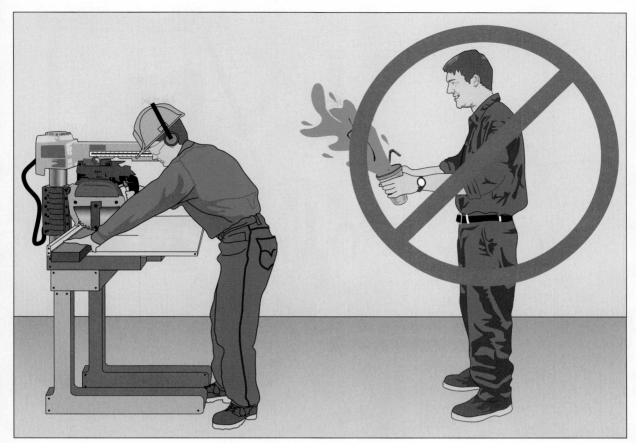

Figure 2 ◆ Horseplay can be dangerous.

2.1.3 Alcohol and Drug Abuse

Alcohol and drug abuse costs the construction industry millions of dollars a year in accidents, lost time, and lost productivity. The true cost of alcohol and drug abuse is much more than just money, of course. Abuse can cost lives. Just as drunk driving kills thousands of people on our highways every year, alcohol and drug abuse kills on the construction site. Examine the person in *Figure 3.* Would you want to be like him or be working near him?

Using alcohol or drugs creates a risk of injury for everyone on a job site. Many states have laws that prevent workers from collecting insurance benefits if they are injured while under the influence of alcohol or illegal drugs.

Would you trust your life to a crane operator who was high on drugs? Would you bet your life on the responses of a co-worker using alcohol or drugs? Alcohol and drug abuse have no place in the construction industry. A person on a construction site who is under the influence of alcohol or drugs is an accident waiting to happen—possibly a fatal accident.

People who work while using alcohol or drugs are at risk of accident or injury, and their co-workers are at risk as well. That's why your employer probably has a formal substance abuse policy. You should know that policy and follow it for your own safety.

You don't have to be abusing illegal drugs such as marijuana, cocaine, or heroin to create a job hazard. Many prescription and over-the-counter drugs, taken for legitimate reasons, can affect your ability to work safely. Amphetamines, barbiturates, and antihistamines are only a few of the legal drugs that can affect your ability to work safely or to operate machinery.

 CAUTION

If your doctor prescribes any medication that you think might affect your job performance, ask about its effects. Your safety and the safety of your co-workers depend on everyone being alert on the job.

101F03.EPS

Figure 3 ◆ How many violations can you identify?

Do yourself and the people you work with a big favor. Be aware of and follow your employer's substance abuse policy. Avoid any substances that can affect your job performance. The life you save could be your own.

? **DID YOU KNOW?**

Quick Quiz

If the man in *Figure 3* doesn't kill himself first, he will almost certainly kill someone else eventually. How many violations can you identify? In this scene alone, the man is

- Consuming alcohol on the job site
- Not following proper safety procedures for operating a motorized vehicle near hazardous materials
- Not using both hands to drive the vehicle
- Not wearing a seat/safety belt
- Not wearing a hard hat
- Not wearing safety glasses or goggles

2.1.4 Lack of Skill

You should learn and practice new skills under careful supervision. Never perform new tasks alone until you've been checked out by a supervisor.

Lack of skill can cause accidents quickly. For example, suppose you are told to cut some 2 × 8 with a circular saw, but you aren't skilled with that tool. A basic rule of circular saw operation is never to cut without a properly functioning guard. Because you haven't been trained, you don't know this. You find that the guard on the saw is slowing you down. So you jam the guard open with a small block of wood. The result could be a serious accident. Proper training can prevent this type of accident.

 WARNING!

Never operate a power tool until you have been trained to use it. You can greatly reduce the chances of accidents by learning safety rules for each task you perform.

2.1.5   Intentional Acts

When someone purposely causes an accident, it is called an intentional act. Sometimes an angry or dissatisfied employee may purposely create a situation that leads to property damage or personal injury. If someone you are working with threatens to get even or pay back someone, let your supervisor know at once.

2.1.6   Unsafe Acts

An unsafe act is a change from an accepted, normal, or correct procedure that usually causes an accident. It can be any conduct that causes unnecessary exposure to a job-site hazard or that makes an activity less safe than usual. Here are examples of unsafe acts:

- Failing to use **personal protective equipment (PPE)**
- Failing to warn co-workers of hazards
- Lifting improperly
- Loading or placing equipment or supplies improperly
- Making safety devices (such as saw guards) inoperable
- Operating equipment at improper speeds
- Operating equipment without authority
- Servicing equipment in motion
- Taking an improper working position
- Using defective equipment
- Using equipment improperly

2.1.7   Rationalizing Risk

Everybody takes risks every day. When you get in your car to drive to work, you know there is a risk of being involved in an accident. Yet when you drive using all the safety practices you have learned, you know that there is a good chance that you will arrive at your destination safely. Driving is an appropriate risk because you have some control over your own safety and that of others.

Some risks are not appropriate. On the job, you must never take risks that endanger yourself or others just because you can make an excuse for doing so. This is called rationalizing risk. Rationalizing risk means ignoring safety warnings and practices. For example, because you are late for work, you might decide to run a red light. By trying to save time, you could cause a serious accident.

The following are common examples of rationalized risks on the job:

- Crossing boundaries because no activity is in sight

- Not wearing gloves because it will take only a minute to make a cut
- Removing your hard hat because you are hot and you cannot see anyone working overhead
- Not tying off your fall protection because you only have to lean over by about a foot

Think about the job before you do it. If you think that it is unsafe, then it is unsafe. Stop working until the job can be done safely. Bring your concerns to the attention of your supervisor. Your health and safety, and that of your co-workers, make it worth taking extra care.

DID YOU KNOW?

Most workers who die from falls were wearing harnesses but had failed to tie off properly. Always follow the manufacturer's instructions when wearing a harness. Know and follow your company's safety procedures when working on roofs, ladders, and other elevated locations.

2.1.8   Unsafe Conditions

An unsafe condition is a physical state that is different from the acceptable, normal, or correct condition found on the job site. It usually causes an accident. It can be anything that reduces the degree of safety normally present. The following are some examples of unsafe conditions:

- Congested workplace
- Defective tools, equipment, or supplies
- Excessive noise
- Fire and explosive hazards
- Hazardous atmospheric conditions (such as gases, dusts, fumes, and vapors)
- Inadequate supports or guards
- Inadequate warning systems
- Poor housekeeping
- Poor lighting
- Poor ventilation
- Radiation exposure
- Unguarded moving parts such as pulleys, drive chains, and belts

2.1.9   Management System Failure

Sometimes the cause of an accident is failure of the management system. The management system should be designed to prevent or correct the acts and conditions that can cause accidents. If the management system did not do these things, that system failure may have caused the accident. What traits could mean the difference between a management system that fails and one that succeeds? A few important traits of a good management system follow:

- The company puts safety policies and procedures in writing.
- The company distributes written safety policies and procedures to each employee.
- The company reviews safety policies and procedures periodically.
- The company enforces all safety policies and procedures fairly and consistently.
- The company evaluates supplies, equipment, and services to see whether they are safe.
- The company provides regular, periodic safety training for employees.

2.2.0 Housekeeping

In construction, housekeeping means keeping your work area clean and free of scraps or spills. It also means being orderly and organized. You must store your materials and supplies safely and label them properly. Arranging your tools and equipment to permit safe, efficient work practices and easy cleaning is also important.

If the work site is indoors, make sure it is well lighted and ventilated. Don't allow aisles and exits to be blocked by materials and equipment. Make sure that flammable liquids are stored in safety cans. Oily rags must be placed only in approved, self-closing metal containers. Remember that the major goal of housekeeping is to prevent accidents. Good housekeeping reduces the chances for slips, fires, explosions, and falling objects.

Here are some good housekeeping rules:

- Remove all scrap material and lumber with nails sticking out from work areas.
- Clean up spills to prevent falls.
- Remove all combustible scrap materials regularly.
- Make sure you have containers for the collection and separation of refuse. Containers for flammable or harmful refuse must be covered.
- Dispose of wastes often.
- Store all tools and equipment when you're finished using them.

Another term for good housekeeping is pride of workmanship. If you take pride in what you are doing, you won't let trash build up around you. The old saying "A place for everything and everything in its place" is the right idea on the job site.

2.3.0 Company Safety Policies and OSHA Regulations

The mission of the Occupational Safety and Health Administration (OSHA) is to save lives, prevent injuries, and protect the health of America's workers. To accomplish this, federal and state governments work in partnership with the 111 million working men and women and their 7 million employers who are covered by the Occupational Safety and Health Act (OSH Act) of 1970.

Nearly every worker in the nation comes under OSHA's jurisdiction. There are some exceptions, such as miners, transportation workers, many public employees, and the self-employed.

2.3.1 The Code of Federal Regulations

The *Code of Federal Regulations* (CFR) *Part 1910* covers the OSHA standards for general industry. *CFR Part 1926* covers the OSHA standards for the construction industry. Either or both may apply to you, depending on where you are working and what you are doing. If a job-site condition is covered in the CFR book, then that standard must be used. However, if a more stringent requirement is listed in *CFR 1910*, it should also be met. Check with your supervisor to find out which standards apply to your job.

If a standard does not specifically address a hazard, the general duty clause must be invoked. This clause, found in *Section 5(a)1* of the OSH Act, summarizes the intent of the law:

> *Each Employer—shall furnish to each of his employees employment and a place of employment which are free from recognized hazards that are causing or are likely to cause death or serious physical harm to his employees.*

DID YOU KNOW?

All of OSHA's safety requirements in the *Code of Federal Regulations* apply to residential as well as commercial construction. In the past, OSHA enforced safety only at commercial sites. The increasing rate of accidents at residential sites led OSHA to enforce safety guidelines for the building of houses and townhouses. Today, however, OSHA still focuses its enforcement efforts on commercial construction.

2.3.2 Violations

Employers who violate OSHA regulations can be fined. The fines are not always high, but they can harm a company's reputation for safety. Fines for serious safety violations can be as high as $70,000 for each violation that was done willfully. In 2002, more than 78,000 fines were levied at a cost of $70,000 per violation.

2.3.3 Compliance

Just as employers are responsible to OSHA for compliance, employees must comply with their company's safety policies and rules. Employers are required to identify hazards and potential hazards within the workplace and eliminate them, control them, or provide protection from them. This can only be done through the combined efforts of the employer and employees. Employers must provide written programs and training on hazards, and employees must follow the procedures. You, as the employee, must read and understand the OSHA poster at your job site explaining your rights and responsibilities. If you are unsure where the OSHA poster is, ask your supervisor.

To help employers provide a safe workplace, OSHA requires companies to provide a **competent person** to ensure the safety of the employees. In *OSHA 29 CFR 1926,* OSHA defines a competent person as follows:

> *A person who can identify working conditions or surroundings that are unsanitary, hazardous, or dangerous to employees and who has authorization to correct or eliminate these conditions promptly.*

In comparison, *OSHA 29 CFR 1926* defines a **qualified person** as follows:

> *Someone who, by possession of a recognized degree, certificate, or professional standing, or who by extensive knowledge, training, and experience, has successfully demonstrated his ability to solve or resolve problems relating to the subject matter, work, or the project.*

In other words, a competent person is experienced and knowledgeable about the specific operation and has the authority from the employer to correct the problem or shut down the operation until it is safe. A qualified person has the knowledge and experience to handle problems. A competent person is not necessarily a qualified person.

These terms will be an important part of your career. It is important for you to know who the competent person is on your job site. OSHA requires a competent person for many of the tasks you may be assigned to perform, such as **confined space** entry, ladder use, and trenching. Different individuals may be assigned as a competent person for different tasks, according to their expertise. To ensure safety for you and your co-workers, work closely with your competent person and supervisor.

2.4.0 Reporting Injuries, Accidents, and Incidents

There are three categories of on-the-job events: injuries, accidents, and incidents. An injury is anything that requires treatment, even minor first aid. An accident is anything that causes an injury or property damage. An incident is anything that could have caused an injury or damage but, because it was caught in time, did not.

You must report all on-the-job injuries, accidents, or incidents, no matter how minor, to your supervisor (see *Figure 4*). Some workers think they will get in trouble if they report minor injuries. That's not true. Small injuries, like cuts and scrapes, can later become big problems because of infection and other complications.

101F04.EPS

Figure 4 ◆ All accidents, injuries, or incidents must be reported to your supervisor.

Many employers are required to maintain a log of significant work-related injuries and illnesses using OSHA Form 300. Employee names can be kept confidential in certain circumstances. A summary of these injuries must be posted at certain intervals, although employers do not need to submit it to OSHA unless requested. Employers can calculate the total number of injuries and illnesses and compare it with the average national rates for similar companies.

By analyzing accidents, companies and OSHA can improve safety policies and procedures. By reporting an accident, you can help keep similar accidents from happening in the future.

Table 2 shows an analysis of the causes of fatal accidents in the construction industry for 1997 through 1998.

Table 2   Causes of Fatal Accidents

Cause	Percentage of Fatalities
Falls from elevation	33%
Struck by . . .	27%
Caught in or caught between . . .	16%
Electrical shock	14%

All other accidents combined accounted for only 10 percent of the total. Because of these findings, OSHA developed its Focused Inspection Program to target these four high-hazard areas. OSHA hopes to reduce accidents, injuries, and fatalities in the construction industry.

Here are explanations of the four leading hazard groups:

- Falls from elevation are accidents involving failure of, failure to provide, or failure to use appropriate fall protection.
- Struck-by accidents involve unsafe operation of equipment, machinery, and vehicles, as well as improper handling of materials, such as through unsafe rigging operations.
- Caught-in or caught-between accidents involve unsafe operation of equipment, machinery, and vehicles, as well as improper safety procedures at **trench** sites and in other confined spaces.
- Electrical shock accidents involve contact with overhead wires, use of defective tools, failure to disconnect power source before repairs, or improper **ground** fault protection.

2.5.0 Evacuation Procedures

In many work environments, specific evacuation procedures are needed. These procedures go into effect when dangerous situations arise, such as fires, chemical spills, and gas leaks. In an emergency, you must know the evacuation procedures. You must also know the signal (usually a horn or siren) that tells workers to evacuate.

When you hear the evacuation signal, follow the evacuation procedures exactly. That usually means taking a certain route to a designated assembly area and telling the person in charge that you are there. If hazardous materials are released into the air, you may have to look at the **wind sock** to see which way the wind is blowing. Different evacuation routes are planned for different wind directions. Taking the right route will keep you from being exposed to the hazardous material.

Section 2.0.0

1. _____ is (are) *not* a main cause of accidents.
   a. Unsafe acts
   b. Alcohol or drug abuse
   c. Weather
   d. Poor work habits

2. Blue signs or markings that provide general information such as No Trespassing are _____ signs.
   a. caution
   b. informational
   c. warning
   d. safety

3. White and green signs or markings that give general instructions or suggestions about first-aid stations, exits, and evacuation routes are _____ signs.
   a. safety
   b. danger
   c. information
   d. MSDS

4. Many states have laws that prevent workers from collecting insurance benefits if they are injured while under the influence of alcohol or illegal drugs.
   a. True
   b. False

5. _____ is an example of an unsafe act.
   a. Taking an improper working position
   b. Radiation exposure
   c. Excessive noise
   d. Using a respirator

6. All of the following are good housekeeping guidelines *except* _____.
   a. keep aisles and exits clear
   b. clean up spills
   c. place oily rags in an uncovered container
   d. dispose of wastes often

7. The _____ summarizes the intent of the *OSHA Act of 1970*.
   a. competent person clause
   b. general duty clause
   c. hazardous duty clause
   d. qualified person clause

8. If a sign has a white background and a red panel with white or gray letters, you might see _____ on it.
   a. Out of Order
   b. Danger
   c. Biological Hazard
   d. Do Not Start

9. _____ must be reported to the employer.
   a. Only major injuries
   b. Only incidents and major injuries
   c. All injuries and incidents
   d. Only incidents in which a death occurred

10. An _____ is anything that could have caused an injury or damage if it hadn't been caught in time.
    a. incident
    b. accident
    c. injury
    d. intentional act

3.0.0 ◆ HAZARDS ON THE CONSTRUCTION JOB SITE

It's impossible to list all the hazards that can exist on a construction job site. This section describes some of the more common hazards and explains how to deal with them. You may want to make a list of other hazards you think could be present on your job site and discuss them with your instructor or supervisor.

For your safety, you must know the specific hazards where you are working and how to prevent accidents and injuries. If you have questions specific to your job site, consult your supervisor.

3.1.0 Welding

Even if you're not welding, you can be injured when you are around a welding operation. The oxygen and acetylene used in gas welding are very dangerous. The cylinders containing oxygen and acetylene must be transported, stored, and handled very carefully. Always follow these safety guidelines:

- Keep the work area clean and free from potentially hazardous items such as combustible materials and grease or petroleum products.

WARNING!
Keep oxygen away from sources of flame and combustible materials, especially substances containing oil, grease, or other petroleum products. Compressed oxygen mixed with oil or grease will explode. Never use petroleum-based products around fittings that serve compressed oxygen lines.

- Use great caution when you handle compressed gas cylinders.
- Store cylinders in an upright position and separate them by metal.

WARNING!
Do not remove the protective cap unless a cylinder is secured. If the cylinder falls over and the nozzle breaks off, the cylinder will shoot off like a rocket, injuring or killing anyone in its path.

- Never look at an **arc welding** operation without wearing the proper eye protection. The **arc** will burn your eyes.

WARNING!
In an arc welding operation, even a reflected arc can harm your eyes. It is extremely important to follow proper safety procedures at and around all welding operations. Serious eye injury or even blindness can result from unsafe conditions.

- If you are welding, use the proper PPE (see *Figure 5*), including the following:
  - Full face shield with proper lens
  - Earplugs to prevent flying sparks from entering your ears
  - All-leather, gauntlet-type welder's gloves
  - High-top leather boots to prevent **slag** from dropping inside your boots
  - Cuffless trousers that cover your ankles and boot tops
  - A respirator, if necessary

CAUTION
When welding on construction job sites, a hard hat with a full face shield may be required.

- If you are welding and other workers are in the area around your work, set up **welding shields.** Make sure everyone wears **flash goggles.** These goggles protect the eyes from the **flash,** which is the sudden bright light associated with starting a welding operation.
- A welder must be protected when the welding shield on the welder's headgear is down, because the shield restricts the welder's field of vision. A helper or monitor must watch the welder and the surrounding area in case of a fire or similar emergency, or rope off the area to prevent collisions and keep other workers away from the area.
- Welded material is hot! Mark it with a sign and stay clear for a while after the welding has been completed.

WARNING!
Post a fire watch when you are welding or cutting. One person other than the welding or cutting operator must constantly scan the work area for fires. Fire watch personnel should have ready access to fire extinguishers and alarms and know how to use them. Welding and cutting operations should never be performed without a fire watch. The area where welding is done must be monitored afterwards until there is no longer a risk of fire.

SAFETY GLASSES

WELDING CAP
(VISOR TURNED BACK)

EAR PLUGS

COTTON OR
WOOL OUTER
GARMENTS

CLEAR OR
SHADED FACE
SHIELD

GAUNTLET-
TYPE WELDING
GLOVES

RESPIRATOR

ALTERNATE
HEAD AND FACE
PROTECTION

PANT LEG EXTENDS
ALL THE WAY TO
THE INSTEP OF THE
BOOT (NO CUFF)

HIGH-TOP
LEATHER BOOTS

101F05.EPS

Figure 5 ◆ Personal protective equipment for welding.

Pay special attention to the safety guidelines about never looking at the arc without proper eye protection. Even a brief exposure to the ultraviolet light from arc welding can cause a **flash burn** and damage your eyes badly. You may not notice the symptoms until some time after the exposure. Here are some symptoms of flash burns to the eye:

- Headache
- Feeling of sand in your eyes
- Red or weeping eyes
- Trouble opening your eyes
- Impaired vision
- Swollen eyes

If you think you may have a flash burn to your eyes, seek medical help at once.

 WARNING!
Never wear contact lenses while you are welding. The ultraviolet rays may dry out the moisture beneath the contact lens, causing it to stick to your eye.

3.2.0 Flame Cutting

Many of the safety guidelines for welding apply to flame cutting as well. Cutting is not dangerous as long as you follow safety precautions. Here are some of the precautions:

- Wear appropriate PPE, including a welding hood with a filter.

- Never open the valve of an acetylene cylinder near an open flame.
- Store oxygen cylinders separately from fuel gas cylinders.
- Store acetylene cylinders in an upright position.
- Always use a friction striker to light a cutting torch.

 WARNING!

Never cut galvanized metal without proper ventilation. The zinc oxide fumes given off as the galvanized material is cut are hazardous. Also, use a respirator when you are cutting galvanized material.

The cutting process results in oxides that mix with molten iron and produce **dross.** The dross is blown from the cut by the jet of cutting oxygen. Hot dross can cause severe injury or can start fires on contact with flammable materials.

Before and during welding and cutting operations, you must follow certain safety procedures. *Figure 6* shows a typical oxyacetylene welding/cutting outfit. As the operator, you must check three things:

- Hoses
- Regulators
- Work area

3.2.1 Hoses and Regulators

Use the proper hose. The fuel gas hose is usually red (sometimes black) and has a left-hand threaded nut for connecting to the torch. The oxygen hose is green and has a right-hand threaded nut for connecting to the torch.

Hoses with leaks, burns, worn places, or other defects that make them unfit for service must be repaired or replaced. When inspecting hoses, look for charred sections close to the torch. These may have been caused by **flashback,** which is the result of a welding flame flaring up and charring the hose near the torch connection. Flashback is caused by improperly mixed fuel. Also check that hoses are not taped up to cover leaks (see *Figure 7*).

 WARNING!

If the torch goes out and begins to hiss, shut off the gas supply to the torch immediately. Otherwise, a flashback could occur. Never relight a torch from hot metal. Doing so could cause an explosion.

New hoses contain talc and loose bits of rubber. These materials must be removed from the hose before the torch is connected. If they are not removed, they will clog the torch needle valves. Common industry practice is to use compressed air to blow these materials out of the hose. Always

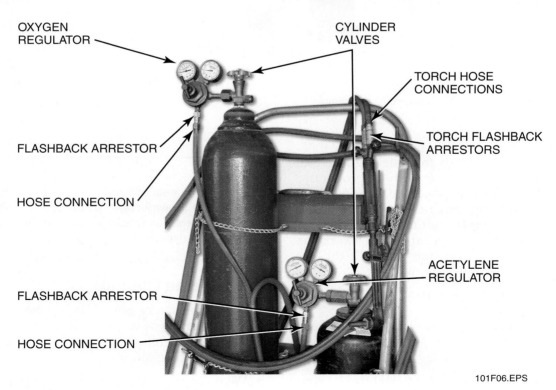

OXYGEN REGULATOR

CYLINDER VALVES

TORCH HOSE CONNECTIONS

FLASHBACK ARRESTOR

TORCH FLASHBACK ARRESTORS

HOSE CONNECTION

FLASHBACK ARRESTOR

ACETYLENE REGULATOR

HOSE CONNECTION

101F06.EPS

Figure 6 ◆ Typical oxyacetylene welding/cutting outfit.

make sure that the regulator valve is turned down to minimal pressures before using compressed air to clean a hose.

WARNING!

Never point a compressed air hose toward anyone. Flying debris and particles of dirt may cause serious injury.

Regulators are attached to the cylinder valve. They lower the high cylinder pressures to the required working pressures and maintain a steady flow of gas from the cylinder.

To prevent damage to regulators, always follow these guidelines:

Never jar or shake regulators, because that can damage the equipment beyond repair.

Always check that the adjusting screw is released before the cylinder valve is turned on.

Always open cylinder valves slowly.

WARNING!

When opening valves, always stand to the side. Dirt that is stuck in the valve may fly out and cause serious injury.

• Once cutting or welding has been completed, fully release the adjusting screw to relieve line pressure.
• Never use oil to lubricate a regulator, because that can cause an explosion.

• Never operate fuel regulators on oxygen cylinders or oxygen regulators on fuel gas cylinders.
• Never use a defective regulator. If a regulator is not working properly, shut off the gas supply and have a qualified person repair the regulator.
• Never operate the fuel regulator above the recommended safe operating pressure.
• Never use pliers or channel locks to install or remove regulators.

3.2.2 Work Area

Before beginning a cutting or welding operation, check the area for fire hazards. Cutting sparks can fly 30 feet or more and can fall several floors. Remove any flammable material in the area or cover it with an approved fire blanket. Have an approved fire extinguisher available before starting your work.

WARNING!

The slag and products that result from cutting and welding operations can start fires and cause severe injuries. Always wear appropriate personal protective equipment, including gloves and eye protection, when cutting or welding. Do not wear clothes made of polyester when welding or cutting. Observe the safety instructions of both the manufacturer and your shop.

Always perform cutting operations in a well-ventilated area. Heating and cutting metals with an oxyfuel torch can create toxic fumes.

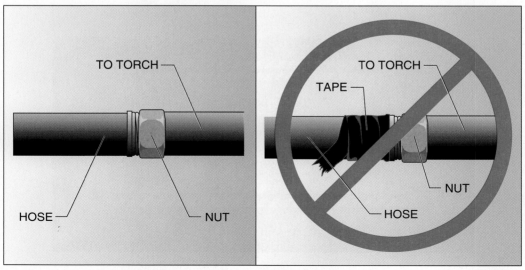

101F07.EPS

Figure 7 ◆ Proper hose connection.

Maintaining a clean and neat work area promotes safety and efficiency. When you are finished welding, be sure to do the following:

- Pick up cutting scraps.
- Sweep up any scraps or debris around the work area.
- Return cylinders and equipment to the proper places.
- Prevent fires by making sure that cut metals and dross are cooled before disposing of them.

3.3.0 Trenches and Excavations

In many construction jobs you will need to work in trenches or excavations. Cave-ins and falling objects are hazards in these areas. Obey the following safety rules when working around trenches and excavations:

- Never put tools, materials, or loose dirt or rocks within 2 feet of the edge of a trench. They can easily fall in and injure the people in the trench. Also, too much weight near the edge of a trench can cause a cave-in.
- Always walk around a trench; never jump over it or straddle it. You could lose your footing and fall in, or your weight could cause a cave-in.
- Never jump into a trench. Always use a ladder to get in and out.
- A stairway, ladder, or ramp must be provided for exit from any trench that is 4 or more feet deep.
- Put barricades around all trenches, as shown in *Figure 8.*

- Always follow OSHA regulations and your employer's procedures for **shoring** up a trench to prevent a cave-in. Never work beyond the shoring.
- Always follow OSHA regulations for determining the maximum allowable slope.

WARNING!
Never work on the face of either sloped excavations or excavations in which concrete slabs were used to flatten the surrounding area at levels above other workers. The workers below you may not be adequately protected from the hazard of falling, rolling, or sliding materials or equipment.

A competent person will inspect excavations daily and decide whether cave-ins or failures of protective systems could occur, and whether there are any other hazardous conditions. The competent person will conduct the inspection before any work begins and as needed throughout the shift. He or she will also inspect the excavations after every rainstorm or other hazard-increasing incident.

You cannot work in excavations that have standing water or in excavations where water is coming in unless you take precautions to protect yourself. A competent person will know what these precautions are. Always ask the competent person on site or your immediate supervisor if you have any questions about proper safety practices.

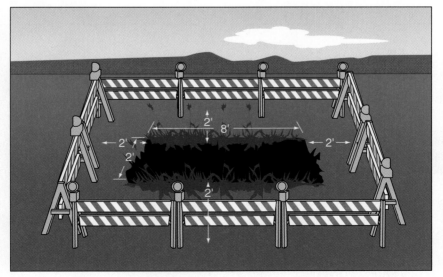

101F08.EPS

Figure 8 ◆ Barricade around a trench.

3.4.0 Proximity Work

Work that is done near a hazard but not in direct contact with it is called **proximity work.** Proximity work requires extra caution and awareness. The hazard may be hot piping, energized electrical equipment, or running motors or machinery (see *Figure 9*). You must do your work so that you do not come into contact with the nearby hazard.

You may need to put up barricades to prevent accidental contact. Lifting and rigging operations may have to be done in a way that minimizes the risk of dropping things on the hazard. A monitor may watch you and alert you if you are in danger of touching the hazard while you work.

Energized electrical equipment is very hazardous. Regulations and policies will tell you the minimum safe working distance from energized electrical conductors. You'll learn more about working with and around energized electrical equipment later in this module.

3.4.1 Pressurized or High-Temperature Systems

In many construction jobs, you must work close to tanks, piping systems, and pumps that contain pressurized or high-temperature fluids. Be aware of these two possible hazards:

- Touching a container of high-temperature fluid can cause burns (see *Figure 10*). Many industrial processes involve fluids that are as hot as several thousand degrees.
- If a container holding pressurized fluids is damaged, it may leak and spray dangerous fluids.

Any work around pressurized or high-temperature systems is proximity work. Barricades, a monitor, or both may be needed for safety (see *Figure 11*).

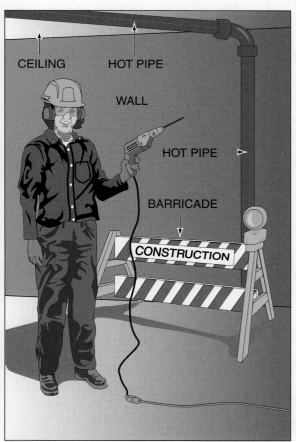

CEILING   HOT PIPE

WALL

HOT PIPE →

BARRICADE

CONSTRUCTION

101F09.EPS

Figure 9 ◆ Proximity work.

DANGER
CONTENTS
HIGH TEMPERATURE

CONSTR

101F10.EPS

Figure 10 ◆ Avoid touching high-temperature components.

BARRICADE

DANGER

CONTENTS
UNDER PRESSURE

CONSTRUCTION

CONSTRUCTION

CONSTRUCTION

101F11.EPS

Figure 11 ◆ Work safely near pressurized or high-temperature systems.

3.5.0 Confined Spaces

Construction and maintenance work isn't always done outdoors. A lot of it is done in confined spaces. A confined space is a space that is large enough to work in but that has limited means of entry or exit. A confined space is not designed for human occupancy, and it has limited ventilation. Examples of confined spaces are tanks, vessels, silos, storage bins, hoppers, vaults, and pits (see *Figure 12*).

A **permit-required confined space** is a type of confined space that has been evaluated by a qualified person and found to have actual or potential hazards (see *Figure 13*). You must have written authorization to enter a permit-required confined space.

When equipment is in operation, many confined spaces contain hazardous gases or fluids. In addition, the work you are doing may introduce hazardous fumes into the space. Welding is an example of such work. For safety, you must take special precautions both before you enter and leave a confined space and while you work there.

Until you have been trained to work in permit-required confined spaces and have taken the needed precautions, you must stay out of them. If you aren't sure whether a confined space require a permit, ask your supervisor. You must alway follow your employer's procedures and your supervisor's instructions. Confined space procedures may include getting clearance from a safety representative before starting the work. You will be told what kinds of hazards are involved and what precautions you need to take. You will also be shown how to use the required PPE. Remember, it is better to be safe than sorry, so ask!

WARNING!

Without proper training, no employee is allowed to enter a permit-required or non-permit-required confined space. Employers are required to have programs to control entry to and hazards in both types of confined spaces.

Never work alone in a confined space. OSHA requires an attendant to remain outside a permit-required confined space. The attendant monitors entry, work, and exit.

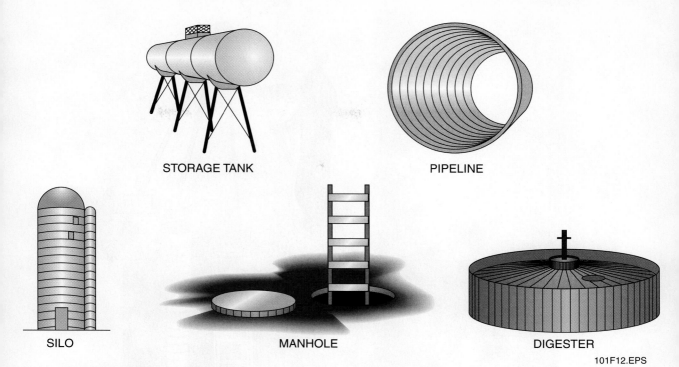

STORAGE TANK

PIPELINE

SILO

MANHOLE

DIGESTER

101F12.EPS

Figure 12 ◆ Examples of confined spaces.

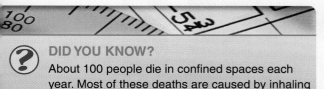
3.6.0 Motorized Vehicles

Motorized vehicles used on job sites include trucks, forklifts, backhoes, cranes, and **trenchers.** Operators must take care when driving vehicles. Helpers, riggers, and anyone else working nearby must also be careful.

If a vehicle is used indoors, ventilation of the work area is especially important. All internal combustion engines give off carbon monoxide as part of their exhaust. You cannot see, smell, or taste carbon monoxide, but it can kill you. Make sure there is good ventilation before you operate any motorized vehicles indoors.

The operator of any vehicle is responsible for the safety of passengers and the protection of the load. Follow these safety guidelines when you operate vehicles on a job site:

- Always wear a seat belt.
- Be sure that each person in the vehicle has a firmly secured seat and seat belt.
- Obey all speed limits. Reduce speed in crowded areas.
- Look to the rear and sound the horn before backing up. If your rear vision is blocked, get a **signaler** to direct you. (Hand signals are covered in the *Rigging* module.)
- Every vehicle must have a backup alarm. Make sure the backup alarm works.
- Always turn off the engine when you are fueling.
- Turn off the engine and set the brakes before you leave the vehicle.
- Never stay on or in a truck that is being loaded by excavating equipment.
- Keep windshields, rearview mirrors, and lights clean and functional.
- Carry road flares, fire extinguishers, and other standard safety equipment at all times.

 WARNING!
Driving a vehicle indoors without good ventilation can make you sick or kill you because of the carbon monoxide given off by the exhaust. Carbon monoxide is especially dangerous because you cannot see, smell, or taste it.

101F13.EPS

Figure 13 ◆ Permit-required confined space.

Section 3.0.0

1. Oil or grease in contact with _____ will cause an explosion.

   a. a gas cylinder
   b. acetylene
   c. compressed oxygen
   d. combustible materials

2. Flash burns are caused by exposing your eyes to _____.

   a. ultraviolet light
   b. oxygen and acetylene
   c. petroleum products
   d. zinc oxide fumes

3. A _____ is attached to a cylinder valve to reduce the high cylinder pressure to the required lower working pressure.

   a. safety valve
   b. regulator
   c. torch assembly
   d. compression hose

4. A confined space _____.

   a. has a limited amount of ventilation
   b. has no means of entry
   c. is too small to work in
   d. may be entered by untrained employees

5. All internal combustion engines give off a deadly odorless, tasteless, invisible gas called _____ as part of their exhaust.

   a. carbon trioxide
   b. carbon monoxide
   c. carbon dioxide
   d. carbon cyanide

4.0.0 ◆ WORKING SAFELY WITH JOB HAZARDS

You can safely handle all the job hazards that you have learned about if you follow the rules. As long as everyone follows safety procedures, there is little risk of being hurt on the job site. In this section, you will learn about procedures and equipment used on construction sites to ensure worker safety.

4.1.0 Lockout/Tagout

A lockout/tagout system safeguards workers from hazardous energy while they work with machines and equipment. A lockout/tagout system protects workers from hazards such as the following:

- Acids
- Air pressure
- Chemicals
- Electricity
- Flammable liquids
- High temperatures
- Hydraulics
- Machinery
- Steam
- Other forms of energy

When people are working on or around any of these hazards, mechanical and other systems are shut down, drained, or de-energized. Tags and locks are placed on each switch, circuit breaker, valve, or other component to make sure that motors aren't started, valves aren't opened or closed, and no other changes are made that would endanger workers. Lockouts and tagouts protect workers from all possible sources of energy, including electrical, mechanical, hydraulic, thermal, pneumatic (air), and high temperature.

Generally, each lock has its own key, and the person who puts the lock on keeps the key. That person is the only one who can remove the lock. Tags have the words DANGER or CLEARANCE (see *Figure 14*).

Follow these rules for a safe lockout/tagout system:

- Never operate any device, valve, switch, or piece of equipment that has a lock or a tag attached to it.
- Use only tags that have been approved for your job site.
- If a device, valve, switch, or piece of equipment is locked out, make sure the proper tag is attached.

101F14.EPS

Figure 14 ◆ Typical safety tags.

- Lock out and tag all electrical systems when they are not in use.
- Lock out and tag pipelines containing acids, explosive fluids, or high-pressure steam during maintenance or repair.
- Tag motorized vehicles and equipment when they are being repaired and before anyone starts work. Also, disconnect or disable the starting devices.

The exact procedures for lockout/tagout may vary at different companies and job sites. Ask your supervisor to explain the lockout/tagout procedure on your job site. You must know and follow this procedure. This is for your safety and the safety of your co-workers. If you have any questions about lockout/tagout procedures, ask your supervisor.

4.2.0 Barriers and Barricades

Any opening in a wall or floor is a safety hazard. There are two types of protection for these openings: (1) they can be **guarded** or (2) they can be covered. Cover any hole in the floor when possible. When it is not practical to cover the hole, use barricades. If the bottom edge of a wall opening is fewer than 3 feet above the floor and would allow someone to fall 4 feet or more, then place guards around the opening.

The types of barriers and barricades used var from job site to job site (see *Figure 15*). There ma also be different procedures for when and hov barricades are put up. Learn and follow the poli cies at your job site.

Several different types of guards are commonl used:

- Railings are used across wall openings or as barrier around floor openings to prevent fall (see *Figure 15a*).
- Warning barricades alert workers to hazard but provide no real protection (see *Figure 15b*, Typical warning barricades are made of plasti tape or rope strung from wire or between posts The tape or rope is color-coded:
  - Red means danger. No one may enter an are with a red warning barricade. A red barri cade is used when there is danger from falling objects or when a load is suspende over an area.
  - Yellow means caution. You may enter an are with a yellow barricade, but be sure yo know what the hazard is, and be careful. Ye low barricades are used around wet areas o areas containing loose dust. Yellow witl black lettering warns of physical hazard such as bumping into something, stumbling or falling.
  - Yellow and purple means radiation warning No one may pass a yellow and purple barri cade without authorization, training, and th appropriate personal protective equipmen These barricades are often used where pip ing welds are being X-rayed.
- Protective barricades give both a visual warn ing and protection from injury (see *Figure 15c* They can be wooden posts and rails, posts an chain, or steel cable. People cannot get past pro tective barricades.
- Blinking lights are placed on barricades so the can be seen at night (see *Figure 15d*).
- Hole covers are used to cover open holes in floor or in the ground (see *Figure 15e*). The must be secured and labeled. They must b strong enough to support twice the weight c anything that may be placed on top of them.

WARNING!

Never remove a barricade unless you have been authorized to do so. Follow your employer's procedures for putting up and removing barricades.

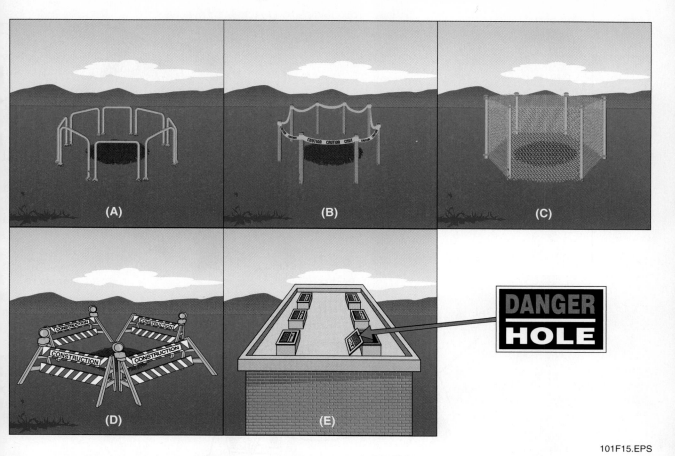

Figure 15 ◆ Common types of barriers and barricades.

101F15.EPS

5.0.0 ◆ PERSONAL PROTECTIVE EQUIPMENT

PPE is designed to protect you from injury. You must keep it in good condition and use it when you need to. Many workers are injured on the job because they are not using PPE.

5.1.0 Personal Protective Equipment Needs

You will not see all the potentially dangerous conditions just by looking around a job site. It's important to stop and consider what type of accidents could happen on any job that you are about to do. Using common sense and knowing how to use PPE will greatly reduce your chance of getting hurt.

5.2.0 Personal Protective Equipment Use and Care

The best protective equipment is of no use to you unless you do the following four things:

Regularly inspect it.
Properly care for it.

- Use it properly when it is needed.
- Never alter or modify it in any way.

The sections that follow describe protective equipment commonly used on construction sites and tell how to use and care for each piece of equipment. Be sure to wear the equipment according to the manufacturer's specifications.

5.2.1 Hard Hat

Figure 16 shows a typical hard hat. The outer shell of the hat can protect your head from a hard blow. The webbing inside the hat keeps space between the shell and your head. Adjust the headband so that the webbing fits your head and there is at least 1 inch of space between your head and the shell. Do not alter your hard hat in any way.

 DID YOU KNOW?
Hard hats used to be made of metal. However, metal conducts electricity, so most hard hats are now made of reinforced plastic or fiberglass.

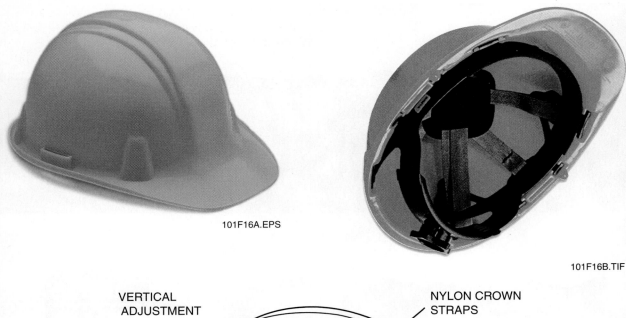

101F16A.EPS

101F16B.TIF

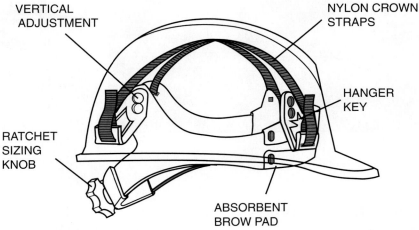

VERTICAL
ADJUSTMENT

NYLON CROWN
STRAPS

HANGER
KEY

RATCHET
SIZING
KNOB

ABSORBENT
BROW PAD

101F16C.EPS

Figure 16 ◆ Typical hard hat.

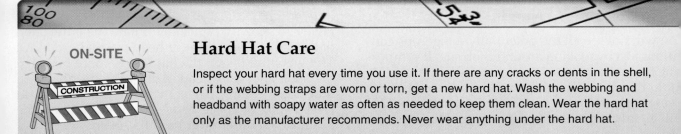

Hard Hat Care

Inspect your hard hat every time you use it. If there are any cracks or dents in the shell, or if the webbing straps are worn or torn, get a new hard hat. Wash the webbing and headband with soapy water as often as needed to keep them clean. Wear the hard hat only as the manufacturer recommends. Never wear anything under the hard hat.

5.2.2 Safety Glasses, Goggles, and Face Shields

Wear eye protection (see *Figure 17*) wherever there is even the slightest chance of an eye injury. Eye and face protection must meet the requirements specified in American National Standards Institute (ANSI) *Standard Z87.1-1968*. Areas where there are potential eye hazards from falling or flying objects are usually identified, but you should always be on the lookout for possible hazards.

Regular safety glasses will protect you from falling objects or from objects flying toward your face. You can add side shields for protection from the sides. In some cases, you may need a face shield. Safety goggles give your eyes the best protection from all directions.

Welders must use tinted goggles or welding hoods. The tinted lenses protect the eyes from the bright welding arc or flame.

 WARNING!

Handle safety glasses and goggles with care. If they get scratched, replace them. The scratches will interfere with your vision. Clean the lenses regularly with lens tissues or a soft cloth.

SAFETY GLASSES

101F17A.TIF

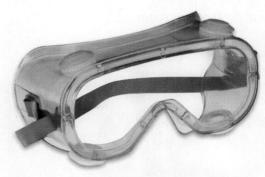

GOGGLES

101F17B.TIF

TINTED HEADBAND
WELDING
FACE SHIELD

CLEAR HEADBAND
SAFETY
FACE SHIELD

101F17C.TIF

Figure 17 ◆ Typical safety glasses, goggles, and full face shields.

5.2.3 Safety Harness

Safety harnesses, like the one in *Figure 18*, are extra-heavy-duty harnesses that buckle around your body. They have leg, shoulder, chest, and pelvic straps.

Safety harnesses have a D-ring attached to one end of a short section of rope called a **lanyard** (see *Figure 19*). The other end of the lanyard should be attached to a strong anchor point located above the work area. (A qualified person will tell you what a strong anchor point is.) The lanyard should be long enough to let you work but short enough to keep you from falling more than 6 feet.

Use a safety harness and lanyard when you are working in the following situations:

- More than 6 feet above ground or according to company policy
- Near a large opening in a floor
- Near a deep hole
- Near protruding rebar

WARNING!

Never use a safety harness and lanyard for anything except their intended purpose. Always follow the manufacturer's instructions for hooking up a safety harness or lanyard.

NOTE

The safety harness and lanyard are parts of a system that is known as the personal fall protection system. Workers must know how to properly inspect, don, and maintain their system.

Treat a safety harness as if your life depends on it, because it does! Carefully inspect the harness each time you use it. Check that the buckles and D-ring are not bent or deeply scratched. Check the harness for any cuts or rough spots. If you find any damage, turn in the harness for testing or replacement.

WARNING!

Always use a safety harness and lanyard properly. More than 70 percent of reported jobsite accidents are caused by improper use of the lanyard and harness.

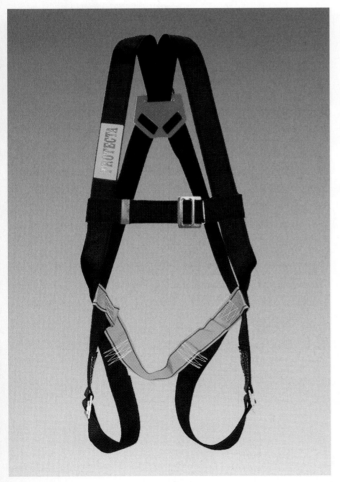

101F18.EPS

Figure 18 ◆ Typical full-body safety harness.

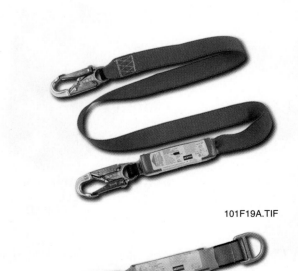

101F19A.TIF

101F19B.TIF

Figure 19 ◆ Lanyards.

5.2.4 Gloves

On many construction jobs, you must wear heavy-duty gloves to protect your hands (see *Figure 20*). Construction work gloves are usually made of cloth, canvas, or leather. Never wear cloth gloves around rotating or moving equipment. They can easily get caught in the equipment.

Gloves help prevent cuts and scrapes when you handle sharp or rough materials. Heat-resistant gloves are sometimes used for hot materials. Electricians use special rubber-insulated gloves when they work on or around live circuits.

Replace gloves when they become worn, torn, or soaked with oil or chemicals. Electrician's rubber-insulated gloves should be tested regularly to make sure they will protect the wearer.

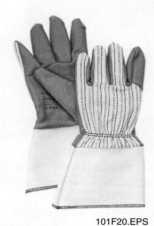

101F20.EPS

Figure 20 ◆ Work gloves.

5.2.5 Safety Shoes

The best shoes to wear on a construction site are ANSI-approved shoes (see *Figure 21*). The steel toe protects your toes from falling objects. The steel sole keeps nails and other sharp objects from puncturing your feet. The next best footwear material is heavy leather. Never wear canvas shoes or sandals on a construction site. They do not provide adequate protection.

Always replace boots or shoes when the sole tread becomes worn or the shoes have holes, even if the holes are on top. Don't wear oil-soaked shoes when you are welding, because of the risk of fire.

101F21.EPS

Figure 21 ◆ Safety shoe.

5.2.6 Hearing Protection

Damage to most parts of the body causes pain. But ear damage does not always cause pain. Exposure to loud noise over a long time can cause hearing loss, even if the noise is not loud enough to cause pain.

Most construction companies follow OSHA rules in deciding when hearing protection must be used. One type of hearing protection is specially designed earplugs that fit into your ears and filter out noise (see *Figure 22*). Clean earplugs regularly with soap and water to prevent ear infection.

Another type of hearing protection is earmuffs, which are large padded covers for the entire ear (see *Figure 23*). You must adjust the headband on earmuffs for a snug fit. If the noise level is very high, you may need to wear both earplugs and earmuffs.

Noise-induced hearing loss can be prevented by using noise control measures and personal protective devices. *Table 3* shows the recommended maximum length of exposure to sound levels rated 90 decibels and higher.

Table 3	Maximum Noise Levels	
Sound Level (decibels)	**Maximum Hours of Continuous Exposure per Day**	**Examples**
90	8	Power lawn mower
92	6	Belt sander
95	4	Tractor
97	3	Hand drill
100	2	Chain saw
102	1.5	Impact wrench
105	1	Spray painter
110	0.5	Power shovel
115	0.25 or less	Hammer drill

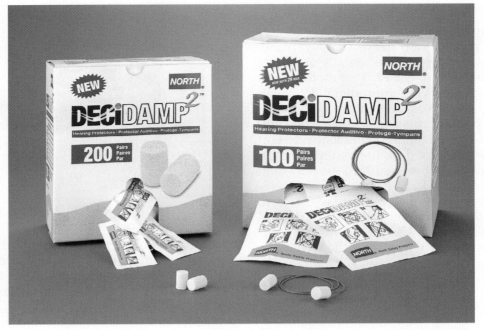

Figure 22 ◆ Earplugs for hearing protection.

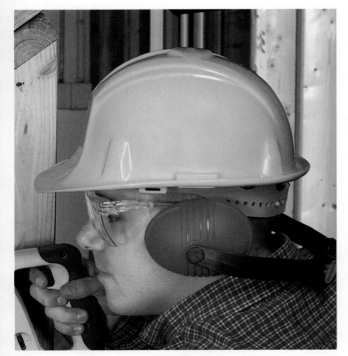

101F23.EPS

Figure 23 ◆ Earmuffs for hearing protection.

5.2.7 Respiratory Protection

Wherever there is danger of an inhalation hazard, you must use a respirator.

Follow company and OSHA procedures when choosing the type of respirator for a particular job.

Also be sure that it is safe for you to wear a respirator. Under OSHA's Respiratory Protection Standard, workers must fill out a questionnaire to determine any potential problems in wearing a respirator. Depending on the answers, a medical exam may be required.

Federal law specifies which type of respirator to use for different types of hazards. There are four general types of respirators (see *Figure 24*):

- Self-contained breathing **apparatus** (SCBA)
- Supplied air mask
- Full facepiece mask with chemical canister (gas mask)
- Half mask or mouthpiece with mechanical filter

An SCBA carries its own air supply in a compressed air tank. It is used where there is not enough oxygen or where there are dangerous gases or fumes in the air.

A supplied air mask uses a remote compressor or air tank. A hose supplies air to the mask. Supplied air masks can be used under the same conditions as SCBAs.

A full facepiece mask with chemical canisters is used to protect against brief exposure to dangerous gases or fumes.

A half mask or mouthpiece with a mechanical filter is used in areas where you might inhale dust or other solid particles. No medical exam is necessary to use this type of general respiratory protection.

101F24A.EPS

SELF-CONTAINED BREATHING APPARATUS

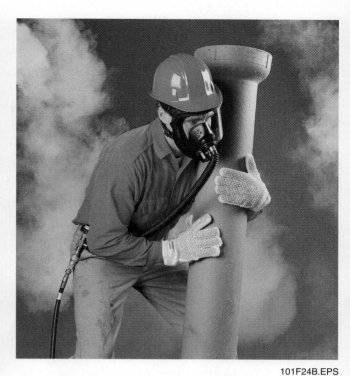

101F24B.EPS

SUPPLIED AIR MASK

101F24C.EPS

FULL FACEPIECE MASK

101F24D.EPS

HALF MASK

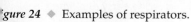

Figure 24 ◆ Examples of respirators.

It is very important to check a respirator carefully for damage and for proper fit. A leaking facepiece can be as dangerous as not wearing a respirator at all. All respirators must be fitted properly, and their facepiece-to-face seal must be checked each time the respirator is used. When conditions prevent a good seal, the respirator cannot be worn. The following conditions will interfere with the respirator's seal:

- Facial hair (such as sideburns or beards)
- Skullcaps that project under the facepiece
- Temple bars on glasses (especially when wearing full-face respirators)
- Absence of upper, lower, or all teeth
- Absence of dentures
- Gum and tobacco chewing

CAUTION

OSHA no longer bans the wearing of contact lenses with respirators (*29 CFR 1910.134 [g][1][ii]*). After sponsoring research and studies on the issue, OSHA recently concluded that wearing contact lenses with respirators does not pose an increased risk to the wearer's safety.

If you wear contact lenses, practice wearing a respirator with your contact lenses to see whether you have any problems. That way, you will identify any problems before you use the respirator under hazardous conditions.

Respirators used by only one person should be cleaned after each day of use, or more often if necessary. Those used by more than one person should be cleaned and disinfected (made germ-free) after each use.

When a respirator is not required, workers may voluntarily use a dust or particle mask for general protection. These masks do not require fit testing or a medical examination.

WARNING!

When a respirator is required, a personal monitoring device is usually also required. This device samples the air to measure the concentration of hazardous chemicals.

6.0.0 ◆ LIFTING

You may be surprised to learn that one-fourth of all occupational injuries happen when workers are handling or moving construction materials, especially lifting heavy objects. There is a right way and a wrong way to lift a heavy object. Lifting the wrong way can land you in the hospital. *Figure 25* shows the right way.

Step 1 Move close to the object you are going to lift. Position your feet in a forward/backward stride, with one foot at the side of the object.

Step 2 Bend your knees and lower your body, keeping your back straight and as upright as possible.

Step 3 Place your hands under the object, wrap your arms around it, or grasp the handles. To get your hands under an object that is flat on the floor, use both hands to lift one corner. Slip one hand under that corner. With one hand under, tilt the object to get the other hand under the opposite side.

Step 4 Draw the object close to your body.

Step 5 Lift by slowly straightening your legs and keeping the object's weight over your legs as much as possible.

Step 6 Pick the object up facing the direction you are going to go, to avoid twisting your knees or back.

These steps let you use your strongest muscles (those in your legs) instead of your weakest ones (those in your back) to lift. Practice with light objects. Then, when you've got it down, move on to heavier ones.

Many employers supply back belts to help reduce back injuries. You should be trained in the right way to use a back belt. Remember, a back belt is no substitute for using proper lifting techniques.

WARNING!

Always check your company's rules and regulations regarding the amount of weight one person is allowed to carry at a time.

Figure 25 ◆ How to lift safely.

101F25.EPS

Sections 4.0.0–6.0.0

1. The _____ keeps the key to a lock used for lockout/tagout.
   a. site supervisor
   b. person who puts on the lock
   c. site safety manager
   d. OSHA inspector

2. You may operate a device that is tagged out if there is no imminent danger.
   a. True
   b. False

3. A yellow and purple warning barricade means _____.
   a. caution
   b. danger
   c. physical danger
   d. radiation hazard

4. Hole covers must be strong enough to support _____ the weight of anything that may be placed on top of them.
   a. exactly
   b. twice
   c. four times
   d. ten times

5. Adjust the webbing of a hard hat so that there is _____ between your head and the shell.
   a. no space
   b. as much space as possible
   c. at least 1 inch of space
   d. less than 1 inch of space

6. _____ provide the best all-around protection for your eyes.
   a. Welding hoods
   b. Face shields
   c. Safety goggles
   d. Strap-on glasses

7. A _____ has its own clean air supply.
   a. half mask
   b. mouthpiece with mechanical filter
   c. self-contained breathing apparatus
   d. full facepiece mask

8. Whenever there is danger of an inhalation hazard, you must use a respirator.
   a. True
   b. False

9. _____ do(es) *not* interfere with the respirator's seal.
   a. Facial hair
   b. Gum and tobacco chewing
   c. Dentures
   d. Temple bars on glasses

10. When lifting heavy objects, keep as much weight as possible over your _____.
    a. hips
    b. shoulders
    c. legs
    d. back

7.0.0 ◆ AERIAL WORK

Working in elevated locations is common in the construction industry. If it is done properly and the proper equipment is used, it is safe. But falls from heights can cause serious injuries or even death. You must always have your supervisor's permission before working in an elevated location. In this section, you will learn about the equipment used for aerial work. You'll learn how to use it, inspect it, and maintain it.

7.1.0 Ladders and Scaffolds

Ladders and scaffolds are used to perform work in elevated locations. Any time work is performed above ground level, there is a risk of accidents. You can reduce this risk by carefully inspecting ladders and scaffolds before you use them and by using them properly.

Overloading means exceeding the maximum intended load of a ladder. Overloading can cause ladder failure, which means that the ladder could buckle, break, or topple, among other possibilities. The maximum intended load is the total weight of all people, equipment, tools, materials, loads that are being carried, and other loads that the ladder can hold at any one time. Check the manufacturer's specifications to determine the maximum intended load. Ladders are usually given a duty rating that indicates their load capacity, as shown in *Table 4*.

WARNING!

When you use a ladder, be sure to maintain three-point contact with the ladder at all times. Three-point contact means that either two feet and one hand or one foot and two hands are always touching the ladder.

WARNING!

Use ladders and scaffolds for their intended uses only. Ladders are not interchangeable, and incorrect use can result in injury or damage.

Table 4   Ladder Duty Ratings and Load Capacities

Duty Ratings	Load Capacities
Type IA	300 lbs., extra-heavy duty/professional use
Type I	250 lbs., heavy duty/industrial use
Type II	225 lbs., medium duty/commercial use
Type III	200 lbs., light duty/household use

7.1.1   Portable Straight Ladders

Straight ladders consist of two rails, rungs between the rails, and safety feet on the bottom of the rails (see *Figure 26*). The straight ladders used in construction are made of wood or fiberglass.

ON-SITE

Fall Protection

Effective February 1995, fall protection must be provided for those working at an elevation above 6 feet or where a drop into a hole or trench is greater than 6 feet. Supervisors must ensure that all walking and working surfaces have the strength and structural integrity to support the workers. Work conducted on an otherwise unprotected side or edge that is 6 feet or more above a lower level must be protected by the use of guardrail systems, safety-net systems, or personal fall-arrest systems.

Effective January 1998, an acceptable personal fall-arrest system is a body harness with a lanyard attached to a D-ring in the center of the back. Body belts are not acceptable as part of a personal fall-arrest system because they unevenly distribute pressure on the wearer's midsection.

All companies are required by law to have a written Fall Protection Plan that addresses site-specific fall hazards and the steps taken to prevent each hazard. This information will normally be included in your training or regularly scheduled safety meetings. If you are unsure of what your company's plan is, or have questions about it, ask your supervisor before performing any aerial work.

Three-Point Contact

When climbing or working from a ladder, you run the risk of falling. An important measure in safeguarding yourself against a fall is to maintain three-point contact with the ladder at all times. This means that you either have two hands and one foot or two feet and one hand touching the ladder constantly. Maintaining three-point contact with the ladder will help prevent you from falling and injuring yourself or a co-worker.

(A)   101SA01A.EPS

(B)   101SA01B.EPS

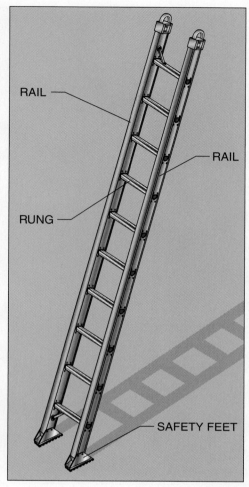

RAIL

RAIL

RUNG

SAFETY FEET

101F26.EPS

Figure 26 ◆ Portable straight ladder.

Metal ladders conduct electricity and should never be used around electrical equipment. Any portable metal ladder must have "Danger. Do Not Use Around Electrical Installations" stenciled on the rails in 2-inch, red letters. Ladders made of dry wood or fiberglass, neither of which conducts electricity, should be used around electrical equipment. Check that any wooden ladder is, in fact, completely dry before using it around electricity. Even a small amount of water will conduct electricity.

Different types of ladders should be used in different situations (see *Figure 27*). Aluminum ladders are corrosion-resistant and can be used where they might be exposed to the elements. They are also lightweight and can be used where they must frequently be lifted and moved. Wooden ladders, which are heavier and sturdier than fiberglass or aluminum ladders, can be used where heavy loads must be moved up and down. Fiberglass ladders are very durable, so they are useful where some amount of rough treatment is unavoidable. Both fiberglass and aluminum are easier to clean than wood.

7.1.2 Inspecting Straight Ladders

Always inspect a ladder before you use it. Check the rails and rungs for cracks or other damage. Also, check for loose rungs. If you find any damage, do not use the ladder. Check the entire ladder for loose nails, screws, brackets, or other hardware. If you find any hardware problems, tighten the loose parts or have the ladder repaired before you use it. OSHA requires regular inspections of all ladders and an inspection just before each use.

 WARNING!
Wooden ladders should never be painted. The paint could hide cracks in the rungs or rails. Clear varnish, shellac, or a preservative oil finish will protect the wood without hiding defects.

Figure 28 shows the safety feet attached to a straight ladder. Make sure the feet are securely attached and that they are not damaged or worn down. Do not use a ladder if its safety feet are not in good working order.

7.1.3 Using Straight Ladders

It is very important to place a straight ladder at the proper angle before using it. A ladder placed at an improper angle will be unstable and could cause you to fall. *Figure 29* shows a properly positioned straight ladder.

The distance between the foot of a ladder and the base of the structure it is leaning against must be one-fourth of the distance between the ground and the point where the ladder touches the structure. For example, if the height of the wall shown in *Figure 29* is 16 feet, the base of the ladder should be 4 feet from the base of the wall. If you are going to step off a ladder onto a platform or roof, the top of the ladder should extend at least 3 feet above the point where the ladder touches the platform or roof.

Ladders should be used only on stable and level surfaces unless they are secured at both the bottom and the top to prevent any accidental movement (see *Figure 30*). Never try to move a ladder while you are on it. If a ladder must be placed in front of a door that opens toward the ladder, the door should be locked or blocked open. Otherwise, the door could be opened into the ladder.

Ladders are made for vertical use only. Never use a ladder as a work platform by placing it horizontally. Make sure the ladder you are about to climb or descend is properly secure before you do so. Check to make sure the ladder's feet are solidly

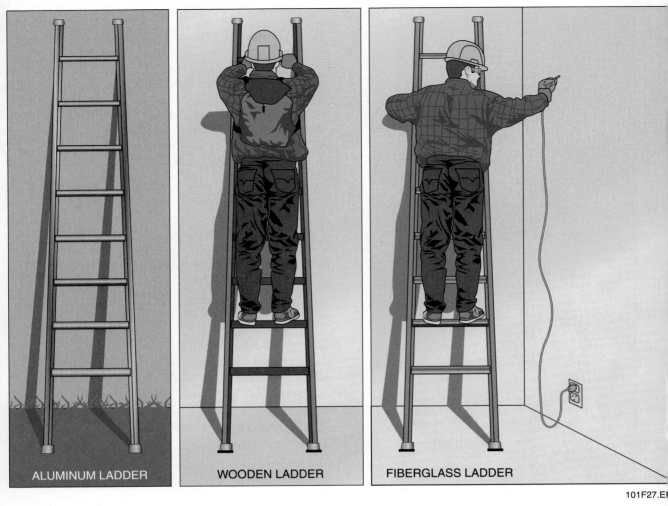

Figure 27 ◆ Different types of ladders and applications.

101F27.E

101F28.EPS

Figure 28 ◆ Ladder safety feet.

positioned on firm, level ground. Also check make sure the top of the ladder is firmly positioned and in no danger of shifting once you begin your climb. Remember that your own weight will affect the ladder's steadiness once you mount it. So it is important to test the ladder first by putting some of your weight on it without actually beginning to climb. This way, you can be sure that the ladder will remain steady as you climb.

When climbing a straight ladder, keep both hands on the rails. Always keep your body weight in the center of the ladder between the rails. Face the ladder at all times. Never go up down a ladder while facing away from it (see *Figure 31*).

To carry a tool while you are on the ladder, use **hand line** or tagline attached to the tool. Climb the ladder and then pull up the tool. Don't carry tool in your hands while you are climbing a ladder.

AT LEAST 3 FEET

16 FEET

4 FEET

101F29.EPS

Figure 29 ◆ Proper positioning of a straight ladder.

101F31.EPS

Figure 31 ◆ Moving up or down a ladder.

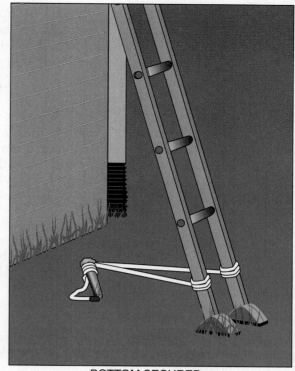

BOTTOM SECURED

TOP SECURED   101F30.EPS

Figure 30 ◆ Securing a ladder.

7.1.4 Extension Ladders

An **extension ladder** is actually two straight ladders. They are connected so you can adjust the overlap between them and change the length of the ladder as needed (see *Figure 32*).

7.1.5 Inspecting Extension Ladders

The same rules for inspecting straight ladders apply to extension ladders. In addition, you should inspect the rope that is used to raise and lower the movable section of the ladder. If the rope is frayed or has worn spots, it should be replaced before the ladder is used.

The rung locks (see *Figure 33*) support the entire weight of the movable section and the person climbing the ladder. Inspect them for damage before each use. If they are damaged, they should be repaired or replaced before the ladder is used.

7.1.6 Using Extension Ladders

Extension ladders are positioned and secured following the same rules as for straight ladders. When you adjust the length of an extension ladder, always reposition the movable section from the bottom, not the top, so you can make sure the rung locks are properly engaged after you make the adjustment. Check to make sure the section locking mechanism is fully hooked over the desired rung. Also check to make sure that all ropes used for raising and lowering the extension are clear and untangled.

RUNG LOCK

101F33.EPS

Figure 33 ◆ Rung locks.

 WARNING!
Extension ladders have a built-in extension stop mechanism. Do not remove it. This could cause the ladder to collapse under a load.

 WARNING!
Haul materials up on a line rather than hand-carrying them up an extension ladder. Use extra caution when carrying anything on a ladder, because it affects your balance.

RUNG LOCK

RUNG LOCK

SAFETY FEET

101F32.EPS

ALUMINUM   FIBERGLASS

Figure 32 ◆ Typical extension ladders.

Never stand above the highest safe standing level on a ladder. The highest safe standing level on an extension ladder is the fourth rung from the top. If you stand higher, you may lose your balance and fall. Some ladders have colored rungs to show where you should not stand.

7.1.7 Stepladders

Stepladders are self-supporting ladders made of two sections hinged at the top (see *Figure 34*).

The section of a stepladder used for climbing consists of rails and rungs like those on straight ladders. The other section consists of rails and braces. Spreaders are hinged arms between the sections that keep the ladder stable and keep it from folding while in use.

7.1.8 Inspecting Stepladders

Inspect stepladders the way you inspect straight and extension ladders. Pay special attention to the hinges and spreaders to be sure they are in good repair. Also, be sure the rungs are clean. A stepladder's rungs are usually flat, so oil, grease, or dirt can build up on them and make them slippery.

7.1.9 Using Stepladders

When you position a stepladder, be sure that all four feet are on a hard, even surface. Otherwise, the ladder can rock from side to side or corner to corner when you climb it. With the ladder in position, be sure the spreaders are locked in the fully open position.

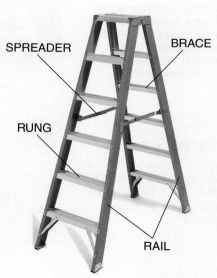

SPREADER

BRACE

RUNG

RAIL

101F34.EPS

Figure 34 ◆ Typical fiberglass stepladder.

Never stand on the top step or the top of a stepladder. Putting your weight this high will make the ladder unstable. The top of the ladder is made to support the hinges, not to be used as a step. And, although the rear braces may look like rungs, they are not designed to support your weight. Never use the braces for climbing. And never climb the back of a stepladder. (For certain jobs, however, there are specially designed two-person ladders with steps on both sides.) *Figure 35* shows common dos and don'ts for using ladders.

7.2.0 Scaffolds

Scaffolds provide safe elevated work platforms for people and materials. They are designed and built to comply with high safety standards, but normal wear and tear or accidentally putting too much weight on them can weaken them and make them unsafe. That's why it is important to inspect every part of a scaffold before each use.

 WARNING!
Never stand on a step with your knees higher than the top of a stepladder. You need to be able to hold on to the ladder with your hand. Also, keep your body centered between the side rails.

Two basic types of scaffolds—manufactured scaffolds and rolling scaffolds—are used in the construction industry. The rules for safe use apply to both of them.

7.2.1 Manufactured Scaffolds

Manufactured scaffolds are made of painted steel, stainless steel, or aluminum (see *Figure 36*). They are stronger and more fire-resistant than wooden scaffolds. They are supplied in ready-made, individual units, which are assembled on site.

7.2.2 Rolling Scaffolds

A rolling scaffold has wheels on its legs so that it can be easily moved (see *Figure 37*). The scaffold wheels have brakes so the scaffold will not move while workers are standing on it.

 CAUTION
Only a competent person has the authority to supervise setting up, moving, and taking down scaffolding. Only a competent person can approve the use of scaffolding on the job site after inspecting the scaffolding.

- Be sure your ladder has been properly set up and is used in accordance with safety instructions and warnings.
- Wear shoes with non-slip soles.

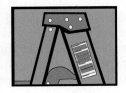

- Keep your body centered on the ladder. Hold the ladder with one hand while working with the other. Never let your belt buckle pass beyond either ladder rail.

- Move materials with extreme caution. Be careful pushing or pulling anything while on a ladder. You may lose your balance or tip the ladder.

- Get help with a ladder that is too heavy to handle alone. If possible, have another person hold the ladder when you are working on it.

- Climb facing the ladder. Center your body between the rails. Maintain a firm grip.
- Always move one step at a time, firmly setting one foot before moving the other.

- Haul materials up on a line rather than carry them up an extension ladder.
- Use extra caution when carrying anything on a ladder.

Read ladder labels for additional information.

- DON'T stand above the highest **safe standing level**.
- DON'T stand above the second step from the top of a stepladder and the 4th rung from the top of an extension ladder. A person standing higher may lose their balance and fall.

- DON'T climb a closed stepladder. It may slip out from under you.
- DON'T climb on the back of a stepladder. It is not designed to hold a person.

- DON'T stand or sit on a stepladder top or pail shelf. They are not designed to carry your weight.
- DON'T climb a ladder if you are not physically and mentally up to the task.

- DON'T exceed the Duty Rating, which is the maximum load capacity of the ladder. Do not permit more than one person on a single-sided stepladder or on any extension ladder.

- DON'T place the base of an extension ladder <u>too close</u> to the building as it may tip over backward.
- DON'T place the base of an extension ladder <u>too far away</u> from the building, as it may slip out at the bottom. **Please refer to the 4 to 1 Ratio Box.**

- DON'T over-reach, lean to one side, or try to move a ladder while on it. You could lose your balance or tip the ladder. **Climb down and then reposition the ladder closer to your work!**

---

4 TO 1 Ratio

Place an extension ladder at a 75-1/2° angle. The set-back ("S") needs to be 1 ft. for each 4 ft. of length ("L") to the upper support point.

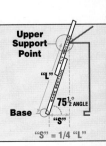

101F35.EPS

Figure 35 ◆ Ladder safety dos and don'ts.

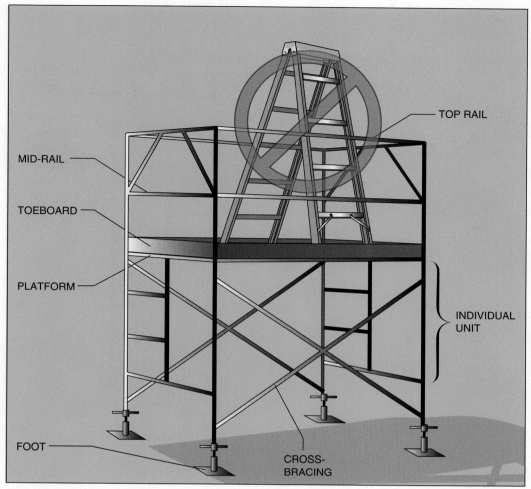

MID-RAIL

TOEBOARD

PLATFORM

FOOT

TOP RAIL

INDIVIDUAL
UNIT

CROSS-
BRACING

101F36.EPS

Figure 36 ◆ Typical manufactured scaffold.

7.2.3 Inspecting Scaffolds

Any scaffold that is assembled on the job site should be tagged. These tags indicate whether the scaffold meets OSHA standards and is safe to use. Three colors of tags are used: green, yellow, and red (see *Figure 38*).

A green tag means the scaffold meets all OSHA standards and is safe to use.

A yellow tag means the scaffold does not meet all OSHA standards. An example is a scaffold on which a railing cannot be installed because of equipment interference. To use a yellow-tagged scaffold, you must wear a safety harness attached to a lanyard. You may have to take other safety measures as well.

A red tag means a scaffold is being put up or taken down. Never use a red-tagged scaffold.

Don't rely on the tags alone. Inspect all scaffolds before you use them. Check for bent, broken, or badly rusted tubes. Check for loose joints where the tubes are connected. Any of these problems must be corrected before the scaffold is used.

Make sure you know the weight limit of any scaffold you will be using. Compare this weight limit to the total weight of the people, tools, equipment, and material you expect to put on the scaffold. Scaffold weight limits must never be exceeded.

If a scaffold is more than 10 feet high, check to see that it is equipped with **top rails, mid-rails,** and **toeboards.** All connections must be pinned. That means they must have a piece of metal inserted through a hole to prevent connections from slipping. **Cross-bracing** must be used. A handrail is not the same as cross-bracing. The working area must be completely **planked.**

If it is possible for people to walk under a scaffold, the space between the toeboard and the top rail must be screened. This prevents objects from falling off the work platform and injuring those below.

When you examine a rolling scaffold, check the condition of the wheels and brakes. Be sure the brakes are working properly and can stop the scaffold from moving while work is in progress. Be sure all brakes are locked before you use the scaffold.

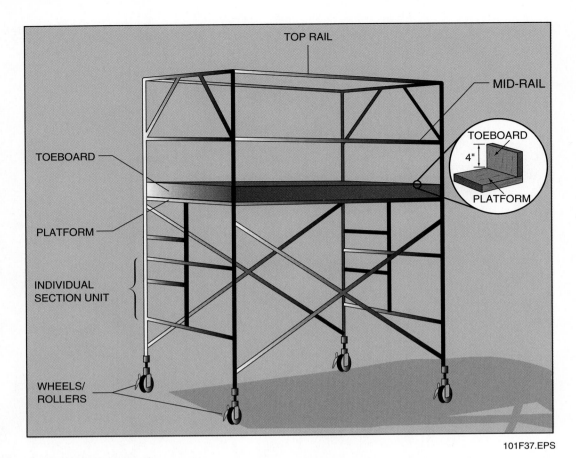

Figure 37 ◆ Typical rolling scaffold.

101F37.EPS

COMPLETE

ERECTED FOR _____
DATE _____
COMPLETE
HANDRAILS _____
TOEBOARDS _____
DECK _____
LADDER _____
LIFE LINE _____
SCAFFOLD OVER _____
LOCATION _____
_____
_____
_____
CHARGE # _____
ERECTION
FOREMAN _____
SIGNATURE
- - - - - - - - - - - - - -
DATE _____
LOCATION _____
SIGNATURE _____

CAUTION

ERECTED FOR _____
DATE _____
INCOMPLETE
HANDRAILS _____
TOEBOARDS _____
DECK _____
LADDER _____
LIFE LINE _____
SCAFFOLD OVER _____
REASON INCOMPLETE
_____
_____
LOCATION _____
CHARGE # _____
ERECTION
FOREMAN _____
SIGNATURE
- - - - - - - - - - - - - -
DATE _____
LOCATION _____
SIGNATURE _____

DANGER

XYZ INC.

SCAFFOLD
INCOMPLETE
TAG

DO NOT USE OR
CLIMB SCAFFOLD
UNTIL COMPLETE

DATE _____
LOCATION _____
SIGNATURE _____

101F38.EPS

Figure 38 ◆ Typical scaffold tags.

7.2.4 Using Scaffolds

Be sure that a competent person inspects the scaffold before you use it.

There should be firm footing under each leg of a scaffold before you put any weight on it. If you are working on loose or soft soil, you can put matting under the scaffold's legs or wheels.

WARNING!
Keep scaffolds a safe distance from power lines in accordance with OSHA guidelines. Refer to *OSHA 1926*.

WARNING!
Falls from scaffolding and falls from ladders each account for 17 percent of deaths among construction workers. Prevent accidents by following OSHA and company guidelines.

When you move a rolling scaffold, always follow these steps:

Step 1 Get off the scaffold.

Step 2 Unlock the wheel brakes.

Step 3 Move the scaffold.

Step 4 Re-lock the wheel brakes.

Step 5 Get back on the scaffold.

WARNING!
Never unlock the wheel brakes of a rolling scaffold while anyone is on it. People on a moving scaffold can lose their balance and fall.

Review Questions

Section 7.0.0

1. Never use a(n) _____ ladder anywhere near electrical current.
   a. fiberglass
   b. aluminum
   c. wooden
   d. straight

2. If you lean a straight ladder against the top of a 16-foot wall, the base of the ladder should be _____ feet from the base of the wall.
   a. 3
   b. 4
   c. 5
   d. 6

3. With a one-person stepladder, it is safe to _____.
   a. stand on the top step
   b. climb the back of it
   c. stand on the rear braces
   d. lock the spreaders in the fully open position

4. Never use a scaffold with a(n) _____ tag.
   a. blue
   b. red
   c. orange
   d. yellow

5. A scaffold must be equipped with top rails, mid-rails, and toeboards if it is more than _____ feet high.
   a. 5
   b. 7
   c. 10
   d. 12

8.0.0 ◆ HAZARD COMMUNICATION STANDARD

OSHA has a rule that affects every worker in the construction industry. It is called the **Hazard Communication Standard (HazCom)**. You may have heard it called the "Right to Know" requirement. It requires all contractors to educate their employees about the hazardous chemicals they may be exposed to on the job site. Employees must be taught how to work safely around these materials.

Many people think that there are very few hazardous chemicals on construction job sites. That isn't true. In the OSHA standard, the term hazardous chemical applies to paint, concrete, and even wood dust, as well as other substances.

8.1.0 Material Safety Data Sheets

A material safety data sheet (MSDS) must accompany every shipment of a hazardous substance and must be available to you on the job site. Use the MSDS to manage, use, and dispose of hazardous materials safely. *Figure 39* shows part of a typical MSDS.

The information on an MSDS includes the following:

- The identity of the substance
- Exposure limits
- Physical and chemical characteristics of the substance

- The kind of hazard the substance presents
- Precautions for safe handling and use
- The reactivity of the substance
- Specific control measures
- Emergency first-aid procedures
- Manufacturer contact for more information

8.2.0 Your Responsibilities Under HazCom

You have the following responsibilities under HazCom:

- Know where MSDSs are on your job site.
- Report any hazards you spot on the job site to your supervisor.
- Know the physical and health hazards of any hazardous materials on your job site, and know and practice the precautions needed to protect yourself from these hazards.
- Know what to do in an emergency.
- Know the location and content of your employer's written hazard communication program.

The final responsibility for your safety rests with you. Your employer must provide you with information about hazards, but you must know this information and follow safety rules.

Material Safety Data Sheet
May be used to comply with OSHA's Hazard Communication Standard, 29 CFR 1910 1200. Standard must be consulted for specific requirements.

U.S. Department of Labor
Occupational Safety and Health Administration
(Non-Mandatory Form)
Form Approved
OMB No. 1218-0072

IDENTITY (as Used on Label and List)	Note: Blank spaces are not permitted. If any item is not applicable or no information is available, the space must be marked to indicate that.

Section I

Manufacturer's name	Emergency Telephone Number
Address (Number, Street, City, State and ZIP Code)	Telephone Number for Information
	Date Prepared
	Signature of Preparer (optional)

Section II—Hazardous Ingredients/Identity Information

Hazardous Components (Specific Chemical Identity, Common Name(s))	OSHA PEL	ACGIH TLV	Other Limits Recommended	% (optional)

Section III—Physical/Chemical Characteristics

Boiling Point		Specific Gravity (H_2O = 1)	
Vapor Pressure (mm Hg)		Melting Point	
Vapor Density (AIR = 1)		Evaporation Rate (Butyl Acetate = 1)	
Solubility in Water			
Appearance and Odor			

Section IV—Fire and Explosion Hazard Data

Flash Point (Method Used)	Flammable Limits	LEL	UEL
Extinguishing Media			
Special Fire Fighting Procedures			
Unusual Fire and Explosion Hazards			

(Reproduce locally)

OSHA 174 Sept. 1985

101F39A.EPS

Figure 39 ◆ Typical MSDS. (1 of 2)

Section V—Reactivity Data

Stability	Unstable		Conditions to Avoid
	Stable		

Incompatibility (Materials to Avoid)

Hazardous Decomposition or Byproducts

Hazardous Polymerization	May Occur		Conditions to Avoid
	Will Not Occur		

Section VI—Health Hazard Data

Route(s) of Entry	Inhalation?	Skin?	Ingestion?

Health Hazards (Acute and Chronic)

Carcinogenicity	NTP?	IARC Monographs?	OSHA Regulated?

Signs and Symptoms of Exposure

Medical Conditions
Generally Aggravated by Exposure

Emergency and First Aid Procedures

Section VII—Precautions for Safe Handling and Use

Steps to Be Taken in Case Material Is Released or Spilled

Waste Disposal Method

Precautions to Be Taken in Handling and Storing

Other Precautions

Section VII—Control Measures

Respiratory Protection (Specify Type)

Ventilation	Local Exhaust		Special
	Mechanical (General)		Other

Protective Gloves	Eye Protection

Other Protective Clothing or Equipment

Work/Hygienic Practices

Figure 39 ◆ Typical MSDS. (2 of 2)

Section 8.0.0

1. OSHA's Hazard Communication Standard (HazCom) rule requires all contractors to _____ on-site hazardous chemicals.

   a. store
   b. clean up
   c. remove all
   d. educate employees about

2. HazCom classifies all paint, concrete, and wood dust as _____ materials.

   a. hazardous
   b. common
   c. inexpensive
   d. nonhazardous

3. The information on an MSDS includes _____.

   a. cost and availability
   b. emergency first-aid procedures
   c. point of origin
   d. warranty limitations

4. Under HazCom, if you spot a hazard on your job site you must _____.

   a. report it to your supervisor
   b. leave immediately
   c. notify your co-workers
   d. clean it up

5. Although your employer must provide you with information about hazardous chemicals, the final responsibility for your safety rests with _____.

   a. your immediate supervisor
   b. your site foreman
   c. you
   d. your co-workers

9.0.0 ◆ FIRE SAFETY

Fire is always a hazard on construction job sites. Many of the materials used in construction are flammable. In addition, welding, grinding, and many other construction activities create heat or sparks that can cause a fire. Fire safety involves two elements: fire prevention and fire fighting.

9.1.0 How Fires Start

For a fire to start, three things are needed in the same place at the same time: fuel, heat, and oxygen. If one of these three is missing, a fire will not start.

Fuel is anything that will combine with oxygen and heat to burn. Oxygen is always present in the air. When pure oxygen is present, such as near a leaking oxygen hose or fitting, material that would not normally be considered fuel (including some metals) will burn.

Heat is anything that will raise a fuel's temperature to the flash point. The flash point is the temperature at which a fuel gives off enough gases (vapors) to burn. The flash points of many fuels are quite low—room temperature or less. When the burning gases raise the temperature of a fuel to the point at which it ignites, the fuel itself will burn—and keep burning—even if the original source of heat is removed.

What is needed for a fire to start can be shown as a fire triangle (see *Figure 40*). If one element of the triangle is missing, a fire cannot start. If a fire has started, removing any one element from the triangle will put it out.

Research has added a fourth side to the fire triangle concept, resulting in the development of a new model called the Fire Tetrahedron. The fourth element involved in the combustion process is referred to as the "chemical chain reaction." Specific chemical chain reactions between fuel and oxygen molecules are essential to sustaining a fire once it has begun.

9.2.0 Fire Prevention

The best way to ensure fire safety is to prevent a fire from starting. The best way to prevent a fire is to make sure that fuel, oxygen, and heat are never present in the same place at the same time.

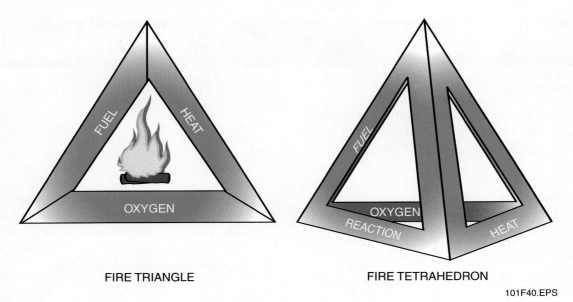

FIRE TRIANGLE   FIRE TETRAHEDRON

101F40.EPS

Figure 40 ◆ Basic fire requirements.

Here are some basic safety guidelines for fire prevention:

- Always work in a well-ventilated area, especially when you are using flammable materials such as shellac, lacquer, paint stripper, or construction adhesives.
- Never smoke or light matches when you are working with or near flammable materials.
- Keep oily rags in approved, self-closing metal containers.
- Store combustible materials only in approved containers.

9.2.1 Flammable and Combustible Liquids

Liquids can be flammable or combustible. Flammable liquids have a flash point below 100°F.

Combustible liquids have a flash point at or abov[e] 100°F. Fire can be prevented by doing the follow[-]ing things:

- *Removing the fuel* – Liquid does not burn. Wha[t] burns are the gases (vapors) given off as the liq[-]uid evaporates. Keeping liquids in an approved sealed container prevents evaporation. If ther[e] is no evaporation, there is no fuel to burn.
- *Removing the heat* – If the liquid is stored or use[d] away from a heat source, it will not be able to ig[-]nite.
- *Removing the oxygen* – The vapor from a liqui[d] will not burn if oxygen is not present. Keepin[g] safety containers tightly sealed prevents oxy[-]gen from coming into contact with the fuel.

Prevention and Preparation Are the Keys to Fire Safety

Any fire in the workplace can cause serious injury or property damage. When chemicals are involved, the risks are even greater. Prevention is the key to eliminating the hazards of fire where you work. Preparation is the key to controlling any fires that do start. Take the following precautions to make sure you are safe from fire in your workplace:

- Keep work areas clean and clutter-free.
- Know how to handle and store chemicals.
- Know what you are expected to do in case of a fire emergency.
- Call for professional help immediately. Don't let a fire get out of control.
- Know what chemicals you work with. You might have to tell firefighters at a chemical fire what kinds of hazardous substances are involved.
- Make sure you are familiar with your company's emergency action plan for fires.
- Use caution when using power tools near flammable substances.

9.2.2 Flammable Gases

Flammable gases used on construction sites include acetylene, hydrogen, ethane, and propane (liquid propane gas, or LPG). To save space, these gases are compressed so that a large amount is stored in a small cylinder or bottle. As long as the gas is kept in the cylinder, oxygen cannot get to it and start a fire. The cylinders should be stored away from sources of heat.

If oxygen is allowed to escape and mix with a flammable gas, the resulting mixture will explode under certain conditions.

> **WARNING!**
>
> Never use grease or oil on the fittings of oxygen bottles and hoses. Never allow greasy or oily rags to come near any part of an oxygen system. Oil and pressurized oxygen form a very dangerous mixture that can ignite at low temperatures.

9.2.3 Ordinary Combustibles

The term ordinary combustibles means paper, wood, cloth, and similar fuels. The easiest way to prevent fire in ordinary combustibles is to keep a neat, clean work area. If there are no scraps of pa-per, cloth, or wood lying around, there will be no fuel for starting a fire. So establish and maintain good housekeeping habits. Use approved storage cabinets and containers for all waste and other ordinary combustibles.

9.3.0 Firefighting

You are not expected to be an expert firefighter. But you may have to deal with a fire to protect your safety and the safety of others. You need to know the locations of firefighting equipment on your job site. You also need to know which equipment to use on different types of fires. However, only qualified personnel are authorized to fight fires.

Most companies tell new employees where fire extinguishers are kept. If you have not been told, be sure to ask. Also ask how to report fires. The telephone number of the nearest fire department should be clearly posted in your work area. If your company has a company fire brigade, learn how to contact them. Learn your company's fire safety procedures. Know what kind of extinguisher to use for different kinds of fires and how to use them. Make sure all extinguishers are fully charged. Never remove the tag from an extinguisher—it shows the date the extinguisher was last serviced and inspected (see *Figure 41*).

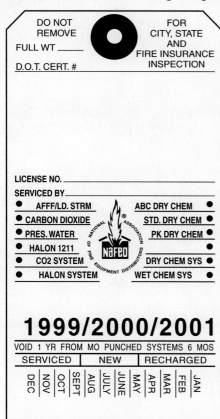

101F41.EPS

Figure 41 ◆ Fire extinguisher tag.

9.3.1 Classes of Fires

Four classes of fuels can be involved in fires (see *Table 5*). You've already learned about liquids, gases, and ordinary combustibles. Another fuel is metal. (You will learn about preventing electrical fires in another module.) Each class of fuel requires a different method of firefighting and a different type of extinguisher.

The label on a fire extinguisher clearly shows the class of fire on which it can be used (see *Figure 42*).

When you check the extinguishers in you work area, you will see that some are rated fo more than one class of fire. You can use an extin guisher that has the three codes A, B, and C on i to fight a class A, B, or C fire. But remember, if th extinguisher has only one code letter, do not use i on any other class of fire, even in an emergency You could make the fire worse and put yourself i great danger.

Table 5	Classes of Fires
Class	**Materials and Proper Fire Extinguisher**
Class A fires 101SA02A.EPS 101SA02B.EPS	These fires involve ordinary combustibles such as wood or paper. Class A fires are fought by cooling the fuel. Class A fire extinguishers contain water. Using a Class A extinguisher on any other type of fire can be very dangerous.
Class B fires 101SA02C.EPS 101SA02D.EPS	These fires involve grease, liquids, or gases. Class B extinguishers contain carbon dioxide (CO_2) or another material that smothers fires by removing oxygen from the fire.
Class C fires 101SA02E.EPS 101SA02F.EPS	These fires are near or involve energized electrical equipment. Class C extinguishers are designed to protect the firefighter from electrical shock. Class C extinguishers smother fires.
Class D fires 101SA02G.EPS	These fires involve metals. Class D extinguishers contain a powder that either forms a crust around the burning metal or gives off gases that prevent oxygen from reaching the fire. Some metals will keep burning even though they have been coated with powder from a Class D extinguisher. The best way to fight these fires is to keep using the extinguisher so the fire will not spread to other fuels.

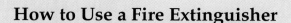

ON-SITE

How to Use a Fire Extinguisher

Step 1 Hold the extinguisher upright.

Step 2 Pull the pin, breaking the plastic seal.

Step 3 Stand back 8 to 10 feet from the fire. Standing any closer may cause burning objects to scatter, spreading the fire.

Step 4 Aim at the base of the fire.

Step 5 Keep the extinguisher upright. Squeeze the handles together to discharge. Sweep from side to side.

Step 6 Move closer as the fire is extinguished (watch for scattering burning material).

Step 7 When the fire is out, watch for reignition.

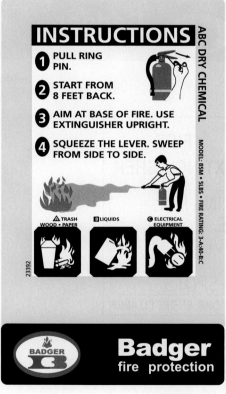

101F42A.EPS

(A)

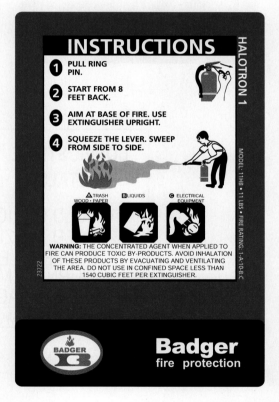

101F42B.EPS

(B)

Figure 42 ◆ Typical fire extinguisher labels. (1 of 2)

(C)   101F42C.EPS

(D)   101F42D.EPS

COMBUSTIBLE METALS   **D**   **FIRE EXTINGUISHER**

1. HOLD UPRIGHT - PULL RING PIN.
2. HOLD NOZZLE OVER FIRE.
3. SQUEEZE LEVER AND COVER ALL BURNING METAL
4. REAPPLY AGENT TO HOT SPOTS.

CAUTION: FIRE MAY RE-IGNITE, ALLOW METAL TO COOL BEFORE CLEANUP.

101F42E.EPS

(E)

Figure 42 ◆ Typical fire extinguisher labels. (2 of 2)

Section 9.0.0

1. _____ must be present in the same place at the same time for a fire to occur.

   a. Oxygen, carbon dioxide, and heat
   b. Oxygen, heat, and fuel
   c. Hydrogen, oxygen, and wood
   d. Grease, liquid, and heat

2. _____ gas is flammable.

   a. Acetylene
   b. Carbon dioxide
   c. Peroxide
   d. Neon

3. A Class D fire involves _____.

   a. grease
   b. wood
   c. electrical equipment
   d. metal

4. Fire extinguishers that contain water for fighting fires involving ordinary combustibles are _____ extinguishers.

   a. Class A
   b. Class B
   c. Class C
   d. Class D

5. For a grease fire, use a _____ extinguisher.

   a. Class A
   b. Class B
   c. Class C
   d. Class D

10.0.0 ◆ ELECTRICAL SAFETY

Some construction workers think that electrical safety matters only to electricians. But on many jobs, no matter what your trade, you will use or work around electrical equipment. Extension cords, power tools, portable lights, and many other pieces of equipment use electricity. If you don't use this equipment safely and properly, the result could be death for you or a co-worker.

Electricity can be described as the flow of electrons through a conductor. This flow of electrons is called electrical current. Some materials—such as silver, copper, steel, and aluminum—are excellent conductors. This means that electrical current flows easily through them. The human body, especially when it is wet, is also a good conductor.

To create an electrical current, a path must be provided in a circular route, or a circuit. If the circuit is interrupted, the electrical current will complete its circular route by flowing along the path of least resistance. This means that it will flow into and through any conductor that is touching it. If it cannot complete its circuit, the electrical current will go to ground. This means that it will find the path of least resistance that allows it to flow as directly as possible into the earth. All of this takes place almost instantly.

If the human body comes in contact with an electrically energized conductor and is in contact with the ground at the same time, the human body becomes the path of least resistance for the electricity. This means the electricity flows through the body in less than the blink of an eye. You can't see that it's about to happen; it just happens. That's why safety precautions are so important when working with and around electrical currents. When a person's body conducts electrical current and the amount of that current is high enough, the person can be electrocuted (killed by electric shock). *Table 6* shows the effects of different amounts of electrical current on the human body and lists some common tools that operate using those currents.

NOTE

Electric shocks or burns are a major cause of accidents in the construction industry. According to the Bureau of Labor Statistics, electrocution is the fourth leading cause of death among construction workers.

WARNING!

All work on electrical equipment should be done with circuits de-energized and cleared or grounded. All conductors, buses, and connections should be considered energized unless proven otherwise.

Table 6   Effects of Electrical Current on the Human Body

Current	Common Item/Tool	Reaction to Current
0.001 amps	Watch battery	Faint tingle
0.005 amps	9-volt battery	Slight shock
0.006–0.025 amps (women)	Christmas tree light bulb	Painful shock. Muscular control is lost.
0.009–0.030 amps (men)		
0.050–0.9 amps	Small electric radio	Extreme pain. Breathing stops; severe muscular contractions occur. Death may result.
1.0–9.9 amps	Jigsaw (4 amps); Sawsall® or Port-a-Band® saw (6 amps); portable drill (3–8 amps)	Ventricular fibrillation and nerve damage occur. Death may result.
10 amps and above	ShopVac® (15-gallon); circular saw	Heart stops beating; severe burns occur. Death may result.

WARNING!
Less than 1 amp of electrical current can kill. Always take precautions when working around electricity.

Here's an example. A craftsperson is operating a portable power drill while standing on damp ground. The power cord inside the drill has become frayed, and the electric wire inside the cord touches the metal drill frame. Three amps of current pass from the wire through the frame, then through the craftsperson's body and into the ground. *Table 6* shows that this craftsperson will probably die.

A good method of protection from accidental electrocution is the use of a ground fault circuit interrupter (GFCI). The GFCI is a fast-acting circuit breaker that senses small (as little as approximately 5 milliamps) imbalances in the circuit caused by current leakage to ground. In as little as 1/40 of a second, the GFCI will interrupt the power.

Not all electrical accidents result in death. There are different types of electrical accidents. Any of the following can happen:

- Burns
- Electric shock
- Explosions
- Falls caused by electric shock
- Fires

10.1.0 Basic Electrical Safety Guidelines

OSHA and your company have specific policies and procedures to keep the workplace safe from electrical hazards. You can do many things to reduce the chance of an electrical accident. If you ever have any questions about electrical safety on the job site, ask your supervisor. Here are the basic job-site electrical safety guidelines:

- Use three-wire extension cords and protect them from damage. Never fasten them with staples, hang them from nails, or suspend them from wires. Never use damaged cords.
- Make sure that panels, switches, outlets, and plugs are grounded.
- Never use bare electrical wire.
- Never use metal ladders near any source of electricity.
- Never wear a metal hard hat.
- Always inspect electrical power tools before you use them.
- Never operate any piece of electrical equipment that has a danger tag or lockout device attached to it.
- Use three-wire cords for portable power tools and make sure they are properly connected (see *Figure 43*). The three-wire system is one of the most common safety grounding systems used to protect you from accidental electrical shock. The third wire is connected to a ground. If the insulation in a tool fails, the current will pass to ground through the third wire—not through your body.

NOTE
It is becoming more common to use double-insulated tools because they are safer than relying on a three-wire cord alone.

- Never use worn or frayed cables (see *Figure 44*).
- Make sure all light bulbs have protective guards to prevent accidental contact (see *Figure 45*).

Electrical Cord Safety

Electrical cords are frequently seen on construction sites, yet they are often overlooked. Use the following safety guidelines to ensure your safety and the safety of other workers.

- Every electrical cord should have an Underwriters Laboratory (UL) label attached to it. Check the UL label for specific wattage. Do not plug more than the specified number of watts into an electrical cord.
- A cord set not marked for outdoor use is to be used indoors only. Check the UL label on the cord for an outdoor marking.
- Do not remove, bend, or modify any metal prongs or pins of an electrical cord.
- Extension cords used with portable tools and equipment must be three-wire type and designated for hard or extra-hard use. Check the UL label for the cord's use designation.
- Avoid overheating an electrical cord. Make sure the cord is uncoiled, and that it does not run under any covering materials, such as tarps, insulation rolls, or lumber.
- Do not run a cord through doorways or through holes in ceilings, walls, and floors, which might pinch the cord. Also, check to see that there are no sharp corners along the cord's path. Any of these situations will lead to cord damage.
- Extension cords are a tripping hazard. They should never be left unattended and should always be put away when not in use.

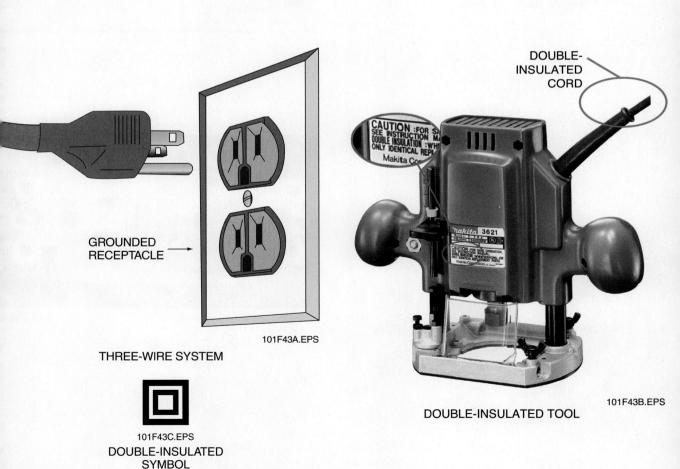

THREE-WIRE SYSTEM

GROUNDED RECEPTACLE

101F43A.EPS

DOUBLE-INSULATED CORD

DOUBLE-INSULATED TOOL

101F43B.EPS

101F43C.EPS

DOUBLE-INSULATED SYMBOL

Figure 43 ◆ Three-wire system and double-insulated tool.

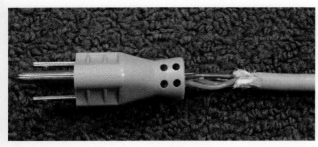

101F44A.EPS

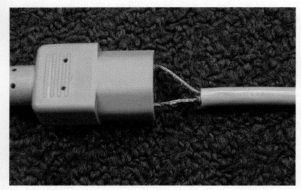

101F44B.EPS

Figure 44 ◆ Never use damaged cords.

- Do not hang temporary lights by their powe
  cords unless they are specifically designed fo
  this use.
- Check the cable and ground prong. Check fo
  cuts in the cords and make sure the cords are
  clean of grease.
- Use only approved **concealed receptacles** fo
  plugs. If different voltages or types of curren
  are used in the same area, the receptacle
  should be designed so that the plugs are not in
  terchangeable.
- Any repairs to cords must be performed by a
  qualified person.
- Use a GFCI (see *Figure 46*) or an assured
  grounding program with every tool.
- Always make sure all tools are grounded before
  use.

CAUTION

All tools used in construction must be ground-fault protected. This helps ensure the safety of workers.

101F45.EPS

Figure 45 ◆ Work light with protective guard.

101F46A.EPS

Figure 46 ◆ GFCI.

10.2.0 Working Near Energized Electrical Equipment

No matter what your trade, your job may include working near exposed electrical equipment or conductors. This is one example of proximity work. Often, **electrical distribution panels**, **switch enclosures**, and other equipment must be left open during construction. This leaves the wires and components in them exposed. Some or all of the wires and components may be energized. Working near exposed electrical equipment can be safe, but only if you keep a safe working distance.

Regulations and company policies tell you the minimum safe working distances from exposed conductors. The safe working distance ranges from a few inches to several feet, depending on the voltage. The higher the voltage, the greater the safe working distance.

You must learn the safe working distance for each situation. Make sure you never get any part of your body or any tool you are using closer to exposed conductors than that distance. You can get information on safe working distances from your instructor, your supervisor, company safety policies, and regulatory documents.

10.3.0 If Someone Is Shocked

If you are there when someone gets an electrical shock, you can save a life by taking immediate action. Here's what to do:

Step 1 Immediately disconnect the circuit.

Step 2 If you can't disconnect the circuit, do not try to separate the victim from the circuit. If you touch a person who is being electrocuted, the current will flow through you, too.

WARNING!

Do not touch the victim or the electrical source with your hand, foot, or any other part of your body or with any object or material. You could become another victim.

Step 3 Once the circuit is disconnected, give first aid and call an ambulance. If you cannot disconnect the circuit, call an ambulance.

Assured Equipment Grounding Program

An assured equipment grounding program is an alternative to GCFIs. It covers all cord sets, receptacles that are not a part of the permanent wiring of the building or structure, and equipment connected by cord and plug that are available for use or used by employees. The requirements that the program must meet are stated in OSHA's *29 CFR 1926.404*, but employers may provide additional tests or procedures.

OSHA requires two tests. One is a continuity test to ensure that the equipment grounding conductor is electrically continuous. It must be performed on all cord sets, receptacles that are not part of the permanent wiring of the building or structure, and cord- and plug-connected equipment that is required to be grounded. This test may be performed using a simple continuity tester, such as a lamp and battery, a bell and battery, an ohmmeter, or a receptacle tester.

The other test must be performed on receptacles and plugs to ensure that the equipment grounding conductor is connected to its proper terminal. This test can be performed with the same equipment used in the first test.

These tests are required before first use, after any repairs, after damage is suspected to have occurred, and at three-month intervals. Cord sets and receptacles that are essentially fixed and not exposed to damage must be tested at regular intervals of no longer than six months. Any equipment that fails to pass the required tests must not be made available to or used by employees.

Section 10.0.0

1. Observing proper safety precautions when working with and around electrical current is important because the human body _____.

   a. resists the electricity's path
   b. can conduct electrical current
   c. won't conduct electricity
   d. doesn't offer electricity a circular route

2. The _____ system is one of the most common safety grounding systems used with portable power tools.

   a. distribution wire
   b. rubber cord
   c. three-wire cord
   d. insulation plug

3. The minimum safe working distance from exposed electrical conductors _____.

   a. depends on the voltage
   b. is at least 1 foot
   c. is a few inches
   d. is unlimited

4. If someone is being electrically shocked, the first thing you should try to do is _____.

   a. use a metal pole to separate the victim from the circuit
   b. disconnect the circuit
   c. give first aid
   d. call your supervisor

5. If someone is being electrically shocked and you cannot disconnect the circuit, the first thing you should do is _____.

   a. call an ambulance
   b. give first aid
   c. pull the victim away with your hands
   d. use a pole to separate the victim from the circuit

Summary

Although the typical construction site has many hazards, it does not have to be a dangerous place to work. Your employer has programs to deal with potential hazards. Basic rules and regulations help protect you and your co-workers from unnecessary risks.

This module has presented many of the basic guidelines you must follow to ensure your safety and the safety of your co-workers. These guidelines fall into the following categories:

- Following safe work practices and procedures
- Inspecting safety equipment before use
- Using safety equipment properly

The basic approach to safety is to eliminate hazards in the equipment and the workplace; to learn the rules and procedures for working safely with and around the remaining hazards; and to apply those rules and procedures. The information covered here offers you the groundwork for a safe, productive, and rewarding construction career.

Notes

Key Terms Quiz

Fill in the blank with the correct key term that you learned from your study of this module.

1. _____ is a formal procedure for taking equipment out of service and ensuring it cannot be operated until a qualified person has returned it to service.

2. _____ is the process of joining metal parts by fusion.

3. Because _____ scrap materials catch fire and burn easily, remove them regularly from the work area.

4. The cutting process results in oxides that mix with molten iron and produce _____.

5. A(n) _____ is any man-made cut, cavity, trench, or depression in an earth surface, formed by removing earth.

6. A(n) _____ identifies unsanitary, hazardous, or dangerous working conditions and has the authority to correct or eliminate them.

7. A(n) _____ is large enough to work in but has limited means of entry or exit; sometimes a permit is required to work in it.

8. Store _____ liquids in safety cans to avoid the risk of fire.

9. If a scaffold is more than 10 feet high, _____—or pieces of wood or metal placed diagonally from the bottom of one rail to the top of another rail that add support to a structure—must be used.

10. The _____ houses the circuits that distribute electricity throughout a structure.

11. A(n) _____ is basically two straight ladders that are connected so the length of the ladder can be changed.

12. Wear _____ to protect your eyes from the _____, which is the sudden, bright light that occurs when you start up a welding operation.

13. To save lives, prevent injuries, and protect the health of America's workers, _____ publishes rules and regulations that employees and employers must follow.

14. If fuel is improperly mixed, it can cause a(n) _____.

15. An opening in a wall or floor is a safety hazard and must be either covered or _____.

16. Even a brief exposure to the ultraviolet light from arc welding can damage your eyes, causing a(n) _____.

17. _____ is an OSHA rule requiring all contractors to educate their employees about the hazardous chemicals they may be exposed to on the job site.

18. The temperature at which a fuel gives off enough gases to burn is called the _____

19. A(n) _____ is the conducting connection between electrical equipment or an electrical circuit and the earth.

20. When climbing a ladder or scaffold, use a tagline or _____ to pull up your tools.

21. SCBA is an example of a(n) _____ , or an assembly of machines used to do a particular job.

22. If a work area is _____ , that means it has pieces of material at least 2 inches thick and 6 inches wide used as flooring, decking, or scaffolding.

23. When doing work more than 6 feet above the ground, you must wear a safety harness with a(n) _____ that is attached to a strong anchor point.

24. A good _____ helps prevent or correct conditions that can cause accidents.

25. To prevent a cave-in, follow OSHA regulations for _____ up a trench.

26. Refer to the _____ to learn about how to handle hazardous substances.

27. Overloading, which means exceeding the _____ of a ladder, can cause ladder failure.

8. If you are operating a vehicle on a job site and cannot see to your rear, get a(n) _____ to direct you.

9. Before working in a(n) _____, you must be trained, obtain written authorization, and take the necessary precautions.

0. A(n) _____ is a narrow excavation made below the surface of the ground that is generally deeper than it is wide.

1. The _____ on a scaffold is placed halfway between the toeboard and the top rail.

2. _____ for welding includes a faceshield, ear plugs, and gloves.

3. A(n) _____ has proven his or her extensive knowledge, training, and experience and has successfully demonstrated the ability to solve problems relating to the work.

4. A(n) _____ provides clean air for breathing.

5. Manufactured and rolling are the two basic types of _____.

6. When doing _____ , you must be careful not to come into contact with the nearby hazard.

7. A(n) _____ is a self-supporting ladder made of two sections hinged at the top.

38. Use only approved _____ for plugs.

39. A(n) _____ is nonadjustable and consists of two rails, rungs between the rails, and safety feet on the bottom of the rails.

40. A vertical barrier called a(n) _____ is used at floor level on scaffolds to prevent materials from falling.

41. A(n) _____ tells you which way the wind is blowing.

42. A horizontal board called a(n) _____ is used at top-level on all open sides of scaffolding and platforms.

43. Never look at the _____ caused by welding without proper eye protection.

44. An excavating machine called a(n) _____ is used to dig trenches, especially for pipeline and cables.

45. When you are welding and other workers are in the area, set up a protective screen called a(n) _____.

46. A(n) _____ houses electrical switches used to regulate and distribute electricity in a building.

47. _____ is the waste material from welding operations.

Key Terms

Apparatus	Flash	Material safety data sheet (MSDS)	Respirator
Arc	Flashback	Maximum intended load	Scaffold
Arc welding	Flash burn	Mid-rail	Shoring
Combustible	Flash goggles	Occupational Safety and Health Administration (OSHA)	Signaler
Competent person	Flash point		Slag
Concealed receptacle	Ground		Stepladder
Confined space	Guarded	Permit-required confined space	Straight ladder
Cross-bracing	Hand line		Switch enclosure
Dross	Hazard Communication Standard (HazCom)	Personal protective equipment (PPE)	Toeboard
Electrical distribution panel	Lanyard		Top rail
Excavation	Lockout/tagout	Planked	Trench
Extension ladder	Management system	Proximity work	Trencher
Flammable		Qualified person	Welding shield
			Wind sock

Doug Garcia

Chairman, Industrial Training Department
Manatee Technical Institute
West Bradenton, Florida

Doug grew up in Fall River, Massachusetts. After completing high school, he began his career as a union construction laborer. He decided to become a welder and worked in the power plant maintenance industry before turning to shipbuilding. Doug built ships at General Dynamics and submarines at Electric Boat. He worked his way up from shipfitter to lead man, foreman, and ultimately ship superintendent, responsible for the delivery of a ship from the keel on up. Doug became a welding instructor at Diman Regional Vocational Technical High School and then Manatee Technical Institute.

Doug has a BA in vocational education from Fitchburg State College and is a U.S. Department of Labor–approved general industry and construction outreach trainer. He is also an American Welding Society (AWS)–certified welding educator and a certified welding inspector, and holds a Level 2 certification from the American Society for Nondestructive Testing.

What aspect of the construction industry appeals to you most?
What I like the most is the personal satisfaction of seeing the finished product. When you look at a completed project, you are really seeing the result of a collaborative effort between a broad spectrum of trades. In the finished product, you can see how they all come together to make a whole.

How did you decide to become an educator?
Over the course of my career, I have really come to appreciate and understand the need for safety training. It bothers me most to see a great career cut short by a needless accident. Safety is one of the most important concerns in the construction industry. As a whole, the industry gives safety the attention it needs, but ultimately the responsibility still falls on the individual. No matter how good a safety program is, it is only as good as the person who's applying it. The company can only do so much; the employee has to finish the job. So I wanted to help people understand and apply safety on the job.

What do you think it takes to be a success in your trade?
I think that it takes a solid work ethic and pride in one's craftsmanship. You must also feel, or want to feel, a sense of satisfaction from seeing a completed project.

What are some of the things you do in your job?
I have a staff of 17 teachers, 2 of whom are approved construction safety instructors and 2 of whom are general industrial safety instructors. I review the existing curriculum and undertake curriculum development tasks. I try to ensure that the curriculum meets the needs of industry and that we remain current with the changes in construction technology and materials. I assist with job placement and maintain contact with area employers. We provide on site training for local area employers and help them to develop and implement procedures that are required by the U.S. Occupational Safety and Health Administration (OSHA).

I teach safety instruction to all students in both the construction and general industry tracks at Manatee. I'm also a mentor for new vocational teachers. And I also coordinate the purchase of equipment and supplies. It's a full-time job, and then some!

What do you like most about your job?
I really enjoy seeing former students become successful. Many of them return to the program to serve on advisory committees. They come back to advise the staff and faculty on current trends in their craft area, and they get to make recommendations for the curricula and the purchase of equipment. That

way, I get to work with them as professional colleagues and not just as students.

What would you say to someone entering the trades today?
In my classes I stress that no matter what your skill level is, if you are not doing your job safely, then you are jeopardizing all your hard work. Even the most talented individuals can't perform their jobs to the best of their ability if they have been injured or hurt.

I have personally witnessed two construction fatalities. The people most affected are usually the families. Your value as a craft worker is the ability to perform for your employer and to provide for your family. If you are injured or incapable of performing your craft, you are not only losing your earning potential and your potential for advancement, but you are also depriving the industry of a trained craft worker and reducing your family's quality of life.

So you have to ask yourself every day, "How would an accident affect my family?" When I tell my students that, it really gets them thinking. The industry has inherent dangers; there's no need for a careless worker to add to them.

Trade Terms
Introduced in This Module

Apparatus: An assembly of machines used together to do a particular job.

Arc: The flow of electrical current through a gas such as air from one pole to another pole.

Arc welding: The joining of metal parts by fusion, in which the necessary heat is produced by means of an electric arc.

Combustible: Capable of easily igniting and rapidly burning; used to describe a fuel with a flash point at or above 100°F.

Competent person: A person who can identify working conditions or surroundings that are unsanitary, hazardous, or dangerous to employees and who has authorization to correct or eliminate these conditions promptly.

Concealed receptacle: The electrical outlet that is placed inside the structural elements of a building, such as inside the walls. The face of the receptacle is flush with the finished wall surface and covered with a plate.

Confined space: A work area large enough for a person to work, but arranged in such a way that an employee must physically enter the space to perform work. A confined space has a limited or restricted means of entry and exit. It is not designed for continuous work. Tanks, vessels, silos, pits, vaults, and hoppers are examples of confined spaces. See also *permit-required confined space.*

Cross-bracing: Braces (metal or wood) placed diagonally from the bottom of one rail to the top of another rail that add support to a structure.

Dross: Waste material resulting from cutting using a thermal process.

Electrical distribution panel: Part of the electrical distribution system that brings electricity from the street source (power poles and transformers) through the service lines to the electrical meter mounted on the outside of the building and to the panel inside the building. The panel houses the circuits that distribute electricity throughout the structure.

Excavation: Any man-made cut, cavity, trench, or depression in an earth surface, formed by removing earth. It can be made for anything from basements to highways. See also *trench.*

Extension ladder: A ladder made of two straight ladders that are connected so that the overall length can be adjusted.

Flammable: Capable of easily igniting and rapidly burning; used to describe a fuel with a flash point below 100°F.

Flash: A sudden bright light associated with starting up a welding torch.

Flashback: A welding flame that flares up and chars the hose at or near the torch connection. It is caused by improperly mixed fuel.

Flash burn: The damage that can be done to eyes after even brief exposure to ultraviolet light from arc welding. A flash burn requires medical attention.

Flash goggles: Eye protective equipment worn during welding operations.

Flash point: The temperature at which fuel gives off enough gases (vapors) to burn.

Ground: The conducting connection between electrical equipment or an electrical circuit and the earth.

Guarded: Enclosed, fenced, covered, or otherwise protected by barriers, rails, covers, or platforms to prevent dangerous contact.

Hand line: A line attached to a tool or object so a worker can pull it up after climbing a ladder or scaffold.

Hazard Communication Standard (HazCom): The Occupational Safety and Health Administration standard that requires contractors to educate employees about hazardous chemicals on the job site and how to work with them safely.

Lanyard: A short section of rope or strap, one end of which is attached to a worker's safety harness and the other to a strong anchor point above the work area.

Lockout/tagout: A formal procedure for taking equipment out of service and ensuring that it cannot be operated until a qualified person has removed the lockout or tagout device (such as a lock or warning tag).

Management system: The organization of a company's management, including reporting procedures, supervisory responsibility, and administration.

Material safety data sheet (MSDS): A document that must accompany any hazardous substance. The MSDS identifies the substance and gives the exposure limits, the physical and chemical characteristics, the kind of hazard it presents, precautions for safe handling and use, and specific control measures.

Maximum intended load: The total weight of all people, equipment, tools, materials, and loads that a ladder can hold at one time.

Mid-rail: Mid-level, horizontal board required on all open sides of scaffolding and platforms that are more than 14 inches from the face of the structure and more than 10 feet above the ground. It is placed halfway between the toe-board and the top rail.

Occupational Safety and Health Administration (OSHA): An agency of the U.S. Department of Labor. Also refers to the Occupational Safety and Health Act of 1970, a law that applies to more than more than 111 million workers and 7 million job sites in the country.

Permit-required confined space: A confined space that has been evaluated and found to have actual or potential hazards, such as a toxic atmosphere or other serious safety or health hazard. Workers need written authorization to enter a permit-required confined space. See also *confined space.*

Personal protective equipment (PPE): Equipment or clothing designed to prevent or reduce injuries.

Planked: Having pieces of material 2 or more inches thick and 6 or more inches wide used as flooring, decking, or scaffolding.

Proximity work: Work done near a hazard but not actually in contact with it.

Qualified person: A person who, by possession of a recognized degree, certificate, or professional standing, or by extensive knowledge, training, and experience, has demonstrated the ability to solve or prevent problems relating to a certain subject, work, or project.

Respirator: A device that provides clean, filtered air for breathing, no matter what is in the surrounding air.

Scaffold: An elevated platform for workers and materials.

Shoring: Using pieces of timber, usually in a diagonal position, to hold a wall in place temporarily.

Signaler: A person who is responsible for directing a vehicle when the driver's vision is blocked in any way.

Slag: Waste material from welding operations.

Stepladder: A self-supporting ladder consisting of two elements hinged at the top.

Straight ladder: A nonadjustable ladder.

Switch enclosure: A box that houses electrical switches used to regulate and distribute electricity in a building.

Toeboard: A vertical barrier at floor level attached along exposed edges of a platform, runway, or ramp to prevent materials and people from falling.

Top rail: A top-level, horizontal board required on all open sides of scaffolding and platforms that are more than 14 inches from the face of the structure and more than 10 feet above the ground.

Trench: A narrow excavation made below the surface of the ground that is generally deeper than it is wide, with a maximum width of 15 feet. See also *excavation.*

Trencher: An excavating machine used to dig trenches, especially for pipeline and cables.

Welding shield: (1) A protective screen set up around a welding operation designed to safeguard workers not directly involved in that operation. (2) A shield that provides eye and face protection for welders by either connecting to helmet-like headgear or attaching directly to a hard hat; also called a welding helmet.

Wind sock: A cloth cone open at both ends mounted in a high place to show which direction the wind is blowing.

This module is intended to present thorough resources for task training. The following reference works are suggested for further study. These are optional materials for continued education rather than for task training.

Construction Back Safety. Videocassette. 10 minutes. Coastal Training Technologies Corp. Virginia Beach, VA.

Construction Confined Space Entry. Videocassette. 10 minutes. Coastal Training Technologies Corp. Virginia Beach, VA.

Construction Electrical Safety. Videocassette. 10 minutes. Coastal Training Technologies Corp. Virginia Beach, VA.

Construction Fall Protection: Get Arrested! Videocassette. 11 minutes. Coastal Training Technologies Corp. Virginia Beach, VA.

Construction Lockout/Tagout. Videocassette. 10 minutes. Coastal Training Technologies Corp. Virginia Beach, VA.

Construction Safety, 1996. Jimmie Hinze. Englewood Cliffs, NJ: Prentice Hall.

Construction Safety Council Home Page, http://buildsafe.org/home.htm.

Construction Safety Manual, 1998. Dave Heberle. New York: McGraw-Hill.

Construction Stairways & Ladders. Videocassette. 10 minutes. Coastal Training Technologies Corp. Virginia Beach, VA.

Construction Welding Safety. Videocassette. 10 minutes. Coastal Training Technologies Corp. Virginia Beach, VA.

Field Safety, 2003. NCCER. Upper Saddle River, NJ: Prentice Hall.

Handbook of OSHA Construction Safety and Health, 1999. James V. Eidson et al. Boca Raton, FL: Lewis Publishers, Inc.

HazCom For Construction. Videocassette. 11 minutes. Coastal Training Technologies Corp. Virginia Beach, VA.

NAHB-OSHA Jobsite Safety Handbook, 1999. Washington, DC: Home Builder Press. Available online at www.osha.gov.

Occupational Safety and Health Standards for the Construction Industry. Washington, DC: Occupational Safety and Health Administration, U.S. Department of Labor, U.S. Government Printing Office.

Safety Orientation, 2003. NCCER. Upper Saddle River, NJ: Prentice Hall.

Safety Technology, 2003. NCCER. Upper Saddle River, NJ: Prentice Hall.

United States Department of Labor, Occupational Safety and Health Administration Home Page, http://www.osha.gov.

CONTREN® LEARNING SERIES — USER FEEDBACK

The NCCER makes every effort to keep these textbooks up-to-date and free of technical errors. We appreciate your help in this process. If you have an idea for improving this textbook, or if you find an error, a typographical mistake, or an inaccuracy in NCCER's *Contren®* textbooks, please write us, using this form or a photocopy. Be sure to include the exact module number, page number, a detailed description, and the correction, if applicable. Your input will be brought to the attention of the Technical Review Committee. Thank you for your assistance.

Instructors – If you found that additional materials were necessary in order to teach this module effectively, please let us know so that we may include them in the Equipment/Materials list in the Annotated Instructor's Guide.

Write: Product Development
National Center for Construction Education and Research
P.O. Box 141104, Gainesville, FL 32614-1104

Fax: 352-334-0932

E-mail: curriculum@nccer.org

Craft _____ Module Name _____

Copyright Date _____ Module Number _____ Page Number(s) _____

Description _____

_____

_____

_____

(Optional) Correction _____

_____

_____

(Optional) Your Name and Address _____

_____

_____

**Build America Winner—
Environmental**

The Genzyme Center in Cambridge, Massachusetts, was built by Turner Construction Company. This building began as a radical concept. The Center is a sustainable "living" building that will set new standards in environmental responsibility, design aesthetics, and workplace well-being. Turner Construction made the Genzyme's vision a reality, creating an office building that will serve as a prototype for sustainable construction for years to come.

00103-04
Introduction to Hand Tools

Topics to be presented in this module include:

Overview

Hand tools are the backbone of the construction trades. Hammers, wrenches, pliers, saws, shovels, and squares are just a few of the hand tools that are used every day on construction sites. Hand tools must be properly used and maintained at all times. Tools that are damaged or don't work are dangerous.

Safety is an important part of using hand tools. This means that tools must always be clean, dry, well-maintained, and used only for the job they were designed to do. Workers must be thoroughly trained in the proper use and maintenance of hand tools. This helps prevent accidents, damages, and injuries.

Take the time to learn how to properly maintain and use tools. It can make the difference between a job well done and the damage of equipment or loss of lives.

Objectives

When you have completed this module, you will be able to do the following:

1. Recognize and identify some of the basic hand tools used in the construction trade.
2. Use hand tools safely.
3. Describe the basic procedures for taking care of hand tools.

Key Trade Terms

Allen wrench	Open-end wrench
Ball peen hammer	Peening
Bell-faced hammer	Pipe wrench
Bevel	Planed
Box-end wrench	Pliers
Carpenter's square	Plumb
Cat's paw	Points
Chisel	Punch
Chisel bar	Rafter angle square
Claw hammer	Ripping bar
Combination square	Round off
Combination wrench	Spud wrench
Crescent wrench	Square
Dowel	Striking (or slugging)
Fastener	wrench
Flat bar	Strip
Flats	Tang
Foot-pounds	Tempered
Inch-pounds	Tenon
Joint	Torque
Kerf	Try square
Level	Vise
Miter joint	Weld
Nail puller	

Required Trainee Materials

1. Appropriate personal protective equipment
2. Sharpened pencils and paper

Prerequisites

Before you begin this module, it is recommended that you successfully complete the following:
Core Curriculum: Introductory Craft Skills, Modules 00101-04 and 00102-04.

This course map shows all of the modules in Core Curriculum: Introductory Craft Skills. The suggested training order begins at the bottom and proceeds up. Skill levels increase as you advance on the course map. The local Training Program Sponsor may adjust the training order.

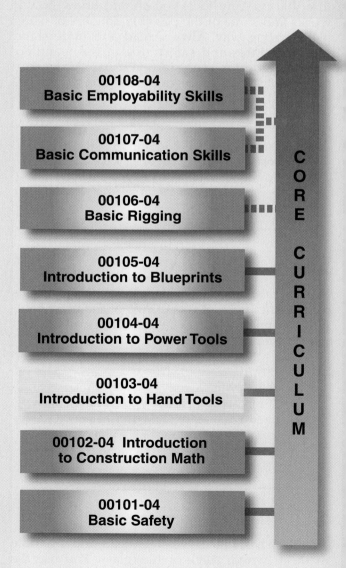

103CMAP.EPS

1.0.0 ◆ INTRODUCTION

Every profession has its tools. A surgeon uses a scalpel, a teacher uses a chalkboard, and an accountant uses a calculator. The construction trade has a whole collection of hand tools, such as hammers, screwdrivers, and **pliers,** that everyone uses. Even if you are already familiar with some of these tools, you need to learn to maintain them and use them safely. The better you use and maintain your tools, the better you will be in your craft.

This module shows you how to safely use and maintain some of the most common hand tools of the construction trade. It also highlights some specialized crafts and uses of hand tools.

1.1.0 Safety

To work safely, you must think about safety. Before you use any tool, you should know how it works and some of the possible dangers of using it the wrong way. Always read and understand the procedures and safety tips in the manufacturer's guide for every tool you use. Make sure every tool you use is in good condition. Never use worn or damaged tools.

WARNING!

Always protect yourself when you are using tools by wearing appropriate personal protective equipment (PPE), such as safety gloves and eye protection.

2.0.0 ◆ HAMMERS

Hammers are made in different sizes and weights for specific types of work. Two of the most common hammers are the **claw hammer** and the **ball peen hammer** (see *Figure 1*).

WARNING!

The most important safety consideration when using a hammer is focusing on the work. If you look away from the work while using a hammer, you may accidentally strike yourself or damage the work.

2.1.0 The Claw Hammer

The claw hammer has a steel head and a handle made of wood, steel, or fiberglass. You use the head to drive nails, wedges, and **dowels.** You use

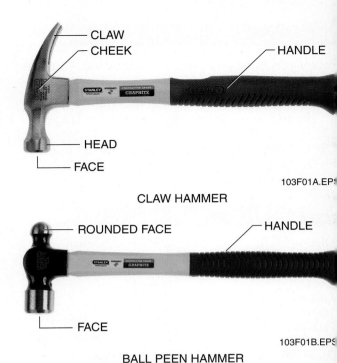

CLAW HAMMER

103F01A.EPS

BALL PEEN HAMMER

103F01B.EPS

Figure 1 ◆ Claw and ball peen hammers.

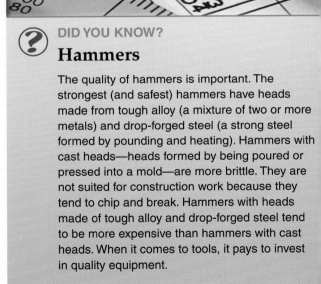

DID YOU KNOW?

Hammers

The quality of hammers is important. The strongest (and safest) hammers have heads made from tough alloy (a mixture of two or more metals) and drop-forged steel (a strong steel formed by pounding and heating). Hammers with cast heads—heads formed by being poured or pressed into a mold—are more brittle. They are not suited for construction work because they tend to chip and break. Hammers with heads made of tough alloy and drop-forged steel tend to be more expensive than hammers with cast heads. When it comes to tools, it pays to invest in quality equipment.

the claw to pull nails out of wood. The face of the hammer may be flat or rounded. It's easier to drive nails with the flat face (plain) claw hammer, but the flat face may leave hammer marks when you drive the head of the nail flush (even) with the surface of the work.

A claw hammer with a slightly rounded (or convex) face is called a **bell-faced hammer.** A skilled worker can use it to drive the nail head flush without damaging the surface of the work.

2.1.1 How to Use a Claw Hammer to Drive a Nail

Follow these simple steps to use a claw hammer properly when driving a nail:

Step 1 Hold the nail straight, at a 90-degree angle to the surface being nailed.

Step 2 Grip the handle of the hammer. Hold the end of the handle even with the lower edge of your palm.

Step 3 Rest the face of the hammer on the nail.

Step 4 Draw the hammer back and give the nail a few light taps to start it.

Step 5 Move your fingers away from the nail and hit the nail firmly with the center of the hammer face. Hold the hammer level with the head of the nail and strike the face squarely (see *Figure 2*). Deliver the blow through your wrist, your elbow, and your shoulder.

2.1.2 How to Use a Claw Hammer to Pull a Nail

Pulling a nail with a claw hammer is as easy as driving one. Follow these steps:

Step 1 Slip the claw of the hammer under the nail head and pull until the handle is nearly straight up (vertical) and the nail is partly drawn out of the wood.

Step 2 Pull the nail straight up from the wood.

2.2.0 The Ball Peen Hammer

A ball peen hammer has a flat face for striking and a rounded face that is used to align brackets. You use this hammer with **chisels** and **punches** (discussed later in this module). In welding operations, the ball peen hammer is used to reduce stress in the **weld** by **peening** or striking the **joint** as it cools. Ball peen hammers are classified by weight. They weigh from 6 ounces to 2½ pounds.

 WARNING!

Do not use a hammer with a cast head. A chip could easily break off and injure you or a co-worker.

Never use a hammer to strike the head of another hammer. Flying fragments from drop-forged alloy steel are dangerous.

2.2.1 How to Use a Ball Peen Hammer

Using a ball peen hammer is not that much different from using a claw hammer. Follow these steps:

Step 1 Grip the handle. Keep the end of the handle flush with the lower edge of your palm. Keep the face of the hammer parallel to the work.

Step 2 Use the face for hammering. Use the ball peen for rounding off (peening) rivets and similar jobs.

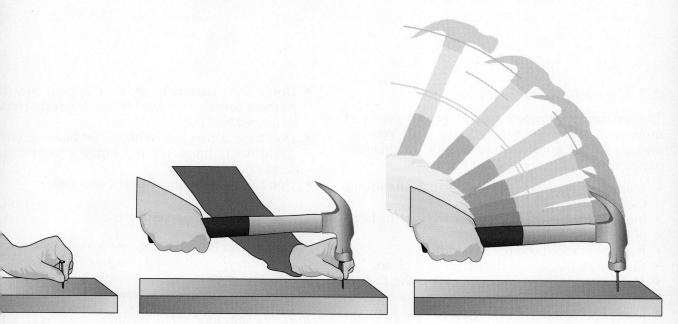

Figure 2 ◆ Proper use of a claw hammer.

103F02.EPS

Weight-Forward Hammers

At 21 ounces, this hammer is a little heavier than most standard hammers. However, its curved, extended handle delivers greater striking force to the square head, so it takes fewer strikes to drive nails into place. That means less fatigue and shock stress for the user. The fiberglass handle (available in 14- or 16-inch lengths) is covered with neoprene rubber to ensure a good grip.

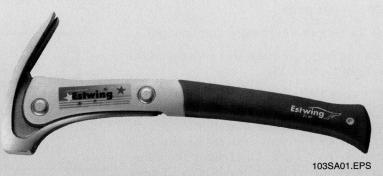

103SA01.EPS

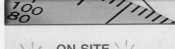

Physics and the Hammer

The hammer is designed to produce a certain amount of force on the object it strikes. If you hold the hammer incorrectly, you cancel out the design factor. Always remember to hold the end of the handle even with the lower edge of your palm. The distance between your hand and the head of the hammer affects the force you use to drive a nail. The closer you hold the hammer to the head, the harder you will need to swing to achieve the desired force. Make it easier on yourself by holding the hammer properly; it takes less effort to drive the nail.

2.3.0 Safety and Maintenance

To keep from hurting yourself or a co-worker, you must focus on your work. Make sure you are aware of these guidelines for safety and maintenance when using all types of hammers:

- Make sure there are no splinters in the handle of the hammer.
- Make sure the handle is set securely in the head of the hammer.
- Replace cracked or broken handles.
- Make sure the face of the hammer is clean.
- Hold the hammer properly. Grasp the handle firmly near the end and hit the nail squarely.
- Don't hit with the cheek or side of the hammer head.

- Don't use hammers with chipped, mush-roomed (overly flattened by use), or otherwis damaged heads.
- Don't use a hammer with a cast head. A chi could easily break off and injure you or a co worker.
- Don't use one hammer to strike another.

3.0.0 ◆ SCREWDRIVERS

A screwdriver is used to tighten or remove screws It is identified by the type of screw it fits. *Figure* shows six common types of screw heads.

The most common screwdrivers are slotte (also known as straight-blade, flat, or standar tip) and Phillips head screwdrivers. You wi also use more specialized screwdrivers such as

Mallets

Mallets, like hammers, generally have short wooden handles, but their heads are made of softer materials, such as plastic, wood, or rubber. Mallets are a hand tool used by many trade specialists, particularly carpenters and stonemasons. When you need to drive another tool, such as a chisel, with great precision, use a mallet. You use a mallet basically the same way you use a hammer, but with much less force. Mallets are perfect for tapping, as well as for striking an object gently but firmly. A mallet is the best tool when it is important to avoid damaging the object you are striking.

Review Questions

Section 2.0.0

1. One of the most commonly used hammers is the _____ hammer.

   a. dowel
   b. bell
   c. claw
   d. wedge

2. The safest hammers are those with heads that are _____.

   a. welded and alloyed
   b. cast steel and chiseled
   c. chiseled and drop forged
   d. alloy and drop-forged steel

3. The claw of the claw hammer is used to _____.

   a. pull nails out of wood
   b. scrape paint from walls
   c. remove loose wires
   d. drive large metal spikes

4. The _____ hammer can drive the nail head flush without damaging the surface of the work.

   a. ball peen
   b. bell-faced claw
   c. flat-faced claw
   d. wedge

5. The rounded face of a ball peen hammer is used for _____.

   a. driving small nails
   b. aligning brackets
   c. making the surface smooth after driving a nail
   d. straightening bent nails

clutch-drive, Torx®, Robertson®, and Allen head (hex). Each is described here.

- *Slotted* – This is the most common type of standard screwdriver. It fits slotted screws.
- *Phillips* – This is the most common type of crosshead screwdriver. It fits Phillips head screws.
- *Clutch-drive* – This screwdriver has an hourglass-shaped tip that is especially useful when you need extra holding power, as when working on cars or appliances.
- *Torx®* – This screwdriver has a star-shaped tip that is useful for replacing such parts as tailgate lenses. It is widely used in automobile

1	2	3
SLOTTED	PHILLIPS	CLUTCH-DRIVE
4	5	6
TORX®	ROBERTSON®	ALLEN

103F03.EPS

Figure 3 ◆ Six common types of screw heads.

repair work. Torx® screws are also used in household appliances, as well as lawn and garden equipment.

- *Robertson® (square)* – This screwdriver has a square drive that provides high **torque** power. Usually color coded according to size, it can reach screws that are sunk below the surface.
- *Allen (hex)* – This screwdriver works with screws that can also be operated with hex keys. It is suitable for socket-head screws that are recessed.

We will focus on slotted and Phillips head screwdrivers (see *Figure 4*) in this module.

To choose the right screwdriver and use it correctly, you have to know a little bit about the sections of a screwdriver. Each section has a name. The handle is designed to give you a firm grip. The shank is the hardened metal portion between the handle and the blade. The shank can withstand a lot of twisting force. The blade is the formed end that fits into the head of a screw. Industrial screwdriver blades are made of **tempered** steel to resist wear and to prevent bending and breaking.

It is important to choose the right screwdriver for the screw. The blade should fit snugly into the screw head and not be too long, short, loose, or tight. If you use the wrong size blade, you might damage the screwdriver or the screw head (see *Figure 5*).

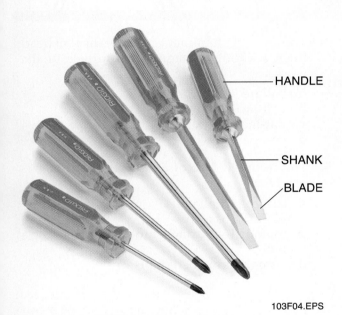

HANDLE

SHANK

BLADE

103F04.EPS

Figure 4 ◆ Slotted and Phillips head screwdrivers.

WARNING!

Keep the screwdriver clean. A dirty or greasy screwdriver can slip out of your hand or out of the screw head and possibly cause injury or equipment damage.

3.1.0 How to Use a Screwdriver

It is very important to use a screwdriver correctly. Using one the wrong way can damage the screwdriver or **strip** the screw head. Follow these steps:

Step 1 Choose the right type of blade for the screw head (see *Figure 4*).

Step 2 Make sure the screwdriver fits the screw correctly, as shown in *Figure 5*.

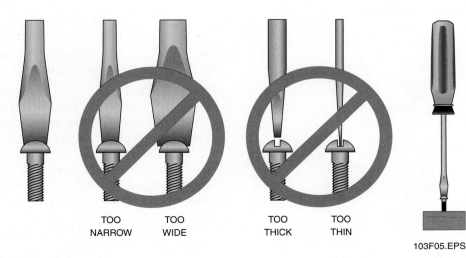

TOO NARROW   TOO WIDE

TOO THICK   TOO THIN

103F05.EPS

Figure 5 ◆ Proper use of a screwdriver.

Screws

Screws hold better than nails in most situations. The spiral ridges (threads) help hold the screw tightly inside the material, unlike the smooth surface of most nails. Self-tapping screws end in a sharp point and have sharp threads. These types of screws cut their own threads in the material, and you do not need to drill a starter hole. In woodworking, however, making a small starter hole with a drill helps keep the wood from splitting.

Wood screws generally have slotted heads and are driven with a slotted-blade screwdriver. Self-tapping screws usually have Phillips heads. Lag screws—very large wood screws—have square or hexagonal (six-sided) heads and are driven with a wrench.

Inspecting Screwdrivers

Visually inspect your screwdriver before using it. The handle should not be worn or damaged. The blade's tip should be straight and smooth. If the handle is worn or damaged, or the tip is not straight and smooth, the screwdriver should be repaired or replaced.

Step 3 Position the shank perpendicular (at a right angle) to your work.

Step 4 Apply firm, steady pressure to the screw head and turn: clockwise to tighten (right is tight); counterclockwise to loosen (left is loose).

WARNING!

When you're starting the screw, it's easy to hurt your fingers if the blade slips. Work with caution.

3.2.0 Safety and Maintenance

If you follow the steps in the section on how to use a screwdriver, you will be effective with a screwdriver. You also want to be safe, though. There are many guidelines you must follow for your own safety and the safety of others, as well as for maintaining your tool, when using a screwdriver. Learn the following usage guidelines for screwdrivers:

- Keep the screwdriver free of dirt, grease, and grit so the blade will not slip out of the screwhead slot.
- File the blade tip to restore a worn straight edge.
- Don't ever use the screwdriver as a punch, chisel, or pry bar.
- Don't ever use a screwdriver near live wires or as an electrical tester.
- Don't expose a screwdriver to excessive heat.
- Don't use a screwdriver that has a worn or broken handle.
- Don't point the screwdriver blade toward yourself or anyone else.

Section 3.0.0

1. A screwdriver is identified by _____.
   a. the length of its handle
   b. its torque
   c. the type of screw it fits
   d. the width of its tip

2. The most common standard screwdriver is the _____ screwdriver.
   a. Phillips
   b. slotted
   c. Robertson®
   d. Allen

3. The most common crosshead screwdriver is the _____ screwdriver.
   a. slotted
   b. Torx®
   c. Robertson®
   d. Phillips

4. For safety's sake, industrial screwdriver blades are made of _____.
   a. tempered steel
   b. Torx®
   c. clutch-driven steel
   d. fiberglass

5. If you use the wrong screwdriver head for the job, you might _____.
   a. strike a live wire
   b. turn the screw counterclockwise
   c. twist the shank of the screwdriver
   d. damage the screw head

? DID YOU KNOW?
Drywall Workers and Lathers

Drywall workers can perform either installation or finishing work. Installers measure, cut, fit, and fasten drywall panels to the inside framework of buildings. They also install the metal or vinyl-beaded edge around the corners. Finishers prepare the panels for painting by taping and finishing joints and imperfections using drywall mud or spackling. They also sand the material lightly using a sanding pole and sanding block. Finishers are respected for their skills in handling the spackling tools, trowels, mud pans, and taping knives.

Lathers apply metal or gypsum lathe to walls, ceilings, or ornamental frameworks to form the support base for plaster coatings. Lathers nail, screw, staple, or wire-tie the lathe directly to the structural framework. Accuracy and precision must be practiced at all times to ensure that the base is prepared properly. The base must be prepared properly; otherwise the plaster will crack and fall off the surface.

4.0.0 ◆ SLEDGEHAMMERS

A sledgehammer is a heavy-duty tool used to drive posts or other large stakes. You can also use it to break up cast iron or concrete. The head of the sledgehammer is made of high-carbon steel and weighs 2 to 20 pounds. The shape of the head depends on the job the sledgehammer is designed to do. Sledgehammers can be either long-handled or short-handled, depending on the jobs for which they are designed.

Figure 6 shows two types of sledgehammers, the double-face and the crosspeen.

4.1.0 How to Use a Sledgehammer

Obviously, a sledgehammer can cause injury to you or to anyone working near you. You must use a sledgehammer the right way, and you must focus on what you are doing the entire time you use one. Follow these steps (see *Figure 7*):

Step 1 Wear appropriate personal protective equipment.

Step 2 Inspect the sledgehammer to ensure that there are no defects.

Step 3 Be sure that no co-workers are standing in the surrounding area.

Step 4 Hold the sledgehammer with both hands (hand over hand).

Getting It Started

You should never use your hand, or anyone else's, to hold an object before you hit it with a sledgehammer. So how do you hold the object you want to strike? If you are driving a stake into the ground, for example, use a mallet to get the stake started. Tap the stake a little way into the ground so that it stands on its own. Then you can step back and use both hands to wield the sledgehammer. For objects that need to be broken up, you can place them in between other objects, such as cinder blocks or broken pieces of concrete or wood, to hold them. If you do this, make sure that you never use anything that might be of value. If you are ever in doubt, ask your instructor or immediate supervisor.

HEAD   HANDLE

103F06A.EPS

DOUBLE-FACE LONG-HANDLED

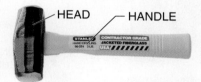

HEAD   HANDLE

103F06B.EPS

DOUBLE-FACE SHORT-HANDLED

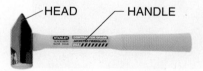

HEAD   HANDLE

103F06C.EPS

CROSSPEEN

Figure 6 ◆ Types of sledgehammers.

tep 5 Stand directly in front of the object you want to drive.

tep 6 Lift the sledgehammer straight up above the target.

tep 7 Set the head of the sledgehammer on the target.

tep 8 Begin delivering short blows to the target and gradually increase the length and force of the stroke.

WARNING!

Hold the sledgehammer with both hands. Never use your hands to hold the object as either you or someone else drives with a sledgehammer. Doing so could result in serious injury, such as crushed or broken bones.

WARNING!

Avoid swinging the sledgehammer behind you or beyond your head. Doing so may cause injury to your back and could limit the control you have directing the blow to the target.

4.2.0 Safety and Maintenance

Remember that using a sledgehammer the correct way not only gets the job done right, but also keeps everyone in the area, including you, safe. Of course, as with all tools, there are other considerations for safety and maintenance when working with this tool. Here are the guidelines for working with a sledgehammer:

- Wear eye protection when you are using a sledgehammer. It's also a good idea to wear safety gloves.
- Replace cracked or broken handles before you use the sledgehammer.
- Make sure the handle is secured firmly at the head.
- Use the right amount of force for the job.
- Keep your hands away from the object you are driving.
- Don't swing until you have checked behind you to make sure you have enough room and no one is behind you.

Figure 7 ◆ Proper use of a long-handled sledgehammer.

103F07.EPS

Section 4.0.0

1. You use a sledgehammer to break up concrete and _____.

   a. remove overhead wires
   b. drive a post or stake
   c. hammer nails
   d. drive bolts

2. Two types of sledgehammers are the double-face and _____.

   a. ball peen
   b. double-edged
   c. crosspeen
   d. round-head

3. The head of a sledgehammer is made of _____.

   a. high-carbon steel
   b. heavy rubber
   c. fiberglass
   d. welded iron

4. The shape of a sledgehammer head depends on _____.

   a. the torque of the sledgehammer
   b. whether the sledgehammer is single-face or double-face
   c. the composition of the head
   d. the job the sledgehammer is intended to do

5. When using a sledgehammer, it is important to _____.

   a. swing from between your knees
   b. wear appropriate personal protective equipment
   c. hold tightly to the object you are driving
   d. place a protective covering over the sledgehammer head

5.0.0 ◆ RIPPING BARS AND NAIL PULLERS

A number of tools are made to rip and pry apart woodwork as well as to pull nails. In this section, you will learn about **ripping bars** and **nail pullers** (see *Figure 8*). These tools are necessary in the construction trade because often the job involves building where something else already exists. The existing structure needs to be torn apart before the building can begin. That is where the ripping bar and the nail puller come in.

5.1.0 Ripping Bars

The ripping bar—also called a pinch, pry, or wrecking bar—can be 12 to 36 inches long. This bar is used for heavy-duty dismantling of woodwork, such as tearing apart building frames or concrete forms. The ripping bar has an octagonal (eight-sided) shaft and two specialized ends. A deeply curved nail claw at one end is used as a nail puller. An angled, wedge-shaped face at the other end is used as a prying tool to pull apart materials that are nailed together.

5.1.1 How to Use a Ripping Bar

Take the following steps when using a ripping bar:

Step 1 Wear appropriate personal protective equipment.

Step 2 Use the angled prying end to force apart pieces of wood or use the heavy claw to pull large nails and spikes.

5.2.0 Nail Pullers

There are three main types of nail-pulling tools: **cat's paw** (also called nail claws and carpenter's pincers), **chisel bars**, and **flat bars.**

The cat's paw is a straight steel rod with a curved claw at one end. It is used to pull nails that have been driven flush with the surface of the wood or slightly below it. You use the cat's paw to pull nails to just above the surface of the wood so they can be pulled completely out with the claw of a hammer or a pry bar.

The chisel bar has a claw at each end and is ground to a chisel-like **bevel** (slant) on both ends. You can use it like a claw hammer to pull nails.

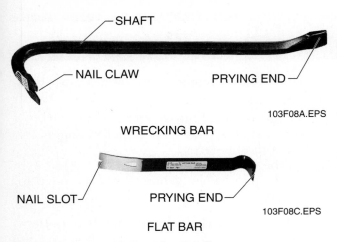

WRECKING BAR

103F08A.EPS

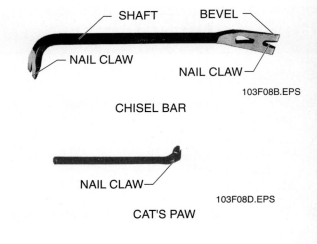

CHISEL BAR

103F08B.EPS

FLAT BAR

103F08C.EPS

CAT'S PAW

103F08D.EPS

Figure 8 ◆ Ripping bars and nail pullers.

You can also drive it into wood to split and rip apart the pieces.

The flat bar (ripping chisel, wonder bar, action bar) has a nail slot at the end to pull nails out from tightly enclosed areas. It can also be used as a small pry bar. The flat bar is usually 2 inches wide and 15 inches long.

 WARNING!

A piece of material can break off and fly through the air when you are using a ripping bar or a nail puller. Wear a hard hat, safety glasses, and gloves to protect yourself from flying debris. Make sure others around you are similarly protected.

5.2.1   *How to Use a Nail Puller (Cat's Paw)*

Take the following steps when using a nail puller:

Step 1 Wear appropriate personal protective equipment.

Step 2 Drive the claw into the wood, grabbing the nail head.

Step 3 Pull the handle of the bar to lift the nail out of the wood.

5.3.0 Safety and Maintenance

Here are the guidelines for ripping and nail pulling:

• Wear appropriate personal protective equipment.

• Use two hands when ripping; this helps ensure you keep even pressure on your back as you pull.
• When nail pulling, be sure the material holding the nail is braced securely before you pull the nail, to keep it from hitting you in the face.

Most accidents with prying tools occur when a pry bar slips and the craftworker falls to the ground. Be sure to keep a balanced footing and a firm grip on the tool. This technique also helps reduce damage to materials that must be reused, such as concrete forms.

? DID YOU KNOW?

Electricians

Electricians read blueprints to install electrical systems in factories, office buildings, homes, and other structures. They may also install coaxial cable for television or fiber-optic cable for computers and telecommunications equipment. Electricians who specialize in residential work may install wire and hardware in a new home, such as electrical panel boxes, receptacles, light switches, and electrical light fixtures, or replace outdated fuse boxes. Those who work in large factories as commercial electricians may install or repair motors, transformers, generators, or electronic controllers on machine tools and industrial robots. They use many hand tools, including pliers, wrenches, screwdrivers, hammers, and saws.

Section 5.0.0

1. The ripping bar is used for _____.
   a. gripping large metal objects for demolition
   b. heavy-duty dismantling of woodwork
   c. hammering nails
   d. breaking up concrete

2. The angled prying end of the ripping bar is used to _____.
   a. rip out nails
   b. drive the claw into the wood
   c. bevel wood
   d. force apart pieces of wood

3. A cat's paw is a kind of _____.
   a. sledgehammer
   b. ripping tool
   c. nail-pulling tool
   d. crushing tool

4. A chisel bar can be used to _____.
   a. pry apart steel beams
   b. split and rip apart pieces of wood
   c. break apart concrete
   d. make ridges in wood beams

5. When using prying tools, be sure to _____.
   a. keep a balanced footing
   b. hold the tool loosely
   c. swing firmly from above
   d. keep the material loosely braced

6.0.0 ◆ PLIERS AND WIRE CUTTERS

Pliers are a special type of adjustable wrench. They are scissor-shaped tools with jaws. The jaws usually have teeth to help grip objects. The jaws are adjustable because the two legs (or handles) move on a pivot. You will generally use pliers to hold, cut, and bend wire and soft metals. Do not use pliers on nuts or bolt heads. They will round off the edges of the hex (six-sided) head, and wrenches will no longer fit properly.

High-quality pliers are made of hardened steel. Pliers come in many different head styles, depending on their use. The following types of pliers are the most commonly used (see *Figure 9*):

- Slip-joint (combination) pliers
- Long-nose (needle-nose) pliers
- Lineman pliers (side cutters)
- Tongue-and-groove (or water pump) pliers
- Vise-Grip® (locking) pliers

You will learn about each type of plier in this module.

6.1.0 Slip-Joint (Combination) Pliers

You use slip-joint (or combination) pliers to hold and bend wire and to grip and hold objects during assembly operations. They have adjustable jaws. There are two jaw settings: one for small materials and one for larger materials.

6.1.1 How to Use Slip-Joint Pliers

When using slip-joint pliers, be sure to wear appropriate personal protective equipment. Take the following steps to use slip-joint pliers properly:

Step 1 Place the jaws on the object to be held.

Step 2 Squeeze the handles until the pliers grip the object.

6.2.0 Long-Nose (Needle-Nose) Pliers

Long-nose (or needle-nose) pliers are used to get into tight places where other pliers won't reach or to grip parts that are too small to hold with your fingers. These pliers are useful for bending angles in wire or narrow metal strips. They have a sharp wire cutter near the pivot. Long-nose pliers, like many other types of pliers, are available with spring openers (see *Figure 9*), which are spring-like devices between the handles that keep the handles apart—and therefore the jaws open—unless you purposely close them. This device can make long-nose pliers easier to use.

6.2.1 How to Use Long-Nose Pliers

Be sure to wear appropriate personal protective equipment when working with long-nose pliers.

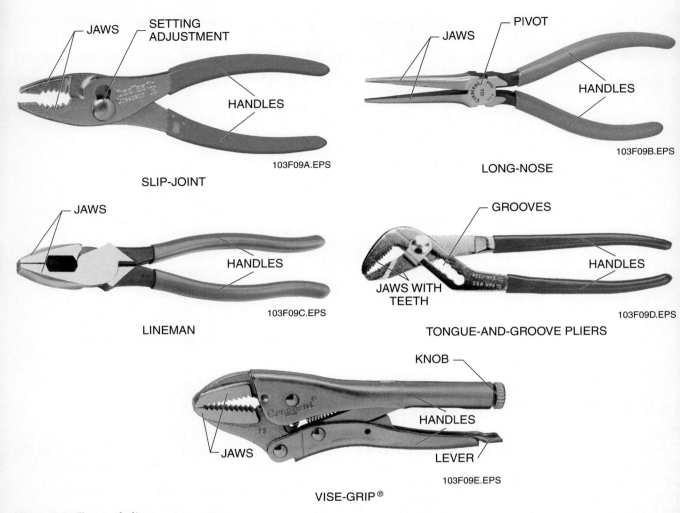

Figure 9 ◆ Types of pliers.

Note the following points in using long-nose pliers properly:

- If the pliers do not have a spring between the handles to keep them open, place your third or little finger inside the handles to keep them open.
- Use the sharp cutter near the pivot for cutting wire.

6.3.0 Lineman Pliers (Side Cutters)

Lineman pliers (or side cutters) have wider jaws than slip-joint pliers do. You use them to cut heavy or large-gauge wire and to hold work. The wedged jaws reduce the chance that wires will slip, and the hook bend in both handles gives you a better grip.

6.3.1 How to Use Lineman Pliers

Be sure to wear appropriate personal protective equipment when working with lineman pliers. Take the following steps to use lineman pliers properly:

Step 1 When you cut wire, always point the loose end of the wire down.

Step 2 Cut at a right angle to the wire.

6.4.0 Tongue-and-Groove Pliers

Tongue-and-groove pliers, manufactured by CHANNELLOCK®, Inc., have serrated teeth that grip flat, square, round, or hexagonal objects. You can set the jaws in up to five positions by slipping the curved ridge into the desired groove (see *Figure 10*). Large tongue-and-groove pliers are often used to hold pipes because the longer handles give more leverage. The jaws stay parallel and give a better grip than slip-joint pliers.

6.4.1 How to Use Tongue-and-Groove Pliers

Be sure to wear appropriate personal protective equipment when using tongue-and-groove pliers. Take the following steps to use tongue-and-groove pliers properly:

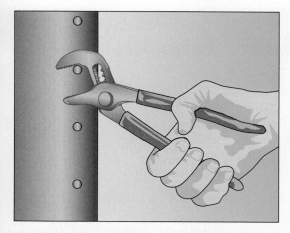

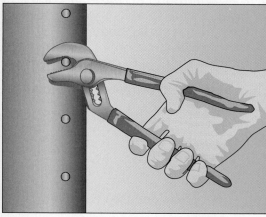

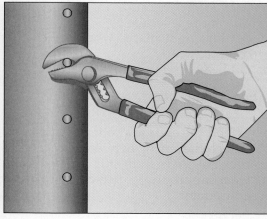

103F10.EPS

igure 10 ◆ Proper use of tongue-and-groove pliers.

tep 1 With pliers open to the widest position, place the jaws on the object to be held.

tep 2 Determine which groove provides the proper position.

tep 3 Squeeze the handles until the pliers grip the object (see *Figure 10*).

6.5.0 Vise-Grip® (Locking) Pliers

Vise-Grip® (locking) pliers clamp firmly onto objects the way a **vise** does. (You will learn about vises later in this module.) A knob in the handle controls the width and tension of the jaws. You close the handles to lock the pliers. You release the pliers by pressing the lever to open the jaws.

6.5.1 How to Use Vise-Grip® Pliers

As with all the types of pliers, be sure to use appropriate personal protective equipment when working with Vise-Grip® pliers. Take the following steps to use Vise-Grip® pliers properly:

Step 1 Place the jaws on the object to be held.

Step 2 Turn the adjusting screw in the handle until the pliers grip the object.

Step 3 Squeeze the handles together to lock the pliers.

Step 4 Squeeze the release lever when you want to remove the pliers (see *Figure 11*).

6.6.0 Safety and Maintenance

You might not think that misusing pliers could cause injury, but it can. Proper safety precautions when using pliers and proper maintenance of your pliers are very important. Here are some guidelines to remember when using pliers:

• Hold pliers close to the end of the handles to avoid pinching your fingers in the hinge.
• Don't extend the length of the handles for greater leverage. Use a larger pair of pliers instead.
• Wear appropriate personal protective equipment, especially when you cut wire.

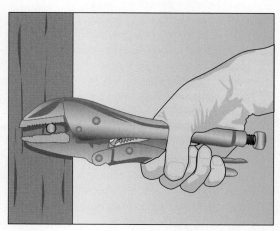

103F11.EPS

Figure 11 ◆ Proper use of Vise-Grip® pliers.

- Hold the short ends of wires to avoid flying metal bits when you cut.
- Always cut at right angles. Don't rock the pliers from side to side or bend the wire back and forth against the cutting blades. Loose wire can fly up and injure you or someone else.
- Oil pliers regularly to prevent rust and to keep them working smoothly.
- Don't use pliers around energized electrical wires. Although the handles may be plastic-coated, they are not insulated against electrical shock.
- Don't expose pliers to extreme heat.
- Don't use pliers to turn nuts or bolts; they are not wrenches.
- Don't use pliers as hammers.

WARNING!

Never rock pliers from side to side when you are cutting. The object you are cutting could fly in your face.

 DID YOU KNOW?

Stonemasons

Stone used to be one of our primary building materials. Because of its strength, stone was often used for dams, bridges, fortresses, foundations, and important buildings. Today, steel and concrete have replaced stone as a basic construction material. Stone is used primarily as sheathing for buildings, for flooring in high-traffic areas, and for decorative uses.

A stonemason's job requires precision. Stones have uneven, rough edges that must be trimmed and finished before each stone can be set. The process of trimming projections and jagged edges is called dressing the stone. This requires skill and experience using specialized hand tools. Many craftworkers consider stonework an art.

Stonemasons build stone walls as well as set stone exteriors and floors, working with natural cut and artificial stones. These include marble, granite, limestone, cast concrete, marble chips, or other masonry materials. Stonemasons usually work on structures such as houses, churches, hotels, and office buildings. Special projects include zoos, theme parks, and movie sets.

Review Questions

Section 6.0.0

1. Pliers are generally used to _____.
   a. pry open objects that are stuck together
   b. turn nuts or bolt heads
   c. hold, cut, and bend wire and soft metals
   d. substitute for wrenches in tight spaces

2. Pliers should not be used on a nut or bolt because _____.
   a. they will round off the edges of the hex head
   b. they are not strong enough
   c. they are designed only for tightening
   d. their jaws will not open wide enough

3. The best-quality pliers are made of _____.
   a. fiberglass
   b. hardened steel
   c. high-carbon steel
   d. alloys

4. Long-nose pliers are used to _____.
   a. clamp objects loosely
   b. hold pipes because the long handles give more leverage
   c. get into tight places where other pliers can't fit
   d. cut heavy or large-gauge wire

5. When using pliers, you should always _____.
   a. extend the ends for better leverage
   b. detach the spring between the handles
   c. rock the pliers from side to side
   d. wear appropriate personal protective equipment

7.0.0 ◆ RULERS AND OTHER MEASURING TOOLS

Craftworkers use four basic types of measuring tools:

- Flat steel rule
- Measuring tape
- Wooden folding rule
- Digital measuring device

When you choose a measuring tool, keep the following in mind:

- It must be accurate.
- It should be easy to use.
- It should be durable.
- The numbers should be easy to read (black on yellow or off-white are good).

7.1.0 Steel Rule

The flat steel rule (see *Figure 12*) is the simplest and most common measuring tool. The flat steel rule is usually 6 or 12 inches long, but longer sizes are available.

Steel rules can be flexible or nonflexible, thin or wide. The thinner the rule, the more accurately it measures, because the division marks are closer to the work.

Generally, a steel rule has four sets of marks, two on each side of the rule. On one side are the inch marks. The longest lines are for 1-inch increments. On one edge of that side, each inch is divided into eight equal spaces of ⅛ inch each. On the other edge of that side, each inch is divided into ¹⁄₁₆-inch spaces. To make counting easier, the ¼-inch and the ½-inch marks are normally longer than the smaller division marks. The other side of the steel rule is divided into 32 and 64 spaces to the inch. Each fourth division in the inch is usually numbered for easier reading.

7.2.0 Measuring Tape

Measuring tapes are available in different lengths. The shorter tapes are usually made with a curved cross section, so they are flexible enough to roll up but stay rigid when they are extended. When using a long, flat tape, lay it along a surface to keep it from sagging in the middle.

Steel measuring tapes (see *Figure 13*) are usually wound into metal cases. A hook at the end of the tape hooks over the object you are measuring. The tape may have a lock that holds the blade open and a rewind spring that returns the blade to the case. Look for a tape that is easy to read. Good-quality tapes have a polyester film bonded to the steel blade to guard against wear.

103F13.EPS

Figure 13 ◆ Steel measuring tape.

103F12.EPS

Figure 12 ◆ Steel rule.

Digital Measuring Devices

Digital measuring devices are becoming increasingly common in the construction industry. They allow you to make very precise and accurate measurements. Precision measuring tools, such as micrometers and calipers, make it possible to accurately measure parts that are being machined to one thousandth of an inch (0.001"). Micrometers can be used for both outside and inside measurements. A standard micrometer's smallest division is 0.001 inch. Digital micrometers are available that can read to 0.00005 inch.

103SA02.EPS

7.2.1 How to Use a Steel Tape

Measuring with a steel tape is simple. Follow these steps to use a steel tape properly:

Step 1 Pull the tape out to the desired length.

Step 2 Place the hook over the edge of the material you are measuring. Lock the tape if necessary (use the lock button on the holder).

Step 3 Mark or record the measurement.

Step 4 Unhook the tape from the edge.

Step 5 Rewind the tape by pressing the rewind button.

7.3.0 Wooden Folding Rule

A wooden folding rule (see *Figure 14*) is usually marked in sixteenths of an inch on both edges of each side. Folding rules come in 6- and 8-foot lengths. Because of its stiffness, a folding rule is better than a cloth or steel tape for measuring vertical distance. This is because, unlike tape, it holds itself straight up. This makes it easier to measure some distances, such as those where you might need a ladder to reach one end.

103F14.EPS

Figure 14 ◆ Wooden folding rule.

7.4.0 Safety and Maintenance

There are some safety concerns, as well as some needed maintenance, for rulers and measuring tools. Here are the guidelines to remember:

- Occasionally apply a few drops of light oil on the spring joints of a wooden folding rule and steel tape.
- Wipe moisture off steel tape to keep it from rusting.
- Don't kink or twist steel tape, because this could cause it to break.
- Don't use steel tape near exposed electrical parts.
- Don't let digital measuring devices get wet.

Section 7.0.0

1. A measuring tool must be accurate and _____.

    a. easy to read
    b. made of strong metal
    c. flat
    d. equipped with a carrying case

2. The simplest and most common measuring tool is the _____.

    a. measuring tape
    b. wooden folding rule
    c. digital measuring device
    d. flat steel rule

3. One side of a steel rule is divided into 32 and 64 spaces to the inch, and the other side shows _____.

    a. vertical distance
    b. digital measurements
    c. inch marks
    d. a curved cross section

4. Steel measuring tapes are usually wound into metal cases and have _____.

    a. inch marks on the cases
    b. a hook at the end of the tape
    c. conversion tables on the cases
    d. markings on both sides of the tape

5. Because of its stiffness, a folding rule is better than a cloth or steel tape for measuring _____.

    a. vertical distance
    b. horizontal distance
    c. plumb
    d. level

8.0.0 ◆ LEVELS

A level is a tool used to determine both how level a horizontal surface is and how **plumb** a vertical surface is. If a surface is described as level, that means it is exactly horizontal. If a surface is described as plumb, that means it is exactly vertical. Levels are used to determine how near to exactly horizontal or exactly vertical a surface is.

Types of levels range from simple spirit levels to electronic and laser instruments. The spirit level (see *Figure 15*) is the most commonly used level in the construction trade.

8.1.0 Spirit Levels

Most levels are made of tough, lightweight metals such as magnesium or aluminum. The spirit level has three vials filled with alcohol. The center vial is used to check for level, and the two end vials are used to check for plumb.

The amount of liquid in each vial is not enough to fill it, so there is always a bubble in the vial. When the bubble is centered between the lines on the vial, the surface is either level or plumb, depending on the vial (see *Figure 16*).

Spirit levels come in a variety of sizes. The longer the level, the greater its accuracy.

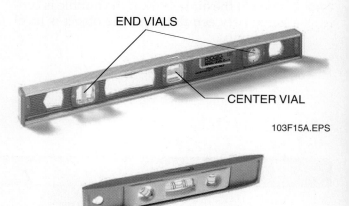

END VIALS

CENTER VIAL

103F15A.EPS

103F15B.EPS

Figure 15 ◆ Spirit levels.

? DID YOU KNOW?

The Spirit Level

The spirit level got its name because the vials in it are filled with alcohol. Alcohol used to be called spirits. Thus, the spirit level.

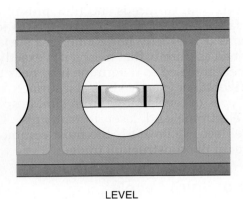

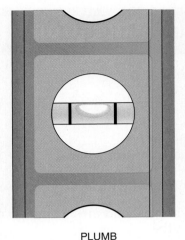

LEVEL

PLUMB

103F16.EPS

Figure 16 ◆ An air bubble centered between the lines shows level or plumb.

8.1.1 *How to Use a Spirit Level*

Using a spirit level is very simple. It just requires a careful eye to be sure you are reading it correctly. Follow these steps to use a spirit level properly:

Step 1 Put the spirit level on the object you are checking.

Step 2 Look at the air bubble. If the bubble is centered between the lines, the object is level or plumb.

8.2.0 Safety and Maintenance

Levels are precision instruments that must be han dled with care. Although there is little chance c personal injury when working with levels, there i a chance of damaging or breaking the level. Her are your guidelines to remember when workin; with levels:

- Replace a level if a crack or break appears i any of the vials.
- Keep levels clean and dry.
- Don't bend or apply too much pressure o your level.
- Don't drop or bump your level.

ON-SITE

Bricklayers

Working with your hands to create buildings is a time-honored craft. People have used bricks for more than 10,000 years. Archeological records prove that bricks were one of the earliest man-made building materials.

In bricklaying, it is important that each course (row) of bricks is level and that the wall is straight. An uneven wall is weak. To ensure that the work stays true, a bricklayer uses a straight level and a plumb line. Bricklayers use trowels to lay bricks individually along the length of the structure.

Today, bricklayers build walls, floors, partitions, fireplaces, chimneys, and other structures with brick, precast masonry panels, concrete block, and other masonry materials. They lay brick for houses, schools, baseball stadiums, office buildings, and other structures. Some bricklayers specialize in installing heat-resistant firebrick linings inside huge industrial furnaces.

Digital (Electronic) Levels

Digital (electronic) levels feature a simulated bubble display plus a digital readout of degrees of slope, inches per foot for rise and run of stairs and roofs, and percentage of slope for drainage problems on decks and masonry. Digital levels, like the one shown here, are becoming more common on construction sites.

103SA03.TIF

Laser Levels

With a laser level, one worker can accurately and quickly establish plumb, level, or square measurements. Levels are used to set foundation levels, establish proper drainage slopes, square framing, and align plumbing and electrical lines. A laser may be mounted on a tripod, fastened onto pipes or framing studs, or suspended from ceiling framing. Levels for professional construction jobs are housed in sturdy casings designed to withstand jobsite conditions. These tools come in a variety of sizes and weights depending on the application.

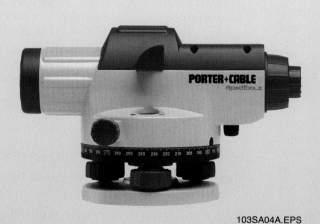

103SA04A.EPS

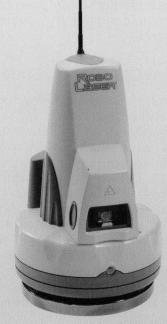

103SA04B.EPS

Section 8.0.0

1. When determining whether a surface is level, you gauge the _____.
   a. vertical surface
   b. spirit
   c. horizontal surface
   d. amount of bubbles

2. When determining whether a surface is plumb, you gauge the _____.
   a. horizontal surface
   b. vertical surface
   c. spirit
   d. degrees of slope

3. The instrument that has three vials and is used to find out if a surface is level or plumb is called a _____.
   a. plumb bob
   b. spirit level
   c. line level
   d. horizontal level

4. The two end vials in a spirit level measure _____.
   a. plumb
   b. level
   c. spirits
   d. horizontal slope

5. When using a spirit level, you know that an object is level if the air bubble _____.
   a. settles at the bottom
   b. disappears
   c. is centered between the lines
   d. sits on the bottom

9.0.0 ◆ SQUARES

Squares (see *Figure 17*) are used for marking, checking, and measuring. The type of square you use depends on the type of job and your preference. Common squares are the **carpenter's square**, **rafter angle square** (also called the speed square or magic square), **try square**, and **combination square**.

9.1.0 The Carpenter's Square

The carpenter's square (framing square) is shaped like an L and is used mainly for squaring up sections of work such as wall studs and sole plates, that is, to ensure that they are at right angles to each other. The carpenter's square has a 24-inch blade and a 16-inch tongue, forming a right (90-degree) angle. The blade and tongue are marked with inches and fractions of an inch. You can use the blade and the tongue as a rule or a straightedge. Tables and formulas are printed on the blade for making quick calculations such as determining area and volume.

The rafter angle square (also called a speed square or magic square) is another type of carpenter's square, frequently made of cast aluminum. It is a combination protractor, try square, and framing square. It is marked with degree gra-

dations for fast, easy layout. The square is small so it's easy to store and carry. By positioning the square on a piece of lumber, you can use it as a guide when cutting with a portable circular saw.

The try square is a fixed, 90-degree angle and is used mainly for woodworking. You can use it to lay out cutting lines at 90-degree angles, to check (or try) the squareness of adjoining surfaces, to check a joint to make sure it is square, and to check if a **planed** piece of lumber is warped or cupped (bowed).

9.1.1 How to Use a Carpenter's Square

Take the following steps to mark a line for cutting:

Step 1 Find and mark the place where the line will be drawn.

Step 2 Place the square so that it lines up with the bottom of the object to be marked (see *Figure 18*).

Step 3 Mark the line and cut off excess material.

To check that joints meet at a 90-degree angle, place the blades of the framing square along the two sides of the angle, as shown in *Figure 19*. If both blades fit there tightly, the material is square. If there is any space between either blade and the side closest to it, the material is not square.

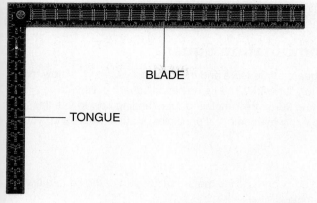

BLADE

TONGUE

103F17A.EPS

CARPENTER'S SQUARE

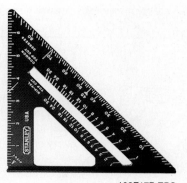

103F17B.EPS

RAFTER ANGLE SQUARE

103F17C.EPS

TRY SQUARE

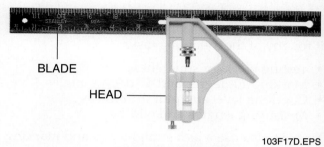

BLADE

HEAD

103F17D.EPS

COMBINATION SQUARE

Figure 17 ◆ Types of squares.

103F18.EPS

Figure 18 ◆ Marking a line for cutting.

103F19.EPS

Figure 19 ◆ Checking squareness.

Take the following steps to check the flatness of material:

Step 1 Place the edge of the blade on the surface to be checked.

Step 2 Look to see if there is light between the square and the surface of the material. If you can see light, the surface is not flat.

9.2.0 The Combination Square

The combination square has a 12-inch blade that moves through a head. The head is marked with 45-degree and 90-degree angle measures. Some squares also contain a small spirit level and a carbide scriber, which is a sharp, pointed tool for marking metal. The combination square is one of

Geometry and the Combination Square

When you use the combination square to measure and mark materials, did you know that you are applying basic geometry to your work? The combination square is used to measure and mark 30-, 45-, 60-, and 90-degree angles. Understanding how to use this hand tool properly requires you to apply mathematical principles. Math is working for you every day!

Angles

To mark angles other than 45 and 90 degrees, slide the protractor part of the square onto the blade and dial in the desired angle.

the most useful tools for layout work. You can use it for any of the following tasks:

- Testing work for squareness
- Marking 90-degree and 45-degree angles
- Checking level and plumb surfaces
- Measuring lengths and widths

You can also use it as a straightedge and marking tool.

Good combination squares have all-metal parts, a blade that slides freely but can be clamped securely in position, and a glass tube spirit level that is truly level and tightly fastened.

9.2.1   How to Use a Combination Square

Take the following steps to mark a 90-degree angle (see *Figure 20*):

Step 1 Set the blade at a right angle (90 degrees)

Step 2 Position the square so that the head fit snugly against the edge of the material t be marked.

Step 3 Starting at the edge of the material, use th blade as a straightedge to guide the mark

Take the following steps to mark a 45-degree angle (see *Figure 21*):

Step 1 Set the blade at a 45-degree angle.

Step 2 Position the square so that the head fit snugly against the edge of the material t be marked.

Step 3 Starting at the edge of the material, use th blade as a straightedge to guide the mark

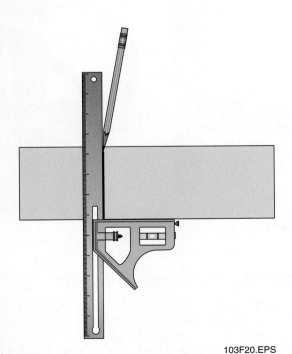

103F20.EPS

Figure 20 ◆ Using a combination square to mark a 90-degree angle.

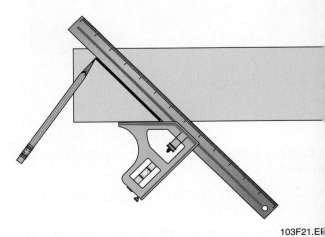

103F21.EP

Figure 21 ◆ Using a combination square to mark a 45-degree angle.

9.3.0 Safety and Maintenance

Here are the guidelines to remember when using squares:

Keep the square dry to prevent it from rusting. Use a light coat of oil on the blade, and occasionally clean the blade's grooves and the setscrew.

Don't use a square for something it wasn't designed for, especially prying or hammering.

Don't bend a square or use one for any kind of horseplay. They are expensive!

Don't drop or strike the square hard enough to change the angle between the blade and the head.

Review Questions

Section 9.0.0

1. Squares are used for marking, checking, and _____.

   a. cutting
   b. bending
   c. twisting
   d. measuring

2. The carpenter's square is used mainly for _____.

   a. squaring up sections of work
   b. placing nails along a beam
   c. measuring 360-degree angles
   d. reaching areas where hammers won't fit

3. The try square is a fixed _____ angle.

   a. 45-degree
   b. 180-degree
   c. 90-degree
   d. 360-degree

4. A combination square can be used to test work for squareness; measure lengths, widths, and angles; and _____.

   a. turn nuts and bolts
   b. check level and plumb surfaces
   c. hold material in place
   d. pry apart objects that are stuck together

5. All of the following are appropriate when using squares *except*_____.

   a. using the square for prying or hammering
   b. wearing the appropriate PPE
   c. keeping the square dry
   d. using a light coat of oil on the blade

10.0.0 ◆ PLUMB BOB

The plumb bob (see *Figure 22*), which is a pointed weight attached to a string, uses the force of gravity to make the line hang vertical, or plumb. Plumb bobs come in different weights: 12 ounces, 8 ounces, and 6 ounces are the most common.

When the weight is allowed to hang freely, the string is plumb (see *Figure 23*). You can use a plumb bob to make sure a wall or a doorjamb is vertical. Or, suppose you want to install a post under a beam. A plumb bob can show what point on the floor is directly under the section of the beam you need to support.

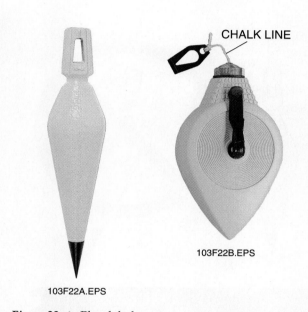

103F22A.EPS

103F22B.EPS

Figure 22 ◆ Plumb bobs.

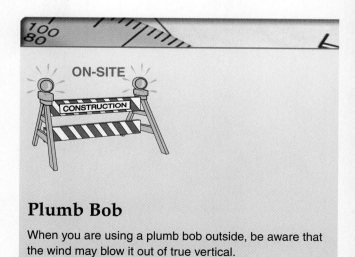

Plumb Bob

When you are using a plumb bob outside, be aware that the wind may blow it out of true vertical.

10.1.0 How to Use a Plumb Bob

Follow these steps to use a plumb bob properly:

Step 1 Make sure the line is attached at the exact top center of the plumb bob.

Step 2 Hang the bob from a horizontal member, such as a doorjamb, joist, or beam.

Step 3 When the weight is allowed to hang freely and stops swinging, the string is plumb (vertical).

Step 4 Mark the point directly below the tip of the plumb bob. This point is precisely below the point where you attached the bob.

> **CAUTION**
>
> Do not drop the plumb bob on its point. A bent or rounded point causes inaccurate readings.

103F23.EPS

Figure 23 ◆ Proper use of a plumb bob.

Review Questions

Section 10.0.0

1. A plumb bob uses _____ to make a line hang vertical.
   a. magnetic forces
   b. a point on the floor
   c. the force of gravity
   d. a spirit level

2. When something is plumb, it is _____.
   a. vertical
   b. horizontal
   c. at a 30-degree angle
   d. bobbed

3. When using a plumb bob outside, remember that _____ may affect the plumb bob.
   a. magnetic forces
   b. wind
   c. noise
   d. the point of suspension

4. When a plumb bob hangs freely, its string is _____.
   a. level
   b. horizontal
   c. vertical
   d. at a 45-degree angle

5. A plumb bob will be damaged if you drop it on its _____.
   a. line
   b. head
   c. joist
   d. point

11.0.0 ◆ CHALK LINES

A chalk line is a piece of string or cord that is coated with chalk. You stretch the line tightly between two points and then snap it to release a chalky line to the surface. You can use a piece of string rubbed with chalk if you need to snap only a couple of lines. But for frequent use, a mechanical self-chalking line is much handier.

A mechanical self-chalking line is a metal box (see *Figure 24*) containing a line on a reel. The box is filled with colored chalk powder. The line is automatically chalked each time you pull it out of the box. Some models have a point on the end of the box so it can be used as a plumb bob also.

11.1.0 How to Use a Chalk Line

Follow these steps to use a chalk line properly:

Step 1 Pull the line from the case. Have a partner hold one end.

Step 2 Stretch the line between the two points to be connected.

Step 3 After the line has been pulled tight, pull straight away from the work and then release. This marks the surface underneath with a straight line of chalk (see *Figure 25*).

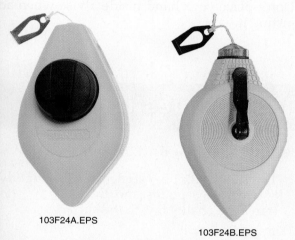

103F24A.EPS

103F24B.EPS

Figure 24 ◆ Mechanical self-chalkers.

CAUTION

Store the chalk line in a dry place. Damp or wet chalk is unusable.

CHALK LINE MARK

103F25.EPS

Figure 25 ◆ Proper use of a chalk line.

12.0.0 ◆ BENCH VISES

Vises are gripping and holding tools. By using a vise, you can do work that would otherwise require two people. Vises are used to secure an object while you work on it. Vises can be portable or fixed, which means they stay in one place.

The bench vise (see *Figure 26*) is a stationary vise with two sets of jaws: one to hold flat work and another to hold round work, such as pipe. Some bench vises have swivel bases so that you can turn the vise in any horizontal direction.

12.1.0 How to Use a Bench Vise

Follow these steps to use a bench vise properly:

Step 1 Place the object in the open clamp of the bench vise.

Step 2 To clamp the object, turn the sliding T-handle screw clockwise.

Step 3 To release the object, turn the T-handle screw counterclockwise.

CAUTION

Never use a hammer to tighten the handle, and never use a piece of pipe for leverage. Doing so may damage both the vise and the object being clamped.

12.2.0 Safety and Maintenance

You can damage a vise or the object it is holding by not using it properly. You can also injure yourself. For example, if the object in the vise is not clamped tightly enough, you could slip while using a saw on the object. Remember these guidelines for using a vise properly:

- Fasten the vise securely to the bench.
- Clamp work evenly in the vise.
- Support the ends of any long piece of wood or other material that is being held in the vise.
- Saw as close as possible to the jaws of the vise when you are sawing an object.
- Keep threaded parts clean.
- Don't use the jaws of the vise as a pounding surface.
- Don't place your hand inside a vise when adjusting it.

Review Questions

Sections 11.0.0 and 12.0.0

1. To use a chalk line, stretch the line tightly between two points and then _____ to transfer a chalky line to the surface.
    a. walk over it
    b. snap it
    c. moisten it
    d. press it

2. A vise is a _____ tool.
    a. measuring and gauging
    b. holding and gripping
    c. slicing and sawing
    d. ripping and prying

3. One set of vise jaws is for holding flat work; the other set is for holding _____ work.
    a. slippery
    b. extra
    c. large
    d. round

4. When using a bench vise, turn the sliding T-handle screw _____ to clamp the object.
    a. clockwise
    b. counterclockwise
    c. downward
    d. upward

5. When sawing an object, you should saw as close as possible to the jaws of the vise.
    a. True
    b. False

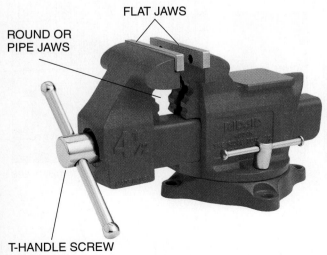

ROUND OR PIPE JAWS

FLAT JAWS

T-HANDLE SCREW

103F26.EPS

Figure 26 ◆ Bench vise.

3.0.0 ◆ CLAMPS

There are many types and sizes of clamps, each designed to solve a different holding problem. Clamps (see *Figure 27*) are sized by the maximum opening of the jaw. They come in sizes from 1 inch to 24 inches. The depth (or throat) of the clamp determines how far from the edge of the work the clamp can be placed. The following are common types of clamps:

C-clamp – This multipurpose clamp has a C-shaped frame. It is used primarily for clamping metalwork. The clamp has a metal shoe at the end of a screw. Using a T-bar, you tighten the clamp so that it holds material between the metal jaw of the frame and the shoe.

Locking C-clamp – This clamp works like vise-grip pliers. A knob in the handle controls the width and tension of the jaws. You close the handles to lock the clamp. You release the clamp by pressing the lever to open the jaws.

Spring clamp – You use your hand to open the spring-operated clamp. When you release the handles, the spring holds the clamp tightly shut, applying even pressure to the material. The jaws are usually made of steel, some with plastic coating to protect the material's surface against scarring.

- *Bar clamp* – A rectangular piece of steel or aluminum is the spine of the bar clamp. It has a fixed jaw at one end and a sliding jaw (tail slide) with a spring-locking device that moves along the bar. You position the fixed jaw against the object you want to hold and then move the sliding jaw into place. The screw set is tightened as with a C-clamp.
- *Pipe clamp* – Although this clamp looks like a bar clamp, the spine is actually a length of pipe. It has a fixed jaw and a movable jaw that work the same way as the bar clamp. The movable jaw has a lever mechanism that you squeeze when sliding the movable jaw along the spine.
- *Hand-screw clamp* – This clamp has wooden jaws. It can spread pressure over a wider area than other clamps can. Each jaw works independently. You can angle the jaws toward or away from each other or keep them parallel. You tighten the clamp using spindles that screw through the jaws.
- *Web (strap, band) clamp* – This clamp uses a belt-like canvas or nylon strap or band to apply even pressure around a piece of material. After looping the band around the work, you use the clamp head to secure the band. Using a wrench or screwdriver, you ratchet (tighten by degrees) the bolt tight in the clamp head. A quick-release device loosens the band after you are finished.

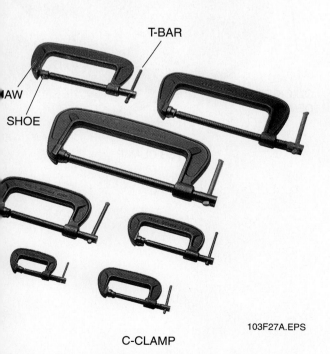

T-BAR

JAW

SHOE

C-CLAMP

103F27A.EPS

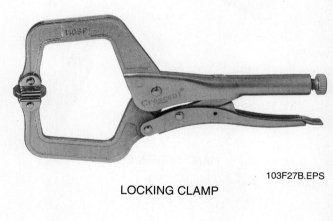

103F27B.EPS

LOCKING CLAMP

Figure 27 ◆ Types of clamps. (1 of 2)

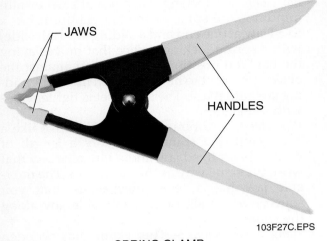

SPRING CLAMP

103F27C.EPS

BAR CLAMP

103F27D.EPS

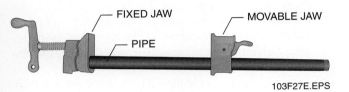

PIPE CLAMP

103F27E.EPS

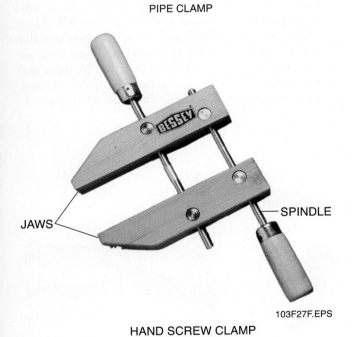

HAND SCREW CLAMP

103F27F.EPS

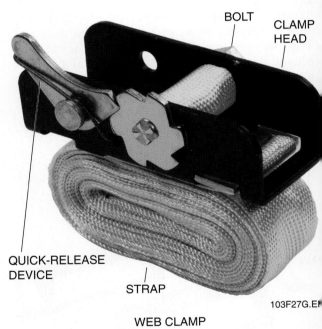

WEB CLAMP

103F27G.EPS

Figure 27 ◆ Types of clamps. (2 of 2)

3.1.0 How to Use a Clamp

Take the following steps to use a clamp properly:

Step 1 When clamping wood or other soft material, place pads or thin blocks of wood between the work piece and the clamp to protect the work (see *Figure 28*).

Step 2 Tighten the clamp's pressure mechanism, such as the T-bar handle. Don't force it.

3.2.0 Safety and Maintenance

Here are some guidelines to remember when using clamps:

Store clamps by clamping them to a rack.
Use pads or thin wood blocks when clamping wood or other soft materials.

CAUTION

When tightening a clamp, do not use pliers or a section of pipe on the handle to extend your grip or gain more leverage. Doing so means you will have less, not more, control over the clamp's tightening mechanism.

If you are clamping work that has been glued, do not tighten the clamps so much that all the glue is squeezed out of the joint.

- Discard clamps with bent frames.
- Clean and oil threads.
- Check the swivel at the end of the screw to make sure it turns freely.
- Don't use a clamp for hoisting (pulling up) work.
- Don't overtighten clamps.

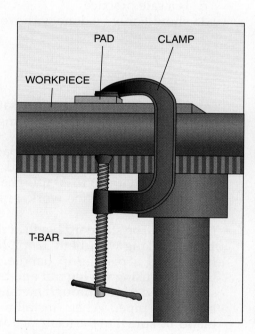
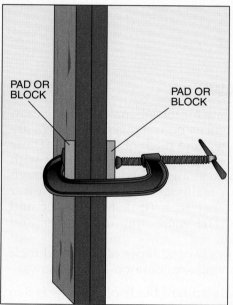

103F28.EPS

Figure 28 ◆ Placing pads and wood blocks.

Section 13.0.0

1. Clamps are sized by the _____.
   a. length of the handles
   b. distance between the metal bar and the shoe
   c. maximum opening of the jaw
   d. kind of pad you insert to protect the work

2. A C-clamp is used mainly for clamping _____.
   a. wood
   b. nylon
   c. T-bars
   d. metal

3. A hand-screw clamp has _____ jaws.
   a. metal
   b. nylon
   c. wooden
   d. fiberglass

4. When clamping soft materials, you need to use _____ to protect the work.
   a. a web
   b. pads
   c. a rack
   d. pipes

5. Using pliers or pipe on the handle of a clamp _____.
   a. gives you less control
   b. gives you more control
   c. is a safe practice
   d. should only be done with woodwork

14.0.0 ◆ SAWS

Using the right saw for the job makes cutting easy. The main differences between types of saws are the shape, number, and pitch of their teeth. These differences make it possible to cut across or with the grain of wood, along curved lines, or through metal, plastic, or wallboard. Generally, the fewer points or teeth per inch (tpi), the coarser and faster the cut. The more tpi, the slower and smoother the cut.

Figure 29 shows several types of saws and their parts. The following are common types of saws:

- *Backsaw* – The standard blade of this saw is 8 to 14 inches long with 11 to 14 tpi. A backsaw has a broad, flat blade and a reinforced back edge. It is used for cutting joints, especially miter joints and tenons.
- *Compass (keyhole) saw* – The standard blade of this saw is 12 to 14 inches long with 7 or 8 tpi. This saw cuts curves quickly in wood, plywood, or wallboard. It is also used to cut holes for large-diameter pipes, vents, and plugs or switch boxes. It can fit in tight places where a larger handsaw will not.
- *Coping saw* – This saw has a narrow, flexible 6¾-inch blade attached to a U-shaped frame. Holders at each end of the frame can be rotated so you can cut at angles. Standard blades range from 10 to 20 tpi. The coping saw is used for making irregular-shaped moldings fit together cleanly.
- *Dovetail saw* – This is a small backsaw with straight handle. The standard blade is 1 inches long with 16 to 20 tpi. The dovetail sa is used for cutting fine work, especially dove tail joints.
- *Hacksaw* – The standard blade of this saw is 8 16 inches long with 14 to 32 tpi. It has a sturd frame and a pistol-grip handle. The blade tightened using a wing nut and bolt. The hac saw is used to cut through metal, such as nail bolts, or pipe. When installing a hacksa blade, be sure that the teeth face away from, n toward, the saw handle. Hacksaws are de signed to cut on the push stroke, not on the pu stroke.
- *Handsaw (crosscut saw or ripsaw)* – The standar blade of this saw is 26 inches long with 8 to 14 t for a crosscut saw and 5 to 9 tpi for a ripsaw. Yo will learn how to use handsaws in this modu

14.1.0 Handsaws

The handsaw's blade is made of tempered steel it will stay sharp and will not bend or buck Handsaws are classified mainly by the numb shape, size, slant, and direction of the teeth. Sa

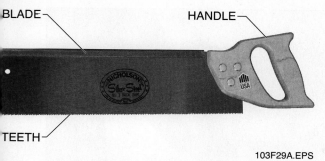

BACKSAW
103F29A.EPS

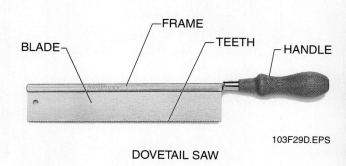

COMPASS SAW
103F29B.EPS

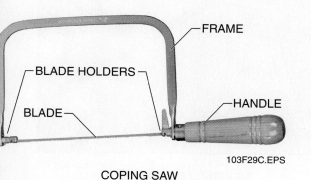

COPING SAW
103F29C.EPS

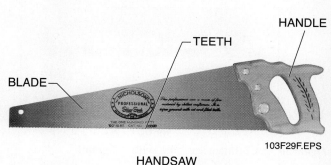

DOVETAIL SAW
103F29D.EPS

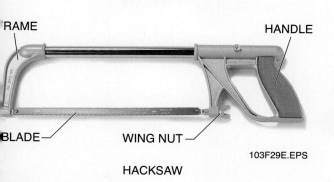

HACKSAW
103F29E.EPS

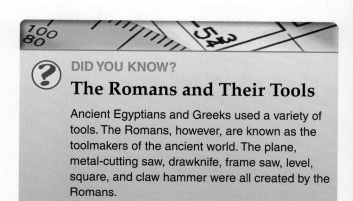

HANDSAW
103F29F.EPS

Figure 29 ◆ Types of saws.

teeth are set or angled alternately in opposite directions to make a cut (or **kerf**) slightly wider than the thickness of the saw blade itself. Two common types of handsaws are the crosscut saw and the ripsaw.

The crosscut saw, which has 8 to 14 tpi, is designed to cut across the grain (the direction of the fibers) of wood. Blade lengths range from 20 inches to 28 inches. For most general uses, 24 inches or 26 inches is a good length.

The ripsaw has 5 to 9 tpi. The ripsaw, designed to cut with the grain (parallel to the wood fibers), meets less resistance than a saw cutting across the grain. *Figure 30* shows how to cut across and with the grain.

? DID YOU KNOW?

The Romans and Their Tools

Ancient Egyptians and Greeks used a variety of tools. The Romans, however, are known as the toolmakers of the ancient world. The plane, metal-cutting saw, drawknife, frame saw, level, square, and claw hammer were all created by the Romans.

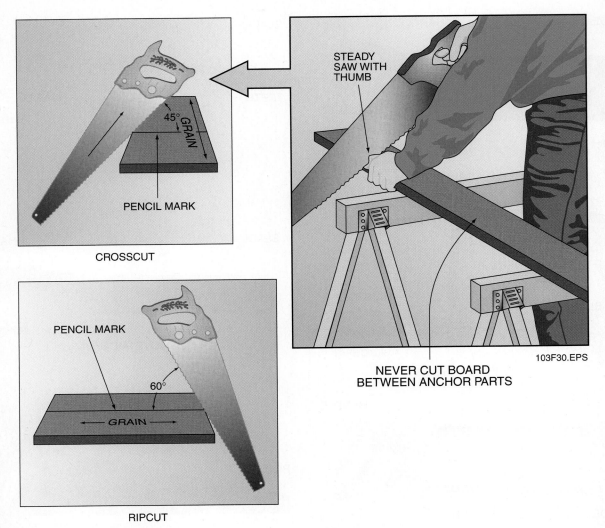

CROSSCUT

RIPCUT

STEADY SAW WITH THUMB

NEVER CUT BOARD BETWEEN ANCHOR PARTS

103F30.EPS

45° GRAIN

PENCIL MARK

PENCIL MARK

60°

GRAIN

Figure 30 ◆ Cutting across and with the grain.

14.1.1 How to Use a Crosscut Saw

Remember, the crosscut saw cuts across the grain of wood and, because it has 8 to 14 tpi, it will cut slowly but smoothly. Follow these steps to use a crosscut saw properly:

Step 1 Mark the cut to be made with a square or other measuring tool.

Step 2 Make sure the piece to be cut is well-supported (on a sawhorse, jack, or other support). Support the scrap end as well as the main part of the wood to keep it from splitting as the kerf nears the edge. With short pieces of wood, you can support the scrap end of the piece with your free hand. With longer pieces, you will need additional support.

Step 3 Place the saw teeth on the edge of the wood farthest from you, just at the outside edge of the mark.

Step 4 Start the cut with the part of the blac closest to the handle-end of the saw, b cause you will pull your first stroke t ward your body.

Step 5 Use the thumb of the hand that is not saw ing to guide the saw so it stays vertical the work.

Step 6 Place the saw at about a 45-degree angle the wood, then pull the saw to make small groove (see *Figure 30*).

Step 7 Start sawing slowly, increasing the leng of the stroke as the kerf deepens.

Step 8 Continue to saw with the blade at a 4 degree angle to the wood.

Using the Saw

Don't push or ride the saw into the wood. Let the weight of the saw set the cutting rate. It's easier to control the saw and less tiring that way.

Keeping the Saw in Line

If the saw starts to wander from the line, angle the blade toward the line. If the saw blade sticks in the kerf, wedge a thin piece of wood into the cut to hold it open.

4.1.2 How to Use a Ripsaw

The ripsaw cuts along the grain of wood. Because it has fewer points (5 to 9 tpi) than the crosscut saw, it will make a coarser, but faster, cut. Follow these steps to use a ripsaw properly:

Step 1 Mark and start a ripping cut the same way you would start cutting with a cross-cut saw.

Step 2 Once you've started the kerf, saw with the blade at a steeper angle to the wood—about 60 degrees.

4.2.0 Safety and Maintenance

You must maintain your saws for them to work properly. Also, it is very important to focus on your work when you are sawing—saws can be dangerous if used incorrectly or if you are not paying attention. Here are the guidelines for working with handsaws:

? DID YOU KNOW?
Emery Cloth

Emery cloth is a maintenance and cleaning tool often used in the construction industry. It is usually used for cleaning tools made of metal, like handsaws. It may be used wet or dry in a manner very similar to sandpaper. Emery cloth is coated with a substance called powdered emery, which is a granular form of pure carborundum.

- Clean your saw blade with a fine emery cloth and apply a coat of light machine oil if it starts to rust—rust ruins the saw blade.
- Always lay a saw down gently.
- Have your saw sharpened by an experienced sharpener.
- Brace yourself when sawing so you are not thrown off balance on the last stroke.
- Don't let saw teeth come in contact with stone, concrete, or metal.

Section 14.0.0

1. The main differences between types of saws relate to their _____.
   a. handles
   b. blades
   c. frames
   d. teeth

2. If you want to cut metal, you would choose the _____.
   a. ripsaw
   b. compass saw
   c. hacksaw
   d. crosscut saw

3. A type of saw that cuts *across* the grain of the wood is the _____.
   a. ripsaw
   b. crosscut saw
   c. hacksaw
   d. coping saw

4. A type of saw that cuts *with* the grain of the wood is the _____.
   a. dovetail saw
   b. ripsaw
   c. crosscut saw
   d. hacksaw

5. If a saw blade sticks in the kerf, you should _____.
   a. wedge a piece of wood in the kerf to keep it open
   b. apply a coat of light machine oil to the kerf
   c. sharpen the saw
   d. switch to a saw with fewer teeth per inch

15.0.0 ◆ FILES AND RASPS

You use files and rasps to cut, smooth, or shape metal parts. You can also use them to finish and shape all metals except hardened steel, and to sharpen many tools.

Files have slanting rows of teeth. Rasps have individual teeth. Files and rasps are usually made from a hardened piece of high-grade steel (see *Figure 31*). Both are sized by the length of the body. The size does not include the handle because the handle is generally separate from the file or rasp. For most sharpening jobs, files and rasps range from 4 inches to 14 inches (see *Figure 32*).

Choose a file or rasp whose shape fits the area you are filing. Files and rasps are available in round, square, flat, half-round, and triangular shapes. For filing large concave (curved inward) or flat surfaces, you might use a half-round shape. For filing small curves or for enlarging and smoothing holes, you might use a round shape with a tapered end, called a rat-tail file. For filing angles, you might use a triangular file.

There is a specific type of file for each of the common soft metals, hard metals, plastics, and wood. In general, the teeth of files for soft materials are very sharp and widely spaced. Those for hard materials are blunter and closer together.

The shape of the teeth also depends on the material to be worked.

If you use a file designed for soft material o hard material, the teeth will quickly chip and dul If you use a file designed for hard material on so material, the teeth will clog.

Most files are sold without a handle. You ca use a single handle for different files. The shar metal point at the end of the file, the **tang,** fits int the handle. You can tighten the handle to preven the tang from coming loose.

Files are classified by the cut of their teeth. Fi classifications include the following:

- Single-cut and double-cut
- Rasp-cut
- Curved-tooth

Table 1 lists types of files and some uses fo each.

Rasps are also classified by the size of the teeth: coarse, medium, and fine.

15.1.0 How to Use a File

Trying to use a file the wrong way will only fru trate you. Follow these steps to use a file properl

Step 1 Mount the work you are filing in a vise about elbow height.

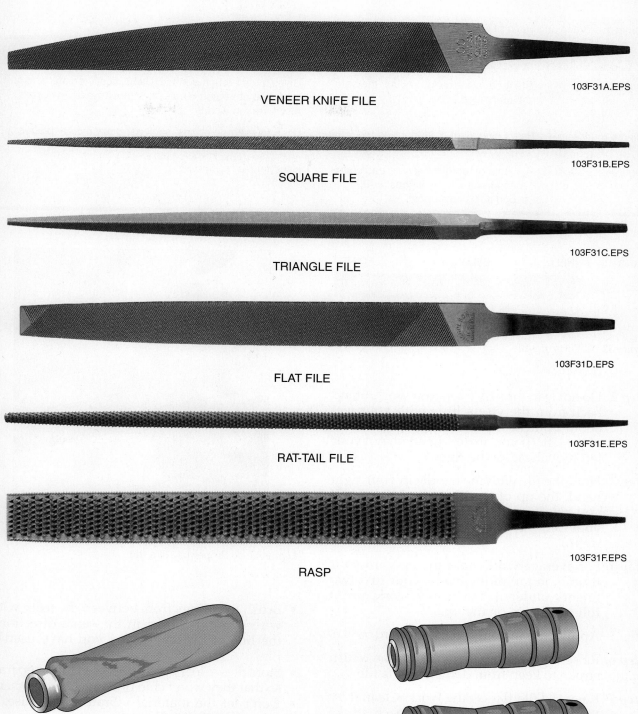

VENEER KNIFE FILE

103F31A.EPS

SQUARE FILE

103F31B.EPS

TRIANGLE FILE

103F31C.EPS

FLAT FILE

103F31D.EPS

RAT-TAIL FILE

103F31E.EPS

RASP

103F31F.EPS

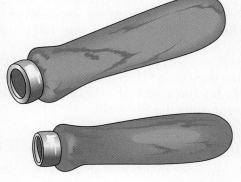

103F31G.EPS

WOODEN FILE HANDLES

103F31H.EPS

PLASTIC FILE HANDLES

Figure 31 ◆ Types of files, rasps, and handles.

Table 1 Types and Uses of Files

Type	Decription	Uses
Rasp-cut file	The teeth are individually cut; they are not connected to each other.	Gives a very rough surface. Used mostly on aluminum, lead, and other soft metals to remove waste materials. Also used on wood.
Single-cut file	Has a single set of straight-edged teeth running across the file at an angle.	Used to sharpen edges, such as rotary mower blades.
Double-cut file	Two sets of teeth crisscross each other. Types are bastard (roughest cut), second cut, and smooth.	Used for fast cutting.

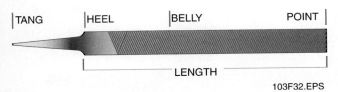

103F32.EPS

Figure 32 ◆ Parts of a file.

Step 2 Do not lean directly over your work. Stand back from the vise a little with your feet about 24 inches apart, the right foot ahead of the left. (If you are left-handed, put your left foot ahead of the right.)

Step 3 Hold the file with the handle in your right hand, the tip of the blade in your left. (If you are left-handed, hold the handle in your left hand and the blade in your right.)

Step 4 For average work, hold the tip with your thumb on top of the blade, your first two fingers under it. For heavy work, use a full-hand grip on the tip.

Step 5 Apply pressure only on the forward stroke.

Step 6 Raise the file from the work on the return stroke to keep from damaging the file.

Step 7 Keep the file flat on the work. Clean it by tapping lightly at the end of each stroke (see *Figure 33*).

15.2.0 Safety and Maintenance

Files will become worthless without proper maintenance. Here are some guidelines for use and maintenance of files:

- Use the correct file for the material being worked.
- Always put a handle on a file before using it—most files have handle attachments.

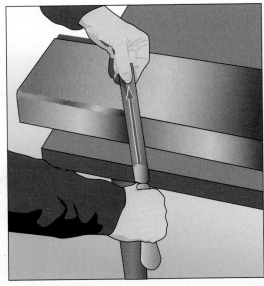

103F33.EPS

Figure 33 ◆ Proper use of a file.

- Brush the filings from between the teeth with wire brush, pushing in the same direction the line of the teeth, after you have used th file.
- Store files in a dry place and keep them separate so that they won't chip or damage each other.
- Don't let the material vibrate in the vise, b cause it dulls the file teeth.

16.0.0 ◆ CHISELS AND PUNCHES

Chisels are used to cut and shape wood, stone, metal. Punches are used to indent metal, dri pins, and align holes.

16.1.0 Chisels

A chisel is a metal tool with a sharpened, bevel (sloped) edge. It is used to cut and shape woc

Section 15.0.0

1. Files and rasps are usually made from _____.

   a. high-grade steel
   b. high-carbon steel
   c. cast aluminum
   d. lead

2. Files are classified by the _____ of their teeth.

   a. width
   b. angle
   c. taper
   d. cut

3. The teeth of files for soft materials are _____.

   a. soft
   b. sharp
   c. loose
   d. dull

4. Files have slanting rows of teeth and rasps have _____ teeth.

   a. smooth
   b. individual
   c. coarse
   d. wire

5. When cleaning files, _____.

   a. brush in the opposite direction of the line of teeth
   b. use an old toothbrush
   c. brush in the same direction as the line of teeth
   d. use soap and water

ON-SITE

CONSTRUCTION

Caring for Hand Tools

You have to use power tools to care for some types of hand tools, such as chisels, screwdrivers, hammers, and punches. If the edge or striking surface of a hand tool is damaged or worn, it should be ground back to its desired shape using a grinder. Grinding a hammer face or a punch point will remove unwanted burrs or mushrooming. For a chisel to cut well, the blade needs to be beveled (sloped) at a precise angle. A grinder can be used to remove nicks. The cutting edge must then be sharpened on an oilstone to produce a keen, precise edge. Screwdriver blades can also be cleaned up using a grinder.

...one, or metal. You will learn about two kinds of ...isels in this section: the wood chisel and the cold ...isel (see *Figure 34*). Both chisels are made from ...eel that is heat-treated to make it harder. A chisel ...n cut any material that is softer than the steel of ...e chisel.

6.1.1   How to Use a Wood Chisel

...ou use the wood chisel to make openings or ...otches in wooden material. For instance, you can ...se it to make a recess for butt-type hinges, such ...s the hinges in a door. Follow these steps to use a ...ood chisel properly:

Step 1 Wear appropriate personal protective equipment.

Step 2 Outline the opening (recess) to be chiseled.

Step 3 Set the chisel at one end of the outline, with its edge on the cross-grain line and the bevel facing the recess to be made.

Step 4 Strike the chisel head lightly with a mallet.

Step 5 Repeat this process at the other end of the outline, again with the bevel of the chisel blade toward the recess. Then make a series of cuts about ¼ inch apart from one end of the recess to the other.

103F34A.EPS

COLD

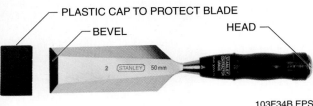

PLASTIC CAP TO PROTECT BLADE

BEVEL

HEAD

2 (STANLEY) 50 mm

103F34B.EPS

WOOD

Figure 34 ◆ Cold and wood chisels.

Step 6 To pare (trim) away the notched wood, hold the chisel bevel-side down to slice inward from the end of the recess (see *Figure 35*).

16.1.2 *How to Use a Cold Chisel*

You use the cold chisel to cut metal. For instance, you can use it to cut rivets, nuts, and bolts made of brass, bronze, copper, or iron. Follow these steps to use a cold chisel properly:

Step 1 Wear appropriate personal protective equipment.

Step 2 Secure the object you want to cut in a vise, if possible.

Step 3 Use a holding tool to hold the chisel in the spot where you want to cut the metal.

Step 4 Using a holding tool, place the blade of the chisel at the spot where you want to cut the material.

Step 5 Hit the chisel handle with a ball peen hammer to force the chisel into and through the material. Use a holding tool to hold material in place. Repeat if necessary.

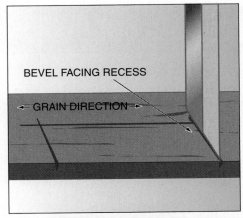

BEVEL FACING RECESS

GRAIN DIRECTION

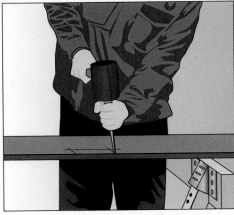

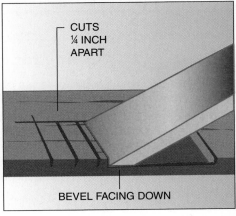

CUTS
¼ INCH
APART

BEVEL FACING DOWN

103F35.EPS

Figure 35 ◆ Proper use of a wood chisel.

16.2.0 Punches

A punch (see *Figure 36*) is used to indent met (from the impact of a hammer) before you drill hole, to drive pins, and to align holes in two par that are mates. Punches are made of hardened an tempered steel. They come in various sizes.

Three common types of punches are the cent punch, the prick punch, and the straight punc The center and prick punches are used to mak small locating points for drilling holes. The straig punch is used to punch holes in thin sheets of met

---

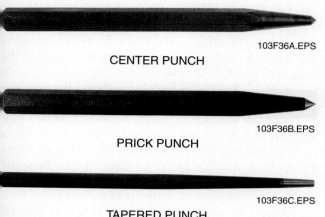

CENTER PUNCH

103F36A.EPS

PRICK PUNCH

103F36B.EPS

TAPERED PUNCH

103F36C.EPS

Figure 36 ◆ Punches.

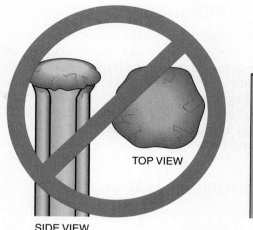

TOP VIEW

SIDE VIEW

MUSHROOMED HEAD

PREFERRED HEAD

103F37.EPS

Figure 37 ◆ Chisel damage.

16.3.0 Safety and Maintenance

Here are the guidelines to remember when you're working with punches and chisels:

Always wear safety goggles.
Make sure the wood chisel blade is beveled at a precise 25-degree angle so it will cut well.
Make sure the cold chisel blade is beveled at a 60-degree angle so it will cut well.
Sharpen the cutting edge of a chisel on an oilstone to produce a keen edge.
Don't use a chisel head or hammer that has become mushroomed or flattened (see *Figure 37*).
Don't use a cold chisel to cut or split stone or concrete.

 WARNING!

Striking a chisel that has a mushroom-shaped head can cause metal chips to break off. These flying chips can cause serious injury. If a chisel has a mushroom-shaped head, it is damaged. Replace the chisel or have a qualified person repair it.

Review Questions

Section 16.0.0

1. A chisel can cut any metal that is _____ than the steel of the chisel.
   a. softer
   b. harder
   c. colder
   d. warmer

2. All of the following are common types of punches *except* the _____.
   a. center punch
   b. prick punch
   c. tempered punch
   d. straight punch

3. A cold chisel is used to cut _____.
   a. wood
   b. plastic
   c. ice
   d. metal

4. You know a chisel head is damaged if it is shaped like a(n) _____.
   a. punch
   b. mushroom
   c. egg
   d. pin

5. A punch is used to _____.
   a. cut metal
   b. cut wood
   c. indent metal
   d. indent oilstone

17.0.0 ◆ WRENCHES

Wrenches are used to hold and turn screws, nuts, bolts, and pipes. There are many types of wrenches, but they fall into two main categories: nonadjustable and adjustable. Nonadjustable wrenches fit only one size nut or bolt. They come in both standard (English) and metric sizes. Adjustable wrenches can be expanded to fit different-sized nuts and bolts.

17.1.0 Nonadjustable Wrenches

Nonadjustable wrenches (see *Figure 38*) include the **open-end wrench**, the **box-end wrench**, the **Allen** (or hex key) **wrench**, the **striking** (or **slugging**) **wrench**, and the **combination wrench**.

The open-end wrench is one of the easiest nonadjustable wrenches to use. It has an opening at each end that determines the size of the wrench. Often, one wrench has two different-sized open-

ings, such as $^7/_{16}$ inch and $^1/_2$ inch, one on each end. These sizes measure the distance between the **flats** (straight sides or jaws of wrench opening) of the wrench and the distance across the head of the **fastener** used. The open end allows you to slide the tool around the fastener when there is not enough room to fit a box-end wrench.

Box-end wrenches form a continuous circle around the head of a fastener. The ends have 6 or 12 **points.** The ends come in different sizes ranging from $^3/_8$ inch to $^{15}/_{16}$ inch. Box-end wrenches offer a firmer grip than open-end wrenches. A box-end wrench is safer to use than an open-end wrench because it will not slip off the sides of certain kinds of bolts. The handles of box-end wrenches are available in a range of lengths.

Striking or slugging wrenches (see *Figure 39*) are similar to box-end wrenches in that they have an enclosed circular opening designed to lock on to the fastener when the wrench is struck. The

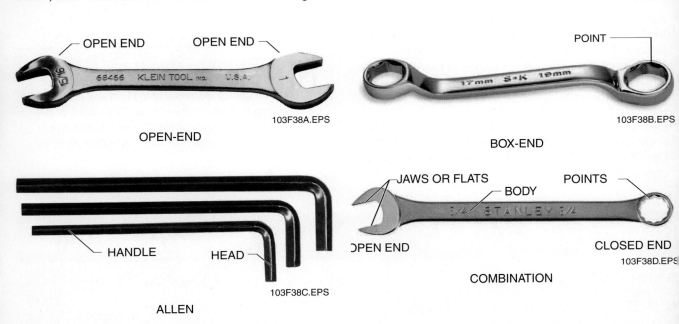

Figure 38 ◆ Nonadjustable wrenches.

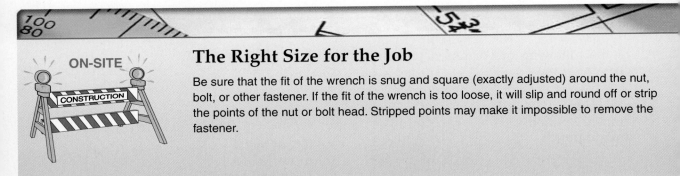

The Right Size for the Job

Be sure that the fit of the wrench is snug and square (exactly adjusted) around the nut, bolt, or other fastener. If the fit of the wrench is too loose, it will slip and round off or strip the points of the nut or bolt head. Stripped points may make it impossible to remove the fastener.

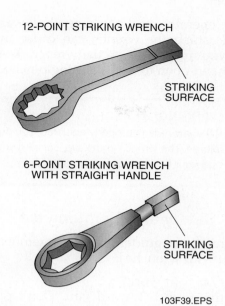

12-POINT STRIKING WRENCH

STRIKING SURFACE

6-POINT STRIKING WRENCH WITH STRAIGHT HANDLE

STRIKING SURFACE

103F39.EPS

Figure 39 ◆ Striking wrenches.

...renches have a large striking surface so you can ...it them more accurately, usually with a mallet or ...andheld sledgehammer. The ends have 6 or 12 ...oints. Striking wrenches are used only in certain ...ituations, such as when a bolt has become stuck ...o another material through rust or corrosion. ...triking wrenches can damage screw threads and ...olt heads. If you are ever in doubt about whether ...r not to use a striking wrench, ask your instruc-...or or immediate supervisor.

Allen or hex key wrenches are L-shaped, hexag-...nal (six-sided) steel bars. Both ends fit the socket ...f a screw or bolt. The shorter length of the L-...hape is called the head, and the longer length is ...e handle. These wrenches generally have a $\frac{1}{16}$-...nch to $\frac{3}{4}$-inch diameter. You might use them with ...etscrews. Setscrews are used in tools and ma-...hinery to set two parts tightly together so they ...on't move from the set position.

Combination wrenches are, as the name im-...lies, a combination of two types of wrenches. ...ne end of the combination wrench is open and ...he other is closed, or box-end. Combination ...renches can speed up your work because you ...on't have to keep changing wrenches.

7.1.1 *How to Use a Nonadjustable Wrench*

...ollow these steps when using a nonadjustable ...rench:

tep 1 Always use the correct size wrench for the nut or bolt.

tep 2 Pull the wrench toward you. Pushing the wrench can cause injury.

17.2.0 Adjustable Wrenches

Adjustable wrenches are used to tighten or re-move nuts and bolts and all types and sizes of pipes. They have one fixed jaw and one movable jaw. The adjusting nut on the wrench joins the teeth in the body of the wrench and moves the ad-justable jaw. These wrenches come in lengths from 4 to 24 inches and open as wide as $2\frac{7}{16}$ inches. Common types of adjustable wrenches include **pipe wrenches**, **spud wrenches**, and **crescent wrenches** (see *Figure 40*). Using an adjustable wrench may save time when you're working with different sizes of nuts and bolts.

Pipe wrenches (often called monkey wrenches) are used to tighten and loosen all types and sizes of threaded pipe. You adjust the upper jaw of the wrench by turning the adjusting nut (see

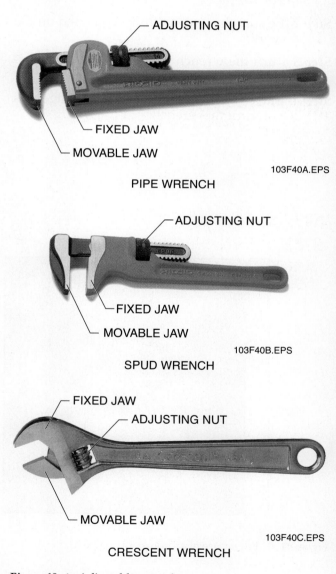

ADJUSTING NUT

FIXED JAW

MOVABLE JAW

103F40A.EPS

PIPE WRENCH

ADJUSTING NUT

FIXED JAW

MOVABLE JAW

103F40B.EPS

SPUD WRENCH

FIXED JAW

ADJUSTING NUT

MOVABLE JAW

103F40C.EPS

CRESCENT WRENCH

Figure 40 ◆ Adjustable wrenches.

Figure 41). Both jaws have serrated teeth for gripping power. The jaw is spring-loaded and slightly angled so you can release the grip and reposition the wrench without having to readjust the jaw.

Spud wrenches loosen and tighten fittings on drain traps, sink strainers, toilet connections, and large, odd-shaped nuts. Spud wrenches have narrow jaws to fit into tight places.

Crescent wrenches are smooth-jawed for turning nuts, bolts, small pipe fittings, and chrome-plated pipe fittings.

17.2.1   *How to Use an Adjustable Wrench*

To use an adjustable wrench properly, follow these steps:

Step 1 Set the jaws to the correct size for the nut, bolt, or pipe.

Step 2 Be sure the jaws are fully tightened on the work.

Step 3 Turn the wrench so you are putting pressure on the fixed jaw (see *Figure 41*).

Step 4 Make sure there is room for your fingers as you turn the wrench.

Step 5 Generally, pull the wrench toward you. Pushing the wrench can cause injury. If you must push on the wrench, keep your hand open to avoid getting pinched.

WARNING!
If the jaws are improperly adjusted, you could be injured. The wrench could slip, causing you to hurt your hand or lose your balance.

17.3.0 Safety and Maintenance

Here are some guidelines to remember when working with wrenches:

- Focus on your work.
- Pull the wrench toward you. Don't push the wrench because that can cause injury.
- Keep adjustable wrenches clean. Don't allow mud or grease to clog the adjusting screw and slide; oil these parts frequently.
- Don't use the wrench as a hammer.
- Don't use any wrench beyond its capacity. For example, never add an extension to increase its leverage. This could cause serious injury.

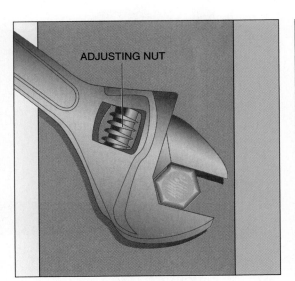
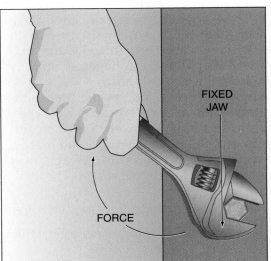

103F41.EPS

Figure 41 ◆ Proper use of an adjustable wrench.

Metrics and Tools

You must know whether the materials you are working with are made using metric or standard measurements. You will not get a proper fit if you use the wrong-size tool. A box-end wrench, for example, may be for metric or standard sizes. If the fit of the wrench is too loose, it will slip and round off the points of the nut or bolt head.

The same is true for socket wrenches. If you use a standard-measure socket on a metric bolt, you may wear the points off the head. You will then have to drill the bolt out to remove it.

Review Questions

Section 17.0.0

1. Wrenches are used to _____.
   a. pound nails into wood
   b. turn screws, nuts, bolts, and pipes
   c. pry open fittings on drains
   d. strip threaded pipe

2. An adjustable wrench _____.
   a. can be used for many purposes, such as hammering or prying
   b. automatically adjusts its jaws
   c. fits only one size of screw, nut, bolt, and pipe
   d. can be used on different sizes of screws, nuts, bolts, and pipes

3. A nonadjustable wrench _____.
   a. fits only one size nut or bolt
   b. can be used on all sizes of screws, nuts, bolts, and pipes
   c. can be used only for hammering
   d. must have its jaws adjusted by hand each time it is used

4. One of the easiest nonadjustable wrenches to use is the _____ wrench.
   a. open-end
   b. box-end
   c. Allen
   d. pipe

5. Using an adjustable wrench can save time when you are working with _____.
   a. nuts and bolts that are all the same size
   b. stripped heads
   c. different sizes of nuts and bolts
   d. nails and plywood

18.0.0 ◆ SOCKETS AND RATCHETS

Socket wrench sets include different combinations of sockets (the part that grips the nut or bolt) and ratchets (handles) that are used to turn the sockets.

Most sockets (see *Figure 42*) have 6 or 12 gripping points. The end of the socket that fits into the handle is square. Sockets also come in different lengths. The long socket is called a deep socket. It is used when normal sockets will not reach down over the end of the bolt to grip the nut.

Socket sets contain different types of handles for different uses. The ratchet handle (see *Figure 43*) has a small lever that you can use to change the turning direction.

18.1.0 How to Use Sockets and Ratchets

Follow these steps to use sockets and ratchets properly:

Step 1 Select a socket that fits the fastener (such as a nut or bolt) you want to tighten or loosen

Step 2 Place the square end of the socket over the spring-loaded button on the ratchet shaft

Step 3 Place the socket over the nut or bolt.

Step 4 Pull on the handle in one direction to turn the nut. (Moving the handle in the other direction has no effect.) To reverse the direction of the socket, use the adjustable lock mechanism.

18.2.0 Safety and Maintenance

Follow these guidelines to maintain your socket and ratchets in good working order:

- Never force the ratchet handle beyond hand-tight. This could break the head off the fastener
- Don't use a cheater pipe (a longer piece of pipe slipped over the ratchet handle to provide more leverage). This could snap the tool or break the head off the bolt or nut.

103F42.EPS

Figure 42 ◆ Sockets.

103F43.EPS

Figure 43 ◆ Ratchet handle.

Review Questions

Section 18.0.0

1. A socket is used to _____.
   a. turn the ratchet
   b. grip a nut or bolt
   c. fasten the ratchet
   d. adjust the lock

2. A ratchet is used to _____.
   a. grip a nut or bolt
   b. fasten the socket
   c. turn the socket
   d. adjust the lock

3. Most sockets have either 6 or 12 _____.
   a. ratchets
   b. locks
   c. handles
   d. gripping points

4. When turning the ratchet, _____.
   a. stop when it is hand-tight
   b. force it just a little past hand-tight
   c. use a wrench to make sure it's very tight
   d. stop just short of making it hand-tight

5. You should never use a(n) _____ with a ratchet handle.
   a. machine-oiled cloth
   b. oilstone
   c. locking bar
   d. cheater pipe

19.0.0 ◆ TORQUE WRENCHES

Torque wrenches (see *Figure 44*) measure resistance to turning. You need them when you are installing fasteners that must be tightened in sequence without distorting the workpiece. You will use a torque wrench only when a torque setting is specified for a particular bolt.

Torque specifications are usually stated in **inch-pounds** for small fasteners or **foot-pounds** for large fasteners.

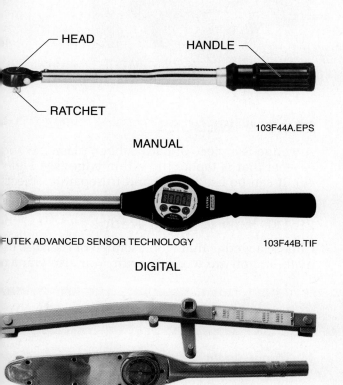

HEAD

HANDLE

RATCHET

103F44A.EPS

MANUAL

FUTEK ADVANCED SENSOR TECHNOLOGY

103F44B.TIF

DIGITAL

103F44C.TIF

TENSIOMETER (WIRE) AND DIAL

Figure 44 ◆ Torque wrenches.

19.1.0 How to Use a Torque Wrench

Take these steps to use a torque wrench properly:

Step 1 Look on the tool to find out how many inch-pounds or foot-pounds you need to torque to. Set the controls on the wrench to the desired torque level (wrench models vary).

Step 2 Find out the torque sequence (which fastener comes first, second, and so on). If you use the wrong sequence, you could damage what you are fastening

Step 3 Place the torque wrench on the object to be fastened, such as a bolt. Hold the head of the wrench with one hand to support the bolt and to make sure it is properly aligned.

Step 4 Watch the torque indicator or listen for the click (depending on the model of the wrench) as you tighten the bolt (see *Figure 45*).

19.2.0 How to Calculate Torque When Using an Adaptor

When you use an adaptor or extension, the torque wrench becomes longer. The extra length and the applied torque will be greater than the torque indicator. Use this formula to determine the correct torque.

$$\text{Preset torque} = \frac{\text{Length of torque wrench} \times \text{desired torque}}{\text{Length of torque wrench} + \text{length of extension}}$$

To determine the length of the torque wrench, measure the distance from the center of the square drive of the wrench to the center of the handle. To determine the length of the extension, measure the distance from the center of the square drive of the extension to the center of the bolt or nut. Be sure to measure only the length that is parallel to the handle.

ON-SITE

CONSTRUCTION

Torque Wrenches

To get accurate settings, make sure all threaded fasteners are clean and undamaged.

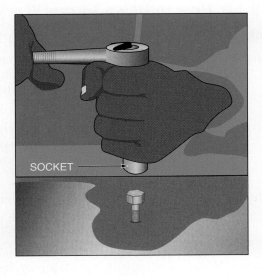
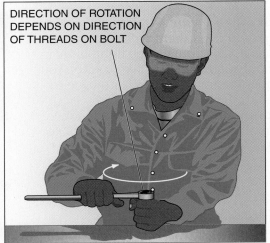

DIRECTION OF ROTATION
DEPENDS ON DIRECTION
OF THREADS ON BOLT

SOCKET

103F45.EPS

Figure 45 ◆ Proper use of a torque wrench.

19.3.0 Safety and Maintenance

A torque wrench can cause property damage and injury if used incorrectly. Follow these guidelines when using your torque wrench:

- Always follow the manufacturer's recommendations for safety, maintenance, and calibration.
- Always store the wrench in its case.
- Never use the wrench as a ratchet or as anything other than its intended purpose.

20.0.0 ◆ WEDGES

A wedge is a piece of hard rubber, plastic, wood, or steel that is tapered to a thin edge (see *Figure 46*). It can be used to lift and to separate objects, among other uses.

20.1.0 How to Use a Wedge

Choose a wedge that won't scratch or damage the material you are working with. You also want to

Review Questions

Section 19.0.0

1. Torque wrenches measure resistance to _____.

   a. accuracy
   b. alignment
   c. turning
   d. plumb

2. Torque specifications for small fasteners are usually specified in _____.

   a. foot-pounds
   b. inch-pounds
   c. wrench widths
   d. threads

3. Torque specifications for large fasteners are usually specified in _____.

   a. foot-pounds
   b. inch-pounds
   c. wrench widths
   d. threads

4. Torque wrenches are used when you need to install _____ that must be tightened in sequence.

   a. torques
   b. clean threads
   c. ratchets
   d. fasteners

5. You should place one hand on the _____ to support the bolt and to make sure it is properly aligned.

   a. vise bench
   b. head of the wrench
   c. plumb bob
   d. head of the bolt

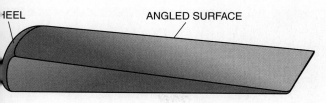

HEEL ANGLED SURFACE

103F46.EPS

Figure 46 ◆ Wedge.

choose one of the proper size so it will lift or separate the material only as far as you need to. Follow these steps to use a wedge properly (see *Figure 47*).

Follow these steps to properly lift an object using a wedge:

Step 1 Place the wedge at the edge of the object.

Step 2 Check to be sure that the object is well supported.

Step 3 Strike the heel of the wedge with a hammer.

Follow these steps to separate two objects using a wedge:

Step 1 Place the wedge between them.

Step 2 Strike the heel of the wedge with a hammer to force the two objects apart.

20.2.0 Safety and Maintenance

A wedge can be dangerous if used without precautions. Remember these guidelines whenever you use a wedge:

● Wear appropriate personal protective equipment, including safety glasses and a face shield, when using a wedge because a piece of it could fly off.

● Keep your hands away from the heel of the wedge when you are striking it.

LIFT AN OBJECT

SEPARATE TWO OBJECTS

103F47.EPS

Figure 47 ◆ Proper use of a wedge.

Section 20.0.0

1. A wedge can be used to lift and _____ objects.

   a. weld
   b. separate
   c. taper
   d. fasten

2. A wedge can be made of _____, plastic, wood, or steel that is tapered to a thin edge.

   a. hard rubber
   b. aluminum
   c. iron
   d. stone

3. When using a wedge, always _____.

   a. wear eye protection
   b. keep your hand close to the heel of the wedge
   c. oil the wedge lightly
   d. sharpen the angled edge first

4. To separate two objects, strike the _____ of the wedge with a hammer.

   a. thin edge
   b. rubber edge
   c. toe
   d. heel

5. Before using a wedge to lift an object, check to make sure the object is _____.

   a. made of the same material as the wedge
   b. well supported
   c. beveled
   d. plumb

21.0.0 ◆ UTILITY KNIVES

A utility knife is used for a variety of purposes including cutting roofing felt, fiberglass or asphalt shingles, vinyl or linoleum floor tiles, fiberboard, and gypsum board. You can also use it for trimming insulation.

The utility knife has a replaceable razor-like blade. It has a handle about 6 inches long, made of cast iron or plastic, to hold the blade. The handle is made in two halves, held together with a screw (see *Figure 48*).

With many utility knives, you can lock the blade in the handle in one, two, or three positions, depending on the type of knife. Models that have a retractable blade (the blade pulls into the handle when not in use) are the safest. Some models have different blades for cutting different materials.

21.1.0 How to Use a Utility Knife

Follow these steps to use a utility knife properly:

Step 1 Unlock the knife blade. Push the blade out.

Step 2 Lock the blade in the open position.

Step 3 Place some scrap, such as a piece of wood, under the object you are cutting. This will protect the surface under the object.

Step 4 Use the sharp side of the blade (the longer side) to cut straight lines.

103F48.EP

Figure 48 ◆ Utility knife.

Step 5 As soon as you have finished cutting, unlock the blade, pull it back to the closed position, and lock the blade.

 WARNING!
Never use a utility knife on live electrical wires. You could be electrocuted.

21.2.0 Safety and Maintenance

Here are some guidelines to remember about your utility knife:

• Don't bother sharpening your utility knife blade (even though you can) because the blades are so inexpensive. It makes more sense to buy new blades.

• Always keep the blade closed and locked when you are not using the knife.

Section 21.0.0

1. A utility knife is used to cut such materials as roofing felt, vinyl floor tiles, and _____.

    a. plastic pipes
    b. gypsum board
    c. electrical wires
    d. porcelain floor tiles

2. The safest kind of utility knife is one with _____.

    a. a leather sheath
    b. a blue blade
    c. at least three blades
    d. a retractable blade

3. When using a utility knife, place a scrap under the object you are cutting in order to _____.

    a. see the object more clearly
    b. keep the blade sharp
    c. protect the surface under the object
    d. automatically unlock the knife blade

4. Once you have pushed the utility knife blade out, always _____.

    a. lock the blade in the closed position
    b. lock the blade in the open position
    c. scuff the blade
    d. sharpen the blade

5. A dull utility knife blade should be sharpened rather than replaced because of the cost of the blade.

    a. True
    b. False

22.0.0 ◆ CHAIN FALLS AND COME-ALONGS

Chain falls and come-alongs are used to move heavy loads safely. A chain fall, also called a chain block or chain hoist, is a tackle device fitted with an endless chain used for hoisting heavy loads by hand. It is usually suspended from an overhead track. A come-along is used to move loads horizontally over the ground for short distances.

22.1.0 Chain Falls

The chain fall (see *Figure 49*) has an automatic brake that holds the load after it is lifted. As the load is lifted, a screw forces fiber discs together to keep the load from slipping. The brake pressure increases as the loads get heavier. The brake holds the load until the lowering chain is pulled. Manual chain falls are operated by hand. Electrical chain falls are operated from an electrical control box.

In a chain fall, the suspension hook is a steel hook used to hang the chain fall. It is one size larger than the load hook. The gear box contains the gears that provide lifting power. The hand chain is a continuous chain used to operate the gearbox. The load chain is attached to the load hook and used to lift loads. A safety latch prevents the load from slipping off the load hook, which is attached to the load.

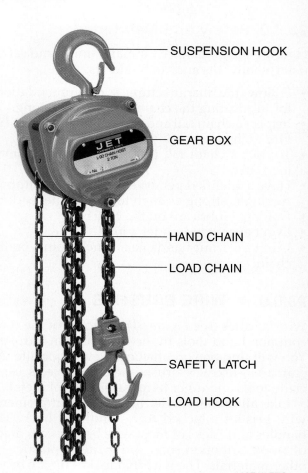

103F49.EPS

Figure 49 ◆ Parts of a manual chain fall.

22.2.0 Come-Alongs

Come-alongs, also called cable pullers, use a ratchet handle to position loads or to move heavy loads horizontally over short distances (see *Figure 50*). They can support loads from 1 to 6 tons. Some come-alongs use a chain for moving their loads; others use wire ropes.

When using a chain come-along, you can use the ratchet handle to take up the chain and the ratchet release to allow the chain to be pulled out. You can also use the fast-wind handle to take up or let out slack in the chain without using the ratchet handle.

103F50A.EPS

CABLE COME-ALONG

 CAUTION

Never use a come-along for vertical overhead lifting. Use a come-along only to move loads horizontally over the ground for short distances. Come-alongs are not equipped with the safety features, such as a pawl to check the ratchet's motion, that would ensure the safety of anyone underneath a load.

103F50B.EPS

CHAIN COME-ALONG

Figure 50 ◆ Come-alongs.

22.3.0 Safety and Maintenance

Here are the guidelines for maintaining and safely using chain falls and come-alongs:

- Follow the manufacturer's recommendations for lubricating the chain fall or come-along.
- Inspect a chain fall and come-along for wear before each use.
- Try out a chain fall or come-along on a small load first.
- Have a qualified person ensure that the support rigging is strong enough to handle the load.
- Don't get lubricant on the clutches.
- Don't ever stand under a load.
- Don't put your hands near pinch-points on the chain.

23.0.0 ◆ WIRE BRUSHES

Wire brushes (see *Figure 51*) are some of the most common hand tools in the construction industry. You will find one on practically every job site. All craft areas use wire brushes to clean objects, especially tools and other hardware made of metal.

Like all brushes, wire brushes are implements with bristles attached to a handle or back. The handles and backs of most wire brushes are made of wood, although some are made of plastic and other materials. The wire that makes up the brush itself is composed of many individual filaments or slender rods of drawn metal. Wire brushes have

103F51.EPS

Figure 51 ◆ Wire brush.

different types of bristles for cleaning different types of metals.

For example, carpenters use wood-handled brushes with stainless steel bristles to clean rusty tools and to remove paint. Pipefitters and plumbers use wire brushes to clean tools and also to clean welds on soldered pipe. Many wire brushes have brass bristles for use on especially heavy-duty jobs. Other types of wire brushes are used to clean wire rope and chains used for rigging operations.

Section 22.0.0

1. Chain falls are used to _____.
   a. transport light loads safely
   b. supplement come-along pulls
   c. rig light loads safely
   d. safely move heavy loads vertically

2. An important feature of the chain fall is the _____.
   a. automatic brake that holds the load after it is lifted
   b. automatic lubricating device
   c. fast-wind handle for lifting or lowering
   d. ratchet handle with automatic release

3. A cable come-along is used to _____.
   a. transport light loads
   b. move heavy loads horizontally over short distances
   c. supplement the work done by a chain fall
   d. hold the load after the chain fall has lifted it

4. You can use the fast-wind handle on a come-along to _____.
   a. perform emergency lifts
   b. transfer the load from the chain fall
   c. take up or let out the chain slack without using the ratchet handle
   d. lift loads weighing more than 6 tons

5. When you lubricate a chain fall or come-along, avoid getting lubricant on the _____.
   a. clutches
   b. chain
   c. ratchet release
   d. jack

23.1.0 How to Use a Wire Brush

Use a wire brush only for its intended purposes. If you are ever in doubt about whether or not a job calls for using a wire brush, ask your instructor or immediate supervisor. Wire brushes can damage many materials, especially wood and plastic. Also, because they are used to keep other tools clean, wire brushes themselves can become quite dirty. Be sure to clean a wire brush properly each time you use it or your work may become soiled or damaged. At this point in your training, you will most likely be relied upon to clean up periodically during and especially at the end of each workday. You'll need to know how to make good use of a wire brush.

CAUTION

Do not use a wire brush for finishing work. It will scratch the surface. Some wire brushes cannot be used on stainless steel.

24.0.0 ◆ SHOVELS

Shovels are used by many different construction trades. An electrician running underground wiring may dig a trench. A concrete mason may dig footers for a foundation. A carpenter may clear dirt from an area for concrete form-building. A plumber may dig a ditch to lay pipe. A welder may use a shovel to clean up scrap metal and slag after the job is finished.

There are three basic shapes of shovel blades: round, square, and spade (see *Figure 52*). Use a round-bladed shovel to dig holes or remove large amounts of soil. Use a square-bladed shovel to move gravel or clean up construction debris. Use a spade to move large amounts of soil or dig trenches that need smooth, straight sides.

Shovels can have wooden or fiberglass handles. They generally come in two lengths. A long handle is usually 47 to 48 inches long. A short handle is usually 27 inches long.

24.1.0 How to Use a Shovel

Follow these steps to shovel properly (see *Figure 53*):

Step 1 Select the type of shovel that is best for the job.

SPADE

ROUND

SQUARE

103F52.EPS

Figure 52 ◆ Shapes of shovel blades.

For a round shovel or spade:

Step 2 Place the tip of the shovel blade or spade at the point where you will begin digging or removing soil.

Step 3 With your foot balanced on the turned step (ridge), press down and cut into the soil with the blade.

For a square shovel:

Step 2 Place the leading edge of the shovel blade against the gravel or construction debris and push until the shovel is loaded.

24.2.0 Safety and Maintenance

Here are some guidelines for working with shovels:

- Always check the handle before using a shovel. There should be no cracks or splits.
- Use appropriate personal protective equipment when digging, trenching, or clearing debris. Wear steel-toed boots to protect your feet from dropped materials.
- Don't let dirt or debris build up on the blade. Always rinse off the shovel blade after using it.

ROUND SHOVEL OR SPADE

SQUARE SHOVEL

103F53.EPS

Figure 53 ◆ Proper use of a shovel.

Sections 23.0.0 and 24.0.0

1. Wire brushes are used for all of the following jobs *except* _____.

    a. removing paint
    b. cleaning rusty tools
    c. cleaning welds
    d. leveling concrete

2. _____ is easily damaged with wire brushes.

    a. Wood
    b. Metal
    c. Concrete
    d. Wire rope

3. A round-bladed shovel is used to _____.

    a. move gravel or clean up construction debris
    b. move large amounts of soil or dig trenches that need straight sides
    c. dig holes or remove large amounts of soil
    d. spread gravel on driveways

4. A square-bladed shovel is used to _____.

    a. move gravel or clean up construction debris
    b. dig holes or remove large amounts of soil
    c. cut roots of plantings
    d. dig footers for a foundation

5. A spade is used to _____.

    a. dig holes or remove large amounts of soil
    b. move gravel or clean up construction debris
    c. tamp down soil along a building's foundation
    d. move large amounts of soil or dig trenches with straight sides

Summary

As a craft professional, your tools are essential to your success. In this module, you learned to identify and work with many of the basic hand tools commonly used in construction. Learning to properly use and maintain your tools is an essential skill for every craftworker. Although you may not work with all of the tools introduced in this module, you will use many of them as you progress in your career, regardless of what craft area you choose to work in.

When you use tools properly, you are working safely and efficiently. You are not only preventing accidents that can cause injuries and equipment damage, you are showing your employer that you are a responsible, safe worker.

The same pride you take in using your tools to do a job well is important when it comes to maintaining your tools. When you maintain your tools properly, they last longer, work better, and function more safely. The simple act of maintaining your tools will help you prevent accidents, make your tools last longer, and help you perform your job better. Taking the time to learn to use and maintain these tools properly now will help keep you safe and save you time and money down the road.

Notes

Key Terms Quiz

Fill in the blank with the correct key term that you learned from your study of this module.

1. Used mainly for woodworking, the _____ is a fixed, 90-degree angle.

2. A(n) _____ is an L-shaped, hexagonal steel bar.

3. The _____ has a flat face for striking and a rounded face that is used to align brackets and drive out bolts.

4. Usually 2 inches wide and 15 inches long, the _____ has a nail slot at the end to pull nails out from tightly enclosed areas.

5. Shaped like an L, the _____ is used to make sure wall studs and sole plates are at right angles to each other.

6. A(n) _____ is a metal tool with a sharpened, beveled edge that is used to cut and shape wood, stone, or metal.

7. The _____ is used to drive nails and to pull nails out of wood.

8. To _____ is to cut on a slant at an angle that is not a right angle.

9. The _____ has a 12-inch blade that moves through a head that is marked with 45-degree and 90-degree angle measures.

10. If you use a screwdriver incorrectly, you can damage the screwdriver or _____ the screw head.

11. Use a(n) _____ to turn nuts, bolts, small pipe fittings, and chrome-plated pipe fittings.

12. To fasten or align two pieces or material, you can use a(n) _____, which is a pin that fits into a corresponding hole.

13. A(n) _____ is a device such as a nut or bolt used to attach one material to another.

14. Use a(n) _____ for heavy-duty dismantling of woodwork.

15. The straight sides or jaws of a wrench opening are called the _____.

16. A(n) _____ is a claw hammer with a slightly rounded face.

17. _____ is a unit of measure used to describe the torque needed to tighten a large object.

18. _____ is a unit of measure used to describe the torque needed to tighten a small object.

19. The point at which members or the edges of members are joined is called the _____.

20. The _____ is the cut or channel made by a saw.

21. Using a(n) _____ can speed up your work because it has an open wrench at one end and a box-end at the other.

22. Use a(n) _____ to determine if a surface is exactly horizontal.

23. You make a(n) _____ by fastening together usually perpendicular parts with the ends cut at an angle.

24. A(n) _____ is a tool used to remove nails.

25. A(n) _____ has an opening at each end that determines its size.

26. To reduce stress in a weld, use a special type of hammer for _____ the joint as it cools.

27. Used for marking, checking, and measuring, a(n) _____ comes in several types: carpenter's, rafter angle, try, and combination.

28. A(n) _____ has serrated teeth on both jaws for gripping power.

29. _____, which is the turning force applied to an object, is measured in inch-pounds or foot-pounds.

30. The _____ is used to pull nails that have been driven flush with the surface of the wood or slightly below it.

31. A box-end wrench has 6 or 12 _____.

32. The _____, a nonadjustable wrench, forms a continuous circle around the head of a fastener.

33. To indent metal before you drill a hole, to drive pins, or to align holes in two parts that are mates, use a(n) _____.

34. Also called a speed square or magic square, the _____ is a combination protractor, try square, and framing square.

35. Using pliers on nuts or bolt heads may _____ the edges of the hex head and cause wrenches to no longer fit properly.

36. Use a(n) _____ to loosen and tighten fittings on drain traps, sink strainers, toilet connections, and large, odd-shaped nuts.

37. The _____ has a claw at each end that can be used to pull nails or split wood.

38. Use a(n) _____ when a bolt has become stuck to another material through rust or corrosion.

39. A special type of adjustable wrench, _____ are scissor-shaped tools with jaws.

40. The _____ fits into a wooden file handle.

41. Some tools are made of _____ steel so that they resist wear and do not bend or break.

42. A(n) _____ piece of lumber is one that has had its surface made smooth.

43. If a surface is _____, it is exactly vertical.

44. A(n) _____ is a piece that projects out of wood so it can be placed into a hole or groove to form a joint.

45. Use a(n) _____ to secure an object while you work on it.

46. A(n) _____ is a joint that has been created by heating pieces of metal.

Key Terms

Allen wrench
Ball peen hammer
Bell-faced hammer
Bevel
Box-end wrench
Carpenter's square
Cat's paw
Chisel
Chisel bar
Claw hammer
Combination square
Combination wrench

Crescent wrench
Dowel
Fastener
Flat bar
Flats
Foot-pounds
Inch-pounds
Joint
Kerf
Level
Miter joint
Nail puller

Open-end wrench
Peening
Pipe wrench
Planed
Pliers
Plumb
Points
Punch
Rafter angle square
Ripping bar
Round off
Spud wrench

Square
Striking (or slugging) wrench
Strip
Tang
Tempered
Tenon
Torque
Try square
Vise
Weld

Jim Evans

Supervisor of Maintenance Training
Calvert Cliffs Nuclear Power Plants
Lusby, Maryland

How did you become interested in the construction industry?
I was born and raised in Baltimore, and I guess I was about 9 years old at the time I first became interested. Our radio broke, and my father threw it out. I dug it out of the trash and got it running again. Ever since then, electrical work has pretty much been my main interest.

Because I expressed so much interest in it as I was growing up, one day my father sat me down with the newspaper and together we looked at the Help Wanted ads. There were a lot of ads for electricians, so it looked like a great field to get into!

I took electronics and shop in high school, and then I went into the Navy and became an electrician's mate. That was my first job in construction. After my discharge, I worked as an electrician at many places, including U.S. Gypsum in Baltimore, Esskay Meats, and the Chessie System railroad.

What drew you to the Calvert Cliffs Nuclear Power Plants?
It was the challenge. The environment and the culture are completely different from any of the other places I've worked. Our number one job is public safety. On that, everything else hinges. For example, you could be working on a motor. When you finish working on it and you walk away from it, you have to know that that motor is going to work exactly when it's supposed to, and work exactly the way it is supposed to. In the nuclear power industry, you can't have a bad day. And I really like that kind of challenge.

What do you think it takes to be a success in your trade?
One word: *learn*. Learn something every day. And when you don't feel like learning any more, then learn some more!

The real challenge of this job is learning how and why things work. I think that it's a fascinating field. It can be an extremely interesting one for you too, but only if you want it to be interesting for you. You really have to enjoy learning to be successful in the electrical industry.

What are some of the things you do in your job?
In maintenance training we try to identify trends before they become a problem, and then train people to perform their tasks more safely. The process begins by identifying what we call a low-level trend. Then we document it, pull data about it, and track it. When we have identified what's behind the trend, we develop the appropriate training to correct the trend.

For example, and this is purely hypothetical, say that we start to see an increased incidence of injuries on the job. We look at the situation and find that people are not using their fall protection properly, because the harnesses are fitted with a new lanyard. So we train everyone how to use the harness properly. After that, the number of fall-related injuries goes back down again.

A constant part of my job is analyzing the performance problems that we're having in the field. We ask ourselves questions such as, "Is the problem that people haven't been trained properly? Is it that they aren't being rewarded enough? Is it the equipment itself?" It could be a knowledge issue; maybe they never learned how to do it. Or maybe they haven't done the task in two years and they need a refresher. Whatever the question is, we identify it and develop appropriate training in response.

What do you like most about your job?
I learn something new every day. I really do. And I really enjoy working with the people I work with. They are professional and knowledgeable, and I learn from them all the time.

What would you say to someone entering the trades today?
I've got quite a few things to say about that, actually! But basically, it all comes down to this: If you come into the craft willing to learn, and you carry that attitude with you, then there is no end to what you can accomplish in your field. I've worked in a lot of places, and I am where I am today because of my willingness to learn and my attitude. With a good attitude, people want to be around you. And that really makes your learning experience better than it would be otherwise.

Trade Terms Introduced in This Module

Allen wrench: A hexagonal steel bar that is bent to form a right angle. Also called a hex key wrench.

Ball peen hammer: A hammer with a flat face that is used to strike cold chisels and punches. The rounded end—the peen—is used to bend and shape soft metal.

Bell-faced hammer: A claw hammer with a slightly rounded, or convex, face.

Bevel: To cut on a slant at an angle that is not a right angle (90 degrees). The angle or inclination of a line or surface that meets another at any angle but 90 degrees.

Box-end wrench: A wrench, usually double-ended, that has a closed socket that fits over the head of a bolt.

Carpenter's square: A flat, steel square commonly used in carpentry.

Cat's paw: A straight steel rod with a curved claw at one end that is used to pull nails that have been driven flush with the surface of the wood or slightly below it.

Chisel: A metal tool with a sharpened, beveled edge used to cut and shape wood, stone, or metal.

Chisel bar: A tool with a claw at each end, commonly used to pull nails.

Claw hammer: A hammer with a flat striking face. The other end of the head is curved and divided into two claws to remove nails.

Combination square: An adjustable carpenter's tool consisting of a steel rule that slides through an adjustable head.

Combination wrench: A wrench with an open end and a closed end.

Crescent wrench: A smooth-jawed adjustable wrench used for turning nuts, bolts, and pipe fittings.

Dowel: A pin, usually round, that fits into a corresponding hole to fasten or align two pieces.

Fastener: A device such as a bolt, clasp, hook, or lock used to attach or secure one material to another.

Flat bar: A prying tool with a nail slot at the end to pull nails out in tightly enclosed areas. It can also be used as a small pry bar.

Flats: The straight sides or jaws of a wrench opening. Also, the sides on a nut or bolt head.

Foot-pounds: Unit of measure used to describe the amount of pressure exerted (torque) to tighten a large object.

Inch-pounds: Unit of measure used to describe the amount of pressure exerted (torque) to tighten a small object.

Joint: The point where members or the edges of members are joined. The types of welding joints are butt joint, corner joint, and T-joint.

Kerf: A cut or channel made by a saw.

Level: Perfectly horizontal; completely flat; a tool used to determine if an object is level.

Miter joint: A joint made by fastening together usually perpendicular parts with the ends cut at an angle.

Nail puller: A tool used to remove nails.

Open-end wrench: A nonadjustable wrench with an opening at each end that determines the size of the wrench.

Peening: The process of bending, shaping, or cutting material by striking it with a tool.

Pipe wrench: A wrench for gripping and turning a pipe or pipe-shaped object; it tightens when turned in one direction.

Planed: Describing a surface made smooth by using a tool called a plane.

Pliers: A scissor-shaped type of adjustable wrench equipped with jaws and teeth to grip objects.

Plumb: Perfectly vertical; the surface is at a right angle (90 degrees) to the horizon or floor and does not bow out at the top or bottom.

Points: Teeth on the gripping part of a wrench. Also refers to the number of teeth per inch on a handsaw.

Punch: A steel tool used to indent metal.

Rafter angle square: A type of carpenter's square made of cast aluminum that combines a protractor, try square, and framing square.

Ripping bar: A tool used for heavy-duty dismantling of woodwork, such as tearing apart building frames or concrete forms.

Round off: To smooth out threads or edges on a screw or nut.

Spud wrench: An adjustable wrench used for fittings on drain traps, sink strainers, toilet connections, and odd-shaped nuts.

Square: Exactly adjusted; any piece of material sawed or cut to be rectangular with equal dimensions on all sides; a tool used to check angles.

Striking (or slugging) wrench: A nonadjustable wrench with an enclosed, circular opening designed to lock on to the fastener when the wrench is struck.

Strip: To damage the threads on a nut or bolt.

Tang: Metal handle-end of a file. The tang fits into a wooden or plastic file handle.

Tempered: Treated with heat to create or restore hardness in steel.

Tenon: A piece that projects out of wood or another material for the purpose of being placed into a hole or groove to form a joint.

Torque: The turning or twisting force applied to an object, such as a nut, bolt, or screw, using a socket wrench or screwdriver to tighten it. Torque is measured in inch-pounds or foot-pounds.

Try square: A square whose legs are fixed at a right angle.

Vise: A holding or gripping tool, fixed or portable, used to secure an object while work is performed on it.

Weld: To heat or fuse two or more pieces of metal so that the finished piece is as strong as the original; a welded joint.

This module is intended to present thorough resources for task training. The following reference
works are suggested for further study. These are
optional materials for continued education rather
than for task training.

Field Safety, 2003. NCCER. Upper Saddle River,
NJ: Prentice Hall.

Hand Tools & Techniques, 1999. Minneapolis, MN:
Handyman Club of America.

The Long and Short of It: How to Take Measurements.
Video. Charleston, WV: Cambridge Vocational
& Technical, 800-468-4227.

Reader's Digest Book of Skills and Tools, 1993. Pleasantville, NY: Reader's Digest.

The NCCER makes every effort to keep these textbooks up-to-date and free of technical errors. We appreciate your help in this process. If you have an idea for improving this textbook, or if you find an error, a typographical mistake, or an inaccuracy in NCCER's *Contren®* textbooks, please write us, using this form or a photocopy. Be sure to include the exact module number, page number, a detailed description, and the correction, if applicable. Your input will be brought to the attention of the Technical Review Committee. Thank you for your assistance.

Instructors – If you found that additional materials were necessary in order to teach this module effectively, please let us know so that we may include them in the Equipment/Materials list in the Annotated Instructor's Guide.

Write: Product Development
National Center for Construction Education and Research
P.O. Box 141104, Gainesville, FL 32614-1104

Fax: 352-334-0932

E-mail: curriculum@nccer.org

Craft

Module Name

Copyright Date

Module Number

Page Number(s)

Description

(Optional) Correction

(Optional) Your Name and Address

Introduction to Power Tools

00104-04

**Excellence in Construction Winner—
Renovation, $10–99 Million**

Manhattan Construction Company and Flintco, Inc.
formed a joint venture to work on the Oklahoma State Capital
Dome in Oklahoma City. This two-phase, design-build project
was the first of its kind awarded by the state of Oklahoma.
Manhattan/Flintco completed restoration of the five-million-
pound dome with two weeks to spare for its unveiling
during Oklahoma Statehood Day.

00104-04
Introduction to Power Tools

Topics to be presented in this module include:

Overview

Power tools are frequently used throughout construction trades. It is very common to see power tools such as drills, saws, grinders, sanders, and nailers on a construction site. These tools are typically powered by electricity, pressurized air, or pressurized fluids.

When power is added to a tool, there is a significant increase in the risks associated with using the tools. For example, you might sustain a serious cut when using a handsaw. However, the same amount of contact with a circular saw could cause a much more severe injury.

Much like the safety precautions required for nonpowered hand tools, anyone using a power tool must be thoroughly trained in the maintenance and proper use of power tools. Power tools should only be used for the work they were designed to do. They should also be kept dry, clean, and in good working order. Never put yourself at risk by using a power tool you don't know how to use or one that isn't safe.

Objectives

When you have completed this module, you will be able to do the following:

1. Identify power tools commonly used in the construction trades.
2. Use power tools safely.
3. Explain how to maintain power tools properly.

Key Trade Terms

Abrasive
AC (alternating current)
Auger
Booster
Carbide
Chuck
Chuck key
Countersink
DC (direct current)
Electric tools
Ferromagnetic
Grit
Ground fault circuit
    interrupter (GFCI)

Ground fault protection
Hazardous materials
Hydraulic tools
Masonry
Pneumatic tools
Reciprocating
Revolutions per minute
    (rpm)
Ring test
Shank
Trigger lock

Required Trainee Materials

1. Appropriate personal protective equipment
2. Sharpened pencils and paper

Prerequisites

Before you begin this module, it is recommended that you successfully complete the following: *Core Curriculum: Introductory Craft Skills,* Modules 00101-04 through 00103-04.

This course map shows all of the modules in *Core Curriculum: Introductory Craft Skills.* The suggested training order begins at the bottom and proceeds up. Skill levels increase as you advance on the course map. The local Training Program Sponsor may adjust the training order.

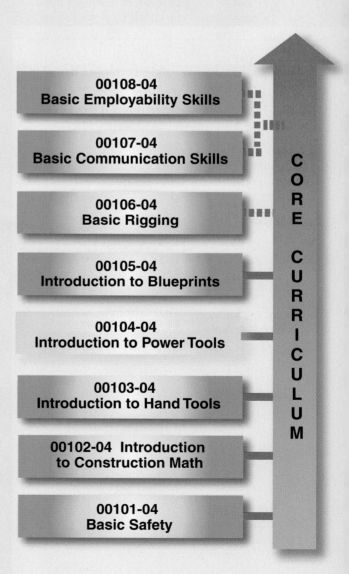

104CMAP.EPS

1.0.0 ◆ INTRODUCTION

Power tools are used to make holes; cut, smooth, and shape materials; and even demolish pavement in almost every construction industry. As a construction worker, you will probably use power tools on the job. Knowing how to identify and use power tools safely and correctly is very important. This module provides an overview of the various types of power tools and how they work. You will also learn the proper safety techniques required to operate these tools.

 WARNING!

If you have not completed the *Basic Safety* module, stop here! You must complete the *Basic Safety* module first. Also, you must wear appropriate personal protective equipment when you operate any power tool or when you are near someone else who is operating a power tool.

2.0.0 ◆ ELECTRIC, PNEUMATIC, AND HYDRAULIC TOOLS

This module introduces three kinds of power tools: electric, pneumatic, and hydraulic.

- *Electric tools* – These tools are powered by electricity. They are operated from either an **alternating current (AC)** source (such as a wall plug) or a **direct current (DC)** source (such as a battery). Belt sanders and circular saws are examples of electric tools.
- *Pneumatic tools* – These tools are powered by air. Electric or gasoline-powered compressors produce the air pressure. Air hammers and pneumatic nailers are examples of pneumatic tools.
- *Hydraulic tools* – These tools are powered by fluid pressure. Hand pumps or electric pumps are used to produce the fluid pressure. Pipe benders and Porta-Powers® are examples of hydraulic tools.

2.1.0 Safety

You must complete the *Basic Safety* module before you take this course. It is easy to hurt yourself or others if you use a power tool incorrectly or unsafely. Safety issues for each tool are covered in this module, but general safety issues—such as safety in the work area, safety equipment, and working with electricity—are covered in the *Basic Safety* module in this book. This information is vital for working with power tools.

One of the most important things about working with power tools is to always disconnect the power source for any tool before you replace parts such as bits, blades, or discs. Always disconnect the power source before you perform maintenance on any power tool. Never activate the **trigger lock** on any power tool.

Review Questions

Section 2.0.0

1. Trigger locks should always be activated when a power tool is in use.

   a. True
   b. False

2. Electric tools get their power from _____.

   a. hand pumps
   b. an AC (wall plug) or DC (battery) source
   c. fluid pressure
   d. a gasoline-powered compressor

3. Pneumatic tools get their power from _____.

   a. air pressure
   b. fluid pressure
   c. hand pumps
   d. AC power sources

4. Hydraulic tools get their power from _____.

   a. rotary engines
   b. air pressure
   c. fluid pressure
   d. solar panels

5. Always disconnect the _____ before you perform maintenance on any power tool.

   a. trigger lock
   b. drill bit
   c. power source
   d. belt sander

.0.0 ◆ POWER DRILLS

he power drill is used often in the construction ndustry. It is most commonly used to make holes y spinning drill bits into wood, metal, plastic, nd other materials. However, with different at- achments and accessories, the power drill can be sed as a sander, polisher, screwdriver, grinder, or ountersink—even as a saw.

.1.0 Types of Power Drills

n this section, you will learn about various types f power drills, including the following:

- Electric drills
- Cordless drills
- Hammer drills
- Electromagnetic drills
- Pneumatic drills (air hammers)
- Electric screwdrivers

Most of these drills are similar, so you will first arn about what they have in common.

Most power drills have a pistol grip with a trig- er switch for controlling power (see *Figure 1*). he harder you pull on the trigger of a variable- peed drill, the faster the speed. Drills also have eversing switches that allow you to back the drill t out if it gets stuck in the material while drilling. Iost drills have replaceable bits for use on differ- nt kinds of jobs (see *Figure 2*). On most power rills, you can insert a screwdriver bit in place of

a drill bit and use the drill as a screwdriver. Be sure to use screwdriver bits that are designed for use in a power drill.

Twist drill bits are used to drill wood and plas- tics at high speeds or to drill metal at a lower speed. A forstner bit is used on wood and is par- ticularly good for boring any part of a circle. A paddle bit or spade bit is also used in wood. The bit size is measured by the paddle's diameter, which generally ranges from ½ inch to 1½ inch. A **masonry** bit, which has a **carbide** tip, is used in concrete, stone, slate, and ceramic. The **auger** drill bit is used for drilling wood and other soft materials, but not for drilling metal. As a rule, the point of a bit should be sharper for softer materi- als than for harder ones. All bits are held in the drill by the drill **chuck**. Chucks can be either keyed or keyless (see *Figure 3*).

CHUCK
CHUCK COLLAR
CHUCK KEY HOLE
CHUCK JAWS
GEAR CASE
TRIGGER SWITCH
PISTOL GRIP HANDLE

104F01.EPS

Figure 1 ◆ Parts of the power drill.

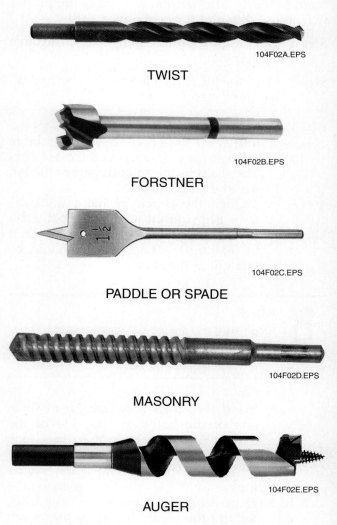

TWIST
104F02A.EPS

FORSTNER
104F02B.EPS

PADDLE OR SPADE
104F02C.EPS

MASONRY
104F02D.EPS

AUGER
104F02E.EPS

Figure 2 ◆ Drill bits.

104F03.EPS

Figure 3 ◆ Chuck key.

3.1.1 How to Use a Power Drill

Power drills can be dangerous if you do not use them properly. This section will show the proper way to use different types of power drills.

Step 1 Wear appropriate personal protective equipment.

Step 2 Load the bit in the electric drill by following these steps:

   a. Disconnect the power. Open the chuck and turn it counterclockwise (to the left) until the chuck opening is large enough for you to insert the bit **shank.** The shank is the smooth part of the bit.

   b. Insert the bit shank.

   c. Tighten the chuck by hand until the jaws grip the bit shank. Keep the bit centered as you tighten it. It should not be leaning to one side but should be straight in the chuck.

NOTE

Stop here if you are using a keyless chuck.

   d. Insert the **chuck key** (see *Figure 4*) in one of the holes on the side of the chuck. You will notice that the chuck key has a grooved ring called a gear. Make sure that the chuck key's gear meshes with the matching gears on the geared end of the chuck. In larger drills, tighten the bit by inserting the chuck key into each of the holes in the three-jawed chuck. This ensures that all the jaws are uniformly tight around the bit.

104F4A.EPS

(A) INSERT THE BIT SHANK INTO THE CHUCK OPENING.

104F04B.EPS

(B) TIGHTEN WITH THE CHUCK KEY.

104F04C.EPS

(C) HOLD THE DRILL PERPENDICULAR TO THE MATERIAL AND START THE DRILL.

Figure 4 ◆ Proper drill use.

 ON-SITE

Drilling Metal

When you are drilling metal, lubricate the bit to help cool the cutting edges and produce a smoother finished hole. A very small amount of cutting oil that is not combustible (capable of catching fire and burning) makes a good lubricant for drilling softer metals. No lubrication is needed for wood drilling. When you are drilling deep holes, pull the drill bit partly out of the hole every so often. This helps to clear the hole of shavings.

e. Turn the chuck key clockwise (right) to tighten the grip on the bit.

f. Remove the key from the chuck.

WARNING!

Always remember to remove the key from the chuck. Otherwise, when you start the drill, the key could fly out and injure you or a co-worker.

Step 3 Make a small indent exactly where you want the hole drilled.

a. In wood, use a small punch to make an indent.

b. In metal, first use a center punch.

Step 4 Firmly clamp or support the work that is being drilled.

Step 5 Hold the drill perpendicular (at a right angle) to the material surface and start the drill motor. Be sure the drill is rotating in the right direction (with the bit facing away from you; it should be turning clockwise). Hold the drill with both hands and apply only moderate pressure when drilling. The drill motor should operate at approximately the same **revolutions per minute (rpm)** as it does when it is not drilling through anything. For power drills, the term *rpm* refers to how many times the drill bit completes one full rotation every minute. *Figure 4(C)* shows the proper way to hold the drill when you are operating it.

Step 6 Lessen the pressure when the bit is about to come through the other side of the work, especially when you are drilling metal. If you are still pressing hard when the bit comes out the other side, the drill itself will hit the surface of your material. This could damage or dent the metal surface. If the drill bit gets stuck in the material while you are drilling, release the

trigger, use the reversing switch to change the direction of the drill, and back it gently out of the material. When you are finished backing it out, switch back to your original drilling position.

 WARNING!

Be sure your hand is not in contact with the drill bit. The spinning bit will cut your hand. Keep an even pressure on the drill to keep the drill from twisting or binding.

 WARNING!

Before you start drilling into or through a wall, find out what is on the other side, and take steps to avoid hitting anything that would endanger your safety or cause damage. Spaces between studs (upright pieces in the walls of a building) often contain electrical wiring, plumbing, or insulation, for instance. If you are not careful, you will drill directly into the wiring, pipes, or insulation.

3.1.2 Safety and Maintenance

In addition to the general safety rules you learned in *Basic Safety*, there are some specific safety rules for working with drills:

• Always wear appropriate personal protective equipment, especially safety glasses.

• To prevent an electrical shock, operate only those tools that are double-insulated electric power tools with proper **ground fault protection.** Using a **ground fault circuit interrupter (GFCI)** device protects the equipment from continued electrical current in case of a circuit fault. The GFCI monitors the current flow and opens the circuit (which stops the flow of electricity) if it detects a difference between positive and negative flow. The interruption typically takes place in less than one-tenth of a second.

- Before you connect to the power source, make sure the trigger is not turned on. It should be off. Always disconnect the power source before you change bits or work on the drill.
- Find out what is inside the wall or on the other side of the work material before you cut through a wall or partition. Avoid hitting water lines or electrical wiring.
- Ensure that electric tools with two-prong plugs are double insulated. If a tool is not double insulated, its plug must have a third prong to provide grounding.
- Ensure that the switch can be operated with one finger.
- Use the right bit for the job.
- Always use a sharp bit.
- Make sure the drill bit is tightened in the chuck before you start the drill.
- Make sure the chuck key is removed from the chuck before you start the drill.
- Hold the drill with both hands and apply steady pressure. Let the drill do the work.
- Never ram the drill while you are drilling. This chips the cutting edge and damages the bearings.
- Never use the trigger lock. The trigger lock is a small lever, switch, or part that you push or pull to lock the trigger in operating mode.
- Drills do not need much maintenance, but they should be kept clean. Many drills have gears and bearings that are lubricated for life. Some drills have a small hole in the case for lubricating the motor bearings. Apply about three drops of oil occasionally, but don't overdo it. Extra lubricant can leak onto electrical contacts and burn the copper surfaces.
- Keep the drill's air vent clean with a small brush or small stick. Airflow is crucial to the maintenance and safety of a drill.
- Attach the chuck key to the power cord when you are not using the key, so it does not get lost.
- Do not overreach when using a power drill while standing on a ladder. You could fall.

 WARNING!

Do not use electric drills around combustible materials. Motors and bits can create sparks, which can cause an explosion.

3.2.0 Cordless Drill

Cordless power drills (see *Figure 5*) are useful for working in awkward spaces or in areas where a power source is hard to find.

Cordless drills usually contain a rechargeabl battery pack that runs the motor. The pack can b detached and plugged into a battery charger an time you are not using the drill. Some chargers ca recharge the battery pack in an hour, while other require more time. Workers who use cordles drills a lot usually carry an extra battery pack wit them. Some cordless drills have adjustabl clutches so that the drill motor can also serve as power screwdriver. Many cordless drills are nov available with keyless chucks.

3.2.1 How to Use a Cordless Drill with a Keyless Chuck

When using a cordless drill with a keyless chuck follow these guidelines:

Step 1 Wear appropriate personal protectiv equipment.

Step 2 To load the bit on a cordless drill with keyless chuck (see *Figure 6*), follow thes steps:
   a. Remove the power pack/battery. Ope the chuck by turning it counterclock wise until the jaws are wide enough fo you to insert the bit shank.
   b. Tighten the chuck by hand until th jaws grip the bit shank. Be sure to kee the bit centered as you tighten it. I should not be leaning to one side, bu should be straight in the chuck.
   c. Grip the chuck in one hand and appl a small amount of pressure to the trig ger. This action spins the drill a littl Resist the drill's spin by holding tightl to the chuck. This locks the bit shan into the chuck.

Step 3 To operate the drill, follow the procedure previously outlined for the power drill.

3.2.2 Safety and Maintenance

Follow the power drill safety practices that yo learned earlier in this module.

3.3.0 Hammer Drill

The hammer drill (see *Figure 7*) has a pounding ac tion that lets you drill into concrete, brick, or til The bit rotates and hammers at the same time, a lowing you to drill much faster than you could wit a regular drill. The depth gauge on a hammer dri can be set to the depth of the hole you want to dri

You need special hammer drill bits that can tak the pounding. Some hammer drills use percu sion and masonry bits (see *Figure 8*).

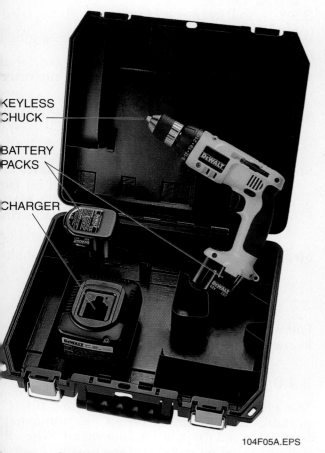

KEYLESS
CHUCK

BATTERY
PACKS

CHARGER

104F05A.EPS

104F05B.EPS

Figure 5 ◆ Cordless drill.

104F06A.EPS

(A) INSERT THE
BIT SHANK.

104F06B.EPS

(B) TIGHTEN THE CHUCK.

Figure 6 ◆ Loading the bit on a cordless drill.

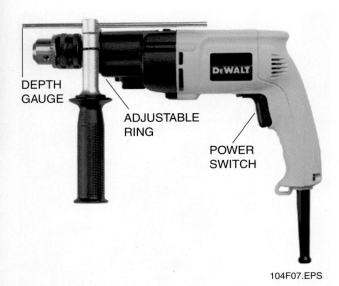

DEPTH
GAUGE

ADJUSTABLE
RING

POWER
SWITCH

104F07.EPS

Figure 7 ◆ Hammer drill.

3.3.1 *How to Use a Hammer Drill*

When using a hammer drill, follow these guide
lines:

Step 1 Wear appropriate personal protectiv
equipment.

Step 2 Follow the procedures for using a powe
drill (which you learned earlier in thi
module).

Step 3 Most hammer drills will not hammer ur
til you put pressure on the drill bit (se
Figure 9). You can adjust the drill's blow
per minute by turning the adjustable rin
(refer to *Figure 7*).

Step 4 The hammer action stops when you sto
applying pressure to the drill.

3.3.2 *Safety and Maintenance*

Follow the power drill safety practices that yo
learned about earlier in this module.

3.4.0 Electromagnetic Drill

The electromagnetic drill (see *Figure 10*) is
portable drill mounted on an electromagneti
base. It is used for drilling thick metal. When th
drill is placed on metal and the power is turne
on, the magnetic base will hold the drill in plac
for drilling. The drill can also be rotated on th
base.

A switch on the junction box controls the elec
tromagnetic base. When the switch is turned or

104F08.EPS

Figure 8 ◆ Hammer drill bits.

104F09.EF

Figure 9 ◆ Proper use of a hammer drill.

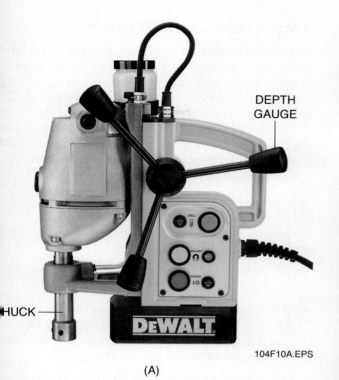

DEPTH
GAUGE

CHUCK

DEWALT

104F10A.EPS

(A)

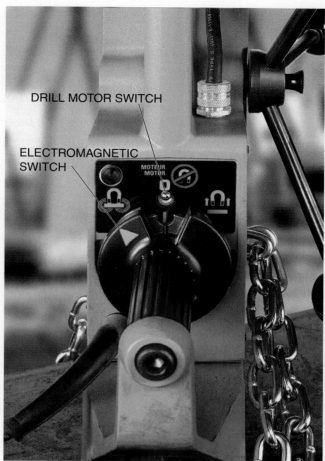

DRILL MOTOR SWITCH

ELECTROMAGNETIC
SWITCH

104F10B.EPS

(B)

CAUTION

DO NOT
UNPLUG

104F10C.EPS

Figure 10 ◆ Electromagnetic drill.

e magnet holds the drill in place on a **ferromag-
etic** metal surface. (Ferromagnetic refers to sub-
ances, especially metals, that have magnetic
roperties.) The switch on the top of the drill turns
e drill on and off. You can also set the depth
uge to the depth of the hole you are drilling.

3.4.1 How to Set Up an Electromagnetic Drill

The use of this tool is explained in detail in the
specific craft areas that use it. For now, you will
learn only the setup procedures for using the electromagnetic drill.

Step 1 Wear appropriate personal protective equipment.

Step 2 Place the drill face down into the metal holder.

Step 3 Put the electromagnetic switch (not the drill) in the ON position. Doing this holds the drill in place by magnetizing the base of the drill directly onto the metal to be drilled.

WARNING!

Expect the unexpected. Use a safety chain to secure the electromagnetic drill in case the power is shut off. If there is no power, you lose the electromagnetic field that holds the base to the metal being drilled.

Step 4 Lock the drill in place.

Step 5 Set the depth gauge to the depth of the hole you are going to drill.

Step 6 Fasten the work securely on the drilling surface with clamps.

Step 7 Proceed to drill.

3.4.2 Safety and Maintenance

In addition to the general safety rules you learned in *Basic Safety,* there are some specific safety rules for working with electromagnetic drills:

- Clamp the material securely. Unsecured materials can become deadly flying objects.
- Make sure the electrical power is not interrupted. Put a DO NOT UNPLUG tag on the cord (refer to *Figure 10*).
- Safety attachments, such as shields to block flying objects and safety lines to keep the drill from falling if the power is cut off, are available. In some states, they are required. Ask your instructor or supervisor about requirements for safety attachments in your area.
- Support the drill before you turn it off. It will fall over if you do not hold it when you turn off the power.

WARNING!

When you are working near combustible materials, be sure to use a nonsparking drill. A drill that gives off sparks could start a fire.

3.5.0 Pneumatic Drill (Air Hammer)

Pneumatic drills (see *Figure 11*), also called air hammers, are powered by compressed air from an air hose. They have many of the same parts, controls and uses as electric drills. The pneumatic drill typically used when there is no source of electricity.

Common sizes of pneumatic drills are ¼, ³⁄ and ½ inch. The size refers to the diameter of the largest shank that can be gripped in the chuck, no the drilling capacity.

3.5.1 How to Use a Pneumatic Drill

Follow these steps to use a pneumatic drill safely and efficiently (see *Figure 12*):

Step 1 Wear appropriate personal protective equipment.

Step 2 Hold the coupler at the end of the air supply line, slide the ring back, and slip the coupler on the connector or nipple that attached to the pneumatic drill.

Step 3 Check to see if you have a good connection. You cannot take apart a good coupling without first sliding the ring back.

Step 4 Once you have a good connection, install whip check as required.

Step 5 Proceed to drill as needed.

Step 6 When your work is completed, disconnect the drill from the hose.

3.5.2 Safety and Maintenance

Follow the power drill safety practices that you learned earlier in this module.

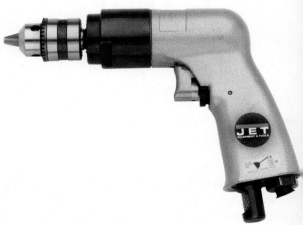

104F11.EPS

Figure 11 ◆ Pneumatic drill.

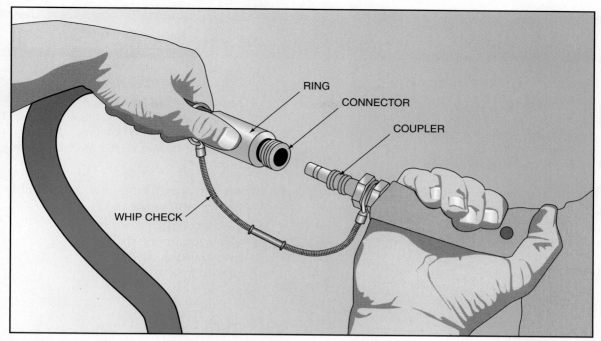

RING

CONNECTOR

COUPLER

WHIP CHECK

104F12.EPS

Figure 12 ◆ Proper use of a pneumatic drill.

Review Questions

Section 3.0.0

1. The most common use of the power drill is to _____.

   a. cut wood, metal, and plastic
   b. drive nails into wood, metal, and plastic
   c. make holes in wood, metal, and plastic
   d. carve letters in wood, metal, and plastic

2. The trigger switch on the variable-speed power drill _____.

   a. controls the speed
   b. shoots nails into walls
   c. blows air to clean the work area
   d. tightens the chuck jaws

3. If the drill bit gets stuck in the material while you are drilling, you should first _____.

   a. unplug the drill
   b. release the trigger switch
   c. back the drill out of the material
   d. use the reversing switch to change directions

4. Before you start drilling, be sure _____ is not in contact with the drill bit.

   a. the bit shank
   b. the material being drilled
   c. the chuck
   d. your hand

5. Before you start drilling through a material, always _____.

   a. find out what is on the other side
   b. disconnect the power source
   c. reinsert the chuck key
   d. drive a nail in first

6. When using a power drill, proper ground fault protection will prevent _____.

   a. drilling into electrical wiring
   b. you from losing your grip
   c. electric shock
   d. excess noise

7. When drilling, hold the drill with _____.
   a. one hand and push it into the material
   b. both hands and apply steady pressure
   c. one hand and the power cord with the other
   d. your arms fully extended

8. Hammer drills are designed to drill into _____.
   a. wood, metal, and plastic
   b. concrete, brick, and tile
   c. drywall
   d. roofing shingles

9. The electromagnetic drill is a _____.
   a. handheld drill used on wood
   b. cordless drill used on masonry and tile
   c. portable drill used on thick metal
   d. pneumatic drill that has a pounding action

10. When you are drilling near combustible materials, be sure to use a(n) _____.
    a. cordless drill
    b. electromagnetic drill
    c. nonsparking drill
    d. masonry bit

4.0.0 ◆ SAWS

Using the right saw for the job will make your work much easier. Always make sure that the blade is right for the material being cut. In this section, you will learn about the following types of power saws:

- Circular saws
- Saber saws
- Reciprocating saws
- Portable handheld bandsaws
- Power miter box saws

4.1.0 Circular Saw

Many years ago a company named Skil® made power-tool history by introducing the portable circular saw. Today many different companies make dozens of models, but a lot of people still call any portable circular saw a *skilsaw*. Other names you might hear are utility saw, electric handsaw, and builder's saw. The portable circular saw (see *Figure 13*) is designed to cut lumber and boards to size for a project.

ON-SITE

CONSTRUCTION

Using Saw Blades

Having a variety of blades will allow you to work on different projects. Blades fall into two categories: standard steel, which must be sharpened regularly, and carbide-tipped. You must use the appropriate type of saw blade for the job. Some common types of saw blades include the following:

- *Rip* – These blades are designed to cut with the grain of the wood. The square chisel teeth cut parallel with the grain and are generally larger than other types of blade teeth.
- *Crosscut* – These blades are designed to cut against the grain of the wood (at a 90-degree angle). Crosscut teeth cut at an angle and are finer than rip blade teeth.
- *Combination* – These blades are designed to cut hard or soft wood, either with or across the grain. The combination blade features both rip and crosscut teeth with deep troughs (gullets) between the teeth.
- *Nail cutter* – This blade has large carbide-tipped teeth that can make rough cuts through nails that may be embedded in the work.
- *Nonferrous metal cutter* – This blade has carbide-tipped teeth for cutting aluminum, copper, lead, and brass. It should be lubricated with oil or wax before each use.

Always follow the manufacturer's instructions when using saw blades.

The Worm-Drive Saw

The worm-drive saw is a heavy-duty type of circular saw. Most circular saws have a direct drive. That is, the blade is mounted on a shaft that is part of the motor. With a worm-drive saw, the motor drives the blade from the rear through two gears. One gear (the worm gear) is cylindrical and threaded like a screw. The worm gear drives a wheel-shaped gear (the worm wheel) that is directly attached to the shaft to which the blade is fastened. This setup delivers much more rotational force (torque), making it easier to cut a double thickness of lumber. The worm-drive saw is almost twice as heavy as a conventional circular saw. This saw should be used only by an experienced craftworker.

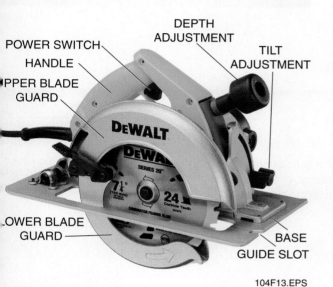

POWER SWITCH
HANDLE
UPPER BLADE GUARD
DEPTH ADJUSTMENT
TILT ADJUSTMENT
LOWER BLADE GUARD
BASE
GUIDE SLOT

104F13.EPS

Figure 13 ◆ Circular saw.

Saw size is measured by the diameter of the circular blade. Saw blade diameters range from 3⅜ to 6¼ inches. The 7¼-inch size is the most popular. A typical circular saw weighs between 9 and 12 pounds. The handle of the circular saw has a trigger switch that starts the saw. The motor is protected by a rigid plastic housing. Blade speed when the blade is not engaged in cutting is given in rpm. The teeth of the blade point in the direction of the rotation. The blade is protected by two guards. On top, a rigid plastic guard protects you from flying debris and from touching the spinning blade if you lean forward accidentally. The lower guard is spring-loaded—as you push the saw forward, it retracts up and under the top guard to allow the saw to cut.

WARNING!

Never use the saw unless the lower blade guard is properly attached. The guard protects you from the blade and from flying particles.

4.1.1 *How to Use a Circular Saw*

Follow these steps to use a circular saw safely and efficiently:

Step 1 Wear appropriate personal protective equipment.

Step 2 Properly secure the material to be cut. If the work isn't heavy enough to stay in position without moving, weight or clamp it down.

Step 3 Make your cut mark with a pencil or other marking tool.

Step 4 Place the front edge of the baseplate on the work so the guide notch is in line with the cut mark.

Step 5 Adjust the blade depth to the thickness of the wood you are cutting plus ¼ inch.

Step 6 Start the saw. After the blade has revved up to full speed, move the saw forward to start cutting. The lower blade guard will automatically rotate up and under the top guard when you push the saw forward.

Step 7 While cutting with the saw, grip the saw handles firmly with two hands, as shown in *Figure 14.*

104F14A.EPS   104F14B.E▊

Figure 14 ◆ Proper use of a circular saw.

ON-SITE

CONSTRUCTION

Cutting

Most circular saw blades have a kerf (a cut or channel) ⅛ inch thick. Be sure to cut on the waste (unused) side of the material, or your finished piece will be ⅛ inch short. Mark an X on the waste side after you make the cut mark. This will help you remember the side of the mark on which to cut.

Step 8 If the saw cuts off the line, stop, back out, and restart the cut. Do not force the saw.

Step 9 As you get to the end of the cut, the guide notch on the baseplate will move off the end of the work. Use the blade as your guide.

Step 10 Release the trigger switch. The blade will stop rotating.

Step 11 Ensure that the work is properly supported.

CAUTION

Make sure the blade is appropriate for the material being cut.

4.1.2 Safety and Maintenance

To use a circular saw safely and ensure its lor life, follow these guidelines:

- Wear appropriate personal protective equi ment.
- Ensure that the blade is tight.
- Check that the blade guard is working correct before you connect the saw to the power sourc
- Before you cut through a wall or partition, fir out what is inside the wall or on the other si of the partition. Avoid hitting water lines electrical wiring.
- Whenever possible, keep both hands on tl saw grips while you are operating the saw.
- Never force the saw through the work. Th causes binding and overheating and m. cause injury.
- Never reach underneath the work while y(are operating the saw.

Never stand directly behind the work. Always stand to one side of it.

Do not use your hands to try to secure small pieces of material to be cut. Use a clamp instead. Know where the power cord is located. You don't want to cut through the power cord by accident and electrocute yourself!

The most important maintenance on a circular saw is at the lower blade guard. Sawdust builds up and causes the guard to stick. If the guard sticks and does not move quickly over the blade after it makes a cut, the bare blade may still be turning when you set the saw down and may cause damage. Remove sawdust from the blade guard area. Remember to always disconnect the power source before you do maintenance.

To avoid injury to you, your materials, and your co-workers, check often to make sure the guard snaps shut quickly and smoothly. To ensure smooth operation of the guard, disconnect the saw from its power source, allow it to cool, and clean foreign material from the track. Be aware of fire hazards when using cleaning liquids such as isopropyl alcohol.

Do not lubricate the guard with oil or grease. This could cause sawdust to stick in the mechanism.

Always keep blades clean and sharp to reduce friction and kickback. Blades can be cleaned with hot water or mineral spirits. Be careful with mineral spirits; they are very flammable.

> **WARNING!**
>
> Never use a circular saw when holding material to be cut with your hands. Doing so violates OSHA regulations.

• Do not hold material to be ripped with your hands.

4.2.0 Saber Saw

Saber saws have very fine blades, which makes the saws great tools for doing delicate and intricate work, such as cutting out patterns or irregular shapes from wood or thin, soft metals. They are also some of the best tools for cutting circles.

The saber saw (see *Figure 15*) is a very useful portable power tool. It can make straight or curved cuts in wood, metal, plastic, wallboard, and other materials. It can also make its own starting hole if a cut must begin in the middle of a board. The saber saw cuts with a blade that moves up and down, unlike the spinning circular saw blade. This means that each cutting stroke (upward) is followed by a return stroke (downward), so the saw is cutting only half the time it is in operation. This is called up-cutting or clean-cutting.

Many models are available with tilting baseplates for cutting beveled edges. Models come with a top handle or a barrel handle. Some cordless models are available.

The saber saw has changeable blades that let it cut many different materials, from wood and metal to wallboard and ceramic tile. Most saber saws can be operated at various blade speeds. Types of saber saws include single-speed, two-speed, and variable-speed. The variable-speed saber saw can cut at low and high speeds. The low-speed setting is for cutting hard materials, and the high-speed setting is for soft materials. An important part of the saber saw is the baseplate (shoeplate or footplate). Its broad surface helps to

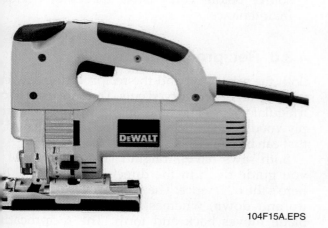

104F15A.EPS

TOP HANDLE

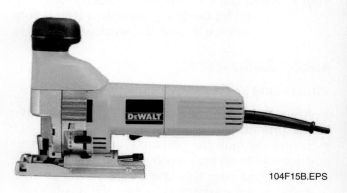

104F15B.EPS

BARREL HANDLE

Figure 15 ◆ Saber saws.

keep the blade lined up. It keeps the work from vibrating and allows the blade teeth to bite into the material.

4.2.1 How to Use a Saber Saw

Follow these steps to ensure that you use a saber saw safely and efficiently:

Step 1 Wear appropriate personal protective equipment.

Step 2 To avoid vibration, clamp the work to a pair of sawhorses or hold the work in a vise.

Step 3 Check the blade to see that it is the right blade for the job and that it is sharp and undamaged.

Step 4 Measure and mark the work.

Step 5 When you cut from the edge of a board or panel, be sure the front of the baseplate is resting firmly on the surface of the work before you start the saw. The blade should not be touching the work at this stage.

Step 6 Start the saw (pull the trigger) and move the blade gently but firmly into the work. Continue feeding the saw into the work as fast as possible without forcing it. Do not push the blade into the work. *Figure 16* shows the proper way to use a saber saw.

CAUTION

Do not lift the blade out of the work while the saw is still running. If you do, the tip of the blade may hit the wood surface, marring the work and possibly breaking the blade.

Step 7 When the cut is finished, release the trigger and let the blade come to a stop before you remove it from the work.

4.2.2 Safety and Maintenance

When using a saber saw, follow these guidelines:

- Always wear appropriate personal protective equipment.
- Secure the material you are working with to reduce vibration and ensure safety.
- Before you plug the saw into a power source, make sure the switch is in the OFF position.
- Before you cut through a wall or partition, find out what is inside the wall or on the other side of the partition. Avoid hitting water lines or electrical wiring.

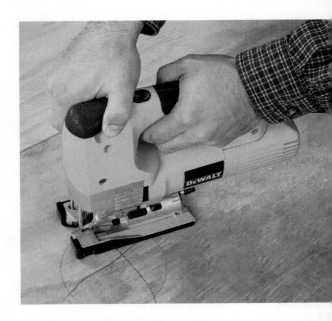

Figure 16 ◆ Proper use of a saber saw.

- Always use a sharp blade and never force th blade through the work.
- Do not force or lean into the blade. You coul lose your balance and fall forward, or you hands could slip onto the work surface and yo could cut yourself.
- When cutting metal pieces, use a metal-cuttin blade. Lubricate the blade with an agent such a beeswax to help make tight turns and to reduc the chance of breaking the blade.
- When you are replacing a broken blade, loc for any pieces of the blade that may be stuck ir side the collar.
- When you install a blade in the saw, make su it is in as far as it will go, and tighten the se screw securely. Always disconnect the pow source before you change blades or perforr maintenance.

4.3.0 Reciprocating Saw

Both the saber saw and the reciprocating saw ca make straight and curved cuts. They are used to c irregular shapes and holes in plaster, plasterboar plywood, studs, metal, and most other materia that can be cut with a saw.

Both saws have straight blades that move you guide them in the direction of the cut. B here's the difference: The saber saw's blade mov up and down, whereas the reciprocating saw blade moves back and forth. The reciprocatir saw is designed for more heavy-duty jobs than t saber saw is. It can use longer and tougher blad

Blade Safety

If you are cutting into the middle of a piece with a saber saw, first make a starter hole using a power drill. Once you have a drilled hole, tip the saber saw forward on the front of its baseplate, positioning the blade over your drilled hole. Press the trigger and slowly tip the baseplate and the blade down toward the surface. When it strikes the surface, the blade may jump. Keep a steady hand, and the gentle pressure will eventually push the blade through the workpiece. Plunging the blade into the work with sudden force is one of the most common causes of broken blades. The other cause of broken blades is pushing a saber saw too fast. The common result of too much pressure too fast is a snapped blade.

---

han a saber saw. Also, because of its design, you an get into more places with it. The reciprocating aw (see *Figure 17*) is used for jobs that require rute strength. It can saw through walls or ceilings nd create openings for windows, plumbing lines, nd more. It is a basic tool in any demolition work.

Like the saber saw, reciprocating saws come n single-speed, two-speed, and variable-speed nodels. The two-speed reciprocating saw can cut t low and high speeds. The low-speed setting is est for metal work. The high-speed setting is for awing wood and other soft materials.

The baseplate (shoeplate or footplate) may ave a swiveling action, or it may be fixed. What-ver the design, the baseplate is there to provide a race or support point for the sawing operation.

.3.1 How to Use a Reciprocating Saw

ollow these steps to use a reciprocating saw afely and efficiently (see *Figure 18*):

tep 1 Wear appropriate personal protective equipment.

tep 2 To avoid vibration, clamp the work to a pair of sawhorses or secure it in a vise.

Step 3 Set the saw to the desired speed. Remember these guidelines:
- Use lower speeds for sawing metal.
- Use higher speeds for sawing wood and other soft materials.

Step 4 Grip the saw with both hands. Place the baseplate firmly against the workpiece.

Step 5 Squeeze the trigger ON switch. The blade moves back and forth, cutting on the backstroke.

CAUTION

Use both hands to grip the saw firmly. Otherwise, the pull created by the blade's grip might jerk the saw out of your grasp.

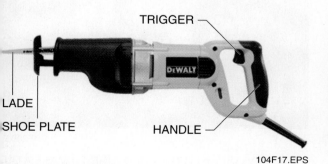

TRIGGER

LADE

SHOE PLATE

HANDLE

104F17.EPS

gure 17 ◆ Reciprocating saw.

104F18.EPS

Figure 18 ◆ Proper use of a reciprocating saw.

4.3.2 Safety and Maintenance

Follow these guidelines to ensure safety for yourself and your nearby co-workers, and a long life for the saw:

- Always wear appropriate personal protective equipment.
- Before you cut through a wall or partition, find out what is inside the wall or on the other side of the partition. Avoid hitting water lines or electrical wiring.
- Always disconnect the power source before you change blades or perform maintenance.

4.4.0 Portable Handheld Bandsaw

The portable handheld bandsaw (see *Figure 19*) is used when it is better to move the saw to the work than to move the work to the saw. The bandsaw can cut pipe, metal, plastics, wood, and irregularly shaped materials. It is especially good for cutting heavy metal, but it will also do fine cutting work.

The bandsaw has a one-piece blade that runs in one direction around guides at either end of the saw. The blade is a thin, flat piece of steel. It is sized according to the diameter of the revolving pulleys that drive and support the blade. The saw often works at various speeds.

4.4.1 How to Use a Portable Bandsaw

Follow these steps to use a bandsaw safely and efficiently:

Step 1 Wear appropriate personal protective equipment.

Step 2 Place the stop firmly against the object to be cut. This will keep the saw from bouncing against the object and breaking the band.

Step 3 Gently pull the trigger. Only a little pressure is needed to make a good clean cut because the weight of the saw gives you more leverage for cutting. *Figure 20* shows the proper way to use a portable bandsaw.

CAUTION

The portable bandsaw cuts on the pull, not the push. You must be especially careful because, in some situations, the saw blade might be moving directly toward your body. Always wear appropriate personal protective equipment and keep your mind focused on the work in front of you.

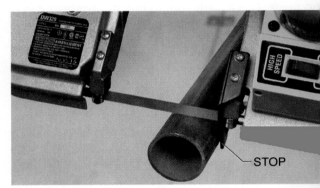

104F20A.EPS

(A) PLACE THE STOP FIRMLY AGAINST THE OBJECT

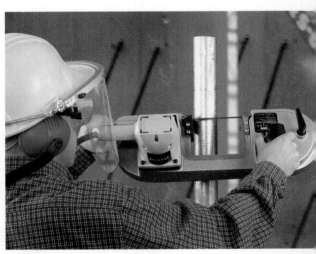

104F20B.EPS

(B) APPLY ONLY A LITTLE PRESSURE TO MAKE A CUT

Figure 20 ◆ Proper use of a portable bandsaw.

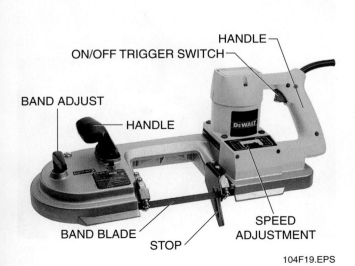

104F19.EPS

Figure 19 ◆ Portable handheld bandsaw.

4.4.2 Safety and Maintenance

Follow these guidelines to ensure safety for yourself and your co-workers, and a long life for the saw:

Always wear appropriate personal protective equipment.
Use only a bandsaw that has a stop.
Before you cut through a wall or partition, find out what is inside the wall or on the other side of the partition. Avoid hitting water lines or electrical wiring.
The blade of a portable bandsaw gets stuck very easily. Never force a portable bandsaw. Let the saw do the cutting.
The blades should be waxed with an appropriate lubricant, such as the one recommended by the blade's manufacturer. Always disconnect the power source before you do maintenance.

4.5.0 Power Miter Box

The power miter saw combines a miter box with a circular saw, allowing it to make straight and miter cuts. There are two types of power miter boxes: power miter saws and compound miter saws.

In a power miter box (see *Figure 21*), the saw blade pivots horizontally from the rear of the table and locks in position to cut angles from 0 degrees to 45 degrees right and left. Stops are set for common angles. The difference between the power miter saw and the compound miter saw is that the blade on the compound miter saw can be tilted vertically, allowing the saw to be used to make a compound cut (combined bevel and miter cut).

4.5.1 How to Use a Power Miter Box

Follow these steps to use a power miter box safely and efficiently:

Step 1 Wear appropriate personal protective equipment.

Step 2 Be sure the saw blade has reached its maximum speed before starting the cut.

Step 3 Hold the workpiece firmly against the fence when making the cut.

Step 4 Turn off the saw immediately after making the cut and use the brake to stop the blade.

> **? DID YOU KNOW?**
>
> ## For Portable Bandsaws, Low Speed Works Best
>
> The portable bandsaw cuts best at a low speed. Using a high speed will cause the blade's teeth to rub rather than cut. This can create heat through friction, which will cause the blade to wear out quickly.

104F21.EPS

Figure 21 ◆ Power miter box saw.

4.5.2 Safety and Maintenance

Follow these guidelines to ensure safety for yourself and your co-workers, and a long life for the miter box:

- Always check the condition of the blade and be sure the blade is secure before starting the saw.
- Keep your fingers clear of the blade.
- Be sure the blade guards are in place and working properly.
- Never make adjustments while the saw is running.
- Never leave a saw until the blade stops.
- Be sure the saw is sitting on a firm base and is properly fastened to the base.
- Be sure the saw is securely locked at the correct angle.
- If working on long stock, have a helper support the end of the stock.

Section 4.0.0

1. Never use a circular saw that doesn't have a lower blade guard because the _____.
   - a. trigger lock won't work properly
   - b. saw blade may fall off
   - c. guard protects you from the blade and from flying particles
   - d. wood will split

2. For circular saws, saw size is measured by the _____.
   - a. diameter of the circular blade
   - b. depth of the upper blade guard
   - c. area of the base
   - d. length of the guide slot

3. When cutting with a circular saw, grip the saw handles _____.
   - a. and pull the saw toward you
   - b. firmly with one hand
   - c. loosely with one hand
   - d. firmly with two hands

4. If the material you are cutting with a circular saw isn't heavy enough to stay in position without moving, _____.
   - a. use a heavier saw
   - b. weight or clamp it down
   - c. hold it down with your free hand
   - d. use a lighter saw

5. To secure small pieces of material when you are cutting them, always use _____.
   - a. a clamp
   - b. your hands
   - c. nails or screws
   - d. the safety guard

6. Saber saws are good for _____.
   - a. heavy-duty materials
   - b. oversized pieces of lumber
   - c. delicate and intricate work
   - d. masonry and concrete

7. When using a saber saw, avoid vibration by _____.
   - a. holding the workpiece down with your free hand.
   - b. setting a heavy object on the workpiece
   - c. using a low-speed setting
   - d. using a clamp or vise to hold the work

8. Before you cut through a wall or partition, always _____.
   - a. remove the lower blade guard
   - b. find out what is on the other side
   - c. increase the revolutions per minute
   - d. lubricate the guard with oil or grease

9. Before you plug any saw into a power source, make sure the _____.
   - a. power switch is in the OFF position
   - b. blade has been loosened
   - c. power switch is in the ON position
   - d. lower blade guard has been removed

10. Use only a bandsaw that has a _____.
    - a. breastplate with a broad surface
    - b. battery pack
    - c. thick, three-piece blade
    - d. stop

5.0.0 ◆ GRINDERS AND SANDERS

Grinding tools can power all kinds of **abrasive** wheels, brushes, buffs, drums, bits, saws, and discs. These wheels come in a variety of materials and **grits.** They can drill, cut, smooth, and polish; shape or sand wood or metal; mark steel and glass; and sharpen or engrave. They can even be used on plastics.

Sanders can shape workpieces, remove imperfections in wood and metal, and create the smooth surfaces needed before finishing work can begin.

Sanding is an essential part of all finish carpentr[y] Sanding gives a smooth, professional look to th[e] completed work regardless of whether it will b[e] painted. You will learn about the following typ[es] of grinders and sanders in this section:

- Angle grinders (side grinders), end grinder[s] detail grinders
- Bench grinders
- Portable belt sanders
- Random orbital sanders (finishing sanders)

5.1.0 Angle Grinders, End Grinders, and Detail Grinders

These types of grinders are grouped together because they are all handheld.

The angle grinder (also called a side grinder) is used to grind away hard, heavy materials and to grind surfaces such as pipes, plates, or welds (see Figure 22).

End grinders (see Figure 23) are also called horizontal grinders or pencil grinders. These smaller grinders are used to smooth the inside of materials such as pipe.

Detail grinders (see Figure 24) use small attachments, also called points, to smooth and polish intricate metallic work. These attachments, some of which are shown in Figure 24, are commonly made in sizes ranging from $1/16$ to $1/4$ inch.

The angle grinder has a rotating grinding disc set at a right angle to the motor shaft. The grinding disc on the end grinder rotates in line with the motor shaft. Grinding is also done with the outside of the grinding disc. The detail grinder has a shank that extends from the motor shaft; points of different sizes and shapes can be mounted on the shank.

5.1.1 How to Use an Angle Grinder, End Grinder, or Detail Grinder

Follow these steps to use an angle, end, or detail grinder safely and efficiently (see Figure 25):

Step 1 Wear appropriate personal protective equipment.

Step 2 If it is not already secured, secure the material in a vise or clamp it to the bench.

Step 3 To use an angle grinder, place one hand on the handle of the grinder and one on the trigger. To use an end grinder or detail grinder, grip the grinder at the shaft end with one hand and cradle the opposite end of the tool in your other hand.

Step 4 Finish the work by removing any loose material with a wire brush.

5.1.2 Safety and Maintenance

Follow these guidelines to ensure safety for yourself and your co-workers, and a long life for the grinder:

- Always wear appropriate personal protective equipment.
- Never use an angle grinder, end grinder, or detail grinder unless it is equipped with the guard that surrounds the grinding wheel.
- Choose a grinding disc that is appropriate for the type of work you are doing.

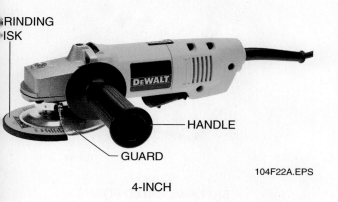

GRINDING DISK

HANDLE

GUARD

4-INCH

104F22A.EPS

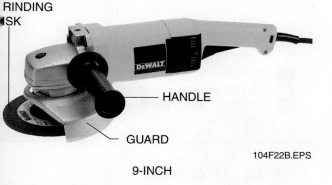

GRINDING DISK

HANDLE

GUARD

9-INCH

104F22B.EPS

Figure 22 ◆ Angle grinders.

GUARD FOR GRINDING DISK

104F23.EPS

Figure 23 ◆ End grinder.

DETAIL GRINDER

104F24A.EPS

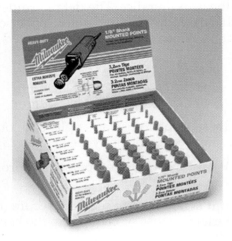

104F24B.EPS

1/8-INCH
SHANK-MOUNTED POINTS

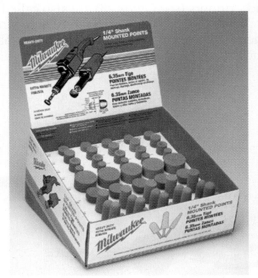

104F24C.EPS

1/4-INCH
SHANK-MOUNTED POINTS

Figure 24 ◆ Detail grinder and points.

- Make sure that you are using a disc that is properly sized for the grinder.
- Before you start the grinder, make sure the grinding disc is secured and is in good condition.
- Make sure all guards are in place.
- Be sure to have firm footing and a firm grip before you use a grinder. Grinders have a tendency to pull you off balance.
- Always hold the grinder with both hands.
- Always use a spark deflector (shield) as well as proper eye protection.
- Direct sparks and debris away from people or from any hazardous materials.
- When you are grinding on a platform, use a flame-retardant blanket to catch falling sparks.
- When you shut off the power, do not leave the tool until the grinding disc has come to a complete stop.
- Always disconnect the power source before you do maintenance.

 WARNING!
Grinding discs can explode if used when they are cracked. Inspect the disc for cracks before using the grinder.

5.2.0 Bench Grinder

Bench grinders (see *Figure 26*) are electricall powered stationary grinding machines. They usu ally have two grinding wheels that are used fo grinding, rust removal, and metal buffing. The are also great for renewing worn edges and mair taining the sharp edges of cutting tools. Remen ber learning about the danger of mushroome cold chisel heads in *Introduction to Hand Tools?* Th bench grinder can smooth these heads.

Heavy-duty grinder wheels range from 6¾ t 10 inches in diameter. Each wheel's maximur speed is given in rpm. Never use a grinding wheel above its rated maximum speed. Bench grinders come with an adjustable tool rest. This is the surface on which you position the material you are grinding, such as cold chisel heads. There should be a distance of only 1/8 inch between the tool rest and the wheel. Attachments for the bench grinder include knot-wire brushes for removing rust, scale, and file marks from metal surfaces, and cloth buffing wheels for polishing and buffing metal surfaces.

5.2.1 How to Use a Bench Grinder

Follow these steps to use a bench grinder safely and efficiently:

Step 1 Wear appropriate personal protective equipment. A face shield is essential.

Step 2 Always use the adjustable tool rest as a support when you are grinding or beveling metal pieces. There should be a maximum gap of 1/8 of an inch between the tool rest and the wheel and 1/4 inch between the top guard and wheel. Make sure the bench grinder is placed on a secure surface.

CAUTION

Never change the adjustment of tool rests when the grinder is on or when the grinding wheels are spinning. Doing so may damage the work.

104F25.EPS

Figure 25 ◆ Proper use of a handheld grinder.

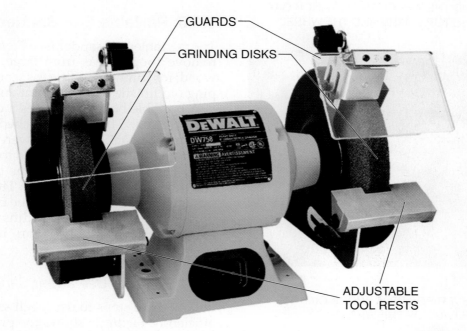

GUARDS

GRINDING DISKS

ADJUSTABLE TOOL RESTS

104F26.EPS

Figure 26 ◆ Bench grinder.

Step 3 Let the wheel come up to full speed before you touch the work.

Step 4 Keep the metal you are grinding cool. If the metal gets too hot, it can destroy the temper (hardness) of the material you are grinding, such as a metal chisel head.

Step 5 Whenever possible, work on the face of the wheel. For many jobs you must work on the side of the wheel, but inspect the wheel frequently to be sure you do not reduce the thickness so much that it can break. *Figure 27* shows the proper way to use a bench grinder.

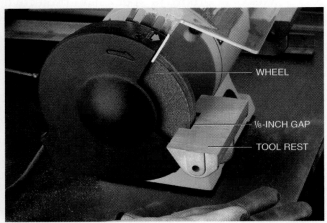

104F27A.EPS

THERE SHOULD BE A ⅛-INCH GAP BETWEEN THE
TOOL REST AND THE WHEEL AND A ¼-INCH GAP
BETWEEN THE TOP GUARD AND THE WHEEL.

104F27B.EPS

WHENEVER POSSIBLE, WORK ON
THE FACE OF THE WHEEL.

Figure 27 ◆ Proper use of a bench grinder.

5.2.2 Safety and Maintenance

Follow these guidelines to ensure safety for yourself and your co-workers, and a long life for the grinder:

- Always wear appropriate personal protective equipment.
- Never wear loose clothing or jewelry when you are grinding. It can get caught in the wheels.
- Grinding metal creates sparks, so keep the area around the grinder clean.
- Always adjust the tool rests so they are within ⅛ inch of the wheel. This reduces the chance of getting the work wedged between the rest and the wheel.
- Keep your hands away from the grinding wheels.
- Let the wheel come up to full speed before you touch the work.
- Never use a grinding wheel above its rated maximum speed.
- When you are finished using the bench grinder, shut it off.
- Always make sure the bench grinder is disconnected before you change grinding wheels.
- Perform a **ring test** before you mount a wheel. After you look for chipped edges and cracks, mount the wheel on a rod that you pass through the wheel hole. Tap the wheel gently on the side with a piece of wood. The wheel will ring clearly if it is in good condition. A dull thud may mean that there is a crack that you can't see. Get rid of the wheel if this happens.

5.3.0 Portable Belt Sander

The portable belt sander (see *Figure 28*) is used to remove rough areas from large, flat sections of wood; for trimming off excess wood; and for stripping old finishes such as paint and varnish.

A portable belt sander uses a continuous-loop abrasive belt that is stretched between two drums. The back roller is powered by the motor; the front roller is spring-loaded to correct belt tension. The longer and wider the belt, the heavier and more powerful the sander. The size of the belt sander refers to the width of the belt. Heavy-duty models usually have belt widths of 3 to 4 inches. All models should have an integrated dust collection bag.

5.3.1 How to Use a Belt Sander

Follow these steps to use a belt sander safely and efficiently. *Figure 29* shows the proper way to use a portable belt sander.

HANDLES

DUST
COLLECTION BAG

HEEL

BACK ROLLER

FRONT
ROLLER

104F28.EPS

Figure 28 ◆ Portable belt sander.

Step 1 Wear appropriate personal protective equipment.

Step 2 Rest the sander on its heel when starting the motor.

Step 3 Once the sander is moving, lower it onto the workpiece.

Step 4 Keep the sander level while you move it across the workpiece.

Step 5 Keep the sander moving whenever it is in contact with the workpiece.

CAUTION

Do not allow the sander to remain stationary. This will create a groove, gouge, or depression in the surface of the workpiece.

Step 6 Tip the sander back on its heel when you finish. Do not set the sander down until the belt stops moving.

5.3.2 Safety and Maintenance

Follow these guidelines to ensure safety for yourself and your co-workers, and a long life for the sander:

- Always wear appropriate personal protective equipment. Use a dust mask, even with models that have a dust-collection system.
- Never wear loose clothing or jewelry when you are sanding. It could get caught in the belt.
- Keep your hands away from the sanding belt.
- Keep the power cord away from the area being sanded.
- Let the belt come up to full speed before you apply it to the workpiece.
- When you are finished using the belt sander, shut it off and unplug it.
- Always make sure the belt sander is disconnected before you change belts.
- Do not light matches when you are sanding in a confined area. Dust from sanding can be explosive.

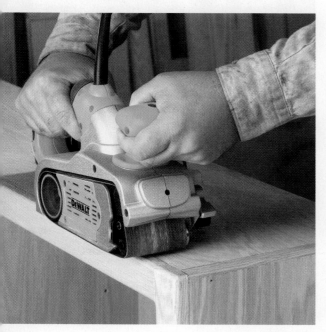

104F29A.EPS

104F29B.EPS

Figure 29 ◆ Proper use of a portable belt sander.

5.4.0 Random Orbital Sander (Finishing Sander)

Finishing sanders are used to create an even, smooth surface, such as one needed for painting. Finishing sander models used to have either orbital (circular) or oscillating (back and forth) movement. The random orbital sander (see *Figure 30*) combines both types of movement.

The random orbital sander's circular motion works together with your own back-and-forth hand motion to eliminate any telltale patterns that orbital sanders tend to leave on the work. Using a fine-grit abrasive paper and moving the sanding disc in a smooth motion over the workpiece maintains a swirl-free finish. Random orbital sanders come in single- and variable-speed models. Many have dust-collection bags attached to the body of the sander.

104F30.EP

Figure 30 ◆ Random orbital sander.

5.4.1 How to Use a Random Orbital Sander

Follow these steps to use a random orbital sander safely and efficiently:

Step 1 Wear appropriate personal protective equipment.

Step 2 Maintain a firm hold when you start the sander.

Step 3 Let the sander come up to full speed before applying it to the surface of the workpiece.

Step 4 Keep the sander level while you move it across the workpiece.

Step 5 Keep the sander moving whenever it is in contact with the workpiece.

CAUTION

Do not let the sander remain in one place. This will create a groove, gouge, or depression in the surface of the workpiece.

Step 6 Lift the sander off the workpiece when you finish. Do not set the sander down until it stops moving. *Figure 31* shows the proper way to use a random orbital sander.

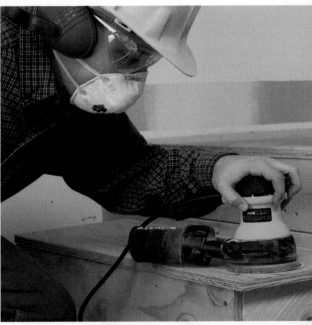

104F31.EP

Figure 31 ◆ Proper use of a random orbital sander.

5.4.2 Safety and Maintenance

Follow the belt-sander safety practices that you learned earlier in this module when using a finishing sander.

Sanding Tips

Always sand with rougher grits of paper first. As you work, change to progressively finer grits for a smoother finish. Before giving wood its final sanding, wipe it down with a damp rag to remove sanding dust from between the grain lines.

Review Questions

Section 5.0.0

1. The angle grinder is used to grind _____.

   a. soft, porous materials
   b. imperfections in wood
   c. hard, heavy materials
   d. nonmetals only

2. The end grinder is used to _____.

   a. polish intricate work
   b. grind surfaces
   c. smooth the work before painting
   d. smooth the inside of materials, such as pipe

3. The _____ is an electrically powered stationary grinding machine.

   a. angle grinder
   b. bench grinder
   c. end grinder
   d. detail grinder

4. A detail grinder uses _____ to smooth and polish intricate metallic work.

   a. points
   b. abrasive paper
   c. wire brushes
   d. grinding wheels

5. When using a grinder, try to work on the _____ of the wheel whenever possible.

   a. face
   b. edge
   c. bottom
   d. side

6. The adjustable tool rest on a bench grinder should be positioned _____ inch from the wheel.

   a. ⅛
   b. ¼
   c. ½
   d. ¾

7. Never use a grinding wheel _____.

   a. to remove rust
   b. above its rated maximum speed
   c. to bevel chiseling tools
   d. on cool metal surfaces

8. The portable belt sander is used to _____.

   a. remove rough areas from wood
   b. maintain sharp edges on cutting tools
   c. sand heavy-duty materials only
   d. sand portable items only

9. When you are sanding, wear _____.

   a. loose clothing
   b. a full face guard
   c. a dust mask
   d. a belt

10. The random orbital sander is used to _____.

    a. strip off paint
    b. bevel the edges of chisel heads
    c. eliminate circular swirls on finished work
    d. remove rust from heavily corroded materials

6.0.0 ◆ MISCELLANEOUS POWER TOOLS

It is very common to see several different types of power tools on a construction site. In this section you will learn about some of the commonly used power tools we haven't yet covered. It is likely you will see them used on your site or use them yourself.

- Pneumatically powered nailers (nail guns)
- Powder-actuated fastening systems
- Air impact wrenches
- Pavement breakers
- Hydraulic jacks

6.1.0 Pneumatically Powered Nailer (Nail Gun)

Pneumatically powered nailers (see *Figure 32*), or nail guns, are commonplace on construction jobs. They greatly speed up the installation of materials such as wallboard, molding, framing members, and shingles.

Nail guns are driven by compressed air traveling through air lines connected to an air compressor. Nailers are designed for specific purposes,

104F32.EPS

Figure 32 ◆ Pneumatic nailer.

such as roofing, framing, siding, flooring, sheathing, trim, and finishing. Nailers use specific types of nails depending on the material to be fastened. The nails come in coils and in strips and are loaded into the nail gun.

Power Nailers

Power nailers come in several types: spring-loaded, electromagnetic, pneumatic, and combustion. All work on the same basic principle. A power source (such as an air compressor) generates enough force to eject fasteners (brads or nails) quickly. As a fastener ejects, another automatically loads, making this tool a good choice for large-scale fastening jobs. Nailers range in weight from 2 to 3 pounds. Most use oil as a lubricant, but some models are oil-free.

104SA01.EPS

Power Screwdrivers

This tool also uses a power source (this model uses a battery) to speed production in a variety of applications, such as drywalling, floor sheathing and underlayment, decking, fencing, and cement board installation. A chain of screws feeds automatically into the firing chamber. Most models incorporate a back-out feature to drive out screws as well as a guide that keeps the screw feed aligned and tangle free. This tool can accept Philips or square slot screws and weighs an average of 6 pounds.

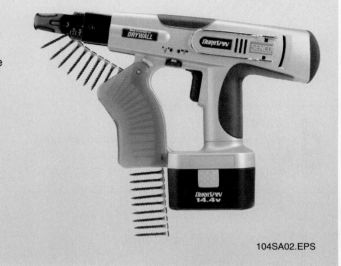

104SA02.EPS

6.1.1 How to Use a Power Nailer

Follow these steps to use a power nailer safely and efficiently:

Step 1 Read the manufacturer's instructions before using a pneumatically powered nailer. Wear all appropriate personal protective equipment.

Step 2 Inspect the nailer for damage and loose connections.

Step 3 Load the nails into the nailer. Be sure to use the correct type of nail for the job.

Step 4 Ensure that hoses are connected properly.

Step 5 Check the air compressor and adjust the pressure.

Step 6 Try a test nail in scrap material. Most nailers operate at pressures of 70 to 120 pounds per square inch (psi).
  a. If nail penetration is too deep, adjust the regulator on the air compressor to get a lower reading on the pressure gauge.
  b. If the nailhead sticks up above the surface, adjust the compressor for higher pressure.

Step 7 When nailing wall materials, locate and mark wall studs before nailing. Otherwise, you won't be able to feel a missed nail that penetrates the wallboard but misses the stud.

Step 8 Hold the nailer firmly against the material to be fastened, then press the trigger (see *Figure 33*).

Step 9 Disconnect the air hose as soon as you finish.

104F33.EPS

Figure 33 ◆ Proper use of a nailer.

Power Nailer Safety

Pneumatic nailers are designed to fire when the trigger is pressed and the tool is pressed against the material being fastened. An important safety feature of all pneumatic nailers is that they will not fire unless pressed against the material.

WARNING!
Never exceed the maximum specified operating pressure of a pneumatic nailer. Doing so will damage the pneumatic nailer and cause injury.

6.1.2 Safety and Maintenance

Follow these guidelines to ensure safety for yourself and your co-workers, and a long life for the nail gun:

- Always wear appropriate personal protective equipment.
- Review the operating manual before using any nailer.
- Keep the nailer oiled. Add a few drops to the air inlet before each use, according to the manufacturer's recommendations.
- Use the correct nailer for the job. Use the correct size and type of nail for the job.
- Never load the nailer with the compressor hose attached.
- Never leave the nailer unattended.
- If the nailer is not firing, disconnect the air hose before you attempt repairs.
- Keep all body parts and co-workers away from the nail path to avoid serious injury. Nails can go through paneling and strike someone on the other side.
- Check for pipes, electrical wiring, vents, and other materials behind wallboard before nailing.

WARNING!
A nail gun is not a toy. Playing with a nail gun can cause serious injury. Nails can pierce a hand, leg, or eye easily. Never point a nail gun at anyone or carry one with your finger on the trigger. Use the nail gun only as directed.

6.2.0 Powder-Actuated Fastening Systems

The use of powder-actuated anchor or fastening systems has been increasing rapidly in recent years. They are used for anchoring static loads to steel and concrete beams, walls, and so forth.

A powder-actuated tool is a low-velocity fastening system powered by gunpowder cartridges called **boosters.** The tools are used to drive steel pins or threaded steel studs directly into masonry and steel (see *Figure 34*).

6.2.1 How to Set Up and Use a Powder-Actuated Fastening Tool

Follow these steps to use a powder-actuated tool safely and efficiently:

Step 1 Wear the appropriate personal protective equipment, including safety goggles, ear protection, and a hard hat.

Step 2 Feed the pin or stud into the piston.

Step 3 Feed the gunpowder cartridge (booster charge) into position.

Step 4 Position the tool in front of the item to be fastened and press it against the mounting surface. This pressure releases the safety lock.

Step 5 Pull the trigger handle to fire the booster charge (see *Figure 34*).

6.2.2 Safety and Maintenance

Follow these guidelines to ensure safety for yourself and your co-workers, and a long life for the powder-actuated tool:

- Always wear appropriate personal protective equipment, including ear protection, safety goggles, and a hard hat.
- Do not use a powder-actuated tool until you are certified on the model you will be using.

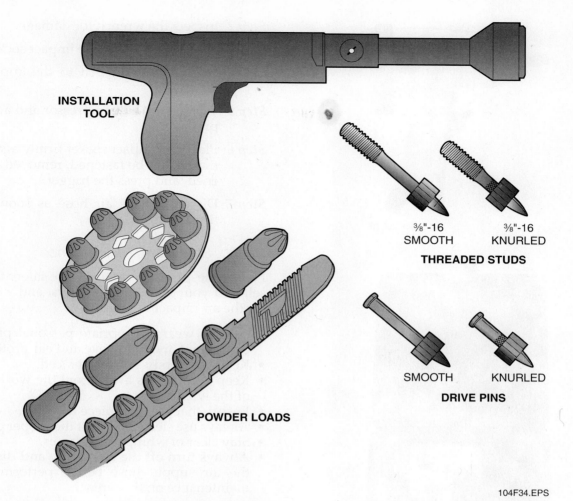

INSTALLATION TOOL

³⁄₈"-16
SMOOTH

³⁄₈"-16
KNURLED

THREADED STUDS

SMOOTH

KNURLED

DRIVE PINS

POWDER LOADS

104F34.EPS

Figure 34 ◆ Powder-actuated fastening system.

Follow all safety precautions in the manufacturer's instruction manual.

Do not load the tool until you are prepared to complete the firing.

Use the proper size pin for the job you are doing. When loading the driver, put the pin in before you load the charge.

Use the correct booster charge according to the manufacturer's instructions for the tool being used.

Never hold the end of the barrel against any part of your body or cock the tool against your hand.

Never hold your hand behind the material you are fastening.

Do not fire the tool close to the edge of concrete. Pieces of concrete may chip off and strike someone, or the projectile could continue past the concrete and strike a co-worker.

Never try to pry the booster out of the magazine with a sharp instrument.

 WARNING!
OSHA requires that all operators of powder-actuated tools be qualified and certified by the manufacturer of the tool. You must carry a certification card when using the tool.

 WARNING!
Avoid firing a powder-actuated tool into easily penetrated materials. The fastener may pass through the material and become a flying missile on the other side.

6.3.0 Air Impact Wrench

Air impact wrenches (see *Figure 35*) are power tools that are used to fasten, tighten, and loosen nuts and bolts. The speed and strength (torque) of

104F35A.TIF

104F35B.TIF

Figure 35 ◆ Air impact wrench.

these wrenches can easily be adjusted depending on the type of job. Air impact wrenches are powered pneumatically (with compressed air). In order to operate an air impact wrench, it must be attached with a hose to an air compressor.

6.3.1 How to Set Up and Use an Air Impact Wrench

Follow these steps to use an air impact wrench safely and efficiently:

Step 1 Read the manufacturer's instructions before using an air impact wrench. Wear all appropriate personal protective equipment.

Step 2 Inspect the wrench for damage.

Step 3 Select the appropriate impact socket.

Step 4 Connect the wrench to the appropriate air hose.

Step 5 Turn on the air compressor and adjust the pressure.

Step 6 Place the impact socket firmly against the material to be fastened, removed, or loosened, and press the trigger.

Step 7 Disconnect the air hose as soon as you finish.

6.3.2 Safety and Maintenance

Follow these guidelines to ensure safety for yourself and your nearby co-workers, and a long life for the air impact wrench:

• Always wear appropriate personal protective equipment, including eye and ear protection.
• Keep your body stance balanced.
• Keep your hands away from the working end of the wrench.
• Ensure that the workpiece is secure.
• Always use clean, dry air at the proper pressure.
• Stay clear of whipping air hoses.
• Always turn off the air supply and disconnect the air supply hose before performing any maintenance on the wrench.

 WARNING!
Using handheld sockets can damage property and cause injury. Use only impact sockets made for air impact wrenches.

6.4.0 Pavement Breaker

Several large-scale demolition tools are frequently used in construction. They include pavement breakers, clay spades, and rock drills (see *Figure 36*). These tools do not rotate like hammer drills. They reciprocate (move back and forth). The name *jackhammer* comes from a trade name, but has come to refer to almost any of the handheld impact tools. There are differences in the tools and their uses, however. In this section, we will look at the pavement breaker.

The pavement breaker is used for large-scale demolition work, such as tearing down brick and concrete walls and breaking up concrete or pavement.

A pavement breaker weighs from 50 to 90 pounds. On most pavement breakers, a throttle is

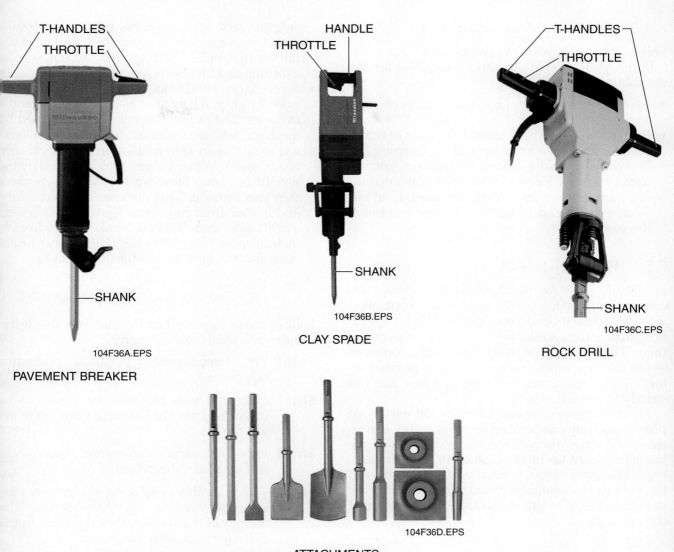

T-HANDLES

THROTTLE

SHANK

104F36A.EPS

PAVEMENT BREAKER

HANDLE

THROTTLE

SHANK

104F36B.EPS

CLAY SPADE

T-HANDLES

THROTTLE

SHANK

104F36C.EPS

ROCK DRILL

104F36D.EPS

ATTACHMENTS

Figure 36 ◆ Three typical demolition tools and attachments.

located on the T-handle. When you push the throttle, compressed air operates a piston inside the tool. The piston drives the steel-cutting shank into the material you want to break up. You can use attachments, such as spades or chisels, for different tasks.

6.4.1 How to Set Up and Use a Pavement Breaker

Follow these steps to use a pavement breaker safely and efficiently:

Step 1 Wear appropriate personal protective equipment.

Step 2 Make sure that the air pressure is shut off at the main air outlet.

Step 3 Hold the coupler at the end of the air supply line, slide the ring back, and slip the

coupler on the connector or nipple that is attached to the air drill.

Step 4 Check to see if you have a good connection. (A good coupling cannot be taken apart without first sliding the ring back.)

Step 5 Add a whip check.

Step 6 Once you have a good connection, turn on the air supply valve. The pavement breaker is now ready to use.

WARNING!

The air hose must be connected properly and securely. An unsecured air hose can come loose and whip around violently, causing serious injury. Some fittings require the use of whip checks to keep them from coming loose.

Follow these guidelines to ensure safety for your-self and your co-workers, and a long life for the demolition tool:

- Always wear appropriate personal protective equipment.
- Because some of these tools make a lot of noise, you must wear hearing protection (earplugs).
- Be aware of what is under the material you are about to break. Know the location of water, gas, electricity, sewer, and telephone lines. Find out what is there and where it is before you break the pavement!

6.5.0 Hydraulic Jack

Hydraulic tools are used when the application calls for extreme force to be applied in a controlled manner. These tools do not operate at high speed, but great care should be used when operating them. The forces generated by hydraulic tools can easily damage equipment or cause personnel injury if the manufacturer's procedures are not strictly followed.

Hydraulic jacks are used for a wide variety of purposes. They can be used to move heavy equipment and other heavy material, to position heavy loads precisely, and to straighten or bend frames. Hydraulic jacks have two basic parts: the pump and the cylinder (sometimes called a ram). There are various types of hydraulic jacks. Some of the most common are:

- *Hydraulic jacks with internal pumps* – This is a general-purpose jack that is available in many different capacities. See *Figure 37*. The pump in-

side the jack applies pressure to the hydrauli fluid when the handle is pumped. The pressur on the hydraulic fluid applies pressure to th cylinder and lifts or moves the load.

- *Porta-Powers®* – This jack consists of a lever-op erated pump, a length of hydraulic hose, and a cylinder. The pump and cylinder are joined by the high-pressure hydraulic hose. Porta-Powers' are available in different capacities. Cylinder are available in many sizes; they are rated by th weight (in tons) they can lift and the distanc they can move it. This distance is called strok and is measured in inches. Hydraulic cylinder can lift more than 500 tons. Strokes range from ½ inch to more than 48 inches. Different cylinde sizes and ratings are used for different jobs.

Follow these steps to ensure that you use a hy draulic jack safely and efficiently:

Step 1 Wear appropriate personal protectiv equipment.

Step 2 Place the jack beneath the object to b lifted. You may have to use a wedge to be gin the lift.

Step 3 Pump the handle down, and then releas it. This raises the cylinder.

Step 4 To lower the jack, open the return pas sage by turning the thumbscrew. Th weight of the load pushes the fluid in th cylinder back into the pump.

Follow these guidelines to ensure safety for your self and your co-workers, and a long life for th hydraulic jack:

- Always wear appropriate personal protectiv equipment.
- Check the fluid level in the pump before using it
- Make sure the hydraulic hose is not twisted o kinked.
- Do not move the pump if the hose is unde pressure.
- Clear the work area when you are making a lift
- When you are lifting, make sure the cylinder i on a secure, level surface to prevent the jacl from kicking out.
- Do not use a cheater bar (extension) on th pump handle.
- Watch for leaks.
- Never use a jack to support a load. Once th load is where you want it, block it up.
- Never exceed the lifting capacity of the jack.

104F37.EPS

Figure 37 ◆ Portable hydraulic jack.

Section 6.0.0

1. Most pneumatic nailers operate at pressures of _____ per square inch (psi).

   a. 70 to 120 grams
   b. 7 to 120 ounces
   c. 7 to 12 pounds
   d. 70 to 120 pounds

2. When loading nails into a pneumatic nailer, _____.

   a. never leave the compressor hose attached
   b. always connect the compressor hose
   c. uncoil the strips
   d. reattach the air lines

3. If a pneumatic nailer is not firing properly, _____ before you attempt repairs.

   a. adjust the compressor
   b. disconnect the air hose
   c. adjust the regulator
   d. load a new coil of nails

4. Some manufacturers suggest adding a _____ to the air inlet each time you use a pneumatic nailer.

   a. few drops of oil
   b. few drops of water
   c. quart of oil
   d. quart of water

5. Powder-actuated fastening systems are used to _____.

   a. penetrate drywall
   b. hammer nails
   c. anchor static loads to steel beams
   d. remove nails

6. Before you begin setting up a pavement breaker for use, make sure that the air pressure is _____.

   a. shut off at the coupler
   b. turned on only halfway
   c. turned on full
   d. shut off at the main air outlet

7. Before you begin using a demolition tool, make sure you _____.

   a. rotate the hammer drill
   b. disconnect the coupler
   c. disconnect the air supply
   d. know what is underneath the material you are breaking up

8. The two basic parts of a hydraulic jack are the _____.

   a. pump and cylinder
   b. reservoir and relief pump
   c. cylinder and hose
   d. hose and pump

9. Porta-Power® cylinders are rated by how much weight they can lift and by _____.

   a. their torque
   b. the amount of electromagnetic material they have
   c. how much they weigh
   d. the distance they can move the weight

10. Before using a Porta-Power®, make sure the hose _____.

   a. reaches to the wall outlet
   b. is connected to the reservoir
   c. is disconnected from the hydraulic jack
   d. is not twisted

Summary

Power tools are a necessity in the construction industry. You might not use all of the tools covered in this module during your career, but it is still important for you to understand how they work and what they do. In fact, it's likely that you'll find yourself working around other craftworkers who use them. You and your co-workers will be safer if everyone is familiar with the tools being used on the job site.

You must also learn how to maintain your power tools properly, whether they belong to you or your employer. The better care you take of your tools, the better and more safely they will function, and the longer they'll last. Proper maintenance of power tools saves you and your employer time and money.

As you progress in your chosen field within the construction industry, you will learn to use the power tools for your specialized area. Although some of these specific tools might not be covered in this module, the basic safety and usage concepts are always applicable. Remember to always read the manufacturer's manual for any new power tool you use and never to use a tool on which you have not been properly trained. Following the basic use and safety guidelines explained in this module, maintaining your tools well, and educating yourself before using any new equipment will help you progress in your career, work efficiently, and stay safe.

Notes

Key Terms Quiz

Fill in the blank with the correct key term that you learned from your study of this module.

1. Activate the _____ to make the trigger stay in operating mode even without your finger on the trigger.

2. _____ reverses its direction at regularly recurring intervals; this type of current is delivered through wall plugs.

3. A(n) _____ saw's straight blades move back and forth.

4. A(n) _____ powers a powder-actuated tool.

5. _____ must be accompanied by material safety data sheets.

6. Masonry bits and nail cutter saw blades have a(n) _____ tip.

7. A(n) _____ is a substance, such as sandpaper, that is used to wear away material.

8. A _____ is used to open and close the chuck on a power drill.

9. _____ is the number of times a drill bit completes one full rotation in a minute.

10. A(n) _____ is used to set the head of a screw at or below the surface of the material.

11. _____ flows in one direction, from the negative to the positive terminal of the source.

12. Belt sanders and circular saws are examples of _____.

13. Use a(n) _____ to bore holes in wood and other materials.

14. An electromagnet holds an electromagnetic drill in place on a(n) _____ metal surface.

15. _____ is applied to the surface of a grinding wheel to give it a nonslip finish.

16. The _____ of the drill holds the drill bit.

17. To prevent an electrical shock, do not operate electric power tools without proper _____.

18. A Porta-Powers® is an example of a(n) _____.

19. _____ refers to building material, including stone, brick, or concrete block.

20. Air hammers and pneumatic nailers are examples of _____.

21. Perform a(n) _____ to check the condition of a grinding wheel.

22. The _____ is the smooth part of a drill bit that fits into the chuck.

23. A(n) _____ protects people from electric shock and protects equipment from damage by interrupting the flow of electricity if a circuit fault occurs.

Key Terms

Abrasive	Countersink	Ground fault protection	Revolutions per minute
AC (alternating current)	DC (direct current)	Hazardous materials	(rpm)
Auger	Electric tools	Hydraulic tools	Ring test
Booster	Ferromagnetic	Masonry	Shank
Carbide	Grit	Pneumatic tools	Trigger lock
Chuck	Ground fault circuit	Reciprocating	
Chuck key	interrupter (GFCI)		

R. P. Hughes

Department Chair for Carpentry and Construction Management
Guilford Technical Community College
Jamestown, North Carolina

R. P. was born in North Carolina and has lived there all his life. After graduating from high school in 1962, R. P. worked in a mill for a year before accepting a job with a residential building company. He enrolled in a construction and apprenticeship program at a local community college, where he quickly came to appreciate the value of education and where he picked up many valuable skills. R. P. worked with the residential builder for 12 years, becoming a superintendent and then becoming a teacher at Guilford Technical Community College.

How did you become interested in the construction industry?
When I graduated from high school, I had neither the money nor the desire to go to college. I was 17 years old, and the only job I could find at that time was in a mill. I was very unhappy about it, and when I had a chance to go into the construction profession with a residential builder, I took it. I started out as a helper.

I saw that construction had the potential to be an excellent career and that it had a promising future. I liked seeing a house going up, and I enjoyed working with my hands. Later, when we finished a house, I enjoyed driving by it and knowing that I had helped to build it.

How did you decide to become an educator?
I got into teaching strictly by accident. At the time, I was working with the residential firm. One day I went to sign up for classes at Guilford. The fellow standing in line ahead of me was applying for the carpentry class, but the person at the desk told him that they weren't going to be able to offer the class because there was no qualified instructor. So I came back the next day and put in my application for carpentry instructor, and I got the job!

What do you think it takes to be a success in your trade?
You need to be able to think problems through and to visualize. You need excellent math skills. You also need strong communication skills to be able to work as part of a team. A lot of people think that it's enough just to know how to drive a nail, but there's so much more involved. You need to be able to deal with subcontractors, with suppliers, and with architects every day. You must have a broad range of skills to be successful in construction.

What are some of the things you do in your job?
A large part of my time is spent teaching. This semester, for example, I am teaching a blueprint class, a safety class, a carpentry class, and an estimating class. Currently in the carpentry class I have 40 students. We established a nonprofit corporation associated with the carpentry program, for which students build a house throughout the year. I supervise the construction of those houses. I try to help individual students determine where their strengths are and then guide them in that direction.

We teach not just the hands-on skills, but also safety skills, estimating techniques, and how to read building codes. If I can teach them to think, then they're well on their way to a successful career in construction. And I think that critical thinking is a skill we are gradually losing. You can punch numbers into a calculator, but you also need to understand what goes on behind those numbers, and how those numbers work the way they do.

I am responsible for two full-time instructors and three or four part-time instructors. I act as a general contractor for the school. I even do the paperwork to see that the bills are paid every month, which is probably one of the least favorite things I have to do!

What do you like most about your job?
I really like the fact that every day is different. You may end up building the same house twice, but you may encounter a unique set of problems each time.

There is a lot of satisfaction that comes from working with your hands. I enjoy going by houses that I built 20 or 30 years ago and seeing them still there. I enjoy giving homeowners a good product and seeing them happy in their homes.

As a teacher and a carpenter, I get both aspects of the profession. I get to build a house, and I get to shape and change some lives and give them some skills that they can work with. Students really develop a lot of skills in a year's time. That's very rewarding to me.

I run into students in the field all the time, and they often come back and ask for my advice on career moves. Often they tell me that, of all the classes they took, one of mine was their favorite and it really meant a lot to them. That makes my job worthwhile. That's why I'm here, why I teach. I could make more money as a builder, but I wouldn't get that reward.

What would you say to someone entering the trades today?

There are so many avenues that you can go into. It depends on your skills and interests. Some students don't mind taking appropriate risks, and they're good at time management. These students could be excellent contractors. Others have more patience and are skilled at detail work. They could do finishing work like trim or cabinets. A lot of students go into framing work and become framing contractors. Whatever you do, you have to want that feeling of accomplishment every day.

There have been some real changes in the industry since I first started. Codes are a lot tougher today, more technical. If you are going to be a success in your chosen field, you need to stay up on your training.

Students today need to be aware of the shortage of skilled workers in the construction industry. A lot of the workers out there are unskilled. The average age of a skilled carpenter today is around 56 years old, I've heard. Someone has to take these people's place when they retire. We see plenty of young, sharp people enter our program, and they need formal training to become skilled workers. You're not going to see skilled jobs like these shipped overseas. People are always going to need a house.

Trade Terms
Introduced in This Module

Abrasive: A substance—such as sandpaper—that is used to wear away material.

AC (alternating current): An electrical current that reverses its direction at regularly recurring intervals; the current delivered through wall plugs.

Auger: A tool with a spiral cutting edge for boring holes in wood and other materials.

Booster: Gunpowder cartridge used to power powder-actuated fastening tools.

Carbide: A very hard material made of carbon and one or more heavy metals. Commonly used in one type of saw blade.

Chuck: A clamping device that holds an attachment; for example, the chuck of the drill holds the drill bit.

Chuck key: A small, T-shaped steel piece used to open and close the chuck on power drills.

Countersink: A bit or drill used to set the head of a screw at or below the surface of the material.

DC (direct current): Electrical current that flows in one direction, from the negative (−) to the positive (+) terminal of the source, such as a battery.

Electric tools: Tools powered by electricity. The electricity is supplied by either an AC source (wall plug) or a DC source (battery).

Ferromagnetic: Having magnetic properties. Substances such as iron, nickel, cobalt, and various alloys are ferromagnetic.

Grit: A granular abrasive used to make sandpaper or applied to the surface of a grinding wheel to give it a nonslip finish. Grit is graded according to its texture. The grit number indicates the number of abrasive granules in a standard size (per inch or per cm). The higher the grit number, the finer the abrasive material.

Ground fault circuit interrupter (GFCI): A circuit breaker designed to protect people from electric shock and to protect equipment from damage by interrupting the flow of electricity if a circuit fault occurs.

Ground fault protection: Protection against short circuits; a safety device cuts power off as soon as it senses any imbalance between incoming and outgoing current.

Hazardous materials: Materials (such as chemicals) that must be transported, stored, applied, handled, and identified according to federal, state, or local regulations. Hazardous materials must be accompanied by material safety data sheets (MSDSs).

Hydraulic tools: Tools powered by fluid pressure. The pressure is produced by hand pumps or electric pumps.

Masonry: Building material, including stone, brick, or concrete block.

Pneumatic tools: Air-powered tools. The power is produced by electric or fuel-powered compressors.

Reciprocating: Moving back and forth.

Revolutions per minute (rpm): The number of times (or rate) a motor component or accessory (drill bit) completes one full rotation every minute.

Ring test: A method of testing the condition of a grinding wheel. The wheel is mounted on a rod and tapped. A clear ring means the wheel is in good condition; a dull thud means the wheel is in poor condition and should be disposed of.

Shank: The smooth part of a drill bit that fits into the chuck.

Trigger lock: A small lever, switch, or part that you push or pull to activate a locking catch or spring. Activating the trigger lock causes the trigger to stay in the operating mode even without your finger on the trigger.

This module is intended to present thorough resources for task training. The following reference works are suggested for further study. These are optional materials for continued education rather than for task training.

29 CFR 1926, OSHA Construction Industry Regulations, latest edition. Washington, DC: Occupational Safety and Health Administration, U.S. Department of Labor, U.S. Government Printing Office.

All About Power Tools. 2002. Des Moines, IA: Meredith Books.

Hand & Power Tool Training. Video. All About OSHA. Surprise, AZ.

Power Tools. 1997. Minnetonka, MN: Handyman Club of America.

Powered Hand Tool Safety: Handle With Care. Video. 20 minutes. Coastal Training Technologies Corp. Virginia Beach, VA.

Reader's Digest Book of Skills and Tools, 1993 edition. Pleasantville, NY: Reader's Digest.

The NCCER makes every effort to keep these textbooks up-to-date and free of technical errors. We appreciate your help in this process. If you have an idea for improving this textbook, or if you find an error, a typographical mistake, or an inaccuracy in NCCER's *Contren®* textbooks, please write us, using this form or a photocopy. Be sure to include the exact module number, page number, a detailed description, and the correction, if applicable. Your input will be brought to the attention of the Technical Review Committee. Thank you for your assistance.

Instructors – If you found that additional materials were necessary in order to teach this module effectively, please let us know so that we may include them in the Equipment/Materials list in the Annotated Instructor's Guide.

Write: Product Development
National Center for Construction Education and Research
P.O. Box 141104, Gainesville, FL 32614-1104

Fax: 352-334-0932

E-mail: curriculum@nccer.org

Craft _____   Module Name _____

Copyright Date _____   Module Number _____   Page Number(s) _____

Description _____

_____

_____

_____

(Optional) Correction _____

_____

_____

(Optional) Your Name and Address _____

_____

_____

Introduction to the
National Electrical Code®
26107-05

Twin Falls Hydroelectric Project

The Snake River is home to numerous hydroelectric power plants that use water power to produce electricity. One such power plant is the Twin Falls Hydroelectric Project in Twin Falls, Idaho. In addition to electricity, it provides many recreational resources, including a boat ramp, overlooks, parks, and picnic areas.

26107-05

Introduction to the National Electrical Code®

Topics to be presented in this module include:

Overview

The primary reference book for safe electrical installations is the *National El trical Code*®, often referred to as the *NEC*®. The *NEC*® states that its prima purpose is "the practical safeguarding of persons and property from hazar arising from the use of electricity." It is not intended to be used as a book of i stallation standards. Every working electrician should include a copy of t current edition in his or her arsenal of tools.

The *NEC*® governs just about every task an electrician does. Therefore, it important to understand the layout of the *NEC*® and be able to naviga through it quickly. The *NEC*® serves as the standard reference book in ma electrical examinations, especially those related to the issuance of journeym and master electrician licenses.

The *NEC*® is updated every three years by a panel of experts. It is importa to keep up to date on the *NEC*®, because each revision contains changes th can affect your work.

Objectives

When you have completed this module, you will be able to do the following:

1. Explain the purpose and history of the *National Electrical Code*®.
2. Describe the layout of the *National Electrical Code*®.
3. Explain how to navigate the *National Electrical Code*®.
4. Describe the purpose of the National Electrical Manufacturers Association and the National Fire Protection Association.
5. Explain the role of testing laboratories.

Trade Terms

Articles
Chapters
Exceptions
Fine print note (FPN)
National Electrical
  Manufacturers
  Association (NEMA)

National Fire Protection
  Association (NFPA)
Nationally Recognized
  Testing Laboratories
  (NRTLs)
Parts
Sections

Required Trainee Materials

1. Paper and pencil
2. Copy of the latest edition of the *National Electrical Code*®

Prerequisites

Before you begin this module, it is recommended that you successfully complete *Core Curriculum* and *Electrical Level One*, Modules 26101-05 through 26105-05.

This course map shows all of the modules in *Electrical Level One*. The suggested training order begins at the bottom and proceeds up. Skill levels increase as you advance on the course map. The Local Training Program Sponsor may adjust the training order.

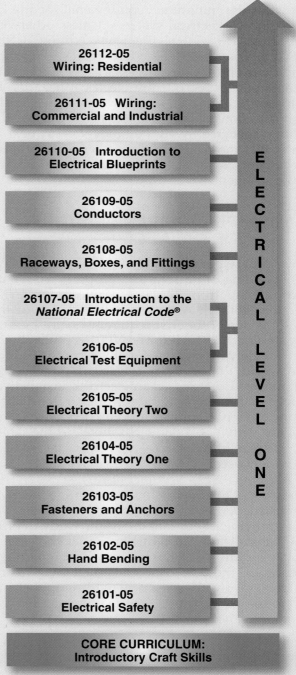

107CMAP.EPS

1.0.0 ◆ INTRODUCTION

The *National Electrical Code®* (*NEC®*) is published by the **National Fire Protection Association (NFPA)**. The *NEC®* is one of the most important tools for the electrician. When used together with the electrical code for your local area, the *NEC®* provides the minimum requirements for the installation of electrical systems. Unless otherwise specified, always use the latest edition of the *NEC®* as your on-the-job reference. It specifies the minimum provisions necessary for protecting people and property from electrical hazards. In some areas, however, local laws may specify different editions of the *NEC®*, so be sure to use the edition specified by your employer. Also, bear in mind that the *NEC®* only specifies minimum requirements, so local or job requirements may be more stringent.

2.0.0 ◆ PURPOSE AND HISTORY OF THE *NEC®*

The primary purpose of the *NEC®* is the practical safeguarding of persons and property from hazards arising from the use of electricity [*NEC Section 90.1(A)*]. A thorough knowledge of the *NEC®* is one of the first requirements for becoming a trained electrician. The *NEC®* is probably the most widely used and generally accepted code in the world. It has been translated into several languages. It is used as an electrical installation, safety, and reference guide in the United States. Many other parts of the world use it as well. Compliance with *NEC®* standards increases the safety of electrical installations—the reason the *NEC®* is so widely used.

Although *NEC Section 90.1(C)* states, "This Code is not intended as a design specification or an instruction manual for untrained persons," it does provide a sound basis for the study of electrical installation procedures—under the proper guidance. The *NEC®* has become the standard reference of the electrical construction industry. Anyone involved in electrical work should obtain an up-to-date copy and refer to it frequently.

Whether you are installing a new electrical system or altering an existing one, all electrical work must comply with the current *NEC®* and all local ordinances. Like most laws, the *NEC®* is easier to work with once you understand the language and know where to look for the information you need.

NOTE

This module is not a substitute for the *NEC®*. You need to acquire a copy of the most recent edition and keep it handy at all times. The more you know about the *NEC®*, the better an electrician you will become.

2.1.0 History

In 1881, the National Association of Fire Engineers met in Richmond, Virginia. From this meeting came the idea to draft the first *National Electrical Code*. The first nationally recommended electrical code was published by the National Board of Fire Underwriters (now the American Insurance Association) in 1895.

In 1896, the National Electric Light Association (NELA) was working to make the requirements of the fire insurance organizations and electrical utilities fit together. NELA succeeded in promoting a conference that would result in producing a standard national code. The NELA code would serve the interests of the insurance industry, operating concerns, manufacturing, and industry.

The conference produced a set of requirements that was unanimously accepted. In 1897, the first edition of the *NEC®* was published, and the *NEC®* became the first cooperatively produced national code. The organization that produced the *NEC®* was known as the *National Conference on Standard Electrical Rules*. This group became a permanent organization, and its job was to develop the *NEC®*.

In 1911, the NFPA took over administration and control of the *NEC®*. However, the National Board of Fire Underwriters continued to publish the *NEC®* until 1962. During the period from 1911 until now, the *NEC®* has experienced several major

The NEC®

Why do you think it's necessary to have a standard set of procedures for electrical installations? Find out who does the electrical inspection in your area. Who determines what will be inspected, when it will be inspected, and who will do the inspection?

What's wrong with these pictures?

107PO701.EPS

107PO702.EPS

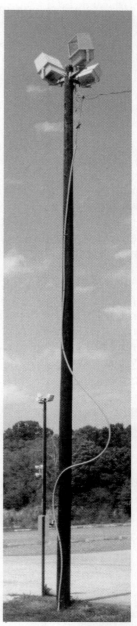

107PO703.EPS

anges, as well as regular three-year updates. In
'23, the *NEC®* was rearranged and rewritten,
d in 1937, it was editorially revised. In 1959, the
EC® was revised to include a numbering system
der which each **section** of each **article** was
entified with an article/section number.

1.1 Who Is Involved?

e creation of a universally accepted set of rules
an involved and complicated process. Rules

made by a committee have the advantage that
they usually do not leave out the interests of any
of the groups represented on the committee.
However, since the rules must represent the interests and requirements of an assortment of
groups, they are often quite complicated and
wordy.

In 1949, the NFPA reorganized the *NEC®* committee into its present structure. The present
structure consists of a Correlating Committee
and twenty Code Making Panels (CMPs). The

Correlating Committee consists of ten principal voting members and six alternates. The principal function of the Correlating Committee is to ensure that:

- No conflict of requirements exists
- Correlation has been achieved
- NFPA regulations governing committee projects have been followed
- A practical schedule of revision and publication is established and maintained

Each of the twenty CMPs have members who are experts on particular subjects and have been assigned certain articles to supervise and revise as required. Members of the CMPs represent such special interest groups as trade associations, electrical contractors, electrical designers and engineers, electrical inspectors, electrical manufacturers and suppliers, electrical testing laboratories, and insurance organizations.

Each panel is structured so that not more than one-third of its members are from a single interest group. The members of the *NEC*® Committee create or revise requirements for the *NEC*® through probing, debating, analyzing, weighing, and reviewing new input. Anyone, including you, can submit pro-

posals to amend the *NEC*®. Sample forms for th purpose may be obtained from the Secretary of t Standards Council at NFPA Headquarters. In add tion to written proposals, the NFPA also hol meetings to discuss code changes and proposals.

The NFPA membership is drawn from the fiel listed above. In addition to publishing the *NEC* the duties of the NFPA include the following:

- Developing, publishing, and distributing sta dards that are intended to minimize the poss bility and effects of fire and explosion
- Conducting fire safety education programs f the general public
- Providing information on fire protection, pr vention, and suppression
- Compiling annual statistics on causes and occ pancies of fires, large-loss fires (over one milli dollars), fire deaths, and firefighter casualties
- Providing field service by specialists on ele tricity, flammable liquids and gases, and m rine fire problems
- Conducting research projects that apply stati tical methods and operations research to d velop computer models and data manageme systems

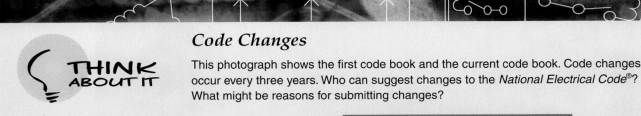

Code Changes

THINK ABOUT IT

This photograph shows the first code book and the current code book. Code changes occur every three years. Who can suggest changes to the *National Electrical Code*®? What might be reasons for submitting changes?

107PO704.EPS

0.0 ◆ THE LAYOUT OF THE *NEC*®

he *NEC*® begins with a brief history. *Figure 1* ows how the *NEC*® is organized.

1.0 Types of Rules

ere are two basic types of rules in the *NEC*®: andatory rules and permissive rules. It is im- rtant to understand these rules as they are de- ed in *NEC Section 90.5*. Mandatory rules ntain the words shall or shall not and must be hered to. Permissive rules identify actions that e allowed but not required and typically cover ctions or alternative methods. Be aware that lo- l ordinances may amend requirements of the EC®. This means that a city or county may have additional requirements or prohibitions that must be followed in that jurisdiction.

3.2.0 *NEC*® Introduction

The main body of the text begins with an *Introduction,* also entitled *NEC Article 90*. This introduction gives you an overview of the *NEC*® (see *Figure 1*). Items included in this section are:

- Purpose of the *NEC*®
- Scope of the code book
- Code arrangement
- Code enforcement
- Mandatory rules and explanatory material
- Formal interpretation
- Examination of equipment for safety
- Wiring planning
- Metric units of measurement

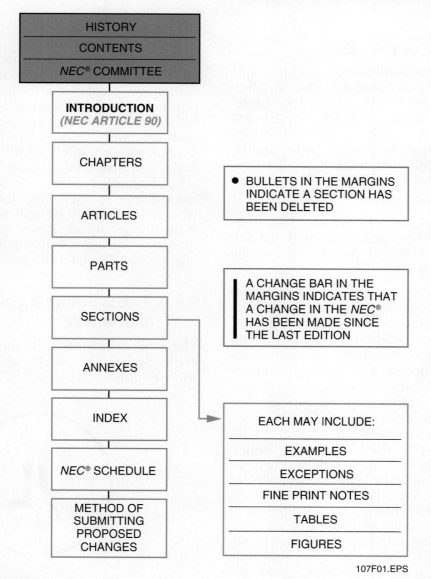

107F01.EPS

ure 1 ◆ The layout of the *NEC*®.

NEC® Layout

Remember, chapters contain a group of articles relating to a broad category. An article is a specific subject within that category, such as *NEC Article 250*, *Grounding and Bonding*, which is in Chapter 2 relating to wiring and protection. When an article applies to different installations in the same category, it will be divided into parts using roman numerals. Any specific requirements in any of the articles may also have exception(s) to the main rules.

The NEC® as a Reference Tool

The *NEC*®, although carefully organized, is a highly technical document; as such, it uses many technical words and phrases. It's crucial for you to understand their meaning—if you don't, you'll have trouble understanding the rules themselves. When using the *NEC*® as a reference tool, you may have to refer to a number of articles to find your answer(s). *NEC*® definitions are covered in *NEC Article 100*. Many issues concerning the *NEC*® may be resolved by simply reviewing the definitions.

3.3.0 The Body of the *NEC*®

The remainder of the book is organized into nine chapters. *NEC Chapter 1* contains a list of definitions used in the *NEC*®. These definitions are referred to as *NEC Article 100*. *NEC Article 110* gives the general requirements for electrical installations. It is important for you to be familiar with this general information and the definitions.

3.3.1 *NEC*® Definitions

There are many definitions included in *NEC Article 100*. You should become familiar with the definitions. Here are two that you should become especially familiar with:

- *Labeled* – "Equipment or materials to which has been attached a label, symbol, or other identifying mark of an organization that is acceptable to the authority having jurisdiction and concerned with product evaluation, that maintains periodic inspection of production of labeled equipment or materials, and by whose labeling the manufacturer indicates compliance with appropriate standards or performance in a specified manner."
- *Listed* – "Equipment, materials, or services included in a list published by an organization that is acceptable to the authority having jurisdiction and concerned with evaluation of products or services, that maintains periodic inspection of production of listed equipment or materials, or periodic evaluation of services, and whose listing states that the equipment, material, or services either meets appropriate designated standards or has been tested and found suitable for use for a specified purpose."

Besides installation rules, you will also have be concerned with the type and quality of mate als that are used in electrical wiring system Nationally recognized testing laboratories a product safety certification laboratories. Unde writers Laboratories, Inc., also called UL, is o such laboratory. These laboratories establish a operate product safety certification programs make sure that items produced under the servi are safeguarded against reasonable foreseeab risks. Some of these organizations maintain worldwide network of field representatives w make unannounced visits to manufacturing fac ities to counter-check products bearing their se of approval. The UL label is shown in *Figure 2*.

3.4.0 The Reference Portion of the *NEC*®

The annexes included with the *NEC*® provide r erence sources that can be used to determine t proper application of the *NEC*® requirements.

107F02.EPS

Figure 2 ◆ Underwriters Laboratories label.

NEC Chapters 1 through 8 each contain numerous articles. Each chapter focuses on a general category of electrical application, such as *NEC Chapter 2, Wiring and Protection*. Each article emphasizes a more specific **part** of that category, such as *NEC Article 210, Branch Circuits, Part I General Provisions*. Each section gives examples of a specific application of the *NEC®*, such as *NEC Section 210.4, Multiwire Branch Circuits*. *NEC Chapter 9* contains tables that are used when referenced by any of the articles in *NEC Chapters 1 through 8*. *Annexes A through F* provide informational material and examples that are helpful when applying *NEC®* requirements.

The chapters of the *NEC®* are organized into four major categories:

- *NEC Chapters 1, 2, 3, and 4* – The first four chapters present the rules for the design and installation of electrical systems. They generally apply to all electrical installations.
- *NEC Chapters 5, 6, and 7* – These chapters are concerned with special occupancies, equipment, and conditions. Rules in these chapters may modify or amend those in the first four chapters.
- *NEC Chapter 8* – This chapter covers communications systems, such as the telephone and telegraph, as well as radio and television receiving equipment. It may also reference other articles, such as the installation of grounding electrode conductor connections as covered in *NEC Section 250.52*.
- *NEC Chapter 9* – This chapter contains tables that are applicable when referenced by other chapters in the *NEC®*.
- *Annexes A through F* – These annexes contain helpful information that is not mandatory.
  - *Annex A* contains a list of product safety standards. These standards provide further references for requirements that are in addition to the *NEC®* requirements for the electrical components mentioned.
  - *Annex B* contains information for determining ampacities of conductors under engineering supervision.
  - *Annex C* contains the conduit fill tables for multiple conductors of the same size and type within the accepted raceways.
  - *Annex D* contains examples of calculations for branch circuits, feeders, and services as well as other loads such as motor circuits.
  - *Annex E* contains information on types of building construction.
  - *Annex F* contains a cross reference index for the articles that were renumbered in the 2005 code.

INSIDE TRACK

Underwriters Laboratories, Inc.

Underwriters Laboratories, Inc. is an internationally recognized authority on product safety testing and safety certification and standards development. It was established in 1893. The Chicago World's Fair was opened and thanks to Edison's introduction of the electric light bulb, the World's Fair lit up the world. But all was not perfect—wires soon sputtered and crackled, and, ironically, the Palace of Electricity caught fire. The fair's insurance company called in a troubleshooting engineer, who, after careful inspection, found faulty and brittle insulation, worn out and deteriorated wiring, bare wires, and overloaded circuits.

He called for standards in the electrical industry, and then set up a testing laboratory above a Chicago firehouse to do just that. Hence, Underwriters Laboratories, Inc. (UL), an independent testing organization, was born.

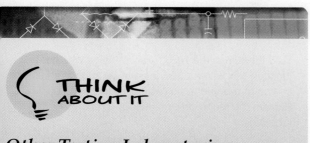

THINK ABOUT IT

Other Testing Laboratories

In addition to UL, there are several other recognized testing laboratories. How many can you name?

3.5.0 Text in the NEC®

When you open the *NEC®*, you will notice several different types of text or printing used. Here is an explanation of each type of text:

- *Bold black letters* – Headings for each *NEC®* application are written in bold black letters.
- *Exceptions* – These explain the circumstances under which a specific part of the *NEC®* does not apply. Exceptions are written in *italics* under that part of the *NEC®* to which they pertain.
- *Fine print notes (FPNs)* – These explain something in an application, suggest other sections to read about the application, or provide tips about the application. These are defined in the text by the term (FPN) shown in parentheses before a paragraph in smaller print.
- *Figures* – These may be included with explanations to give you a picture of what your application may look like.
- *Tables* – These are often included when there is more than one possible application of the *NEC®*. You would use a table to look up the specifications of your application.

4.0.0 ◆ NAVIGATING THE *NEC®*

To locate information for a particular procedure being performed, use the following steps:

Step 1 Familiarize yourself with *NEC Articles 90, 100, and 110* to gain an understanding of the material covered in the *NEC®* and the definitions used in it.

Step 2 Turn to the *Table of Contents* at the beginning of the *NEC®*.

Step 3 Locate the chapter that focuses on the desired category.

Step 4 Find the article pertaining to your specific application.

Step 5 Turn to the page indicated. Each application will begin with a bold heading.

NOTE

An index is provided at the end of the *NEC®*. The index lists specific topics and provides a reference to the location of the material within the *NEC®*. The index is helpful when you are looking for a specific topic rather than a general category.

Once you are familiar with *NEC Articles 9 100, and 110,* you can move on to the rest of th *NEC®*. There are several key sections used often servicing electrical systems.

- *Wiring and protection* – *NEC Chapter 2* di cusses wiring design and protection, the i formation electrical technicians need mo often. It covers the use and identificatic of grounded conductors, branch circuit feeders, calculations, services, overcurre protection, and grounding. This is essenti information for all types of electrical system If you run into a problem related to the desig or installation of a conventional electrical sy tem, you can probably find a solution for it this chapter.
- *Wiring methods and materials* – *NEC Chapter* lists the rules on wiring methods and material The materials and procedures to use on a pa ticular system depend on the type of buildir construction, the type of occupancy, the loc tion of the wiring in the building, the type of a mosphere in the building or in the ar surrounding the building, mechanical facto and the relative costs of different wiring met ods. The general requirements for conducto and wiring methods that form an integral pa of manufactured equipment are not included the requirements of *NEC Article 300.1(B)*.

THINK ABOUT IT

Junction Boxes

Find the rule in the *NEC®* that explains whether a junction box without devices can be supported solely by two or more lengths of rigid metal conduit (RMC). Explain the technical terminology in everyday language.

NEC® Article 90

After you've familiarized yourself with *NEC Article 90,* explain its intent. What part of electrical installation does it not cover?

NEC Article 300 provides the general requirements for all wiring methods, including information such as minimum burial depths and permitted wiring methods for areas above suspended ceilings.

NEC Article 310 contains a description of acceptable conductors for the wiring methods contained in *NEC Chapter 3*.

NEC Articles 312 and 314 give rules for raceways, boxes, cabinets, and raceway fittings. Outlet boxes vary in size and shape, depending on their use, the size of the raceway, the number of conductors entering the box, the type of building construction, and the atmospheric conditions of the area. These articles should answer most questions on the selection and use of these items.

The *NEC®* does not describe in detail all types and sizes of outlet boxes. However, the manufacturers of outlet boxes provide excellent catalogs showing their products. Collect these catalogs, since these items are essential to your work.

NEC Articles 320 through 340 cover sheathed cables of two or more conductors, such as nonmetallic-sheathed and metal-clad cable.

NEC Articles 342 through 356 cover raceway wiring systems, such as rigid and flexible metal and nonmetallic conduit.

NEC Articles 358 through 362 cover tubing wiring methods, such as electrical metallic and nonmetallic tubing.

NEC Articles 366 through 390 cover other wiring methods, such as busways and wireways. Cable trays are a system of support for the wiring methods found not only in *NEC Article 392*, but also in *NEC Chapters 4, 7, and 8*.

1.0 Equipment for General Use

NEC Chapter 4 begins with the use and installation of flexible cords and cables, including the trade name, type letter, wire size, number of conductors, conductor insulation, outer covering, and use of each. This chapter also covers fixture wires, again giving the trade name, type letter, and other important details.

NEC Article 404 covers the requirements for the uses and installation of switches, switching devices, and circuit breakers where used as switches.

NEC Article 406 gives the rules for the ratings, types, and installation of receptacles, cord connectors, and attachment plugs (cord caps).

NEC Article 410 on lighting fixtures is especially important. It gives installation procedures for fixtures in specific locations. For example, it covers fixtures near combustible material and fixtures in closets. However, the *NEC®* does not describe how many fixtures will be needed in a given area to provide a certain amount of illumination.

NEC Article 430 covers electric motors, including mounting the motor and making electrical connections to it. Motor controls and overload protection are also covered.

NEC Articles 440 through 460 cover air conditioning and heating equipment, generators, transformers, phase converters, and capacitors.

NEC Article 480 provides requirements related to battery-operated electrical systems. Storage batteries are seldom thought of as part of a conventional electrical system, but they often provide standby emergency lighting service. They may also supply power to security systems that are separate from the main AC electrical system.

4.2.0 Special Occupancies

NEC Chapter 5 covers special occupancy areas. These are areas where the sparks generated by electrical equipment may cause an explosion or fire. The hazard may be due to the atmosphere of the area or the presence of a volatile material in the area. Commercial garages, aircraft hangars, and service stations are typical special occupancy locations.

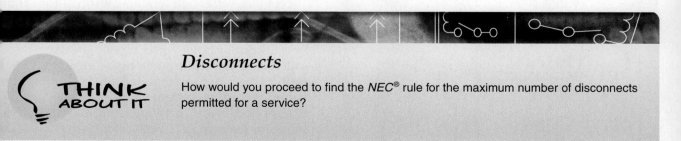

Disconnects

THINK ABOUT IT

How would you proceed to find the *NEC®* rule for the maximum number of disconnects permitted for a service?

NEC Article 500 covers the different types of special occupancy atmospheres where an explosion is possible. The atmospheric groups were established to make it easy to test and approve equipment for various types of uses.

NEC Articles 501.10, 502.10, and 503.10 cover the installation of explosion-proof wiring. An explosion-proof system is designed to prevent the ignition of a surrounding explosive atmosphere when arcing occurs within the electrical system.

There are three main classes of special occupancy location:

- *Class I* – Areas containing flammable gases or vapors in the air. Class I areas include paint spray booths, dyeing plants where hazardous liquids are used, and gas generator rooms *(NEC Article 501)*.
- *Class II* – Areas where combustible dust is present, such as grain-handling and storage plants, dust and stock collector areas, and sugar-pulverizing plants *(NEC Article 502)*. These are areas where, under normal operating conditions, there may be enough combustible dust in the air to produce explosive or ignitable mixtures.
- *Class III* – Areas that are hazardous because of the presence of easily ignitable fibers or other particles in the air, although not in large enough quantities to produce ignitable mixtures *(NEC Article 503)*. Class III locations include cotton mills, rayon mills, and clothing manufacturing plants.

NEC Articles 511 and 514 regulate garages and similar locations where volatile or flammable liquids are used. While these areas are not always considered critically hazardous locations, there may be enough danger to require special precautions in the electrical installation. In these areas, the *NEC*® requires that volatile gases be confined to an area not more than four feet above the floor.

So in most cases, conventional raceway systems are permitted above this level. If the area is judged to be critically hazardous, explosion-proof wiring (including seal-offs) may be required.

NEC Article 520 regulates theaters and similar occupancies where fire and panic can cause hazards to life and property. Drive-in theaters do not present the same hazards as enclosed auditoriums, but the projection rooms and adjacent areas must be properly ventilated and wired for the protection of operating personnel and others using the area.

NEC Chapter 5 also covers service stations, bulk storage plants, health care facilities, mobile homes and parks, and temporary installations.

4.3.0 Special Equipment

Residential electrical workers will seldom need to refer to the articles in *NEC Chapter 6,* but this chapter is of great concern to commercial and industrial electrical workers.

NEC Article 600 covers electric signs and outline lighting. *NEC Article 610* applies to cranes and hoists. *NEC Article 620* covers the majority of the electrical work involved in the installation and operation of elevators, dumbwaiters, escalators, and moving walks. The manufacturer is responsible for most of this work. The electrician usually just furnishes a feeder terminating in a disconnect means in the bottom of the elevator shaft. The electrician may also be responsible for a lighting circuit to a junction box midway in the elevator shaft for connecting the elevator cage lighting cable and exhaust fans. The articles in this chapter list most of the requirements for these installations.

NEC Article 630 regulates electric welding equipment. It is normally treated as a piece of industrial power equipment requiring a special power outlet, but there are special conditions that apply to the circuits supplying welding equipment. These are outlined in detail in this chapter.

NEC Article 640 covers wiring for sound recording and similar equipment. This type of equipment normally requires low-voltage wiring. Special outlet boxes or cabinets are usually provided with the equipment, but some items may be mounted in or on standard outlet boxes. Some sound recording systems require direct current. It is supplied from rectifying equipment, batteries, or motor generators. Low-voltage alternating current comes from relatively small transformers connected on the primary side to a 120V circuit within the building.

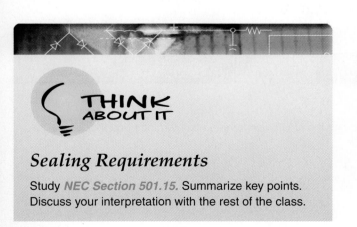

THINK ABOUT IT

Sealing Requirements

Study *NEC Section 501.15.* Summarize key points. Discuss your interpretation with the rest of the class.

Other items covered in *NEC Chapter 6* include ray equipment *(NEC Article 660)*, induction d dielectric heat-generating equipment *(NEC rticle 665),* and industrial machinery *(NEC Arti- 670).*

If you ever have work that involves *NEC apter 6,* study the chapter before work begins. at can save a lot of installation time. Another ay to cut down on labor hours and prevent in- allation error is to acquire a set of rough-in awings of the equipment being installed. It is sy to install the wrong outlet box or to install the ht box in the wrong place. Having a set of ugh-in drawings can prevent these simple but stly errors.

4.0 Special Conditions

most commercial buildings, the *NEC®* and local dinances require a means of lighting public oms, halls, stairways, and entrances. There ust be enough light to allow the occupants to it from the building if the general building light- g is interrupted. Exit doors must be clearly indi- ted by illuminated exit signs.

NEC Chapter 7 covers the installation of emer- ncy systems. These circuits should be arranged that they can automatically transfer to an alter- te source of current, usually storage batteries or gasoline-driven generators. As an alternative in some types of occupancies, you can connect them to the supply side of the main service, so discon- necting the main service switch would not dis- connect the emergency circuits. This chapter also covers fire alarms and a variety of other equip- ment, systems, and conditions that are not easily categorized elsewhere in the *NEC®*.

NEC Chapter 8 is a special category for wiring associated with electronic communications sys- tems including telephone and telegraph, radio and TV, and community antenna systems.

4.5.0 Examples of Navigating the *NEC®*

4.5.1 Installing Type SE Cable

Suppose you are installing Type SE (service- entrance) cable on the side of a home. You know that this cable must be secured, but you are not sure of the spacing between cable clamps. To find out this information, use the following procedure:

Step 1 Look in the *NEC® Table of Contents* and fol- low down the list until you find an appro- priate category. (Or you can use the index at the end of the book.)

Step 2 *NEC Article 230* will probably catch your eye first, so turn to the page where it begins.

Step 3 Scan down through the section numbers until you come to *NEC Section 230.51, Mounting Supports.* Upon reading this sec- tion, you will find in paragraph *(a) Service- Entrance Cables* that "service cables shall be supported by straps or other approved means within 300 mm (12 in) of every service head, gooseneck, or connection to a raceway or other enclosure and at inter- vals not exceeding 750 mm (30 in)."

After reading this section, you will know that a cable strap is required within 12 inches of the ser- vice head and within 12 inches of the meter base. Furthermore, the cable must be secured in be- tween these two termination points at intervals not exceeding 30 inches.

INSIDE TRACK

Different Interpretations

For as many trainees in class with you today, there will be as many different interpretations of the *NEC®*. However, a difference of opinion is not always a problem—discussing the *NEC®* with your peers will allow you to expand your own understanding of it. In your previous discussion about *NEC Section 501.15*, what differences of interpretation did you have to resolve?

4.5.2 Installing Track Lighting

Assume that you are installing track lighting in a residential occupancy. The owners want the track located behind the curtain of their sliding glass patio doors. To determine if this is an *NEC®* violation, follow these steps:

Step 1 Look in the *NEC® Table of Contents* and find the chapter that contains information about the general application you are working on. *NEC Chapter 4, Equipment for General Use,* covers track lighting.

Step 2 Now look for the article that fits the specific category you are working on. In this case, *NEC Article 410* covers lighting fixtures, lampholders, lamps, and receptacles.

Step 3 Next locate the section within *NEC Article 410* that deals with the specific application. For this example, refer to *Part XV, Lighting Track.*

Step 4 Turn to the page listed.

Step 5 Read *NEC Section 410.100, Definitions,* to become familiar with track lighting. Continue down the page with *NEC Section 410.101* and read the information contained therein. Note that paragraph *(c) Locations Not Permitted* under *NEC Section 410.101* states the following: "Lighting track shall not be installed in the following locations: (1) where likely to be subjected to physical damage; (2) in wet or damp locations; (3) where subject to corrosive vapors; (4) in storage battery rooms; (5) in hazardous (classified) locations; (6) where concealed; (7) where extended through walls or partitions; (8) less than 1.5 m (5 ft)

above the finished floor except where pr tected from physical damage or tra operating at less than 30 volts rms ope circuit voltage; (9) where prohibited l *NEC Section 410.4(D)*."

Step 6 Read *NEC Section 410.101(C)* carefully. I you see any conditions that would viola any *NEC®* requirements if the track ligh ing is installed in the area specified? checking these items, you will probab note condition (6), "where concealed Since the track lighting is to be install behind a curtain, this sounds like an *NE* violation. We need to check further.

Step 7 You need the *NEC®* definition of co cealed. Therefore, turn to *NEC Article 1 Definitions* and find the main term co cealed. It reads: "Concealed. Rendered i accessible by the structure or finish of t building …"

Step 8 Although the track lighting may be out sight if the curtain is drawn, it will still readily accessible for maintenance. Cons quently, the track lighting is really not co cealed according to the *NEC®* definition

When using the *NEC®* to determine electri installation requirements, keep in mind that y will nearly always have to refer to more than o section. Sometimes the *NEC®* itself refers t reader to other articles and sections. In sor cases, the user will have to be familiar enou with the *NEC®* to know what other sections pe tain to the installation at hand. It can be a co fusing situation, but time and experience using the *NEC®* will make it much easier. A p torial road map of some *NEC®* topics is shown *Figure 3*.

Conformance and Electrical Equipment

THINK ABOUT IT

What other resources are available for finding information about the use of electrical equipment and materials?

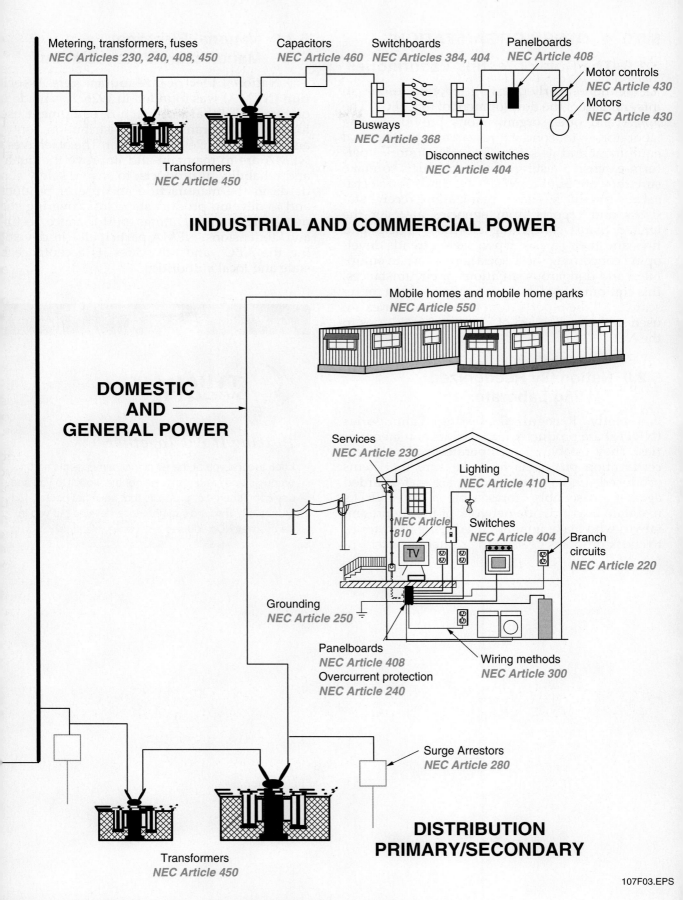

Metering, transformers, fuses
NEC Articles 230, 240, 408, 450

Capacitors
NEC Article 460

Switchboards
NEC Articles 384, 404

Panelboards
NEC Article 408

Motor controls
NEC Article 430

Motors
NEC Article 430

Busways
NEC Article 368

Transformers
NEC Article 450

Disconnect switches
NEC Article 404

INDUSTRIAL AND COMMERCIAL POWER

Mobile homes and mobile home parks
NEC Article 550

DOMESTIC AND GENERAL POWER

Services
NEC Article 230

Lighting
NEC Article 410

NEC Article 810

Switches
NEC Article 404

Branch circuits
NEC Article 220

TV

Grounding
NEC Article 250

Panelboards
NEC Article 408

Overcurrent protection
NEC Article 240

Wiring methods
NEC Article 300

Surge Arrestors
NEC Article 280

DISTRIBUTION PRIMARY/SECONDARY

Transformers
NEC Article 450

107F03.EPS

Figure 3 ◆ *NEC*® references for industrial, commercial, and residential power.

5.0.0 ◆ OTHER ORGANIZATIONS

5.1.0 The Role of Testing Laboratories

As mentioned earlier, testing laboratories are an integral part of the development of the *NEC*®. The NFPA and other organizations provide testing laboratories to conduct research into electrical equipment and its safety. These laboratories perform extensive testing of new products to make sure they are built to *NEC*® standards for electrical and fire safety. These organizations receive statistics and reports from agencies all over the United States concerning electrical shocks and fires and their causes. Upon seeing trends developing concerning the association of certain equipment and dangerous situations or circumstances, this equipment will be specifically targeted for research. All the reports from these laboratories are used in the generation of changes or revisions to the *NEC*®.

5.2.0 Nationally Recognized Testing Laboratories

Nationally Recognized Testing Laboratories (NRTLs) are product safety certification laboratories. They establish and operate product safety certification programs to make sure that items produced under the service are safeguarded against reasonably foreseeable risks. NRTLs maintain a worldwide network of field representatives who make unannounced visits to factories to check products bearing their safety marks.

5.3.0 National Electrical Manufacturers Association

The **National Electrical Manufacturers Association (NEMA)** was founded in 1926. It is made up of companies that manufacture equipment used for generation, transmission, distribution, control, and utilization of electric power. The objectives of NEMA are to maintain and improve the quality and reliability of products; to ensure safety standards in the manufacture and use of products; and to develop product standards covering such matters as naming, ratings, performance, testing, and dimensions. NEMA participates in developing the *NEC*® and advocates its acceptance by state and local authorities.

THINK ABOUT IT

Putting It All Together

Look around you at the electrical components and products used and the quality of the work. Do you see any components or products that have not been listed or labeled? If so, how might these devices put you in harm's way? Do you see any code violations?

1. The *NEC®* provides the _____ requirements for the installation of electrical systems.
   a. minimum
   b. most stringent
   c. design specification
   d. complete

2. All of the following groups are usually represented on the Code Making Panels *except* _____.
   a. trade associations
   b. electrical inspectors
   c. insurance organizations
   d. government lobbyists

3. Mandatory and permissive rules are defined in _____.
   a. *NEC Article 90*
   b. *NEC Article 100*
   c. *NEC Article 110*
   d. *NEC Article 200*

4. *NEC Article 110* covers _____.
   a. branch circuits
   b. definitions
   c. general requirements for electrical installations
   d. wiring design and protection

5. The general design and installation of electrical systems is covered in _____.
   a. *NEC Chapters 1, 2, and 7*
   b. *NEC Chapters 1, 2, 3, 4, and 9*
   c. *NEC Chapters 6, 7, and 9*
   d. *NEC Chapters 5, 6, 7, and 9*

6. Devices such as radios, televisions, and telephones are covered in _____.
   a. *NEC Chapter 8*
   b. *NEC Chapter 7*
   c. *NEC Chapter 6*
   d. *NEC Chapter 5*

7. Busways are covered in _____.
   a. *NEC Article 330*
   b. *NEC Article 342*
   c. *NEC Article 368*
   d. *NEC Article 378*

8. Installation procedures for lighting fixtures in specific locations are provided in _____.
   a. *NEC Article 410*
   b. *NEC Article 501*
   c. *NEC Article 366*
   d. *NEC Article 460*

9. Theaters are covered in _____.
   a. *NEC Article 338*
   b. *NEC Article 110*
   c. *NEC Article 430*
   d. *NEC Article 520*

10. *NEC Article 600* covers _____.
    a. track lighting
    b. electric signs and outline lighting
    c. X-ray equipment
    d. emergency lighting systems

Summary

The *NEC*® specifies the minimum provisions necessary for protecting people and property from hazards arising from the use of electricity and electrical equipment. As an electrician, you must be aware of how to use and apply the *NEC*® on the job site. Using the *NEC*® will help you to safely install and maintain the electrical equipment and systems you come into contact with.

Notes

Trade Terms Quiz

_____ are the main topics of the *NEC®*.

Nine _____ form the broad structure of the *NEC®*.

Certain articles in the *NEC®* are subdivided into lettered _____.

Parts and articles are subdivided into numbered _____.

Although they follow the applicable sections of the *NEC®*, _____ allow alternative methods to be used under specific conditions.

6. A(n) _____ is explanatory material that follows specific *NEC®* sections.

7. The _____ is an organization that maintains and improves the quality and reliability of electrical products.

8. The _____ publishes the *NEC®*; it also develops standards to minimize the possibility and effects of fire.

9. _____ are organizations that are responsible for testing and certifying electrical equipment.

ade Terms

rticles
hapters
xceptions
ne print note (FPN)

National Electrical
  Manufacturers
  Association (NEMA)
National Fire Protection
  Association (NFPA)

Nationally Recognized
  Testing Laboratories
  (NRTLs)

Parts
Sections

Christine Thorstensen Porter

Intertek Testing Services

How did you choose a career in the electrical field?
It was "in the blood" literally. My father had his own electrical contracting company and was an instructor for our apprenticeship/training program. One day, my husband, who also worked for my dad, gave me a tool belt and sent me through the Construction Industry Training Council's (CITC) apprenticeship program in Seattle, Washington. Since my father taught many of the classes, the pressure was on. I felt that I had to perform well. My father was a major influence on me both as an electrician, and as a student leader. Eventually, I went into the estimating side of things in my dad's business.

In the fourth year of my apprenticeship program I was taking a lot of estimating and project management courses and applying the skills I gained in the field. My dad's business was high-end residential and some small commercial work. We'd have a crew on site from six months to a year until the projects were complete. A lot of the installations we did were data systems and computer-controlled security systems. When I took the Administrator's exam, that gave me my qualifications to supervise.

What positions have you held in the industry?
In 1981 I was a teaching assistant. That teacher started a new review class for electricians needing to pass journeyman and administrative exams; I took over his second-year apprenticeship/trainee class. To better prepare myself for my new teaching role, I took various classes offered by the International Association of Electrical Inspectors (IAEI), but I was dismayed and disappointed with the instructor because he merely read the *NEC®* to us, instead of giving us any insights as to how the *NEC®* could impact our installations, or why any particular *NEC®*

rule was in place. So I also ended up getting involve with teaching classes for the IAEI.

My experience with IAEI gave me a solid grounding in the Code. It also led to more local involvement. In fact, I'm now the chairman of the city's Electrical Code Advisory Committee. I have also served on the Technical Advisory Committee fo our state amendments to the *NEC®*.

What does your current job involve?
I teach the second-year electrical training program a CITC. I teach courses for IAEI. I perform inspections for Intertek Testing Services, and I serve on a variety of committees. In addition to chairing the Electrical Code Advisory Committtee, I'm a Senior Associate member of the Puget Sound Chapter of IAEI; I sit on the city of Seattle's Construction Codes Advisory Board and am a subject matter expert for NCCER's *Contren®* Electrical Curriculum.

Do you have any advice for someone just entering th trade?
I'd tell them that the electrical trade is extremely rich and diverse. There is so much that you can do. From installing all different types of systems, to project management, and to estimating, the field is wide open. The job never stays dull. The field changes wit all the changes in technology. Because of that, there are so many new and emerging jobs within the trade As far as becoming a success, I'd say to keep abreast of changes—changes in the Code and in technology-and stay connected. A good way to do that is to join associations such as IAEI. Network and continue you training. It never ends in this field. Also, spend time mentoring others. You learn more that way, by givin yourself.

Trade Terms
Introduced in This Module

Articles: The articles are the main topics of the *NEC®*, beginning with *NEC Article 90*, *Introduction*, and ending with *NEC Article 830*, *Network-Powered Broadband Communications Systems.*

Chapters: Nine chapters form the broad structure of the *NEC®*.

Exceptions: Exceptions follow the applicable sections of the *NEC®* and allow alternative methods to be used under specific conditions.

Fine print note (FPN): Explanatory material that follows specific *NEC®* sections.

National Electrical Manufacturers Association (NEMA): The association that maintains and improves the quality and reliability of electrical products.

National Fire Protection Association (NFPA): The publishers of the *NEC®*. The NFPA develops standards to minimize the possibility and effects of fire.

Nationally Recognized Testing Laboratories (NRTLs): Product safety certification laboratories that are responsible for testing and certifying electrical equipment.

Parts: Certain articles in the *NEC®* are subdivided into parts. Parts have letter designations (e.g., Part A).

Sections: Parts and articles are subdivided into sections. Sections have numeric designations that follow the article number and are preceded by a period (e.g., 501.4).

Additional Resources

This module is intended to present thorough resources for task training. The following reference work is suggested for further study. This is optional material for continued education rather than for task training.

National Electrical Code® Handbook, Latest Edition. Quincy, MA: National Fire Protection Association.

The NCCER makes every effort to keep these textbooks up-to-date and free of technical errors. We appreciate your help in this process. If you have an idea for improving this textbook, or if you find an error, a typographical mistake, or an inaccuracy in NCCER's *Contren®* textbooks, please write us, using this form or a photocopy. Be sure to include the exact module number, page number, a detailed description, and the correction, if applicable. Your input will be brought to the attention of the Technical Review Committee. Thank you for your assistance.

Instructors – If you found that additional materials were necessary in order to teach this module effectively, please let us know so that we may include them in the Equipment/Materials list in the Annotated Instructor's Guide.

Write: Product Development
National Center for Construction Education and Research
P.O. Box 141104, Gainesville, FL 32614-1104

Fax: 352-334-0932

E-mail: curriculum@nccer.org

Craft

Module Name

Copyright Date

Module Number

Page Number(s)

Description

(Optional) Correction

(Optional) Your Name and Address

Bayside Power Station

Bayside Power Station in Tampa, Florida, is the result of a decision to reconfigure an existing facility from coal to natural gas. This project integrated seven new combustion turbines and seven heat-recovery steam generators into two of the plants' existing steam turbines to reliably and cost effectively produce 1,800 megawatts of power. By using natural gas along with high-efficiency, state-of-the-art controls, emissions are significantly reduced, and growing energy needs will be met well into the future.

26110-05
Introduction to Electrical Blueprints

Topics to be presented in this module include:

Overview

The electrician on a job is usually handed a set of blueprints and a book or [
of specifications for the job before conduit is installed, wire is pulled,
equipment is mounted. A set of blueprints tells the electrician how the c
tomer wants the building wired. Specifications spell out the type and qual
of material, components, and equipment that the customer wants, and p
vides specific instructions for installing them. Blueprints and specifications
gether create the roadmap to a successful installation and a satisfied custom

An electrician must be able to read any set of blueprints, even though t
style may vary from designer to designer. Standardized symbols are us
throughout the industry to represent types of material, raceways, conducto
equipment, and circuit connections. It is the electrician's responsibility to a
curately interpret a set of blueprints, and to be familiar with the standardiz
numbering system used in specifications to identify electrical components a
their installation.

Note: *National Electrical Code*® and *NEC*® are registered trademarks of the National Fire Protection Association, Inc., Quincy, MA 02269.
All *National Electrical Code*® and *NEC*® references in this module refer to the 2005 edition of the *National Electrical Code*®.

Objectives

When you have completed this module, you will be able to do the following:

1. Explain the basic layout of a blueprint.
2. Describe the information included in the title block of a blueprint.
3. Identify the types of lines used on blueprints.
4. Identify common symbols used on blueprints.
5. Understand the use of architect's and engineer's scales.
6. Interpret electrical drawings, including site plans, floor plans, and detail drawings.
7. Read equipment schedules found on electrical blueprints.
8. Describe the type of information included in electrical specifications.

Trade Terms

Architectural drawings
Block diagram
Blueprint
Detail drawing
Dimensions
Electrical drawing
Elevation drawing
Floor plan
One-line diagram

Plan view
Power-riser diagram
Scale
Schedule
Schematic diagram
Sectional view
Shop drawing
Site plan
Written specifications

Required Trainee Materials

1. Paper and pencil
2. Copy of the latest edition of the *National Electrical Code®*
3. Appropriate personal protective equipment

Prerequisites

Before you begin this module, it is recommended that you successfully complete *Core Curriculum* and *Electrical Level One*, Modules 26101-05 through 26109-05.

This course map shows all of the modules in *Electrical Level One*. The suggested training order begins at the bottom and proceeds up. Skill levels increase as you advance on the course map. The Local Training Program Sponsor may adjust the training order.

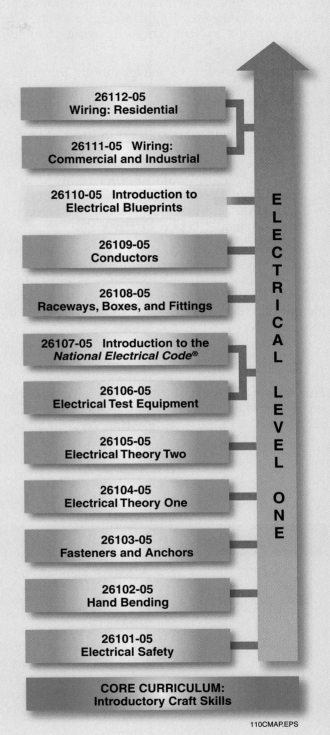

26112-05
Wiring: Residential

26111-05   Wiring:
Commercial and Industrial

26110-05   Introduction to
Electrical Blueprints

26109-05
Conductors

26108-05
Raceways, Boxes, and Fittings

26107-05   Introduction to the
National Electrical Code®

26106-05
Electrical Test Equipment

26105-05
Electrical Theory Two

26104-05
Electrical Theory One

26103-05
Fasteners and Anchors

26102-05
Hand Bending

26101-05
Electrical Safety

CORE CURRICULUM:
Introductory Craft Skills

ELECTRICAL LEVEL ONE

110CMAP.EPS

1.0.0 ◆ INTRODUCTION TO BLUEPRINT READING

In all large construction projects and in many of the smaller ones, an architect is commissioned to prepare complete working drawings and specifications for the project. These drawings usually include:

- A site plan indicating the location of the building on the property.
- Floor plans showing the walls and partitions for each floor or level.
- Elevations of all exterior faces of the building.
- Several vertical cross sections to indicate clearly the various floor levels and details of the footings, foundation, walls, floors, ceilings, and roof construction.
- Large-scale detail drawings showing such construction details as may be required.

For projects of any consequence, the architect usually hires consulting engineers to prepare structural, electrical, and mechanical drawings, with the latter encompassing pipe-fitting, instrumentation, plumbing, heating, ventilating, and air conditioning drawings.

1.1.0 Site Plan

This type of plan of the building site looks as if the site is viewed from an airplane and shows the property boundaries, the existing contour lines, the new contour lines (after grading), the locati of the building on the property, new and existi roadways, all utility lines, and other pertinent tails. The drawing scale is also shown. Descripti notes may also be found on the site (plot) plan li ing names of adjacent property owners, the la surveyor, and the date of the survey. A legend symbol list is also included so that anyone w must work with the site plan can readily read t information. See *Figure 1*.

1.2.0 Floor Plans

The plan view of any object is a drawing showi the outline and all details as seen when looking rectly down on the object. It shows only two di ensions, length and width. The floor plan of building is drawn as if a horizontal cut were ma through the building—at about window height and then the top portion removed to reveal t bottom part. See *Figure 2*.

If a plan view of a home's basement is neede the part of the house above the middle of the bas ment windows is imagined to be cut away. By loc ing down on the uncovered portion, every det and partition can be seen. Likewise, imagine t part above the middle of the first floor windows k ing cut away. A drawing that looks straight dov at the remaining part would be called the first flo plan or lower level. A cut through the second flo windows would be called the second floor plan upper level. See *Figure 3*.

Then and Now

Years ago, blueprints were created by placing a hand drawing against light-sensitive paper and then exposing it to ultraviolet light. The light would turn the paper blue except where lines were drawn on the original. The light-sensitive paper was then developed, and the resulting print had white lines against a blue background. Modern blueprints are usually blue or black lines against a white background and are generated using computer-aided design programs. Newer programs offer three-dimensional modeling and other enhanced features.

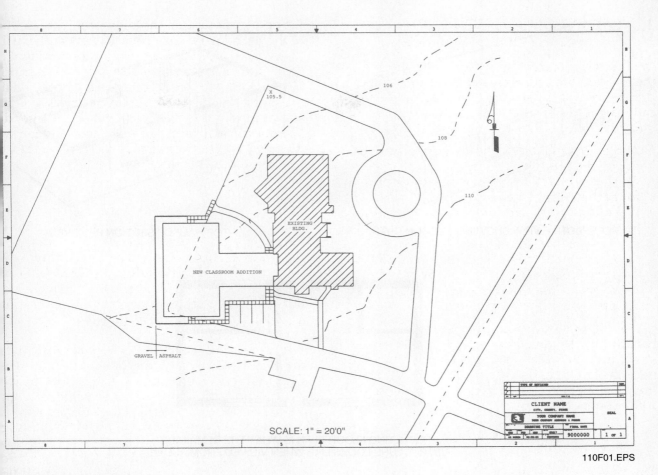

SCALE: 1" = 20'0"

110F01.EPS

Figure 1 ◆ Typical site plan.

Using a Drawing Set

Always treat a drawing set with care. It is best to keep two sets, one for the office and one for field use. After you use a sheet from a set of drawings, be sure to refold the sheet with the title block facing up.

PERSPECTIVE VIEW SHOWING SECTION CUTS

TOP HALF OF SECTION REMOVED

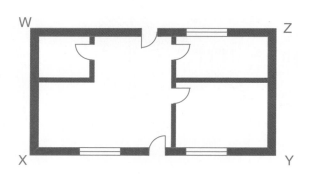

RESULTING FLOOR PLAN IS WHAT THE REMAINING
STRUCTURE LOOKS LIKE WHEN VIEWED FROM ABOVE

110F02

Figure 2 ◆ Principles of floor plan layout.

1.3.0 Elevations

The elevation is an outline of an object that shows heights and may show the length or width of a particular side, but not depth. *Figures 4* and *5* show **elevation drawings** for a building.

> **NOTE**
>
> These elevation drawings show the heights of windows, doors, and porches, the pitch of roofs, etc., because all of these measurements cannot be shown conveniently on floor plans.

1.4.0 Sections

A section or **sectional view** (*Figure 6*) is a cutaway view that allows the viewer to see the inside of a structure. The point on the plan or elevation showing where the imaginary cut has been made is indicated by the section line, which is usually a dashed line. The section line shows the location the section on the plan or elevation. It is necessa to know which of the cutaway parts is represent in the sectional drawing. To show this, arr points are placed at the ends of the section line

In **architectural drawings**, it is often necessa to show more than one section on the same dra ing. The different section lines must be dist guished by letters, numbers, or other designatic placed at the ends of the lines. These section l ters are generally large so as to stand out on t drawings. To further avoid confusion, the sa letter is usually placed at each end of the secti line. The section is named according to these l ters (e.g., Section A-A, Section B-B, and so forth

A longitudinal section is taken lengthw while a cross section is usually taken straig across the width of an object. Sometimes, ho ever, a section is not taken along one straight lii It is often taken along a zigzag line to show i portant parts of the object.

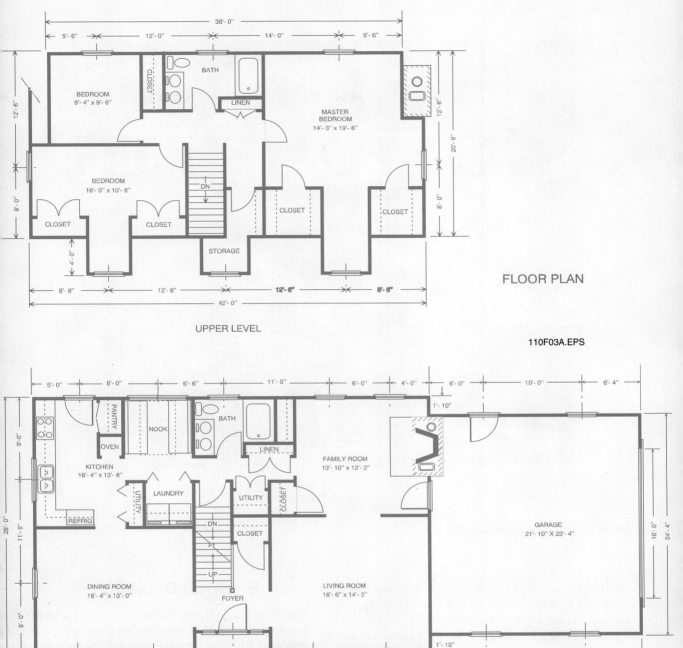

FLOOR PLAN

UPPER LEVEL

110F03A.EPS

LOWER LEVEL

110F03B.EPS

Figure 3 ◆ Floor plans of a building.

FRONT ELEVATION

REAR ELEVATION

110F04.EPS

Figure 4 ◆ Front and rear elevations.

A sectional view, as applied to architectural drawings, is a drawing showing the building, or portion of a building, as though it were cut through on some imaginary line. This line may be either vertical (straight up and down) or horizontal. Wall sections are nearly always made vertically so that the cut edge is exposed from top to bottom. In some ways, the wall section is one of the most important of all the drawings to construction workers, because it answers the questions as to how a structure should be built. The floor plans of a building show how each floor is arranged, but the wall sections tell how each part is constructed and usually indicate the material to be used. The electrician needs to know this information when determining wiring methods that comply with the *NEC*®.

1.5.0 Electrical Drawings

Electrical drawings show in a clear, concise man ner exactly what is required of the electricians. Th amount of data shown on such drawings shou be sufficient, but not overdone. This means tha complete set of electrical drawings could consist only one 8½" × 11" sheet, or it could consist of se eral dozen 24" × 36" (or larger) sheets, dependi on the size and complexity of a given project. shop drawing, for example, may contain details only one piece of equipment, while a set of wor ing drawings for an industrial installation m contain dozens of drawing sheets detailing t electrical system for lighting and power, alo with equipment, motor controls, wiring diagram schematic diagrams, equipment schedules, and host of other pertinent data.

LEFT ELEVATION

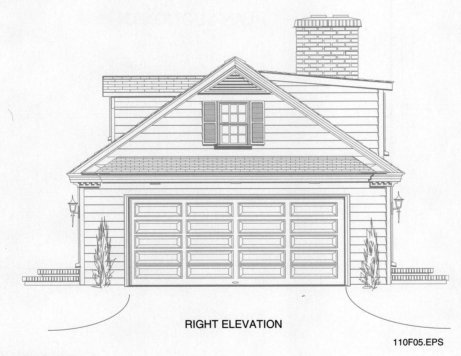

RIGHT ELEVATION

110F05.EPS

Figure 5 ◆ Left and right elevations.

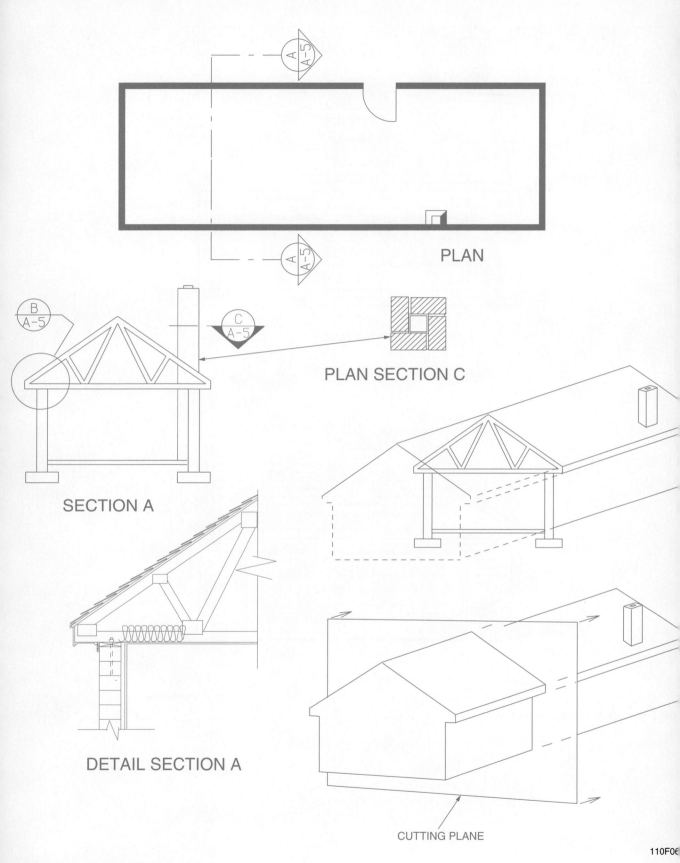

PLAN

PLAN SECTION C

SECTION A

DETAIL SECTION A

CUTTING PLANE

110F06

Figure 6 ◆ Sectional drawing.

Orient Yourself

INSIDE TRACK

When reading a drawing, find the north arrow to orient yourself to the structure. Knowing where north is enables you to accurately describe the locations of walls and other parts of the building.

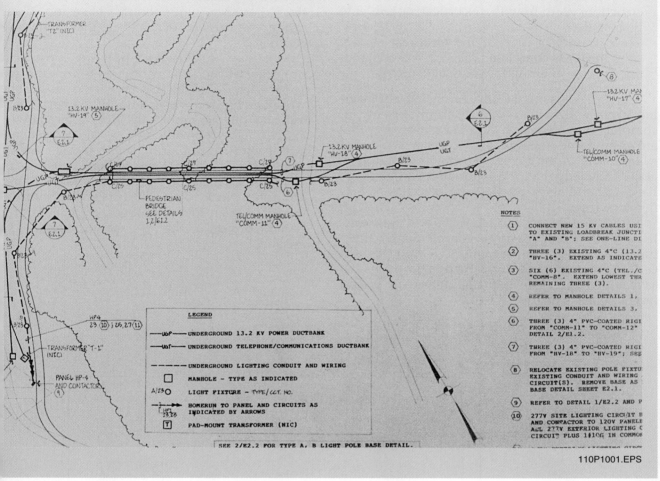

110P1001.EPS

Using All of the Drawings

Look back over the information on floor plans, elevations, and sections. What kinds of information would an electrician get from each of these drawings? What could a sectional drawing show that a floor plan could not?

In general, the electrical working drawings for a given project serve three distinct functions:

- They provide electrical contractors with an exact description of the project so that materials and labor may be estimated to project a total cost of the project for bidding purposes.
- They provide workers on the project with instructions as to how the electrical system is to be installed.
- They provide a map of the electrical system once the job is completed to aid in maintenance and troubleshooting for years to come.

Electrical drawings from consulting engineering firms will vary in quality from sketchy, incomplete drawings to neat, precise drawings that are easy to understand. Few, however, will cover every detail of the electrical system. Therefore, a good knowledge of installation practices must go hand-in-hand with interpreting electrical working drawings.

Sometimes electrical contractors will have electrical drafters prepare special supplemental drawings for use by the contractors' employees. On certain projects, these supplemental drawings can save supervision time in the field once the project has begun.

2.0.0 ◆ BLUEPRINT LAYOUT

Although a strong effort has been made to sta dardize drawing practices in the building co struction industry, **blueprints** prepared different architectural or engineering firms w rarely be identical. Similarities, however, will e ist between most sets of blueprints, and with a l tle experience, you should have no troub interpreting any set of drawings that might be e countered.

Most drawings used for building constructi projects will be drawn on sheets ranging fro 11" × 17" to 24" × 36" in size. Each drawing she will have border lines framing the overall draw ing and one or more title blocks, as shown *Figure 7*. The type and size of title blocks vari with each firm preparing the drawings. In add tion, some drawing sheets will also contain a r vision block near the title block, and perhaps approval block. This information is normal found on each drawing sheet, regardless of t type of project or the information contained the sheet.

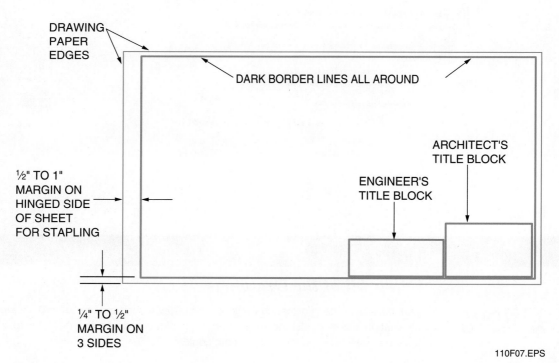

Figure 7 ◆ Typical blueprint layout.

1.0 Title Block

e architect's title block for a blueprint is usually
xed in the lower right-hand corner of the draw-
; sheet; the size of the block varies with the size
the drawing and with the information required.
Figure 8.

In general, the title block of an electrical draw-
; should contain the following information:

Name of the project
Address of the project
Name of the owner or client
Name of the architectural firm
Date of completion
Scale(s)
Initials of the drafter, checker, and designer,
with dates under each
Job number
Sheet number
General description of the drawing

Interpreting Electrical Drawings

A good example of when an electrician must interpret
the drawings is when wiring a log cabin. The drawings
will show the receptacle and switch locations in
branch circuits as usual, but the electrician must
figure out how to route wires and install boxes where
there is no hollow wall and sometimes no ceiling
space.

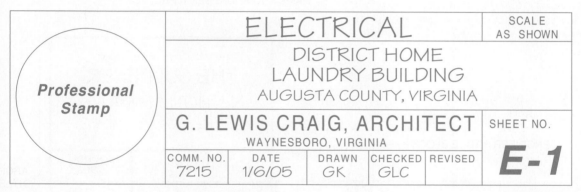

110F08.EPS

ure 8 ◆ Typical architect's title block.

Check the Title Block

Always refer to the title block for scale and be aware that it often changes from drawing
to drawing within the same set. Also check for the current revision, and when you
replace a drawing with a new revision, be sure to remove and file the older version.

Applying Your Skills

Once you learn how to interpret blueprints, you can apply that knowledge to any type of construction, from simple residential applications to large industrial complexes.

Every architectural firm has its own standard for drawing titles, and they are often preprinted directly on the tracing paper or else printed on a sticker, which is placed on the drawing.

Often, the consulting engineering firm will also be listed, which means that an additional title block will be applied to the drawing, usually next to the architect's title block. *Figure 9* shows completed architectural and engineering title blocks as they appear on an actual drawing.

2.2.0 Approval Block

The approval block, in most cases, will appear the drawing sheet as shown in *Figure 10*. The v ious types of approval blocks (drawn, check etc.) will be initialed by the appropriate persc nel. This type of approval block is usually part the title block and appears on each drawing she

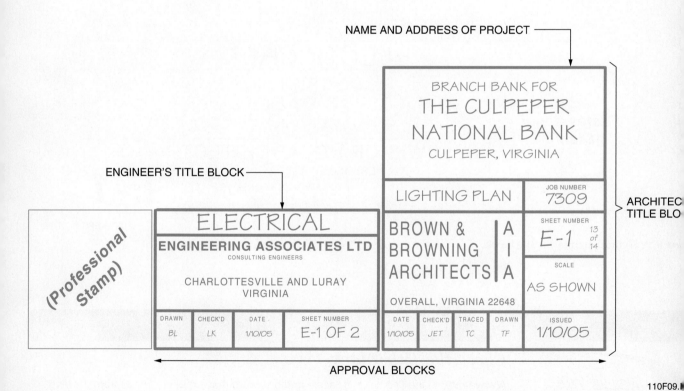

Figure 9 ◆ Title blocks.

Figure 10 ◆ Typical approval block.

On some projects, authorized signatures are required before certain systems may be installed, or
even before the project begins. An approval block
such as the one shown in *Figure 11* indicates that
the required personnel have checked the drawings
for accuracy, and that the set meets with everyone's approval. Such an approval block usually
appears on the front sheet of the blueprint set and
may include:

Professional stamp – Registered seal of approval
by the architect or consulting engineer.
Design supervisor – Signature of the person who
is overseeing the design.
Drawn (by) – Signature or initials of the person
who drafted the drawing and the date it was
completed.
Checked (by) – Signature or initials of the person
who reviewed the drawing and the date of
approval.
Approved – Signature or initials of the architect/
engineer and the date of the approval.
Owner's approval – Signature of the project
owner or the owner's representative along with
the date signed.

3.0 Revision Block

Sometimes electrical drawings will have to be partially redrawn or modified during the construction of a project. It is extremely important that
such modifications are noted and dated on the

drawings to ensure that the workers have an up-
to-date set of drawings to work from. In some situations, sufficient space is left near the title block
for dates and descriptions of revisions, as shown
in *Figure 12*. In other cases, a revision block is provided (again, near the title block), as shown in
Figure 13.

NOTE

Architects, engineers, designers, and drafters
have their own methods of showing revisions, so
expect to find deviations from those shown here.

CAUTION

When a set of electrical working drawings has
been revised, always make certain that the most
up-to-date set is used for all future layout work.
Either destroy the old, obsolete set of drawings or
else clearly mark on the affected sheets,
Obsolete Drawing—Do Not Use. Also, when
working with a set of working drawings and
written specifications for the first time, thoroughly
check each page to see if any revisions or
modifications have been made to the originals.
Doing so can save much time and expense to all
concerned with the project.

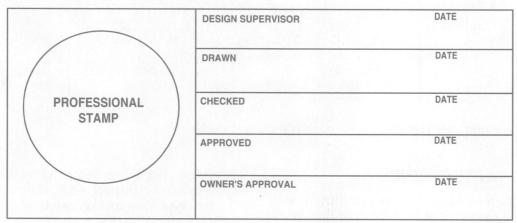

110F11.EPS

Figure 11 ◆ Alternate approval block.

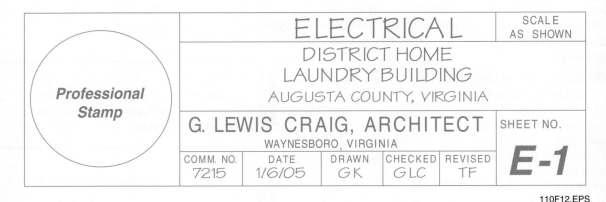

Figure 12 ◆ One method of showing revisions on working drawings.

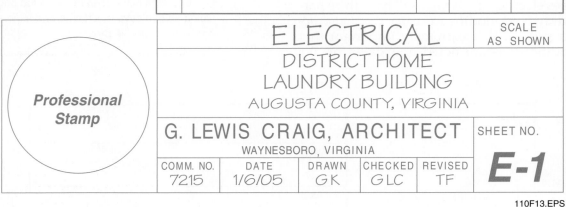

Figure 13 ◆ Alternative method of showing revisions on working drawings.

3.0.0 ◆ DRAFTING LINES

You will encounter many types of drafting lines. To specify the meaning of each type of line, contrasting lines can be made by varying the width of the lines or breaking the lines in a uniform way.

Figure 14 shows common lines used on architectural drawings. However, these lines can vary. Architects and engineers have strived for a common standard for the past century, but unfortunately, their goal has yet to be reached. Therefore, you will find variations in lines and symbols from drawing to drawing, so always consult the legend or symbol list when referring to any drawin Also, carefully inspect each drawing to ensu that line types are used consistently.

The drafting lines shown in *Figure 14* are us as follows:

- *Light full line* – This line is used for secti lines, building background (outlines), a similar uses where the object to be drawn secondary to the system being shown (e. HVAC or electrical).
- *Medium full line* – This type of line is frequen used for hand lettering on drawings. It

LIGHT FULL LINE	—————————————
MEDIUM FULL LINE	—————————————
HEAVY FULL LINE	━━━━━━━━━━━━━
EXTRA HEAVY FULL LINE	━━━━━━━━━━━━━
CENTERLINE	— · — · — · — · —
HIDDEN LINE	· · · · · · · · · · · · · · · · · ·
DIMENSION LINE	←————— 3.00" —————→
SHORT BREAK LINE	
LONG BREAK LINE	
MATCH LINE	━ ━ ━ ━ ━ ━ ━
SECONDARY LINE	— — — — — —
PROPERTY LINE	— · — · — · — · —

110F14.EPS

ure 14 ◆ Typical drafting lines.

further used for some drawing symbols, circuit lines, etc.

Heavy full line – This line is used for borders around title blocks, schedules, and for hand lettering drawing titles. Some types of symbols are frequently drawn with a heavy full line.

Extra heavy full line – This line is used for border lines on architectural/engineering drawings.

- *Centerline* – A centerline is a broken line made up of alternately spaced long and short dashes. It indicates the centers of objects such as holes, pillars, or fixtures. Sometimes, the centerline indicates the dimensions of a finished floor.
- *Hidden line* – A hidden line consists of a series of short dashes that are closely and evenly spaced. It shows the edges of objects that are not visible in a particular view. The object

Check the Legend

Be sure to check the legend on every drawing set. Symbols and abbreviations often vary widely from drawing set to drawing set.

outlined by hidden lines in one drawing is often fully pictured in another drawing.

- *Dimension line* – These are thin lines used to show the extent and direction of dimensions. The dimension is usually placed in a break inside the dimension lines. Normal practice is to place the dimension lines outside the object's outline. However, it may sometimes be necessary to draw the dimensions inside the outline.
- *Short break line* – This line is usually drawn freehand and is used for short breaks.
- *Long break line* – This line, which is drawn partly with a straightedge and partly with freehand zigzags, is used for long breaks.
- *Match line* – This line is used to show the position of the cutting plane. Therefore, it is also called the cutting plane line. A match or cutting plane line is a heavy line with long dashes alternating with two short dashes. It is used on drawings of large structures to show where one drawing stops and the next drawing starts.
- *Secondary line* – This line is frequently used to outline pieces of equipment or to indicate reference points of a drawing that are secondary to the drawing's purpose.
- *Property line* – This is a light line made up of one long and two short dashes that are alternately spaced. It indicates land boundaries on the site plan.

Other uses of the lines just mentioned include the following:

- *Extension lines*–Extension lines are lightweight lines that start about ⅟₁₆ inch away from the edge of an object and extend out. A common use of extension lines is to create a boundary for dimension lines. Dimension lines meet extension lines with arrowheads, slashes, or dots. Extension lines that point from a note or other reference to a particular feature on a drawing are called leaders. They usually end in either an arrowhead or a dot and may include an explanatory note at the end.
- *Section lines*–These are often referred to as *cross-hatch lines*. Drawn at a 45° angle, these lines show where an object has been cut away to reveal the inside.
- *Phantom lines*–Phantom lines are solid, light lines that show where an object will be installed. A future door opening or a future piece of equipment can be shown with phantom lines.

3.1.0 Electrical Drafting Lines

Besides the architectural lines shown in *Figure 14*, consulting electrical engineers, designers, and

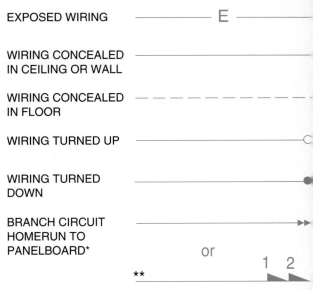

* Number of arrowheads indicates number of circuits. A numb at each arrowhead may be used to identify circuit numbers.

** Half arrowheads are sometimes used for homeruns to avo confusing them with drawing callouts.

110F15.E

Figure 15 ◆ Electrical drafting lines.

drafters use additional lines to represent circu and their related components. Again, these lir may vary from drawing to drawing, so check t symbol list or legend for the exact meaning lines on the drawing with which you are workir *Figure 15* shows lines used on some electric drawings.

4.0.0 ◆ ELECTRICAL SYMBOLS

The electrician must be able to correctly read a understand electrical working drawings. This cludes a thorough knowledge of electrical sy bols and their applications.

An electrical symbol is a figure or mark th stands for a component used in the electrical s tem. *Figure 16* shows a list of electrical symbol that are currently recommended by the Americ National Standards Institute (ANSI). It is evide from this list of symbols that many have the sar basic form, but, because of some slight differen their meaning changes. For example, the recep cle symbols in *Figure 17* each have the same ba form (a circle), but the addition of a line or an abreviation gives each an individual meaning. good procedure to follow in learning symbols is first learn the basic form and then apply the va ations for obtaining different meanings.

It would be much simpler if all architects, en neers, electrical designers, and drafters used t

SWITCH OUTLETS

Single-Pole Switch

Double-Pole Switch

Three-Way Switch

Four-Way Switch

Key-Operated Switch

Switch w/Pilot

Low-Voltage Switch

Switch & Single Receptacle

Switch & Duplex Receptacle

Door Switch

Momentary Contact Switch

RECEPTACLE OUTLETS

Single Receptacle

Duplex Receptacle

Triplex Receptacle

Split-Wired Duplex Recep.

Single Special Purpose Recep.

Duplex Special Purpose Recep.

Range Receptacle

Special Purpose Connection or Provision for Connection. Subscript letters indicate Function DW - Dishwasher; CD - Clothes Dryer, etc.)

Clock Receptacle w/Hanger

Fan Receptacle w/Hanger

Single Floor Receptacle

A numeral or letter within the symbol or as a subscript keyed to the list of symbols indicates type of receptacle or usage.

LIGHTING OUTLETS

	Ceiling	Wall

Surface Fixture

Surface Fixt. w/Pull Switch

Recessed Fixture

Surface or Pendant Fluorescent Fixture

Recessed Fluor. Fixture

Surface or Pendant Continuous Row Fluor. Fixtures

Recessed Continuous Row Fluorescent Fixtures

Surface Exit Light

Recessed Exit Light

Blanked Outlet

Junction Box

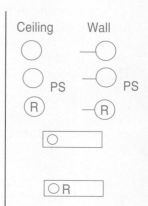

CIRCUITING

Wiring Concealed in Ceiling or Wall

Wiring Concealed in Floor

Wiring Exposed

Branch Circuit Homerun to Panelboard. Number of arrows indicates number of circuits in run. Note: Any circuit without further identification is 2-wire. A greater number of wires is indicated by cross lines as shown below. Wire size is sometimes shown with numerals placed above or below cross lines.

3-Wire

4-Wire

110F16.EPS

Figure 16 ◆ ANSI electrical symbols.

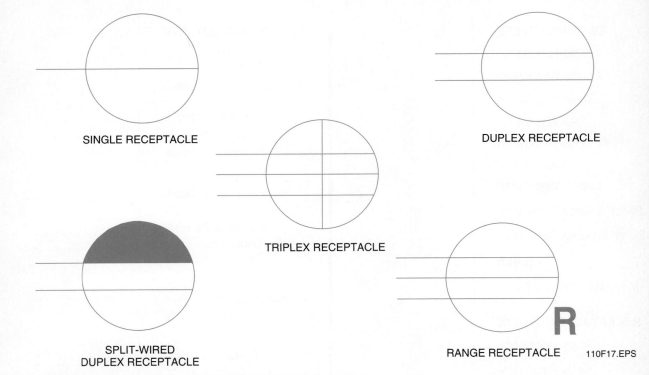

SINGLE RECEPTACLE

DUPLEX RECEPTACLE

TRIPLEX RECEPTACLE

SPLIT-WIRED
DUPLEX RECEPTACLE

RANGE RECEPTACLE

110F17.EPS

Figure 17 ◆ Various receptacle symbols used on electrical drawings.

same symbols; however, this is not the case. Although standardization is getting closer to a reality, existing symbols are still modified, and new symbols are created for almost every new project.

The electrical symbols described in the following paragraphs represent those found on actual electrical working drawings throughout the United States and Canada. Many are similar to those recommended by ANSI and the Consulting Engineers Council/US; others are not. Understanding how these symbols were devised will help you to interpret unknown electrical symbols in the future.

Some of the symbols used on electrical drawings are abbreviations, such as WP for weatherproof and AFF for above finished floor. Others are simplified pictographs, such as (A) in *Figure 18* for a double floodlight fixture or (B) for an infrared electric heater with two quartz lamps.

In some cases, the symbols are combinations of abbreviations and pictographs, such as (C) in *Figure 18* for a fusible safety switch, (D) for a nonfusible safety switch, and (E) for a double-throw safety switch. In each example, a pictograph of a

switch enclosure has been combined with an breviation: F (fusible), DT (double-throw), and (nonfusible), respectively.

Lighting outlet symbols have been devised t represent incandescent, fluorescent, and hi intensity discharge lighting; a circle usually rep sents an incandescent fixture, and a rectangle used to represent a fluorescent fixture. These sy bols are designed to indicate the physical shape a particular fixture, and while the circles rep senting incandescent lamps are frequently larged somewhat, symbols for fluorescent fixtu are usually drawn as close to scale as possible. T type of mounting used for all lighting fixture usually indicated in a lighting fixture schedu which is shown on the drawings or in the writ specifications.

The type of lighting fixture is identified by a meral placed inside a triangle or other symb and placed near the fixture to be identified complete description of the fixtures identified the symbols must be given in the lighting fixt schedule and should include the manufactu catalog number, number and type of lam

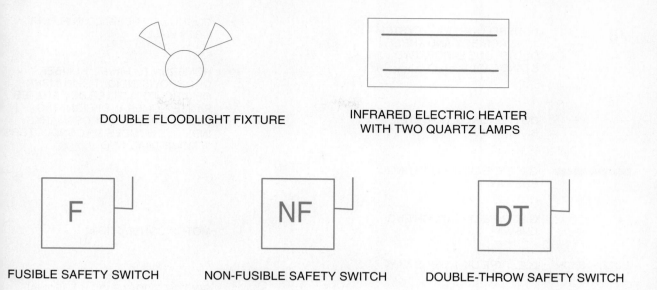

DOUBLE FLOODLIGHT FIXTURE

INFRARED ELECTRIC HEATER
WITH TWO QUARTZ LAMPS

F

FUSIBLE SAFETY SWITCH

NF

NON-FUSIBLE SAFETY SWITCH

DT

DOUBLE-THROW SAFETY SWITCH

110F18.EPS

re 18 ◆ General types of symbols used on electrical drawings.

tage, finish, mounting, and any other informa-
1 needed for proper installation of the fixture.
witches used to control lighting fixtures are
) indicated by symbols (usually the letter S
owed by numerals or letters to define the ex-
type of switch). For example, S_3 indicates a
ee-way switch; S_4 identifies a four-way
tch; and S_P indicates a single-pole switch with
ilot light.
Main distribution centers, panelboards, trans-
ners, safety switches, and other similar electri-
components are indicated by electrical symbols
floor plans and by a combination of symbols
l semipictorial drawings in riser diagrams.
A detailed description of the service equipment
sually given in the panelboard schedule or in
written specifications. However, on small
jects, the service equipment is sometimes indi-
ed only by notes on the drawings.
Circuit and feeder wiring symbols are getting
ser to being standardized. Most circuits con-
led in the ceiling or wall are indicated by a
d line; a broken line is used for circuits con-
led in the floor or ceiling below; and exposed
eways are indicated by short dashes or else the
er *E* placed in the same plane with the circuit
 at various intervals. The number of conduc-

tors in a conduit or raceway system may be indicated in the panelboard schedule under the appropriate column, or the information may be
shown on the floor plan.

Symbols for communication and signal systems, as well as symbols for light and power, are
drawn to an appropriate scale and accurately located with respect to the building. This reduces
the number of references made to the architectural
drawings. Where extreme accuracy is required in
locating outlets and equipment, exact dimensions
are given on larger-scale drawings and shown on
the plans.

Each different category in an electrical system is
usually represented by a basic distinguishing
symbol. To further identify items of equipment or
outlets in the category, a numeral or other identifying mark is placed within the open basic symbol. In addition, all such individual symbols used
on the drawings should be included in the symbol
list or legend. The electrical symbols shown in
Figure 19 were modified by a consulting engineering firm for use on a small industrial electrical installation. The symbols shown in *Figure 20* are
those recommended by the Consulting Engineers
Council/US. You should become familiar with
these symbols.

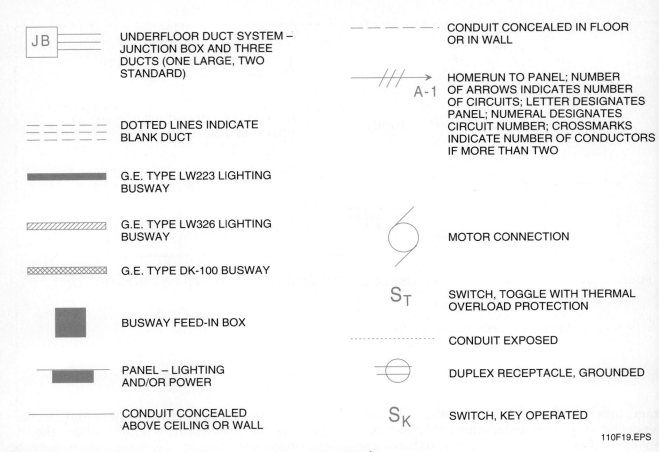

Figure 19 ◆ Electrical symbols used by one consulting engineering firm.

SWITCH OUTLETS

Single Pole Switch	S
Double Pole Switch	S_2
Three-Way Switch	S_3
Four-Way Switch	S_4
Key-Operated Switch	S_K
Switch and Fusestat Holder	$S_F H$
Switch and Pilot Lamp	S_P
Fan Switch	S_F
Switch for Low-Voltage Switching System	S_L
Master Switch for Low-Voltage Switching System	S_{LM}
Switch and Single Receptacle	⊖ S
Switch and Duplex Receptacle	⊖ S
Door Switch	S_D
Time Switch	S_T
Momentary Contact Switch	S_{MC}
Ceiling Pull Switch	Ⓢ
"Hand-Off-Auto" Control Switch	HOA
Multi-Speed Control Switch	M
Pushbutton	⊡

RECEPTACLE OUTLETS

Where weatherproof, explosionproof, or other specific types of devices are to be required, use the upper-case subscript letters to specify. For example, weatherproof single or duplex receptacles would have the upper-case WP subscript letters noted alongside the symbol. All outlets must be grounded.

Single Receptacle Outlet	
Duplex Receptacle Outlet	
Triplex Receptacle Outlet	
Quadruplex Receptacle Outlet	
Duplex Receptacle Outlet Split Wired	
Triplex Receptacle Outlet Split Wired	
250-Volt Receptacle/Single Phase Use Subscript Letter to Indicate Function (DW - Dishwasher, RA - Range) or Numerals (with explanation in symbols schedule)	
250-Volt Receptacle/Three Phase	
Clock Receptacle	Ⓒ
Fan Receptacle	Ⓕ
Floor Single Receptacle Outlet	
Floor Duplex Receptacle Outlet	
Floor Special-Purpose Outlet	*
Floor Telephone Outlet - Public	◀
Floor Telephone Outlet - Private	◁

* Use numeral keyed explanation of symbol usage

ure 20 ◆ Recommended electrical symbols (1 of 7).

110F20A.EPS

Example of the use of several floor outlet symbols to identify a 2, 3, or more gang outlet:

Underfloor duct and junction box for triple, double, or single duct system as indicated by the number of parallel lines

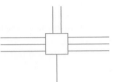

Example of the use of various symbols to identify the location of different types of outlets or connections for underfloor duct or cellular floor systems:

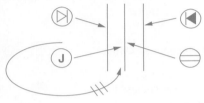

Cellular Floor Heater Duct

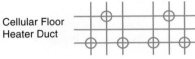

CIRCUITING

Wiring Exposed (not in conduit)	—— E ——
Wiring Concealed in Ceiling or Wall	————
Wiring Concealed in Floor	– – – – –
Wiring Existing*	- - - - - - - - -
Wiring Turned Up	———○
Wiring Turned Down	———●
Branch Circuit Homerun to Panelboard	2 1 →

Number of arrows indicates number of circuits. (A number at each arrow may be used to identify the circuit number.)**

BUS DUCTS AND WIREWAYS

Trolley Duct***	T	T
Busway (Service, Feeder or Plug-in)***	B	B
Cable Trough Ladder or Channel***	C	C
Wireway***	W	W

PANELBOARDS, SWITCHBOARDS AND RELATED EQUIPMENT

Flush Mounted Panelboard and Cabinet***	
Surface Mounted Panelboard and Cabinet***	
Switchboard, Power Control Center, Unit Substation (Should be drawn to scale)***	/////////
Flush Mounted Terminal Cabinet (In small scale drawings the TC may be indicated alongside the symbol)***	TC
Surface Mounted Terminal Cabinet (In small scale drawings the TC may be indicated alongside the symbol)***	TC
Pull Box (Identify in relation to Wiring System Section and Size)	■
Motor or Other Power Controller May be a starter or contactor***	⊠
Externally Operated Disconnection Switch***	▭
Combination Controller and Disconnection Means***	⊠

*Note: Use heavy-weight line to identify service and feeders. Indicate empty conduit by notation CO.

**Note: Any circuit without further identification indicates two-wire circuit. For a greater number of wires, indicate with cross lines, e.g.:

3 wires   ——┤┤├——   4 wires, etc.   ——┤┤┤├——

Neutral wire may be shown longer. Unless indicated otherwise, the wire size of the circuit is the minimum size required by the specification. Identify different functions of wiring system (e.g., signaling system) by notation or other means.

***Identify by Notation or Schedule

110F20B.EF

Figure 20 ◆ Recommended electrical symbols (2 of 7).

POWER EQUIPMENT

Electric Motor (HP as Indicated)   1/4

Power Transformer

Pothead (Cable Termination)

Circuit Element
  e.g. Circuit Breaker   CB

Circuit Breaker

Fusible Element

Single-Throw Knife Switch

Double-Throw Knife Switch

Ground

Battery

Contactor   C

Photoelectric Cell   PE

Voltage Cycles, Phase   EX: 480/60/3

Relay   R

Equipment Connection (as noted)

REMOTE CONTROL STATIONS FOR MOTORS OR OTHER EQUIPMENT

Pushbutton Station   PB

Float Switch - Mechanical   F

Limit Switch - Mechanical   L

Pneumatic Switch - Mechanical   P

Electric Eye - Beam Source

Electric Eye - Relay

Temperature Control Relay
  Connection (3 Denotes Quantity)   R 3

Solenoid Control Valve Connection   S

Pressure Switch Connection   P

Aquastat Connection   A

Vacuum Switch Connection   V

Gas Solenoid Valve Connection   G

Flow Switch Connection   F

Timer Connection   T

Limit Switch Connection   L

LIGHTING OUTLETS

	Ceiling	Wall
Incandescent Fixture (Surface or Pendant)		
Incandescent Fixture with Pull Chain (Surface or Pendant)	PC	PC

Figure 20 ◆ Recommended electrical symbols (3 of 7).

110F20C.EPS

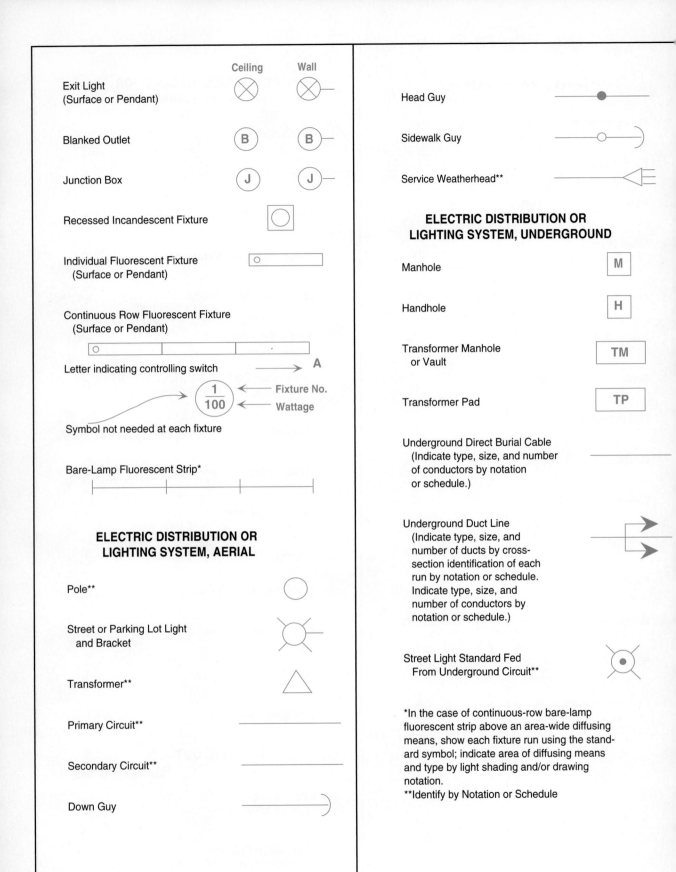

Exit Light
(Surface or Pendant)

Ceiling   Wall

Blanked Outlet   B   B

Junction Box   J   J

Recessed Incandescent Fixture

Individual Fluorescent Fixture
(Surface or Pendant)

Continuous Row Fluorescent Fixture
(Surface or Pendant)

Letter indicating controlling switch   A

1/100   Fixture No.
Wattage

Symbol not needed at each fixture

Bare-Lamp Fluorescent Strip*

**ELECTRIC DISTRIBUTION OR
LIGHTING SYSTEM, AERIAL**

Pole**

Street or Parking Lot Light
and Bracket

Transformer**

Primary Circuit**

Secondary Circuit**

Down Guy

Head Guy

Sidewalk Guy

Service Weatherhead**

**ELECTRIC DISTRIBUTION OR
LIGHTING SYSTEM, UNDERGROUND**

Manhole   M

Handhole   H

Transformer Manhole
or Vault   TM

Transformer Pad   TP

Underground Direct Burial Cable
(Indicate type, size, and number
of conductors by notation
or schedule.)

Underground Duct Line
(Indicate type, size, and
number of ducts by cross-
section identification of each
run by notation or schedule.
Indicate type, size, and
number of conductors by
notation or schedule.)

Street Light Standard Fed
From Underground Circuit**

*In the case of continuous-row bare-lamp
fluorescent strip above an area-wide diffusing
means, show each fixture run using the standard symbol; indicate area of diffusing means
and type by light shading and/or drawing
notation.
**Identify by Notation or Schedule

110F20D.E

Figure 20 ◆ Recommended electrical symbols (4 of 7).

SIGNALLING SYSTEM OUTLETS

INSTITUTIONAL, COMMERCIAL, AND INDUSTRIAL OCCUPANCIES

I NURSE CALL SYSTEM DEVICES (Any Type)

Basic Symbol

(Examples of Individual Item Identification Not a Part of Standard)

Nurses' Annunciator
(Add a number after it as
—① 24 to indicate number
of lamps)   —①

Call Station, Single Cord,
Pilot Light   —②

Call Station, Double Cord,
Microphone Speaker   —③

Corridor Dome Light
1 Lamp   —④

Transformer   —⑤

Any Other Item On Same
System Use Number As
Required   —⑥

II PAGING SYSTEM DEVICES

Basic Symbol

(Examples of Individual Item Identification Not a Part of Standard)

Keyboard   ◇1

Flush Annunciator   ◇2

2-Face Annunciator   ◇3

Any Other Item On Same
System Use Numbers As
Required   ◇4

III FIRE ALARM SYSTEM DEVICES (Any Type) Including Smoke and Sprinkler Alarm Devices

Basic Symbol

(Examples of Individual Item Identification. Not a Part of Standard)

Control Panel   —□1

Station   —□2

10" Gong   —□3

Pre-Signal Chime   —□4

Any Other Item On Same System
Use Numbers As Required   —□5

IV STAFF REGISTER SYSTEM DEVICES (Any Type)

Basic Symbol

(Examples of Individual Item Identification. Not a Part of Standard)

Phone Operators' Register   ◇1

Entrance Register - Flush   ◇2

Staff Room Register   ◇3

Transformer   ◇4

Any Other Item On Same System
Use Numbers As Required   ◇5

V ELECTRIC CLOCK SYSTEM DEVICES (Any Type)

Basic Symbol

(Examples of Individual Item Identification. Not a Part of Standard)

re 20 ◆ Recommended electrical symbols (5 of 7).

110F20E.EPS

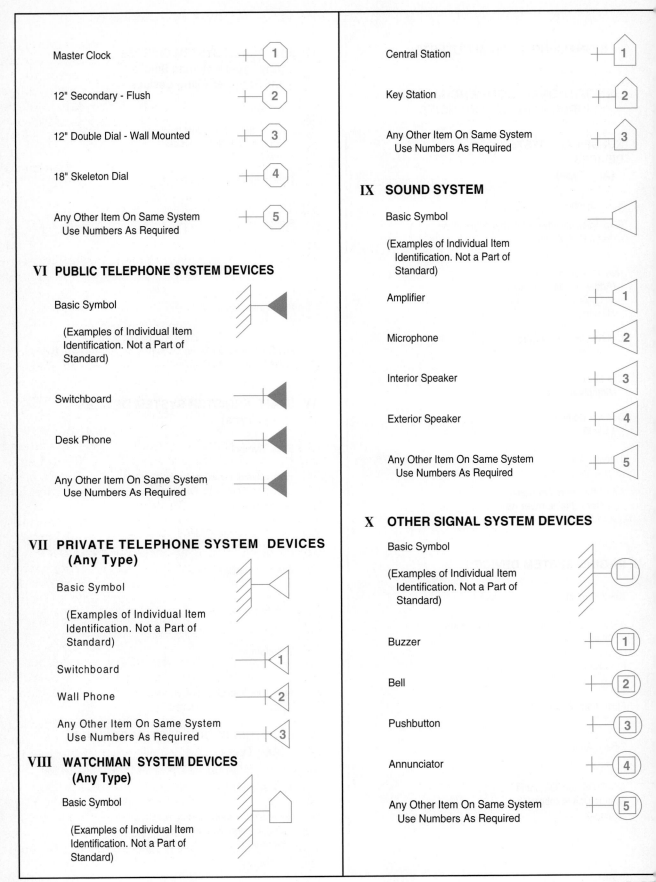

Master Clock	1
12" Secondary - Flush	2
12" Double Dial - Wall Mounted	3
18" Skeleton Dial	4
Any Other Item On Same System Use Numbers As Required	5

VI PUBLIC TELEPHONE SYSTEM DEVICES

Basic Symbol

(Examples of Individual Item Identification. Not a Part of Standard)

Switchboard

Desk Phone

Any Other Item On Same System Use Numbers As Required

VII PRIVATE TELEPHONE SYSTEM DEVICES (Any Type)

Basic Symbol

(Examples of Individual Item Identification. Not a Part of Standard)

Switchboard   1

Wall Phone   2

Any Other Item On Same System Use Numbers As Required   3

VIII WATCHMAN SYSTEM DEVICES (Any Type)

Basic Symbol

(Examples of Individual Item Identification. Not a Part of Standard)

Central Station	1
Key Station	2
Any Other Item On Same System Use Numbers As Required	3

IX SOUND SYSTEM

Basic Symbol

(Examples of Individual Item Identification. Not a Part of Standard)

Amplifier	1
Microphone	2
Interior Speaker	3
Exterior Speaker	4
Any Other Item On Same System Use Numbers As Required	5

X OTHER SIGNAL SYSTEM DEVICES

Basic Symbol

(Examples of Individual Item Identification. Not a Part of Standard)

Buzzer	1
Bell	2
Pushbutton	3
Annunciator	4
Any Other Item On Same System Use Numbers As Required	5

Figure 20 ◆ Recommended electrical symbols (6 of 7).

110F20F.E

RESIDENTIAL OCCUPANCIES

Signalling system symbols for use in identifying standardized residential-type signal system items on residential drawings where a descriptive symbol list is not included on the drawing. When other signal system items are to be identified, use the above basic symbols for such items together with a descriptive symbol list.

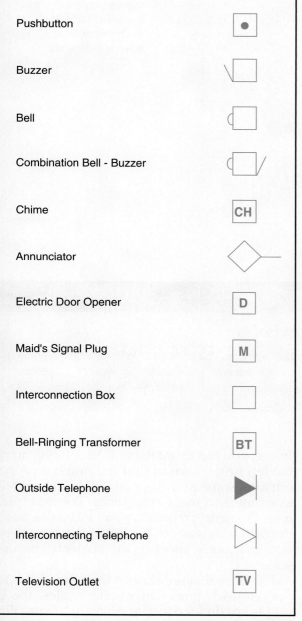

Pushbutton	
Buzzer	
Bell	
Combination Bell - Buzzer	
Chime	CH
Annunciator	
Electric Door Opener	D
Maid's Signal Plug	M
Interconnection Box	
Bell-Ringing Transformer	BT
Outside Telephone	
Interconnecting Telephone	
Television Outlet	TV

110F20G.EPS

Figure 20 ◆ Recommended electrical symbols (7 of 7).

5.0.0 ◆ SCALE DRAWINGS

In most electrical drawings, the components are so large that it would be impossible to draw them actual size. Consequently, drawings are made to some reduced *scale*; that is, all the distances are drawn smaller than the actual dimensions of the object itself, with all dimensions being reduced in the same proportion. For example, if a floor plan of a building is to be drawn to a scale of ¼" = 1'–0", each ¼" on the drawing would equal 1 foot on the building itself; if the scale is ⅛" = 1'–0", each ⅛" on the drawing equals 1 foot on the building, and so forth.

When architectural and engineering drawings are produced, the selected scale is very important. Where dimensions must be held to extreme accuracy, the scale drawings should be made as large as practical with dimension lines added. Where dimensions require only reasonable accuracy, the object may be drawn to a smaller scale (with dimension lines possibly omitted).

In dimensioning drawings, the dimensions written on the drawing are the actual dimensions of the building, not the distances that are measured on the drawing. To further illustrate this point, look at the floor plan in *Figure 21;* it is drawn to a scale of ½" = 1'–0". One of the walls is drawn to an actual length of 3½" on the drawing paper, but since the scale is ½" = 1'–0" and since 3½" contains 7 halves of an inch (7 × ½ = 3½"), the dimension shown on the drawing will therefore be 7'–0" on the actual building.

As shown in the previous example, the most common method of reducing all the dimensions (in feet and inches) in the same proportion is to choose a certain distance and let that distance represent one foot. This distance can then be divided into 12 parts, each of which represents an inch. If half inches are required, these twelfths are further subdivided into halves, etc. Now the scale represents the common foot rule with its subdivisions into inches and fractions, except that the scaled foot is smaller than the distance known as a foot and, likewise, its subdivisions are proportionately smaller.

When a measurement is made on the drawing, it is made with the reduced foot rule or scale; when a measurement is made on the building, it is made with the standard foot rule. The most common reduced foot rules or scales used in electrical drawings are the architect's scale and the engineer's scale. Drawings may sometimes be encountered that use a metric scale, but using this scale is similar to using the architect's or engineer's scales.

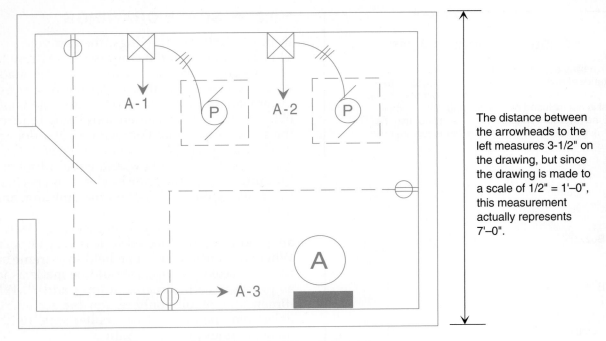

The distance between the arrowheads to the left measures 3-1/2" on the drawing, but since the drawing is made to a scale of 1/2" = 1'–0", this measurement actually represents 7'–0".

PUMP HOUSE FLOOR PLAN

1/2" = 1'–0"

110F21.EPS

Figure 21 ◆ Typical floor plan showing drawing scale.

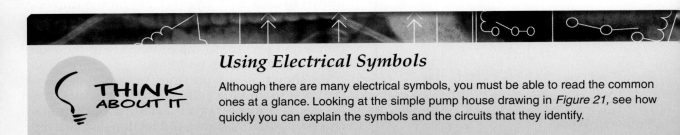

Using Electrical Symbols

THINK ABOUT IT

Although there are many electrical symbols, you must be able to read the common ones at a glance. Looking at the simple pump house drawing in *Figure 21*, see how quickly you can explain the symbols and the circuits that they identify.

5.1.0 Architect's Scale

Figure 22 shows two configurations of architect's scales. The one on the top is designed so that 1" = 1'–0", and the one on the bottom has graduations spaced to represent ⅛" = 1'–0".

Note that on the one-inch scale in *Figure 23*, the longer marks to the right of the zero (with a numeral beneath) represent feet. Therefore, the distance between the zero and the numeral 1 equals one foot. The shorter mark between the zero and 1 represents ½ of a foot, or six inches.

Referring again to *Figure 23*, look at the marks to the left of the zero. The numbered marks are spaced three scaled inches apart and have the numerals 0, 3, 6, and 9 for use as reference points. The other lines of the same length also represent scaled inches, but are not marked with numerals.

In use, you can count the number of long marks the left of the zero to find the number of inch but after some practice, you will be able to tell exact measurement at a glance. For example, measurement A represents five inches because i the fifth inch mark to the left of the zero; it is a one inch mark short of the six-inch line on scale.

The lines that are shorter than the inch line the half-inch lines. On smaller scales, the ba unit is not divided into as many divisions. For ample, the smallest subdivision on some sca represents two inches.

5.1.1 Types of Architect's Scales

Architect's scales are available in several typ but the most common include the triangl

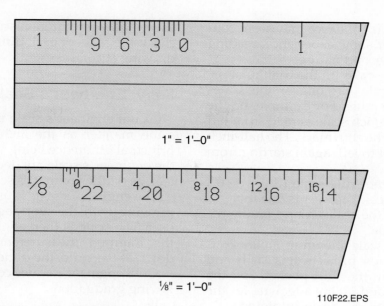

1" = 1'–0"

⅛" = 1'–0"

110F22.EPS

Figure 22 ◆ Two different configurations of architect's scales.

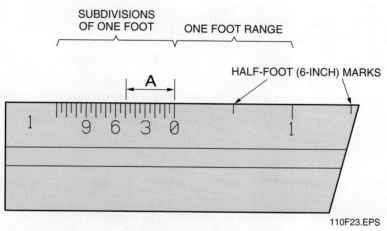

SUBDIVISIONS OF ONE FOOT

ONE FOOT RANGE

HALF-FOOT (6-INCH) MARKS

A

110F23.EPS

Figure 23 ◆ One-inch architect's scale.

scale (*Figure 24*) and the flat scale. The quality of architect's scales also varies from cheap plastic models (costing a dollar or two) to high-quality wooden-laminated tools that are calibrated to precise standards.

The triangular scale (*Figure 24*) is frequently found in drafting and estimating departments or

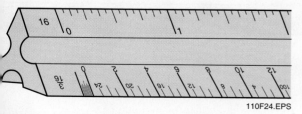

110F24.EPS

Figure 24 ◆ Typical triangular architect's scale.

engineering and electrical contracting firms, while the flat scales are more convenient to carry on the job site.

Triangular architect's scales have 12 different scales—two on each edge—as follows:

- Common foot rule (12 inches)
- $\frac{1}{16}$" = 1'–0"
- $\frac{3}{32}$" = 1'–0"
- $\frac{3}{16}$" = 1'–0"
- $\frac{1}{8}$" = 1'–0"
- $\frac{1}{4}$" = 1'–0"
- $\frac{3}{8}$" = 1'–0"
- $\frac{3}{4}$" = 1'–0"
- 1" = 1'–0"
- $\frac{1}{2}$" = 1'–0"
- $1\frac{1}{2}$" = 1'–0"
- 3" = 1'–0"

Two separate scales on one face may seem confusing at first, but after some experience, reading these scales becomes second nature.

In all but one of the scales on the triangular architect's scale, each face has one of the scales placed opposite to the other. For example, on the one-inch face, the one-inch scale is read from left to right, starting from the zero mark. The half-inch scale is read from right to left, again starting from the zero mark.

On the remaining foot-rule scale (1/16" = 1'–0") each 1/16" mark on the scale represents one foot.

Figure 25 shows all the scales found on the triangular architect's scale.

The flat architect's scale shown in *Figure 26* is ideal for workers on most projects. It is easily and conveniently carried in the shirt pocket, and the four scales (1/8", 1/4", 1/2", and 1") are adequate for the majority of projects that will be encountered.

The partial floor plan shown in *Figure 26* is drawn to a scale of 1/8" = 1'–0". The dimension in question is found by placing the 1/8" architect's scale on the drawing and reading the figures. It can be seen that the dimension reads 24'–6".

Every drawing should have the scale to which it is drawn plainly marked on it as part of the drawing title. However, it is not uncommon to have several different drawings on one blueprint sheet—all with different scales. Therefore, alwa check the scale of each different view found o drawing sheet.

5.2.0 Engineer's Scale

The civil engineer's scale is used in basically same manner as the architect's scale, with principal difference being that the graduations the engineer's scale are decimal units rather th feet, as on the architect's scale.

The engineer's scale is used by placing it on drawing with the working edge away from user. The scale is then aligned in the direction the required measurement. Then, by look down at the scale, the dimension is read.

Civil engineer's scales commonly show the lowing graduations:

- 1" = 10 units
- 1" = 20 units
- 1" = 30 units
- 1" = 40 units
- 1" = 60 units
- 1" = 80 units
- 1" = 100 units

The purpose of this scale is to transfer the r tive dimensions of an object to the drawing or

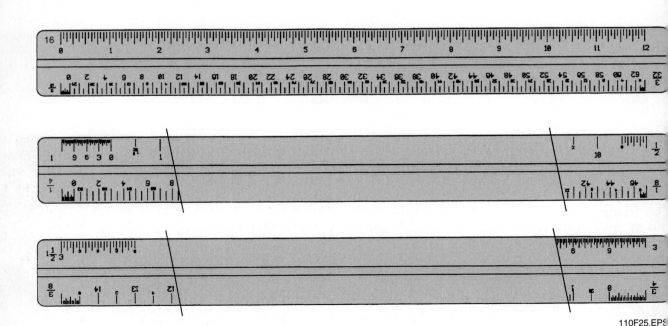

Figure 25 ◆ Various scales on a triangular architect's scale.

110F25.EPS

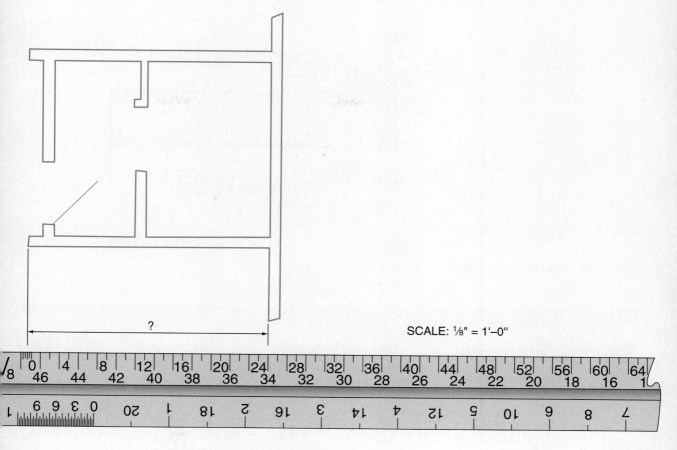

SCALE: ⅛" = 1'–0"

110F26.EPS

Figure 26 ◆ Using the ⅛" architect's scale to determine the dimensions on a drawing.

ersa. It is used mainly on site plans to determine .stances between property lines, manholes, duct ins, direct-burial cable runs, and the like.

Site plans are drawn to scale using the engi-eer's scale rather than the architect's scale. On nall lots, a scale of 1 inch = 10 feet or 1 inch = 20 et is used. For a 1:10 scale, this means that one ch (the actual measurement on the drawing) is jual to 10 feet on the land itself.

On larger drawings, where a large area must be vered, the scale could be 1 inch = 100 feet or 1 ch = 1,000 feet, or any other integral power of . On drawings with the scale in multiples of 10, e engineer's scale marked 10 is used. If the scale 1 inch = 200 feet, the engineer's scale marked 20 used, and so on.

Although site plans appear reduced in scale, pending on the size of the object and the size of e drawing sheet to be used, the actual dimen-ons must be shown on the drawings at all times.

When you are reading the drawing plans to scale, think of each dimension in its full size and not in the reduced scale it happens to be on the drawing (*Figure 27*).

5.3.0 Metric Scale

Metric scales are calibrated in units of 10 (*Figure 28*). The two common length measurements used in the metric scale or architectural drawings are the meter and the millimeter, the millimeter being ¹⁄₁,₀₀₀ of a meter. On drawings drawn to scales be-tween 1:1 and 1:100, the millimeter is typically used. On drawings drawn to scales between 1:200 and 1:2,000, the meter is generally used. Many con-tracting firms that deal in international trade have adopted a dual-dimensioning system expressed in both metric and English symbols. Drawings pre-pared for government projects may also require metric dimensions. See also *Appendix A*.

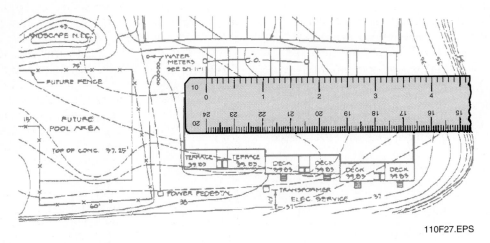

Figure 27 ◆ Practical use of the engineer's scale.

Figure 28 ◆ Typical metric scale.

6.0.0 ◆ ANALYZING ELECTRICAL DRAWINGS

The most practical way to learn how to read electrical construction documents is to analyze an existing set of drawings prepared by consulting or industrial engineers.

Engineers or electrical designers are responsible for the complete layout of electrical systems for most projects. Electrical drafters then transform the engineer's designs into working drawings, using either manual drafting instruments or computer-aided design (CAD) systems. The following is a brief outline of what usually takes place in the preparation of electrical design and working drawings:

- The engineer meets with the architect and owner to discuss the electrical needs of the building or project and to discuss various recommendations made by all parties.
- After that, an outline of the architect's floor plan is laid out.
- The engineer then calculates the required power and lighting outlets for the project; these are later transferred to the working drawings.
- All communications and alarm systems are located on the floor plan, along with lighting and power panelboards.

- Circuit calculations are made to determine wi[re] size and overcurrent protection.
- The main electric service and related com[ponents] ponents are determined and shown on th[e] drawings.
- Schedules are then placed on the drawings identify various pieces of equipment.
- Wiring diagrams are made to show the worke[r] how various electrical components are to [be] connected.
- A legend or electrical symbol list is drafted ar[d] shown on the drawings to identify all symbo[ls] used to indicate electrical outlets or equipmer[t]
- Various large-scale electrical details are i[n]cluded, if necessary, to show exactly what is r[e]quired of the electricians.
- Written specifications are then made to give[?] description of the materials and installatio[n] methods.

6.1.0 Development of Site Plans

In general practice, it is usually the owner's r[e]sponsibility to furnish the architect/engineer wi[th] property and topographic surveys, which a[re] made by a certified land surveyor or civil eng[i]neer. These surveys show:

All property lines
Existing public utilities and their location on or near the property (e.g., electrical lines, sanitary sewer lines, gas lines, water-supply lines, storm sewers, manholes, telephone lines, etc.)

A land surveyor does the property survey from information obtained from a deed description of the property. A property survey shows only the property lines and their lengths, as if the property were perfectly flat.

The topographic survey shows both the property lines and the physical characteristics of the land by using contour lines, notes, and symbols. The physical characteristics may include:

The direction of the land slope
Whether the land is flat, hilly, wooded, swampy, high, or low, and other features of its physical nature

All of this information is necessary so that the architect can properly design a building to fit the property. The electrical engineer also needs this information to locate existing electrical utilities and to route the new service to the building, provide outdoor lighting and circuits, etc.

Electrical site work is sometimes shown on the architect's plot plan. However, when site work involves many trades and several utilities (e.g., gas, telephone, electric, television, water, and sewage), it can become confusing if all details are shown on the drawing sheet. In cases like these, it is best to have a separate drawing devoted entirely to the electrical work, as shown in *Figure 29*. This project is an office/warehouse building for Virginia Electric, Inc. The electrical drawings consist of four 24" × 36" drawing sheets, along with a set of written specifications, which will be discussed later in this module.

The electrical site or plot plan shown in *Figure* has the conventional architect's and engineer's title blocks in the lower right-hand corner of the drawing. These blocks identify the project and project owners, the architect, and the engineer. They also show how this drawing sheet relates to the entire set of drawings. Note the engineer's professional stamp of approval to the left of the engineer's title block. Similar blocks appear on all four of the electrical drawing sheets.

When examining a set of electrical drawings for the first time, always look at the area around the title block. This is where most revision blocks or revision notes are placed. If revisions have been made to the drawings, make certain that you have a clear understanding of what has taken place before proceeding with the work.

Refer again to the drawing in *Figure 29* and note the North Arrow in the upper left corner. A North Arrow shows the direction of true north to help you orient the drawing to the site. Look directly down from the North Arrow to the bottom of the page and notice the drawing title, *Plot Utilities*. Directly beneath the drawing title you can see that the drawing scale of 1" = 30' is shown. This means that each inch on the drawing represents 30 feet on the actual job site. This scale holds true for all drawings on the page unless otherwise noted.

An outline of the proposed building is indicated on the drawing by cross-hatched rectangles along with a callout, *Proposed Bldg. Fin. Flr. Elev. 590.0.* This means that the finished floor level of the building is to be 590 feet above sea level, which in this part of the country will be about two feet above finished grade around the building. This information helps the electrician locate conduit sleeves and stub-ups to the correct height before the finished concrete floor is poured.

The shaded area represents asphalt paving for the access road, drives, and parking lot. Note that the access road leads into a highway, which is designated Route 35. This information further helps workers to orient the drawing to the building site.

Existing manholes are indicated by a solid circle, while an open circle is used to show the position of the five new pole-mounted lighting fixtures that are to be installed around the new building. Existing power lines are shown with a light solid line with the letter E placed at intervals along the line. The new underground electric service is shown in the same way, except the lines are somewhat wider and darker on the drawing. Note that this new high-voltage cable terminates into a padmount transformer near the proposed building. New telephone lines are similar except the letter T is used to identify the telephone lines.

The direct-burial underground cable supplying the exterior lighting fixtures is indicated with dashed lines on the drawing—shown connecting the open circles. A homerun for this circuit is also shown to a time clock.

The manhole detail shown to the right of the North Arrow may seem to serve very little purpose on this drawing since the manholes have already been installed. However, the dimensions and details of their construction will help the electrical contractor or supervisor to better plan the pulling of the high-voltage cable. The same is true of the cross section shown of the duct bank. The electrical contractor knows that three empty ducts are available if it is discovered that one of them is damaged when the work begins.

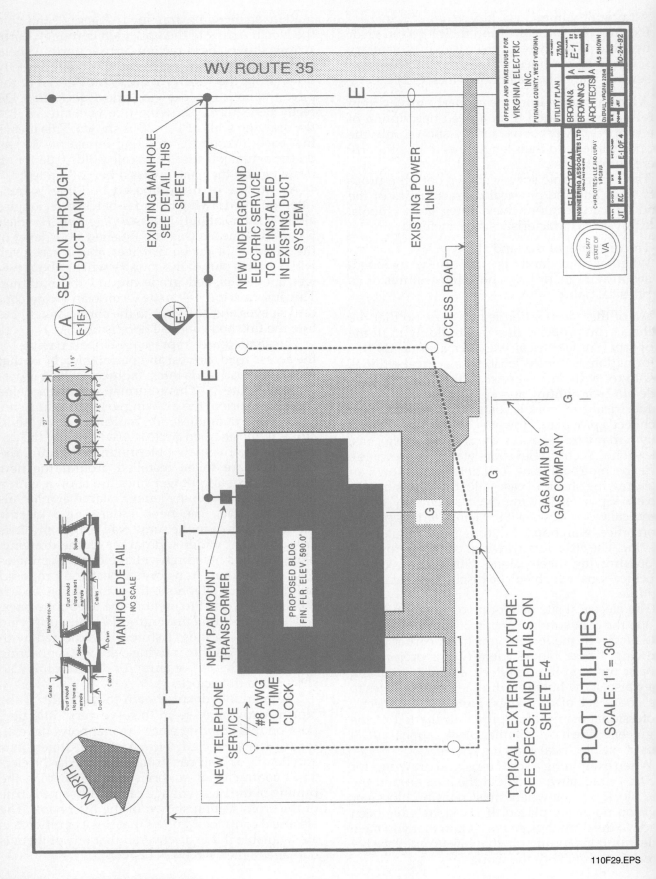

Figure 29 ◆ Typical electrical site plan.

110F29.EPS

Interpreting Site Plans

Study *Figure 29* and explain as many of its features as you can. How much can be understood using common sense? What features require special information?

Although the electrical work will not involve working with gas, the main gas line is shown on the electrical drawing to let the electrical workers know its approximate location while they are installing the direct-burial conductors for the exterior lighting fixtures.

0.0 ◆ POWER PLANS

The electrical power plan (*Figure 30*) shows the complete floor plan of the office/warehouse building with all interior partitions drawn to scale. Sometimes, the physical locations of all wiring and outlets are shown on one drawing; that is, outlets for lighting, power, signal and com-

munications, special electrical systems, and related equipment are shown on the same plan. However, on complex installations, the drawing would become cluttered if both lighting and power were shown on the same floor plan. Therefore, most projects will have a separate drawing for power and another for lighting. Riser diagrams and details may be shown on yet another drawing sheet, or if room permits, they may be shown on the lighting or power floor plan sheets.

A closer look at this drawing reveals the title blocks in the lower right corner of the drawing sheet. These blocks list both the architectural and engineering firms, along with information to identify the project and drawing sheet. Also note

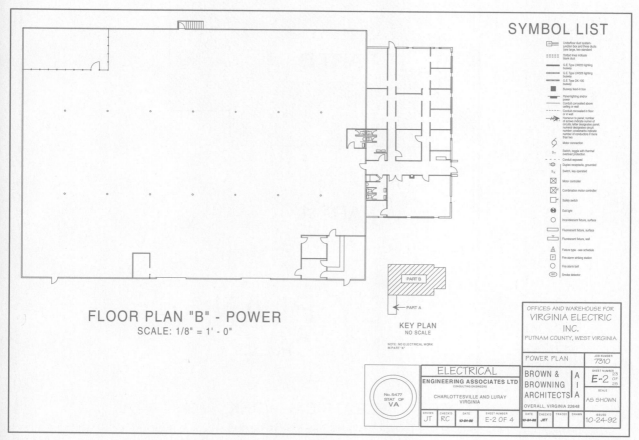

Figure 30 ◆ Electrical power plan.

110F30.EPS

that the floor plan is titled *Floor Plan "B"—Power* and is drawn to a scale of ⅛" = 1'–0". There are no revisions shown on this drawing sheet.

7.1.0 Key Plan

A key plan appears on the drawing sheet immediately above the engineer's title block (*Figure 31*). The purpose of this key plan is to identify that part of the project to which this sheet applies. In this case, the project involves two buildings: Building A and Building B. Since the outline of Building B is cross-hatched in the key plan, this is the building to which this drawing applies. Note that this key plan is not drawn to scale—only its approximate shape.

Although Building A is also shown on this key plan, a note below the key plan title states that there is no electrical work required in Building A.

On some larger installations, the overall project may involve several buildings requiring appropriate key plans on each drawing to help the workers orient the drawings to the appropriate building. In some cases, separate drawing sheets

may be used for each room or area in an industri[al] project—again requiring key plans on each draw[-]ing sheet to identify applicable drawings for eac[h] room.

7.2.0 Symbol List

A symbol list appears on the electrical power pla[n] (immediately above the architect's title block) [to] identify the various symbols used for both pow[er] and lighting on this project. In most cases, the on[ly] symbols listed are those that apply to the partic[u-]lar project. In other cases, however, a standard li[st] of symbols is used for all projects with the follow[-]ing note:

These are standard symbols and may not all appe[ar] on the project drawings; however, wherever the symb[ol] on the project drawings occurs, the item shall be pr[o-]vided and installed.

Only electrical symbols that are actually use[d] for the office/warehouse drawings are show[n] in the list on the example electrical power pla[n.] A close-up look at these symbols appears [in] *Figure 32.*

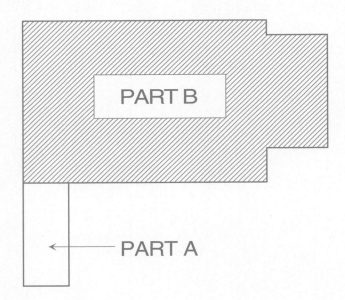

KEY PLAN
NO SCALE

NOTE: NO ELECTRICAL WORK
IN PART "A"

110F31.EPS

Figure 31 ◆ Key plan appearing on electrical power plan.

JB	Underfloor duct system – junction box and three ducts (one large, two standard)	··········	Conduit exposed
☰☰☰	Dotted lines indicate blank duct	⊖	Duplex receptacle, grounded
	G.E. Type LW223 lighting busway	S_K	Switch, key operated
	G.E. Type LW326 lighting busway	⊠	Motor controller
	G.E. Type DK-100 busway	⊠⊣	Combination motor controller
■	Busway feed-in box	⊓	Safety switch
▬	Panel-lighting and/or power	⊗	Exit light
	Conduit concealed above ceiling or wall	○	Incandescent fixture, surface
	Conduit concealed in floor or in wall	▭	Fluorescent fixture, surface
➤➤ A-1	Homerun to panel; number of arrows indicates number of circuits; letter designates panel; numeral designates circuit number; crossmarks indicate number of conductors if more than two	⊤	Fluorescent fixture, wall
⌀	Motor connection	Ⓐ	Fixture type – see schedule
		F	Fire alarm striking station
S_T	Switch, toggle with thermal overload protection	○	Fire alarm bell
		SD	Smoke detector

110F32.EPS

Figure 32 ◆ Sample electrical symbols list.

.3.0 Floor Plan

somewhat enlarged view of the electrical floor an drawing is shown in *Figure 33*. However, due the size of the drawing in comparison with the size of the pages in this module, it is still difficult to see very much detail. This illustration is meant to show the overall layout of the floor plan and how the symbols and notes are arranged.

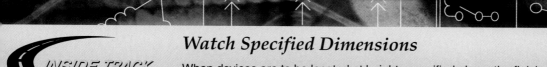

Watch Specified Dimensions

When devices are to be located at heights specified above the finished floor (AFF), be sure to find out the actual height of the flooring to be installed. Some materials, such as ceramic tile, can add significantly to the height of the finished floor.

Power Plans

Study *Figure 33*. Where does the power enter, and how is it distributed and controlled? What is meant by each of the symbols and lines? Is every electrical connection marked or are some left to the discretion of the electrician?

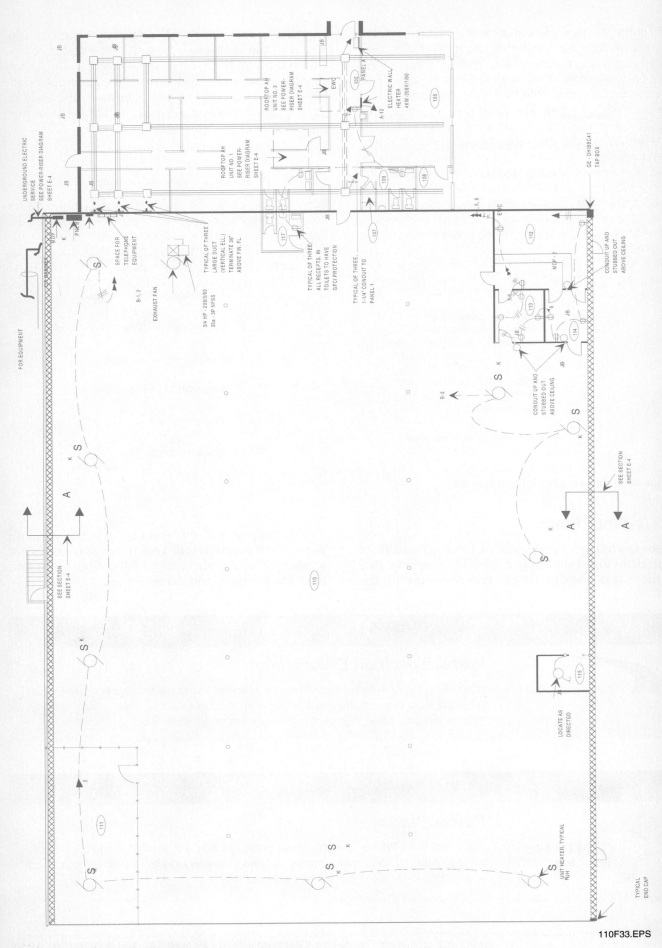

Figure 33 ◆ Power plan for office/warehouse building.

110F33.EPS

In general, this plan shows the service equipment (in plan view), receptacles, underfloor duct system, motor connections, motor controllers, electric heat, busways, and similar details. The electric panels and other service equipment are drawn close to scale. The locations of other electrical outlets and similar components are only approximated on the drawings because they have to be exaggerated to show up on the prints. To illustrate, a common duplex receptacle is only about three inches wide. If such a receptacle were to be located on the floor plan of this building (drawn at a scale of ⅛" = 1'–0"), even a small dot on the drawing would be too large to draw the receptacle exactly to scale. Therefore, the receptacle symbol is exaggerated. When such receptacles are scaled on the drawings to determine the proper

location, a measurement is usually taken to the center of the symbol to determine the distance between outlets. Junction boxes, switches, and other electrical connections shown on the floor plan will be exaggerated in a similar manner. The partial floor plan drawing in *Figure 34* allows a better view of the drawing details.

7.3.1 Notes and Building Symbols

Referring again to *Figure 33*, you will notice numbers placed inside an oval symbol in each room. These numbered ovals represent the room name or type and correspond to a room schedule in the architectural drawings. For example, room number 112 is designated as the lobby in the room

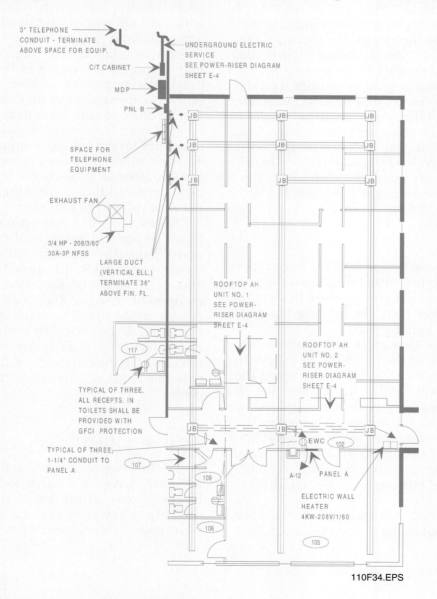

110F34.EPS

Figure 34 ◆ Partial floor plan for office/warehouse building.

Reading Notes

The notes are crucial elements of the drawing set. Receptacles, for example, are hard to position precisely based on a scaled drawing alone, and yet the designer may call for exact locations. For example, the designer may want receptacles exactly 6" above the kitchen counter backsplash and centered on the sink.

schedule (not shown), room number 113 is designated as office No. 1, etc. On some drawings, these room symbols are omitted and the room names are written out on the drawings.

There are also several notes appearing at various places on the floor plan. These notes offer additional information to clarify certain aspects of the drawing. For example, only one electric heater is to be installed by the electrical contractor; this heater is located in the building's vestibule. Rather than have a symbol in the symbol list for this one heater, a note is used to identify it on the drawing. Other notes on this drawing describe how certain parts of the system are to be installed. For example, in the office area (rooms 112, 113, and 114), you will see the following note: *CONDUIT UP AND STUBBED OUT ABOVE CEILING.* This empty conduit is for telephone/communications cables that will be installed later by the telephone company.

7.3.2 Busways

The office/warehouse project utilizes three types of busways: two types of lighting busways and one power busway. Only the power busway is shown on the power plan; the lighting busways will appear on the lighting plan.

Figure 33 shows two runs of busways: one running the length of the building on the south end (top wall on drawing), and one running the length of the north wall. The symbol list in *Figure 32* shows this busway to be designated by two parallel lines with a series of X's inside. The symbol list further describes the busway as General Electric Type DK-100. These busways are fed from the main distribution panel (circuits MDP-1 and MDP-2) through GE No. DHIBBC41 tap boxes.

The *NEC®* defines a busway as a grounded metal enclosure containing factory-mounted, bare

or insulated conductors, which are usually copper or aluminum bars, rods, or tubes.

The relationship of the busway and hangers the building construction should be checked prior to commencing the installation so that any problems due to space conflicts, inadequate or inappropriate supporting structure, openings through walls, etc. are worked out in advance so as not to incur lost time.

For example, the drawings and specifications may call for the busway to be suspended from brackets clamped or welded to steel columns. However, the spacing of the columns may be such that additional supplementary hanger rods suspended from the ceiling or roof structure may be necessary for the adequate support of the busway. To offer more assistance to workers on the office/warehouse project, the engineer may also provide an additional drawing that shows how the busway is to be mounted.

Other details that appear on the floor plan Figure 34 include the general arrangement of the underfloor duct system, junction boxes and feeder conduit for the underfloor duct system, and plan views of the service and telephone equipment, along with duplex receptacle outlets. A note on the drawing requires all receptacles the toilets to be provided with ground fault circuit interrupter (GFCI) protection. The letters EWC next to the receptacle in the vestibule designate this receptacle for use with an electric water cooler.

8.0.0 ◆ LIGHTING FLOOR PLAN

A skeleton view of a lighting floor plan is shown in *Figure 35*. Again, the architect's/engineer's title blocks appear in the lower right corner of the drawing. A key plan, as discussed previously, appears above the engineer's title block. This plan

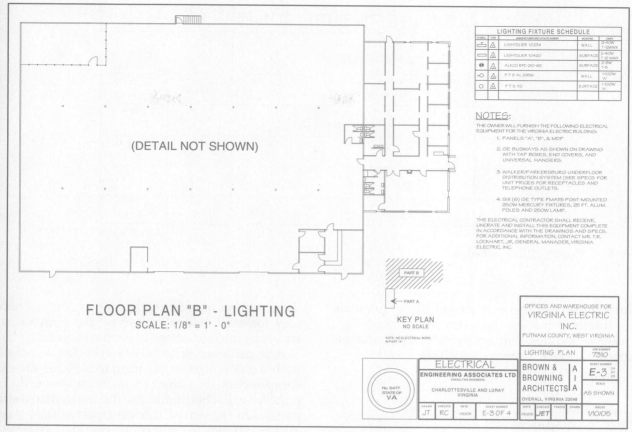

(DETAIL NOT SHOWN)

FLOOR PLAN "B" - LIGHTING
SCALE: 1/8" = 1' - 0"

LIGHTING FIXTURE SCHEDULE

SYMBOL	TYPE	MANUFACTURER AND CATALOG NUMBER	MOUNTING	LAMPS
		LIGHTOLIER 10234	WALL	2-40W T-12WWX
		LIGHTOLIER 10420	SURFACE	2-40W T-12 WWX
		ALKCO RPC-20-6E	SURFACE	2-8W T-8
		F 7 S AL 2356	WALL	1-100W 'A'
O		F 7 S 110	SURFACE	1-100W 'A'

NOTES:

THE OWNER WILL FURNISH THE FOLLOWING ELECTRICAL EQUIPMENT FOR THE VIRGINIA ELECTRIC BUILDING:

1. PANELS "A", "B", & MDP

2. GE BUSWAYS AS SHOWN ON DRAWING WITH TAP BOXES, END COVERS, AND UNIVERSAL HANGERS.

3. WALKER/PARKERSBURG UNDERFLOOR DISTRIBUTION SYSTEM (SEE SPECS FOR UNIT PRICES FOR RECEPTACLES AND TELEPHONE OUTLETS.

4. SIX (6) GE TYPE PMA115 POST-MOUNTED 250W MERCURY FIXTURES, 25 FT. ALUM. POLES AND 250W LAMP.

THE ELECTRICAL CONTRACTOR SHALL RECEIVE, UNCRATE AND INSTALL THIS EQUIPMENT COMPLETE IN ACCORDANCE WITH THE DRAWINGS AND SPECS. FOR ADDITIONAL INFORMATION, CONTACT MR. T.R. LOCKHART, JR, GENERAL MANAGER, VIRGINIA ELECTRIC, INC.

PART B

PART A

KEY PLAN
NO SCALE

NOTE: NO ELECTRICAL WORK IN PART "A"

OFFICES AND WAREHOUSE FOR
VIRGINIA ELECTRIC INC.
PUTNAM COUNTY, WEST VIRGINIA

| LIGHTING PLAN | JOB NUMBER 7310 |

ELECTRICAL ENGINEERING ASSOCIATES LTD CONSULTING ENGINEERS CHARLOTTESVILLE AND LURAY VIRGINIA	BROWN & BROWNING ARCHITECTS OVERALL, VIRGINIA 22648

No. 5477 STATE OF VA

SHEET NUMBER E-3 24 OF 20
SCALE AS SHOWN

| DRAWN JT | CHECKED RC | DATE 1/10/05 | SHEET NUMBER E-3 OF 4 |

| DATE | CHECKO | TRACED | DRAWN JET |
| ISSUED 1/10/05 |

110F35.EPS

Figure 35 ◆ Sample lighting plan.

...rawn to the same scale as the power plan; that is, ... = 1'-0". A lighting fixture schedule appears in ...e upper right corner of the drawing and some ...stallation notes appear below the schedule.

The lighting outlet symbols found on the draw-...g for the office/warehouse building represent ...th incandescent and fluorescent types; a circle ... most electrical drawings usually represents an ...candescent fixture, and a rectangle represents a ...uorescent one. All of these symbols are designed ... indicate the physical shape of a particular fix-...re and are usually drawn to scale.

The type of mounting used for all lighting fix-...res is usually indicated in a lighting fixture ...hedule, which in this case is shown on the draw-...gs. On some projects, the schedule may be ...und only in the written specifications.

The type of lighting fixture is identified by a ...meral placed inside a triangle near each light-...g fixture. If one type of fixture is used exclu-...vely in one room or area, the triangular indicator ...ed only appear once with the word ALL lettered ... the bottom of the triangle.

8.1.0 Drawing Schedules

A schedule is a systematic method of presenting notes or lists of equipment on a drawing in tabular form. When properly organized and thoroughly understood, schedules are powerful timesaving devices for both those preparing the drawings and workers on the job.

For example, the lighting fixture schedule shown in *Figure 36* lists the fixture and identifies each fixture type on the drawing by number. The manufacturer and catalog number of each type are given along with the number, size, and type of lamp for each.

At times, all of the same information found in schedules will be duplicated in the written specifications, but combing through page after page of written specifications can be time consuming, and workers do not always have access to the specifications while working, whereas they usually do have access to the working drawings. Therefore, the schedule is an excellent means of providing essential information in a clear and accurate

LIGHTING FIXTURE SCHEDULE

SYMBOL	TYPE	MANUFACTURER AND CATALOG NUMBER	MOUNTING	LAMPS
⊢—T—⊣	Ⓐ	LIGHTOLIER 10234	WALL	2-40W T-12WWX
▭	Ⓑ	LIGHTOLIER 10420	SURFACE	2-40W T-12 WWX
⊗	Ⓒ	ALKCO RPC-210-6E	SURFACE	2-8W T-5
⊢○	Ⓓ	P 7 S AL 2936	WALL	1-100W 'A'
○	Ⓔ	P 7 S 110	SURFACE	1-100W 'A'

110F36.EPS

Figure 36 ◆ Lighting fixture schedule.

manner, allowing the workers to carry out their assignments in the least amount of time.

Other schedules that are frequently found on electrical working drawings include:

- Connected load schedule
- Panelboard schedule
- Electric heat schedule
- Kitchen equipment schedule
- Schedule of receptacle types

There are also other schedules found on electrical drawings, depending upon the type of project. However, most will deal with lists of equipment such as motors, motor controllers, and similar items.

9.0.0 ◆ ELECTRICAL DETAILS AND DIAGRAMS

Electrical diagrams are drawings that are intended to show electrical components and their related connections. They show the electrical association of the different components, but are seldom, if ever, drawn to scale.

9.1.0 Power-Riser Diagrams

One-line (single-line) block diagrams are used extensively to show the arrangement of electric service equipment. The power-riser diagram in *Figure 37*, for example, was used on the office/warehouse building under discussion and is typical of such drawings. The drawing shows all pieces of electrical equipment as well as the connecting lines used to indicate service-entrance conductors and feeders. Notes are used to identify

the equipment, indicate the size of conduit nece sary for each feeder, and show the number, siz and type of conductors in each conduit.

A panelboard schedule (*Figure 38*) is include with the power-riser diagram to indicate the exa components contained in each panelboard. Th panelboard schedule is for the main distributic panel. On the actual drawings, schedules wou also be shown for the other two panels (PNL and PNL B).

In general, panelboard schedules usually ind cate the panel number, type of cabinet (eith flush- or surface-mounted), panel mains (ampe and voltage rating), phase (single- or thre phase), and number of wires. A four-wire pane for example, indicates that a solid neutral exists the panel. Branches indicate the type of overcu rent protection; that is, they indicate the numb of poles, trip rating, and frame size. The items f by each overcurrent device are also indicated.

9.2.0 Schematic Diagrams

Complete schematic wiring diagrams are no mally used only in complicated electrical system such as control circuits. Components are repr sented by symbols, and every wire is either show by itself or included in an assembly of sever wires, which appear as one line on the drawin Each wire should be numbered when it enters a assembly and should keep the same numbe when it comes out again to be connected to son electrical component in the system. *Figure* shows a complete schematic wiring diagram for three-phase, AC magnetic non-reversing mot starter.

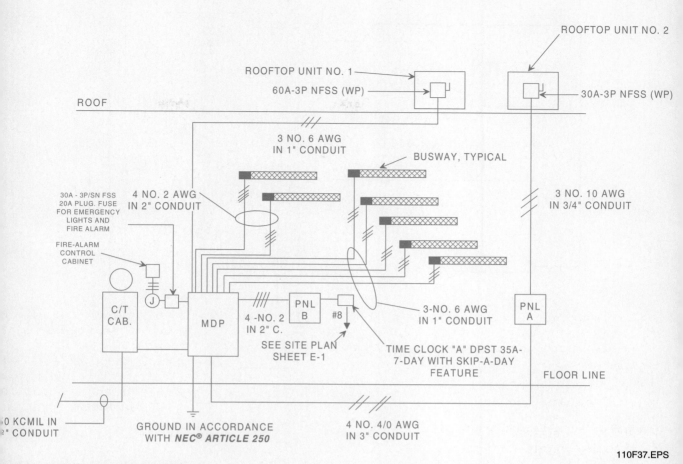

Figure 37 ◆ Typical power-riser diagram.

PANELBOARD SCHEDULE

PANEL No.	CABINET TYPE	PANEL MAINS			BRANCHES					ITEMS FED OR REMARKS
		AMPS	VOLTS	PHASE	1P	2P	3P	PROT.	FRAME	
MDP	SURFACE	600A	120/208	3φ,4-W	-	-	1	225A	25,000	PANEL "A"
					-	-	1	100A	18,000	PANEL "B"
					-	-	1	100A		POWER BUSWAY
					-	-	1	60A		LIGHTING BUSWAY
					-	-	1	70A		ROOFTOP UNIT #1
					-	-	1	70A	↓	SPARE
					-	-	1	600A	42,000	MAIN CIRCUIT BRKR

110F38.EPS

Figure 38 ◆ Typical panelboard schedule.

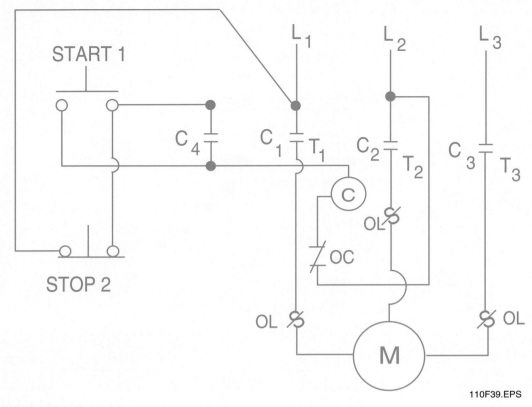

110F39.EPS

Figure 39 ◆ Wiring diagram.

Note that this diagram shows the various devices in symbol form and indicates the actual connections of all wires between the devices. The three-wire supply lines are indicated by L_1, L_2, and L_3; the motor terminals of motor M are indicated by T_1, T_2, and T_3. Lines L_1, L_2, and L_3 each have a thermal overload protection device (OL) connected in series with normally open line contacts C_1 and C_3, respectively, which are both controlled by the magnetic starter coil, C. The control station, consisting of start pushbutton 1 and stop pushbutton 2, is connected across lines L_1 and L_2. Auxiliary contacts (C_4) are connected in series with the stop pushbutton and in parallel with the start pushbutton. The control circuit also has normally closed overload contacts (OC) connected in series with the magnetic starter coil (C).

Any number of additional pushbutton stations may be added to this control circuit similarly to the way in which three-way and four-way switches are added to control a lighting circuit. When adding pushbutton stations, the stop buttons are always connected in series and the start buttons are always connected in parallel. *Figure 40* shows the same motor starter circuit in *Figure 39*, but this time it is controlled by two sets of start/stop buttons.

Schematic wiring diagrams have only been touched upon in this module; there are many other details that you will need to know to perform your work in a proficient manner. Later modules cover wiring diagrams in more detail.

9.3.0 Drawing Details

A detail drawing is a drawing of a separate item or portion of an electrical system, giving a complete and exact description of its use and all the details needed to show the electrician exactly what is required for its installation. For example, the power plan for the office/warehouse has a sectional cut through the busduct. This is a good example of where an extra, detailed drawing is desirable.

A set of electrical drawings will sometimes require large-scale drawings of certain areas that are not indicated with sufficient clarity on the small-scale drawings. For example, the site plan may show exterior pole-mounted lighting fixtures that are to be installed by the contractor.

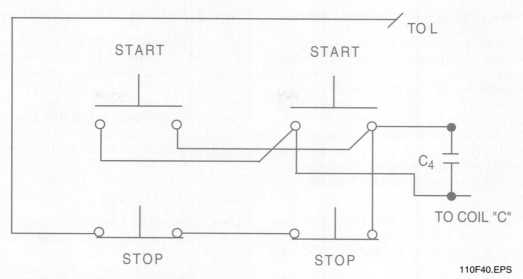

110F40.EPS

Figure 40 ◆ Circuit being controlled by two sets of start/stop buttons.

Understanding Contact Symbols

When a drawing shows normally open or normally closed contacts, the word normally refers to the condition of the contacts in their de-energized or shelf state.

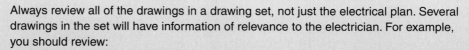

Don't Just Check the Electrical Plan

Always review all of the drawings in a drawing set, not just the electrical plan. Several drawings in the set will have information of relevance to the electrician. For example, you should review:

- Site plans for utility lines and elevation information
- Mechanical drawings for routing, clearances, and HVAC equipment and controls
- Architectural drawings for the type of construction (block, wood, metal stud, etc.), fire ratings, and special details.
- Finish drawings (e.g., reflected ceiling plans) for locations of fixtures, fans, and other devices
- Room finish schedules for ceiling heights and floor and wall finishing details
- Plumbing drawings for pumps, water service, and sprinklers

10.0.0 ◆ WRITTEN SPECIFICATIONS

The written specifications for a building or project are the written descriptions of work and duties required of the owner, architect, and consulting engineer. Together with the working drawings, these specifications form the basis of the contract requirements for the construction of the building or project. Those who use the construction drawings and specifications must always be alert to discrepancies between the working drawings and the written specifications. Such discrepancies may occur when:

- Architects or engineers use standard or prototype specifications and attempt to apply them without any modification to specific working drawings.
- Previously prepared standard drawings are changed or amended by reference in the specifications only and the drawings themselves are not changed.
- Items are duplicated in both the drawings and specifications, but an item is subsequently amended in one and overlooked in the other contract document.

In such instances, the person in charge of the project has the responsibility to ascertain whether the drawings or the specifications take precedence. Such questions must be resolved, preferably before the work begins, to avoid added cost to the owner, architect/engineer, or contractor.

10.1.0 How Specifications Are Written

Writing accurate and complete specifications for building construction is a serious responsibility for those who design the buildings because the specifications, combined with the working drawings, govern practically all important decisions made during the construction span of every project. Compiling and writing these specifications is not a simple task, even for those who have had considerable experience in preparing such documents. A set of written specifications for a single project will usually contain thousands of products, parts, and components, and the methods of installing them, all of which must be covered in either the drawings and/or specifications. No one can memorize all of the necessary items required to accurately describe the various areas of construction. One must rely upon reference materials such as manufacturer's data, catalogs, checklists, and, most of all, a high-quality master specification.

10.2.0 Format of Specifications

For convenience in writing, speed in estimating and ease of reference, the most suitable organization of the specifications is a series of sections dealing successively with the different trades. All the work of each trade should be incorporated into the section devoted to that trade. Those people who use the specifications must be able to find all information needed without spending too much time looking for it.

10.2.1 CSI Format

The Construction Specification Institute (CSI) has developed the Uniform Construction Index which allows all specifications, product information, and cost data to be arranged into a uniform system. This format is followed on most large construction projects in North America. All construction is divided into 16 divisions, and each division has several sections and subsections. The following outline describes the various divisions normally included in a set of specifications for building construction.

Division 1: General Requirements – This division summarizes the work, alternatives, project meetings, submissions, quality control, temporary facilities and controls, products, and the project closeout. Every responsible person involved with the project should become familiar with this division.

Division 2: Site Work – This division outlines work involving such items as paving, sidewalks, outside utility lines (electrical, plumbing, gas, telephone, etc.), landscaping, grading, and other items pertaining to the outside of the building.

Division 3: Concrete – This division covers work involving footings, concrete formwork, expansion and contraction joints, cast-in-place concrete, specially finished concrete, precast concrete, concrete slabs, and similar items.

Division 4: Masonry – This division covers concrete, mortar, stone, masonry accessories, and similar items.

Division 5: Metals – Metal roofs, structural metal framing, metal joists, metal decking, ornamental metal, and expansion control normally fall under this division.

Division 6: Carpentry – Items falling under this division include rough carpentry, heavy timber construction, trestles, prefabricated structural wood, finish carpentry, wood treatment, architectural woodwork, and the like. Plastic fabrication may also be included in this division.

Division 7: Thermal and Moisture Protection – Waterproofing is the main topic discussed under this division. Other related items such as dampproofing, building insulation, shingles and roofing tiles, preformed roofing and siding, membrane roofing, sheet metal work, wall flashing, roof accessories, and sealants are also included.

Division 8: Doors and Windows – All types of doors and frames are included under this division: metal, plastic, wood, etc. Windows and framing are also included, along with hardware and other window and door accessories.

Division 9: Finishes – Included in this division are the types, quality, and workmanship of lath and plaster, gypsum wallboard, tile, terrazzo, acoustical treatment, ceiling suspension systems, wood flooring, floor treatment, special coatings, painting, and wallcovering.

Division 10: Specialties – Specialty items such as chalkboards and tackboards, compartments and cubicles, louvers and vents that are not connected with the mechanical system, wall and corner guards, access flooring, specialty modules, pest control, fireplaces, flagpoles, identifying devices, lockers, protective covers, postal specialties, partitions, scales, storage shelving, wardrobe specialties, and similar items are covered in this division of the specifications.

Division 11: Equipment – The equipment included in this division could include central vacuum cleaning systems, bank vaults, darkrooms, food service, vending machines, laundry equipment, and many similar items.

Division 12: Furnishing – Items such as cabinets and storage files, fabrics, furniture, rugs and mats, seating, and similar furnishings are included under this division.

Division 13: Special Construction – Such items as air-supported structures, incinerators, and other special items will fall under this division.

Division 14: Conveying Systems – This division covers conveying apparatus such as dumbwaiters, elevators, hoists and cranes, lifts, material-handling systems, turntables, moving stairs and walks, pneumatic tube systems, and power scaffolding.

Division 15: Mechanical – This division includes plumbing, heating, ventilating, and air conditioning and related work. Electric heat is sometimes covered under Division 16, especially if individual baseboard heating units are used in each room or area of the building.

Division 16: Electrical – This division covers all electrical requirements for the building including lighting, power, alarm and communications systems, special electrical systems, and related electrical equipment. This is the division that electricians will use the most.

A sample set of electrical specifications is shown in *Figure 41*.

NOTE

In June 2004, CSI issued a new specification format (see *Appendix B*) but it was not in common use at the time of this revision. Be aware that future specifications will follow this new format.

NOTE

The above specifications refer to color coding. Please refer to *NEC Sections 200.6 and 210.5(C)* for specific requirements.

Putting It All Together

Study the specifications in *Figure 41*. How would you need to combine information from the drawings and the written specifications to create a finished installation?

1 <u>SECTION 16011 - ELECTRICAL OUTLINE OF WORK</u>
2
3 <u>PART 1 - GENERAL</u>
4
5
6 The work included in Division 16 electrical includes, but is not necessarily limited to the following
7 items and systems:
8
9 .   Two new 480/277 volt, 3 phase underground services from Duke Power Company pad
10   mounted transformer.
11 .   Connection to power company transformers.
12 .   Concrete pad for power company transformers.
13 .   Installation of new power company meter box.
14 .   All coordination, labor and materials required to connect new chiller service to existing
15   Duke Power Company pad mounted transformer.
16 .   Motor control center.
17 .   Lighting and receptacle panelboard.
18 .   Feeder circuits, including conduits, conductors, troughs and fittings.
19 .   Branch circuits, including conduits, conductors, outlets, boxes, receptacles, switches and
20   fittings.
21 .   Lighting fixtures including lamps.
22 .   Equipment tests.
23 .   Wiring devices
24 .   Grounding systems.
25 .   Safety switches.
26 .   Power connection to all equipment requiring power.
27 .   Provide new lay-in ceiling in corridor of Building 'B'.
28 .   Remove existing ceiling in part of Guidance Area of Building 'A' and provide new lay-in
29   ceiling throughout the entire Guidance Area.
30
31
32 END OF SECTION
33

16011-1

110F41A.T

Figure 41 ◆ Sample electrical specifications (1 of 12).

SECTION 16110 - RACEWAYS

PART 1 - GENERAL:

GENERAL

All wiring shall be in rigid metal conduit, 'RMC', except as otherwise noted.

Electric metallic tubing 'EMT' may be used for concealed and exposed work, except as listed below.

> (1) Exposed to the weather, or in damp location.
> (2) In earth or stone.
> (3) In concrete slabs on grade.
> (4) Where obviously subject to mechanical injury.
> (5) Where specified otherwise.

EMT may be used in lieu of 'RMC' in the following sizes, 1/2 inch through 2-inch for power circuits, 1/2 inch through 4 inch for communications circuits and control wiring as applicable, subject to the use limitations specified above. Intermediate metal conduit 'IMC' may be used for 'RMC'.

Rigid non-metallic conduit (RNC) may be used in in the following applications only. (All stub-ups shall be 'RMC' or 'IMC' elbows.)

> Below slab, encased all around in not less than three inches of concrete and not less than 18 inches of ground cover for power service and power feeders, under building. Except, that conduit under building foundation, or conduit run through footings or foundations, shall be rigid steel conduit.

> Underground, buried not less than 30" below grade for area lighting circuits.

> In concrete slab on grade for branch circuits utilizing 3/4 inch or smaller conduit when encased by at least 2-inches of concrete all around.

Flexible metallic conduit shall not be used as a wiring method, other than when specifically noted to be used, without prior permission of the Architect/Engineer.

Type AC (BX) armored cable is not permitted in this project.

SLEEVES AND PENETRATIONS:

See Section 16115 for required sleeves and method of achieving raceway penetrations.

APPLICABLE SPECIFICATIONS AND STANDARDS:

The materials specified here shall meet the following specifications and standards in their current edition.

16110-1

110F41B.TIF

Figure 41 ◆ Sample electrical specifications (2 of 12).

        (1) UL Standards

                Electric metallic Tubing
                Flexible Metal Conduits-UL-1
                Rigid Metal Conduit UL-6
                Intermediate Metal Conduit UL-1242

        (2) NEMA Standards

                Electric plastic conduit-TC-2

        (3) ANSI Standards

                Specifications for Rigid Steel Conduit, Zinc Coated,
                ANSI C80.1.

PART 2 - PRODUCTS:

RACEWAYS:

General: Minimum size conduit shall be 1/2 inch.

Rigid Metal Conduit:

Rigid metal conduit shall be schedule 40, of the best quality steel.

The interior and exterior surfaces of the conduit shall be protected with a metallic zinc coating. Rigid steel conduit shall be galvanized by the Hot-Dip process in accordance with ASTM A 123.

Fittings for 'RMC' shall be threaded UL listed.

Electric Metallic Tubing:

Electrical metallic tubing shall be rigid metal conduit of the thin-wall type in straight lengths, elbows or bends for use as raceways for wire or cables in an electrical system.

 Electrical metallic tubing shall utilize hexagonal steel type compression threadless fittings of galvanized steel throughout. All fittings shall be UL listed for concrete-tight and rain-tight construction. All EMT entrance fittings shall be provided with insulated throats.

Flexible Metallic Conduit:

Flexible metallic conduit shall conform to UL standard 'Flexible Steel Conduit'. All steel used in the fabrication of the conduit shall be zinc coated.

Liquid-tight flexible steel conduit shall be provided with a protective jacket of polyvinyl chloride extruded over a flexible interlocked galvanized steel core to protect wiring against moisture, oil, chemicals and corrosive fumes.

Flexible conduit connectors shall be UL listed T & B nylon-insulated "Tite-Bite", or equivalent from "Blackhawk.'

16110-2

110F41C.TIF

Figure 41 ◆ Sample electrical specifications (3 of 12).

Rigid Non-Metallic Conduit:

Schedule 40 (EPC-40), heavy wall polyvinyl chloride plastic conduit and fittings, UL listed, suitable for 90 degree C. conductors.

Minimum size RNC conduit shall be 3/4-inch.

Intermediate Metal Conduit:

Intermediate metal conduit 'IMC' shall be zinc coated steel, UL listed and labeled.

Fittings shall be the same type as for 'RMC.'

Wireways and Troughs:

Wireways or troughs shall be of the size noted on the drawings or as required by the NEC of code gauge galvanized steel. Sizes 6 inch x 6 inch and smaller wireways and all troughs shall be of the hinged cover type except as otherwise noted on the drawings. Larger sized wireways shall be of the flangeless screw cover lay-in type. All shall be without knockout, and shall be provided with fittings, supports, and apurtenances as required.

PART 3 - EXECUTION:

INSTALLATION OF CONDUIT AND TUBING:

Metallic raceways shall not be stored exposed to the weather.

Conduits shall be concealed within the walls, ceilings, and floors, where possible, and shall be kept at least 6 inches from parallel runs of flues, steam pipes, or hot water pipes. Exposed runs of conduit or tubing, and conduit or tubing run above suspended ceilings, shall have supports spaced not more than 8 feet apart and shall be installed with runs parallel or perpendicular to walls, structural members, or intersections of vertical planes and ceilings with right-angle turns consisting of cast metal fittings or symmetrical bends. All raceways shall be run in a neat and orderly fashion. Conduits or tubing run in diagonal or disorganized way shall be removed from the premises if so instructed by the A/E. Bends and offsets shall be avoided where possible, but where necessary shall be made with an approved hickey or conduit bending machine. Conduit or tubing which has been crushed or deformed in any way shall not be installed.

Conduit and tubing shall be supported on approved types of galvanized wall brackets, ceiling trapezes, strap hangers, or pipe straps, secured by means of toggle bolts on hollow masonry units, expansion bolts in concrete or brick, machine screws on metal surfaces, and wood screws on wood construction. Nails shall not be used as the means of fastening boxes on conduits. Wooden plugs inserted in masonry or concrete shall not be used as a base to secure conduit supports.

Conduits shall be installed in such manner as to insure against trouble from the collection of trapped condensation, and all runs of conduit shall be arranged so as to be devoid of traps where feasible. The contractor shall exercise the necessary precautions to prevent the lodgment of dirt, plaster, or trash in conduit, tubing, fittings, and boxes during the course of installation by the use of T & B pushpennies, appleton pennies, or equal closures. A run of conduit or tubing which has become clogged shall be entirely freed of these accumulations or shall be replaced.

16110-3

110F41D.TIF

Figure 41 ◆ Sample electrical specifications (4 of 12).

1	Conduit shall be securely fastened to all sheet metal enclosures with double galvanized locknuts
2	and insulated bushings, care being observed to see that full number of threads project through to
3	permit the bushing to be drawn tight against the end of conduit, after which the locknuts shall be
4	made up sufficiently tight to insure positive ground continuity between conduit and box.
5	
6	Double locknuts shall be used on all feeder and motor circuit conduits and where insulated
7	bushings are used. Insulated bushings of molded bakelite shall be used on all conduit entrances,
8	one inch over in size, into junction boxes, panel boxes and motors starters having sheet metal
9	enclosures. Galvanized steel insulated throat fittings shall be used for EMT work.
10	
11	Rigid metal conduit 'RMC' installed underground 5 feet or more from the building shall have a
12	minimum cover of three feet. 'RMC' directly installed underground shall be coated with two coats
13	of bitumastic or asphalt paint. Conduit installed underground or in concrete on ground shall be
14	made watertight by wrapping the joints with 'Teflon' tape.
15	
16	EXPANSION FITTINGS:
17	
18	Conduit crossing expansion joints in concrete slabs shall be provided with suitable expansion
19	fittings, or other suitable means shall be provided to compensate for the building expansion and
20	contraction.
21	
22	PULL WIRE:
23	
24	Nylon pull wire not less than 5/32 inches in diameter shall be installed in all empty conduit longer
25	than 10 feet. Pull wire shall be secured at each end and tagged for identification of the use of the
26	conduit.
27	
28	
29	END OF SECTION
30	

16110-4

Figure 41 ◆ Sample electrical specifications (5 of 12).

```
1    SECTION 16120 - CONDUCTORS
2
3    PART 1 - GENERAL
4
5    SCOPE:
6
7    This Section applies to secondary conductors for systems rated 600 volts and below.
8
9    A complete system of conductors shall be installed in the raceway systems as specified here and
10   shown on drawings.
11
12   APPLICABLE SPECIFICATIONS AND STANDARDS:
13
14   Compliance:
15
16   The materials specified here shall meet the following specifications and standards in their current
17   edition.
18
19        (1)  UL Standards:
20
21             Insulation tape
22             Wire Connectors and Soldering lugs
23
24        (2)  NEMA Standards:
25
26             Thermoplastic - Insulated WC 5 (IPCEA S-61-402)
27
28   PART 2  PRODUCTS
29
30   CONDUCTORS:
31
32   All conductors shall be made of copper.
33
34   Conductors, unless otherwise noted, shall be heat and moisture resistant grade, thermoplastic
35   insulated. Conductors No. 8 AWG and larger shall be stranded copper conductors, dual rated, Type
36   THHN-THWN; Conductors No. 10 and smaller shall be solid copper, Type THHN-THWN (dual
37   rated), unless otherwise required below. Branch circuit conductors for all other lighting fixtures
38   shall have a temperature rating of not less than what is required by the UL listing of the fixture
39   with a minimum rating of 90 degrees C.
40
41   Conductors for signal and control circuits above 50 volts AC may be THWN-THHN as permitted
42   by NEC, No. 14 AWG.  Conductors for signal and control circuits below 50 volts AC may be 300-
43   volt, PVC insulated, No. 14 AWG.
44
45   Branch circuit conductors shall be not smaller than No. 12 AWG, except that conductors for branch
46   circuits whose length from panel to center of load exceeds 75 feet for the 280/120 volt system,
47   or 150 feet for 277/480 volt system, shall not be smaller than No. 10 AWG from the panel to the
48   first outlet box in the circuit regardless of what is scheduled on panelboard schedule.
49
50   Conductors being connected to transformers and other equipment shall have a temperature rating
51   as required by the transformer or equipment manufacturer.
52
53   PART 3 - EXECUTION:
54
```

16120-1

Figure 41 ◆ Sample electrical specifications (6 of 12).

1 SPLICES:
2
3 Solid Conductor Splices:
4
5 Solid conductors namely those sized #10, #12, and #14 AWG copper, and smaller, shall be spliced
6 by twisting securely and by means of hot-dipped solder plus gum rubber tape, plus friction tape,
7 or plastic tape approved as a substitute for friction tape. The contractor shall use Ideal "wire-nuts"
8 for recessed lighting fixture lead splices to branch circuit conductors.
9
10 Stranded Conductor Splices:
11
12 Namely #8 AWG and larger, shall be spliced by approved mechanical connectors plus gum tape,
13 plus friction or plastic tape. Solderless mechanical connectors, for splices and taps provided with
14 U.L. approval insulating covers, may be used instead of mechanical connectors plus tape.
15
16 INSTALLATION OF CONDUCTORS:
17
18 Conductors shall be continuous from outlet to outlet, and no splices shall be made except within
19 outlet or junction boxes, troughs and gutters. Junction boxes may be utilized where required. No
20 'condulet' type fitting shall be used on any service conduits. If other than long radius bends are
21 required, pull boxes sized in accordance with the NEC shall be used.
22
23 Home runs may be combined in one conduit, provided all connections are in accordance with
24 National Electrical Code requirements, and the maximum unbalanced current in the neutral does
25 not extend the capacity of the conductor, and the conductors are not required to be derated to
26 below circuit capacity.
27
28 Conductors in vertical runs shall be supported as required by NEC 300.19.
29
30 COLOR CODING:
31
32 Conductors, feeders, and branch circuits shall be color coded by phases as follows:
33
34 480/277-volt systems: Phase A-brown; Phase B-orange; Phase C-yellow; Neutral - white with
35 identifiable color stripe, other than green; grounding wire - green.
36
37 208/120-volt systems: Phase A-black; Phase B-red; Phase C-blue; neutral-white; Grounding wire-
38 green.
39
40 Insulating tape of proper color shall be used to identify the phase conductors No. 6 AWG and
41 larger conductors.
42
43 All feeders, sub-feeds to panels, motors, etc., shall be completely phased out as to sequence
44 and rotation. Phase sequence shall be A-B-C from front to rear, top to bottom, left to right when
45 facing equipment.
46
47

16120-2

110F41G.TIF

Figure 41 ◆ Sample electrical specifications (7 of 12).

SECTION 16136 - WIRING DEVICES, BOXES & ENCLOSURES

PART 1 GENERAL

WORK INCLUDED:

Work under this Section includes but is not necessarily limited to the following.

Receptacles, toggle switches, dimmers and photoelectric switching devices.
Outlet Boxes
Cabinets and Enclosures

APPLICABLE SPECIFICATIONS AND STANDARDS:

Equipment specified in this Section shall meet the following specifications and standards.

 (1) UL Standards

   Attachment Plug and Receptacles
   Electric Cabinet and Boxes
   Outlet Boxes and Fittings
   Snap Switches

 (2) NEMA Standards

   Boxes, OS1
   Wiring Devices, General - Purpose, WD1
   Wiring Devices, Specific - Purpose, WD5

PART 2 PRODUCTS

OUTLET BOXES, PULL BOXES, CABINETS AND ENCLOSURES:

Boxes:

Boxes shall have sufficient volume to accomodate the number of conductors entering the box in accordance with the requirements of NFPA 70, Article 314. Boxes that are exposed to the weather or that are in normally wet locations shall be of the cast-metal type having threaded hubs. Boxes shall be of suitable construction for installation in the environment of their location. Unless otherwise specifically stated all boxes shall be metallic boxes.

Zinc-coated or cadium-plated sheet steel boxes, or a class to satisfy the conditions of each outlet, shall be used in concealed work or in exposed work above eight feet from floor.

Fixture outlet boxes on ceiling shall be not less than 4 inch octagonal. Fixture outlet boxes in concrete ceiling shall be of the 4 inch octagonal concrete type, set flush with the finished surface. Fixture outlet boxes on plastered ceilings shall be fitted with open covers set to come flush with the finished surface.

Switch and receptacle outlet boxes in dry walls, plastered walls and pour-in concrete walls shall be not less than 4 inches square cut with appropriate extension to set flush with the finished surface. One-piece gang or gangable boxes not less than 2 inches deep shall be utilized where the

16136-1

Figure 41 ◆ Sample electrical specifications (8 of 12).

use of 4-inch square boxes is not feasible.

Unless otherwise noted on the drawings, outlet, junction or pull boxes not larger than 5 inches square and within eight feet from floor level in exposed work shall be of cast steel or alloy with threaded hubs and appropriate covers.

Outlet boxes in unplastered masonry and gypsum drywall walls shall be tile type.

Outlet boxes for use with conduit and tubing systems shall be not less than 1-1/2 inches deep.

A device plate or cover shall be provided for each outlet to suit the outlet.

Pull Boxes:

Pull boxes shall be constructed of code-gauge galvanized sheet metal. Boxes shall be of not less than the minimum size required by the National Electrical Code and shall be furnished with screw fastened covers. When several feeders pass through a common pull box they shall be tagged to indicate clearly their electrical characteristics, circuit numbers and panel designations.

Pull boxes shall be furnished and installed where necessary in the raceway system to facilitate conductor installation. Except as otherwise noted for telephone raceways, conduit runs longer than 150 feet, or with more than 360 degrees compound angle bends, shall have a pull box insalled at a convenient intermediate location. Normally, when feeder routing is shown on drawings, pull boxes are not acceptable. It is the responsibility of the electrical contractor to provide pull boxes as necessary to meet the stated requirements.

Cabinets:

Cabinet boxes shall be constructed of zinc-coated sheet steel and shall conform with the requirements of Underwriters' Laboratories "Standards for Cabinets and Cutout Boxes". Unless otherwise noted, surface mounted cabinet trims shall have a corrosion inhibiting primer and a lacquer finish. Flush mounted cabinets shall be factory primed ready for finish painting by the General Contractor. Cabinets shall be of suitable construction for installation in the environment of their locations.

Systems cabinet, if shown, shall be provided with interior dimensions not less than those indicated on the drawings. Trims shall provide maximum size openings to the box interiors. Cabinets shall be provided with 5/8 inch fire retardant plywood back-boards having an insulating varnish finish.

Device Plates:

A device plate shall be provided for each outlet (including telephone and computer system outlets) to suit the device installed. Screws shall be of metal with countersunk heads, with finish to match the finish of the plate.

Device plates shall be of the one-piece type, of suitable shape for the devices to be covered. The use of sectional device plates will not be permitted. Plates shall be as follows:

- . Plates on surface boxes in unfinished areas shall be of galvanized steel with beveled edges.
- . All plates on walls with flush switches or receptacles shall be 302 stainless steel, 0.32" nominal thickness.

16136-2

110F41I.TIF

Figure 41 ◆ Sample electrical specifications (9 of 12).

Plates on surface boxes in finished areas shall be as for flush outlets.

Switches and Receptacles:

Switches and receptacles shall be as shown on the drawings and in the symbol schedule, and shall meet the latest federal specifications W-S 896 or W-C 596 as verified by UL. Devices shall be the product of one of the following manufacturers complying with referenced NEMA Standards - Arrow-Hart Electric Company, Bryant Electric Company, General Electric Company, Harvey Hubbell, Inc., Slater Electric, Inc., Pass & Seymour, Inc., Sierra Electric, or Leviton. 20-ampere and 15 ampere receptacles shall be heavy duty, hospital grade with nylon body. Switches shall be 20-ampere, specification grade.

Color of switches and receptacles shall be gray.

Receptacles with ground fault interrupting (GFI) Protection.

GFI receptacles shall be NEMA 5-15R configuration, UL listed with "noise-suppressed" circuitry to eliminate false trippings. GFI receptacles shall provide protection to all other receptacles installed "downstream" on the same branch circuit. Provide separate neutral conductor for GFI receptacle circuit.

Wiring Device Schedule

For clarity and to identify the class and type of devices required, refer to the following schedule of devices by Pass & Seymour (P&S). Device color shall be as previous specified.

Switches:	Catalogue Number
Single Pole	20 AC 1
Double Pole	20 AC 2
Three Way	20 AC 3

Receptacles:

NEMA Configuration	P&S Catalogue Number
5-15R	5262
5-20R	5362
5-30R	3802
5-50R	3803
6-20R	5862
6-30R	3801
6-50R	3804
10-30R	3860
10-50R	3890
14-30R	3864
15-20R	3821
15-30R	5740
18-20R	3822
L5-20R	L520-R
L5-30R	L530-R
L6-20R	L620-R

16136-3

Figure 41 ◆ Sample electrical specifications (10 of 12).

110F41J.TIF

1	L6-30R	L630-R
2	L15-20R	L1520-R
3	L15-30R	L1530-R

4

MULTI-OUTLET ASSEMBLIES AND SURFACE METAL RACEWAYS:

6

7 Surface metal raceways shall be provided as indicated on the drawings, complete with all
8 appropriate fittings as required, to provide a safe and complete installation. All components shall
9 be UL listed. Raceways shall be supported on approximately 18" centers with #8 flat lead
10 fasteners. The entire installation shall meet the requirements of Articles 380 and 386 of the NEC
11 All field cuts of the raceway shall be made square and shall have no rough edges.

12

PART 3 - EXECUTION:

14

INSTALLATION OF OUTLETS:

16

17 Location of outlets shown on drawings, other than those dimensioned, are only approximate, the
18 Owner shall have the right to make slight changes in the position of outlets if the Contractor is
19 notified before roughing-in is done. The Contractor shall study the general building plans in relation
20 to the spaces surrounding each outlet in order that his work may fit the other work required by
21 these specifications. When necessary, the Contractor shall relocate outlets of junction boxes so
22 that, when fixtures or other fittings are installed, they will be symmetrically located according to
23 room layout and will not interfere with other work or equipment. Do not install outlets back to
24 back. Outlets flush mounted in fire or sound wall shall be mounted not closer than 24" apart
25 horizontally when on same face of wall and 12" apart horizontally when mounted on opposite sides
26 of wall. For those outlets in fire or sound rated walls that must be closer than 24" apart, provide
27 Nelson Firestop system 'putty pads' all around outlets to maintain fire rating.

28

29 Minimum length of conduit connecting to adjacent flush in sound rated walls outlets sound rated
30 walls shall be 18".

31

32 Boxes shall be installed in a rigid and satisfactory manner, either by wood screws on wood,
33 expansion shields on masonry, or machine screws on steel work.

34

35 Recessed boxes in dry wall type construction shall be supported from both adjacent studs, or by
36 the use of metal stud brackets as manufactured by E-Z Mount Bracket Co., or equivalent.

37

PLATES:

39

40 Plates for receptacles and switches shall be installed with all four edges in continuous contact with
41 the finished wall surfaces without the use of mats or similar devices. Plaster fillings will not be
42 permitted. Plates shall be installed vertically and with an alignment tolerance of 1/16 inch.

43

SURFACE METAL RACEWAYS

45

46 Surface metal raceways shall be installed where noted on the drawings. Support on approximately
47 30" centers with #8 flat head screws. In addition, couplings, fittings and boxes shall be supported
48 independent of the raceway.

49

INSTALLATION OF PULL BOXES

51

52 Pull boxes shall be installed overhead or on walls at locations free of interference with equipment,

16136-4

110F41K.TIF

Figure 41 ◆ Sample electrical specifications (11 of 12).

ducts, piping and activities being carried out at the premises. Pull boxes with covers larger than 4 square feet shall be provided with two handles.

END OF SECTION

16136-5

110F41L.TIF

gure 41 ◆ Sample electrical specifications (12 of 12).

Questions 1 through 7 refer to the seven electrical symbols shown below. In the spaces provided, place the letter corresponding to the correct answer found in the list.

_____ 1.

_____ 2.

_____ 3.

PC   PC

_____ 4.

_____ 5.

Ceiling   Wall

_____ 6.

_____ 7.

a. Single receptacle outlet

b. Duplex receptacle outlet

c. Triplex receptacle outlet

d. Incandescent fixture
   (surface or pendant)

e. Incandescent fixture
   with pull chain
   (surface or pendant)

f. Head guy

g. Sidewalk guy

110RQ01.EPS

Questions 8 through 10 refer to the sample electrical specifications shown in Figure 41.

8. Which of the following tasks is *not* covered under Division 16?
   a. Lighting fixtures
   b. New lay-in ceiling in the corridor of Building B
   c. Concrete pad for power company transformers
   d. Telephone cable

9. What is the minimum size RNC allowed by the specifications?
   a. ½ inch
   b. ¾ inch
   c. 1 inch
   d. ⁵⁄₁₆ inch

10. The color code specified for a 208/120V system is _____.
    a. phase A—black; phase B—red; phase C—blue; neutral—white; grounding wire—green
    b. the same as that for a 480/277V system
    c. phase A—brown; phase B—orange; phase C—yellow; neutral—white; grounding wire—green
    d. any color but green or green with a yellow stripe

Summary

this module, you learned the symbols and con-
ntions used on architectural and engineering
awings. As an electrician, you need to know
w to recognize the basic symbols used on elec-
cal drawings and other drawings used in the
ilding construction industry. You should also
ow where to find the meaning of symbols that
you do not immediately recognize. Schedules, diagrams, and specifications often provide detailed
information that is not included on the working
drawings.

Reading architectural and engineering drawings takes practice and study. Now that you have
the basic skills, take the time to master them.

Notes

Trade Terms Quiz

1. A(n) _____ drawing typically includes the following information: a site plan, floor plans, elevations of all exterior faces of the building, and large-scale detail drawings.

2. A(n) _____ is an exact copy or reproduction of an original drawing.

3. A simple, single-line diagram used to show electrical equipment and related connections is a(n) _____ diagram.

4. A(n) _____ shows the path of an electrical circuit or system of circuits, along with the circuit components.

5. To convey a substantial amount of detailed information to installation electricians, an engineer will use a(n) _____ drawing.

6. Shown in a separate view, a(n) _____ view is an enlarged, detailed view taken from an area of a drawing.

7. A cutaway drawing that shows the inside of an object or building is a(n) _____ drawing.

8. The sizes or measurements that are printed on a drawing are called _____.

9. The relationship between an object's size in a drawing and the object's actual size is the _____.

10. The height of the front, rear, or sides of a building is shown in a(n) _____ drawing.

11. A building's location on the site is shown in a(n) _____ plan.

12. A drawing that has a top-down view of a building is a(n) _____ plan.

13. A drawing that has a top-down view of a single object is a(n) _____ view.

14. A(n) _____ diagram is a single-line block diagram used to indicate the electric service equipment, service conductors and feeders, and subpanels.

15. Owners, architects, and engineers use written _____ to specify material and workmanship requirements.

16. A(n) _____ is a systematic way of presenting equipment lists on a drawing in tabular form.

17. Complicated circuits, such as control circuits, are shown in a(n) _____ diagram.

18. Usually developed by manufacturers, fabricators, or contractors, a(n) _____ drawing shows specific dimensions and other information about a piece of equipment and its installation methods.

Trade Terms

Architectural drawings	Electrical drawing	Power-riser diagram	Sectional view
Block diagram	Elevation drawing	Scale	Shop drawing
Blueprint	Floor plan	Schedule	Site plan
Detail drawing	One-line diagram	Schematic diagram	Written specifications
Dimensions	Plan view		

Wayne Stratton

Associated Builders and Contractors

How did you choose a career in the electrical field?
Three events in my childhood created the desire to learn the electrical trade. At age six, the farmhouse we lived in was totally destroyed by fire. The cause was electrical. As a young teen, a local electrician had incorrectly wired a heating element and electrocuted several pigs. In 1973, my father hired this electrician to install a motor starter on a grain conveyor. He could not figure it out. I wanted to learn how to do this type of work and do it safely.

Tell us about your apprenticeship experience.
My education is from a technical school. I have attended several manufacturers' training sessions. I had to gain the hands-on experience after learning the trade. My observation of the apprenticeship programs is this: you get hands-on experience while you learn.

What positions have you held in the industry?
I worked as a plant industrial electrician responsible for motor control, DC motors, co-generation, and medium voltage distribution. Later, I began working for an electrical contractor who wanted to expand his business into the industrial field. I worked as a PLC

technician designing and installing control systems. In 1987, I began teaching apprenticeship classes.

What would you say is the primary factor in achieving success?
The desire to learn all that I can learn, the ability to think outside the box, and the opportunities to gain a variety of experiences. All this helps me continue to learn and share with trainees.

What does your current job involve?
I teach electrical apprenticeship levels one through four at two different locations in Iowa. My other responsibilities involve task training for electrical licensing, fire alarm, and code updates.

Do you have any advice for someone just entering the trade?
Continue to learn. Completing an apprenticeship program or acquiring an electrician's license is not the end of learning. With code changes every 3 years, there is always more to learn. If you don't understand something, ask! Observe and learn from experienced individuals.

Trade Terms
Introduced in This Module

Architectural drawings: Working drawings consisting of plans, elevations, details, and other information necessary for the construction of a building. Architectural drawings usually include:

- A site (plot) plan indicating the location of the building on the property
- Floor plans showing the walls and partitions for each floor or level
- Elevations of all exterior faces of the building
- Several vertical cross sections to indicate clearly the various floor levels and details of the footings, foundations, walls, floors, ceilings, and roof construction
- Large-scale detail drawings showing such construction details as may be required

Block diagram: A single-line diagram used to show electrical equipment and related connections. See *power-riser diagram.*

Blueprint: An exact copy or reproduction of an original drawing.

Detail drawing: An enlarged, detailed view taken from an area of a drawing and shown in a separate view.

Dimensions: Sizes or measurements printed on a drawing.

Electrical drawing: A means of conveying a large amount of exact, detailed information in an abbreviated language. Consists of lines, symbols, dimensions, and notations to accurately convey an engineer's designs to electricians who install the electrical system on a job.

Elevation drawing: An architectural drawing showing height, but not depth; usually the front, rear, and sides of a building or object.

Floor plan: A drawing of a building as if a horizontal cut were made through a building at about window level, and the top portion removed. The floor plan is what would appear if the remaining structure were viewed from above.

One-line diagram: A drawing that shows, by means of lines and symbols, the path of an electrical circuit or system of circuits along with the various circuit components. Also called a single-line diagram.

Plan view: A drawing made as though the viewer were looking straight down (from above) on an object.

Power-riser diagram: A single-line block diagram used to indicate the electric service equipment, service conductors and feeders, and subpanels. Notes are used on power-riser diagrams to identify the equipment; indicate the size of conduit; show the number, size, and type of conductors; and list related materials. A panelboard schedule is usually included with power-riser diagrams to indicate the exact components (panel type and size), along with fuses, circuit breakers, etc., contained in each panelboard.

Scale: On a drawing, the size relationship between an object's actual size and the size it is drawn. Scale also refers to the measuring tool used to determine this relationship.

Schedule: A systematic method of presenting equipment lists on a drawing in tabular form.

Schematic diagram: A detailed diagram showing complicated circuits, such as control circuits.

Sectional view: A cutaway drawing that shows the inside of an object or building.

Shop drawing: A drawing that is usually developed by manufacturers, fabricators, or contractors to show specific dimensions and other pertinent information concerning a particular piece of equipment and its installation methods.

Site plan: A drawing showing the location of a building or buildings on the building site. Such drawings frequently show topographical lines, electrical and communication lines, water and sewer lines, sidewalks, driveways, and similar information.

Written specifications: A written description of what is required by the owner, architect, and engineer in the way of materials and workmanship. Together with working drawings, the specifications form the basis of the contract requirements for construction.

Metric Conversion Chart

inches (fractions)	inches (decimals)	m m
–	.0004	.01
–	.004	.10
–	.01	.25
1/64	.0156	.397
–	.0197	.50
–	.0295	.75
1/32	.03125	.794
–	.0394	1.
3/64	.0469	1.191
–	.059	1.5
1/16	.062	1.588
5/64	.0781	1.984
–	.0787	2.
3/32	.094	2.381
–	.0984	2.5
7/64	.109	2.778
–	.1181	3.
1/8	.125	3.175
–	.1378	3.5
9/64	.141	3.572
5/32	.156	3.969
–	.1575	4.
11/64	.172	4.366
–	.177	4.5
3/16	.1875	4.763
–	.1969	5.
13/64	.203	5.159
–	.2165	5.5
7/32	.219	5.556
15/64	.234	5.953
–	.2362	6.
1/4	.250	6.350
–	.2559	6.5
17/64	.2656	6.747
–	.2756	7.
9/32	.281	7.144
–	.2953	7.5
19/64	.297	7.541
5/16	.312	7.938
–	.315	8.
21/64	.328	8.334
–	.335	8.5
11/32	.344	8.731
–	.3543	9.
23/64	.359	9.128
–	.374	9.5
3/8	.375	9.525
25/64	.391	9.922
–	.3937	10.
13/32	.406	10.319
–	.413	10.5
27/64	.422	10.716
–	.4331	11.
7/16	.438	11.113
29/64	.453	11.509
15/32	.469	11.906
–	.4724	12.
31/64	.484	12.303
–	.492	12.5
1/2	.500	12.700
–	.5118	13.
33/64	.5156	13.097
17/32	.531	13.494
35/64	.547	13.891
–	.5512	14.
9/16	.563	14.288
–	.571	14.5
37/64	.578	14.684
–	.5906	15.
19/32	.594	15.081
39/64	.609	15.478
5/8	.625	15.875
–	.6299	16.
41/64	.6406	16.272
–	.6496	16.5
21/32	.656	16.669
–	.6693	17.
43/64	.672	17.066
11/16	.6875	17.463
45/64	.703	17.859
–	.7087	18.
23/32	.719	18.256
–	.7283	18.5
47/64	.734	18.653
–	.7480	19.
3/4	.750	19.050
49/64	.7656	19.447

inches (fractions)	inches (decimals)	m m
25/32	.781	19.844
–	.7874	20.
51/64	.797	20.241
13/16	.8125	20.638
–	.8268	21.
53/64	.828	21.034
27/32	.844	21.431
55/64	.859	21.828
–	.8661	22.
7/8	.875	22.225
57/64	.8906	22.622
–	.9055	23.
29/32	.9062	23.019
59/64	.922	23.416
15/16	.9375	23.813
–	.9449	24.
61/64	.953	24.209
31/32	.969	24.606
–	.9843	25.
63/64	.9844	25.003
1	1.000	25.400
–	1.0236	26.
1-1/32	1.0312	26.194
1-1/16	1.062	26.988
–	1.063	27.
1-3/32	1.094	27.781
–	1.1024	28.
1-1/8	1.125	28.575
–	1.1417	29.
1-5/32	1.156	29.369
–	1.1811	30.
1-3/16	1.1875	30.163
1-7/32	1.219	30.956
–	1.2205	31.
1-1/4	1.250	31.750
–	1.2598	32.
1-9/32	1.281	32.544
–	1.2992	33.
1-5/16	1.312	33.338
–	1.3386	34.
1-11/32	1.344	34.131
1-3/8	1.375	34.925
–	1.3779	35.
1-13/32	1.406	35.719
–	1.4173	36.
1-7/16	1.438	36.513
–	1.4567	37.
1-15/32	1.469	37.306
–	1.4961	38.
1-1/2	1.500	38.100
1-17/32	1.531	38.894
–	1.5354	39.
1-9/16	1.562	39.688
–	1.5748	40.
1-19/32	1.594	40.481
–	1.6142	41.
1-5/8	1.625	41.275
–	1.6535	42.
1-21/32	1.6562	42.069
1-11/16	1.6875	42.863
–	1.6929	43.
1-23/32	1.719	43.656
–	1.7323	44.
1-3/4	1.750	44.450
–	1.7717	45.
1-25/32	1.781	45.244
–	1.8110	46.
1-13/16	1.8125	46.038
1-27/32	1.844	46.831
–	1.8504	47.
1-7/8	1.875	47.625
–	1.8898	48.
1-29/32	1.9062	48.419
–	1.9291	49.
1-15/16	1.9375	49.213
–	1.9685	50.
1-31/32	1.969	50.006
2	2.000	50.800
–	2.0079	51.
2-1/32	2.03125	51.594
–	2.0472	52.
2-1/16	2.062	52.388
–	2.0866	53.
2-3/32	2.094	53.181
2-1/8	2.125	53.975
–	2.126	54.
2-5/32	2.156	54.769

inches (fractions)	inches (decimals)	m m
–	2.165	55.
2-3/16	2.1875	55.563
–	2.2047	56.
2-7/32	2.219	56.356
–	2.244	57.
2-1/4	2.250	57.150
2-9/32	2.281	57.944
–	2.2835	58.
2-5/16	2.312	58.738
–	2.3228	59.
2-11/32	2.344	59.531
–	2.3622	60.
2-3/8	2.375	60.325
–	2.4016	61.
2-13/32	2.406	61.119
2-7/16	2.438	61.913
–	2.4409	62.
2-15/32	2.469	62.706
–	2.4803	63.
2-1/2	2.500	63.500
–	2.5197	64.
2-17/32	2.531	64.294
–	2.559	65.
2-9/16	2.562	65.088
2-19/32	2.594	65.881
–	2.5984	66.
2-5/8	2.625	66.675
–	2.638	67.
2-21/32	2.656	67.469
–	2.6772	68.
2-11/16	2.6875	68.263
–	2.7165	69.
2-23/32	2.719	69.056
2-3/4	2.750	69.850
–	2.7559	70.
2-25/32	2.781	70.6439
–	2.7953	71.
2-13/16	2.8125	71.4376
–	2.8346	72.
2-27/32	2.844	72.2314
–	2.8740	73.
2-7/8	2.875	73.025
2-29/32	2.9062	73.819
–	2.9134	74.
2-15/16	2.9375	74.613
–	2.9527	75.
2-31/32	2.969	75.406
–	2.9921	76.
3	3.000	76.200
3-1/32	3.0312	76.994
–	3.0315	77.
3-1/16	3.062	77.788
–	3.0709	78.
3-3/32	3.094	78.581
–	3.1102	79.
3-1/8	3.125	79.375
–	3.1496	80.
3-5/32	3.156	80.169
3-3/16	3.1875	80.963
–	3.1890	81.
3-7/32	3.219	81.756
–	3.2283	82.
3-1/4	3.250	82.550
–	3.2677	83.
3-9/32	3.281	83.344
–	3.3071	84.
3-5/16	3.312	84.1377
3-11/32	3.344	84.9314
–	3.3464	85.
3-3/8	3.375	85.725
–	3.3858	86.
3-13/32	3.406	86.519
–	3.4252	87.
3-7/16	3.438	87.313
–	3.4646	88.
3-15/32	3.469	88.106
3-1/2	3.500	88.900
–	3.5039	89.
3-17/32	3.531	89.694
–	3.5433	90.
3-9/16	3.562	90.4877
–	3.5827	91.
3-19/32	3.594	91.281
–	3.622	92.
3-5/8	3.625	92.075
3-21/32	3.656	92.869
–	3.6614	93.

inches (fractions)	inches (decimals)	m m
3-11/16	3.6875	93.663
–	3.7008	94.
3-23/32	3.719	94.456
–	3.7401	95.
3-3/4	3.750	95.250
–	3.7795	96.
3-25/32	3.781	96.044
3-13/16	3.8125	96.838
–	3.8189	97.
3-27/32	3.844	97.631
–	3.8583	98.
3-7/8	3.875	98.425
–	3.8976	99.
3-29/32	3.9062	99.219
–	3.9370	100.
3-15/16	3.9375	100.013
3-31/32	3.969	100.806
–	3.9764	101.
4	4.000	101.600
4-1/16	4.062	103.188
4-1/8	4.125	104.775
–	4.1338	105.
4-3/16	4.1875	106.363
4-1/4	4.250	107.950
4-5/16	4.312	109.538
–	4.3307	110.
4-3/8	4.375	111.125
4-7/16	4.438	112.713
4-1/2	4.500	114.300
–	4.5275	115.
4-9/16	4.562	115.888
4-5/8	4.625	117.475
4-11/16	4.6875	119.063
–	4.7244	120.
4-3/4	4.750	120.650
4-13/16	4.8125	122.238
4-7/8	4.875	123.825
–	4.9212	125.
4-15/16	4.9375	125.413
5	5.000	127.000
–	5.1181	130.
5-1/4	5.250	133.350
5-1/2	5.500	139.700
–	5.5118	140.
5-3/4	5.750	146.050
–	5.9055	150.
6	6.000	152.400
6-1/4	6.250	158.750
–	6.2992	160.
6-1/2	6.500	165.100
–	6.6929	170.
6-3/4	6.750	171.450
7	7.000	177.800
–	7.0866	180.
–	7.4803	190.
7-1/2	7.500	190.500
–	7.8740	200.
8	8.000	203.200
–	8.2677	210.
8-1/2	8.500	215.900
–	8.6614	220.
9	9.000	228.600
–	9.0551	230.
–	9.4488	240.
9-1/2	9.500	241.300
–	9.8425	250.
10	10.000	254.001
–	10.2362	260.
–	10.6299	270.
11	11.000	279.401
–	11.0236	280.
–	11.4173	290.
–	11.8110	300.
12	12.000	304.801
13	13.000	330.201
–	13.7795	350.
14	14.000	355.601
15	15.000	381.001
–	15.7480	400.
16	16.000	406.401
17	17.000	431.801
–	17.7165	450.
18	18.000	457.201
19	19.000	482.601
–	19.6850	500.
20	20.000	508.001

110A01.TIF

Breakdown of CSI Divisions

Division Numbers and Titles

PROCUREMENT AND CONTRACTING REQUIREMENTS GROUP
 Division 00 Procurement and Contracting Requirements

SPECIFICATIONS GROUP

 GENERAL REQUIREMENTS SUBGROUP
  Division 01 General Requirements

 FACILITY CONSTRUCTION SUBGROUP
  Division 02 Existing Conditions
  Division 03 Concrete
  Division 04 Masonry
  Division 05 Metals
  Division 06 Wood, Plastics, and Composites
  Division 07 Thermal and Moisture Protection
  Division 08 Openings
  Division 09 Finishes
  Division 10 Specialties
  Division 11 Equipment
  Division 12 Furnishings
  Division 13 Special Construction
  Division 14 Conveying Equipment
  Division 15 Reserved
  Division 16 Reserved
  Division 17 Reserved
  Division 18 Reserved
  Division 19 Reserved

 FACILITY SERVICES SUBGROUP
  Division 20 Reserved
  Division 21 Fire Suppression
  Division 22 Plumbing
  Division 23 Heating, Ventilating, and Air Conditioning
  Division 24 Reserved
  Division 25 Integrated Automation
  Division 26 Electrical
  Division 27 Communications
  Division 28 Electronic Safety and Security
  Division 29 Reserved

 SITE AND INFRASTRUCTURE SUBGROUP
  Division 30 Reserved
  Division 31 Earthwork
  Division 32 Exterior Improvements
  Division 33 Utilities
  Division 34 Transportation
  Division 35 Waterway and Marine Construction
  Division 36 Reserved
  Division 37 Reserved
  Division 38 Reserved
  Division 39 Reserved

 PROCESS EQUIPMENT SUBGROUP
  Division 40 Process Integration
  Division 41 Material Processing and Handling Equipment
  Division 42 Process Heating, Cooling, and Drying Equipment
  Division 43 Process Gas and Liquid Handling, Purification, and Storage Equipment
  Division 44 Pollution Control Equipment
  Division 45 Industry-Specific Manufacturing Equipment
  Division 46 Reserved
  Division 47 Reserved
  Division 48 Electrical Power Generation
  Division 49 Reserved

Div Numbers - 1

110A02.EPS

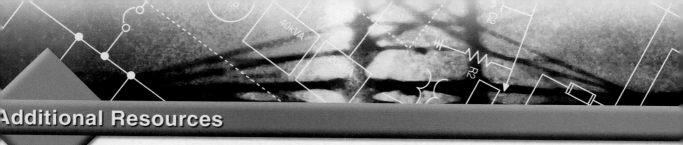

This module is intended to present thorough resources for task training. The following reference works are suggested for further study. These are additional materials for continued education rather than for task training.

American Electrician's Handbook. Terrell Croft and Wilford I. Summers. New York: McGraw-Hill.

National Electrical Code® Handbook, Latest Edition. Quincy, MA: National Fire Protection Association.

CONTREN® LEARNING SERIES — USER FEEDBACK

The NCCER makes every effort to keep these textbooks up-to-date and free of technical errors. We appreciate your help in this process. If you have an idea for improving this textbook, or if you find an error, a typographical mistake, or an inaccuracy in NCCER's *Contren®* textbooks, please write us, using this form or a photocopy. Be sure to include the exact module number, page number, a detailed description, and the correction, if applicable. Your input will be brought to the attention of the Technical Review Committee. Thank you for your assistance.

Instructors – If you found that additional materials were necessary in order to teach this module effectively, please let us know so that we may include them in the Equipment/Materials list in the Annotated Instructor's Guide.

Write: Product Development
National Center for Construction Education and Research
P.O. Box 141104, Gainesville, FL 32614-1104

Fax: 352-334-0932

E-mail: curriculum@nccer.org

Craft   Module Name
_____

Copyright Date   Module Number   Page Number(s)
_____

Description
_____

_____

_____

_____

_____

(Optional) Correction
_____

_____

_____

(Optional) Your Name and Address
_____

_____

_____

Walt Disney World's Wilderness Lodge

Walt Disney World's Wilderness Lodge is modeled after the Old Faithful Inn that was built inside Yellowstone National Park in 1902; it even includes a functional reproduction of Old Faithful Geyser. Installation of the electrical work involved highly detailed coordination to ensure that the various lighting and power systems would be concealed and not detract from the period feel of the building.

26112-05
Wiring: Residential

Topics to be presented in this module include:

Overview

The first step in residential wiring is a complete review of the floor plan lay out. Electrical floor plans show approximate locations of panels, switches, receptacles, lighting, and other outlets. They do not show, however, the routing of the wiring that interconnects these devices, as this task is generally left up to the electrician.

If the design engineer has not performed the load calculations, the electrician must determine the connected load for the residence, and then size the electrical service accordingly. In order to figure total connected load, certain formulas must be applied based on livable square footage of the house and other factors. Residential electricians must know how to perform load calculations accurately.

Specific wiring methods, grounding requirements, and ground fault circuit interrupting techniques for residences are strictly regulated by the *National Electrical Code®* because building occupants are constantly exposed to the hazards associated with electrical systems and devices. If the *NEC®* and local codes are not strictly followed, the inspector will not sign off on the installation. This will cause construction delays and rework expenses.

Objectives

When you have completed this module, you will be able to do the following:

1. Describe how to determine electric service requirements for dwellings.
2. Explain the grounding requirements of a residential electric service.
3. Calculate and select service-entrance equipment.
4. Select the proper wiring methods for various types of residences.
5. Explain the role of the *National Electrical Code®* in residential wiring.
6. Compute branch circuit loads and explain their installation requirements.
7. Explain the types and purposes of equipment grounding conductors.
8. Explain the purpose of ground-fault circuit interrupters and tell where they must be installed.
9. Size outlet boxes and select the proper type for different wiring methods.
10. Describe rules for installing electric space heating and HVAC equipment.
11. Describe the installation rules for electrical systems around swimming pools, spas, and hot tubs.
12. Explain how wiring devices are selected and installed.
13. Describe the installation and control of lighting fixtures.

Trade Terms

Appliance
Armored (Type AC) cable
Bonding bushing
Bonding jumper
Branch circuit
BX®
Feeder
Load center
Nonmetallic-sheathed (Type NM) cable
Romex®

Roughing in
Service drop
Service entrance
Service-entrance conductors
Service-entrance equipment
Service lateral
Switch
Switch leg

Required Trainee Materials

1. Paper and pencil
2. Copy of the latest edition of the *National Electrical Code®*
3. Appropriate personal protective equipment

Prerequisites

Before you begin this module, it is recommended that you successfully complete *Core Curriculum* and *Electrical Level One*, Modules 26101-05 through 26110-05.

This course map shows all of the modules in *Electrical Level One*. The suggested training order begins at the bottom and proceeds up. Skill levels increase as you advance on the course map. The local Training Program Sponsor may adjust the training order.

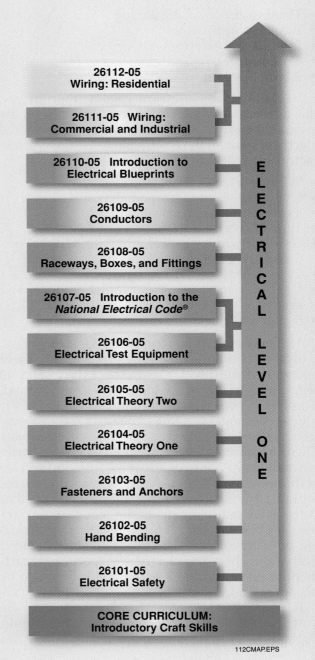

26112-05
Wiring: Residential

26111-05 Wiring:
Commercial and Industrial

26110-05 Introduction to
Electrical Blueprints

26109-05
Conductors

26108-05
Raceways, Boxes, and Fittings

26107-05 Introduction to the
National Electrical Code®

26106-05
Electrical Test Equipment

26105-05
Electrical Theory Two

26104-05
Electrical Theory One

26103-05
Fasteners and Anchors

26102-05
Hand Bending

26101-05
Electrical Safety

CORE CURRICULUM:
Introductory Craft Skills

ELECTRICAL LEVEL ONE

112CMAP.EPS

1.0.0 ◆ INTRODUCTION

The use of electricity in houses began shortly after the opening of the California Electric Light Company in 1879 and Thomas Edison's Pearl Street Station in New York City in 1882. These two companies were the first to enter the business of producing and selling electric service to the public. In 1886, the Westinghouse Electric Company secured patents that resulted in the development and introduction of alternating current; this paved the way for rapid acceleration in the use of electricity.

The primary use of early home electrical systems was to provide interior lighting, but today's uses of electricity include:

- Heating and air conditioning
- Electrical **appliances**
- Interior and exterior lighting
- Communications systems
- Alarm systems

In planning any electrical system, there are certain general steps to be followed, regardless of the type of construction. In planning a residential electrical system, the electrician must take certain factors into consideration. These include:

- Wiring method
- Overhead or underground electrical service
- Type of building construction
- Type of **service entrance** and equipment
- Grade of wiring devices and lighting fixtures
- Selection of lighting fixtures
- Type of heating and cooling system
- Control wiring for the heating and cooling system
- Signal and alarm systems

The experienced electrician readily recognizes, within certain limits, the type of system that will be required. However, always check the local code requirements when selecting a wiring method. The *NEC*® provides minimum requirements for the practical safeguarding of persons and property from hazards arising from the use of electricity. These minimum requirements are not necessarily efficient, convenient, or adequate for good service or future expansion of electrical use. Some local building codes require electrical installations that surpass the requirements of the *NEC*®. For example, *NEC Section 230.51(A)* requires that service cable be secured by means of cable straps placed every 30 inches. The electrical inspection department in one area requires these cable straps to be placed at a minimum distance of 18 inches.

If more than one wiring method may be practical, a decision as to which type to use should be made prior to beginning the installation.

NOTE

See the Appendix for a general reference to other codes and electrical standards that apply to residential electrical installations.

In a residential occupancy, the electrician should know that a 120/240-volt (V), single-phase service entrance will invariably be provided by the utility company. The electrician knows that the service and **feeders** will be three-wire, that the **branch circuits** will be either two- or three-wire, and that the safety **switches**, service equipment, and panelboards will be three-wire, solid neutral. On each project, however, the electrician must consult with the local utility to determine the point of attachment for overhead connections and the location of the metering equipment.

2.0.0 ◆ SIZING THE ELECTRICAL SERVICE

It may be difficult to decide at times which comes first, the layout of the outlets or the sizing of the electric service. In many cases, the service (main disconnect, panelboard, service conductors, etc.) can be sized using the *NEC*® before the outlets are actually located. In other cases, the outlets will have to be laid out first. However, in either case, the service entrance and panelboard locations will have to be determined before the circuits can be installed—so the electrician will know in which direction (and to what points) the circuit homeruns will terminate. In this module, an actual residence will be used as a model to size the electric service according to the latest edition of the *NEC*®.

2.1.0 Floor Plans

A floor plan is a drawing that shows the length and width of a building and the rooms that it contains. A separate plan is made for each floor.

Figure 1 shows how a floor plan is developed. An imaginary cut is made through the building as shown in the view on the left. The top half of the cut is removed (bottom view), and the resulting floor plan is what the remaining structure looks like when viewed directly from above.

The floor plan for a small residence is shown in *Figure 2*. This building is constructed on a concrete slab with no basement or crawl space. There is an unfinished attic above the living area and an open carport just outside the kitchen entrance. Appl

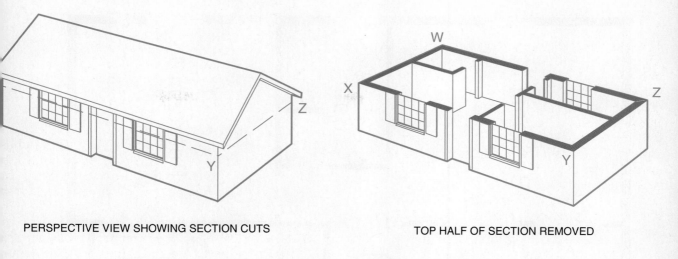

PERSPECTIVE VIEW SHOWING SECTION CUTS

TOP HALF OF SECTION REMOVED

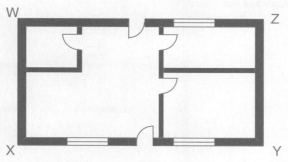

RESULTING FLOOR PLAN IS WHAT THE REMAINING
STRUCTURE LOOKS LIKE WHEN VIEWED FROM ABOVE

112F01.EPS

Figure 1 ◆ Principles of floor plan layout.

...ces include a 12 kilovolt-ampere (kVA) electric
...nge, a 4.5kVA water heater, a ½hp 120V disposal,
...d a 1.5kVA dishwasher.

There is also a washer/dryer (rated at 5.5kVA)
...the utility room. A gas furnace with a ⅓hp 120V
...ower supplies the heating. In this module, the
...ectrical requirements of this example building
...ill be computed.

2.0 General Lighting Loads

...eneral lighting loads are calculated on the basis
... *NEC Table 220.12.* For residential occupancies,
...ree volt-amperes (watts) per square foot of liv-
...g space is the figure to use. This includes non-
...ppliance duplex receptacles into which lamps,
...levisions, etc. may be connected. Therefore, the
...ea of the building must be calculated first. If the
...uilding is under construction, the dimensions
...n be determined by scaling the working draw-
...gs used by the builder. If the residence is an ex-
...ting building, with no drawings, actual
...easurements will have to be made on the site.

Using the floor plan of the residence in *Figure 2*
as a guide, an architect's scale is used to measure
the longest width of the building (using outside
dimensions). It is determined to be 33 feet. The
longest length of the building is 48 feet. These
two measurements multiplied together give 33 ×
48 = 1,584 square feet of living area. However,
there is an open carport on the lower left of the
drawing. This carport area will have to be calculated and then deducted from 1,584 to give the
true amount of living space. This open area (carport) is 12 feet wide by 19.5 feet long: 12 × 19.5 =
234 square feet. Subtract the carport area from
1,584 square feet: 1,584 − 234 = 1,350 square feet
of living area.

When using the square-foot method to determine lighting loads for buildings, *NEC Section
220.12* requires the floor area for each floor to be
computed from the outside dimensions. When
calculating lighting loads for residences, the computed floor area must not include open porches,
carports, garages, or unused or unfinished spaces
that are not adaptable to future use.

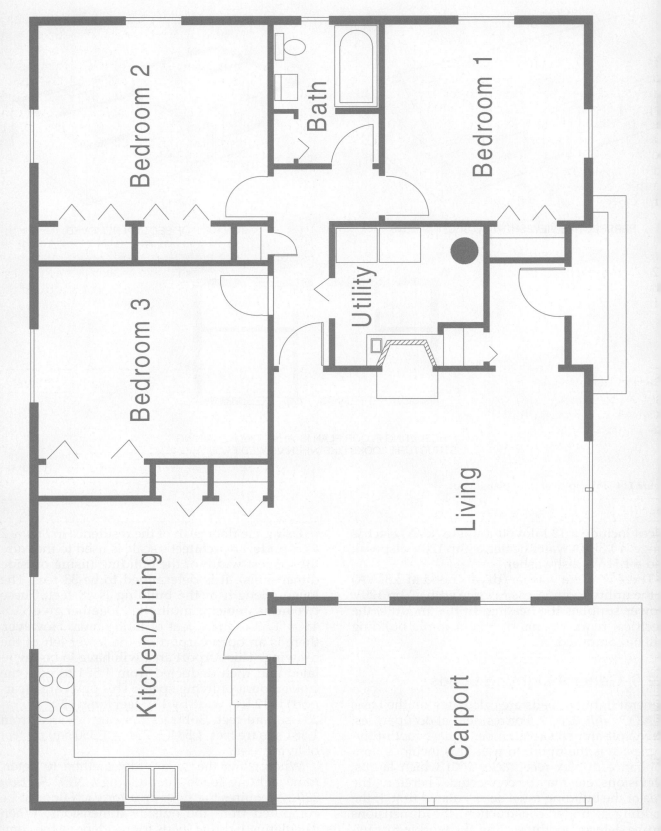

Figure 2 ◆ Floor plan of a typical residence.

2.3.0 Calculating the Electric Service Load

Figure 3 shows a standard calculation worksheet for a single-family dwelling. This form contains numbered blank spaces to be filled in while making the service calculation. Using this worksheet as a guide, the total area of our sample dwelling has been previously determined to be 1,350 square feet of living space. This figure is entered in the appropriate space (Box 1) on the form and multiplied by 3 volt-amperes (VA) for a total general lighting load of 4,050VA (Box 2).

2.3.1 Small Appliance Loads

NEC Section 210.11(C)(1) requires at least two 120V, 20A small appliance branch circuits to be installed for the small appliance loads in each kitchen area of a dwelling. Kitchen areas include the dining area, breakfast nook, pantry, and similar areas where small appliances will be used. *NEC Section 220.52* gives further requirements for residential small appliance circuits; that is, the load for those circuits is to be computed at 1,500VA each. Since our example dwelling has only one kitchen area, the number 2 is entered in Box 3 for the number of required kitchen small appliance branch circuits. Multiply the number of these circuits by 1,500 and enter the result in Box 4.

2.3.2 Laundry Circuit

NEC Section 210.11(C)(2) requires an additional 20A branch circuit to be provided for the exclusive use of the laundry area (Box 5). This circuit must not have any other outlets connected except for the laundry receptacle(s). Therefore, enter 1,500VA in Box 6 on the form.

General Lighting Load						Phase		Neutral
Square footage of the dwelling	[1] 1350	× 3VA =	[2] 4050					
Kitchen small appliance circuits	[3] 2	× 1500 =	[4] 3000					
Laundry branch circuit	[5] 1	× 1500 =	[6] 1500					
Subtotal of gen. lighting loads per *NEC Section 220.52* =			[7] 8550					
Subtract 1st 3000VA per *NEC Section 220.42*			[8] 3000	× 100% =	[9] 3000			
Remaining VA times 35% per *NEC Section 220.42*			[10] 5550	× 35% =	[11] 1943			
Total demand for general lighting loads =						[12] 4943	[13]	

Fixed Appliance Loads (Nameplate or NEC FLA of motors) per *NEC Section 220.53*			Phase		Neutral
Hot water tank, 4.5kVA, 240V		[14] 4500			
Dishwasher 1.5kVA, 120V		[15] 1500			
Disposal 1/2HP, 120V per *NEC Table 430.248* = 9.8A		[16] 1176			
Blower 1/3HP, 120V per *NEC Table 430.248* = 7.2A		[17] 864			
		[18]			
		[19]			
Subtotal of fixed appliances	[20] 8040				
If 3 or less fixed appliances take @ 100% =			[21]		[22]
If 4 or more fixed appliances take @ 75% =			[23] 6030		[24]

Other Loads per *NEC Section 220.14*		Phase		Neutral
Electric Range per *NEC Section 220.55* (neutral @ 70% per *NEC Section 220.61*)		[25] 8000		[26]
Electric Dryer per *NEC Section 220.54* (neutral @ 70% per *NEC Section 220.61*)		[27] 5500		[28]
Electric Heat per *NEC Section 220.51*				
Air Conditioning	omit smaller load per *NEC Section 220.60*	[29]		[30]
Largest Motor = 1176	× 25% (per *NEC Section 430.24*) =	[31] 294		[32]
Total VA Demand =		[33] 24767		[34]
(VA divided by 240 volts) Amps =		[35] 103		[36]
Service OCD and minimum size grounding electrode conductor		[37] 125		[38]
AWG per *NEC Sections 310.15(B)(6)* and *310.16* for neutral		[39]		[40]

112F03.EPS

Figure 3 ◆ Calculation worksheet for residential requirements.

So far, there is enough information to complete the first portion of the service calculation form:

- General lighting   4,050VA (Box 2)
- Small appliance load   3,000VA (Box 4)
- Laundry load   1,500VA (Box 6)
- Total general lighting and
  appliance loads   8,550VA (Box 7)

2.3.3 Lighting Demand Factors

All residential electrical outlets are never used at one time. There may be a rare instance when all the lighting may be on for a short time every night, but even so, all the small appliances and receptacles throughout the house will never be used simultaneously. Knowing this, *NEC Section 220.42* allows a diversity or demand factor to be used when computing the general lighting load for services. Our calculation continues as follows:

- The first 3,000VA is rated
  at 100%   3,000VA (Box 8)
- The remaining 5,550VA
  (Box 10) may be rated at
  35% (the allowable
  demand factor)
  Therefore, 5,550 × 0.35 =   1,943VA (Box 11)
- Net general lighting and
  small appliance load   4,943VA (Box 12)
  (rounded off)

2.3.4 Fixed Appliances

NEC Section 220.53 permits the loads for fixed appliances to be computed at 75% as long as they are not electric heating, air conditioning, electric cooking, or electric clothes dryer loads. To compute the load of the fixed appliances in this dwelling, list all the fixed appliances that meet *NEC Section 220.53*. Enter the nameplate rating of the appliance or VA for motors by using *NEC Table 430.298* to find the FLA of each motor. *NEC Section 220.5(A)* tells us to use 120V (not 115V) for calculation purposes. The fixed appliances would be as follows:

- Hot water tank   4,500VA (Box 14)
- Dishwasher   1,500VA (Box 15)
- ½hp 120V disposal
  (9.8A × 120V)   1,176VA (Box 16)
- Gas furnace blower
  (7.2A × 120V)   864VA (Box 17)
- Add the loads for the
  fixed appliances   8,040VA (Box 20)
- Since there are four or
  more fixed appliances,
  multiply the total in
  Box 20 by 75%   6,030VA (Box 23)

2.3.5 Other Loads

The remaining loads of the dwelling are now computed in the Other Loads section in *Figure 3*. *NEC Section 220.14* allows electric dryers to be computed as permitted in *NEC Table 220.54* and electric cooking appliances to be computed per *NEC Table 220.56*. For a single range rated over 8.75kVA, but not over 12kVA, Column C of *NEC Table 220.56* permits a demand of 8kVA for the range in this dwelling. Enter 8,000VA in Box 25.

The electric dryer must be computed at 5,000VA or the nameplate, whichever is greater according to *NEC Section 220.54.* Up to four electric dryers must be taken at 100%. Enter 5,500VA in Box 27.

If this dwelling had electric space heating and/or air conditioning, it would be computed in this section using the larger of the two loads. Since these are typical noncoincidental loads, *NEC Section 220.60* permits the smaller of those loads to be omitted. There are no demand factors for either electric heating or air conditioning; therefore, the larger of the two loads would be computed at 100%.

The final step in this calculation is to add in 25% of the largest motor in the dwelling. This dwelling unit has two motors: the disposal at 9.8A and the blower at 7.2A. (See *NEC Section 430.17.*) In this case, the larger motor is the disposal; therefore, we must add 25% of the rating to meet the requirements of *NEC Section 430.24.* Enter 294VA (1,176 × 25%) in Box 31. Adding together the individual loads as computed, we have a minimum demand of 24,767VA (Box 33) for the phase conductors.

2.3.6 Required Service Size

The conventional electric service for residential use is 120/240V, three-wire, single-phase. Services are sized in amperes, and when the volt-amperes are known on single-phase services, amperes may be found by dividing the highest voltage into the total volt-amperes. For example:

24,767VA ÷ 240V = 103A (Box 35)

The **service-entrance conductors** have now been calculated and must be rated at a minimum of 110A, which is a standard rating for overcurrent protection. However, this is not a typical trade size; therefore, we will use the more common rating of 125A as the size of our service.

If the demand for our dwelling unit had resulted in a load of less than 100A, *NEC Section 230.79(C)* would have required that the minimum rating of the service disconnect be 100A. *NEC Section 230.42(B)* would have required the ampacity of the service conductors to be equal to the rating of the 100A disconnect as well.

.4.0 Demand Factors

NEC Article 220, Part III provides the rules regarding the application of demand factors to certain types of loads. Recall that a demand factor is the maximum amount of volt-amp load expected at any given time compared to the total connected load of the circuit. The maximum demand of a feeder circuit is equal to the connected load times the demand factor. The loads to which demand factors apply can be found in the *NEC*® as follows:

Lighting loads	*NEC Table 220.42*
Receptacle loads	*NEC Table 220.44*
Dryer loads	*NEC Table 220.54*
Range loads	*NEC Table 220.55*
Kitchen equipment loads	*NEC Table 220.56*

In addition to those demand factors listed in *NEC Article 220, Part III,* alternative (optional) methods for computing loads can be found in *NEC Article 220, Part IV.* They include the following:

Dwelling unit loads	*NEC Table 220.82*
Existing dwelling unit loads	*NEC Section 220.83*
Multi-family dwelling unit loads	*NEC Section 220.84*

.5.0 General Lighting and Receptacle Load Demand Factors

NEC Table 220.42 provides the demand factors allowed for various types of lighting situations.

.6.0 Small Appliance and Laundry Loads for Dwelling Units

The small appliance branch circuits required by *NEC Section 210.11(C)* for small appliances supplied by 15A or 20A receptacles on 20A branch circuits for each kitchen area served are calculated at 1,500VA. If a dwelling has more than one kitchen area, the *NEC*® will require two small appliance branch circuits computed at 1,500VA for each kitchen area served. Where a dwelling with only one kitchen area has more than the required two small appliance branch circuits installed to serve a single kitchen area, only the first two required circuits need be computed. Additional circuits for countertops or refrigeration provide a separation of load, not additional loads. If a dwelling has two kitchen areas, then the total small appliance branch circuits required would be four at 1,500VA each. These loads are permitted to be included with the general lighting load and subjected to the demand factors of *NEC Table 220.42.*

2.6.1 Laundry Circuit Load

A 1,500VA feeder load is added to load calculations for each two-wire laundry branch circuit installed in a home. The branch circuit is required by *NEC Section 210.11(C)(2).* This load may also be added to the general lighting load and subjected to the same demand factors provided in *NEC Section 220.42.*

2.6.2 Dryer Load

The dryer load for each electric clothes dryer is 5,000VA or the actual nameplate value of the dryer, whichever is larger. Demand factors listed in *NEC Table 220.54* may be applied for more than one dryer in the same dwelling. If two or more single-phase dryers are supplied by a three-phase, four-wire feeder, the total load is computed by using twice the maximum number connected between any two phases.

2.6.3 Range Load

Range loads and other cooking appliances are covered under *NEC Section 220.55.* The feeder demand loads for household electric ranges, wall-mounted ovens, countertop cooking units, and other similar household appliances individually rated over 1¾kW are permitted to be computed in accordance with *NEC Table 220.55.* If two or more single-phase ranges are supplied by a three-phase, four-wire feeder, the total load is computed by using twice the maximum number connected between any two phases.

Demand Factors

Examine *NEC Table 220.55.* Why does the demand factor decrease as the number of appliances increases? Why does the demand factor decrease more for larger ranges than it does for smaller ones?

2.6.4 Demand Loads for Electric Ranges

Ranges can be computed in various ways that depend on which part of *NEC Article 220* you are using and the occupancy type for the ranges involved. Note the demand factors permitted for the following occupancy types:

- Dwelling units per Part III   *NEC Section 220.55*
- Dwelling units per Part IV   *NEC Section 220.82*
- Additions to existing dwellings per Part IV   *NEC Section 220.83*
- Multi-family dwellings per Part III   *NEC Section 220.55*
- Multi-family dwellings per Part IV   *NEC Section 220.84*
- Restaurant loads per Part III   *NEC Section 220.56*
- Restaurant loads per Part IV   *NEC Section 220.88*

2.7.0 Demand Factors for Neutral Conductors

The neutral conductor of electrical systems generally carries only the maximum current imbalance of the phase conductors. For example, in a single-phase feeder circuit with one phase conductor carrying 50A and the other carrying 40A, the neutral conductor would carry 10A. Since the neutral in many cases will never be required to carry as much current as the phase conductors, the *NEC®* allows us to apply a demand factor. (See *NEC Section 220.61*.) Note that in certain circumstances such as electrical discharge lighting, data processing equipment, and other similar equipment, a demand factor cannot be applied to the neutral conductors because these types of equipment produce harmonic currents that increase the heating effect in the neutral conductor.

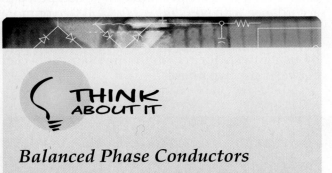

THINK ABOUT IT

Balanced Phase Conductors

The word phase is used in these modules to refer to a hot wire rather than a neutral one. Some electricians call these legs rather than phases. Why must the two phase conductors be balanced?

3.0.0 ◆ SIZING RESIDENTIAL NEUTRAL CONDUCTORS

The neutral conductor in a three-wire, single-phase service carries only the unbalanced load between the two ungrounded (hot) wires or legs. Since there are several 240V loads in the above calculations, these 240V loads will be balanced and therefore reduce the load on the service neutral conductor. Consequently, in most cases, the service neutral does not have to be as large as the ungrounded (hot) conductors.

In the previous example, the water heater does not have to be included in the neutral conductor calculation, since it is strictly 240V with no 120V loads. This takes the total number of fixed appliances on the neutral conductor down to three appliances. Therefore, each of the fixed appliance loads on the neutral must be computed at 100% (dishwasher at 1,500VA, plus disposal at 1,176VA, plus the blower at 864VA). The neutral loads of the electric range and clothes dryer are permitted by *NEC Section 220.61* to be computed at 70% of the demand for the phase conductors since these appliances have both 120V and 240V loads. In this case, the largest motor is the same for the neutral conductors as it is for the phase conductors; therefore, it is computed in the same manner. Using this information, the neutral conductor may be sized accordingly:

- Net general lighting and small appliance load   4,943VA (Box 13)
- Fixed appliance loads   3,540VA (Box 22)
- Electric range (8,000VA × 0.70)   5,600VA (Box 26)
- Clothes dryer (5,500VA × 0.70)   3,850VA (Box 28)
- Largest motor   294VA (Box 32)
- Total   18,227VA (Box 34)

To find the total phase-to-phase amperes, divide the total volt-amperes by the voltage between phases:

$$18,227VA \div 240V = 75.9A \text{ or } 76A$$

The service-entrance conductors have now been calculated and are rated at 125A with a neutral conductor rated for at least 76A. See *Figure* for a completed calculation form for the example residence.

In *NEC Section 310.15(B)(6)*, special consideration is given to 120/240V, single-phase residential services and feeders. Conductor sizes are shown in *NEC Table 310.15(B)(6)*. Reference to this table shows that the *NEC®* allows a No. 2 AWG copper or a 1/0 AWG aluminum conductor for a 125

General Lighting Load

					Phase		Neutral	
Square footage of the dwelling	[1] 1350	× 3VA =	[2] 4050					
Kitchen small appliance circuits	[3] 2	× 1500 =	[4] 3000					
Laundry branch circuit	[5] 1	× 1500 =	[6] 1500					
Subtotal of gen. lighting loads per *NEC Section 220.52* =			[7] 8550					
Subtract 1st 3000VA per *NEC Section 220.42*			[8] 3000	× 100% =	[9] 3000			
Remaining VA times 35% per *NEC Section 220.42*			[10] 5550	× 35% =	[11] 1943			
Total demand for general lighting loads =					[12] 4943		[13] 4943	

Fixed Appliance Loads (Nameplate or NEC FLA of motors) per *NEC Section 220.53*

		Phase	Neutral
Hot water tank, 4.5kVA, 240V	[14] 4500		
Dishwasher 1.5kVA, 120V	[15] 1500		
Disposal 1/2HP, 120V per *NEC Table 430.248* = 9.8A	[16] 1176		
Blower 1/3HP, 120V per *NEC Table 430.248* = 7.2A	[17] 864		
	[18]		
	[19]		
Subtotal of fixed appliances	[20] 8040		
If 3 or less fixed appliances take @ 100% =		[21]	[22] 3540
If 4 or more fixed appliances take @ 75% =		[23] 6030	[24]

Other Loads per *NEC Section 220.14*

		Phase	Neutral
Electric Range per *NEC Section 220.55* (neutral @ 70% per *NEC Section 220.61*)		[25] 8000	[26] 5600
Electric Dryer per *NEC Section 220.54* (neutral @ 70% per *NEC Section 220.61*)		[27] 5500	[28] 3850
Electric Heat per *NEC Section 220.51*			
Air Conditioning	omit smaller load per *NEC Section 220.60*	[29]	[30]
Largest Motor = 1176	× 25% (per *NEC Section 430.24*) =	[31] 294	[32] 294
Total VA Demand =		[33] 24767	[34] 18227
(VA divided by 240 volts) **Amps** =		[35] **103**	[36] **76**
Service OCD and minimum size grounding electrode conductor		[37] 125	[38] 8 AWG
AWG per *NEC Sections 310.15(B)(6) and 310.16* for neutral		[39] 2 AWG	[40] 4 AWG

112F04.EPS

Figure 4 ◆ Completed calculation form.

service. The neutral conductor is sized per *NEC Tables 310.15(B)(6) or 310.16* using the appropriate column for the markings on the service equipment per *NEC Section 110.14(C)*. Assuming our service panel is marked as suitable for use with 75°C-rated conductors, the minimum size of the neutral would be a No. 4 AWG copper or No. 2 AWG aluminum.

When sizing the grounded conductor for services, the provisions stated in *NEC Sections 215.2, 220.61, and 230.42* must be met, along with other applicable sections.

10.0.0 ◆ SIZING THE LOAD CENTER

Each ungrounded conductor in all circuits must be provided with overcurrent protection in the form of either fuses or circuit breakers. If more than six such devices are used, a means of discon-

necting the entire service must be provided using either a main disconnect switch or a main circuit breaker.

To calculate the number of fuse holders or circuit breakers required in the sample residence, look at the general lighting load first. The total general lighting load of 4,050VA can be divided by 120V to find the amperage:

$$4,050VA \div 120V = 33.75A$$

Either 15A or 20A circuits may be used for the lighting load. Two 20A circuits (2 × 20) equal 40A, so two 20A circuits would be adequate for the lighting. However, two 15A circuits total only 30A and 33.75A are needed. Therefore, if 15A circuits are used, three will be required for the total lighting load. In this example, three 15A circuits will be used.

In addition to the lighting circuits, the sample residence will require a minimum of two 20A

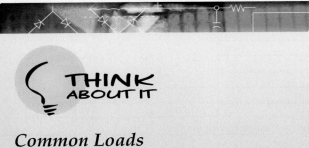

THINK ABOUT IT

Common Loads

Which of the following devices uses the most power?

- Giant-screen television
- Typical hair dryer
- Curling iron
- Crockpot

circuits for the small appliance load and one 20A circuit for the laundry. So far, the following branch circuits can be counted:

- General lighting load — Three 15A circuits
- Small appliance load — Two 20A circuits
- Laundry load — One 20A circuit
- Total — Six branch circuits

Most **load centers** and panelboards are provided with an even number of circuit breaker spaces or fuse holders (for example, four, six, eight, or ten). But before the panelboard can be selected, space must be provided for the remaining loads. Each 240V load will require two spaces. In some existing installations, you might find a two-pole fuse block containing two cartridge fuses being used to feed a residential electric range. Each 120V load will require one space each. Thus, the remaining number of circuits for this example is as follows:

- Hot water heater — One two-pole breaker
- Dishwasher — One single-pole breaker
- Disposal — One single-pole breaker
- Blower — One single-pole breaker
- Electric range — One two-pole breaker
- Electric dryer — One two-pole breaker

These additional appliances will therefore require an additional nine spaces in the load center or panelboard. *NEC Section 210.11(C)(3)* requires that a separate 20A branch circuit be provided for the bathroom receptacles. While this circuit requires extra space within a load center, it does not add to the demand on the service for a dwelling unit. Adding the nine spaces for the other loads in the dwelling, plus one for a bathroom circuit, to the six required for the general lighting and small appliance loads requires at least a 16-space load center to handle the circuits.

4.1.0 Ground-Fault Circuit Interrupters

Under certain conditions, the amount of current takes to open an overcurrent protective device ca be critical. You should remember from the *Electrical Safety* module that when persons are subjec to very low current values (less than one full am pere), it can be fatal. The overcurrent protectio installed on services, feeders, and branch circuits protects only the conductors and equipment.

Because of this fact, the *NEC*® requires groun fault circuit interrupter (GFCI) protection fo receptacle outlets and/or equipment in many lo cations and occupancies. The *NEC*® defines GFCI as "a device intended for the protection of personnel that functions to de-energize a circuit portion thereof within an established period time when a current to ground exceeds the value established for a Class A device." Class A GFC trip when the current to ground has a value in the range of 4mA to 6mA.

For dwelling units, the majority of require ments to provide protection for 15A or 20A, 125V rated receptacles can be found in *NEC Sectio 210.8(A)*. Further requirements for GFCI prote tion at dwelling units can be found in other *NEC* articles such as *NEC Article 590* for temporar construction sites; *NEC Article 620* for speci equipment such as elevators; or in *NEC Artic 680* for special equipment such as swimmin pools, hot tubs, and hydromassage tubs. These a ticles may also expand the requirements for GFC protection to include circuits rated at more tha 20A or operating at 240V.

According to *NEC Section 210.8(A)*, the 15 and 20A, 125V-rated receptacles in our dwellin that require GFCI protection will be those recep tacles located in the following areas:

- Bathrooms
- Outdoor receptacles (except those provided d dedicated circuits for snow melting and de icing equipment)
- Receptacles that serve the countertops kitchens

Further requirements for GFCI protection dwelling units are as follows:

- Readily accessible receptacles within garag and accessory buildings, such as storage shed or workshops, or similar uses that have a floo located at or below grade level
- Readily accessible receptacles in unfinishe basements
- Crawl spaces at or below grade level
- Receptacles that serve countertops and a within 6' of wet bar sinks, utility, or laundry sin
- Boathouses

One way to provide this GFCI protection is through the use of a GFCI circuit breaker. GFCI circuit breakers require the same mounting space as standard single-pole circuit breakers and provide the same branch circuit wiring protection as standard circuit breakers. They also provide Class A ground fault protection.

Listed GFCI circuit breakers are available in single- and two-pole construction; 15A, 20A, 25A, and 30A, 50A, and 60A ratings; and have a 10,000A interrupting capacity. Single-pole units are rated at 120VAC; two-pole units are rated at 120/240VAC.

GFCI breakers can be used not only in load centers and panelboards, but they are also available factory-installed in meter pedestals and power outlet panels for recreational vehicle (RV) parks and construction sites.

The GFCI sensor continuously monitors the current balance in the ungrounded or energized (hot) load conductor and the neutral load conductor. If the current in the neutral load wire becomes less than the current in the hot load wire, then a ground fault exists, since a portion of the current is returning to the source by some means other than the neutral load wire. When a current imbalance occurs, the sensor, which is a differential current transformer, sends a signal to the solid-state circuit, which activates the ground trip solenoid mechanism and breaks the hot load connection (*Figure 5*). A current imbalance as low as four milliamps (4mA) will cause the circuit breaker to interrupt the circuit. This is indicated by the trip indicator on the front of the device.

The two-pole GFCI breaker (*Figure 6*) continuously monitors the current balance between the two hot conductors and the neutral conductor. As long as the sum of these three currents is zero, the device will not trip; that is, if the A load wire is carrying 10A of current, the neutral is carrying 5A, and the B load wire is carrying 5A, then the sensor is balanced and will not produce a signal. A current imbalance from a ground fault condition as low as 4mA will cause the sensor to produce a signal of sufficient magnitude to trip the device.

4.1.1 Single-Pole GFCI Circuit Breakers

The single-pole GFCI breaker has two load lugs and a white wire pigtail in addition to the line side plug-on or bolt-on connector. The line side hot connection is made by installing the GFCI breaker in the panel just as any other circuit breaker is installed. The white wire pigtail is attached to the panel neutral (S/N) assembly. Both the neutral and hot wires of the branch circuit being protected are terminated in the GFCI breaker. These two load lugs are clearly marked LOAD POWER and LOAD NEUTRAL in the breaker case. Also in the case is the identifying marking for the pigtail, PANEL NEUTRAL.

Single-pole GFCI circuit breakers must be installed on independent circuits. Circuits that employ a neutral common to more than one hot conductor cannot be protected against ground faults by a single-pole breaker because a common neutral cannot be split and retain the necessary hot wire to neutral wire balance under normal use to prevent the GFCI breaker from tripping.

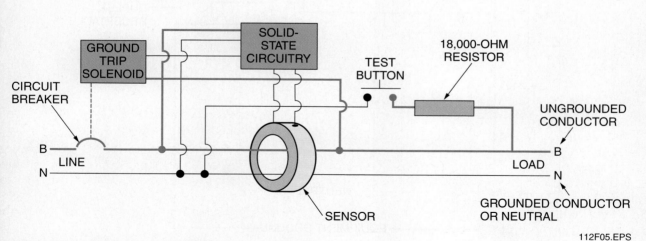

112F05.EPS

Figure 5 ◆ Operating circuitry of a typical GFCI.

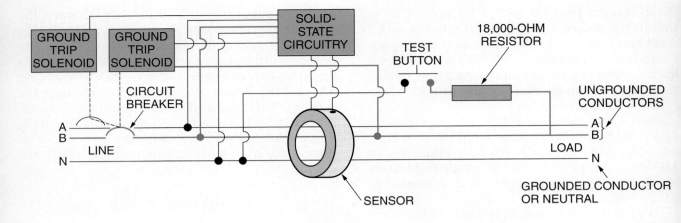

Figure 6 ◆ Operating characteristics of a two-pole GFCI.

Care should be exercised when installing GFCI breakers in existing panels. Be sure that the neutral wire for the branch circuit corresponds with the hot wire of the same circuit. Always remember that unless the current in the neutral wire is equal to that in the hot wire (within 4mA), the GFCI breaker senses this as being a possible ground fault (see *Figure 7*).

4.1.2 *Two-Pole GFCI Circuit Breakers*

A two-pole GFCI circuit breaker can be installed on a 120/240VAC single-phase, three-wire sys-

tem; the 120/240VAC portion of a 120/240VA three-phase, four-wire system; or the two phase and neutral of a 120/208VAC three-phase, fou wire system. Regardless of the application, the ir stallation of the breaker is the same—connection are made to two hot buses and the panel neutra assembly. When installed on these system protection is provided for two-wire 240VA or 208VAC circuits, three-wire 120/240VA or 120/208VAC circuits, and 120VAC multiwi circuits.

The circuit in *Figure 8* illustrates the problem that are encountered when a common load neutr.

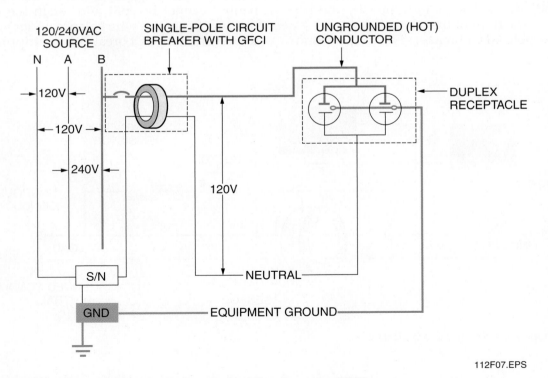

Figure 7 ◆ Operating characteristics of a single-pole circuit breaker with a GFCI.

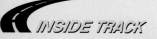

GFCI Circuit Breaker

This GFCI breaker shows the markings for the panel neutral and load neutral.

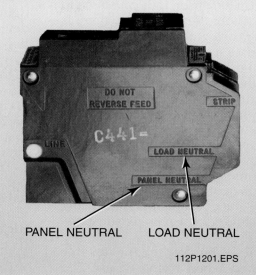

PANEL NEUTRAL   LOAD NEUTRAL

112P1201.EPS

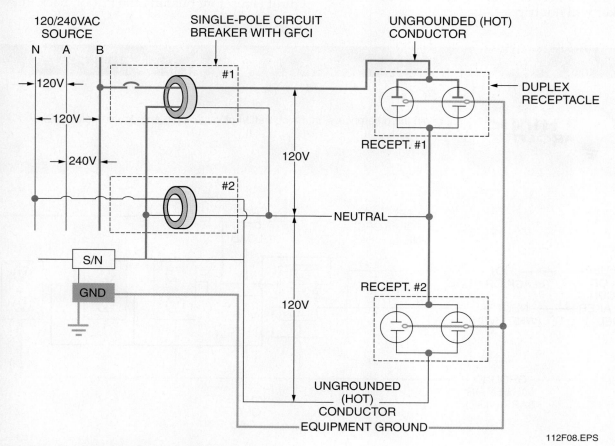

Figure 8 ◆ Circuit depicting the common load neutral.

112F08.EPS

is used for two single-pole GFCI breakers. Either or both breakers will trip when a load is applied at the #2 duplex receptacle. The neutral current from the #2 duplex receptacle flows through breaker #1; this increase in neutral current through breaker #1 causes an imbalance in its sensor, thus causing it to produce a fault signal. At the same time, there is no neutral current flowing through breaker #2; therefore, it also senses a current imbalance. If a load is applied at the #1 duplex receptacle, and there is no load at the #2 duplex receptacle, then neither breaker will trip because neither breaker will sense a current imbalance.

Junction boxes can also present problems when they are used to provide taps for more than one branch circuit. Even though the circuits are not wired using a common neutral, sometimes all neutral conductors are connected together. Thus, parallel neutral paths are established, producing an imbalance in each GFCI breaker sensor, causing them to trip.

The two-pole GFCI breaker eliminates the problems encountered when trying to use two single-pole GFCI breakers with a common neutral. Because both hot currents and the neutral current pass through the same sensor, no imbalance occurs between the three currents, and the breaker will not trip.

4.1.3 Direct-Wired GFCI Receptacles

Direct-wired GFCI receptacles provide Class ground fault protection on 120VAC circuits. The are available in both 15A and 20A arrangemen The 15A unit has a NEMA 5-15R receptacle co figuration for use with 15A plugs only. The 20 device has a NEMA 5-20R receptacle configur tion for use with 15A or 20A plugs. Both 15A ar 20A units have a 120VAC, 20A circuit rating. Th is to comply with *NEC Table 210.24,* which quires that 15A circuits use 15A receptacles b permits the use of either 15A or 20A receptac on 20A circuits. Therefore, GFCI receptacle un that contain a 15A receptacle may be used on 20 circuits.

These receptacles have line terminals for t hot, neutral, and ground wires. In addition, th have load terminals that can be used to provi ground fault protection for other receptacles ele trically downstream on the same branch circ (*Figure 9*). All terminals will accept No. 14 to 10 AWG copper wire.

GFCI receptacles have a two-pole trippi mechanism that breaks both the hot and the ne tral load connections.

When tripped, the RESET button pops out. T unit is reset by pushing the button back in.

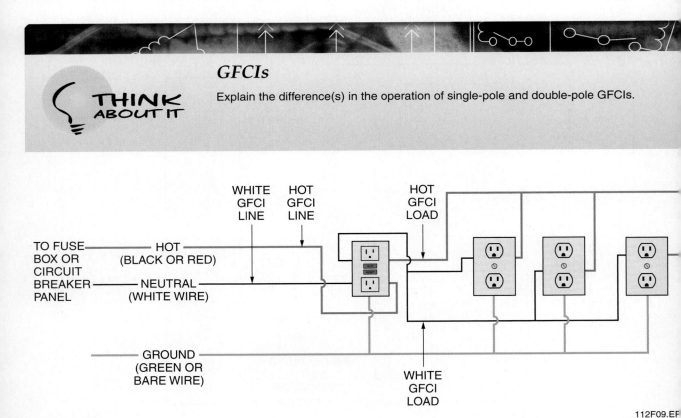

GFCIs

THINK ABOUT IT

Explain the difference(s) in the operation of single-pole and double-pole GFCIs.

WHITE GFCI LINE | HOT GFCI LINE | HOT GFCI LOAD

TO FUSE BOX OR CIRCUIT BREAKER PANEL

HOT (BLACK OR RED)

NEUTRAL (WHITE WIRE)

GROUND (GREEN OR BARE WIRE)

WHITE GFCI LOAD

112F09.EF

Figure 9 ◆ GFCI receptacle used to protect other outlets on the same circuit.

GFCI receptacles have the additional benefit of noise suppression. Noise suppression minimizes false tripping due to spurious line voltages or radio frequency (RF) signals between 10 and 500 megahertz (MHz).

GFCI receptacles can be mounted without adapters in wall outlet boxes that are at least 1.5 inches deep.

0.0 ◆ GROUNDING ELECTRIC SERVICES

NEC Section 250.4(A) provides the general requirements for grounding and bonding of grounded electrical systems. In order to ensure systems are properly grounded and bonded, the prescriptive requirements of *NEC Article 250* must be followed.

The grounding system is a major part of the electrical system. Its purpose is to protect people and equipment against the various electrical faults that can occur. It is sometimes possible for higher-than-normal voltages to appear at certain points in an electrical system or in the electrical equipment connected to the system. Proper grounding ensures that the electrical charges that cause these higher voltages are channeled to the earth or ground and that an effective ground fault path is provided throughout the system so that overcurrent devices will open before people are endangered or equipment is damaged.

The word ground refers to ground potential or earth ground. If a conductor is connected to the earth or some conducting body that serves in place of the earth, such as a driven ground rod (electrode), the conductor is said to be grounded. The neutral conductor in a three- or four-wire service, for example, is intentionally grounded, and therefore becomes a grounded conductor. This is the path back to the source of supply for all ground faults in an electrical system. This conductor is intended not only to carry the unbalanced loads of an installation, but also to provide

the low-impedance path back to the source so that enough current will flow in the system to open the overcurrent devices. A wire that is used to connect this neutral conductor to a grounding electrode or electrodes is referred to as a grounding electrode conductor (GEC). Note the difference in the two meanings: one is grounded, while the other provides a means for grounding.

There are two general classifications of protective grounding:

- System grounding
- Equipment grounding

The system ground relates to the **service-entrance equipment** and its interrelated and bonded components; that is, the system and circuit conductors are grounded to limit voltages due to lightning, line surges, or unintentional contact with higher voltage and to stabilize the voltage to ground during normal operation per *NEC Sections 250.4(A)(1) and (2)*.

The noncurrent-carrying conductive parts of materials enclosing electrical conductors or equipment, or forming a part of such equipment, and electrically conductive materials that are likely to become energized are all connected together to the supply source in a manner that establishes an effective ground fault path per *NEC Sections 250.4(A)(3) and (4)*.

NEC Section 250.4(A)(5) defines the requirements for an effective ground path. It requires that electrical equipment and wiring and other electrically conductive materials likely to become energized shall be installed in a manner that creates a permanent, low-impedance circuit capable of safely carrying the maximum ground-fault current likely to be imposed on it from any point on the wiring system where a ground fault may occur to the electrical supply source. The earth shall not be used as the sole equipment grounding conductor or effective ground-fault current path.

To better understand a complete grounding system, a conventional residential system will be

Grounding

Systematic grounding wasn't required by the *NEC*® until the mid-1950s; even then, electricians commonly grounded an outlet by wrapping an uninsulated wire around a cold-water pipe and taping it. Three-hole receptacles with grounding terminals became common in the 1960s, but in many older houses, you cannot assume that receptacles are grounded, even when you see a three-hole receptacle. Sometimes, new receptacles have simply been screwed onto old boxes where there is no equipment grounding conductor.

examined, beginning at the power company's high-voltage lines and transformer, as shown in *Figure 10*. The pole-mounted transformer is fed with a two-wire, single-phase 7,200V system, which is transformed and stepped down to a three-wired, 120/240V, single-phase electric service suitable for residential use. Note that the voltage between line A and line B is 240V. However, by connecting a third (neutral) wire on the secondary winding of the transformer—between the other two—the 240V is split in half, providing 120V between either line A or line B and the neutral conductor. Consequently, 240V is available for household appliances such as ranges, hot water heaters, and clothes dryers, while 120V is available for lights and small appliances.

Referring again to *Figure 10*, conductors A and B are ungrounded conductors, while the neutral is a grounded conductor. If only 240V loads were connected, the neutral (grounded conductor) would carry no current. In this instance, the neutral would be used to carry any ground-fault currents from the load side of the service back to the utility instead of depending on the earth as the path back to the source. However, since 120V loads are present, the neutral will carry the unbalanced load and become a current-carrying conductor. For example, if line A carries 60A and line

B carries 50A, the neutral would carry only 10A (60A − 50A = 10A). This is why the *NEC*® allow the neutral conductor in an electric service to b smaller than the ungrounded conductors. How ever, *NEC Section 250.24(C)(1)* requires that must be sufficient to carry fault currents back the source and, therefore, must not be less than th required grounding electrode conductor usin *NEC Table 250.66* for service conductors up 1,100 kcmil and not less than 12.5% of the area the service-entrance conductors (or equivalen larger than 1,100 kcmil. The typical pole-mounte service drop conductors are normally routed by messenger cable from a point on the pole to point on the building being served, terminating the point where service-entrance conductors exi weatherhead. Service-entrance conductors a then typically routed through metering equip ment into the service disconnecting means. This the point where most services are grounded. S *Figure 11*. *NEC Section 250.24(A)(1)* requires th the grounding electrode for the structure conne tion to the neutral (grounded conductor) be at an accessible point from the load end of the servi drop or **service lateral** to and including the term nal or bus to which the neutral (grounded servi conductor) is connected to the service disconnec ing means.

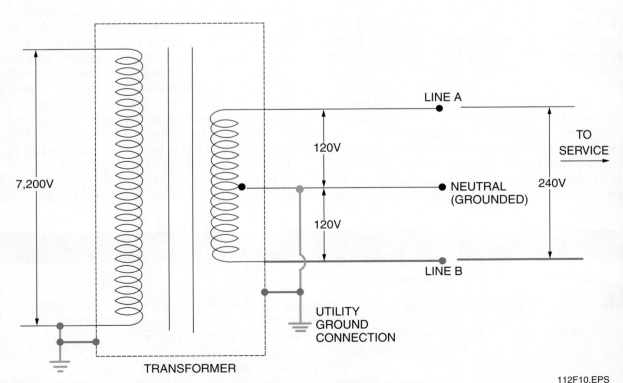

Figure 10 ◆ Wiring diagram of a 7,200V to 120/240V, single-phase transformer connection.

112F10.EPS

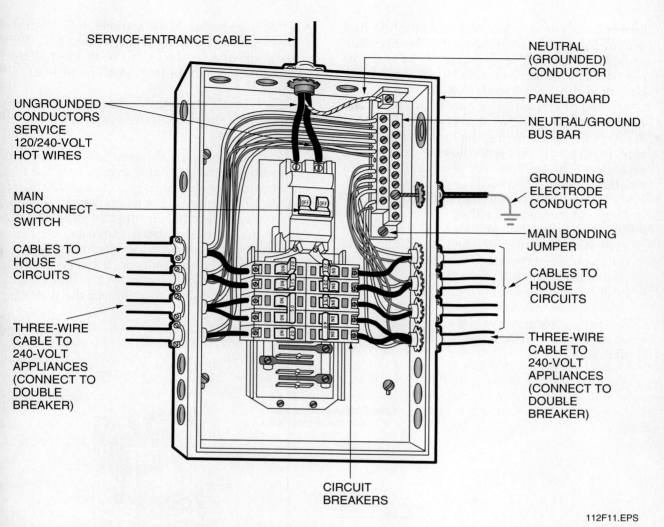

SERVICE-ENTRANCE CABLE

NEUTRAL (GROUNDED) CONDUCTOR

UNGROUNDED CONDUCTORS SERVICE 120/240-VOLT HOT WIRES

PANELBOARD

NEUTRAL/GROUND BUS BAR

GROUNDING ELECTRODE CONDUCTOR

MAIN DISCONNECT SWITCH

MAIN BONDING JUMPER

CABLES TO HOUSE CIRCUITS

CABLES TO HOUSE CIRCUITS

THREE-WIRE CABLE TO 240-VOLT APPLIANCES (CONNECT TO DOUBLE BREAKER)

THREE-WIRE CABLE TO 240-VOLT APPLIANCES (CONNECT TO DOUBLE BREAKER)

CIRCUIT BREAKERS

112F11.EPS

gure 11 ◆ Interior view of panelboard showing connections.

NOTE

Effectively grounded means intentionally connected to earth through one or more ground connection(s) of sufficiently low impedance and having sufficient current-carrying capacity to prevent the buildup of voltages that may result in a hazard to people or connected equipment.

.1.0 Grounding Electrodes

EC Article 250, Part III provides the require-
ents for connecting an electric service to the
rounding electrode system of a building or struc-
re. *NEC Section 250.50* requires, in general, that
l of the electrodes described in *NEC Section
0.52(A)* be used (if present), and they must be
nded together to form the grounding electrode

system. The electrodes listed in *NEC Section 250.52(A)* are as follows:

- Metal underground water pipe in direct contact with the earth for 10' or more and electrically continuous (or made electrically continuous by bonding around insulating joints or insulating pipe) to the points of connection of the grounding electrode conductor and the bonding conductors. Interior metal water piping located more than 5' from the point of entrance to the building shall not be used as part of the grounding electrode system or as a conductor to interconnect electrodes that are part of the grounding electrode system.
- Metal frame of the building or structure that complies with *NEC Section 250.52(A)(2)*.
- An electrode encased by at least 2" of concrete may be used if it is located within and near the

bottom of a concrete foundation or footing that is in direct contact with the earth. The electrode must be at least 20' long and must be made of electrically conductive coated steel reinforcing bars or rods of not less than ½" in diameter, or consisting of at least 20' of bare copper conductor not smaller than No. 4 AWG wire size.

- A ground ring encircling the building or structure, in direct contact with the earth, consisting of at least 20' of bare copper conductor not smaller than No. 2 AWG.
- Rod and pipe electrodes shall not be less than 8' in length and consist of either:
  - Pipe or conduit not smaller than trade size ¾ and, where of iron or steel, shall have the outer surface galvanized or otherwise metal-coated for corrosion protection.
  - Rods of iron or steel not smaller than ⅝" in diameter. Stainless steel rods less than ⅝" in diameter, nonferrous rods, or their equivalent shall be listed and not less than ½" in diameter.

- Plate electrodes shall expose less than tw[o] square feet of surface to exterior soil. Plate[s] made of iron or steel shall be at least ¼" thic[k.] Nonferrous metal plates shall be at least 0.0[6] thick.
- Other local metal underground systems [or] structures such as piping systems and unde[r]ground tanks.

Often in residential construction, the onl[y] grounding electrode that is available is the met[al] underground water piping system. *NEC Sectio[n] 250.53(D)(2)* requires that whenever water pipin[g] is used as an electrode, it must be supplemente[d.] Any of the electrodes listed above can be used [to] supplement the water pipe electrode. *Figure 1[2]* shows a typical residential electric service and th[e] available grounding electrodes for this structu[re] using a ground rod to supplement the water pip[e] electrode.

This house also has a metal underground g[as] piping system, but this may not be used as an ele[c]trode per *NEC Section 250.52(B)*. In some case[s]

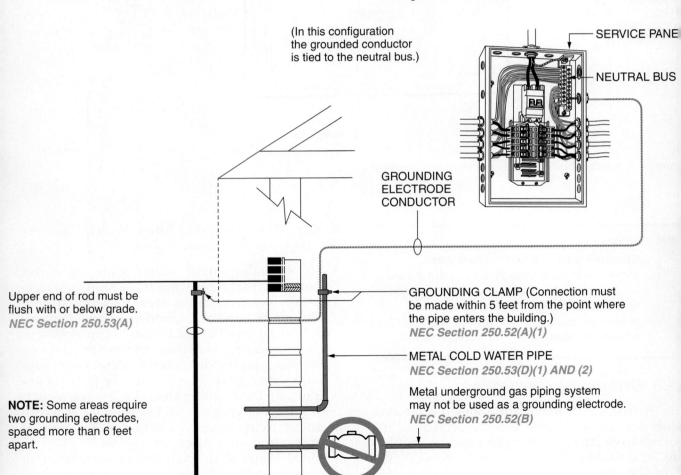

(In this configuration the grounded conductor is tied to the neutral bus.)

SERVICE PANE[L]

NEUTRAL BUS

GROUNDING ELECTRODE CONDUCTOR

Upper end of rod must be flush with or below grade.
NEC Section 250.53(A)

GROUNDING CLAMP (Connection must be made within 5 feet from the point where the pipe enters the building.)
NEC Section 250.52(A)(1)

METAL COLD WATER PIPE
NEC Section 250.53(D)(1) AND (2)

Metal underground gas piping system may not be used as a grounding electrode.
NEC Section 250.52(B)

NOTE: Some areas require two grounding electrodes, spaced more than 6 feet apart.

112F1[...]

Figure 12 ◆ Components of a residential grounding system.

water pipe electrode, building steel, and a ncrete-encased electrode are not available to be ed as a part of the grounding electrode system. r example, a building may be fed by plastic wa- r piping, be constructed of wood, and an electri- an may not be present at the site when the undation for the structure is poured. When that ppens, *NEC Section 250.50* requires that rod, pe, plate, or other local metal underground uctures be used.

Some local jurisdictions do not recognize water ping as an electrode due to the rise in the use of nmetallic piping for both new and replacement ater systems. They do not want to rely on the aintained viability of an existing metallic water rvice and therefore require the use of other elec- odes such as the concrete-encased or rod elec- odes. This means electricians must be involved th the construction prior to the foundation be- g poured in order to utilize concrete-encased ctrodes.

In most cases, the supplemental electrode used r a water pipe electrode will consist of either a iven rod or pipe electrode, the specifications for iich are shown in *Figure 13*.

WARNING!
A metal underground gas piping system must never be used as a grounding electrode.

5.1.1 Grounding Electrode Installations

NEC Section 250.53(A) requires that rod, pipe, and plate electrodes, where practical, be buried below the permanent moisture level and that they are free from any nonconductive coatings, such as paint or enamel. This section also requires that each electrode system used for a structure be at least 6' from other electrode systems, such as those for lightning protection.

NEC Section 250.53(G) permits a rod or pipe electrode to be driven at a 45-degree angle if rock bottom is encountered and prevents the rod or pipe from being driven vertically for at least 8'. Where driving a rod or pipe electrode at a 45-degree angle will not work, it is permitted to lay a rod or pipe horizontally in a trench that is at least 30" deep. For rod or pipe electrodes longer than 8',

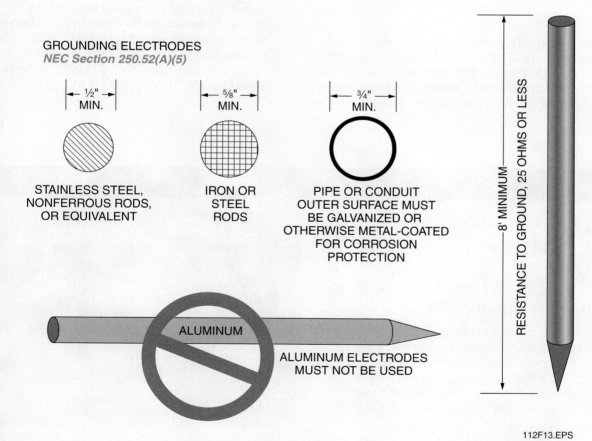

112F13.EPS

ure 13 ◆ Specifications for rod and pipe grounding electrodes.

it is permitted to have the upper end above ground level if a suitable means of protection is provided for the grounding electrode conductor attachment; otherwise, the upper end must be flush with the earth surface.

NEC Section 250.56 requires that a single rod, pipe, or plate electrode that does not have a resistance to ground of 25Ω or less shall be augmented by one additional electrode of any of the types specified by *NEC Sections 250.52(A)(2) through (7)*. In fact, many local jurisdictions require two electrodes regardless of the resistance to ground. Always check with the local inspection authority, including the local utility, for rules that surpass the requirements of the *NEC®*.

- Where multiple rod, pipe, or plate electrodes are installed to meet the requirements of this section, they shall not be less than 6' apart.
- Plate electrodes must be buried at least 30" below the surface of the earth, according to *NEC Section 250.53(H)*.
- Where two or more electrodes are effectively bonded together, they are treated as a single electrode system.

5.1.2 Grounding Electrode Conductors (GECs)

The grounding electrode conductor (GEC) connecting the neutral (grounded conductor of the service) at the panelboard neutral bus to the grounding electrodes must meet the requirements of *NEC Section 250.62*. This requires that it be made of copper, aluminum, or copper-clad aluminu[m]. The material selected must be suitably protect[ed] against corrosion. The GEC may be either solid [or] stranded, covered or bare. Note that the GEC is n[ot] an equipment grounding conductor, and thus [is] not required to be identified by the use of the col[or] green or green with yellow stripes, if insulated.

5.1.3 Installation of GECs

NEC Section 250.64 provides the installation [re]quirements for GECs and does not permit ba[re] aluminum or copper-clad aluminum groundi[ng] conductors to be used where in direct contact wi[th] masonry, the earth, where subject to corrosi[ve] conditions, or where used outside within 18" [of] the earth at the termination point. Other *NEC®* [re]quirements include the following:

- A GEC or its enclosure is required to be secure[ly] fastened to the surface on which it is carried.
- A No. 4 AWG or larger copper or aluminu[m] GEC is required to be protected where it will [be] exposed to severe physical damage.
- A No. 6 AWG or larger GEC that is free from e[x]posure to physical damage is permitted to [be] run along the surface of the building witho[ut] metal covering or protection where it is s[e]curely fastened to the building. Otherwise, [it] must be installed in RMC, IMC, RNC, EMT, [or] a cable armor.
- GECs smaller than No. 6 AWG must be p[ro]tected by RMC, IMC, RNC, EMT, or cable arm[or]

THINK ABOUT IT

Grounding Conductors

This residential application has a grounding electrode connected to a rod that travels through the floor and into the ground at least 8'. In addition, it is also connected to a metal cold-water pipe (not shown). What type of grounding system is provided at your home? Does it meet *NEC®* requirements?

112P1202.EPS

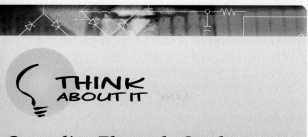

Grounding Electrode Conductors

Which table would you use to size the minimum GEC required for a typical residential service?

The GEC shall be installed in one continuous length without a splice or joint, unless spliced only by irreversible compression-type connectors listed for the purpose or by an exothermic welding process. Connecting sections of busbars together to form a GEC is not considered to be a splice.

Where a service consists of more than a single enclosure, it is permissible to connect taps to the GEC, provided each tap extends all the way into the inside of each such enclosure. The tap conductors shall be connected to the GEC in such a manner that the GEC remains without a splice.

Metal enclosures for the GEC are required to be electrically continuous from the point of attachment to metal cabinets or metallic equipment enclosures to the GEC. They must also be securely fastened to the ground clamp or fitting.

Metal enclosures for the GEC that are not physically continuous from a metal cabinet or metallic equipment enclosure to the grounding electrode must be made electrically continuous by bonding each to the enclosed GEC.

GECs may be run to any convenient grounding electrode available in the grounding electrode system, or to one or more grounding electrode(s) individually. The GEC shall be sized for the largest grounding electrode conductor required among all the electrodes connected together.

5.1.4 Methods of Connecting GECs

NEC Section 250.70 requires the GEC to be connected to electrodes using exothermic welding, listed pressure connectors, listed clamps, listed lugs, or other listed means. Connections that depend on solder must never be used. To prevent corrosion, the ground clamp must be listed for the material of the grounding electrode and the GEC.

Where used on a pipe, ground rod, or other buried electrodes, the fitting must be listed for direct soil burial or concrete encasement. More than one conductor is not permitted to be connected to the grounding electrode using a single clamp or fitting unless the clamp or fitting is specifically listed for the connection of more than one conductor.

For the connection to an electrode, you must use one of the following:

- A listed, bolted clamp of cast bronze or brass, or plain or malleable iron
- A pipe fitting, pipe plug, or other approved device that is screwed into a pipe or pipe fitting
- For indoor telecommunication purposes only, a listed sheet metal strap-type ground clamp with a rigid metal base that seats on the electrode with a strap that will not stretch during or after installation
- An equally substantial approved means

The connection of a GEC or a **bonding jumper** to a grounding electrode must be accessible unless that connection is to the concrete-encased or buried grounding electrodes permitted in *NEC Section 250.68*. Where it is necessary to ensure the grounding path for metal piping used as a grounding electrode, effective bonding shall be provided around insulated joints and around any equipment likely to be disconnected for repairs or replacement. Bonding conductors shall be of sufficient length to permit removal of such equipment while retaining the integrity of the bond. Coatings on metal piping systems must be removed to ensure that a permanent and effective grounding path is provided.

> **NOTE**
>
> The UL listing states that "strap-type ground clamps are not suitable for attachment of the grounding electrode conductor of an interior wiring system to a grounding electrode."

For the example house, the point of connection to the water piping is shown in *Figure 12* and would be required to be accessible after any wall coverings are installed. Any nonconductive coatings on the water piping would also have been scraped off or removed prior to installing the clamp on the water pipe.

5.1.5 Sizing GECs

Grounding electrode conductors must be sized per *NEC Section 250.66,* which uses the area of the largest service-entrance conductor (or equivalent area for paralleled conductors). Except as noted below, *NEC Table 250.66* will provide the minimum size GEC and any bonding jumpers used to interconnect grounding electrodes used.

- Where connected to rod, pipe, or plate electrodes, that portion of the GEC that is the sole connection to the grounding electrode shall not be required to be larger than No. 6 AWG copper or No. 4 AWG aluminum.
- Where connected to a concrete-encased electrode, that portion of the GEC that is the sole connection to the grounding electrode shall not be required to be larger than No. 4 AWG copper wire.
- Where the GEC is connected to a ground ring, that portion of the conductor that is the sole connection to the grounding electrode shall not be required to be larger than the conductor used for the ground ring.
- Where multiple sets of service-entrance conductors are used as permitted in *NEC Section 230.40, Exception 2,* the equivalent size of the largest service-entrance conductor is required to be determined by the largest sum of the areas of the corresponding conductors of each set.
- Where there are no service-entrance conductors, the GEC size is required to be determined by the equivalent size of the largest service-entrance conductor required for the load to be served.

For our sample dwelling unit, the size of the service-entrance conductors is No. 2 AWG. Using *NEC Table 250.66,* we can determine that the size of the conductor coming from the service panel to the water pipe (the GEC) must be at least No. 8 AWG copper. This No. 8 AWG may continue on without a splice to the ground rod, as shown in *Figure 12,* or a separate No. 6 AWG could be installed for the ground rod(s). This conductor would have to be connected to the service panel as an individual run or with a separate connector to any portion of the No. 8 AWG. It may not be connected directly to the water piping.

5.1.6 Air Terminals

Air terminal conductors and driven pipes, rods, or plate electrodes used for grounding air terminals are not permitted to be used in lieu of the grounding electrodes covered in *NEC Section 250.50* for grounding wiring systems and equipment. However, *NEC Section 250.106* requires that they be bonded to the wiring and equipment grounding electrode system for the structure.

5.2.0 Main Bonding Jumper

NEC Section 250.24(B) requires that an unspliced main bonding jumper (MBJ) shall be used to connect the equipment grounding conductor(s) and the service disconnect enclosure to the grounded conductor (neutral) of the system within the enclosure of each service disconnect.

The MBJ must be of copper or other corrosion-resistant material. An MBJ may be in the form of a wire, bus, screw, or similar suitable conductor.

Where an MBJ is in the form of a screw, it is required to be identified with a green finish so that the head of the screw is visible for inspection. An MBJ must be attached using exothermic welding, a listed pressure connector, listed clamp, or other listed means. Sheet metal screws shall not be used for any grounding connections.

The MBJ cannot be smaller than the sizes given in *NEC Table 250.66* for grounding electrode conductors. See *NEC Section 250.28(D)* for service conductors that exceed 1,100 kcmil.

INSIDE TRACK

What Does a Lightning Rod Do?

An interesting fact about grounding is that a lightning rod (air terminal) isn't meant to bring a bolt of lightning to ground. To do this, its conductors would have to be several feet in diameter. The purpose of the rod is to dissipate the negative static charge that would cause the positive lightning charge to strike the house.

The MBJ is the means by which any ground fault in the branch circuits and feeders of the electrical system travels back to the source of supply the utility. A ground fault will travel along the equipment conductors of the circuits back to the service disconnecting means. Where metallic raceways are used as equipment grounding conductors, there will be no connection to the grounded conductor at the service. Without the MBJ, the path back to the source would be through the grounding electrode system and the earth. This does not provide a low-impedance path, and thus will not allow enough current to flow in the circuit to let the overcurrent devices open.

For example, suppose a phase conductor makes contact with the metallic housing of a 120V, 15A appliance that was wired using EMT. Further suppose that the total combined resistance of the EMT being used as the equipment grounding conductor connected to the appliance and the resistance of the metal water piping and our ground rod in the sample house is 20Ω (less than the 25Ω permitted in *NEC Section 250.56*). The amount of current that could flow back to the utility source would be 120V ÷ 20 = 6A. The smallest overcurrent device in our electrical system is 15A, and would not trip. With the MBJ installed, the path back to the utility source is through the MBJ to the grounded conductor of the service. This resistance will be much less than 1Ω, and thus would allow enough current to flow to open up the overcurrent devices within the system. The MBJ provides the path back to the source for faults that occur within the service disconnect means.

2.1 Bonding at the Service

Electrical continuity is required at the service per *NEC Section 250.92(A)*, which states that all of the following must be bonded:

The service raceways, auxiliary gutters, or service cable armor or sheaths, except for underground metallic sheaths of continuously underground cables as noted in *NEC Section 250.84*

All service enclosures containing service-entrance conductors, including meter fittings, boxes, or the like interposed in the service raceway or armor

Any metallic raceway or armor enclosing a grounding electrode conductor as specified in *NEC Section 250.64(E)*

Bonding shall apply at each end and to all intervening raceways, boxes, and enclosures between the service equipment and the grounding electrode.

The items that typically require bonding include the mast and weatherhead, the meter enclosure, the armor of the SE cable (if it has armor), and the service disconnect.

5.2.2 Methods of Bonding at the Service

The electrical continuity of the service equipment, raceways, and enclosures will be ensured per *NEC Section 250.92(B)* through the use of the following methods:

- Bonding equipment to the grounded service conductor in a manner provided in *NEC Section 250.8*
- Connections utilizing threaded couplings or threaded bosses on enclosures where made up wrenchtight
- Threadless couplings and connectors where made up tight for metal raceways and metal-clad cables
- Other approved devices, such as bonding-type locknuts and **bonding bushings**

Bonding jumpers must be used around concentric or eccentric knockouts that are punched or otherwise formed so as to impair the electrical connection to ground. Standard locknuts or bushings shall not be the sole means for bonding.

5.2.3 Bonding and Grounding Requirements for Other Systems

An accessible means external to the service equipment enclosure is required for connecting intersystem bonding and grounding conductors and connections for the communications, radio and television (TV), community antenna television (CATV), and network-powered broadband communication system. This can be accomplished by using at least one of the following:

- An exposed metallic service raceway
- An exposed grounding electrode conductor
- A No. 6 AWG copper conductor that is not shorter than 6" and is bonded to the metallic service raceway or service equipment enclosure using a listed and identified fitting

If a copper conductor is used, the other end of this conductor must be accessible and must be located on the exterior wall so that an external connection of the intersystem bonding or grounding conductor can be made as required by *NEC Sections 800.100, 810.21, 820.100, and 830.100.*

5.2.4 Bonding of Water Piping Systems

Metallic water piping systems in or on a structure must be bonded as required by *NEC Section*

250.104(A). The metallic water piping system(s) must be bonded by means of a bonding jumper sized in accordance with *NEC Table 250.66* and connected to one of the following:

- The service-entrance enclosures
- The grounded (neutral) conductor at the service
- The grounding electrode conductor where of sufficient size
- The grounding electrode(s) used

The points of attachment of the bonding jumper(s) shall be accessible. It shall be installed in accordance with *NEC Section 250.64(A), (B), and (E).* Note that while this conductor is sized in the same manner as if the water piping system is a grounding electrode, the point of attachment to the water piping is permitted to be at any convenient point on the water piping system and not just within the first 5' of where the water enters the building.

NEC Section 250.104(A)(2) states that in multifamily dwelling units (or other multiple occupancy buildings) where the metal water piping system(s) installed in or attached to a building or structure for the individual occupancies is metallically isolated from all other occupancies by use of nonmetallic water piping, the metal water piping system(s) for each occupancy shall be permitted to be bonded to the equipment grounding terminal of the panelboard or switchboard enclosure (other than service equipment) supplying that occupancy. The bonding jumper shall be sized in accordance with *NEC Table 250.122.*

5.2.5 *Bonding of Other Piping Systems*

NEC Section 250.104(B) requires that other piping systems, where installed in or attached to a building or structure, including gas piping, that may become energized shall be bonded to one of the following:

- The service equipment enclosure
- The grounded conductor at the service
- The grounding electrode conductor where of sufficient size
- One or more grounding electrodes used

The bonding jumper(s) shall be sized in accordance with *NEC Table 250.122* using the rating of the circuit that may energize the piping system(s). The equipment grounding conductor for the circuit that may energize the piping shall be permitted to serve as the bonding means. The points of attachment of the bonding jumper(s) shall be accessible.

NOTE

Bonding all piping and metal air ducts within the premises will provide additional safety.

6.0.0 ◆ INSTALLING THE SERVICE ENTRANCE

In practical applications, the electric service is normally one of the last components of an electrical system to be installed. However, it is one of the first considerations when laying out a residential electrical system. For instance:

- The electrician must know in which direction and to what location to route the circuit homeruns while **roughing in** the electrical wiring.
- Provisions must be made for sleeves through footings and foundations in cases where underground systems (service laterals) are used.
- The local power company must be notified as to the approximate size of service required so that may plan the best way to furnish a **service drop** to the property.

6.1.0 Service Drop Locations

The location of the service drop, electric meter, and load center should be considered first. It is always wise to consult the local power company to obtain their requirements; where you want the service drop and where they want it may not coincide. A brief meeting with the power company about the location of the service drop can prevent problems later on.

The service drop must be routed so that the service drop conductors have a clearance of not less than 3' horizontally and below windows that open, doors, porches, fire escapes, or similar locations. In addition, they must have a 10' vertical clearance that extends 3' horizontally from porches, fire escapes, balconies, and so forth, required in *NEC Section 230.9.* Where service drop conductors pass over rooftops, driveways, yards, and so forth, they must have clearances specified in *NEC Section 230.24.*

A plot plan (also called a site plan) is often available for new construction. The plot plan shows the entire property, with the building or buildings drawn in their proper location on the plot of land. It also shows sidewalks, driveways, streets, and existing utilities—both overhead and underground.

A plot plan of the sample residence is shown in Figure 14. In reviewing this drawing, you can see that the closest power pole is located across a public street from the house. By consulting with the local power company, it is learned that the service will be brought to the house from this pole by triplex cable, which will connect to the residence at a point on its left (west) end. The steel uninsulated conductor of triplex cable acts as both the grounded conductor (neutral) and as a support for the insulated (ungrounded) conductors. It is also suitable for overhead use.

When service-entrance cable is used, it will run directly from the point of attachment and service head to the meter base. However, since the carport is located on the west side of the building, a service mast (Figure 15) will have to be installed.

The NEC® requires a clearance of not less than 8' over rooftops, unless the roof has a slope of 4" in 12" or greater, in which case the clearance may be reduced to 3'. Where the service drop conductors pass over only the overhang (eaves) of a roof, the clearance may be reduced to 18" as long as no more than 6' of the conductors travel over no more than 4' of the overhang (eave). This minimum height requirement extends beyond the roof for a distance of not less than 3' in all directions, except the final portion of the span where the service drop conductors attach to the sides of a building.

6.2.0 Vertical Clearances of Service Drop

NEC Section 230.24(B) specifies the distances by which service drop conductors must clear the ground. These distances vary according to the surrounding conditions.

In general, the *NEC®* states that the vertical clearances of all service drop conductors that carry 600V or under are based on a conductor temperature of 60°F (15°C) with no wind and with the final unloaded sag in the wire, conductor, or cable. Service drop conductors must be at least 10' above the ground or other accessible surfaces at all times. More distance is required under most conditions. For example, if the service conductors pass over residential property and driveways or commercial property that is not subject to truck traffic, the conductors must be at least 15' above the ground. However, this distance may be reduced to 12' when the voltage is limited to 300V to ground.

In other areas, such as public streets, alleys, roads, parking areas subject to truck traffic, driveways on other-than-residential property, the minimum vertical distance is 18'. The conditions of the sample residence are shown in *Figure 16*.

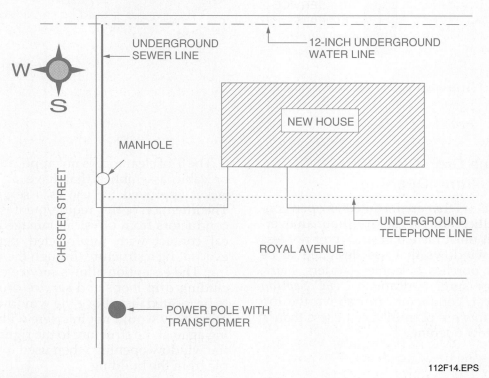

112F14.EPS

Figure 14 ◆ Plot plan of the sample residence.

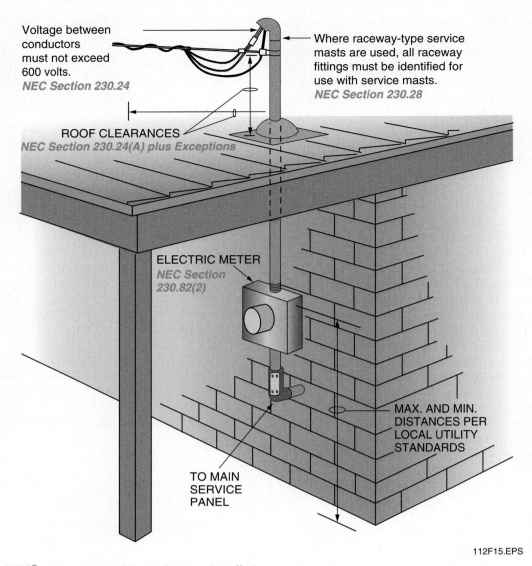

Voltage between conductors must not exceed 600 volts.
NEC Section 230.24

Where raceway-type service masts are used, all raceway fittings must be identified for use with service masts.
NEC Section 230.28

ROOF CLEARANCES
NEC Section 230.24(A) plus Exceptions

ELECTRIC METER
NEC Section 230.82(2)

MAX. AND MIN. DISTANCES PER LOCAL UTILITY STANDARDS

TO MAIN SERVICE PANEL

112F15.EPS

Figure 15 ◆ *NEC® sections governing service mast installations.*

6.3.0 Service Drop Clearances for Building Openings

Service conductors that are installed as open conductors or multiconductor cable without an overall outer jacket must have a clearance of not less than 3' from windows that are designed to be opened, doors, porches, balconies, ladders, stairs, fire escapes, or similar locations (*NEC Section 230.9*). However, conductors run above the top level of a window are permitted to be less than 3' from the window opening.

The 3' of clearance is not applicable to racewa or cable assemblies that have an overall out jacket approved for use as a service conducto The intention of this requirement is to protect t conductors from physical damage and/or phys cal contact with unprotected personnel whe evacuating a structure through the window ope ing. The exception allows service conductors, i cluding drip loops and service drop conducto to be located just above the window openings b cause they would not interfere with ladders lea ing against the structure to the right, left, or belo the window opening when used to evacuate pe ple from the building.

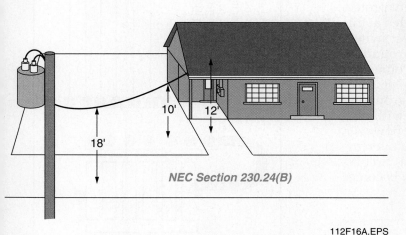

112F16A.EPS

112F16B.EPS

Figure 16 ◆ Vertical clearances for service drop conductors.

Failure to De-energize Panelboard

A 31-year-old electrician was finishing the installation of an outdoor floodlight on a new home. He borrowed an aluminum ladder from another contractor and then proceeded with his task. He did not verify that power was removed at the panelboard, and when he used his wire strippers to remove the conductor insulation, his right thumb and index finger contacted a 110V circuit. He received a fatal shock.

The Bottom Line: Always de-energize circuits at the panelboard before beginning any electrical task, and never use aluminum ladders while working in or near electrical devices. In this case, the ladder provided a path to ground.

7.0.0 ◆ PANELBOARD LOCATION

The main service disconnect or panelboard is normally located in a portion of an unfinished basement or utility room on an outside wall so that the service cable coming from the electric meter can terminate immediately into the switch or panelboard when the cable enters the building. In the example home, however, there is no basement and the utility room is located in the center of the house with no outside walls. Consequently, a somewhat different arrangement will have to be used. A load center is a type of panelboard that is normally located at the service entrance of a residential installation. The load center usually contains a main circuit breaker, which is the main disconnect. Circuit breakers are provided for equipment such as electric water heaters, ranges, dryers, air conditioning and heating units, and breakers that feed subpanels such as lighting panels.

NEC Section 230.70 requires that the service disconnecting means be installed in a readily accessible location—either outside or inside the building. If located inside the building, it must be located nearest the point of entrance of the service conductors. In the sample home, there are at least two methods of installing the panelboard in the utility room that will comply with this *NEC®* regulation, as well as the requirements in *NEC Sections 110.26 and 240.24.*

The first method utilizes a weatherproof 100A disconnect (safety switch or circuit breaker enclosure) mounted next to the meter base on the outside of the building. With this method, service conductors are provided with overcurrent protection; the neutral conductor is also grounded at this point, as this becomes the main disconnect switch. Three-wire cable with an additional grounding wire is then routed from this main disconnect to the panelboard in the utility room. All three current-carrying conductors (two ungrounded and one neutral) must be insulated with this arrangement; the equipment ground, however, may be bare. The panelboard containing overcurrent protection devices for the branch circuits, which is located in the utility room, now becomes a subpanel. See *Figure 17.*

NOTE

Local ordinances in some areas may require a disconnect at the meter base, making the panel in the utility room a subpanel.

An alternate method utilizes conduit from the meter base that is routed under the concrete slab and then up to a main panelboard located in the utility room. *NEC Section 230.6* considers conductors to be outside of a building when they are installed under not less than 2" of concrete beneath a building or installed in a conduit not less than 18" deep beneath a building. The sample residence has a 4"-thick reinforced concrete slab—well within the *NEC®* regulations. Therefore, the service conductors from the meter base that are installed under the concrete slab in conduit are considered to be outside the house, and no disconnect is required at the meter base. When this conduit emerges in the utility room, it will run straight up into the bottom of the panelboard, again meeting the *NEC®* requirement that the panel be located nearest the point of entrance of the service conductors. Always check with your local authority having jurisdiction for specific requirements about where services are to be located. Details of this service arrangement are shown in *Figure 18.*

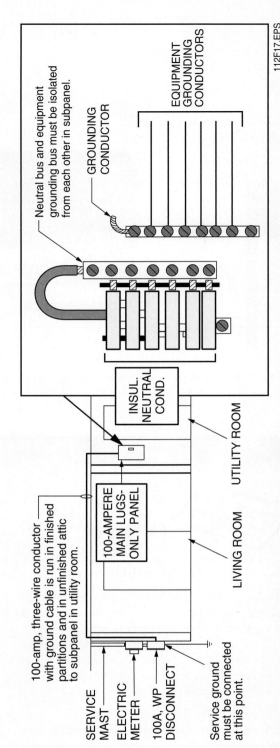

Figure 17 ◆ One method of wiring a panelboard for the sample residence.

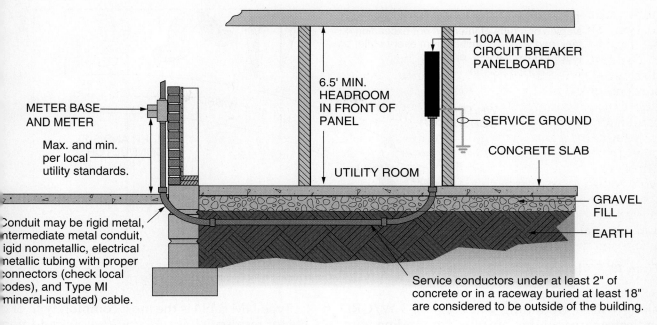

Figure 18 ◆ Alternate method of service installation for the sample residence.

0.0 ◆ WIRING METHODS

...anch circuits and feeders are used in residential ...nstruction to provide power wiring to operate ...mponents and equipment, and control wiring ...regulate the equipment. Wiring may be further ...bdivided into either open or concealed wiring.

In open wiring systems, the cable and/or race-...ays are installed on the surface of the walls, ceil-...gs, columns, and other areas where they are in ...ew and are readily accessible. Open wiring is of-...n used in areas where appearance is not impor-...nt, such as in unfinished basements, attics, and ...rages.

Concealed wiring systems are installed inside ...alls, partitions, ceilings, columns, and behind ...seboards or moldings where they are out of ...ew and are not readily accessible. This type of ...iring is generally used in all new construction ...ith finished interior walls, ceilings, and floors, ...d it is the preferred type of wiring where ap-...earance is important.

In general, there are two basic wiring methods ...ed in the majority of modern residential electri-...l systems. They are:

Sheathed cables of two or more conductors
Raceway (conduit) systems

The method used on a given job is determined ... the requirements of the *NEC*®, any amend-...ents made by local authorities, the type of build-ing construction, and the location of the wiring in the building. In most applications, either of the two methods may be used, and both methods are frequently used in combination.

8.1.0 Cable Systems

Several types of cable are used in wiring systems to feed or supply power to equipment. These include nonmetallic-sheathed cable, armored cable, underground feeder cable, and service-entrance cable.

8.1.1 Nonmetallic-Sheathed Cable

Nonmetallic-sheathed (Type NM) cable *(NEC Article 334)* is manufactured in two- or three-wire configurations with varying sizes of conductors. In both two- and three-wire cables, conductors are color-coded: one conductor is black while the other is white in two-wire cable; in three-wire cable, the additional conductor is red. Both types also have a grounding conductor, which is usually bare, but it is sometimes covered with green plastic insulation, depending upon the manufacturer. The jacket or covering consists of rubber, plastic, or fiber. Most also have markings on this jacket giving the manufacturer's name or trademark, wire size, and number of conductors (see *Figure 19*). For example, NM 12-2 W/GRD indicates that the jacket contains two No. 12 AWG conductors

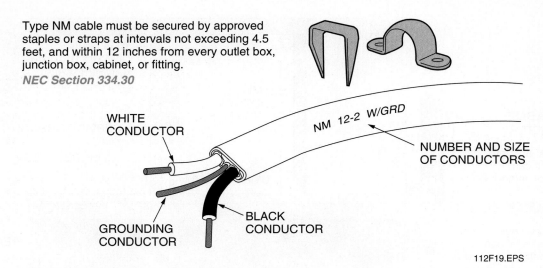

Type NM cable must be secured by approved staples or straps at intervals not exceeding 4.5 feet, and within 12 inches from every outlet box, junction box, cabinet, or fitting.
NEC Section 334.30

WHITE CONDUCTOR

NM 12-2 W/GRD

NUMBER AND SIZE OF CONDUCTORS

GROUNDING CONDUCTOR

BLACK CONDUCTOR

112F19.EPS

Figure 19 ◆ Characteristics of Type NM cable.

along with a grounding wire; NM 12-3 W/GRD indicates three conductors plus a grounding wire. Type NM cable is often referred to as **Romex**®.

NEC Section 334.10 permits Type NM cable to be used in the following applications:

• One- and two-family dwelling units
• Multi-family dwellings when they are of Types III, IV, and V construction
• Other structures if concealed behind a 15-minute finish barrier and are of Types III, IV, and V construction

NEC Section 334.12 prohibits the use of Type NM cable in the following applications:

• As open runs in dropped or suspended ceilings in other than dwelling units
• As service-entrance cable
• In commercial garages that have hazardous (classified) areas
• In theaters and similar locations, except as permitted by *NEC Section 518.4*
• In motion picture studios
• In storage battery rooms
• In hoistways or on elevators or escalators
• Embedded in poured cement, concrete, or aggregate
• In hazardous (classified) areas except as permitted in *NEC Sections 501.10(B)(3), 502.10(B)(3), and 504.20*
• Where exposed to corrosive fumes or vapors
• Embedded in masonry, adobe, fill, or plaster
• In a shallow chase in masonry, concrete, or adobe and covered with plaster, adobe, or similar finish
• Where exposed or subject to excessive moisture or dampness

Type NM cable is the most common type of cable for residential use. *Figure 20* shows additional *NEC*® regulations pertaining to the installation of Type NM cable.

8.1.2 Armored Cable

Armored (Type AC) cable, commonly called **BX**®, is manufactured in two-, three-, and four-wire assemblies with varying sizes of conductors, and is used in locations similar to those where Type NM cable is allowed.

NOTE

In some areas, BX® may not be allowed and metal-clad (MC) cable must be used. MC cable has a plastic wrapping to protect the conductors and does not require an insulating insert.

The metallic spiral covering on Type AC cable offers a greater degree of mechanical protection than with Type NM cable and also provides a continuous grounding bond without the need for additional grounding conductors.

Type AC cable may be embedded in plaster finish, brick, or other masonry, except in damp or wet locations. It may also be run in the air voids of masonry block or tile walls, except where such walls are exposed or subject to excessive moisture or dampness. See *Figures 21* and *22*.

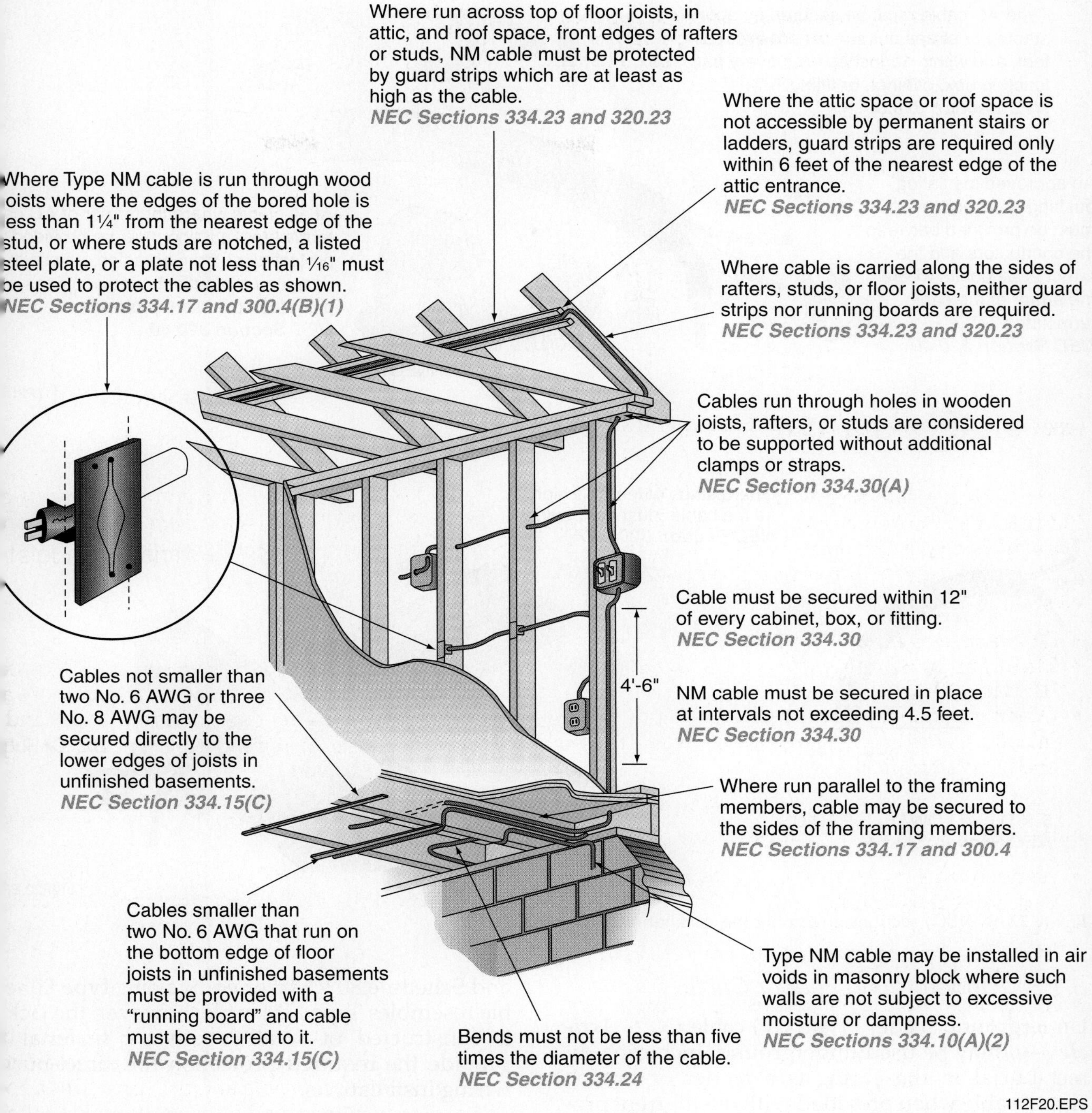

Where run across top of floor joists, in attic, and roof space, front edges of rafters or studs, NM cable must be protected by guard strips which are at least as high as the cable.
NEC Sections 334.23 and 320.23

Where the attic space or roof space is not accessible by permanent stairs or ladders, guard strips are required only within 6 feet of the nearest edge of the attic entrance.
NEC Sections 334.23 and 320.23

Where Type NM cable is run through wood joists where the edges of the bored hole is less than 1¼" from the nearest edge of the stud, or where studs are notched, a listed steel plate, or a plate not less than ¹⁄₁₆" must be used to protect the cables as shown.
NEC Sections 334.17 and 300.4(B)(1)

Where cable is carried along the sides of rafters, studs, or floor joists, neither guard strips nor running boards are required.
NEC Sections 334.23 and 320.23

Cables run through holes in wooden joists, rafters, or studs are considered to be supported without additional clamps or straps.
NEC Section 334.30(A)

Cable must be secured within 12" of every cabinet, box, or fitting.
NEC Section 334.30

Cables not smaller than two No. 6 AWG or three No. 8 AWG may be secured directly to the lower edges of joists in unfinished basements.
NEC Section 334.15(C)

4'-6"

NM cable must be secured in place at intervals not exceeding 4.5 feet.
NEC Section 334.30

Where run parallel to the framing members, cable may be secured to the sides of the framing members.
NEC Sections 334.17 and 300.4

Cables smaller than two No. 6 AWG that run on the bottom edge of floor joists in unfinished basements must be provided with a "running board" and cable must be secured to it.
NEC Section 334.15(C)

Bends must not be less than five times the diameter of the cable.
NEC Section 334.24

Type NM cable may be installed in air voids in masonry block where such walls are not subject to excessive moisture or dampness.
NEC Sections 334.10(A)(2)

112F20.EPS

Figure 20 ◆ *NEC® sections governing the installation of Type NM cable.*

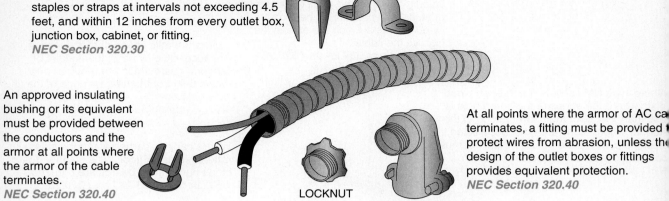

Type AC cable must be secured by approved staples or straps at intervals not exceeding 4.5 feet, and within 12 inches from every outlet box, junction box, cabinet, or fitting.
NEC Section 320.30

An approved insulating bushing or its equivalent must be provided between the conductors and the armor at all points where the armor of the cable terminates.
NEC Section 320.40

LOCKNUT

CONNECTOR

At all points where the armor of AC ca terminates, a fitting must be provided protect wires from abrasion, unless the design of the outlet boxes or fittings provides equivalent protection.
NEC Section 320.40

112F21.

Figure 21 ◆ Characteristics of Type AC cable.

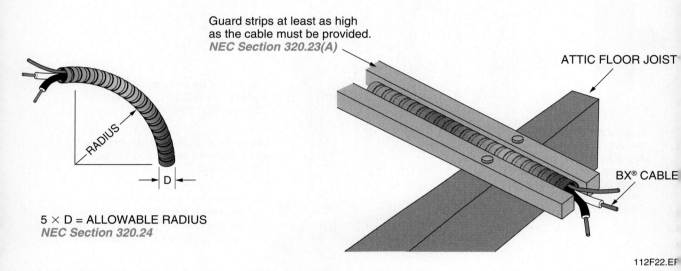

Guard strips at least as high as the cable must be provided.
NEC Section 320.23(A)

ATTIC FLOOR JOIST

RADIUS

D

5 × D = ALLOWABLE RADIUS
NEC Section 320.24

BX® CABLE

112F22.EF

Figure 22 ◆ *NEC®* sections governing the installation of Type AC cable.

8.1.3 Underground Feeder Cable

Underground feeder (Type UF) cable *(NEC Article 340)* may be used underground, including direct burial in the earth, as a feeder or branch circuit cable when provided with overcurrent protection at the rated ampacity as required by the *NEC®*. When Type UF cable is used above grade where it will come in direct contact with the rays of the sun, its outer covering must be sun-resistant. Furthermore, where Type UF cable emerges from the ground, some means of mechanical protection must be provided. This protection may be in the form of conduit or guard strips. *NEC Section 300.5(D)(1)* requires that the protection extend from the minimum burial depth below grade to a point at least 8' above grade. *NEC 300.5(D)(4)* states that if conduit is used as protection, the permitted types are RMC, IMC,

and Schedule 80 RNC, or equivalent. Type UF c ble resembles Type NM cable; however, the jack is constructed of weather-resistant material provide the required protection for direct-buri wiring installations.

8.1.4 Service-Entrance Cable

Service-entrance (Type SE) and undergroun service-entrance (Type USE) cable, when used f electrical services, must be installed as specified *NEC Articles 230 and 338.* Service-entrance cab is available with the grounded conductor bare f outside service conductors, and also with an ins lated grounded conductor for interior wirin systems.

Type SE cable is permitted for use on bran circuits or feeders provided that all curren carrying conductors are insulated; this include

Romex® Cable

This picture shows most of the Romex® cables for the house wiring run through a series of large holes drilled through the joists. Is this a code violation?

112P1203.EPS

ne grounded or neutral conductor. Where a con-uctor in the cable is not insulated, it is only per-mitted to be used as an equipment grounding onductor for branch circuits or feeders. Where sed as an interior wiring method, the installation equirements of *NEC Article 334* must be fol-owed, except for determining the ampacity of the able. Where installed as exterior wiring, the re-uirements of *NEC Article 225* must be met, with ne supports for the cable in accordance with *NEC ection 334.30.*

SE Style R (SER) cable is used in residential pplications for subfeeds for ranges, and it is lso used for service laterals in multi-family wellings.

Figure 23 summarizes the installation rules for ype SE cable for both exterior and interior viring.

.2.0 Raceways

 raceway is any channel that is designed and sed solely for the purpose of holding wires, ca-les, or busbars. Types of raceways include rigid etal conduit, intermediate metal conduit, rigid nonmetallic conduit, flexible metallic conduit, electrical metallic tubing, and auxiliary gutters. Raceways are constructed of either metal or insu-lating material, such as polyvinyl chloride or PVC (plastic). Metal raceways are joined using threaded, compression, or setscrew couplings; nonmetallic raceways are joined using cement-coated couplings. Where a raceway terminates in an outlet box, junction box, or other enclosure, an approved connector must be used.

Raceways provide mechanical protection for the conductors that run in them and also prevent accidental damage to insulation and the conduct-ing material. They also protect conductors from corrosive atmospheres and prevent fire hazards to life and property by confining arcs and flames that may occur due to faults in the wiring system. Conduits or raceways are used in residential ap-plications for service masts, underground wiring embedded in concrete, and sometimes in unfin-ished basements, shops, or garage areas.

Another function of metal raceways is to pro-vide a continuous equipment grounding system throughout the electrical system. To maintain this feature, it is extremely important that all raceway systems be securely bonded together into a

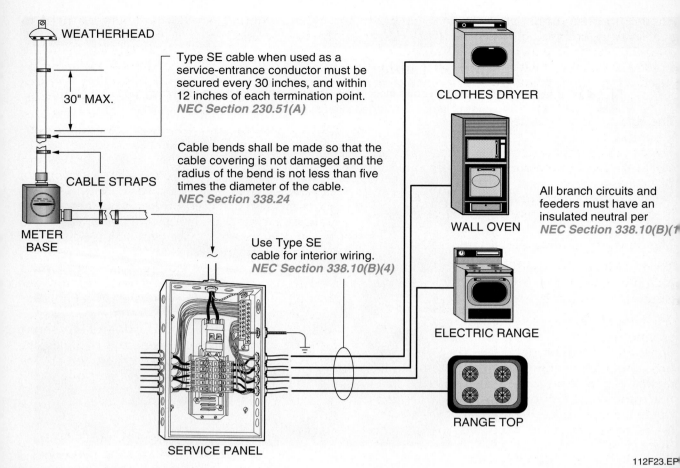

WEATHERHEAD

30" MAX.

Type SE cable when used as a service-entrance conductor must be secured every 30 inches, and within 12 inches of each termination point. *NEC Section 230.51(A)*

CABLE STRAPS

METER BASE

Cable bends shall be made so that the cable covering is not damaged and the radius of the bend is not less than five times the diameter of the cable. *NEC Section 338.24*

Use Type SE cable for interior wiring. *NEC Section 338.10(B)(4)*

SERVICE PANEL

CLOTHES DRYER

WALL OVEN

All branch circuits and feeders must have an insulated neutral per *NEC Section 338.10(B)(1*

ELECTRIC RANGE

RANGE TOP

112F23.EP

Figure 23 ◆ *NEC® sections governing Type SE cable.*

continuous conductive path and properly connected to the system ground. The following section explains how this is accomplished.

9.0.0 ◆ EQUIPMENT GROUNDING SYSTEM

NEC Article 250, Part IV generally requires that all metallic enclosures, raceways, and cable armor be grounded. The exceptions in *NEC Sections 250.80 and 250.86* allow metal enclosures or short sections of raceways that are used to provide support or physical protection to be ungrounded under specific conditions.

NEC Article 250, Part VI covers equipment grounding and equipment grounding conductors. This section generally requires that the exposed noncurrent-carrying metal parts of fixed equipment likely to become energized be grounded under the following conditions:

- Where within 8' vertically or 5' horizontally of ground or grounded metal objects and subject to contact by occupants or others

- Where located in wet or damp locations
- Where in electrical contact with metal
- Where in hazardous (classified) locations covered by *NEC Articles 500 through 517*
- Where supplied by a metal-clad, metal sheathed, or metal raceway, or other wiring method that provides an equipment ground
- Where equipment operates with any termina at over 150V to ground

Specific equipment that is required to b grounded regardless of the voltage is listed i *NEC Section 250.112* and includes equipmen such as motors, motor controllers, and light fi tures. Types of cord- and plug-connected equi ment in dwelling units that are required to b grounded are found in *NEC Section 250.114* an include equipment such as refrigerators, freezer air conditioners, information technology equip ment (computers), clothes washers, clothes dr ers, and dishwashing machines.

The types of equipment grounding conducto that are acceptable to be used are found in *NE Section 250.118.* Note that among the list of wirir ethods approved for use as equipment grounding conductors, both flexible metal conduit (FMC) and liquidtight flexible metal conduit (LFMC) are permitted to be used. Listed FMC is permitted to be used as an equipment grounding conductor only when the following conditions are met:

The conduit is terminated in fittings listed for grounding.
The circuit conductors contained in the conduit are protected by overcurrent devices rated at 20A or less.
The combined length of FMC, FMT, and LFMC in the same ground return path does not exceed 6'.
The conduit is not installed for flexibility.

Type LFMC is also used in dwelling units and has slightly different requirements when used as an equipment grounding conductor:

The conduit is terminated in fittings listed for grounding.
For trade sizes ⅜ through ½, the circuit conductors contained in the conduit are protected by overcurrent devices rated at 20A or less.
For trade sizes ¾ through 1¼, the circuit conductors contained in the conduit are protected by overcurrent devices rated at 60A or less and there is no FMC, FMT, or LFMC in trade sizes ⅜ through ½ in the grounding path.
The combined length of FMC, FMT, and LFMC in the same ground return path does not exceed 6'.
The conduit is not used for flexibility.

Where external bonding jumpers are used to provide the continuity of the fault current path, *NEC Section 250.102(E)* limits the length to not more than 6', except at outside pole locations for the purposes of bonding or grounding the isolated sections of metal raceways or elbows installed in exposed risers at those pole locations. When installing an equipment grounding conductor in a raceway, *NEC Table 250.122* is used to determine the size of the equipment grounding conductor. It is permitted to install one equipment grounding conductor in a raceway that has several circuits. In that case, the size of the equipment grounding conductor is based on the rating of the largest overcurrent device protecting the circuits contained in the raceway.

NEC Section 250.148 requires that where circuit conductors are spliced within a box, or terminated on equipment within or supported by a box, separate equipment grounding conductors associated with those circuit conductors shall be spliced or joined within the box or to the box with devices suitable for the use. *Figure 24* shows several types of fittings that are suitable for this purpose.

NOTE
NEC Section 250.8 prohibits the use of sheet metal screws to connect grounding conductors. This precludes the use of screw(s) to secure the equipment cover(s), screw-on connectors, and so forth.

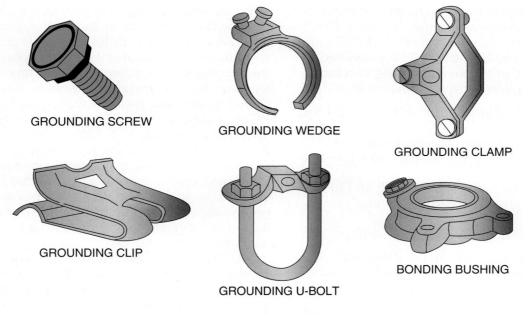

GROUNDING SCREW

GROUNDING WEDGE

GROUNDING CLAMP

GROUNDING CLIP

GROUNDING U-BOLT

BONDING BUSHING

Where splices are made in
a junction box, the grounding
conductors must be spliced to
the metal junction box.
NEC Section 250.148

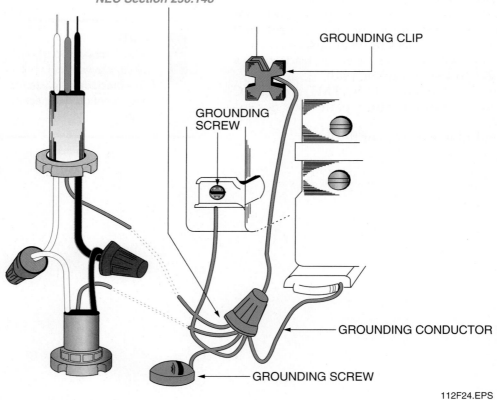

GROUNDING CLIP

GROUNDING
SCREW

GROUNDING CONDUCTOR

GROUNDING SCREW

112F24.EPS

Figure 24 ◆ Equipment grounding methods.

0.0.0 ◆ BRANCH CIRCUIT LAYOUT FOR POWER

The point at which electrical equipment is connected to the wiring system is commonly called an outlet. There are many classifications of outlets: lighting, receptacle, motor, appliance, and so forth. This section, however, deals with the power outlets normally found in residential electrical wiring systems.

When viewing an electrical drawing, outlets are indicated by symbols (usually a small circle with appropriate markings to indicate the type of outlet). The most common symbols for receptacles are shown in *Figure 25*.

0.1.0 Branch Circuits and Feeders

The conductors that extend from the panelboard to the various outlets are called branch circuits and are defined by the *NEC*® as the point of a wiring system that extends beyond the final overcurrent device protecting the circuit. See *Figure 26*.

A feeder consists of all conductors between the service equipment and the final overcurrent device. See *Figure 27*.

In general, the size of the branch circuit conductors varies depending upon the load requirements of the electrically operated equipment connected to the outlet. For residential use, most branch circuits consist of either No. 14 AWG, No. 12 AWG, No. 10 AWG, or No. 8 AWG conductors.

The basic branch circuit requires two wires or conductors to provide a continuous path for the flow of electric current, plus a third wire for equipment grounding. The usual receptacle branch circuit operates at 120V.

Fractional horsepower motors and small electric heaters usually operate at 120V and are connected to 120V branch circuits by means of a receptacle, junction box, or direct connection.

With the exception of very large residences and tract-development houses, the size of the average residential electrical system of the past has not been large enough to justify the expense of preparing complete electrical working drawings and specifications. Such electrical systems were usually laid out by the architect in the form of a sketchy outlet arrangement or else laid out by the electrician on the job, often only as the work progressed. However, many technical developments in residential electrical use—such as electric heat

 THINK ABOUT IT

Grounding Devices

Identify each of the devices pictured here and explain their function(s). Which of these devices would *not* be used for equipment grounding?

112P1204.EPS

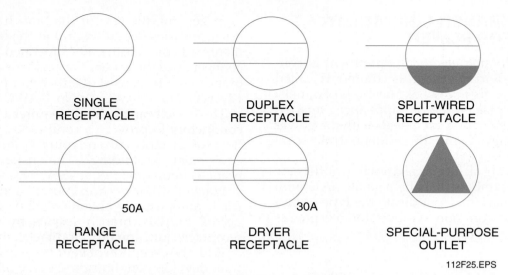

Figure 25 ◆ Typical outlet symbols appearing in electrical drawings.

SINGLE
RECEPTACLE

DUPLEX
RECEPTACLE

SPLIT-WIRED
RECEPTACLE

50A
RANGE
RECEPTACLE

30A
DRYER
RECEPTACLE

SPECIAL-PURPOSE
OUTLET

112F25.EPS

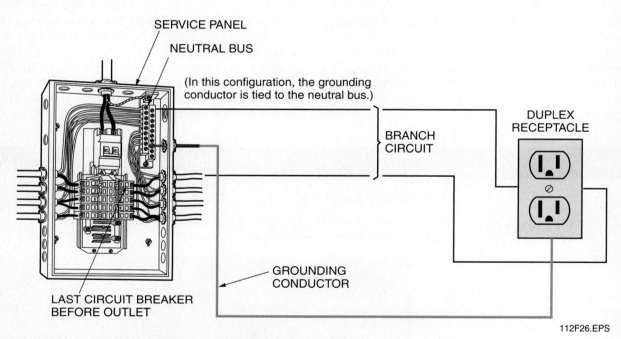

SERVICE PANEL

NEUTRAL BUS

(In this configuration, the grounding
conductor is tied to the neutral bus.)

BRANCH
CIRCUIT

DUPLEX
RECEPTACLE

GROUNDING
CONDUCTOR

LAST CIRCUIT BREAKER
BEFORE OUTLET

112F26.EPS

Figure 26 ◆ Components of a duplex receptacle branch circuit.

with sophisticated control wiring, increased use of electrical appliances, various electronic alarm systems, new lighting techniques, and the need for energy conservation techniques—have greatly expanded the demand and extended the complexity of today's residential electrical systems.

Each year, the number of homes with electrical systems designed by consulting engineering firms increases. Such homes are provided with complete electrical working drawings and specifications, similar to those frequently provided for commercial and industrial projects. Still, these are more the exception than the rule. Most residential projects will not have a complete set of drawings.

Circuit layout is provided on the drawings to follow for several reasons:

• They provide a visual layout of house wiring circuitry.
• They provide a sample of electrical residential drawings that are prepared by consulting engineering firms, although the number may still be limited.
• They introduce the method of showing electrical systems on working drawings so that you will have a better foundation for tackling advanced electrical systems.

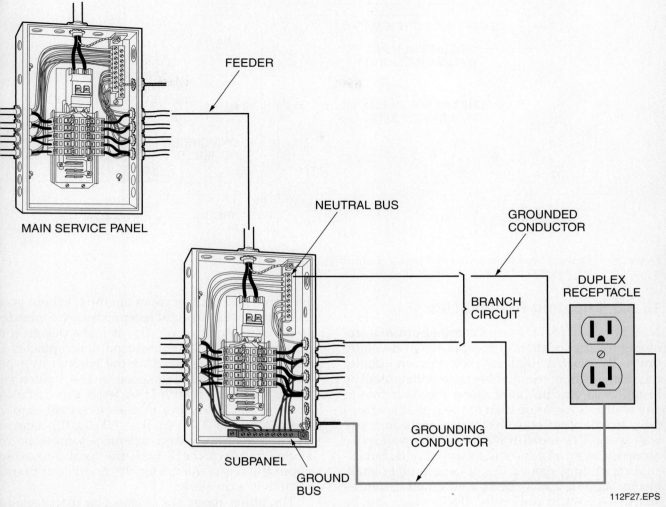

FEEDER

MAIN SERVICE PANEL

NEUTRAL BUS

GROUNDED CONDUCTOR

BRANCH CIRCUIT

DUPLEX RECEPTACLE

SUBPANEL

GROUND BUS

GROUNDING CONDUCTOR

112F27.EPS

Figure 27 ◆ A feeder being used to feed a subpanel from the main service panel.

Branch circuits are shown on electrical draw-ings by means of a single line drawn from the pan-elboard (or by homerun arrowheads indicating that the circuit goes to the panelboard) to the out-let or from outlet to outlet where there is more than one outlet on the circuit.

The lines indicating branch circuits can be solid to show that the conductors are to be run con-cealed in the ceiling or wall, dashed to show that the conductors are to be run in the floor or ceiling below, or dotted to show that the wiring is to be run exposed. *Figure 28* shows examples of these three types of branch circuit lines.

In *Figure 28*, No. 12 indicates the wire size. The slash marks shown through the circuits in *Figure 28* indicate the number of current-carrying conductors in the circuit. Although two

slash marks are shown, in actual practice, a branch circuit containing only two conductors usually contains no slash marks; that is, any cir-cuit with no slash marks is assumed to have two conductors. However, three or more conductors are always indicated on electrical working drawings—either by slash marks for each con-ductor, or else by a note.

Never assume that you know the meaning of any electrical symbol. Although great efforts have been made in recent years to standardize drawing symbols, architects, consulting engineers, and electrical drafters still modify existing symbols or devise new ones to meet their own needs. Always consult the symbol list or legend on electrical working drawings for an exact interpretation of the symbols used.

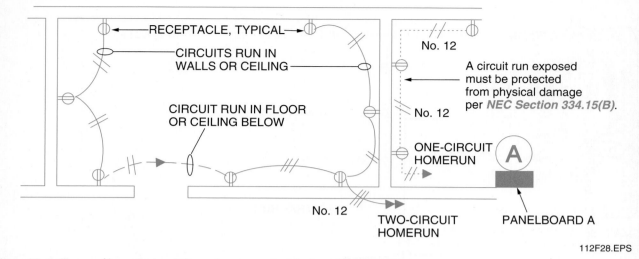

Figure 28 ◆ Types of branch circuit lines shown on electrical working drawings.

10.2.0 Locating Receptacles

NEC Section 210.52 states the minimum requirements for the location of receptacles in dwelling units. It specifies that in each kitchen, family room, and dining room, receptacle outlets shall be installed so that no point along the floor line in any wall space is more than 6', measured horizontally, from an outlet in that space, including any wall space 2' or more in width and the wall space occupied by fixed panels in exterior walls, but excluding sliding panels. Receptacle outlets shall, insofar as practicable, be spaced equal distances apart. Receptacle outlets in floors shall not be counted as part of the required number of receptacle outlets unless located within 18" of the wall.

The *NEC*® defines wall space as a wall that is unbroken along the floor line by doorways, fireplaces, or similar openings. Each wall space that is two feet or more in width must be treated individually and separately from other wall spaces within the room.

The purpose of *NEC Section 210.52* is to minimize the use of cords across doorways, fireplaces, and similar openings.

With this *NEC*® requirement in mind, outlets for our sample residence will be laid out (see *Figure 29*). In laying out these receptacle outlets, the floor line of the wall is measured (also around corners), but not across doorways, fireplaces, passageways, or other spaces where a flexible cord extended across the space would be unsuitable.

In general, duplex receptacle outlets must be no more than 12' apart. When spaced in this manner, a 6' extension cord will reach a receptacle from any point along the wall line.

Note that at no point along the wall line are any receptacles more than 12' apart or more than six

feet from any door or room opening. Where practical, no more than eight receptacles are connected to one circuit. However, this is just a design consideration since general-purpose receptacles in dwelling units are sized on the basis of 3VA per square foot of dwelling space. A 15A branch circuit is rated at 1,800VA (15A × 120V = 1,800VA) and the *NEC*® requires that for every 600 square feet (1,800VA ÷ 3VA/sq. ft. = 600 sq. ft.), a circuit to supply lighting and receptacles must be installed. Always check with the local authorities about the requirements for the number of branch circuits in a dwelling.

The utility room has at least one receptacle for the laundry on a separate circuit in order to comply with *NEC Sections 210.11(C)(2) and 210.52(F)*.

One duplex receptacle is located in the vestibule for cleaning purposes, such as feeding a portable vacuum cleaner or similar appliance. It is connected to the living room circuit. An additional duplex receptacle is required per *NEC Section 210.52(H)* in hallways of 10' or more.

Although this is not shown in the figure, the living room outlets could be split-wired (the lower half of each duplex receptacle is energized all the time, while the upper half can be switched on or off). The reason for this is that a great deal of the illumination for this area will be provided by portable table lamps, and the split-wired receptacles provide a means to control these lamps from several locations, such as at each entry to the living room, if desired. Split receptacles are discussed in more detail in the next section.

To comply with *NEC Sections 210.11(C)(1) and 210.52(B)*, the kitchen receptacles are laid out as follows. In addition to the number of branch circuits determined previously, two or more 20A small appliance branch circuits must be provided

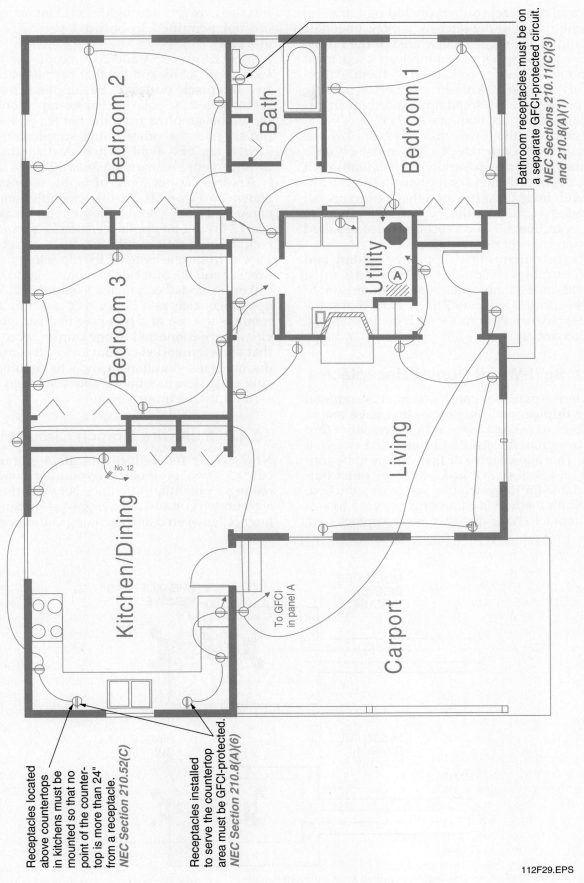

Bathroom receptacles must be on a separate GFCI-protected circuit. *NEC Sections 210.11(C)(3) and 210.8(A)(1)*

Bedroom 2

Bath

Bedroom 1

Bedroom 3

Utility

(A)

No. 12

Kitchen/Dining

Living

To GFCI in panel A

Carport

Receptacles located above countertops in kitchens must be mounted so that no point of the countertop is more than 24" from a receptacle. *NEC Section 210.52(C)*

Receptacles installed to serve the countertop area must be GFCI-protected. *NEC Section 210.8(A)(6)*

112F29.EPS

Figure 29 ◆ Floor plan of the sample residence.

to serve all receptacle outlets (including refrigeration equipment) in the kitchen, pantry, breakfast room, dining room, or similar area of the house. Such circuits, whether two or more are used, must have no other outlets connected to them. All receptacles serving a kitchen countertop require GFCI protection. No small appliance branch circuit shall serve more than one kitchen.

To comply with *NEC Sections 210.11(C)(3) and 210.52(D),* bathroom receptacle(s) must be on a separate branch circuit supplying only bathroom receptacles or on a circuit supplying a single bathroom with no loads other than that bathroom. All receptacles located within a bathroom require GFCI protection. GFCI protection is also required on garage and exterior receptacles.

All branch circuits that supply the lighting and general-purpose receptacles in bedrooms must have arc-fault circuit interrupter protection to comply with *NEC Section 210.12.* Note that some localities have exceptions for such items as smoke detection outlets.

10.3.0 Split-Wired Duplex Receptacles

In modern residential construction, it is common to have duplex wall receptacles that have one of the outlets wired as a standard duplex outlet (hot all the time) and the other half controlled by a wall switch. This allows table or floor lamps to be controlled by a wall switch and leaves the other outlet available for items that are not to be switched. This wiring method is commonly referred to as a split receptacle. Note that switched receptacles are

installed to provide lighting. Dimmer switches are not permitted to be used per *NEC Section 404.14(E).*

Most duplex 15A and 20A receptacles are provided with a breakoff tab that permits each of the two receptacle outlets to be supplied from a different source or polarity. For example, one outlet would be supplied from the hot leg of a series of outlets and the other outlet supplied from the switch leg of a light switch. A diagram of this arrangement is shown in *Figure 30.*

Another application of split receptacles is shown in *Figure 31.* In this example, one outlet connected from a double-pole circuit breaker supplies 240V for an appliance such as a window air conditioning unit, while the other outlet is connected from one pole of the double-pole circuit breaker and the other side is connected to the neutral or grounded conductor to supply 120V for a appliance such as a lamp. *NEC Section 210.4(B)* requires the use of a two-pole breaker when two circuits are connected to one duplex receptacle so that all ungrounded conductors of the circuit are disconnected simultaneously. This circuit and the split receptacle mentioned above are both considered multiwire branch circuits.

10.4.0 Multiwire Branch Circuits

NEC Article 100 defines a multiwire branch circuit as "two or more ungrounded conductors having a potential difference between them, and a grounded conductor having equal potential difference between it and each ungrounded conductor

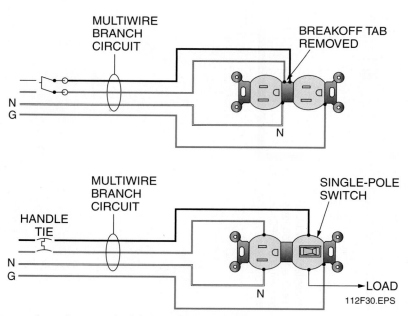

Figure 30 ◆ Two 120V receptacle outlets supplied from different sources.

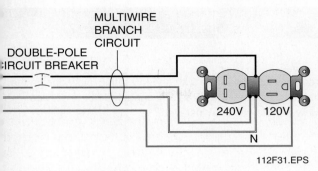

MULTIWIRE
BRANCH
CIRCUIT

DOUBLE-POLE
CIRCUIT BREAKER

240V   120V

N

112F31.EPS

gure 31 ◆ Combination receptacle.

or of the circuit and that is connected to the neu-
al conductor of the system."

Multiwire branch circuits have many advan-
ges, such as three wires doing the work of four
n place of two two-wire branch circuits), less
aceway fill, easier balancing and phasing of a
ystem, and less voltage drop.

0.5.0 240-Volt Circuits

he electric range, clothes dryer, and water heater
n the sample residence all operate at 240VAC.
ach will be fed by a separate circuit and con-
ected to a two-pole circuit breaker of the approriate rating in the panelboard. To determine the
onductor size and overcurrent protection for the
ange, proceed as follows:

tep 1 Find the nameplate rating of the electric
range. This has previously been determined to be 12kVA.

tep 2 Refer to *NEC Table 220.55.* Since Column
A of this table applies to ranges rated at
12kVA (12kW) and under, this will be the
column to use in this example.

tep 3 Under the Number of Appliances column,
locate the appropriate number of appliances (one in this case), and find the maximum demand given for it in Column A.
Column A states that the circuit should be
sized for 8kVA (not the nameplate rating
of 12kVA).

tep 4 Calculate the required conductor ampacity as follows:

$$\frac{8,000VA}{240V} = 33.33A$$

The minimum branch circuit must be rated at
40A since common residential circuit breakers are
rated in steps of 15A, 20A, 30A, 40A, and so forth.
A 30A circuit breaker is too small, so a 40A circuit
breaker is selected. The conductors must have a
current-carrying capacity that is equal to or
greater than the overcurrent protection. Therefore, No. 8 AWG conductors will be used.

If a cooktop and wall oven were used instead of
the electric range, the circuit would be sized
similarly. The *NEC*® specifies that a branch circuit
for a counter-mounted cooking unit and not more
than two wall-mounted ovens, all supplied from a
single branch circuit and located in the same
room, is computed by adding the nameplate ratings of the individual appliances and treating this
total as equivalent to one range. Therefore, two
appliances of 6kVA each may be treated as a single range with a 12kVA nameplate rating.

Figure 32 shows how the electric range circuit
may appear on an electrical drawing. The connection may be made directly to the range junction
box, but more often a 50A range receptacle is
mounted at the range location and a range cord-
and-plug set is used to make the connection. This
facilitates moving the appliance later for maintenance or cleaning.

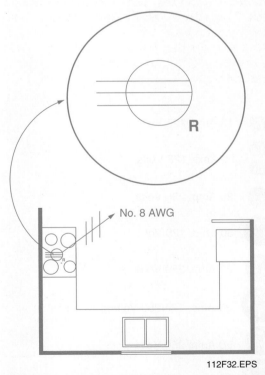

No. 8 AWG

112F32.EPS

Figure 32 ◆ Range circuits shown on an electrical drawing.

240V Circuits

THINK ABOUT IT

Calculate the ampacity required for a kitchen range with an 8kW rating. Now design the practical wiring in a labeled diagram. How will the wires be connected at the service panel and at the appliance? How will the cable be installed?

Figure 33 shows several types of receptacle configurations used in residential wiring applications. You will eventually recognize these configurations at a glance.

The branch circuit for the water heater in the sample residence must be sized for its full capacity because there is no diversity or demand factor for this appliance. Since the nameplate rating on the water heater indicates two heating elements of 4,500W each, the first inclination would be to size the circuit for a total load of 9,000W

(volt-amperes). However, only one of the two elements operates at a time. See *Figure 34*. Note that each element is controlled by a separate thermostat. The lower element becomes energized when the thermostat calls for heat, and at the same time, the thermostat opens a set of contacts to prevent the upper element from operating. When the lower element's thermostat is satisfied, the lower contacts open, and at the same time, the thermostat closes the contacts for the upper element to become energized to maintain the water temperature.

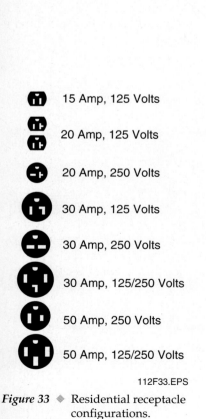

15 Amp, 125 Volts

20 Amp, 125 Volts

20 Amp, 250 Volts

30 Amp, 125 Volts

30 Amp, 250 Volts

30 Amp, 125/250 Volts

50 Amp, 250 Volts

50 Amp, 125/250 Volts

112F33.EPS

Figure 33 ◆ Residential receptacle configurations.

Figure 34 ◆ Wiring diagram of water heater controls.

112F34.EPS

With this information in hand, the circuit for the water heater may be sized as follows:

$$\frac{4,500VA}{240V} = 18.75A \times 1.25 = 23.44A$$

NEC Section 422.13 requires that the branch circuits that supply storage type water heaters having a capacity of 120 gallons or less be rated not less than 125% of the nameplate rating of the water heater. Our calculation shows this to be not less than 23A. Normally, this would require a maximum rating for the branch circuit to be not more than 25A. (See standard ratings of overcurrent devices in *NEC Section 240.6*.) However, *NEC Section 422.11(E)* permits a single nonmotor-operated appliance to be protected by overcurrent devices rated up to 150% of the nameplate rating of the appliance. In this case, $4,500VA \div 240V = 18.75A \times 150\% = 28.125A$. Since the next standard rating is 30A, the water heater will be wired with No. 10 AWG conductors protected by a 30A overcurrent device.

The *NEC*® specifies that electric clothes dryers must be rated at 5kVA or the nameplate rating, whichever is greater. In this case, the dryer is rated at 5.5kVA, and the conductor current-carrying capacity is calculated as follows:

$$\frac{5,500VA}{240V} = 22.92A$$

A three-wire, 30A circuit will be provided (No. 10 AWG wire). It is protected by a 30A circuit breaker. The dryer may be connected directly, but a 30A dryer receptacle is normally provided for the same reasons as mentioned for the electric range.

Large appliance outlets rated at 240V are frequently shown on electrical drawings using lines and symbols to indicate the outlets and circuits. In some cases, no drawings are provided.

1.0.0 ◆ BRANCH CIRCUIT LAYOUT FOR LIGHTING

A simple lighting branch circuit requires two conductors to provide a continuous path for current flow. The usual lighting branch circuit operates at 120V; the white (grounded) circuit conductor is therefore connected to the neutral bus in the panelboard, while the black (ungrounded) circuit conductor is connected to an overcurrent protection device.

Lighting branch circuits and outlets are shown on electrical drawings by means of lines and symbols; that is, a single line is drawn from outlet to outlet and then terminated with an arrowhead to indicate a homerun to the panelboard. Several methods are used to indicate the number and size of conductors, but the most common is to indicate the number of conductors in the circuit by using slash marks through the circuit lines and then indicate the wire size by a notation adjacent to these slash marks. For example, two slash marks indicate two conductors; three slash marks indicate three conductors. Some electrical designers omit slash marks for two-conductor circuits. In this case, the conductor size is usually indicated in the symbol list or legend.

The circuits used to feed residential lighting must conform to standards established by the *NEC*® as well as by local and state ordinances. Most of the lighting circuits should be calculated to include the total load, although at times this is not possible because the electrician cannot be certain of the exact wattage that might be used by the homeowner. For example, an electrician may install four porcelain lampholders for the unfinished basement area, each to contain one 100-watt (100W) incandescent lamp. However, the homeowners may eventually replace the original lamps with others rated at 150W or even 200W. Thus, if the electrician initially loads the lighting circuit to full capacity, the circuit will probably become overloaded in the future.

It is recommended that no residential branch circuit be loaded to more than 80% of its rated capacity. Since most circuits used for lighting are rated at 15A, the total ampacity (in volt-amperes) for the circuit is as follows:

$$15A \times 120V = 1,800VA$$

Therefore, if the circuit is to be loaded to only 80% of its rated capacity, the maximum initial connected load should be no more than 1,440VA.

Figure 35 shows one possible lighting arrangement for the sample residence. All lighting fixtures are shown in their approximate physical location as they should be installed.

Electrical symbols are used to show the fixture types. Switches and lighting branch circuits are also shown by appropriate lines and symbols. The meanings of the symbols used on this drawing are explained in the symbol list in *Figure 36*.

In actual practice, the location of lighting fixtures and their related switches will probably be the extent of the information shown on working drawings. The circuits shown in *Figure 35* are meant to illustrate how lighting circuits are routed, not to imply that such drawings are typical for residential construction. If fixtures are used in a closet, they must meet the requirements of *NEC Section 410.8* and be provided with a lens.

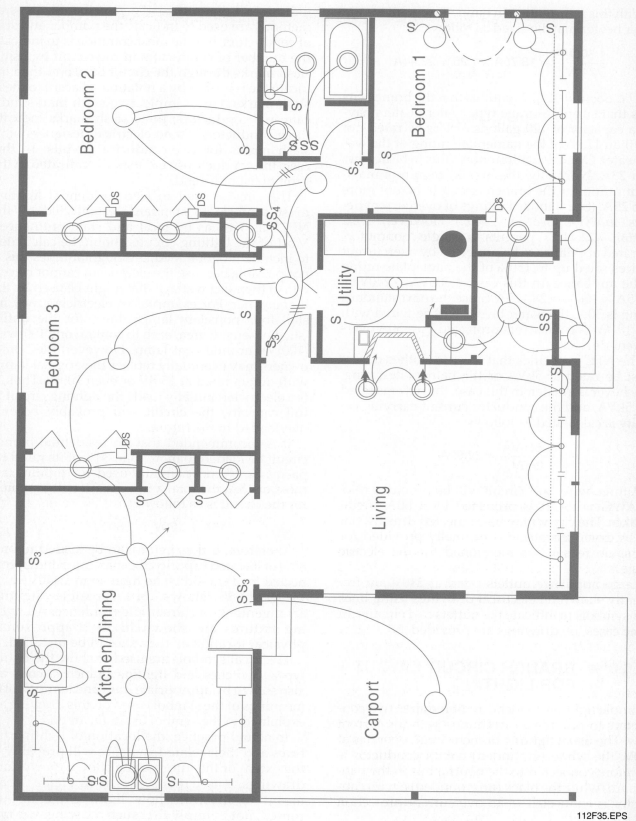

Figure 35 ◆ Lighting layout of the sample residence.

112F35.EPS

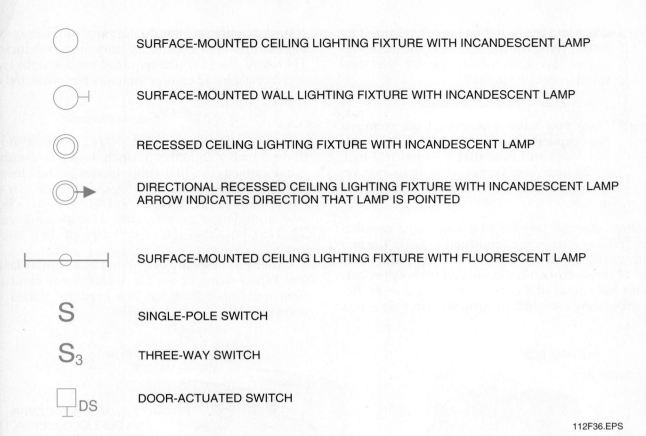

SURFACE-MOUNTED CEILING LIGHTING FIXTURE WITH INCANDESCENT LAMP

SURFACE-MOUNTED WALL LIGHTING FIXTURE WITH INCANDESCENT LAMP

RECESSED CEILING LIGHTING FIXTURE WITH INCANDESCENT LAMP

DIRECTIONAL RECESSED CEILING LIGHTING FIXTURE WITH INCANDESCENT LAMP
ARROW INDICATES DIRECTION THAT LAMP IS POINTED

SURFACE-MOUNTED CEILING LIGHTING FIXTURE WITH FLUORESCENT LAMP

S   SINGLE-POLE SWITCH

S₃   THREE-WAY SWITCH

DS   DOOR-ACTUATED SWITCH

112F36.EPS

Figure 36 ◆ Symbols.

2.0.0 ◆ OUTLET BOXES

Electricians installing residential electrical systems must be familiar with outlet box capacities, means of supporting outlet boxes, and other requirements of the *NEC*®. Boxes were discussed in detail in an earlier module, but a general review of the rules and necessary calculations is provided here.

The maximum numbers of conductors of the same size permitted in standard outlet boxes are listed in *NEC Table 314.16(A).* These figures apply where no fittings or devices such as fixture studs, cable clamps, switches, or receptacles are contained in the box and where no grounding conductors are part of the wiring within the box. Obviously, in all modern residential wiring systems there will be one or more of these items contained in every outlet box installed. Therefore, where one or more of the above-mentioned items are present, the total number of conductors will be less than that shown in the table. Also, if the box contains a looped, unbroken conductor 12" or more in length, it must be counted twice.

For example, a deduction of two conductors must be made for each strap containing a wiring device entering the box (based on the largest size conductor connected to the device) such as a switch or duplex receptacle; a further deduction of one conductor must be made for one or more equipment grounding conductors entering the box (based on the largest size grounding conductor). For instance, a 3-inch × 2-inch × 2¾-inch box is listed in the table as containing a maximum of six No. 12 wires. If the box contains cable clamps and a duplex receptacle, three wires will have to be deducted from the total of six, providing for only three No. 12 wires. If a ground wire is used, which is always the case in residential wiring, only two No. 12 wires may be used.

For example, to size a metallic outlet box for two No. 12 AWG conductors with a ground wire, cable clamp, and receptacle, proceed as follows:

Step 1 Calculate the total number of conductors and equivalents [*NEC Section 314.16(B)*]. One ground wire plus one cable clamp plus one receptacle (two wires) plus two No. 12 conductors equals a total of six No. 12 conductors.

Step 2 Determine the amount of space required for each conductor. *NEC Table 314.16(B)* gives the box volume required for each conductor. No. 12 AWG equals 2.25 cubic inches.

Step 3 Calculate the outlet box space required by multiplying the number of cubic inches required for each conductor by the total number of conductors:

$$6 \times 2.25 = 13.5 \text{ cubic inches}$$

Step 4 Once you have determined the required box capacity, again refer to *NEC Table 314.16(A)* and note that a 3-inch × 2-inch × 2¾-inch box comes closest to our requirements. This box is rated for 14 cubic inches.

Now, size the box for two additional conductors. Where four No. 12 conductors enter the box with two ground wires, only the two additional No. 12 conductors must be added to our previous count for a total of 8 conductors (6 + 2 = 8). Remember, any number of ground wires in a box counts as only one conductor; any number of ca[ble] clamps also counts as only one conducto[r.] Therefore, the box size required for use with tw[o] additional No. 12 conductors may be calculated a[s] follows:

$$8 \times 2.25 = 18 \text{ cubic inches}$$

Again, refer to *NEC Table 314.16(A)* and not[e] that a 3-inch × 2-inch × 3½-inch device box with [a] rated capacity of 18.0 cubic inches is the close[st] device box that meets *NEC*® requirements. An a[l]ternative is to use a 4-inch × 1¼-inch square bo[x] with a single-gang plaster ring, as shown in *Figu[re]* 37. This box also has a capacity of 18.0 cub[ic] inches.

Other box sizes are calculated in a similar fash[]ion. When sizing boxes for different size condu[c]tors, remember that the box capacity varies a[s] shown in *NEC Table 314.16(B)*.

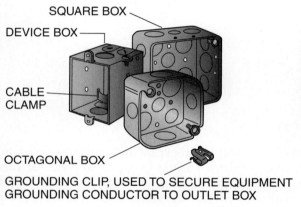

SQUARE BOX
DEVICE BOX
CABLE CLAMP
OCTAGONAL BOX
GROUNDING CLIP, USED TO SECURE EQUIPMENT GROUNDING CONDUCTOR TO OUTLET BOX

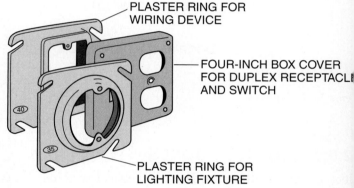

PLASTER RING FOR WIRING DEVICE
FOUR-INCH BOX COVER FOR DUPLEX RECEPTACL[E] AND SWITCH
PLASTER RING FOR LIGHTING FIXTURE

112F37A.EP[S]

112F37B.EPS

Figure 37 ◆ Typical metallic outlet boxes with extension (plaster) rings.

Calculating Conductors

In a 4" × 4" × 1½" metal box, one 14/3 cable with ground feeds three 14/2 cables with ground wires. The red wire of the 14/3 cable feeds a receptacle, and the black wire feeds the 14/2 black wires. All of the white wires are spliced together, with one brought out to the receptacle terminal. The ground wires are all spliced, with one brought out to the grounding terminal on the receptacle and one to the ground clip on the box. All four cables are connected with box connectors rather than internal clamps. Using *NEC Section 314.16,* decide whether this wiring violates the code.

112P1205.EPS

2.1.0 Mounting Outlet Boxes

utlet box configurations are almost endless, and you research the various methods of mounting ese boxes, you will be astonished. In this section, some common outlet boxes and their mounting considerations will be reviewed.

The conventional metallic device box, which is sed for residential duplex receptacles and witches for lighting control, may be mounted to all studs using 16d (penny) nails placed through e round mounting holes passing through the inrior of the box. The nails are then driven into the all stud. When nails are used for mounting out-t boxes in this manner, the nails must be located ithin ¼" of the back or ends of the enclosure.

Nonmetallic boxes normally have mounting ails fitted to the box for mounting. Other boxes ave mounting brackets. When mounting outlet oxes with brackets, use either wide-head roofing nails or box nails about 1¼" in length. *Figure 38* shows various methods of mounting outlet boxes.

Before mounting any boxes during the rough wiring process, first find out what type and thickness of finish will be used on the walls. This will dictate the depth to which the boxes must be mounted to comply with *NEC*® regulations. For example, the finish on plastered walls or ceilings is normally ½" thick; gypsum board or drywall is either ½" or ⅝" thick; and wood paneling is normally only ¼" thick. (Some tongue-and-groove wood paneling is ½" to ⅝" thick.)

The *NEC*® specifies the amount of space permitted from the edge of the outlet box to the finished wall. When a noncombustible wall finish (such as plaster, masonry, or tile) is used, the box may be recessed ¼". However, when combustible finishes are used (such as wood paneling), the box must be flush (even) with the finished wall or ceiling. See *Figure 39* and *NEC Section 314.20.*

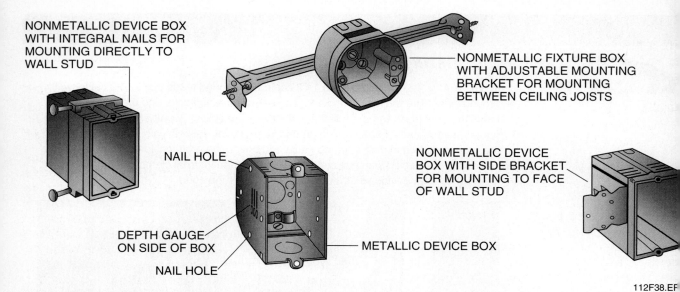

NONMETALLIC DEVICE BOX WITH INTEGRAL NAILS FOR MOUNTING DIRECTLY TO WALL STUD

NONMETALLIC FIXTURE BOX WITH ADJUSTABLE MOUNTING BRACKET FOR MOUNTING BETWEEN CEILING JOISTS

NAIL HOLE

NONMETALLIC DEVICE BOX WITH SIDE BRACKET FOR MOUNTING TO FACE OF WALL STUD

DEPTH GAUGE ON SIDE OF BOX

METALLIC DEVICE BOX

NAIL HOLE

112F38.EP

Figure 38 ◆ Several methods of mounting outlet boxes.

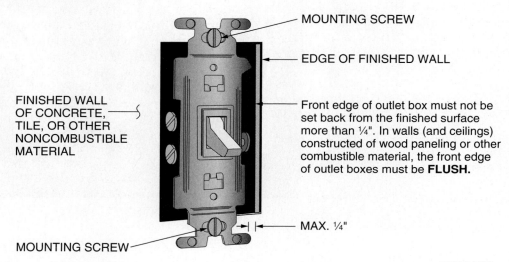

MOUNTING SCREW

EDGE OF FINISHED WALL

FINISHED WALL OF CONCRETE, TILE, OR OTHER NONCOMBUSTIBLE MATERIAL

Front edge of outlet box must not be set back from the finished surface more than ¼". In walls (and ceilings) constructed of wood paneling or other combustible material, the front edge of outlet boxes must be **FLUSH.**

MAX. ¼"

MOUNTING SCREW

112F39.EPS

Figure 39 ◆ Outlet box installation.

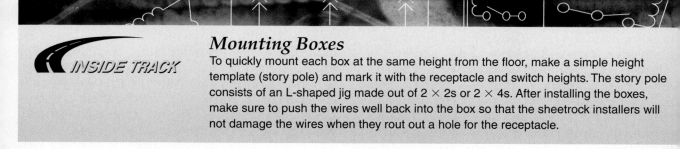

Mounting Boxes

To quickly mount each box at the same height from the floor, make a simple height template (story pole) and mark it with the receptacle and switch heights. The story pole consists of an L-shaped jig made out of 2 × 2s or 2 × 4s. After installing the boxes, make sure to push the wires well back into the box so that the sheetrock installers will not damage the wires when they rout out a hole for the receptacle.

When Type NM cable is used in either metallic or nonmetallic outlet boxes, the cable assembly, including the sheath, must extend into the box by not less than ¼" [*NEC Section 314.17(C)*]. In all instances, all permitted wiring methods must be secured to the boxes by means of either cable clamps or approved connectors. The one exception to th rule is where Type NM cable is used with 2¼-inc × 4-inch (or smaller) nonmetallic boxes where th cable is fastened within eight inches of the box. I this case, the cable does not have to be secured t the box. See *NEC Section 314.17(C), Exception.*

3.0.0 ◆ WIRING DEVICES

iring devices include various types of recepta-
es and switches, the latter being used for light-
g control. Switches are covered in *NEC Article
4,* while regulations for receptacles may be
und in *NEC Article 406.*

3.1.0 Receptacles

ceptacles are rated by voltage and amperage ca-
city. *NEC Section 406.3* requires that receptacles
nnected to a 15A or 20A circuit have the correct
ltage and current rating for the application, and
· of the grounding type.

Where there is only one outlet on a circuit, the
ceptacle's rating must be equal to or greater
an the capacity of the conductors feeding it per
EC Section 210.21(B)(1). For example, if one re-
ptacle is connected to a 20A residential laundry
rcuit, the receptacle must be rated at 20A or
ore. When more than one outlet is on a circuit,
e total connected load must be equal to or less
an the capacity of the branch circuit conductors
eding the receptacles.

Refer to *Figure 40* for some of the characteristics
a standard 125V, 15A duplex receptacle. Note
at the terminals are color coded as follows:

Green – Connection for the equipment grounding conductor
Silver – Connection for the neutral or grounded
conductor
Brass – Connection for the ungrounded
conductor

A standard 125V, 15A receptacle is also typically imprinted with the following symbols:

- *UL* – Underwriters Laboratories, Inc., listing
- *CSA* – Canadian Standards Association
- *CO/ALR* – Designed for use with both copper
  and aluminum wire
- *15A* – Receptacle rated for a maximum of 15A
- *125V* – Receptacle rated for a maximum of 125V

The UL label means that the receptacle has un-
dergone testing by Underwriters Laboratories,
Inc., and meets minimum safety requirements.
Underwriters Laboratories, Inc., was created by
the National Board of Fire Underwriters to test
electrical devices and materials. The UL label is a
safety rating only and does not mean that the device or equipment meets any type of quality standard. The CSA label means that the receptacle is
approved by the Canadian Standards Association,
the Canadian equivalent to Underwriters Laboratories, Inc. The CSA label means that the receptacle is acceptable for use in Canada.

The CO/ALR symbol means that the device is
suitable for use with copper, aluminum, or
copper-clad aluminum wire. The CO in the symbol stands for copper while ALR stands for aluminum revised. The CO/ALR symbol replaces
the earlier CU/AL mark, which appeared on
wiring devices that were later found to be inadequate for use with aluminum wire in the 15A to
20A range. Therefore, any receptacle or wall
switch marked with the CU/AL configuration or
anything other than CO/ALR should be used
only for copper wire.

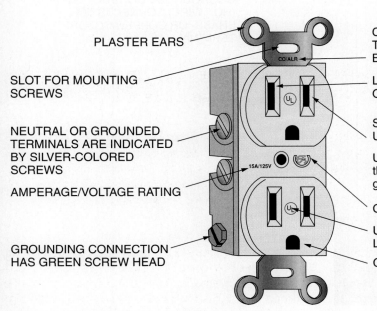

PLASTER EARS

SLOT FOR MOUNTING
SCREWS

NEUTRAL OR GROUNDED
TERMINALS ARE INDICATED
BY SILVER-COLORED
SCREWS

AMPERAGE/VOLTAGE RATING

GROUNDING CONNECTION
HAS GREEN SCREW HEAD

CO/ALR DESIGNATION INDICATES THAT
THE SWITCH IS DESIGNED FOR USE WITH
BOTH COPPER AND ALUMINUM WIRE

LONGER SLOT INDICATES NEUTRAL
OR GROUNDED CONDUCTOR

SMALL SLOT INDICATES
UNGROUNDED CONDUCTOR

Ungrounded conductors are connected to
the brass screws on opposite side from
grounded conductor screws.

CANADIAN STANDARDS ASSOCIATION

UNDERWRITERS LABORATORIES, INC.,
LISTING

GROUNDING SLOT

112F40.EPS

gure 40 ◆ Standard 125V, 15A duplex receptacle.

These same configurations also apply to wall switches used for lighting control. These will be discussed next.

14.0.0 ◆ LIGHTING CONTROL

There are many types of lighting control devices. These devices have been designed to make the best use of the lighting equipment provided by the lighting industry. They include:

- Automatic timing devices for outdoor lighting
- Dimmers for residential lighting
- Common single-pole, three-way, and four-way switches

For the purposes of this module, a switch is defined as a device that is used on branch circuits to control lighting. Switches fall into the following basic categories:

- Snap-action switches
- Quiet switches

A single-pole snap-action switch consists of device containing two stationary current-carryi elements, a moving current-carrying element, toggle handle, a spring, and a housing. When t contacts are open, as shown in *Figure 41*, the c cuit is broken and no current flows. When t moving element is closed by manually flippi the toggle handle, the contacts complete the c cuit and the lamp is energized. See *Figure 42*.

The quiet switch (*Figure 43*) is the most co mon switch for use in lighting applications. Its o eration is much quieter than the snap-acti switch.

The quiet switch consists of a stationary conta and a moving contact that are close together wh the switch is open. Only a short, gentle moveme is required to open and close the switch, produ ing very little noise. This type of switch may used only on alternating current.

Quiet switches are common for loads from 1(to 20A, and are available in single-pole, three-wa and four-way configurations.

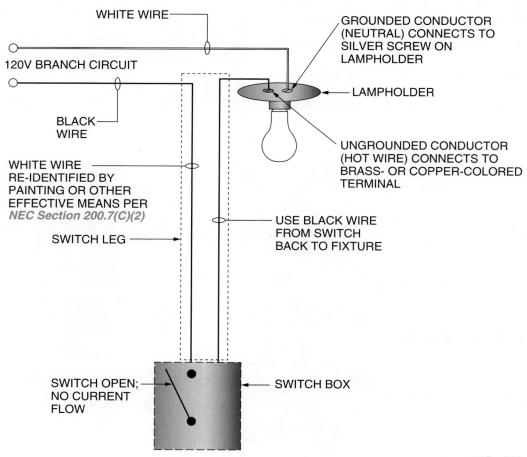

Figure 41 ◆ Switch operation, contacts open.

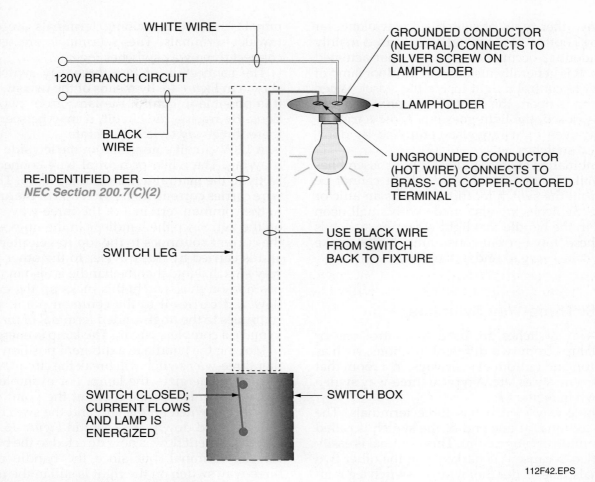

WHITE WIRE

GROUNDED CONDUCTOR (NEUTRAL) CONNECTS TO SILVER SCREW ON LAMPHOLDER

120V BRANCH CIRCUIT

LAMPHOLDER

BLACK WIRE

UNGROUNDED CONDUCTOR (HOT WIRE) CONNECTS TO BRASS- OR COPPER-COLORED TERMINAL

RE-IDENTIFIED PER *NEC Section 200.7(C)(2)*

USE BLACK WIRE FROM SWITCH BACK TO FIXTURE

SWITCH LEG

SWITCH CLOSED; CURRENT FLOWS AND LAMP IS ENERGIZED

SWITCH BOX

112F42.EPS

gure 42 ◆ Switch operation, contacts closed.

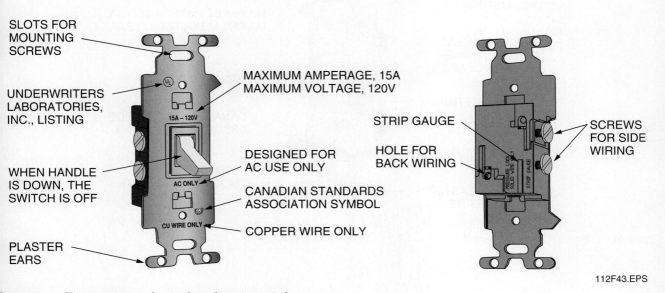

SLOTS FOR MOUNTING SCREWS

MAXIMUM AMPERAGE, 15A MAXIMUM VOLTAGE, 120V

UNDERWRITERS LABORATORIES, INC., LISTING

STRIP GAUGE

SCREWS FOR SIDE WIRING

HOLE FOR BACK WIRING

DESIGNED FOR AC USE ONLY

WHEN HANDLE IS DOWN, THE SWITCH IS OFF

CANADIAN STANDARDS ASSOCIATION SYMBOL

COPPER WIRE ONLY

PLASTER EARS

112F43.EPS

gure 43 ◆ Characteristics of a single-pole quiet switch.

Many other types of switches are available for lighting control. One type of switch used mainly in residential occupancies is the door-actuated switch. It is generally installed in the door jamb of a closet to control a light inside the closet. When the door is open, the light comes on; when the door is closed, the light goes out. Most refrigerator and oven lights are also controlled by door-actuated switches.

Combination switch/indicator light assemblies are available for use where the light cannot be seen from the switch location, such as an attic or garage. Switches are also made with small neon lamps in the handle that light when the switch is off. These low-current-consuming lamps make the switches easy to find in the dark.

14.1.0 Three-Way Switches

Three-way switches are used to control one or more lamps from two different locations, such as at the top and bottom of stairways, in a room that has two entrances, etc. A typical three-way switch is shown in *Figure 44*.

A three-way switch has three terminals. The single terminal at one end of the switch is called the common or hinge point. This terminal is easily identified because it is darker than the other two terminals. The feeder (hot wire) or switch leg is always connected to the common dark or black ter-

minal. The two remaining terminals are calle[d] traveler terminals. These terminals are used [to] connect three-way switches together.

The connection of two three-way switches [is] shown in *Figure 45*. By means of the two switche[s] it is possible to control the lamp from two loc[a]tions. By tracing the circuit, it may be seen ho[w] these three-way switches operate.

A 120V circuit emerges from the left side of t[he] drawing. The white or neutral wire connects [di]rectly to the neutral terminal of the lamp. The h[ot] wire carries current, in the direction of the arrow[s,] to the common terminal of the three-way swit[ch] on the left. Since the handle is in the up positio[n,] the current continues to the top traveler termin[al] and is carried by this traveler to the other thre[e-] way switch. Note that the handle is also in the u[p] position on this switch; this picks up the curre[nt] flow and carries it to the common point, whi[ch] continues to the ungrounded terminal of the lam[p] to make a complete circuit. The lamp is energize[d.]

Moving the handle to a different position on e[i]ther three-way switch will break the circuit, whi[ch] in turn deenergizes the lamp. For example, let[']s say a person leaves the room at the point of t[he] three-way switch on the left, and the switch ha[n]dle is flipped down, as shown in *Figure 46*. No[te] that the current flow is now directed to the botto[m] traveler terminal, but since the handle of t[he] three-way switch on the right is still in the up p[o]sition, no current will flow to the lamp.

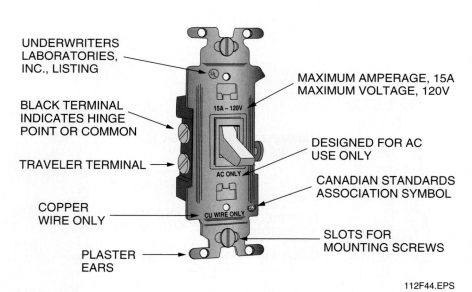

UNDERWRITERS LABORATORIES, INC., LISTING

MAXIMUM AMPERAGE, 15A
MAXIMUM VOLTAGE, 120V

BLACK TERMINAL INDICATES HINGE POINT OR COMMON

TRAVELER TERMINAL

DESIGNED FOR AC USE ONLY

CANADIAN STANDARDS ASSOCIATION SYMBOL

COPPER WIRE ONLY

SLOTS FOR MOUNTING SCREWS

PLASTER EARS

112F44.EPS

Figure 44 ◆ Typical three-way switch.

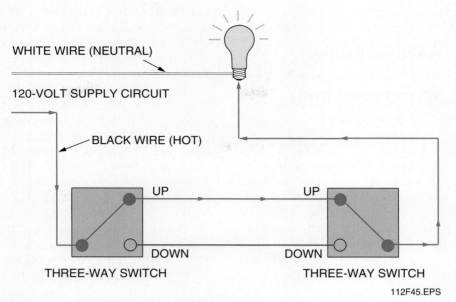

WHITE WIRE (NEUTRAL)

120-VOLT SUPPLY CIRCUIT

BLACK WIRE (HOT)

UP   UP

DOWN   DOWN

THREE-WAY SWITCH   THREE-WAY SWITCH

112F45.EPS

Figure 45 ◆ Three-way switches in the ON position; both handles are up.

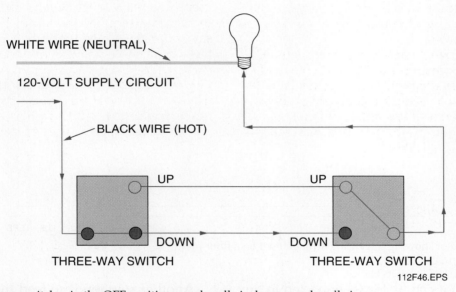

WHITE WIRE (NEUTRAL)

120-VOLT SUPPLY CIRCUIT

BLACK WIRE (HOT)

UP   UP

DOWN   DOWN

THREE-WAY SWITCH   THREE-WAY SWITCH

112F46.EPS

Figure 46 ◆ Three-way switches in the OFF position; one handle is down, one handle is up.

If another person enters the room at the location of the three-way switch on the right, and the handle is flipped downward, as shown in *Figure 47*, this change provides a complete circuit to the lamp, which causes it to be energized. In this example, current flow is on the bottom traveler. Again, changing the position of the switch handle (pivot point) on either three-way switch will deenergize the lamp.

In actual practice, the exact wiring of the two three-way switches to control the operation of a lamp will be slightly different from the routing shown in these three diagrams. There are several ways that two three-way switches may be connected. One solution is shown in *Figure 48*. In this case, two-wire, Type NM cable is fed to the three-way switch on the left.

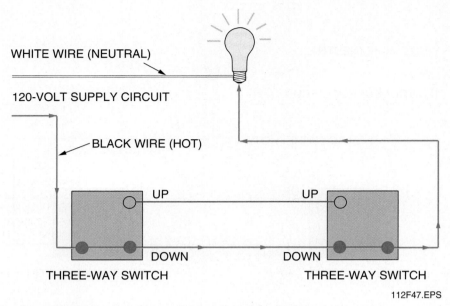

WHITE WIRE (NEUTRAL)

120-VOLT SUPPLY CIRCUIT

BLACK WIRE (HOT)

UP

UP

DOWN

DOWN

THREE-WAY SWITCH

THREE-WAY SWITCH

112F47.EPS

Figure 47 ◆ Three-way switches with both handles down; the light is energized.

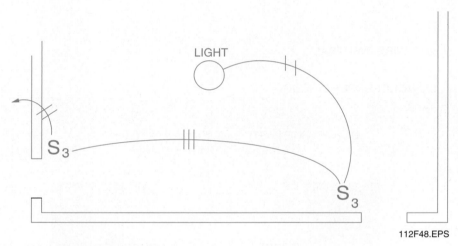

LIGHT

S₃

S₃

112F48.EPS

Figure 48 ◆ Method of showing the wiring arrangement on a floor plan.

The black or hot conductor is connected to the common terminal on the switch, while the white or neutral conductor is spliced to the white conductor of the three-wire, Type NM cable leaving the switch. This three-wire cable is necessary to carry the two travelers plus the neutral to the three-way switch on the right. At this point, the black and red wires connect to the two traveler terminals, respectively. The white or neutral wire is again spliced—this time to the white wire of another two-wire, Type NM cable. The neutral wire is never connected to the switch itself. The black wire of the two-wire, Type NM cable connects to the common terminal on the three-way switch. This cable, carrying the hot and neutral conductors, is routed to the lighting fixture outlet for connection to the fixture.

Another solution is to feed the lighting fixtu outlet with two-wire cable. Run another two-wi cable carrying the hot and neutral conductors one of the three-way switches. A three-wire cab is pulled between the two three-way switche and then another two-wire cable is routed fro the other three-way switch to the lighting fixtu outlet.

Some electricians use a shortcut method th eliminates one of the two-wire cables in the pr ceding method. In this case, a two-wire cable run from the lighting fixture outlet to one thre way switch. Three-wire cable is pulled betwee the two three-way switches—two of the wires f travelers and the third for the common point turn. This method is shown in *Figure 49*.

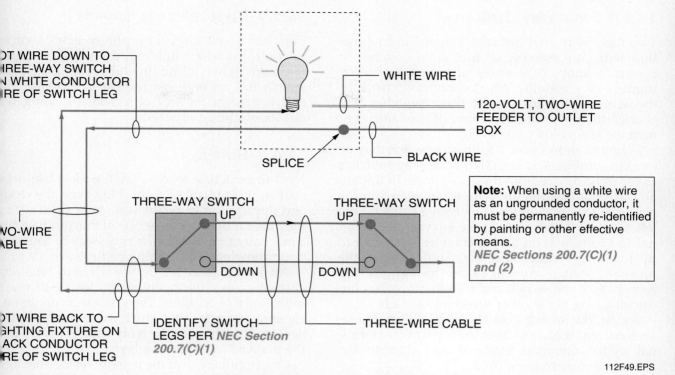

HOT WIRE DOWN TO
THREE-WAY SWITCH
ON WHITE CONDUCTOR
WIRE OF SWITCH LEG

WHITE WIRE

120-VOLT, TWO-WIRE
FEEDER TO OUTLET
BOX

SPLICE

BLACK WIRE

TWO-WIRE
CABLE

THREE-WAY SWITCH
UP

THREE-WAY SWITCH
UP

DOWN

DOWN

Note: When using a white wire
as an ungrounded conductor, it
must be permanently re-identified
by painting or other effective
means.
*NEC Sections 200.7(C)(1)
and (2)*

HOT WIRE BACK TO
LIGHTING FIXTURE ON
BLACK CONDUCTOR
WIRE OF SWITCH LEG

IDENTIFY SWITCH
LEGS PER *NEC Section
200.7(C)(1)*

THREE-WIRE CABLE

112F49.EPS

Figure 49 ◆ One way to connect a pair of three-way switches to control one lighting fixture.

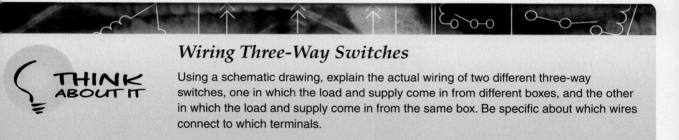

Wiring Three-Way Switches

Using a schematic drawing, explain the actual wiring of two different three-way
switches, one in which the load and supply come in from different boxes, and the other
in which the load and supply come in from the same box. Be specific about which wires
connect to which terminals.

14.2.0 Four-Way Switches

Two three-way switches may be used in conjunction with any number of four-way switches to control a lamp, or a series of lamps, from any number of positions. When connected correctly, the actuation of any one of these switches will change the operating condition of the lamp (i.e., turn the lamp either on or off).

Figure 50 shows how a four-way switch may be used in combination with two three-way switches to control a device from three locations. In this example, note that the hot wire is connected to the common terminal on the three-way switch on the left. Current then travels to the top traveler terminal and continues on the top traveler conductor to the four-way switch. Since the handle is up on the four-way switch, current flows through the top terminals of the switch and into the traveler conductor going to the other three-way switch.

Again, the switch is in the up position. Therefore, current is carried from the top traveler terminal to the common terminal and then to the lighting fixture to energize it.

If the position of any one of the three switch handles is changed, the circuit will be broken and no current will flow to the lamp. For example, assume that the four-way switch handle is flipped downward. The circuit will now appear as shown in *Figure 51*, and the light will be out.

Remember, any number of four-way switches may be used in combination with two three-way switches, but two three-way switches are always necessary for the correct operation of one or more four-way switches.

14.3.0 Photoelectric Switch

The chief application of the photoelectric switch to control outdoor lighting, especially the dus to-dawn lights found in suburban areas. Th switch has an endless number of possible us and is a great tool for electricians dealing wi outdoor lighting situations.

14.4.0 Relays

Next to switches, relays play the most importa part in the control of light. However, the desi; and application of relays is a study in itself, ar they are far beyond the scope of this module. St a brief mention of relays is necessary to round c your knowledge of lighting controls.

An electric relay is a device whereby an elect current causes the opening or closing of one more pairs of contacts. These contacts are usua. capable of controlling much more power than necessary to operate the relay itself. This is one the main advantages of relays.

One popular use of the relay in residential ligh ing systems is that of remote control lighting. this type of system, all relays are designed to o erate on a 24V circuit and are used to control 12(lighting circuits. They are rated at 20A, which sufficient to control the full load of a normal ligh ing branch circuit, if desired.

Remote control switching makes it possible install a switch wherever it is convenient and pr tical to do so or wherever there is an obvious ne for a switch, no matter how remote it is from t lamp or lamps it is to control. This method enabl

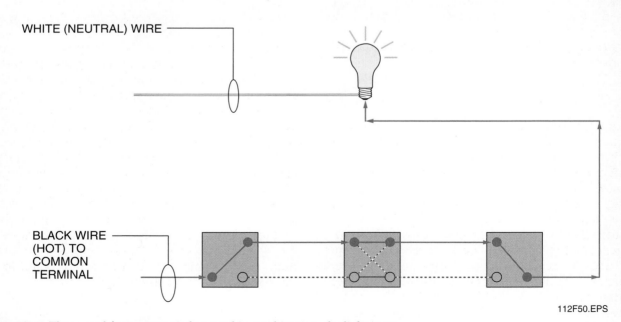

112F50.EPS

Figure 50 ◆ Three- and four-way switches used in combination; the light is on.

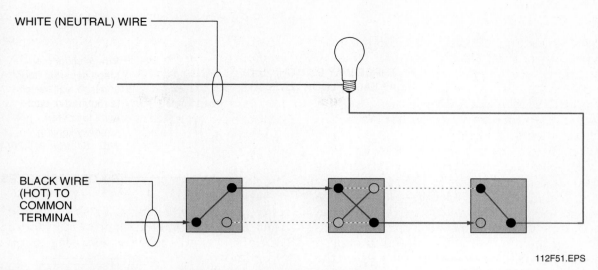

WHITE (NEUTRAL) WIRE

BLACK WIRE
(HOT) TO
COMMON
TERMINAL

112F51.EPS

ure 51 ◆ Three- and four-way switches used in combination; the light is off.

hting designs to achieve new advances in light-
g control convenience at a reasonable cost. Re-
ote control switching is also ideal for rewiring
isting homes with finished walls and ceilings.

One relay is required for each fixture or each
oup of fixtures that are controlled together.
vitch locations for remote control follow the
me rules as for conventional direct switching.
owever, since it is easy to add switches to con-
ol a given relay, no opportunities should be
erlooked for adding a switch to improve the
nvenience of control.

Remote control lighting also has the advantage
using selector switches at central locations. For
ample, selector switches located in the master
droom or in the kitchen of a home enable the
vner to control every lighting fixture on the
operty from this location. For example, the sector switch may be used to control outside or
sement lights that might otherwise be left on in-
lvertently.

.5.0 Dimmers

mming a lighting system provides control of
e quantity of illumination. It may be done to cre-
e certain moods or to blend the lighting from
fferent sources for various lighting effects.

For example, in homes with formal dining
oms, a chandelier mounted directly above the
ning table and controlled by a dimmer switch
comes the centerpiece of the room while provid-
g general illumination. The dimmer adds versa-
ity since it can set the mood for the activity—low
illiance (candlelight effect) for formal dining or
ight for an evening of playing cards. When chan-
liers with exposed lamps are used, the dimmer
essential to avoid a garish and uncomfortable at-

mosphere. The chandelier should be sized in proportion to the dining area.

NOTE

It is very important that dimmers be matched to
the wattage of the application. Check the
manufacturer's data.

14.6.0 Switch Locations

Although the location of wall switches is usually
provided for convenience, the *NEC*® also stipu-
lates certain mandatory locations for lighting
fixtures and wall switches. See *NEC Section
210.70(A)* for specific switch locations in dwelling
units. These locations are deemed necessary for
added safety in the home for both the occupants
and service personnel.

For example, the *NEC*® requires adequate
light in areas where heating, ventilating, and air
conditioning (HVAC) equipment is placed. Furthermore, these lights must be conveniently controlled so that homeowners and service personnel
do not have to enter a dark area where they might
come in contact with dangerous equipment.
Three-way switches are required under certain
conditions. The *NEC*® also specifies regulations
governing lighting fixtures in clothes closets,
along with those governing lighting fixtures that
may be mounted directly to the outlet box without
further support. *Figure 52* summarizes some of the
NEC® requirements for light and switch placement in the home. For further details, refer to the
appropriate sections in the *NEC*®.

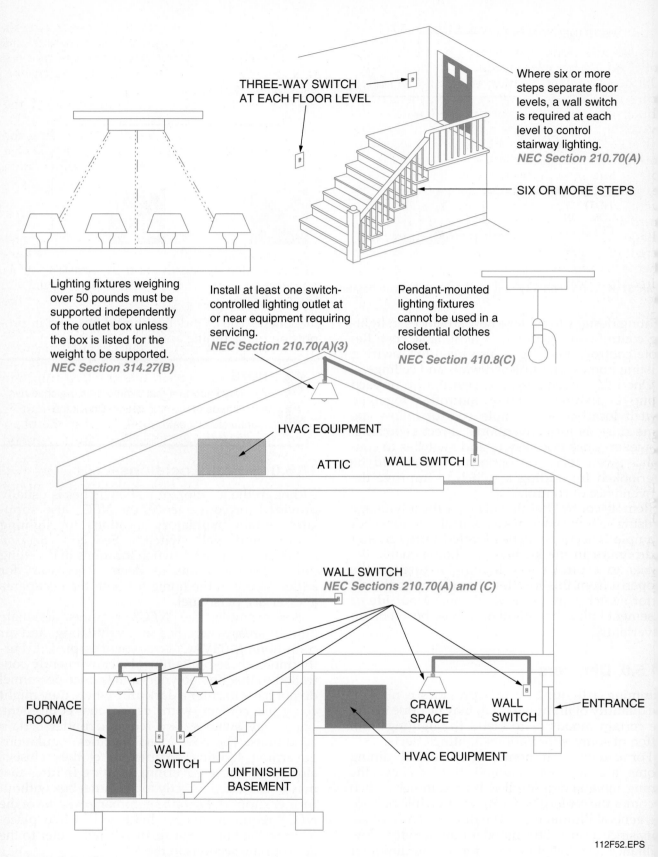

THREE-WAY SWITCH
AT EACH FLOOR LEVEL

Where six or more
steps separate floor
levels, a wall switch
is required at each
level to control
stairway lighting.
NEC Section 210.70(A)

SIX OR MORE STEPS

Lighting fixtures weighing
over 50 pounds must be
supported independently
of the outlet box unless
the box is listed for the
weight to be supported.
NEC Section 314.27(B)

Install at least one switch-
controlled lighting outlet at
or near equipment requiring
servicing.
NEC Section 210.70(A)(3)

Pendant-mounted
lighting fixtures
cannot be used in a
residential clothes
closet.
NEC Section 410.8(C)

HVAC EQUIPMENT

ATTIC   WALL SWITCH

WALL SWITCH
NEC Sections 210.70(A) and (C)

FURNACE
ROOM

CRAWL
SPACE

WALL
SWITCH

ENTRANCE

WALL
SWITCH

HVAC EQUIPMENT

UNFINISHED
BASEMENT

112F52.EPS

Figure 52 ◆ *NEC*® requirements for light and switch placement.

.7.0 Low-Voltage Electrical Systems

nventional lighting systems operate and are
ntrolled by the same system voltage, generally
)V in residential lighting circuits. The *NEC*®
rmits the use of low-voltage systems to control
hting circuits. There are some advantages to
v-voltage systems. One advantage is that the
ntrol of lighting from several different locations
more easily accomplished, such as with the re-
ote control system discussed earlier. For exam-
, outside flood lighting can be controlled from
veral different rooms in a house. The cost of the
ntrol wiring is less in that it is rated for a lower
ltage and only carries a minimum amount of
rrent compared to a standard lighting system.
hen extensive or complex lighting control is re-
ired, low-voltage systems are preferred. Also,
ice these circuits are low-energy circuits, circuit
otection is not required.

.7.1 NEC® Requirements for Low-Voltage Systems

C Article 725 governs the installation of low-
ltage system wiring. These provisions apply to
note control circuits, low-voltage relay switch-
;, low-energy power circuits, and low-voltage
cuits. The *NEC*® divides these circuits into three
egories:

Remote control
Signaling
Power-limited circuits

As mentioned earlier, circuit protection of the
v-voltage circuit is not required; however, the
;h-voltage side of the transformer that supplies
e low-voltage system must be protected. *NEC*

Chapter 9, Tables 11(A) and 11(B) cover circuits
that are inherently limited in power output and
therefore require no overcurrent protection or are
limited by a combination of power source and
overcurrent protection.

There are a number of requirements of the
power systems described in *NEC Chapter 9, Tables 11(A) and 11(B)* and the notes preceding the
tables. You should read and study all applicable
portions of the *NEC*® before installing low-
voltage power systems.

14.7.2 Relays

A low-voltage remote control wiring system is relay operated. The relay is controlled by a low-
voltage switching system and in turn it controls
the power circuit that is connected to it (*Figure 53*).
The low-voltage, split coil relay is the heart of the
low-voltage remote control system (*Figure 54*).
When the ON coil of the relay is energized, the solenoid mechanism causes the contacts to move
into the ON position to complete the power circuit. The contacts stay in this position until the
OFF coil is energized. When this occurs, the contacts are withdrawn and the power circuit is
opened. The red wire is the ON wire; the black
wire is the OFF wire, and the blue wire is common
to the transformer.

The low-voltage relay is available in two
mounting styles. One type is designed to mount
through a ½-inch knockout opening (*Figure 55*).
For a ¾-inch knockout, a rubber grommet is inserted to isolate the relay from the metal. This
practice should ensure quieter relay operation.

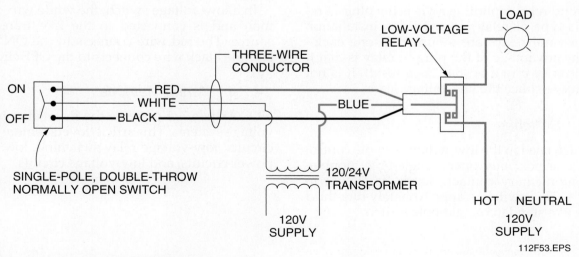

ure 53 ◆ Low-voltage remote control system.

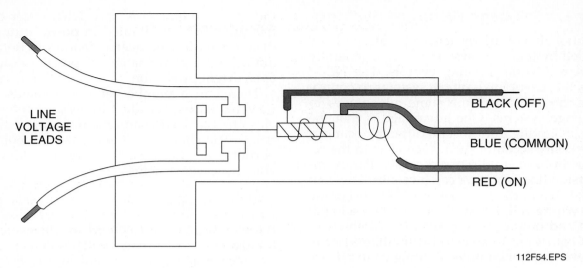

Figure 54 ◆ Low-voltage relay diagram.

LINE
VOLTAGE
LEADS

BLACK (OFF)

BLUE (COMMON)

RED (ON)

112F54.EPS

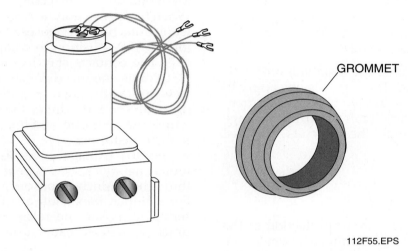

GROMMET

112F55.EPS

Figure 55 ◆ Low-voltage relay.

The second relay mounting style is the plug-in relay. This type of relay is used in an installation where several relays are mounted in one enclosure. The advantage of the plug-in relay is that it plugs directly into a busbar. As a result, it is not necessary to splice the line voltage leads.

14.7.3 Switches

The switch used in the low-voltage remote control system is a normally open, single-pole, double-throw, momentary contact switch, as shown in *Figure 56*. This switch is approximately one-third the size of a standard single-pole switch.

In a low-voltage switch, the white wire is common and is connected to the 24V transformer source. The red wire connects to the ON circuit and the black wire connects to the OFF circuit.

14.7.4 Wiring Methods

NEC Article 725 governs the installation of low-voltage systems. This article covers remote control circuits, low-voltage relay switching, low-energy power circuits, and low-voltage circuits.

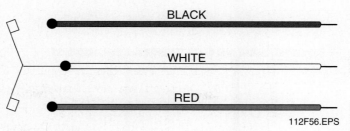

BLACK
WHITE
RED

112F56.EPS

Figure 56 ◆ Single-pole, double-throw switch.

.0.0 ◆ ELECTRIC HEATING

he use of electric heating in residential occupancies has risen tremendously over the past decade or so, and the practice will no doubt continue. This is due to the following advantages of electric heat over most other heating systems:

Electric heat is noncombustible and is therefore safer than combustible fuels.
It requires no storage space, fuel tanks, or chimneys.
It requires little maintenance.
The initial installation cost is relatively inexpensive when compared to other types of heating systems.
The comfort level may be improved since each room may be controlled separately by its own thermostat.

There are also some disadvantages to using electric baseboard heat, especially in northern climates. Some of these disadvantages include:

Electric heat is often more expensive to operate than other types of fuels.
Receptacles must not be installed above electric baseboard heaters.
Electric baseboard heaters tend to discolor the wall area immediately above the heater, especially if there are smokers in the home.

> **NOTE**
>
> It is very important to calculate the extra electric load of an electric heater installation (especially in an add-on situation). Ensure that the extra load does not exceed the maximum amperage draw of either the circuit or the panel.

The type of electric heating system used for a given residence will usually depend on the structural conditions, the kind of room, and the activities for which the room will be used. The homeowner's preference will also enter into the final decision.

Electric heating equipment is available in baseboard, wall, ceiling, kick space, and floor units; in resistance cable embedded in the ceiling or concrete floor; in forced-air duct systems similar to conventional oil- or gas-fired hot air systems; and in electric boilers for hot water baseboard heat.

Electric heat pumps have also become popular for HVAC systems in certain parts of the country. The term heat pump, as applied to a year-round air conditioning system, commonly denotes a system in which refrigeration equipment is used in such a manner that heat is taken from a heat source and transferred to the conditioned space when heating is desired; heat is removed from the space and discharged to a heat sink when cooling and dehumidification are desired.

A heat pump has the unique ability to furnish more energy than it consumes. This is due to the fact that under certain outdoor conditions, electrical energy is required only to move the refrigerant and run the fan; thus, a heat pump can attain a heating efficiency of two or more to one; that is, it will put out an equivalent of two or three watts of heat for every watt consumed. For this reason, its use is highly desirable for the conservation of energy.

In general, electric baseboard heating equipment should be located on the outside wall near the areas where the greatest heat loss will occur, such as under windows, etc. The controls for wall-mounted thermostats should be located on an interior wall, about 50 inches above the floor to sense the average room temperature. *Figure 57* shows an electric heating arrangement for the sample residence. *NEC*® regulations governing the installation of these units are also noted.

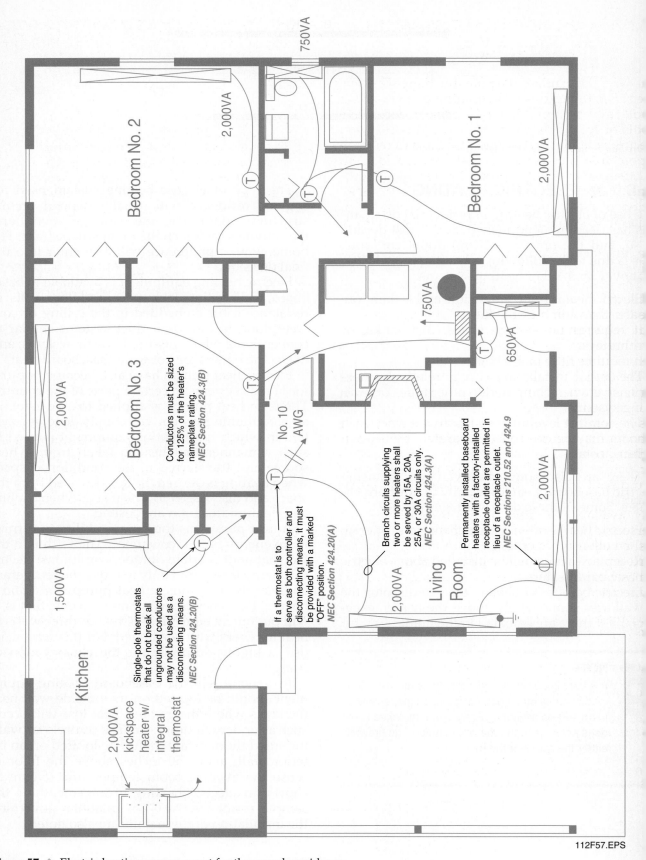

750VA

2,000VA

Bedroom No. 1

2,000VA

2,000VA

Bedroom No. 2

750VA

650VA

2,000VA

2,000VA

Bedroom No. 3

Conductors must be sized for 125% of the heater's nameplate rating.
NEC Section 424.3(B)

No. 10 AWG

Branch circuits supplying two or more heaters shall be served by 15A, 20A, 25A, or 30A circuits only.
NEC Section 424.3(A)

Permanently installed baseboard heaters with a factory-installed receptacle outlet are permitted in lieu of a receptacle outlet.
NEC Sections 210.52 and 424.9

2,000VA

Living Room

If a thermostat is to serve as both controller and disconnecting means, it must be provided with a marked "OFF" position.
NEC Section 424.20(A)

Single-pole thermostats that do not break all ungrounded conductors may not be used as a disconnecting means.
NEC Section 424.20(B)

1,500VA

Kitchen

2,000VA kickspace heater w/ integral thermostat

112F57.EPS

Figure 57 ◆ Electric heating arrangement for the sample residence.

6.0.0 ◆ RESIDENTIAL SWIMMING POOLS, SPAS, AND HOT TUBS

The NEC® recognizes the potential danger of electric shock to persons in swimming pools, wading pools, and therapeutic pools, or near decorative pools or fountains. This shock could occur from electric potential in the water itself or as a result of a person in the water or a wet area touching an enclosure that is not at ground potential. Accordingly, the NEC® provides rules for the safe installation of electrical equipment and wiring in or adjacent to swimming pools and similar locations. NEC Article 680 covers the specific rules governing the installation and maintenance of swimming pools, spas, and hot tubs.

The electrical installation procedures for hot tubs and swimming pools are too vast to be covered in detail in this module. However, the general requirements for the installation of outlets, overhead fans and lighting fixtures, and other items are summarized in Figure 58.

Besides NEC Article 680, another good source for learning more about electrical installations in and around swimming pools is from manufacturers of swimming pool equipment, including those who manufacture and distribute underwater lighting fixtures. Many of these manufacturers offer pamphlets detailing the installation of their equipment with helpful illustrations, code explanations, and similar details. This literature is usually available at little or no cost to qualified personnel. You can write directly to manufacturers to request information about available literature, or contact your local electrical supplier or contractor who specializes in installing residential swimming pools. See Figure 59.

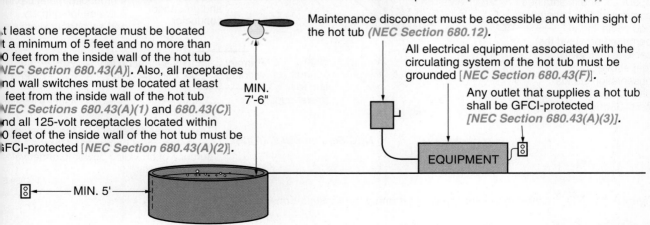

All lighting fixtures, lighting outlets, and ceiling fans located over the hot tub or within 5 feet from its inside walls shall be a minimum of 7 feet 6 inches above the maximum water level and shall be GFCI-protected [NEC Section 680.43(B)].

At least one receptacle must be located at a minimum of 5 feet and no more than 10 feet from the inside wall of the hot tub [NEC Section 680.43(A)]. Also, all receptacles and wall switches must be located at least 5 feet from the inside wall of the hot tub [NEC Sections 680.43(A)(1) and 680.43(C)] and all 125-volt receptacles located within 10 feet of the inside wall of the hot tub must be GFCI-protected [NEC Section 680.43(A)(2)].

Maintenance disconnect must be accessible and within sight of the hot tub (NEC Section 680.12).

All electrical equipment associated with the circulating system of the hot tub must be grounded [NEC Section 680.43(F)].

Any outlet that supplies a hot tub shall be GFCI-protected [NEC Section 680.43(A)(3)].

MIN. 7'-6"

EQUIPMENT

MIN. 5'

112F58.EPS

Figure 58 ◆ NEC® requirements for packaged indoor hot tubs.

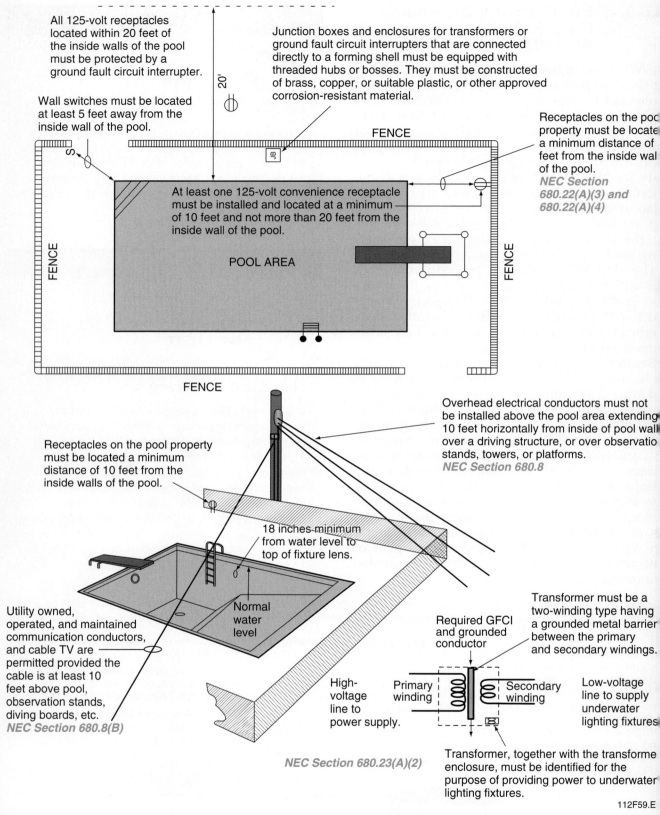

All 125-volt receptacles located within 20 feet of the inside walls of the pool must be protected by a ground fault circuit interrupter.

Wall switches must be located at least 5 feet away from the inside wall of the pool.

Junction boxes and enclosures for transformers or ground fault circuit interrupters that are connected directly to a forming shell must be equipped with threaded hubs or bosses. They must be constructed of brass, copper, or suitable plastic, or other approved corrosion-resistant material.

FENCE

JB

20'

At least one 125-volt convenience receptacle must be installed and located at a minimum of 10 feet and not more than 20 feet from the inside wall of the pool.

POOL AREA

FENCE

FENCE

Receptacles on the pool property must be located a minimum distance of feet from the inside wall of the pool.
NEC Section 680.22(A)(3) and 680.22(A)(4)

FENCE

Overhead electrical conductors must not be installed above the pool area extending 10 feet horizontally from inside of pool wall over a driving structure, or over observation stands, towers, or platforms.
NEC Section 680.8

Receptacles on the pool property must be located a minimum distance of 10 feet from the inside walls of the pool.

18 inches minimum from water level to top of fixture lens.

Normal water level

Utility owned, operated, and maintained communication conductors, and cable TV are permitted provided the cable is at least 10 feet above pool, observation stands, diving boards, etc.
NEC Section 680.8(B)

High-voltage line to power supply.

Primary winding

Required GFCI and grounded conductor

Secondary winding

Transformer must be a two-winding type having a grounded metal barrier between the primary and secondary windings.

Low-voltage line to supply underwater lighting fixtures

NEC Section 680.23(A)(2)

Transformer, together with the transformer enclosure, must be identified for the purpose of providing power to underwater lighting fixtures.

112F59.E

Figure 59 ◆ *NEC® requirements for typical swimming pool installations.*

1. When sizing electrical services, at what percentage is the first 3,000VA rated?
a. 20%
b. 45%
c. 80%
d. 100%

2. What section of the *NEC®* requires that fittings be identified for use with service masts?
a. *NEC Section 230.28*
b. *NEC Section 230.40*
c. *NEC Section 250.46*
d. *NEC Section 250.83*

3. A service conductor without an overall jacket must have a clearance of not less than _____ above a window that can be opened.
a. two feet
b. three feet
c. eight feet
d. ten feet

4. *NEC Section 230.6* considers conductors installed under at least _____ inch(es) of concrete to be outside the building.
a. one
b. two
c. four
d. five

5. Type NM cable may not be used in _____.
a. shallow chases of masonry used for below-grade walls
b. the framework of a building
c. protective strips
d. attic spaces

6. Type AC cable may not be used in _____.
a. concrete or plaster where dry
b. dry masonry
c. attic spaces
d. wet locations

7. Type SE cable is available with _____ for interior wiring systems.
a. a non-insulated ground or neutral conductor
b. an insulated grounded conductor
c. no ground conductor
d. guard strips

8. Type SER cable may be used _____.
a. in overhead applications
b. underground
c. as a subfeed under certain conditions
d. in hazardous locations

Identify the following receptacles by numbers shown below for each receptacle.

9. _____ Single receptacle

10. _____ Split-wired receptacle

11. _____ Dryer receptacle

12. _____ Range receptacle

13. _____ Duplex receptacle

14. _____ Special-purpose outlet

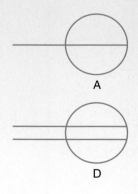

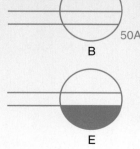

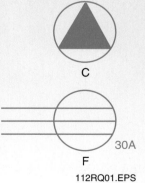

112RQ01.EPS

15. Using *NEC Table 314.16(A),* calculate the cubic inches required for the receptacle outlets shown the table below. Then, indicate the size of the metallic box that should be used.

Number and Size of Conductors in Box	Free Space within Box for Each Conductor	Total Cubic Inches of Box Space Required	What Size Metallic Box May Be Used?
A. Six No. 12 conductors and three ground wires	2.25	_____	_____
B. Seven No. 12 conductors and three ground wires with one receptacle	2.25	_____	_____
C. Two No. 14 conductors and one ground wire	2.0	_____	_____
D. Four No. 14 conductors and two ground wires	2.0	_____	_____
E. Six No. 14 conductors and three ground wires with one receptacle	2.0	_____	_____

Summary

This module covered the basics of residential wiring, including switches, outlets, conductor sizes, and service sizes. A thorough knowledge of the *NEC*® is essential to the successful installation of residential wiring systems.

Notes

Trade Terms Quiz

1. _____ consists of wires with a spiral-wound, flexible steel outer jacketing; it is also called _____.

2. A type of cable that is popular in residential and small commercial wiring systems, _____ may be used for both exposed and concealed work in normally dry locations; this type of cable is also referred to as _____.

3. A(n) _____ is a piece of equipment that has been designed for a particular purpose.

4. A(n) _____ is used for turning an electrical circuit on and off.

5. The circuit that is routed to a switch box for controlling electric lights is known as a(n) _____.

6. A(n) _____ is equipped with a conductor terminal to take a bonding jumper.

7. A(n) _____ is a bare or green insulated conductor used to ensure conductivity between metal parts that are required to be electrically connected.

8. The _____ is comprised of the conductors that extend from the last power company pole to the point of connection at the service facilities.

9. The _____ is the point where power is supplied to a building.

10. _____ lie between the point of termination of the overhead service drop or underground service lateral and the main disconnecting device in the building.

11. _____ mainly provides overcurrent protection to the feeder and service conductors.

12. A(n) _____ is comprised of the underground conductors through which service is supplied between the power company's distribution facilities and their first point of connection to the building.

13. The portion of a wiring system that extends beyond the final overcurrent device is the _____.

14. A(n) _____ is a circuit that carries current from the service equipment to a subpanel or a branch circuit panel or to some point in the wiring system.

15. Normally located at the service entrance of a residential installation, a(n) _____ usually contains the main disconnect.

16. Raceway, cable, wires, boxes, and other equipment are installed during _____.

Trade Terms

Appliance
Armored (Type AC) cable
Bonding bushing
Bonding jumper
Branch circuit
BX®

Feeder
Load center
Nonmetallic-sheathed
  (Type NM) cable
Romex®
Roughing in

Service drop
Service entrance
Service-entrance
  conductors
Service-entrance
  equipment

Service lateral
Switch
Switch leg

Dan Lamphear

Associated Builders and Contractors, Inc.

ke many other people, Dan Lamphear just fell into career as an electrician. But once he discovered the ctrical trade, he knew he had found a home. Since n, he has progressed from a helper to an prentice, a journeyman, an independent contractor, inventor, and finally, a teacher.

It was as much luck as anything else that led Dan vard a career as a professional electrician more than o decades ago. He wasn't sure what he wanted to with his life after graduating from high school. owever, after watching an electrician perform a mmercial wiring job at a friend's business—and oviding a helping hand—he was hooked. "It emed like a challenging career, and I was curious to rn more about how electricity works," he recalls.

Dan was hired by that same electrician, under hom he apprenticed for several years before hearing out the NCCER program. He jumped at the chance further his skills through the program. "Like they , knowledge is money," he smiles.

After graduating from the program, Dan struck t on his own as an independent electrician,

specializing in plant maintenance, industrial, and commercial work. His ability to diagnose and repair electrical problems in factory machinery soon made him a valuable contractor in Milwaukee's industrial sector.

He also discovered his knack for invention, and he has designed and built specialized machinery for a company that hired him as its full-time electrical maintenance supervisor. "Knowing the electrical side of machinery allowed me to understand how they operate mechanically," he says of his work as an inventor.

Dan later returned to the Associated Builders and Contractors (ABC) chapter, which trains out of a local community college, to repay the favor that helped him embark on his career. He teaches Electrical Level 2 courses for students who represent the next generation of professional electricians.

"Knowing how to use test instruments is perhaps the most important aspect of the job," he notes. "I still have some of the same meters I started out with."

Trade Terms
Introduced in This Module

Appliance: Equipment designed for a particular purpose (for example, using electricity to produce heat, light, or mechanical motion). Appliances are usually self-contained, are generally available for applications other than industrial use, and are normally produced in standard sizes or types.

Armored (Type AC) cable: Cable that consists of wires with a spiral-wound, flexible steel outer jacketing. *See BX®*.

Bonding bushing: A special conduit bushing equipped with a conductor terminal to take a bonding jumper. It also has a screw or other sharp device to bite into the enclosure wall to bond the conduit to the enclosure without a jumper when there are no concentric knockouts left in the wall of the enclosure.

Bonding jumper: A bare or green insulated conductor used to ensure the required electrical conductivity between metal parts required to be electrically connected. Bonding jumpers are frequently used from a bonding bushing to the service-equipment enclosure to provide a path around concentric knockouts in an enclosure wall, and they may also be used to bond one raceway to another.

Branch circuit: The portion of a wiring system extending beyond the final overcurrent device protecting a circuit.

BX®: A name for armored cable; although used generically, BX® is a registered trademark of the General Electric Company.

Feeder: A circuit, such as conductors in conduit or a cable run, that carries current from the service equipment to a subpanel or a branch circuit panel or to some point in the wiring system.

Load center: A type of panelboard that is normally located at the service entrance of a residential installation. It usually contains the main disconnect.

Nonmetallic-sheathed (Type NM) cable: A type of cable that is popular for use in residential and small commercial wiring systems. In general, it may be used for both exposed and concealed work in normally dry location. *See Romex®*.

Romex®: General Cable's trade name for Typ NM cable; however, it is often used generically to refer to any nonmetallic-sheathe cable.

Roughing in: The first stage of an electrical installation, when the raceway, cable, wire boxes, and other equipment are installed. Thi is the electrical work that must be done befor any finishing work can be done.

Service drop: The overhead conductors through which electrical service is supplied between the last power company pole and th point of their connection to the service facilities located at the building.

Service entrance: The point where power is supplied to a building (including the equipmen used for this purpose). The service entrance includes the service main switch or panelboard metering devices, overcurrent protective devices, and conductors/raceways for connecting to the power company's conductors.

Service-entrance conductors: The conductor between the point of termination of the overhead service drop or underground service lateral and the main disconnecting device in th building.

Service-entrance equipment: Equipment tha provides overcurrent protection to the feede and service conductors, a means of disconnecting the feeders from energized servic conductors, and a means of measuring the energy used.

Service lateral: The underground conductor through which service is supplied between the power company's distribution facilities and the first point of their connection to the building or area service facilities located at the building.

Switch: A mechanical device used for turning an electrical circuit on and off.

Switch leg: A circuit routed to a switch box for controlling electric lights.

Reference Information—Other Codes and Electrical Standards That Apply to Electrical Installations

until 2000, there were three model building des. These included the following:

Standard Building Code (SBC) – Published by the Southern Building Code Congress International.
BOCA National Building Code (NBC) – Published by the Building Officials and Code Administrators.
Uniform Building Code (UBC) – Published by the International Conference of Building Officials.

The three code writing groups, SBCCI, BOCA, d UBC, combined into one organization called e International Code Council with the purpose writing one nationally accepted family of build-g and fire codes. The first edition of the *Inter-tional Building Code* was published in 2000 and e second edition in 2003. It is intended to con-ue on a three-year cycle.

In 2002, the NFPA published its own building de, *NFPA 5000*. There are now two nationally cognized codes competing for adoption by the states.

For your reference, information is included re on several other codes and standards that ap-y to electrical installations in residential struc-res. It is suggested that to be thoroughly mpetent in the electrical trade, you should be-me familiar with the contents of these codes and e terminology used in them.

> **NOTE**
> This information is provided as a general reference only. Refer to operative local codes and the latest editions of codes in effect in your area.

UMC—UNIFORM MECHANICAL CODE

Installation of Appliances

Appliances installed in garages, warehouses, or other areas where they may be subjected to mechanical damage are required to be suitably guarded against such damage by being installed behind protective barriers or by being elevated or located out of the normal path of vehicles. Heating and cooling equipment that generates a glow, spark, or flame that is capable of igniting flammable vapors located in a garage is required to be installed with the pilots and burners or heating elements and switches at least 18 inches above the floor level.

Where such appliances are installed within a garage and are enclosed in a separate approved compartment, having access only from outside the garage, they are permitted to be installed at floor level only where the required combustion air is taken from and discharged to the exterior of the garage. See *UMC Section 508*.

Disconnecting Means, Receptacle and Lighting Outlets

Equipment requiring electrical connections of more than 50 volts must have a positive means of disconnect. This disconnect must be adjacent to, and in sight from, the equipment served. A 120-volt receptacle is required to be located within 25 feet of the equipment for service and maintenance purposes. The receptacle is not required to be located on the same level as the equipment.

Where installed within a structure, low-voltage wiring of 50 volts or less is required to be installed in a manner to prevent physical damage. See *UMC Section 509*.

Where a furnace is installed in an attic, a permanent electric outlet and switch-controlled lighting fixture is required to be located at the required passageway opening. This lighting fixture is required to be installed at or near the furnace. See *UMC Section 708.*

Where a warm air furnace is located in an under-floor space, a permanent electric outlet and switch-controlled lighting fixture is required to be located at the required passageway opening. This lighting fixture is required to be installed at or near the furnace. See *UMC Section 709(5).*

Cooling Systems Lighting in Concealed Spaces

Where access is required to equipment located in an under-floor space, attic, or furred space, a permanent electric light outlet and lighting fixture must be installed at or near the equipment. The light must be controlled by a switch located at the required passageway opening.

Exception: Lighting fixtures are not required to be installed where the fixed lighting in the building will provide sufficient light for safe servicing of the equipment. See *UMC Section 1203.*

Where cooling system equipment requires access for service or maintenance, it must be provided with an unobstructed working space on the control or servicing side of the equipment. This space cannot be less than 30 inches in depth and not less than 6 feet 6 inches in height. Note: Also see the Electrical Code for working space requirements about electrical equipment. See *UMC Sections 1202* and *Section 1204, Exception.*

A cooling system includes all equipment intended or installed for the purpose of cooling air by mechanical means and discharging such air into any room or space. This definition does not include any evaporative cooler. See *UMC—91.*

BOCA—NATIONAL MECHANICAL CODE

Convenience Outlet

A 125-volt AC grounding-type outlet must be available for all appliances (see definition later in this chapter). The convenience outlet must be located on the same level within 75 feet of the appliance. The outlet must not be connected to the load side of the appliance disconnect switch. See *BOCA Section M-407.2.*

Lighting

Permanent lighting must be provided to illuminate the area in which an appliance is located. For remote locations, the light switch must be located

near the access opening leading to the applian. See *BOCA M-407.3.*

SBCCI—STANDARD MECHANICAL CODE

Air Conditioning, Heating, and Ventilating Equipment

Every appliance must be located with respect building construction and other equipment so to permit access for service of the appliance. Su cient clearance must be maintained to per cleaning of heating surfaces, the replacement filters, blowers, motors, burners, controls, a vent connections; the lubrication of moving pa where required; and the adjustment and cleani of burners and pilots.

SBCCI Mechanical Code Section 303.2.1— Outdoor Installations

Appliances listed for outdoor installations a permitted to be installed without protection in a cordance with the provisions of their listing a must be accessible for servicing. Appliances list for outdoor installation only must not be install inside a building. See *SBCCI Mechanical Co Section 303.2.2.*

Attic Installations

Every attic or furred space in which mechanic equipment is installed must be accessible by opening and passageway as large as the large piece of the equipment and in no case less than × 36 inches continuous from the opening to t equipment and its controls. The opening to t passageway must be located not more than 20 from the equipment measured along the cent line of such passageway. Every passageway mu be unobstructed and shall have solid continuo flooring not less than 24 inches wide from the e trance opening to the equipment. On the contr side and other sides where access is necessary f servicing the equipment, a level working platfor extending a minimum of 30 inches from the ed of the equipment with a 36-inch-high clear wor ing space must be provided. Top or bottom servi equipment must have a full clearance above or b low the unit for component removal. See *SBC Mechanical Code Section 303.4.1.*

A permanent electric light outlet and lighti fixture must be provided at, or near, the mechar cal equipment and controlled by a switch locat at the required passageway opening. See *SBC Mechanical Code Section 303.4.5.*

Roof or Exterior Wall Installation

Mechanical equipment installations on roofs or exterior walls of buildings must comply with the requirements for roof and wall structures as specified in the *Standard Building Code,* and must be listed and approved for such use. See *SBCCI Mechanical Code Section 303.6.1.* Each appliance must have an accessible weatherproof disconnect switch and a 110- to 120-volt AC grounding-type convenience outlet on the roof adjacent to the appliance. The convenience outlet must be on the supply side of the disconnect switch. See *SBCCI Mechanical Code Section 303.6.2.*

Nameplate Marking

Every electric comfort heating appliance must bear a permanent and legible factory-applied nameplate that must include the following:

- Name and trademark of the manufacturer
- The catalog (model) number or equivalent
- The electric rating in volts, ampacity, and phase
- BTU output rating
- Individual marking for each electrical component in amperes or watts, volts and phase
- Required clearances from combustibles
- A seal indicating approval of the appliance by an approved testing agency (see *SBCCI Mechanical Code Section 303.11.2*)

Panel Heating Systems

Panel heating is a method of radiant space heating in which heat is supplied by large heated areas of room surfaces. The heating element usually consists of warm water piping, warm air ducts, or electrical resistance elements embedded in or located behind ceiling, wall, or floor surfaces. See *SBCCI Mechanical Code Section 303.12.1.*

The installation of panel heating systems must be designed and installed in strict accordance with the accepted engineering practices and the requirements of the *SBCCI Mechanical Code Section 303.12.2.*

SBCCI—STANDARD GAS CODE

Electrical Connections for Electrical Ignition and Control Devices

Devices employing or depending upon an electrical current must not be used to control or ignite a gas supply if of such character that failure of the electrical current could result in the escape of unburned gas or in failure to reduce the supply of gas under conditions which would normally result in its reduction unless other means are provided to prevent the development of dangerous temperatures, pressures, or the escape of gas. See *SBCCI Standard Gas Code Section 404.2.*

Switches in Air Conditioning Electrical Supply Line

Means for interrupting the electrical supply to the air conditioning appliance and to its associated cooling tower (if supplied and installed in a location remote from the air conditioner) must be provided within sight of and not over 50 feet from the air conditioner and cooling tower. See *SBCCI Standard Gas Code Section 508.5.*

Electric Ignition Systems

Electric ignition systems must ignite only a pilot. The input to the pilot shall not exceed 3% of the maximum input to the main burner as fired. If ignition of the pilot is not obtained within 15 seconds, the gas must shut off automatically. See *SBCCI Standard Gas Code Section 807.3.*

SBCCI—STANDARD PLUMBING CODE

Existing Metallic Water Service Piping

Existing metallic water service piping used for electrical grounding must not be replaced with nonmetallic pipe or tubing until other grounding means are provided which are satisfactory to the proper administrative authority having jurisdiction. See *SBCCI Standard Plumbing Code Section 504.3.3.*

IAPMO—UNIFORM PLUMBING CODE

Water Heater Locations

Attic and under-floor water heater locations must be provided with an electric light at or near the water heater. Such light must be controlled by a switch located adjacent to the opening or trap door. See *Section 1311(e) IAPMO—UPC—91.*

The International Association of Plumbing and Mechanical Officials include their Installation Standards in *IAPMO—UPC—91.* These standards are not considered as part of the *Uniform Plumbing Code* (*UPC*) unless they are formally adopted as such. Some sections include the following.

Recessed light fixtures: Polybutylene (PB) tubing shall not be installed within 12 inches of a recessed light fixture.

Identification: A permanent sign with the legible words THIS BUILDING HAS NONMETALLIC INTERIOR WATER PIPING must be fastened on or inside the main electric service panel.

UBC—UNIFORM BUILDING CODE

Requirements for Group R Occupancies

A Group R occupancy includes Division 3—Dwellings and Lodging Houses. A complete code for construction of detached one- and two-family dwellings is located in Appendix Chapter 12 of the UBC. See *UBC Section 1201.*

Smoke Detectors

Smoke detectors are required in dwelling units that are used for sleeping purposes. They must be installed in accordance with the manufacturer's instructions.

The power source used for a smoke detector must be by a permanently connected wiring method and must be provided with a battery backup where installed in new construction. This supply cannot be operated by any type of switching device or other disconnecting means. This restriction does not include branch-circuit overcurrent protection.

A smoke detector must be installed in all sleeping rooms. Additional smoke detectors must be installed so they are located centrally in the corridor or area giving access to each separate sleeping area. See *UBC Section 1210.*

Heating

Dwelling units must be provided with heating facilities capable of maintaining a room temperature of 70°F at a point three feet above the floor in all habitable rooms. See *UBC Section 1212.*

Exterior openings exposed to the weather must be protected and must be flashed in such a manner as to make them weatherproof. See *UBC Section 1708(b).*

Cutting and Notching Wood

In exterior walls and bearing partitions, any wood stud may be cut or notched to a depth not exceeding 25 percent of its width. Cutting or notching of studs to a depth not greater than 40 percent of the width of the stud is permitted in nonbearing partitions supporting no loads other than the weight of the partition. See *UBC Section 2517(g)(8).*

Bored Holes in Wooden Studs

A hole not greater in diameter than 40 percent of the stud width may be bored in any wood stud. Bored holes not greater than 60 percent of the width of the stud are permitted in nonbearing partitions or in any wall where each bored stud is doubled, provided not more than two such successive doubled studs are so bored.

In no case shall the edge of the bored hole nearer than ⅝ inch to the edge of the stud. Bore holes must not be located at the same section stud as a cut or notch. See *UBC Section 2517(g)(9*

Wall and Ceiling Coverings

Where electrical radiant heat cables are installe on ceilings, the stripping, if conductive, may omitted a distance not to exceed 12 inches fro the wall. See *UBC Section 4705(a).*

BOCA—NATIONAL BUILDING CODE

Bathroom and Toilet Room Lighting

Every bathroom and toilet room must be pr vided with artificial light. The illumination mu have an average intensity of three footcandl measured at a level of 30 inches above the floc See *BOCA Section 703.1.1.*

Grounding Metal Veneers

Grounding of metal veneers on all buildings mu comply with the requirements of *BOCA Article* and *NFPA 70.* See *BOCA Section 2103.4.3.* See *NE Section 250.116 (FPN).*

SBCCI Standard Building Code

Underground inspection: To be made after trench or ditches are excavated, conduit or cable i stalled, and before any backfill is put in place.

Rough-in inspection: To be made after the roo framing, fireblocking, and bracing is in plac and prior to the installation of wall or ceilin membranes.

Final inspection: To be made after the building complete, all required electrical fixtures are place and properly connected or protected, an the structure is ready for occupancy. See *SBCC Section 103.8.6.*

Separation Between Townhouses

Where not more than three stories in height, towr houses (which are defined as a single famil dwelling constructed in a series or group of a tached units with property lines separating eac unit) may be separated by a single wall meetin the following requirements.

The wall is required to provide not less than two-hour fire resistance rating. Plumbing, pipinε ducts, and electrical or other building services ar not permitted to be installed within or through th two-hour wall, unless such materials and methoc of penetration have been tested in accordance wit *SBCCI Section 1001.1.* See *SBCCI Section 403.5.2.*

etal Veneers

etal veneers fastened to supporting elements hich are not a part of the grounded metal fram-; of a building must be made electrically ntinuous by contact or interconnection of indi-lual units and must be effectively grounded. e conductor used to ground the veneer must ve no greater resistance than the conductor ed to ground the electrical system within the ilding. Where a metal veneer is applied to a ilding with no electrical wiring system, punding is required only if determined to be cessary by the Building Official. See *SBCCI ction 811.4.6.*

alls, Floors, and Partitions

hen walls, floors, and partitions are required to ve a minimum of one hour or greater fire resis-nce rating, cabinets, bathroom components, hting, and other fixtures must be so installed ch that the required fire resistance will not be luced.

NOTE

This requirement must be coordinated with the electrical inspector as well. See *NEC Section 250.116 (FPN)*.

Exception: Fixtures which are listed for such stallation are permitted. See *SBCCI Section 01.3.7.*

UMMARY OF APPLICABLE EFINITIONS FROM BUILDING ODES ABOVE

ie following definitions are selected from the des referenced above and that relate to ectrical installations in residential structures. here the code definitions differ, each definition included.

ACCESSIBLE – Having access to, but which rst may require the removal of, a panel, door, or milar obstruction. *BOCA—MECH—90; SBCCI— ECH—91; SBCCI—91; SBCCI—91—GAS; BC/UMC—91*

AIR CONDITIONING – The treatment of air as to control simultaneously its temperature, imidity, cleanliness, and distribution to meet the quirements of a conditioned space. *BOCA— ECH—90; SBCCI—MECH—91; SBCCI—91— AS*

AIR CONDITIONING SYSTEM – An air conditioning system consists of heat exchangers, blowers, filters, supply, exhaust, and return ducts, and shall include any apparatus installed in connection therewith. *BOCA—MECH—90; SBCCI—CI—MECH—91*

AIR-HANDLING UNIT – A blower or fan used for the purpose of distributing supply air to a room, space, or area. *UBC/UMC—91*

ALLEY – Any public way or thoroughfare less than 16 feet but not less than 10 feet in width which has been dedicated or deeded to the public for public use. *UBC—91*

ALTERATION – A change in an air conditioning, heating, ventilating, or refrigeration system that involves an extension, addition, or change to the arrangement, type, or purpose of the original installation. *SBCCI—MECH—91*

AND/OR – In a choice of two code provisions, signifies that use of both provisions will satisfy the code requirement and use of either provision is acceptable also. *SBCCI 91—GAS*

APPLIANCE – A device which utilizes fuel or other forms of energy to produce light, heat, power, refrigeration, or air conditioning. This definition also shall include a vented decorative appliance. *UBC/UMC—91*

APPLIANCE – Utilization equipment normally built in standardized sizes which is installed or connected as a unit to perform one or more functions. *SBCCI—MECH—GAS—91*

APPLIANCE, AUTOMATICALLY CONTROLLED – Appliances equipped with an automatic burner which accomplish complete turn-on and shut-off of the gas to the main burner or burners, and graduate the gas supply to the burner or burners (they do not affect complete shut-off of the gas). *SBCCI—91—GAS*

APPLIANCE (MECHANICAL) – A device or apparatus—including any attachments or apparatus designed to be attached—which is manufactured and designed to use electricity, natural gas, manufactured gas, mixed gas, liquefied petroleum products, solid fuel, oil, or any gas as a fuel for heating, cooling, or developing light or power. *BOCA—MECH—90*

ATTIC – The space between the ceiling beams of the top story and the roof rafters. *BOCA—90*

ATTIC, HABITABLE – A habitable attic is an attic which has a stairway as a means of access and egress and in which the ceiling area at a height of $7\frac{1}{3}$ feet above the attic floor is not more than one third of the area of the next floor below. *BOCA—90*

BASEMENT – Any building story having a floor below grade. *SBCCI—91*

BASEMENT – Any floor level below the first story in a building, except that a floor level in a building having only one floor level must be classified as a basement unless such floor level qualifies as a first story as defined herein. *UBC—91*

BASEMENT – That portion of a building which is partly or completely below grade (see Story above grade). *BOCA—90*

BATHROOM – A room containing a bathtub or shower for use by a person to bathe or cleanse one's self, located in or adjacent to a residence, apartment, hotel, motel, or similar type building. *SBCCI—91—GAS*

BATHROOM – A room equipped with a shower or bathtub. *IAPMO—UPC—91*

BUILDING – A building is a structure built, erected, and framed of component structural parts designed for the housing, shelter, enclosure, or support of persons, animals, or property of any kind. *IAPMO—UPC—91*

BUILDING – Any structure that encloses a space used for sheltering any occupancy. Each portion of a building separated from other portions by a fire wall must be considered as a separate building. *SBCCI—91*

BUILDING – Any structure used or intended for supporting or sheltering any use or occupancy. *UBC—91*

BUILDING – Any structure used or intended for supporting or sheltering any use or occupancy. For application of this code, each portion of a building which is completely separated from other portions by fire wall complying with *Section 907.0* must be considered as a separate building. *BOCA—90*

BUILDING CODE – The *Uniform Building Code* promulgated by the International Conference of Building Officials, as adopted by this jurisdiction. *ICBO ELECTRICAL CODE*

BUILDING, EXISTING – Any structure erected prior to the adoption of the appropriate code, or one for which a legal building permit has been issued. *BOCA—90; SBCCI—91; UBC—91*

BUILDING SERVICE EQUIPMENT – The mechanical, electrical, and elevator equipment including piping, wiring, fixtures, and other accessories, which provides sanitation, lighting, heating, ventilation, fire-fighting, and transportation facilities essential for the habitable occupancy of the building or structure for its designated use and occupancy. *BOCA—90*

COMBUSTIBLE CONSTRUCTION – A w or surface constructed of wood, composition, o wooden studding and lath and plaster. *SBCC 91—GAS*

COMBUSTION – The rapid oxidation of f gases accompanied by the production of heat, heat and light. *SBCCI—91—GAS*

DWELLING – A building occupied exc sively for residential purposes by not more th two families, unless qualified otherwise in c text. *SBCCI—91*

DWELLING – Any building or portion there which contains not more than two dwelling un *UBC—91*

DWELLING UNIT – Any building or porti thereof which contains living facilities, includi provisions for sleeping, eating, cooking, and sa tation, as required by this code, for not more th one family, or a congregate residence for 10 fewer persons. *UBC—91*

DWELLING UNIT – A single unit providi complete, independent living facilities for one more persons, including permanent provisio for living, sleeping, eating, cooking, and sani tion. *BOCA—90; SBCCI—91*

DWELLING, ONE-FAMILY – A building c taining one dwelling unit with not more than fi lodgers or boarders. *BOCA—90*

DWELLING, TWO-FAMILY – A buildi containing two dwelling units with not more th five lodgers or boarders per family. *BOCA—90*

EFFICIENCY DWELLING UNIT – dwelling unit containing only one habitable roo *UBC—91*

ELECTRIC HEATING APPLIANCE – A d vice which produces heat energy to create a war environment by the application of electric pow to resistance elements, refrigerant compressors, dissimilar material junctions. *Section 407 UBC/UMC—91*

ELECTRIC SPACE HEATERS, PORTABLE Heaters not intended for permanent connection a structure or to electric wiring. *SBCCI—MECH 91*

ELECTRIC SPACE HEATERS, STATIONAR – Heaters permanently mounted in a structure (a duct system) and which are permanently co nected to electric wiring. *SBCCI—MECH—91*

EQUIPMENT, EXISTING – Any equipme covered by this code which was installed prior the effective date of this code, or for which an a plication for permit to install was filed with t code official prior thereto. *BOCA—90*

EXISTING WORK – A mechanical system, or y part thereof, installed prior to the effective te of this code. *BOCA—MECH—90*

EXIT – See *Section 3301(b)* Definitions of: Bal- ny, Exterior Exit; Exit; Exit Court; Exit Passage- ry; and Horizontal Exit. *UBC—91*

FIRE PROTECTION – The provision of con- uction safeguards and exit facilities; and the in- llation of fire alarm, fire detecting, and fire tinguishing service equipment, to reduce the e risk and the conflagration hazard. *BOCA—90*

FLOOR AREA – The area included within the rounding exterior walls of a building or por- n thereof, exclusive of vent shafts and courts. e floor area of a building, or portion thereof, not ovided with surrounding exterior walls must be e usable area under the horizontal projection of e roof or floor above. *UBC—91*

FURNACE – A completely self-contained unit at produces heat by utilizing electric energy or burning fuel. *SBCCI—MECH—91*

FURNACE, CENTRAL – A self-contained in- rect fired or electrically heated appliance de- ned to supply heated air through ducts to aces remote from or adjacent to the appliance. *BCCI—MECH—91*

GARAGE, PRIVATE – A building or a portion a building, not more than 1,000 square feet in ea, in which only motor vehicles used by the nants of the building or buildings on the prem- es are stored or kept (see *UBC Chapter 11*). *BC—91*

GARAGE, PRIVATE – A garage for four or ss passenger motor vehicles without provision r repairing or servicing such vehicles for profit ee *Section 608.0*). *BOCA—90*

GRADE – A reference plane representing the verage of finished ground level adjoining the uilding at all exterior walls. When the finished round level slopes away from the exterior walls, e reference plane must be established by the west points within the area between the build- g and the lot line or between the building and a oint six feet from the building, whichever is oser to the building. *SBCCI—91*

HABITABLE SPACE – A space in a structure r living, sleeping, eating, or cooking. Bath- oms, toilet compartments, closets, halls, storage utility spaces, and similar areas are not consid- red habitable spaces. *BOCA—90; SBCCI—91*

HABITABLE SPACE (ROOM) – Space in a ructure for living, sleeping, eating, or cooking. athrooms, toilet compartments, closets, halls, torage or utility spaces, and similar areas, are not considered habitable spaces. *UBC—91; BOCA— 90*

HEAT PUMP – An appliance having heating or heating/cooling capability and which uses re- frigerants to extract heat from air, liquid, or earth sources. *UBC/UMC—91*

HEATING EQUIPMENT – Includes all warm- air furnaces, warm-air heaters, combustion prod- ucts vents, heating air distribution ducts and fans, all steam and hot water piping, together with all control devices and accessories installed as part of, or in connection with, any environmental heat- ing system or appliance regulated by this code. *UBC/UMC Section 410*

HEATING SYSTEM – A warm-air heating plant consisting of a heat exchanger enclosed in a casing, from which the heated air is distributed through ducts to various rooms and areas. A heat- ing system includes the outside air, return air, and supply air system, and all accessory apparatus and equipment installed in connection therewith. *UBC/UMC—91*

HEATING SYSTEM, CENTRAL WARM AIR – A heating system consisting of an air heating appliance from which the heated air is distributed by means of ducts, pipes, or plenums including any accessory apparatus and equipment installed in connection therewith. *SBCCI—MECH—91*

LISTED and LISTING – Terms referring to equipment and materials which are shown in a list published by an approved testing agency, quali- fied and equipped for experimental testing and maintaining an adequate periodic inspection of current productions. The listing states that the material or equipment complies with accepted na- tional standards which are approved or standards which have been evaluated for conformity with approved standards.

MASONRY – That form of construction com- posed of stone, brick, concrete, gypsum, hollow clay tile, concrete block or tile, glass block or other similar building units or materials, or a combina- tion of these materials laid up by unit and set in mortar. *UBC—91*

READILY ACCESSIBLE – Having direct ac- cess without the need of removing or moving any panel, door or similar obstruction. *BOCA— MECH—90*

READILY ACCESSIBLE – Having direct ac- cess without the need of removing any panel, door, or similar covering of the item described, and without requiring the use of portable ladders, chairs, etc. *SBCCI—MECH—GAS—91*

SINGLE-FAMILY DWELLING – A single-family dwelling shall mean a building designed to be used as a home by the owner of such building, and must be the only dwelling located on a parcel of ground with the usual accessory buildings. *IAPMO—UPC—91*

SMOKE DETECTOR – An approved device that senses visible or invisible particles of combustion. *UBC—91*

SMOKE DETECTOR – An approved listed detector sensing either visible or invisible particles of combustion. *SBCCI—91*

STAIRWAY – One or more flights of stairs, either exterior or interior, with the necessary landings and platforms connecting them, to form a continuous and uninterrupted passage from one level to another in a building or structure. *SBCCI—91*

STRUCTURE – That which is built or constructed, an edifice or building of any kind, or a piece of work artificially built up or composed of parts joined together in some definite manner. *UBC—91*

TOWNHOUSE – A single-family dwelling constructed in a series or group of attached units with property lines separating each unit. *SBCCI—91*

USABLE CRAWL SPACE – A crawl space designed to be used for equipment or storage. *SBCCI—91*

WATER HEATER – An appliance designed primarily to supply hot water and equipped with automatic controls limiting water temperature to a maximum of 210°F. *UBC—91*

This module is intended to present thorough re-sources for task training. The following reference work is suggested for further study. This is op-ional material for continued education rather an for task training.

National Electrical Code® Handbook, Latest Edition. Quincy, MA: National Fire Protection Association.

The NCCER makes every effort to keep these textbooks up-to-date and free of technical errors. We appreciate your help in this process. If you have an idea for improving this textbook, or if you find an error, a typographical mistake, or an inaccuracy in NCCER's *Contren®* textbooks, please write us, using this form or a photocopy. Be sure to include the exact module number, page number, a detailed description, and the correction, if applicable. Your input will be brought to the attention of the Technical Review Committee. Thank you for your assistance.

Instructors – If you found that additional materials were necessary in order to teach this module effectively, please let us know so that we may include them in the Equipment/Materials list in the Annotated Instructor's Guide.

Write: Product Development
National Center for Construction Education and Research
P.O. Box 141104, Gainesville, FL 32614-1104

Fax: 352-334-0932

E-mail: curriculum@nccer.org

Craft

Module Name

Copyright Date

Module Number

Page Number(s)

Description

(Optional) Correction

(Optional) Your Name and Address